The Electroco Therapy Workbook

Electroconvulsive Therapy (ECT) remains one of the most effective forms of neurostimulation for severe mental illness. Sound scientific research underpins contemporary practice challenging the complex history and stigma that surround this treatment.

The Electroconvulsive Therapy Workbook integrates the history of ECT with major advances in practice, including ultrabrief ECT, in a hands-on workbook format. Novel forms of neurostimulation are reviewed, highlighting the future directions of practice in this exciting area. The book is also richly illustrated with historical and technical images and includes 'clinical wisdom' sections that provide the reader with clinical insights into ECT practice. Online eResources are also available, featuring a wide range of questions and answers related to each chapter to help test and consolidate readers' understanding of ECT, as well as regionally specific legislation governing ECT practice in Australia and New Zealand.

This comprehensive introduction to ECT is a must-read for doctors in training, psychiatrists who require credentialing in this procedure, anaesthetists, nursing staff who work in ECT and other professionals who have an interest in ECT as well as consumer and carer networks.

Alan Weiss is conjoint senior lecturer at the University of Newcastle, Australia. He is also a fellow of the Royal Australian and New Zealand College of Psychiatrists (RANZCP) and chair of the Colleges Section for ECT and Neurostimulation (SEN); clinical director of the neurostimulation programme for the Hunter New England Local Health District; chair of the expert committee to revise 2010 NSW ECT Guidelines; and foundation director of neurostimulation at two private hospitals in Newcastle. Dr Weiss is a member of the International Society for ECT and Neurostimulation and the American Psychiatric Association.

The Electroconvulsive Therapy Workbook

Clinical Applications

Alan Weiss

Routledge
Taylor & Francis Group

LONDON AND NEW YORK

First published 2018
by Routledge
2 Park Square, Milton Park, Abingdon, Oxon OX14 4RN

and by Routledge
711 Third Avenue, New York, NY 10017

Routledge is an imprint of the Taylor and Francis Group, an informa business

British Library Cataloguing-in-Publication Data
A catalogue record for this book is available from the British Library

Library of Congress Cataloging-in-Publication Data
Names: Weiss, Alan, 1955 July 9– author.
Title: The electroconvulsive therapy workbook :
clinical applications / Alan Weiss.
Description: Abingdon, Oxon ; New York, NY : Routledge, 2018. |
Includes bibliographical references.
Identifiers: LCCN 2017056040 | ISBN 9781138713369 (hardback) |
ISBN 9781138713376 (pbk.) | ISBN 9781315198897 (ebook)
Subjects: | MESH: Electroconvulsive Therapy – methods
Classification: LCC RC485 | NLM WM 412 | DDC 616.89/122 – dc23
LC record available at https://lccn.loc.gov/2017056040

ISBN: 978-1-138-71336-9 (hbk)
ISBN: 978-1-138-71337-6 (pbk)
ISBN: 978-1-315-19889-7 (ebk)

Typeset in Palatino and Bell Gothic
by Florence Production Ltd, Stoodleigh, Devon, UK

eResources are available at www.routledge.com/9781138713376/

MIX
Paper from
responsible sources
FSC® C013985
Printed in the United Kingdom
by Henry Ling Limited

Contents

Preface

Electroconvulsive Therapy (ECT) remains one of the most effective treatments for severe mental illness. It has a complex history that continues to stigmatise and distract from the large number of changes in technology and methods that have made it a modern treatment. Modern ECT practice is based upon sound scientific research generating a substantial evidence base that guides treatment. However, there continues to be a gap between the clinicians who administer ECT and its consumers and a failure of ECT practitioners to implement novel techniques.

Training provided to doctors administering ECT worldwide has been inadequate and highly variable. International audits have highlighted a lack of expertise and resources in this area. In 2003, the UK's National Institute for Health and Clinical Excellence (NICE) Guidance Document for ECT was very critical of ECT practice, stating that ECT should be a "treatment of the last resort", a criticism that may have merit owing to the vast difference between clinicians' and consumers' perspectives of ECT. Staff administering ECT often have superficial training before they are expected to administer the treatment in their hospital.

The Electroconvulsive Therapy Workbook is a book for clinicians and trainees of all disciplines who practise ECT. It is not a Royal College or Association clinical practice guideline or an academic work but a comprehensive approach to ECT that emphasises knowledge in an environment that challenges prejudice and stigma, incorporates new techniques to minimise unwanted side effects and maximise the benefits of ECT.

The Electroconvulsive Therapy Workbook has been the result of two major influences: 22 years of listening to patients undergoing ECT and using their experiences to change practice through the development of a competency-based ECT training programme for doctors, nurses and students working in the area of ECT. The competency-based learning model provides a structured approach to ensure that trainees who complete the ECT Entrustable Professional Activities (EPA) programme have a high level of technical skills and the ability to engage with patients undergoing ECT in an empathic manner, closely monitoring progress and making changes in treatment to minimise adverse reactions. There is an emphasis on training in a multidisciplinary setting that places the ECT team at the core of treatment. *The ECT Workbook* is an integral part of this programme, anchoring learning in sound clinical practice.

The ECT Workbook offers practical information, supported by recent evidence, concerning the clinical application of ECT in psychiatric practice throughout the world. Information is broken down into relevant sections using a workbook format: overview, definition, knowledge (ranging from past history to major advances), mechanism of action, clinical indications, efficacy, neurostimulation techniques, organisational and administrative skills, clinical skills, technical skills, anaesthesia, maintenance ECT, the lived experience, the role of the ECT nurse and detailed scenario-based problems.

Relevant chapters are illustrated with historical, technical photos and figures to aid learning with a question and answer format following most chapters. Many sections include a "clinical wisdom" insert that offers advice where there is limited evidence to guide treatment drawing upon extensive practice-based experience in the administration of ECT.

After reading this volume it is anticipated that the reader will have a comprehensive understanding of current ECT practice and feel equipped to challenge stigma by implementing change into the way ECT is delivered in their service.

Dr Alan Weiss
Newcastle, NSW, Australia

Acknowledgements

The Electroconvulsive Therapy Workbook would not have been possible if it were not for the tireless and unyielding support from my wife, Ann, and my three daughters, Ella, Danika and Petra. Thank you Ella and Caitlin for your early inspiration and your support in helping me type and design the original manuscript that provided the framework for *The Electroconvulsive Therapy Workbook*.

I would like to thank all of the patients that I have treated with ECT over many years who have shared their lived experience, inspiring me to develop an ECT service and training programme with a strong focus on eliminating stigma, using modern techniques that minimise cognitive impairment while striving to achieve complete remission. In particular, I would like to thank Alirra for bravely agreeing to share her moving and personal account of ECT from the first moments through to maintenance treatment.

A big thank you goes to Shane and the ECT team at the Mater Hospital, Newcastle, Australia. This team forms the basis of the ECT training programme. Shane has provided endless support over many years to myself and countless trainees and has become a vast store of clinical wisdom concerning ECT practice. I am indebted to Shane who helped me write the chapter on the ECT nurse and his inspiration and encouragement to continue with this large and at times overwhelming project.

A special thank you goes to Doctor Michael, a vibrant and enthusiastic senior psychiatry fellow who is passionate about his patients, ECT and neurostimulation. Doctor Michael's enthusiasm and support has been inspirational in the writing of *The Electroconvulsive Therapy* Workbook, reinforcing my own passion to administer ECT in a manner that minimises stigma, is patient-focused and patient-responsive, and has a strong evidence base with the capacity to incorporate practice-based experience to ensure that patients benefit from this powerful treatment with the least possible side effects.

The Electroconvulsive Therapy Workbook would not have been as colourful and informative if it were not for Luke, who generously consented to model for all photographs in this volume. It is refreshing to incorporate the difference in his presentation between the two photo shoots that occurred many months apart echoing the enormous diagnostic, psychosocial and cultural difference in patients who are given ECT.

I am most grateful to Doctor John Fluit for opening up his fantastic medical history museum and providing all of the historical photos that grace this Workbook. I am indebted to him for assisting in writing Section 2.1 History: treatment of mental illness.

I would like to acknowledge and thank Amber for her inspiration and innovation in the drawings and figures that are used to simplify and clearly explain different concepts used in this *Workbook*.

I am indebted to the staff at Hudson Street Specialist Centre, who provided support and assistance during the long period of time it has taken to complete this work.

I would like to thank the staff and psychiatrists who work at Lakeside Clinic, Warner's Bay Private Hospital, Newcastle, Australia, who have provided encouragement and support, reinforcing that the techniques incorporated in *The Electroconvulsive Therapy Workbook* are effective in reducing stigma, minimising cognitive problems and achieving remission in a patient-focused supportive environment that is responsive to clinical change.

I would like to thank Robin, CEO MECTA Corporation, for generously providing photographs and historical content that enhances this *Workbook*.

I wish to acknowledge Magventure for making available a photograph of their new Magpro MST device.

Finally I wish to make a posthumous acknowledgement to Mr Ian Maudsley, the foundation ECT coordinator within Hunter New England Local Health District, NSW, Australia. Ian's huge drive and tireless work have irreversibly changed the role of nurses in ECT services internationally. His willingness to step up to the challenge and engage with nurses from around the world was instrumental in nursing becoming a valued member of the International Society for ECT and Neurostimulation (ISEN). If it were not for his contribution, the prominence of nursing in the local ECT training programme for medical and nursing staff would not have been as great. Ian Maudsley inspired me to describe the ECT coordinator as the "powerhouse" of the ECT team. Thank you from the bottom of my heart. I miss your charm, humour and sophistication.

Dr Alan Weiss

CHAPTER 1

Introduction

Overview

PURPOSE

Electroconvulsive Therapy (ECT) is a treatment that has a complex history. It was first used in 1938. Since that time, many advances have been made in the practice of ECT and the science behind this very effective treatment for severe mental illness.

For many years, the training of doctors and other staff administering ECT was inadequate and highly variable. Medical staff administering this treatment often had very superficial training before they were expected to administer the treatment in their hospital.

Duffett and Lelliott (1998) commented that after a 20-year period only modest improvements in the local practice of ECT within England and Wales were demonstrated, after the Royal College of Psychiatrists (RCP) completed its third large-scale audit. These audits were very extensive and were followed by specific recommendations for change highlighting a lack of expertise and resources that were allocated to the provision of ECT.

Significant changes have been made since the release of National Institute for Health and Care Excellence (2003) guidance on ECT for depressive illness, schizophrenia, catatonia and mania. This document was based upon two systematic reviews sponsored by the Department of Health; UK ECT Review Group (2003) and Rose, Fleischmann, Wykes, Leese and Bindman (2003) highlighted the consumer's viewpoint. Following these reviews, the guidance for ECT was very critical, stating:

ECT should be used only to achieve rapid and short-term improvement of severe symptoms after adequate trials of other treatments have failed when the condition is considered to be potentially life-threatening with, severe depressive illness, catatonia or a prolonged or severe manic episode. The current state of the evidence does not allow the general use of ECT on the management of schizophrenia to be recommended as the long-term benefits and risk of ECT have not been clearly established, it is not recommended as a maintenance therapy in depressive illness. ECT should be used as a treatment of last resort.

(NICE, 2003)

This guidance was met with strong criticism from psychiatrists within the UK and around the world, as they were not consistent with the common clinical use of ECT in the everyday treatment of depression. The *ECT Handbook*, 2nd edition (Scott, 2005) was revised to address the criticisms raised by the NICE guidance document and released as *The ECT Handbook*, 3rd edition (Waite and Easton, 2013).

More recently, the Royal College of Psychiatrists released the *ECT Accreditation Service (ECTAS): Standards for the Administration of ECT*, 12th edition (Royal College of Psychiatrists, 2015), which specifies minimum standards of practice. Australia and New Zealand have followed this lead, with many states making a considerable effort to review ECT practice by developing minimum standards guidelines (Chief Psychiatrist of Western Australia, 2015; NSW Health, 2010; SA Health, 2014; Victorian Government, 2014).

It was within this environment that *The Electroconvulsive Therapy Workbook* evolved over a 16-year period as part of a competency-based ECT training programme for staff working in this area.

CLINICAL WISDOM 1.1.1

One of the most distressing encounters that junior house staff and psychiatric registrars have to deal with when completing studies in psychiatry is their encounter with the relevant mental health legislation, which often involves dealing with an independent mental health review tribunal (MHRT) in the state/territory in which they practise. In many instances this creates significant ethical concerns within the individual about the pros and cons of administering psychiatric treatment to patients who are unable to provide informed consent.

The adversarial model is particularly paramount in some jurisdictions where the consumer/patient is entitled to legal representation whereas the medical arguments are often presented by a junior member of the medical team. The medical argument necessarily involves breaking the confidence of the patient by expanding the content of significant past events, psychotic delusions or self-harming behaviour. This process can create distress in the doctor who has limited academic knowledge, clinical and legal experience and a superficial understanding of complex clinical details.

The dilemma is magnified when the doctor is also required to ask for a determination to administer a course of ECT. It is not until some time later, when the doctor has followed a number of patients through a course of ECT, that they understand the marked and rapid clinical improvement that occurs with this treatment, providing meaning to what can often be a hostile and unpleasant experience.

The process becomes even more complex as the adversarial model challenges the fundamental core skill of psychiatry, namely establishing a good therapeutic alliance with the patient (Bellis, 2016; Martin, Garske and Davis, 2000). The registrar is obliged to reveal complex, detailed personal information in a semi-legal setting to enable the tribunal to make a determination. This fundamental breach of confidence usually results in the patient resenting the doctor, and often will be reluctant to speak to them for the remainder of the admission if the tribunal has determined that ECT is necessary.

The junior psychiatric registrar can be left feeling disillusioned, confused and angry as this process is at odds with their early impression of psychiatry as a profession that is altruistic, nurturing and caring. The ethical challenge is so intense that it often leads to early withdrawal from the training programme.

This phenomenon is well recognised and has led to the development of some innovative strategies to empathise with the new trainee, like *The Hitchhikers Guide to Psychiatry* (Varmos, 2008).

There are four guiding principles that can assist in navigating this difficult road. These principles are guided by the basic tenets of ethics (Bloch and Singh, 2001). They include:

- Beneficence: do good; maximise efficacy.
- Non-maleficence: do no harm; minimise side effects and reduce stigma.
- Autonomy: respect patient; ensure that individual wishes and differences are considered.
- Justice: equality; ensure that there is equal opportunity for treatment regardless of age, gender, colour, religion or wealth in the least restrictive environment (Bloch and Singh, 2001).

Application of these principles has formed the basis of clinical practice over many years, particularly in ECT, enabling difficult situations, ethical dilemmas and conflict situations to be overcome and resolved. Fink (2009) provides a more detailed and helpful discussion of these principles as they apply to ECT.

All medical practice seeks to optimise benefits and minimise risks by ensuring a high level of competency in staff administering the treatment. The ECT technique can have a substantial impact on clinical outcome, particularly cognitive impairment (Sackeim et al., 2007). The benefits of modern ECT are well defined and substantial, offering severely unwell patients a chance to recover in modern settings that provides autonomy, justice and beneficence.

ECT worked for me, not that it will work for everyone. . . . We need to face up to ECT's risk and try to reduce them, but we need to acknowledge its potential benefits. . . . There are too many people in desperate need of a workable treatment to limit any viable options.

(Dukakis and Tye, 2006)

AIMS

The aims of the Electroconvulsive Therapy training programme are set out in Table 1.1.1.

OBJECTIVES

The objectives of the Electroconvulsive Therapy training programme are set out in Table 1.1.2.

A COMPETENCY-BASED ECT PROGRAMME

A recent initiative in postgraduate medical education is competency-based learning with the use of modules incorporating entrustable professional activities (EPA) (Cate and Sheele, 2007). An EPA is defined as an activity or procedure that should only be carried out by a trained specialist who achieves a level of competency in a range of special skills that are fundamental to the procedure. ECT is a good example of an EPA. Such a programme was first described in the Netherlands to help supervisors determine the competency of their trainees (Scheele et al., 2008). Supervisors consider whether or not to delegate professional activities to trainees by determining whether they feel confident to trust a trainee to perform a specialised task with specific independence. At completion the trainee knows when to ask for additional help and can be trusted to seek assistance in a timely manner (Cohen and Port, 2012).

Competency-based training and assessment is the term used in the education literature that closely examines what actual tasks a person has to perform in the "workplace" in the role for which they are being trained and then ensuring that the required

Table 1.1.1 Aims

- Provide an overview of the historical context surrounding the practice of ECT
- Provide an understanding of how the community has been influenced by the media, resulting in shame, stigma and marginalisation of ECT practice
- Identify the changes that have occurred in ECT practice since its inception as the first neurostimulation technique
- Understand the science and research that underpin modern ECT practice
- Understand local protocols and procedures that determine ECT practice
- Understand the legal principals as they apply to the relevant Mental Health Act that governs the practice of ECT in the local region, with an emphasis on adequate informed consent
- Understand the clinical context in which modern ECT is utilised
- Understand the indications for ECT as well as the necessity for a comprehensive history, physical examination, appropriated investigations and mandatory cognitive and diagnostic measures
- Understand how to proceed with high-risk populations and special precautions that are required
- Be familiar with all aspects of anaesthesia
- Understand the rationale for monitor, role of the "time out procedure" and evaluation during and after the treatment
- Understand dosing protocols, procedures and rationale for different electrode placements
- Develop confidence in interaction with patients, careers and the ECT team
- Demonstrate an ability to obtain informed consent and the importance of involving family and careers when treatment is voluntary
- Ability to present a patient to the relevant mental health review tribunal to request an authorization to commence ECT

skills are taught and assessed in training (Cate and Sheele, 2007; Cohen and Port, 2012; Scheele et al., 2008). In particular, competency refers to the demonstrated ability of the person being trained to actually perform the important learned tasks, at the required level in the workplace (Cate and Sheele, 2007). It is known that knowledge alone does not ensure a competent practitioner. It also requires the right attitude and a number of practical skills for the task required.

In recent years this approach to medical education has been applied to ECT. The ECT competency-based training programme has been designed to provide "hands-on" learning for candidates over a six-week period. In addition to having hands-on experience treating many patients, there is also a self-discovery or experiential session with the aim of giving the trainee the experience of being the patient. This "getting your hands dirty" session is conducted once during the training period (often

when the patient list is short). The aim is to give each trainee the experience of being the psychiatrist administering the treatment and then being the patient by simulating ECT treatment in theatre.

The ECT team has found that this experience provides the trainee with a personal experience of simulating ECT practice in situ as well as a snapshot of the patient's experience of the treatment. Feedback from trainees has consistently highlighted the value of this programme component, which is practical and a lot of fun.

At completion of the EPA the trainee will be proficient in the modern use of ECT, demonstrating proficiency in all of the expected tasks associated with the prescription, administration and monitoring of ECT and able to complete the medical competency form.

The ECT Workbook provides the framework for an ECT EPA where trainees have to complete a case-based discussion (CbD) critically examining

Table 1.1.2 Objectives

- Describe the history and recent innovations in ECT practice and treatment
- Describe brain neuromodulation with specific reference to neurostimulation
- Define ECT, highlighting its benefits and limitations in a concise way to challenge public perceptions of this very effective but misunderstood treatment
- Describe the indications and contraindications for ECT
- Demonstrate an awareness of and appropriate management of medical comorbidities
- Describe situations of increased risk associated with ECT and how to manage them
- Describe complications of ECT and their management
- Describe the principles of stimulus dose titration, the strengths and limitations of this technique and alternative dosing strategies
- Demonstrate a detailed knowledge of the techniques in administering different types of ECT
- Demonstrate an ability to identify and measure the correct anatomical sites for recording and treatment electrodes for different types of ECT
- Demonstrate an ability to adequately prepare all electrode and treatment sites for all forms of electrode placement
- Describe the difference between different electrode placements, highlighting strengths and weakness
- Describe the different types of ECT highlighting the benefits and limitations of each method
- Understand potential drug interactions with ECT
- Understand the basic science and research evidence that underpin ECT
- Administer different types of ECT in a competent and professional manner
- Demonstrate basic knowledge of EEG monitoring and the relevant parameters involved in clinical decision-making
- Demonstrate an ability to work with the ECT team, recognising the specific tasks and roles of each team member
- Identify the challenges that are encountered in setting up an ECT service
- Describe the principles involved with ECT anaesthesia and recovery
- Describe the rationale behind using different induction agents and their impact on the quality of ECT administered
- Demonstrate an ability to liaise with inpatient and community teams concerning relevant issues involved with the delivery of ECT

the use of ECT in either an acute or chronic patient. At completion of the module the ECT coordinator conducts a workplace assessment by completing a direct observation of procedural skills (DOPS) form. The candidate gives a PowerPoint presentation on a ECT topic that is clinically relevant and of interest to them. The final assessment is the completion of an open book exam followed by an interactive discussion of the results. All questions are taken out of *The Electroconvulsive Therapy Workbook*. Robust discussion is more important to complete the EPA than the final test score.

CLINICAL WISDOM 1.1.2

It is not an exaggeration to say that ECT has opened a new reality for me. I used to deny when a depressive episode was coming on, to others and myself. I just could not face it. I thought if I ignored it, it might go away on its own. Now I know there is something that will work and work quickly. It takes away the anticipation and the fear. . . . It has given me a sense of control, of hope.

(Dukakis and Tye, 2006)

Table 1.1.3 Medical Competency Checklist

Competency criterion	Competent	(tick)	Comments
Knowledge			
History	_____	____	_____
Recent developments	_____	____	_____
Legal aspects/legislation	_____	____	_____
Drug interactions	_____	____	_____
Clinical indications	_____	____	_____
Risk situations	_____	____	_____
The sequence of ECT	_____	____	_____
Adverse events	_____	____	_____
Anaesthesia	_____	____	_____
Other	_____	____	_____
Administrative skills			
Clinical governance	_____	____	_____
Treatment schedule	_____	____	_____
ECT facilities	_____	____	_____
ECT documentation	_____	____	_____
Clinical skills			
Patient interaction	_____	____	_____
Staff interactions	_____	____	_____
Informed consent	_____	____	_____
Patient rapport	_____	____	_____
Communication with staff	_____	____	_____
Technical skills			
ECT clinical pathway	_____	____	_____
ECT technique	_____	____	_____
Equipment	_____	____	_____
Basic steps			
Set dose/charge	_____	____	_____
Skin preparation	_____	____	_____
Cuff monitoring/ILT	_____	____	_____
Monitoring lead placement	_____	____	_____
Treatment lead placement	_____	____	_____
Testing impedance	_____	____	_____
Baseline determination	_____	____	_____
Labelling the trace	_____	____	_____
Role of anaesthetic agents	_____	____	_____
Team consultation about current treatment	_____	____	_____
Pre deep tendon knee reflex (DTKR)	_____	____	_____
Observe fasciculations	_____	____	_____
Post DTKR	_____	____	_____
Recheck impedance	_____	____	_____
Ensure mouth guard placement	_____	____	_____
Team consent to treat	_____	____	_____
Administer ECT	_____	____	_____

Table 1.1.3 continued

Competency criterion	Competent	(tick)	Comments
Stimulus dosing			
Titration protocol	_____	____	_____
Determining dose/charge	_____	____	_____
Dosing strategies:			
Stimulus dose titration	_____	____	_____
Stimulus parameters:			
Pulse width	_____	____	_____
Seizure threshold	_____	____	_____
Subconvulsive stimulation	_____	____	_____
Electroencephalogram (EEG)			
EEG wave forms	_____	____	_____
Phases of EEG	_____	____	_____
Interpretation of EEG	_____	____	_____
When to change dose	_____	____	_____
Markers of seizure adequacy:			
• Postictal suppression index (PSI)	_____	____	_____
• Average seizure energy index (SEI)	_____	____	_____
• Maximum sustained power (MSP)	_____	____	_____
• Maximum sustained coherence (MSC)	_____	____	_____
Impedance – static/dynamic	_____	____	_____
EEPRS	_____	____	_____
EEG artefacts	_____	____	_____
Electrode placement (EP)			
Choice of EP	_____	____	_____
Right/left unilateral	_____	____	_____
Bifrontal	_____	____	_____
Bitemporal	_____	____	_____
Left anterior right temporal	_____	____	_____
Criteria for altering EP	_____	____	_____
New directions			
Magnetic seizure therapy	_____	____	_____
Transcranial magnetic stimulation	_____	____	_____

Trainee comments: _____

_____

Signature: _____

Director of ECT comments: _____

_____

Signature: _____

ECT coordinator's comments: _____

_____

Signature: _____

Date: _____

REFERENCES

Cate, O.T., and Sheele, F. (2007). Entrustable professional activities. (EPA). *Academic Medicine, 82*, 542–547.

Chief Psychiatrist of Western Australia. (2015). Chief Psychiatrist's practice standards for the administration of electroconvulsive therapy. Retrieved from www.chief psychiatrist.wa.gov.au/wp-content/uploads/2015/2/ CP_ECT_Standards_2015.pdf.

Cohen, M., and Port, N. (2012). Competency based fellowship program (CBFP) for supervisors workshop: overview of the CBFP. Hunter New England Local Health District, Newcastle, Australia. Retrieved from www.ranzcp.org/trainingprogram.aspx.

Duffett, R., and Lelliott, P. (1998). Auditing electroconvulsive therapy. The third cycle. *British Journal of Psychiatry, 172*(5), 401–405. Retrieved from www.ncbi.nlm.nih.gov/pubmed/ 9747401.

NICE. (2003). *Guidance on the Use of Electroconvulsive Therapy (Vol. Guidance Number 59)*. London: National Institute for Health and Care Excellence; National Health Service.

NSW Health. (2010). ECT minimum standard of practice NSW. Retrieved from www.health.nsw.gov.au/policies/pd/2011/ pdf/PD2011_003.pdf.

Rose, D., Fleischmann, P., Wykes, T., Leese, M., and Bindman, J. (2003). Patients' perspectives on electroconvulsive therapy: systematic review. *British Medical Journal, 326*(7403), 1363. doi:10.1136/bmj.326.7403.1363.

Royal College of Psychiatrists. (2015). *ECT Accreditation Service (ECTAS): Standards for the Administration of ECT,* 12th edition. London: Royal College of Psychiatrists.

SA Health. (2014). South Australian guidelines for electroconvulsive therapy. Retrieved from www.sahealth.sa.gov.au/ wps/wcm/connect/0608270046ad5b01b89.

Scheele, F., Teunissen, P., Van Luijk, S., Heineman, E., Fluit, L., Mulder, H., ... Hummel, T. (2008). Introducing competency-based postgraduate medical education in the Netherlands. *Medical Teaching, 30*(3), 248–253. doi:10.1080/ 01421590801993022.

Scott, A.I.F. (2005). *The ECT Handbook,* 2nd edition. London: Royal College of Psychiatrists.

UK ECT Review Group. (2003). Efficacy and safety of electroconvulsive therapy in depressive disorders: a systematic review and meta-analysis. *Lancet, 361*, 799–808.

Victorian Government. (2014). Mental Health Act 2014 handbook. Retrieved from www.health.vic.gov.au/mental health/mhact2014.

Waite, J., and Easton, A. (2013). *The ECT Handbook,* 3rd edition. London: Royal College of Psychiatrists.

Definition

ECT is a treatment that has spaned nearly 80 years. During that time it has been given many different names, including Electroconvulsive Therapy (ECT), electroseizure therapy (EST), electoshock and convulsive therapy (CT) (Fink, 2009). Some of these names were not accurate and contributed significantly to the stigma associated with the treatment. Fink (2009) notes that electroshock is not an accurate term as there is no shock involved in ECT. It originated in 1933, when insulin was first used to treat schizophrenia and patients did show classic signs of "surgical shock", including sweating, pallor and lowered levels of consciousness, and it was called insulin shock treatment. Seizure therapy, known as convulsion therapy, followed a year later, with the electrical induction of seizures in 1938 being termed "Electroshock" (Fink, 2009). Electroconvulsive Therapy (ECT), now the preferred name, has been used more recently to describe the treatment.

Over the years, the term shock treatment has remained popular and used by the media to gain immediate attention and instant recognition following its use in the movie *One Flew Over the Cuckoo's Nest* (Kesey, 1962). The term continues to be used by the media to stigmatise and denigrate the treatment (Bucci, 2009; De Brito, 2004) or portray a more balanced report (Brockie, 2013; Morrison, 2009). The popularity of the term is reflected in the book *Shock: The Healing Power of Electroconvulsive Therapy* (Dukakis and Tye, 2006), which provides a balanced view of ECT, interweaving the history of

ECT with a positive account of a consumers personal experience of the treatment that saved her life. Unfortunately the term "shock" carries with it the notion that the treatment is painful, an image that is widely used by the Citizens Commission on Human Rights, established in 1969, to "investigate and expose criminal and abusive practices of psychiatrists" (Church of Scientology, 2015).

Painful electric shocks were used as aversion therapy as part of the early developments of operant conditioning (Wilson and Davison, 1969). Operant conditioning was a technique that used positive stimuli to reward positive behaviours and negative stimuli to inhibit unwanted or negative behaviours like headbanging, unwanted screaming in intellectually disabled patients and self-injurious behaviours. The initial stimulus for aversion conditioning was chemical and its move into painful electric shocks was controversial (Wilson and Davison, 1969).

As the science of psychology progressed, aversion therapy was applied to a range of other "deviant" behaviours: homosexuality and other sexual deviations (Feldman, 1966), compulsive gambling (Barker and Miller, 1968) and changing the sexual object choice through controlling masturbation (Marquis, 1970). The stigma associated with these abandoned and now discredited treatments fuels the persistent stigma associated with ECT (Torpey, 2016).

Further confusion comes from "electroconvulsive shock" (ECS), a term used to describe the

CLINICAL WISDOM 1.2.1

One of the biggest challenges that ECT faces in modern times is the stigma that remains prevalent throughout the community. The multiple terms and definitions that have been applied to this treatment have actively contributed to this prejudice. The advent of neuromodulation and more specifically neurostimulation has placed ECT into a context that enhances understanding of how it works challenging misinformation enabling the development of new and more focal techniques like Focal Electrical Administered Seizure Therapy (FEAST).

Photo 1.2.1 *Aversion stimulator*

experimental induction of seizures in animals models that were designed to maximise the concordance of experimental animal studies with the clinical use of ECT (Nutt and Glue, 1993).

The journal *Convulsive Therapy* was established in April 1985 to provide a scientific platform for ECT research and discussion (McCall, Kellner and Fink, 2014). The foundation editor focused on convulsive therapy rather than other, more stylish areas of research because the practice was being actively challenged by both professionals and public attacks. Governments in many states and countries around the world condemned the practice enthused by the many new drugs and new forms of psychotherapy that were being developed to treat depression and psychosis (McCall et al., 2014).

The journal was called *Convulsive Therapy* as this was the most descriptive and least pejorative term when compared to other common terms used to describe ECT at that time, "shock therapy, electroshock and seizure therapy" (McCall et al., 2014). The goal of the journal was to provide a forum for ongoing debate and argument, systematic observation, comparison, deduction and verification of experiences with seizures and psychotic behaviour (Fink, 1985). Over the years, ECT has embraced modern anaesthetic practice, which has largely abolished the convulsion, the outward

muscular manifestations of a seizure. Acknowledging this change in clinical practice and the increased trend to call the procedure ECT to overcome stigma, the journal changed its name to the *Journal of ECT* in 1998 (McCall et al., 2014).

Electroconvulsive Therapy has been defined as a medical procedure that involves the electrical induction of a series of generalised grand mal seizures, under general anaesthesia, with the specific aim of bringing about therapeutic remission in patients suffering from episodes of specific mental disorders such as major depression, mania and certain types of schizophrenia. Contrary to the views expressed by critics of the procedure, ECT is not subconvulsive electrical stimulation of the brain, or administration of aversive electrical stimuli for behaviour modification treatment. It is not invasive, no tissue is incised or removed, and therefore it is not a surgical procedure. It does not result in any gross anatomical or histological lesions producing permanent brain damage.

It is believed that the brain's control of the seizure may be what makes ECT efficacious (Abrams, 2002). Seizure induction as a treatment for psychiatric illness was based upon early observations that symptoms of dementia praecox (schizophrenia) were diminished when patients developed epilepsy and that patients with epilepsy had a low incidence of psychosis (Mankad, Beyer, Weiner and Krystal, 2010).

Recent neuroscience reports have verified that repeated seizures create new neurons and enhance gliosis providing a further explanation as to why induced seizures are highly antimelancholic (Bolwig and Madsen, 2007).

REFERENCES

Abrams, R. (2002). *Electroconvulsive Therapy,* 4th edition. New York: Oxford University Press.

Barker, J.C., and Miller, M. (1968). Aversion therapy for compulsive gambling. *The Journal of Nervous and Mental Disease, 146*(4), 285–302. Retrieved from http://journals.lww. com/jonmd/Fulltext/1968/04000/AVERSION_THERAPY_ FOR_COMPULSIVE_GAMBLING_.2.aspx.

Bolwig, T.G., and Madsen, T.M. (2007). Electroconvulsive therapy in melancholia: the role of hippocampal neurogenesis. *Acta Psychiatrica Scandinavica Suppl, 433*, 130–135. doi:10.1111/j.1600-0447.2007.00971.x.

Brockie, J. (2013). Electro-shock. *SBS Insight.* Retrieved from www.sbs.com.au/news/insight/tvepisode/electroshock.

Bucci, N. (2009). Patient fears shock therapy. Retrieved from www.bendigoadvertiser.com.au/story/705391/patient-fears-shock-therapy.

Church of Scientology. (2015). Citizens Commission on Human Rights (CCHR). Retrieved from www.cchr.org/cchr-reports/ citizen-commission-on-human-rights/introduction.html.

De Brito, K. (2004). It has a brutal history. We don't know if it works. So why are we still using electric shock therapy? *Australian Report Marie Claire Magazine.*

Dukakis, K., and Tye, L. (2006). *Shock: The Healing Power of Electroconvulsive Therapy.* New York: Penguin.

Feldman, M.P. (1966). Aversion therapy for sexual deviations: A critical review. *Psychological Bulletin, 62*(2), 65–79. doi:10.1037/h0022913.

Fink, M. (1985). Convulsive therapy. *Convulsive Therapy, 1*(1), 1–3.

Fink, M. (2009). *Electroconvulsive Therapy: A Guide for Professionals and Their Patients.* New York: Oxford University Press.

Kesey, K. (1962). *One Flew Over the Cuckoo's Nest.* Retrieved from www.goodreads.com/author/show/7285.Ken_Kesey.

McCall, W.V., Kellner, C.H., and Fink, M. (2014). Convulsive therapy and the *Journal of ECT*: 30 years of publication and continuing. *Journal of ECT, 30*(1), 1–2. doi:10.1097/YCT. 0000000000000107.

Mankad, M.V., Beyer, J.L., Weiner, R.D., and Krystal, A. (2010). *Clinical Manual of Electroconvulsive Therapy.* Washington, DC: American Psychiatric Publishing.

Marquis, J.N. (1970). Orgasmic reconditioning: changing sexual object choice through controlling masturbation fantasies. *Journal of Behavior Therapy and Experimental Psychiatry, 1*(4), 263–271. doi:10.1016/0005-7916(70)90050-9.

Morrison, L. (2009). ECT: shocked beyond belief. *Australasian Psychiatry, 17*(2), 164–167. doi:10.1080/10398560802 596090.

Nutt, D.J., and Glue, P. (1993). The neurobiology of ECT: animal studies. In Coffey, E.C. (Ed.), *The Clinical Science of Electroconvulsive Therapy* (Vol. 38, pp. 213–234). Washington, DC: American Psychiatric Press.

Torpey, N. (2016). Special investigation: Shock treatment: Alarming spike in risky electroconvulsive therapy on children. *Sunday Mail* (Brisbane, Australia).

Wilson, G.T., and Davison, G.C. (1969). Aversion techniques in behavior therapy: some theoretical and metatheoretical considerations. *Journal of Consulting and Clinical Psychology, 33*(3), 327–329. doi:10.1037/h0027597.

Equipment

HISTORY: ECT DEVICES

Cerletti and Bini designed and built the first ECT device in Rome, Italy, in 1937 (Metastasio and Dodwell, 2013). In 1941, Dr H.M. Birch, with the assistance of C.R.Paul from the physics department at the University of Adelaide, built the first ECT device in Australia, which was used to treat patients with manic depression and schizophrenia at Glenside Hospital in South Australia (Website for the Virtual Museum, 2015).

C.R. Paul manufactured a second device in 1943 for Dr Dibden, who also worked at Glenside Hospital.

Dr H.M. Birch published an article in the *Medical Journal of Australia* on 20 June 1942 describing the physics involved in constructing the device, including a circuit diagram and a review of the first nine months of clinical use (Website for the Virtual Museum, 2015). The device used contemporary telecommunications technology incorporating a telephone dial that allowed the stimulus length to be varied. There were a number of different device manufacturers in Australia.

Photo 1.3.1 illustrates an ECT device manufactured by Techtron Appliances in Melbourne, while Photo 1.3.2 illustrates an ECT device manufactured by "BOTH" and sold in Adelaide and Sydney.

Dr H.M. Birch recognised that the effective dose of the alternating current may differ between

Photo 1.3.1 *Dial-up ECT device*

Source: Rodman & Kelame electro medical instrument makers, Sydney

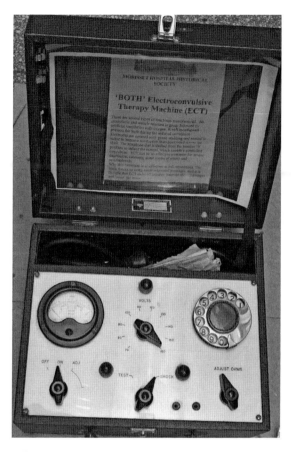

"There are several types of machines manufactured. An anaesthetic and muscle relaxant is given followed by artificial ventilation with oxygen. A soft mouth guard protects the teeth during the induced convulsion. Electrodes are covered with gauze wadding and soaked in saline to improve conduction then positioned across the skull. The telephone dial is dialed from the number '9' position to induce the current, which causes a controlled convulsion. ECT can be an effective treatment for severe depression, catatonia, some forms of mania and schizophrenia.

Why this treatment is so effective is still mysterious. The brain functions using electrochemical messages, and it is thought that ECT-induced seizures interrupt these messages and 'reset' the brain."

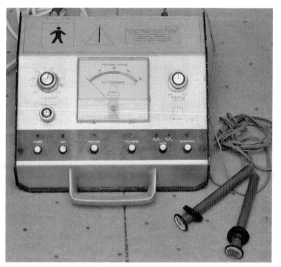

■ **Photo 1.3.3** *Sine wave ECT device*

patients owing to the impact of the skin, tissue and bony structures, allowing the stimulus to be adjusted, an early acknowledgement of seizure threshold (Website for the Virtual Museum, 2015).

The telephone dial-up device from the 1950s illustrated in Photos 1.3.1and 1.3.2 was used at Morisset Hospital until the 1960s, when it was replaced by a sine wave ECT device shown in Photo 1.3.3.

Sine wave devices such as that illustrated in Photo 1.3.3 replaced the dial-up instrument in most

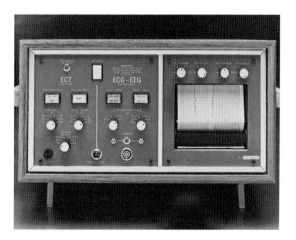

■ **Photo 1.3.4** *MECTA Model C*

hospitals administering ECT at that time around the world.

Oregon Health Sciences University (OHSU), Portland, Oregon, developed the original MECTA, an acronym meaning Monitored Electro-Convulsive Therapy Apparatus, to counter the ECT stigma that had ramped up against ECT in the 1970s within the USA. Dr Paul Blachly was concerned that patients were getting inferior treatment and required a new device with built-in safety features: a self-test to assure adequate patient electrode connections before being allowed to treat to avoid skin burns, a bidirectional pulse width one tenth of the energy of competitive Medcraft and Reider sine wave devices, and two monitoring channels. MECTA (MECTA Corporation, 2015). Such innovation changed the practice of ECT. What is disturbing but common in the development of ECT is how slowly new technology gets incorporated into clinical practice. This is well illustrated in the community study of ECT, where some centres continued to use sine wave devices across the state of New York even after the year 2000 (Sackeim et al., 2007).

The original MECTA Model C device, illustrated in Photo 1.3.4, was developed in 1973 by Oregon Health Sciences University and sold by the MECTA Corporation from 1980. The instrument was innovative as it was the first device to incorporate monitored electroencephalogram (EEG) and electrocardiogram (EKG) brief pulse into an ECT device. MECTA Model D, shown in Photo 1.3.5, was developed by the MECTA Corporation and introduced in 1981 and was quickly followed by

Photo 1.3.6 *MECTA Model JR-1*

Models JR-1, shown in Photo 1.3.6, JR-2, SR-1, illustrated in Photo 1.3.7, and SR-2, which were developed by MECTA in collaboration with the Columbia University and released in 1985, a collaboration that lasted until 2006. These devices dominated the US market for 13 years and lead to substantial improvement in clinical practice. These devices were eventually replaced by new devices in 1998 (MECTA Corporation, 2015).

In the United Kingdom, the device market was dominated by ECTRON Limited, which was set up by a psychiatrist, Robert Russell, in 1950. Devices have evolved from the Ectnos and Ectonustim series to the current model Ectonustim Series 6+ ECT device (ECRON Limited, 2016). In more recent years, the UK, like many other ECT services worldwide, has incorporated Thymatron and MECTA devices into their practice.

Photo 1.3.5 *MECTA Model D*

Photo 1.3.7 *MECTA Model SR-1*

In Australia, the sine wave devices were replaced with a Kabtronics unit, which incorporated brief-pulse, square wave technology, an innovation that reduced the level of cognitive impairment in patients having ECT (Spanis and Squire, 1981). The Kabtronics device is illustrated in Photo 1.3.8.

It was manufactured locally using electrical fittings manufactured by Clipsal, a large Australian company. The device utilised a Y-shaped, fixed handheld unilateral electrode that incorporated both mental discs with a switch built into the top of the yoke, allowing the stimulus to be delivered by direct pressure from the thumb, illustrated in Photo 1.3.9. In many centres, these electrodes replaced the rubber band and metal disc system that was commonly used at that time and is illustrated in Photo 1.3.10.

Theoretically it was a useful innovation; however, the electrodes could not be adjusted to suit

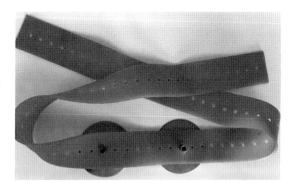

Photo 1.3.10 *Rubber band and metal electrodes*

Photo 1.3.11 *Thymatron DGx ECT device*

individual patient variability, with treatment often being administered using the wrong electrode site, Lancester rather than the d'Elia position (d'Elia, 1970; Lancester, Steinert and Frost, 1958). There were safety issues concerning the built-in switch, which could be easily pushed accidentally.

Incorporating an EEG into the ECT instrument increased the clinical power to deliver effective ECT rather than sole reliance on the length of motor end point, a feature that has failed to have clinical utility (Abrams, 2002; Mayer, 2006).

The EEG facilitates discrimination between electrode positions and different stimulus doses. It can predict treatment response and changes in the EEG that may indicate threshold changes highlighting the need to increase the stimulus dose or reduce the anaesthetic induction agent. Postictal suppression or electrical silence is an important feature of the EEG that has strong clinical relevance as it has been shown to correlate with treatment efficacy (Mayer, 2006), illustrated in EEG 5.5.9.

Photos 1.3.11 and 1.3.12 illustrate two models of the Thymatron DGx device, which incorporated a two-channel EEG that was stored on a dual graph

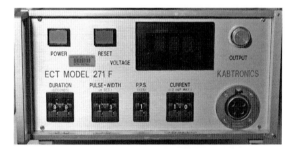

Photo 1.3.8 *Kabtronics ECT device*

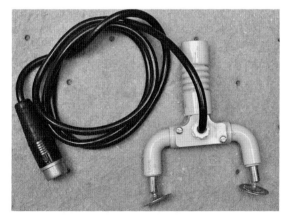

Photo 1.3.9 *Kabtronics ECT electrodes*

Photo 1.3.12 *More recent Thymatron DGx ECT device*

paper trace, developed in the late 1980s by Somatics, a US-based company (Somatics L.L.C., 2015). This was the first device widely used in Australia that incorporated an EEG with a stimulus that had a constant-current, square wave with a pulse width of 1.5 milliseconds (ms). A few years after it was released, Somatics released the Flexidial, which plugged into the back of the device, as shown in Photo 1.3.13. The Flexidial enabled the operator to change the frequency and pulse width and allowed the device to administer stimuli up to double the millicoulombs (mC) from 504 mC to 1008 mC (Somatics L.L.C., 2015).

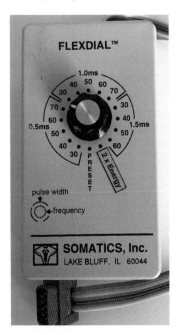

Photo 1.3.13 *Flexidial for Thymatron DGx ECT device*

It incorporated one- or two-channel EEG recording and calculated objective markers of seizure adequacy that were printed out at the end of the seizure when the recording device was turned off. It was the first attempt to provide objective measures to aid the clinician in determining whether a seizure had been of good quality or not. In the mid-1990s the Thymatron System IV replaced the Thymatron DGx. This device is illustrated in Photo 1.3.14.

In 1998, the MECTA Corporation released a series of competitive devices, the spECTrum 4000 and 5000M and Q, which replaced the SR and JR models. Like the Thymatron, these devices incorporated EEG data analysis to aid the clinician. The spECTrum 4000 was fully featured except it did not have EEG capacity, whereas the 5000 models had the capacity for six-channel recording. An early spECTrum 5000M device is illustrated in Photo 1.3.15.

The MECTA spECTrum 4000M and 5000M devices were similar to the Thymatron System IV, changing all of the stimulus parameters with a single dial to determine the stimulus charge. The MECTA spECTrum 4000Q and 5000Q required the ECT practitioner to set each stimulus parameter –

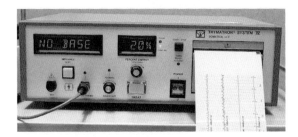

Photo 1.3.14 *Thymatron System IV ECT device*

Photo 1.3.15 *MECTA spECTrum 5000M ECT device*

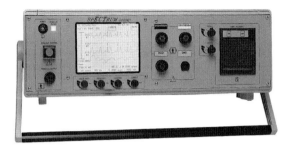

Photo 1.3.16 *MECTA spECTrum 5000Q ECT device*

pulse width, duration, frequency and voltage – separately. The spECTrum 5000Q is illustrated in Photo 1.3.16. Photo 1.3.17 illustrates the MECTA spECTrum 5000 digital display options.

In Australia, the common use of MECTA devices in clinical practice has been a recent phenomenon with the release of the spECTrum 5000M and Q. MECTA SR and JR devices were used in a few centres but there were no ELCRON devices sold, with the market being dominated by a locally produced device made by Kabtronics.

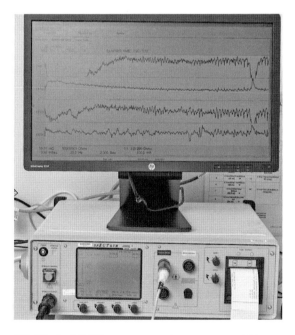

Photo 1.3.17 *MECTA spECTrum 5000Q ECT device with digital display*

The new Thymatron System IV device had other features that were clinically useful. "System IV" referred to the capacity to record information from four different channels, generating a more comprehensive trace: two EEG channels as well as channels for an electromyogram (EMG) and an electrocardiogram (ECG). The Thymatron System IV device generated a larger number of markers of seizure adequacy, which were designed to assist the clinician in assessing the adequacy of the seizure obtained. Tables 5.5.1 and 5.5.2 illustrate the markers of seizure adequacy for the Thymatron DGx and Table 5.5.3 for the MECTA spECTrum 5000 devices.

ECT DEVICE CHARACTERISTICS

The Thymatron System IV, MECTA spECTrum 5000 and Ectonustim Series 6 share similar specifications. They all deliver a constant current while the voltage varies according to the impedance (electrical resistance) offered by the head of the patient during the application of the electrical stimulus. The advantage of a constant-current delivery system is that the clinician is guaranteed a predetermined charge, independent of fluctuations and impedance. The delivered charge will be inversely proportional to the impedance in the circuit, following Ohm's law (American Psychiatric Association, 2001). Careful skin preparation of all sites is required to maximise electrode contact before the electrodes are attached to minimise the impedance and reduce voltage and the risk of burns. All devices offer handheld electrodes, with the ECRON and MECTA incorporating the treatment button within the handle of one treating electrode so that the stimulus can be applied without touching the device. Care must be taken not to accidentally hit the switch prematurely. The Thymatron System IV is the only device to offer disposable treatment electrodes, an innovation that reduces stigma, heralding ECT as a modern medical practice.

All devices have the potential for recording an EEG. The Ectonustim Series 6 device and the MECTA 4000 series do not have built-in EEG recording facilities. Both the MECTA 5000 series and the Thymatron System IV device have built-in channels for recording. All MECTA 5000 devices print only two recorded channels but have the capacity to store six channels of information. By contrast, the Thymatron "System IV" refers to its capacity to record information from four different channels generating a more comprehensive trace: two EEG channels as well as channels for an electro-myogram (EMG) and an electrocardiogram (ECG). The device also generated a larger number of markers of seizure adequacy, which were designed to assist the clinician in assessing the adequacy of the seizure obtained.

All devices offer simular stimulus ranges. The Ectonustim Series 6 offers a range from 50 to 1000 millicoulombs and claims to have a feature called Auto Crescendo, which delivers an advanced 0.25-second auto crescendo onset that gently eases the patients into ECT (ECRON Limited, 2016). This device also claims an advantage over the other devices with its split pulse technology, where each pulse group consists of a single 1-millisecond (ms) pulse followed by two pulses of 0.6 ms as well as offering a mode for non-convulsive stimulation, a low-voltage unidirectional sine wave stimulus that may be used to give a counter-stimulus after ECT. The Ectonustim Series 6+ delivers different ranges of ECT output: low range, 50 to 750 mC at 750 mA, and high range, 200 to 1000 mC at 900 mA (ECRON Limited, 2016).

The MECTA spECTrum 5000 has a stimulus range from 22.9 to 1152 millicoulombs, whereas the Thymatron System IV range is from 25 to 1008 millicoulombs.

All devices have the capacity to measure static and dynamic impedance to ensure effective treatment. Static impedance needs to be manually assessed through pushing a button on the Thymatron device, whereas it is automatically displayed on the other two devices.

REFERENCES

Abrams, R. (2002). *Electroconvulsive Therapy*, 4th edition. New York: Oxford University Press.

American Psychiatric Association. (2001). *The Practice of Electroconvulsive Therapy: Recommendations for Treatment, Training and Privileging: A Task Force Report*, 2nd edition. Washington, DC: American Psychiatric Association.

d'Elia, G. (1970). Unilateral electroconvulsive therapy. *Acta Psychiatrica Scandinavica, Supplement 215*, 1–98.

ECRON Limited. (2016). Ectonustim Series 6+.

Lancester, N.P., Steinert, R.R., and Frost, I. (1958). Unilateral electro-convulsive therapy. *Journal of Mental Science, 104*, 221–227.

Mayer, P. (2006). Ictal electroencephalographic characteristics during electroconvulsive therapy: a review of determination and clinical relevance. *Journal of ECT, 22*(3), 213–217.

MECTA Corporation. (2015). spECTrum 5000Q – MECTA Corp. Retrieved from www.mectacorp.com/spectrum-5000Q.html.

Metastasio, A., and Dodwell, D. (2013). A translation of "L'Elettroshock" by Cerletti and Bini, with an introduction. *The European Journal of Psychiatry, 27*(4). doi:10.4321/S0213-61632013000400001.

Sackeim, H.A., Prudic, J., Fuller, R., Keilp, J., Lavori, P.W., and Olfson, M. (2007). The cognitive effects of electro-convulsive therapy in community settings. *Neuropsycho-pharmacology, 32*(1), 244–254. doi:10.1038/sj.npp.1301180.

Somatics L.L.C. (2015). Somatics, LLC – manufacturer of the Thymatron ECT machine. Retrieved from www.thymatron.com/main_home.asp.

Spanis, C.W., and Squire, L.R. (1981). Memory and convulsive stimulation: effects of stimulus waveform. *American Journal of Psychiatry, 138*(9), 1177–1181. Retrieved from www.ncbi.nlm.nih.gov/pubmed/7270720.

Website for the Virtual Museum. (2015). Electroconvulsive therapy (ECT): The South Australian experience: 1942. Retrieved from http://samhs.org.au/Virtual Museum/Medicine/drugs_nonsurg/ect/ect.html.

CHAPTER 2

Knowledge

History: treatment of mental illness

From very early times, physicians, witch doctors, apothecaries and charlatans have searched for methods of understanding and improving people's general health and sense of well-being or treating mental illness specifically. The principal methods employed included: trepanning, phlebotomy/purging, pharmacology, phrenology and electricity.

TREPANNING: EARLY PSYCHOSURGERY?

Trepanning was a technique that involved cutting holes into the skull. Trepanning tools, a skull and a photograph of the outcome are illustrated in Photos 2.1.1. and 2.1.2. From ancient times, trepanning had an enthusiastic following for many years and we know it was carried out successfully as trepanned skulls of early man have been found with healed bone edges. Although still used for

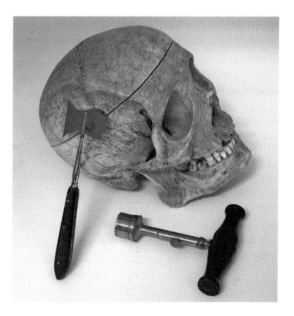

Photo 2.1.1 *Trepanning with skull*

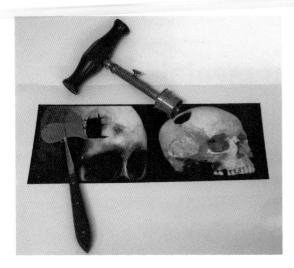

Photo 2.1.2 *Trepanning with tools and image*

legitimate reasons – for example, depressed fractures, removing blood clots and neurosurgery – it was particularly popular in the middle ages for treatment of vague headaches and to release evil spirits that were blamed for causing various derangements of the mind. It continued to be practised regularly, well into the eighteenth century.

The piece of bone removed was even pulverised and drunk as a therapeutic elixir when mixed with various liquids! There is no evidence that trepanation actually had any benefit for treatment of mental illness and in the early days of primitive instruments, no anaesthetic and poor hygiene the risks would have far outweighed any possible benefit.

BLOODLETTING

Bloodletting tools and a map that was used to guide treatment are illustrated in Photo 2.1.3. Bloodletting was one of medicine's earliest and most widely practised treatments. Even before the fifth century AD, surgeons and barbers practised bloodletting, which is reflected in the barber's red and white pole, red signifying blood and white the tourniquet.

"Cutting of a vein", or "airing a vein", was a logical treatment when based on a prevailing theory of four bodily "humours" – blood, phlegm, yellow

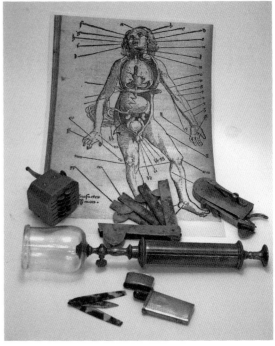

Photo 2.1.3 *Bloodletting*

bile and black bile. Excessive humours caused fever, inflammation and general debility so purging or bloodletting would rid the patient of this excess and restore the balance. Good health was just a lancet puncture away.

It was particularly popular in the eighteenth and nineteenth centuries and is still used in some cultures, where it is often combined with "cupping", where the application of a heated "cup" results in an engorged area on the skin due to the vacuum created as the air in the cup cooled.

Generally an artery or vein was punctured with a lancet for a good yield and an average quantity of 500–900 ml to get rid of bad humours continued to the point of faintness. It was often permanent; for example, King Charles II succumbed to bleeding by physicians in 1685. On 14 December 1799, George Washington went to his death with a throat infection after receiving a series of medical procedures including draining nearly 40% (9 pints) of his blood.

Various instruments were used, the oldest being just a lancet. The lancet was a simple blade, sharp stick or a piece of bone. In order of chronology and complexity then came a fleam. The fleam was a selection of blades in a brass or horn sheath that was hit with a fleam-stick. The next was a spring lancet, a spring-loaded single blade, and finally the "scarifier". The scarifier was the epitome of sophisticated and efficient bleeding as it was equipped with multiple spring-loaded blades.

Charts were produced that instructed the operator where the most productive sites for bloodletting were in the body. For a time leeches were a popular way of blood letting, especially in

the mid-1800s. However, man-made instruments, sometimes known as "mechanical leeches", were more efficient and more popular.

Bloodletting was often combined with purging with various emetics to induce vomiting or enemas to flush out toxins. Purging practices were popular and still have a limited following in modern times. Photo 2.1.4 shows various bottles of different purges and emetics, with Photo 2.1.5 displaying a sophisticated enema tool.

None of these treatments demonstrated any significant benefit for treatment of any illness, let alone mental illness, except for a placebo effect.

PHARMACOLOGY

For many centuries, natural healers and physicians used various plant preparations that continue to form the base from which most of our current traditional and alternative medicines originate. Many of these drugs had some benefit in treating a range of conditions. Photo 2.1.6 illustrates a range of different products.

The nineteenth century brought an age of "science" but despite many advances these were mostly in the area of diagnosing disease rather than treating it. People became jaded with doctors, who arrived weighed down by the dignity and mystery of an ancient profession and murmured "there is no cure for this disease" as they took their fees.

Photo 2.1.4 Bottles of purges and emetics

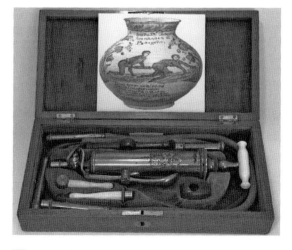

Photo 2.1.5 Enema tool

Photo 2.1.6 Medicines and remedies

With high mortality and difficult or expensive access to doctors and hospitals, for many sickness was the final tragedy.

In this context and in an age that enshrined free enterprise and the law being far from clear as to who could practise medicine, the stage was set for the most outrageous and unethical practices, which were cruel and exploited human suffering. Quack cures of no or minimal pharmacological benefit were pedalled from door to door all over the country and for the modest fee of £1 you could even have a consultation by mail. For example, one newspaper in the 1880s had advertisements for 54 medicines, 15 quack cures and 12 abortionists. An example is Dr Williams' Pink Pills, illustrated in Photo 2.1.7:

> If you are quickly tired, lack energy, feel weak in the back and always want something to lean upon; if you do not care for your food and cannot relish your work; if you are nervous and have headaches, Dr Williams' Pink Pills are the best tonic in the world—cannot harm the most delicate. They are not a purgative. They make people strong.

Practitioners with bogus qualification from bogus establishments made outrageous claims with little regard for the truth and testimonials were bought or faked. The modus operandi of the so-called "specialists" was to first terrify the patient with a list of ominous symptoms and then guarantee a cure at a price.

Positive outcomes were possible as many specialists claimed to cure "nervous ailments and the private results of youthful indiscretions", setting the scene for effective placebo treatments. Many such pharmacological cures at best did no harm, though most gave relief via alcohol or narcotics. The popular "woman's tonic" of *c*. 1900 had 16.8% alcohol and "Mrs Winslow's Soothing Syrup" for babies, 1850–1930, contained an opiate. The more the infant cried the more he got until . . . he stopped.

It was not until 1930–40s that pharmacological treatment of disease gained credibility and could be used reliably.

PHRENOLOGY

A German physician, Franz Joseph Gall, pictured in Photo 2.1.8, developed phrenology in 1796 (van Wyhe, 2002). It had some influence through to the late 1800s throughout Britain and Europe. Gall's hypothesis was that the brain is an organ of the mind and has various functions that relate to

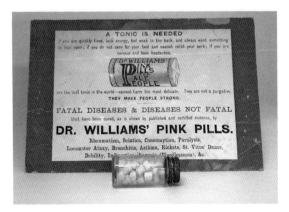

Photo 2.1.7 *Dr Williams' Pink Pills*

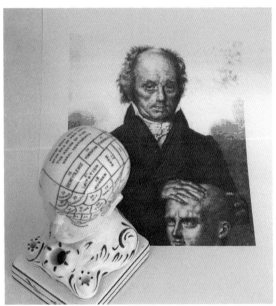

Photo 2.1.8 *Phrenology application*

different areas of the brain. These areas develop independently and are scientifically measurable by observing the contours of the skull after it has fused over the brain. Observation of the topography of the skull could be used to assess the state of various mental functions and give credence to various moral philosophies concerning the mentally ill, the superiority of various races, criminality and other things. Photo 2.1.9 shows a list of the phrenological faculties developed by Spurzheim in 1834, with a skull highlighting the location of each. The faculties were divided into two types, affective

and intellectual. There were two affective subtypes: propensities, which had 11 elements, and sentiments, with 12 parts. Likewise, intellectual faculties had two parts: perceptive, with 12 elements, and reflective, which contained comparison and causality.

Gall and his supporters used their observations to focus attempts to modify behaviour and, although his observations and treatments had little efficacy, his belief that various parts of the brain have different functions was a forerunner of modern neuropsychiatry.

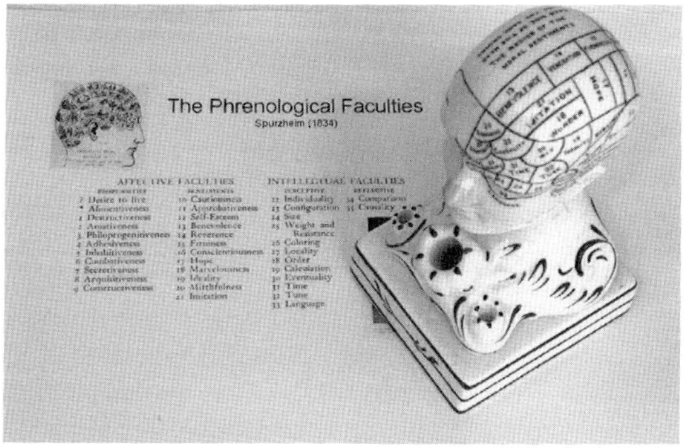

EARLY 1800s

Life was tough in the early 1800s, in stark contrast to today's world. Horses and carts abounded and the leading cause of death was infectious disease, accounting for 25% of all deaths (Fluit, 2006). Life expectancy was very short in the 1840s and medical care was rudimentary.

Fluit (2006) notes that only utter hopelessness or intense suffering would bring someone to seek surgical treatment. Dr Robert Liston 1840 is a good example of an early West End surgeon who developed a fearsome reputation for amputation using a surgical kit, as in Photo 2.1.10, and syringes, as in Photo 2.1.11 (Mental Floss, 2012). Other early equipment was beginning to appear, like the auriscope (Photo 2.1.12), stethoscopes (Photo 2.1.13) and slings (Photo 2.1.14).

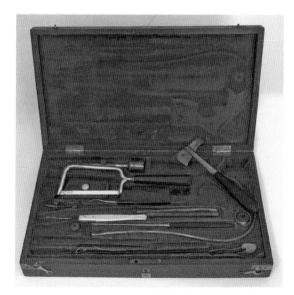

Photo 2.1.9 *The phrenological faculties*

Photo 2.1.10 *Surgical kit*

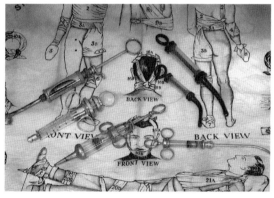

Photo 2.1.11 *Syringes*

Photo 2.1.12 *Auriscope*

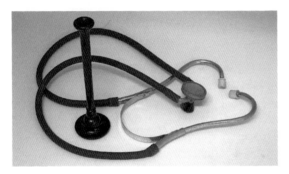

Photo 2.1.13 *Stethoscopes*

Anaesthesia was very basic, consisting of "a good soaking of the internal organs with brandy and opium that was often shared by the assistants", with a typical outcome being fatal for more than just the patient (Fluit, 2006) Anaesthetic agents and techniques progressed with the advent of chloroform (Photo 2.1.15). In the late nineteenth century, surgery took place in a room with spectators sitting on benches rising in a semicircle around the table, giving rise to the term operating "theatre". There was no concept of sterility or infection control.

In August 1865, Dr Joseph Lister applied a piece of lint dipped in carbolic acid solution onto a wound of an 11-year-old boy who had sustained a compound fracture after a cart wheel had passed over his leg. The treatment prevented infection and allowed the boy's bones to fuse back together. Following this success, the treatment spread and different applicators were developed to apply the soap (Photo 2.1.16).

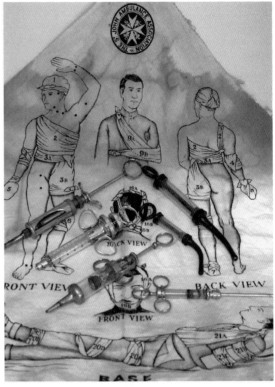

Photo 2.1.14 *Slings*

Photo 2.1.15 *Chloroform anaesthesia*

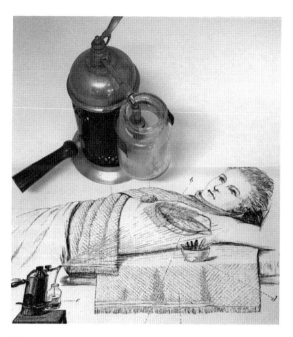

Photo 2.1.16 *Carbolic treatment*

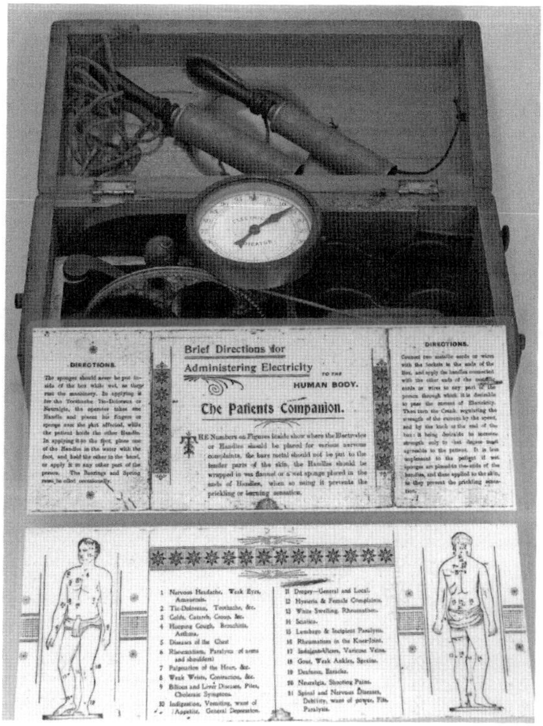

Photo 2.1.17 *Electrical stimulator*

ELECTRICITY

In order to understand the origins of ECT, it is useful to understand the history of electricity. Scribonius Largus, a Roman physician, described the first recorded use of electricity to treat human conditions (Scribonius Largus, AD 43). Headaches were treated by placing a large Mediterranean electrical sting ray, *torpedo mamorata* (Torpedo Mamorata, 1810), across the forehead of a patient and allowing the fish to discharge its "electricity until the patient's senses were a bit numbed". Placing the fish under the patient's foot before the electricity was discharged treated gout. Galan also used the shock of the torpedo fish to treat headaches and other pains and was enthusiastic about using it as a remedy for epilepsy (Finger, 2001).

In 1809, Humphry Davy, an English chemist, invented the first electric light; in 1875 the first electric light bulb was invented (Bellis, 2016) and the first electric trains appeared in England and Germany in 1885 (Duffy, 2003).

Everyone wanted to be part of this new phenomenon. Conventional doctors and quacks produced a wide variety of therapeutic electrical devices to replace the very common technique of bloodletting. The principle behind the new electrical devices was to administer an electrical stimulus with different intensities for different ailments. Photo 2.1.17 illustrates an early electrical stimulator with specific instructions:

Brief directions for administering electricity to the human body. The patients companion.

The Numbers on Figures inside show where the Electrodes or Handles should be placed for various nervous complaints, the bare metal should not be put to the tender parts of the skin, the Handles should be wrapped in wet flanuel or a wet sponge placed in the ends of Handles, when so using it to prevents the prickling or burning sensation.

Photo 2.1.18 *Galvanic stimulator*

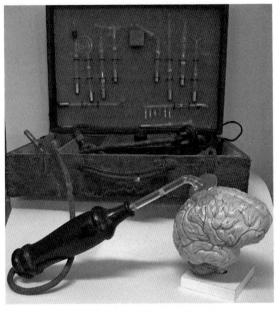

Photo 2.1.20 *Violet stimulator*

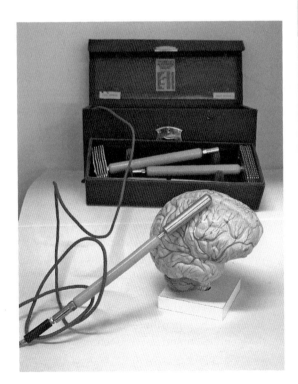

Photo 2.1.19 *Overbeck stimulator*

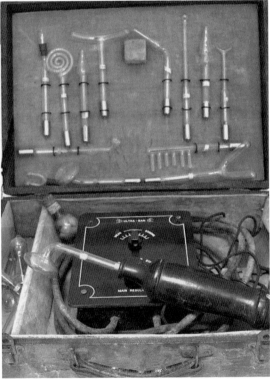

Photo 2.1.21 *Violet stimulation tray*

Photo 2.1.22 Griggs stimulator

Photo 2.1.23 Dr Scott's electric hair curler

Photo 2.1.24 White's electric comb

Over the next few years, newer and more elaborate devices developed: the galvanic stimulator (Photo 2.1.18), the Overbeck stimulator (Photo 2.1.19), the violet stimulator (Photo 2.1.20), the violet stimulator tray (Photo 2.1.21) and the Griggs stimulator (Photo 2.1.22).

Such devices could cure "nervousness, depression, brain fatigue, hysteria, functional irregularities, dyspepsia, kidney disorders and arthritis".

Photo 2.1.23 shows Dr Scott's electric hair curler and Photo 2.1.24 shows an electrical comb that was used to treat headaches. Other things available from a "Dr Scott" were electrical inner soles and an electric stomach pad. A *"Dr Carter Moford"* released a range of electrical applications for failing health. In particular, he had a "his and hers" electric belt.

In the latter half of the nineteenth century, British asylum doctors began to use various electrical methods to treat their patients. Clinical enthusiasm for electricity arose owing to the major developments during the Victorian era. These developments subsequently had a major impact on people's everyday lives. As a result, doctors were keen to harness the therapeutic purposes.

Asylum doctors believed that "electrotherapy might provide a technique that would distinguish themselves as serious men of science and strengthen their claim that they were the appropriate agents to provide the care of the mentally ill" (Fluit, 2006). Asylum doctors were facing an increasing number of patients being admitted to their institutions but lacked effective treatment. Doctors were also working hard to establish their professional credentials and social standing with the general public. However, the clinical application of electricity produced inconsistent and often disappointing results, with the technique being largely abandoned by the medical fraternity by the close of the nineteenth century (Beveridge and Renvoize, 1988).

REFERENCES

Bellis, M. (2016). The history of the incandescent lightbulb. Retrieved from http://inventors.about.com/od/famousinventions/fl/The-History-of-the-Incandescent-Light-Bulb.htm.

Beveridge, A., and Renvoize, E. (1988). Electricity: the history of its use and the treatment of mental illness in Britain in the second half of the nineteenth century. *British Journal of Psychiatry, 153,* 157–162.

Duffy, D.C. (2003). *Electric Trains 1880–1990.* London: The Institution of Engineering and Technology.

Finger, S. (2001). *Origins of Neuroscience: A History of Explorations into Brain Function.* London: Oxford University Press.

Fluit, J. (2006). Medical history: PowerPoint presentation; medical history 1800–1900.

Mental Floss. (2012). On the table with one of history's most infamous surgeons. Retrieved from http://mentalfloss.com/article/31514/table-one-history%E2%80%99s-most-infamous-surgeons.

Scribonius Largus. (AD 43). A physician and pharmacologist. Retrieved from http://penelope.uchicago.edu/~grout/encyclopaedia_romana/aconite/largus.html.

Torpedo Mamorata. (1810). Marbled electric ray. Retrieved from www.fishbase.org/summary/Torpedo-marmorata.html.

van Wyhe, J. (2002). The history of phrenology on the web. Retrieved from www.historyofphrenology.org.uk/fjgall.html.

History: ECT

Electroconvulsive Therapy has been an important and effective treatment in psychiatry for nearly three quarters of a century. Its effectiveness in a variety of psychiatric conditions has been established beyond doubt (Abrams, 2002). However, it remains a controversial treatment owing to its colourful history, intense stigma and, until recently, lack of systematic research (Editorial, 2003).

In 2006, Kitty Dukakis, wife of former Massachusetts governor and 1988 Democratic presidential nominee Michael Dukakis, collaborated with Larry Tye (a journalist) to write a book called *Shock: The Healing Power of Electroconvulsive Therapy* (Dukakis and Tye, 2006). The book cleverly documents the science of ECT and its origins over the last 80 years, interspersed with Kitty's own journey in beating the challenges of depression, addictions to alcohol and diet pills. They highlight that ECT continues to be a serious option for treating life-threatening illnesses. Kitty stated, "now I know that there is something that will work and work quickly. It takes away the anticipation and fear . . . it has given me a sense of control, of hope."

The book identifies three aspects of ECT that contribute to the stigma associated with the treatment. It identifies the "unholy trinity": electricity, convulsions and memory loss. It goes on to say: "Each are powerful and frightening images . . . multiply by three and you have already made horror . . . toddlers are told never to put fingers near electrical socket . . . epileptics are treated like lepers . . . Alzheimer's disease is the scariest disease of all". These images dramatically illustrate the intense feelings and emotions that are associated with ECT treatment. Further examples of these emotions are demonstrated in the following excerpts of poetry taken from Walter, Fisher and Harte (2002): "Fear they want to jump start me!";

"Confusion, will she forget everything?"; "Secrecy, nobody must know"; "Hope, the scent of fruit and the buzz of honey bees return to me . . . my brain begins to rev, the starter motor works."

The book by Dukakis and Tye (2006) provides further clarity about ECT, highlighting the historical and scientific point of view as well as providing a moving and real-life account of its clinical applications.

These issues are developed further by Kivler (2010), in her book *Will I Ever Be the Same Again? Transforming the Face of ECT (Shock Therapy)*. In this book she recalls her first response to the thought of having ECT: "Shock therapy? Are you kidding me? No way!" It's "barbaric", "Something only the craziest and most unstable people would undergo". Thoughts of the movie *One Flew Over the Cuckoo's Nest* filled her mind as she commented "people who get that treatment end up staring into space forever. . . . They sit and rock and drool."

However, once they experience the healing power of the treatment they conclude, "ECT has not only saved my life, but has turned my life around" (Kivler, 2010). Kitty Dukakis said after her first session of seizure therapy that "I feel good – I feel alive . . . Feeling this good is truly amazing". Kitty's husband said, "ECT is our miracle" (Dukakis and Tye, 2006).

MENTAL ILLNESS AND CONVULSIONS

Paracelsus described the idea that convulsions might influence a course of mental illnesses as early as the sixteenth century (The European Graduate School, 2015). In the 1920s there was an unfounded belief that epilepsy was negatively correlated and that there might be an antagonism between them (Brain and Mind, 2015b). Ladislas J. Von Meduna, a Hungarian neurologist and neuropathologist (Brain and Mind, 2015b), correlated the brains of people with schizophrenia and epilepsy and concluded that there appeared to be a "biological antagonism" between the two brain diseases. He reasoned that "pure artificially induced epileptic convulsions would be able to cure schizophrenia" (Sabbatini, 2015; Stinson, 2006).

Many agents were trialled to see whether they could produce seizures consistently and effectively. In the eighteenth and nineteenth centuries, camphor was injected intramuscularly to induce a seizure (Kilogh, Smith and Johnson, 1988; Stinson, 2006). Complications included intense tremor and fear in patients owing to its delayed onset.

Sabbatini (2015) highlights that in Europe, between 1917 and 1935, four methods for producing physiological shock were discovered, tested and used in psychiatric practice.

Julius Wagner Von Jauregg, a Viennese neurologist, noted that "insane patients" improved considerably if they survived severe infective illnesses like typhoid fever, erisipella or tuberculosis (Brain and Mind, 2015a). He began a series of experiments aimed at inducing fevers in patients with "incurable diseases" like paresis (dementia paralyticus), caused by tertiary syphilis. It was a disease that was accompanied by marked neurological and mental disability (paranoia, delusions, loss of memory and disorientation), resulting in high numbers being admitted to the asylums of the day. At that time the cause of syphilis was unknown.

Initially, Julius Wagner Von Jauregg's experiments were unsuccessful, but in 1917 he inoculated nine patients who had paresis with blood taken from a soldier infected with malaria to give them a regular fever. Four patients achieved complete recovery and improvement was noted in two others, with a reduction in the intensity of the psychosis and physical symptoms (Sabbatini, 2015; Stinson, 2006).

Julius Wagner Von Jauregg then proceeded to devise and test a complex treatment protocol in 275 syphilitic patients who were at risk for paresis (Sabbatini, 2015). Out of this group of patients, the techniques he developed resulted in an 83% success rate. The technique was heralded as being a breakthrough in science and he received the 1927 Nobel Prize for Medicine for his work.

His work has been replaced by the discovery of the spirochetes and antibiotics. Nyiro and Jablonzky, who in 1932 took blood from people with schizophrenia and transferred it into patients with epilepsy with the aim of curing the epilepsy, developed the technique further. However, this technique was not successful (Kilogh et al., 1988; Stinson, 2006).

The second breakthough in using physical treatments to induce a seizure was in 1927. A young Polish neurophysiologist and neuropsychiatrist, Manfred J. Sakel, induced by injecting insulin a superficial coma in a woman addicted to morphine, who was able to recovery her mental facilities (Kilogh et al., 1988). Sakel's accidental discovery that an overdose of insulin causing a convulsion in patients with mental illness could improve patients who had psychosis and schizophrenia led to the development of the Sakel technique. The technique was perfected in Vienna, with 70% of patients improving. It was introduced to the USA in 1934, where two further studies were completed, leading to its spread worldwide. However, enthusiasm for the technique waned in favour of ECT as inducing a hypoglycaemic coma was dangerous and required constant medical care for five hours following each daily injection (Stinson, 2006).

In 1934, Ladislas J. Von Meduna, a Hungarian neurologist and neuropathologist, found that camphor was difficult to use as it resulted in terrible complications for the patient. After trialling various other drugs, he had success with pentilenetetrazol (cardiazol or mertrazol), an intravenous agent that had a faster onset of action and was less likely to cause multiple fits. Meduna began to apply the technique to patients with schizophrenia and affective psychosis (Sabbatini, 2015). However, the onset of the seizure was still delayed, resulting in intense fear and mounting anxiety in the patient prior to the loss of consciousness, making it a difficult procedure to administer (Sabbatini, 2015; Stinson, 2006).

In Rome in the 1930s, Ugo Cerletti, a neuropsychiatrist, and his registrar, Lucio Bini, began experimenting with using electricity to induce a seizure. They initially experimented with dogs using the ano-oral electrode placement technique.

However, this technique was dangerous as the electricity passed through the heart before entering the brain, resulting in the death of the dog (Kilogh et al., 1988). The technique was not safe for humans. Bini discovered a much safer technique after he visited the Rome abattoir. Here pigs were slaughtered in a more humane manner after being stunned with an electrical shock administered using electrodes that were placed in the bitemporal position. Once applied to dogs, they quickly realised that this position was safe and very effective and could be applied to humans, as examination of the canine brain did not reveal any histological damage (Stinson, 2006).

In March 1938, a 42-year-old man was brought into the neuropsychiatry hospital in Rome after being found wandering aimlessly at the railway station. He was psychotic, confused, incoherent, hallucinating and in a highly agitated distressed state. Cerletti and Bini made the diagnosis of schizophrenia. They determined that the patient should be treated with their new technique, called "electroshock treatment". The first treatment was administered on 11 April 1938. Three stimuli were applied with no effect. There was significant fear among staff about the technique and they put pressure on Cerletti and Bini not to do it again. However, this was overruled and the second attempt was made three days later using a higher dose of electricity that resulted in a grand mal seizure (Kilogh et al., 1988).

It was noted soon after recovery that the man was more lucid and coherent, able to engage in regular conversations. He was then given 11 further electroshock treatments with a very good outcome. After 11 treatments he made a full recovery and went back to work and his family. Cerletti and Bini demonstrated that electricity was a safe, simple and convenient technique that was easy to use compared to other earlier methods of chemical induction.

The discovery by Cerletti and Bini led to the rapid spread of ECT throughout the world. It was first given in Paris in 1939, in the US in 1940 and in the UK in 1944. It was first administered in Australia in 1941. Dr H.M. Birch, the superintendent at the large psychiatric institution in South Australia, developed an ECT device with the assistance of the physics department of the University of Adelaide.

It was not possible to import a device from Europe owing to the imminent threat of war. The original device remains on display in the Glenside Hospital Museum, Adelaide, South Australia (Emdler, 1988; Website for the Virtual Museum, 2015). After numerous problems, including overcoming power surges within the hospital, Dr Birch was able to successfully administer the treatment. By the end of the 1940s, ECT was widely administered throughout Australia and manufactured by Techtron and BOTH companies, which used Dr Birch's design, illustrated in Photos 1.3.1 and 1.3.2. Kilogh et al. (1988) noted that "physical treatments rendered curable, some who were formally incurable". However, not everyone agreed with this statement.

NEGATIVE IMAGES EMERGE

Over the next few years, people became worried about the morbidity associated with ECT, particularly with regard to broken bones or torn muscles (Kilogh et al., 1988). The reception of ECT into the United States was controversial owing to the strong influence of psychoanalysis and the disinclination of psychiatrists to use physical treatments (Emdler, 1988).

The distortion of public perception and the poor reputation of ECT was heightened by reports that ECT had been used as punishment (Kingman, 1993). There was also confusion between ECT and the use of electricity for non-convulsive purposes (Metastasio and Dodwell, 2013). In the 1960s, non-convulsive electricity was used clinically as an aversive stimulus in behaviour modification (Bancroft and Marks, 1968) and had been applied to gain conformity and obedience (Milgram, 1963).

There are reports that non-convulsive electricity was used for non-clinical purposes as torture in the 1950s and 1960s (Rejali, 2012).

In the 1960s and 70s, strong anti-psychiatry lobby groups appeared. ECT was described as "an assault on the vulnerable" (Szasz, 1961). For decades, Szasz (1973) publicly challenged "the excesses that obscure reason". He is known for his quote, "If you talk to God, you are praying; If God talks to you, you have schizophrenia" (Szasz, 1973).

In the 1960s, ECT was modified with the introduction of anaesthesia and muscle relaxants. However, some hospitals were slow to embrace this new approach, heightening the stigma associated with the procedure. At the same time, ECT went out of favour owing to the impact of new antipsychotic and antidepressant medication (Sabbatini, 2015). ECT re-emerged in the 1970s as psychiatrists sought ways to help the mentally ill who were unresponsive to psychotropic drugs and psychotherapy. Today, pharmacotherapy remains the first-line treatment for all serious psychiatric illness, with ECT being relegated to a treatment of "last resort" (NICE, 2003, Modified 2009; Waite and Easton, 2013).

In the 1960s, Ronald Hubble established the Church of Scientology (Russell Miller's "Bare-Faced Messiah", 2005). In 1969, the Citizens Commission on Human Rights (CCHR) was established (Church of Scientology, 2015). The CCHR is an international organisation with 125 chapters in 28 nations. Its mandate is to "investigate and expose the criminal abusive practices by psychiatrists". It collects ECT data from "the writings and testimonies of physicians, scientists and other experts highlighting the archetypical representation of biological psychiatry without consideration of humanity" (Church of Scientology, 2015). The group publishes regular monthly magazines that have graphic images with highly emotive titles like "ECT promotes breast cancer" and "Psychiatry Destroys Minds".

THE MEDIA FANS NEGATIVITY

ECT's reputation has been further challenged by its portrayal in the media over many years. Movies have left long-standing scars upon public attitudes even though the form of ECT depicted is no longer used. Media is the principal source of the community perspective. Portrayals of ECT in the media reflect and influence public attitudes. ECT has been depicted in many fiction and non-fiction films, songs and books. The depiction is usually extremely negative and dramatic. An example is an article by De Brito (2004) that featured in the popular magazine *Marie Claire* called the "Australian Report". This article has very dramatic and graphic photographs that are set to shock but the article lacks substance as it is based upon two case reports. It included a statement on the title page, "it has a brutal history. We don't know if it works. So why are we still using electroshock therapy?"(De Brito, 2004).

One of the first movies that depicted ECT was *The Snake Pit* by Antotole Litivak in 1948 (Lounsbery, 2013). This followed the path to recovery of Virginia Cunningham, a young writer who developed a psychosis soon after getting married. The true story of Jim Piersall, a baseball player who suffered a catatonic breakdown, is recounted in the 1957 movie *Fear Strikes Out* (Pakula, 1957). In both of these movies, ECT was portrayed as being helpful and adjunctive to psychotherapy.

One of the most powerful depictions of the use of ECT was portrayed in the 1975 *One Flew over the Cuckoo's Nest*, in which Jack Nicholson was given an Oscar for best actor (Filmsite Movie Review, 1975). The movie was based upon the 1962 book written by Ken Kessey (Kesey, 1962). The film went global and influenced community views for generations.

Psychiatry and ECT were portrayed in a negative and unsympathetic manner. The impact was unprecedented owing to its worldwide audience. In 1990, Janet Frame's life story was depicted in the movie *An Angel at my Table* (Campion, 1991).

Frame was a writer from New Zealand who wrote an autobiography of the time she spent in a psychiatric institution in New Zealand. As a child, Janet was different, described as a "funny-looking due to bad teeth and a mope of unruly scarlet hair" (Campion, 1991). She found it hard to socialise or date and was described as a loner. In the movie, she gets work as a teacher but things go wrong when a

school inspector comes into her class. A "panic attack" is misdiagnosed as schizophrenia and she is committed to a mental home for eight years. During that time she received over 200 ECT treatments, finding it hard to convince staff that she was "sane" and should be released from hospital.

Requiem for a Dream (2000) is a recent movie depicting the horrifying side of drug addition as it follows the desperation of four addicts chasing "the dragon" (Ebert, 2000). ECT is depicted as a grim and horrifying treatment, adding to the disturbing power of the movie.

In 2001, the film *A Beautiful Mind* portrayed Dr Nash, a brilliant mathematician who suffered from schizophrenia (Howard, 2001). The film depicts him having unmodified ECT but history suggests that he had insulin coma therapy instead (Brain and Mind, 2015c). This treatment was less dramatic and not a very good visual spectacle.

McDonald and Walter (2001) identify 22 American films from 1948 to 2000 that depicted ECT. Initially, ECT was portrayed as a severe intervention to relieve distress but gradually over time Hollywood has brutalised the treatment, making it more negative and cruel, leaving the observer with the impression that ECT is "brutal, harmful and abusive manoeuvre with no therapeutic benefit". McDonald and Walter highlight that the media has a powerful impact of social attitude and that it has done little to promote ECT as being a helpful therapeutic treatment. Instead, movies like *One Few Over the Cuckoo's Nest* put people off the treatment and promote high level of resistance in the majority of people (Walter and McDonald, 2004).

UNMODIFIED ECT

Unmodified ECT, or direct ECT, was a term given to ECT utilised in the 1940s and 50s that involved inducing a seizure without the use of muscle relaxation or anaesthesia (Chittaranjan et al., 2012). It is surprising, however, to note that unmodified ECT was still used in Western countries well after the development of suitable anaesthetic agents and muscle relaxants that could be used to modify the treatment. Thiopentone was discovered in 1934, methohexitone was first used by Stoelting in 1957 (Royal Adelaide Hospital, 2015) and suxamethonium developed in the 1940s and was widely used in the 1950s (Dorkins, 1982). However, it was not until the 1960s that unmodified ECT was abandoned in Western countries. It was the slow uptake of these agents that resulted in many of the long-standing scars on public attitudes, a history that has been difficult to overcome.

Unmodified ECT is still used in Third World countries owing to the scarcity and high cost of anaesthetic resources. Currently, in India there is intense debate about the continued use of this technique (Chittaranjan et al., 2012; Oliver Talks, January 2014; Skukla, 2000). A survey conducted by the Indian Psychiatric Society found that during 1991–1992 only 44.2% of respondents always administered modified treatments, 24.2% always administered unmodified treatments and the remainder administered modified or unmodified treatment (Chittaranjan et al., 2012). Little had changed in a more recent survey completed in 2001–2002, where unmodified ECT treatment was given in 52% of treatments administered in 66 university teaching hospitals (Chittaranjan et al., 2012; Oliver Talks, January 2014). The number of treatments administered are large, with 10,234 patients receiving 52,450 unmodified ECT treatments, 46% of treatments administered at 33 institutions (Chittaranjan et al., 2012).

Chittaranjan et al. (2012), identified six reasons why unmodified ECT continues to be popular:

- lack of anaesthetic support for ECT for any of a variety of reasons:
  - lack of facilities for anaesthetic practice at the ECT clinic,
  - absence of qualified anaesthetists in the geographical vicinity of the centre,
  - monopoly of anaesthetists by surgical specialities,

  - lack of interest of anaesthetists in a minor procedure that is poorly remunerative,
  - lack of infrastructure and funding.
- urgent need for ECT, associated with a lack of time for or delay in obtaining anaesthetic clearance for ECT,
- inability to administer anaesthesia because of inaccessibility of veins for intravenous administration of anaesthesia and muscle relaxant,
- contraindication for use of anaesthesia owing to cardiorespiratory disorders,
- contraindications for use of succinylcholine (e.g. in patients with burns or neuromuscular disease),
- unaffordability of anaesthetic support.

The Indian position statement extensively details the complications that occur when a seizure is induced without anaesthesia. The report concludes that unmodified ECT is associated with a wide range of adverse consequences and should be administered in exceptional circumstances only (Chittaranjan et al., 2012). The issues raised in the Indian position statement that are used to support unmodified ECT remain some of the commonest challenges in delivering modern ECT services in the world today.

THE CHANGING FACE OF THE MEDIA

In 2013, the *SBS Insight* programme focused on ECT (Brockie, 2013). The show was based around three patients who had gained considerable benefit from the treatment. They spoke about their personal experiences that were juxtaposed against Australian ECT experts and John Reed, a highly vocal anti-ECT proponent. The show provided a very useful discussion about the positive and negative aspects of the treatment. It left the observer with a deep understanding of the detrimental effects of depression in individuals and their families.

For Michael, ECT gave him remission of symptoms with minimal cognitive side effects and he had maintenance ECT to stay well. This was in contrast to the experience of Natalie, who reported that ECT had saved her life even though she had profound memory problems: "It doesn't have to be perfect to work. If it saves your life, isn't that more important?" (Brockie, 2013).

ECT and psychiatry in general have been presented in a balanced way by ABC TV in the documentary series *Changing Minds: The Inside Story* (ABC TV, 2014). This series goes into a busy mental health facility in Sydney's west to explore the realities of twenty-first-century psychiatric treatment. The show aims to challenge the stigma and taboos that exist around mental illness by spending time with real patients and their treating teams. It achieves its aim y presenting a comprehensive view of how large public psychiatric hospitals in NSW operate. The show follows patients through their experience with the Mental Health Review Tribunal (MHRT) as an involuntary patient.

It discusses modern drug approaches with treating teams and witnesses the recovery made by patients who were treated with pharmacotherapy, changing from involuntary to voluntary status and eventually going home. It also follows patients with bipolar depression and unipolar depression who are granted ECT by the MHRT into theatre to witness the administration of ECT, which is modern and very effective, resulting in remission of symptoms and discharge home.

In 2015 there was a media release that portrays modern ECT as being a modern treatment that is based upon extensive research (Worthington, 2015). The media release highlights research published in the *Journal of Clinical Psychiatry* in July 2015, as being one of the "most significant developments in depression treatment in decades". It reviewed the published meta-analysis that compared brief versus ultrabrief ECT and found that ultrabrief ECT had less cognitive side effects and was almost as effective as brief-pulse ECT (Tor et al., 2015).

However, negative images persist. The *Canadian Medical Association Journal* published an image associated with the Food and Drug Administration hearing on the reclassification of ECT devices in 2011 (Benac, 2011). The image depicts a man, with wide-eyed stare, injected conjunctivae and crumpled electrodes, suggesting that the man was in a very bad state after having ECT. This image has since that time appeared in a box on the lower right-hand corner of the reputable PubMed pages. This posting is an insidious attack on ECT and somewhat surprising that it is linked to such a reputable online site (Kellner, Schwartz, Geduldig and Ahle, 2015).

THE BOLAM TEST

In 1957, legal action was taken by a patient who sustained fractures to both hips in August 1954 from unmodified ECT at the Friern Hospital in London (*Bolam v Friern*, 1957). Dr Allfrey administered ECT under the supervision of Dr Baste. Mr Bolam argued that the hospital and the doctors were negligent owing to their not informing him of the risks associated with ECT, failing to use muscle relaxants, or not utilising better manual controls to prevent injury beyond shoulder control, support of the chin and placing a pillow under his back (*Bolam v Friern*, 1957). Litigation proceeded, resulting in the case of *Bolam v The Friern Hospital Management Committee* in 1957.

Mr Bolam lost the case as it was argued that unmodified ECT was considered to be best practice in that time. Muscle relaxants were very new and not everyone used more extensive physical restrains to ensure patient safety. "We must not condemn as negligence that which is only misadventure!" (*Bolam v Friern*, 1957). This decision had far-reaching consequences and formed the Bolam test, one of the rules used to determine the issue of professional negligence in the English law of tort.

REFERENCES

ABC TV. (2014). Changing minds – the inside story. Retrieved from www.abc.net.au/tv/programs/changing-minds-the-inside-story.

Abrams, R. (2002). *Electroconvulsive Therapy*, 4th edition. New York: Oxford University Press.

Bancroft, J., and Marks, I. (1968). Electric aversion therapy of sexual deviations. *Proceedings of the Royal Society of*

Medicine, 61(8), 796–799. Retrieved from www.ncbi.nlm.nih. gov/pubmed/5673410.

Benac, N. (2011). United States reviews safety of electro-convulsive therapy. *Canadian Medical Association Journal, 183*(5), E269–270. doi:10.1503/cmaj.109-3817.

Bolam v Friern Hospital Management Committee. (1957). *Bolam v Friern*. Retrieved from xcheps.new.ox.ac.uk/casebook/ Resources/BOLAMV_1%20DOC.pdf.

Brain and Mind. (2015a). Julius Wagner von Jauregg: a brief biography. Retrieved from www.cerebromente.org.br/n04/ historia/jauregg_i.htm.

Brain and Mind. (2015b). Ladislas J. von Meduna: a brief biography. Retrieved from www.cerebromente.org.br/n04/ historia/meduna_i.htm.

Brain and Mind. (2015c). Manfred J. Sakel: a brief biography. Retrieved from www.cerebromente.org.br/n04/historia/ sakel_i.htm.

Brockie, J. (2013). Electro-shock. *SBS Insight*. Retrieved from www.sbs.com.au/news/insight/tvepisode/electroshock.

Campion, J. (1991). An angel at my table. Retrieved from www.rogerebert.com/reviews/an-angel-at-my-table-1991.

Chittaranjan, A.N., Shah, P., Tharyan, M.S., Reddy, M., Thirunavukarasu, R.A., Kallivayalil, R., . . . Mohandas, E. (2012). Position statement and guidelines on unmodified electroconvulsive therapy. *Indian Journal of Psychiatry, 54*(2), 119–133. doi:10.4103/0019-5545.99530.

Church of Scientology. (2005). Russell Miller's "Bare-Faced Messiah". *The Riverside Dictionary of Biography*. Retrieved from www.ronthenut.org/va-scam.htm.

Church of Scientology. (2015). Citizens Commission on Human Rights (CCHR). Retrieved from www.cchr.org/cchr-reports/citizen-commission-on-human-rights/introduction. html.

De Brito, K. (2004). It has a brutal history. We don't know if it works. So why are we still using electric shock therapy? *Australian Report, Marie Claire Magazine*.

Dorkins, H.R. (1982). Suxamethonium: the development of a modern drug from 1906 to the present day. *Medical History, 26*(2), 145–168.

Dukakis, K., and Tye, L. (2006). *Shock: The Healing Power of Electroconvulsive Therapy*. New York: Penguin.

Ebert, R. (2000). Requiem for a Dream: movie review. Retrieved from www.rogerebert.com/reviews/requiem-for-a-dream-2000.

Editorial. (2003). Electroconvulsive therapy. *British Medical Journal, 326*(June), 1343–1344.

Emdler, N.S. (1988). The origins of electroconvulsive therapy (ECT). *Convulsive Therapy, 4*(1), 5–23.

Filmsite Movie Review. (1975). One Flew Over the Cuckoo's Nest (1975). Retrieved from www.filmsite.org/onef.html.

Howard, R. (2001). A beautiful mind. Retrieved from www.abeautifulmind.com.

Kellner, C.H., Schwartz, E.K., Geduldig, E.T., and Ahle, G.M. (2015). Electroconvulsive therapy. Image on Pubmed. *Journal of ECT, 31*(3), 141–142.

Kesey, K. (1962). *One Flew Over the Cuckoo's Nest*. Retrieved from www.goodreads.com/author/show/7285.Ken_Kesey.

Kilogh, L.G., Smith, S., and Johnson, G.F. (1988). *Physical Treatments in Psychiatry*. Melbourne, Australia: Blackwell.

Kingman, S. (1993). Psychiatrist accused of contravening Mental Health Act. *Bristish Medical Journal, 306*(6870), 85. Retrieved from www.ncbi.nlm.nih.gov/pubmed/11643095.

Kivler, C.A. (2010). *Will I Ever Be the Same Again?: Transforming the Face of ECT (Shock Therapy)*. New York: Three Gem/Kivler.

Lounsbery, A. (2013). The Snake Pit (13 November 1948). Retrieved from http://ocdviewer.com/2013/08/21/the-snake-pit-nov-13–1948.

McDonald, A., and Walter, G. (2001). The portrayal of ECT in American movies. *Journal of ECT, 17*(4), 264–274. Retrieved from www.ncbi.nlm.nih.gov/pubmed/11731728.

Metastasio, A., and Dodwell, D. (2013). A translation of "L'Elettroshock" by Cerletti and Bini, with an introduction. *The European Journal of Psychiatry, 27*(4). doi:10.4321/ S0213-61632013000400001.

Milgram, S. (1963). Behavioral study of obedience. *Journal of Abnormal Psychology, 67*, 371–378. Retrieved from www.ncbi.nlm.nih.gov/pubmed/14049516.

NICE. (2003, Modified 2009). *Guidance on the use of electroconvulsive therapy (Vol. Guidance Number 59)*. London: National Institute for Health and Care Excellence; National Health Service.

Oliver Talks. (January 2014). Torture or abandonment: unmodified ECT and the shocking position of Indian and global psychiatric leaders. Retrieved from www.mdac.info/en/ olivertalks/2014/01/15/torture-or-abandonment-unmodified-ect-and-shocking-position-indian-and-global.

Pakula, A.J. (1957). Fear Strikes Out (1957). Retrieved from www.tcm.com/this-month/article/118146%7C0/Fear-Strikes-Out.html.

Rejali, D. (2012). Electric torture: a global history of a torture technology. Retrieved from http://humanrights. uchicago.edu/documents/Torture Conference/Rejali.htm.

Royal Adelaide Hospital. (2015). Intravenous anaesthetics – RAH – intensive care unit. Retrieved from www.icuadelaide. com.au/files/primary/pharmacology/intravenous.pdf.

Sabbatini, R.M.E. (2015). The history of shock therapy in psychiatry. *Brain and Mind*. Retrieved from www.cerebromente.org.br/n04/historia/shock_i.htm.

Skukla, G.D. (2000). Modified versus unmodified ECT. *Indian Journal of Psychiatry, 42*(4), 445–446.

Stinson, V. (2006). Electricity as a cure for madness: the development of electroconvulsive therapy. Retrieved from www.blinkingburro.com/sremsarodnn/ECT.html.

Szasz, T.S. (1961). *The Myth of Mental Illness: Foundations of a Theory of Personal Conduct*. New York: Syracuse.

Szasz, T.S. (1973). *The Second Sin*. Garden City, NY: Anchor/Doubleday.

The European Graduate School. (2015). Paracelsus – biography. Retrieved from www.egs.edu/library/paracelsus/biography.

Tor, P.C., Bautovich, A., Wang, M.J., Martin, D., Harvey, S.B., and Loo, C. (2015). A systematic review and meta-analysis of brief versus ultrabrief right unilateral electroconvulsive therapy for depression. *Journal of Clinical Psychiatry, 10*(4088). doi:10.4088/JCP.14r09145.

Waite, J., and Easton, A. (2013). *The ECT Handbook,* 3rd edition. London: Royal College of Psychiatrists.

Walter, G., and McDonald, A. (2004). About to have ECT? Fine, but don't watch it in the movies: a sorry portrayal of ECT in film. *Psychiatric Times, June*.

Major advances in ECT practice

Criticism of ECT has arisen from the failure to incorporate into clinical practice the major advances in research over the last 80 years (American Psychiatric Association, 2001; NICE, 2003, Modified 2009; Scott, 2005). The epitome of this criticism is highlighted in the current debate in India, where unmodified ECT is still widely practised (Chittaranjan et al., 2012). Western countries have also been criticised for their failure to incorporate new developments in ECT (Carney and Geddes, 2003). Sackeim et al. (2007), in a six-month prospective study of 347 patients covering seven different sites in New York City, found that there were considerable variations in clinical practice between hospitals, leading to significant differences in cognitive deficits that persisted for more than six months after the last ECT treatment. Those that performed bilateral ECT and used sine wave devices had the worst outcome.

Cognitive data highlighting the detrimental effects of sine wave versus brief-pulse ECT, bilateral versus unilateral electrode placement and a high stimulus dose has been known for many years (Carney, Rogan, Sebastian et al., 1976; Valentine, Keddie and Dunne, 1968).

INTRODUCTION OF ANAESTHESIA

A major advance has been the development of a range of anaesthetic agents that have revolutionised ECT practice, making it a safe and humane treatment.

Induction agents

Until well into the twentieth century, anaesthesia, hypnosis, analgesia and muscle relaxation were provided by single inhalation agents, ether or chloroform (Royal Adelaide Hospital, 2015).

1932 marked the start of changes to anaesthetic drugs with the release of barbiturates like hexobarbital or hexobaritone (Citopan, Evipan and Tobinal), closely followed by Sodium Pentothal (trademark), thiopental or thiopentone (preferred term) in 1934. The use of thiopentone was met with many early disasters. Its use as an induction and maintenance of anaesthesia agent for casualties in Pearl Harbor resulted in its description as "an ideal method of euthanasia" (Royal Adelaide Hospital, 2015).

By the 1950s, the pharmacokinetics and pharmacodynamics of the barbiturates were better understood and methohexitone or methohexital (preferred term) was first used by Stoelting in 1957 and is still used today in many countries around the world (Royal Adelaide Hospital, 2015).

The phencyclidine derivative ketamine was introduced in 1965 and became known as the "dissociative anaesthesia" (Royal Adelaide Hospital, 2015). Ketamine continues to have relevance to the ECT practice (Folk, Kellner, Beale, Conray and Duc, 2000; Galvez, McGuirk and Loo, 2016).

Propofol, first used in clinical trials in 1977 by Kay and Rolly (Royal Adelaide Hospital, 2015), has become the primary ECT induction agent used in many centres following the limited supply of thiopentone around the world (Folk et al., 2000; Walker, Bowley and Walker, 2013).

Muscle relaxants

The development of muscle relaxants has been another major breakthrough in ECT treatment. Curare was used for centuries by South American Indians to hunt game. The high demand for suitable agents during World War II led to its development as a muscle relaxant suitable for trauma surgery (Raghavendra, 2002).

Suxamethonium chloride, also known as suxamethonium (preferred term used in this book) or succinylcholine, was first trialled unsuccessfully as a cardiovascular agent in 1905, with the neuromuscular properties being discovered much later in 1949 (Lee, 2009). It was introduced into clinical anaesthesia in Europe in 1951 and in the United States in 1952. Suxamethonium has been associated with life-threatening adverse events like malignant hyperthermia and hyperkalemia (Folk et al., 2000). This has lead to the development of at least 11 different non-depolarising agents, with most having a slow onset and offset of action. However, even to this day, of the non-depolarising agents suxamethonium continues to be the primary muscle relaxant used in ECT owing to its rapid onset and quick time to recovery (Lee, 2009).

HYPEROXYGENATION AND HYPERVENTILATION

There is growing evidence that hyperventilation lowers seizure threshold (Loo, Simpson and MacPherson, 2010) prolongs seizures (Swayama, Takahashi and Inoue, 2008) and reduces the severity of cognitive impairment (Haeck, Gillmann, Janouschek and Grözinger, 2011). One study failed to show any benefit from hyperventilation on seizure adequacy but did show that hyperventilation was superior to normal treatment, with 34% quicker reorientation time compared to controls (Mayur, Bray, Fernandes, Bythe and Gilbett, 2010). Inadequate oxygenation increases the risk of hypoxia, cerebral dysfunction and CVS complications (American Psychiatric Association, 2001; Waite and Easton, 2013).

All ECT guidelines now recommend adequate pre-oxygenation, usually three to four minutes before the anaesthetic agents have been administered and immediately before the stimulus has been administered (American Psychiatric Association, 2001; NSW Health, 2010; SA Health, 2014; Tiller and Lyndon, 2003; Waite and Easton, 2013).

ELECTRODE PLACEMENT

Over many years there has been considerable work examining the efficacy and memory effects of different electrode placements (Fink, 2009). These placements are illustrated in Figure 2.3.1.

In 1938, Cerletti and Bini pioneered the temporal position that has become known as bitemporal electrode placement (Position 1 on both sides of head). It has been extensively investigated over many years and remains the strongest form of ECT, with early onset of recovery and a reduced rate of rehospitalisation (Little, Munday, Atkins and Khalid, 2004). However, it is associated with considerable cognitive impairment compared to

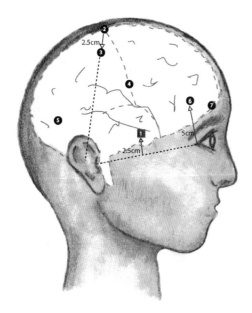

Figure 2.3.1 *Electrode placement*
Source: Adapted from Weiner, 1980

other electrode placements (Bailine et al., 2000; Kellner et al., 2010; Metastasio and Dodwell, 2013; Sackeim et al., 2000).

The right temporal position became the reference point for many other electrode placements. Friedman and Wilcox (1942) investigated the temporal-vertex position (Position 2), postulating that this position would reduce cognitive impairment by avoiding the speech area of the brain. The Lancaster position (Position 4) was similar to the d'Elia electrode placement (Position 3) but the "vertex" electrode was half way between the vertex and temporal electrode position. Lancaster coined the term "unilateral ECT" (Lancaster, Steinert and Frost, 1958). McAndrew placed the "vertex" electrode behind the ear near the occiput (Position 5) (McAndrew, Berkley and Matthews, 1967), while Muller placed it on the forehead midpoint above the left orbit (Position 7) (Muller, 1971).

The work by d'Elia in the 1970s demonstrated that unilateral electrode placement, usually on the right side, had less cognitive impairment than bilateral electrode positions. The d'Elia position has become the "gold standard" placement for unilateral ECT (d'Elia, 1970, 1976).

Bifrontal electrode placement (Position 6) was first proposed by Abrams and Fink (1972). Since then, a number of trials have been conducted highlighting that it may have similar efficacy to bitemporal ECT, similar cognitive impairment to unilateral ECT and reduced brain stem stimulation resulting in less cardiac effects (Bailine et al., 2000; Letemendia et al., 1993; Ranjkesh, Barekatain and Akuchakian, 2005).

Left anterior right temporal position (LART) was developed by Swartz (1994), illustrated in Figure 2.3.1 as Position 1 (right) and Position 7 (left). Swartz proposed that an asymmetrical electrode placement would decrease the cognitive adverse effects compared to symmetrically placed electrodes. The left electrode placed in the fully anterior position separated it from the temporal lobe and was positioned over the dorsolateral prefrontal cortex (Manley and Swartz, 1994; Swartz, 2006; Swartz and Evans, 1996).

There has been some confusion with this electrode placement, with LART being used interchangeably with left frontal right temporal electrode placement (LFRT) (Weiss, Hansen, Safranko and Hughes, 2015). In LFRT, the electrodes are placed in Position 1 (right) and Position 6 (left), as illustrated in Figure 2.3.1. Like many of the other electrode placements noted above, data supporting their use is limited.

In conclusion, non-dominant right unilateral electrode placement in the d'Elia position is frequently recommended as the initial electrode placement for an index course of treatment owing to strong evidence supporting its efficacy and reduced cognitive impairment (Kolshus, Jelovac and McLoughlin, 2017; Sackeim et al., 1993; Sackeim et al., 2000).

ULTRABRIEF ECT

In 2008, the first published study of ultrabrief ECT, pulse width 0.3 ms, highlighted the marked reduction in cognitive impairment with only a small reduction in efficacy compared to standard brief-pulse ECT (Sackeim et al., 2008). Ultrabrief right unilateral ECT has been proposed as a preferred alternative for routine clinical treatment owing to less cognitive impairment.

Randomised controlled trials have shown that it is less efficacious and may not be the preferred choice when urgency is a factor (Loo et al., 2014; Mayer, Byth and Harris, 2013; Sackeim et al., 2008; Spaans, Verwijk and Comijs, 2013). In this situation, bifrontal ECT should be considered. Bifrontal ECT has become the preferred electrode placement when there is treatment failure or a rapid response is required and less cognitive impairment is desirable compared to bitemporal ECT (Dunne and McLoughlin, 2012).

A recent large trial involving 240 elderly patients reinforced the benefits of ultrabrief ECT when combined with venlafaxine, with 61.7% meeting remission criteria (Kellner et al., 2016). This study reinforces the current recommendation that ultrabrief ECT be the default form of ECT offered owing to its cognitive advantage with stronger types proposed when a rapid clinical response is required (Tor et al., 2015).

STIMULUS WAVE FORMS

A major advance in ECT practice has been the development of the stimulus used to elicit the seizure in ECT. In 1938, Cerletti and Bini made the first ECT device. This device was innovative as it included a separate circuit to test the pre-stimulus impedance using a low level signal to aid the estimation of the stimulus current based upon Ohm's law (Weiner, 1988). However, it was not a reliable estimation of treatment impedance and the feature was largely abandoned by manufacturers until modern times (Weiner, 1988). Although in demand, very few of these devices were made or exported owing to the impact of World War II. Each country was forced to develop its own device in consultation with appropriate electrical instrument companies (Weiner, 1988).

In Great Britain, the Edison Electric Company made the first device in 1940. In the same year, the Rahm device was manufactured in the USA (Weiner, 1988). In 1941, Dr H.M. Birch made the first device in Australia with the assistance of the University of Adelaide Physics Department (South Australian Medical Heritage Society Inc, 2015). Over the next 10 years there were a large variety of different devices available worldwide, which all relied on a sine wave stimulator. These stimulators delivered a continuous flow of electrons in alternating positive and negative deflections producing a slow rising current to generate a seizure.

Early on it was noted that a sine wave current might not be the most efficient stimulus owing to the severity of the amnesia and confusion that often accompanied a course of treatment. Friedman and Wilcox (1942) were the first group to develop a device that delivered a monophasic sine wave with part of the polarity removed. These techniques were developed further by Liberson (1948), who did trials using a brief-pulse, square wave stimulus measuring seizure threshold, clinical response, memory and the electroencephalogram (ECG). Extremely short pulse widths (0.3 ms or less) were first used to most closely approximate optimum stimulation of the neuron physiology (Liberson and Wilcox, 1945). The differences between sine waveforms and brief-pulse waveform are illustrated in Photos 5.4.2 and 5.4.3.

Early trials were limited by technical difficulties when very short pulse widths were used owing to the need to generate very high peak current levels to reliably produce a seizure with a complete ictal response and pulse widths between 0.5–1.0 ms were recommended (Weiner, 1988). New technology has made delivering an ultrabrief pulse reliable, confirming the early observations that this type of ECT had less cognitive impairment (Tor et al., 2015).

Resistance to incorporating new innovations into clinical practice is not a new phenomenon. Cerletti (1950) noted that the prevailing belief of the day was that sine waves were safe and there was a strong push by leaders in the field to simplify devices eliminating many of the early safety features. In comparison, low-energy ECT devices were costly and complex and were less effective in inducing seizures resulting in less patient acceptance (Weiner, 1988). This debate continued for many years (Valentine et al., 1968; Weaver et al., 1977).

Blachly (1976) modified the brief-pulse device with successful results. Over the next 15 years, evidence continued to grow that brief-pulse, constant-current devices produced significantly less cognitive impairment, leading the American Psychiatric Association (1990) to recommend it as the preferred device for all ECT treatments. By 2001, the American Psychiatric Association (APA) had recommended that a brief-pulse stimulus should be used for all treatments. The continued use of sine wave stimulation is not justified "because of the potential aggravation of cognitive side effects and the lack of evidence of any therapeutic advantage" (American Psychiatric Association, 2001). Further, the APA recommended that all devices should deliver a constant-current stimulus with no advantage in the use of constant-voltage

devices. Recent guidelines published by the Royal College of Psychiatrists reinforce these recommendations (Dunn and McLoughlin, 2013). Translating recommendations into clinical practice remains challenging as sine wave devices were still being used in some centres in New York City in 2007 (Sackeim et al., 2007).

SEIZURE THRESHOLD AND STIMULUS DOSE TITRATION

Seizure threshold has changed the conceptualisation of the role of seizures in the efficacy of ECT. Sackeim, Decina, Prohovnik and Malitz (1987) first elucidated a structured stimulus dosing strategy to determine seizure threshold. It was noted by the American Psychiatric Association (1990) that the estimation of seizure threshold can guide the dose of the stimulus required for ECT. Coffey, Lucke, Weiner, Krystal and Aque (1995) used a structured stimulus dosing procedure to measure initial seizure threshold in 111 depressed patients using brief-pulse, constant-current ECT. They demonstrated a 6 times difference across patients.

Differences in seizure threshold can be accounted for by:

- age and sex (Sackeim et al., 1987),
- electrode placement (Heikman, Tuunainen and Kuoppasalmi, 1999; Sackeim, Decina, Kanzler, Kerr and Malitz, 1987),
- anaesthetic agents (Christensen et al., 1986; Galvez, Hadzi-Pavlovic, Smith and Loo, 2015),
- medications (Boylan, Haskett, Mulsant et al., 2000),
- frequency of treatment (Sackeim et al., 1987; Weiner, 1980), and
- stimulus characteristics (Devanand et al., 1998; Peterchev, Rosa, Deng, Prudic and Lisanby, 2010; Swartz and Larson, 1989; Swartz, 1994).

The structured stimulus dosing strategy, now called "stimulus dose titration", was incorporated into clinical practice worldwide after it was demonstrated that not all seizures were effective. Dose relative to threshold was an important requirement that contributed to clinically effective seizures, with low-dose ECT ineffective (Sackeim et al., 1993). Low-dose right unilateral ECT was ineffective, whereas high- and low-dose bitemporal electrode placement was effective (Sackeim et al., 1993). This technique is now used routinely in many centres around the world during the first ECT treatment to determine seizure threshold, thereby establishing the effective dose required for subsequent treatments.

Not everyone agreed that stimulus dose titration is the best way to determine the stimulus used in ECT (Abrams, 2002a; Swartz and Larson, 1989; Swartz, 1994). High fixed dose strategies have been proposed (Abrams, Swartz and Vedak, 1991) as well as using a formula based upon a particular factor that predicts seizure threshold. "Age-based" dosing has been put forward as a simple and convenient way of determining dose (Abrams, 2002b; Abrams, Swartz and Vedak, 1989). However, this method has been criticised for administering excessive stimulation, causing increased levels of cognitive effects. In response, "Half-age-based" dosing strategy has been proposed as an alternative (Petrides and Fink, 1996). Half-age-based dosing has been shown to stimulate 30% higher than using a titration method contributing to increased cognitive impairment (Petrides and Fink, 1996; Tiller and Ingram, 2006).

In summary, stimulus dose titration is the most effective way of determining stimulus intensity as other methods are less accurate in clinical practice, contributing to excessive cognitive impairment (Dunn and McLoughlin, 2013).

ELECTROENCEPHALOGRAM (EEG)

Adding the electroencephalogram (EEG) to an ECT device demonstrated that the seizure recorded by the EEG is often considerably longer than the motor fit measured by the isolated limb technique and it enabled closer clinical monitoring to prevent missed seizures (Fink and Johnson, 1982). Further

evaluation of the EEG generated by different types of ECT demonstrated that the most effective form of ECT, bitemporal electrode placement, generated a more intense alteration in seizure expression when compared to unilateral ECT, suggesting that the EEG may be a useful marker of seizure adequacy (Krystal et al., 1993).

Further work suggested that slowing of the EEG and a rhythmic spike wave pattern may be useful clinical predictors (Folkerts, 1996). Multivariate modelling and manual ratings of the ictal EEG data from treatments with right unilateral electrode placement predicted rising seizure threshold with a high degree of accuracy causing decreased seizure intensity over the course of ECT (Krystal, Coffey, Weiner and Holsinger, 1998; Mayer, 2006). EEG monitoring led to a better understanding that seizure threshold monitoring anticipated a rise in seizure threshold as seen on the EEG, allowing changes in dose to be made before there was a missed seizure and treatment failure.

The ictal EEG indices have been shown to have considerable potential for predicting stimulus intensity changes and their effect on therapeutic outcome (Krystal et al., 1998). Sackeim et al. (1996) showed that the induction of slow wave activity in the prefrontal cortex was predictive of therapeutic efficacy. This work was replicated in a further study that showed that more intense seizure expression in the prefrontal regions is linked to clinical efficacy (Luber et al., 2000). Ictal EEG indices have considerable potential for predicting stimulus intensity changes and their effect on therapeutic outcome (Andrew, Coffey, Richard and Tracey, 1998). However, not all studies support this finding (Nobler et al., 2000). A recent review confirmed that analysing the EEG during ECT is clinically useful, offering the ECT practitioner markers that can aid treatment response like postictal suppression (Mayer, 2006). Further analyses of the EEG characteristics are required to develop a clinically useful, reliable and repeatable ECT algorithm (Mayer, 2006).

In summary, although the ictal EEG is not an ideal indicator of treatment adequacy and an assessment algorithm does not exist, the ictal EEG provides guidance of treatment adequacy, in addition to that afforded by patient clinical response, allowing a timely change to ECT dose.

ECT: MINIMUM STANDARDS AND AUDIT

One of the most important recent challenges confronting ECT practitioners has been the pressing need to provide minimum standards to guide clinical practice. In the past, efforts to change clinical practice have been unsuccessful.

In the 1990s, the United Kingdom ran three audits of ECT practice, in 1991, 1992 and 1996 (Duffett and Lelliott, 1998). After each audit, new guidelines were written and training in ECT was offered by the Royal College of Psychiatrists. The 1996 audit highlighted that previous attempts to change clinical practice had failed, with only 33% of clinics meeting the guideline standards and 41% using outdated equipment. The responsible consultant attended their weekly ECT treatment session in only 16% of cases, with only one third having clear policies to guide and train junior doctors to administer ECT effectively. The audit concluded that only 33% of clinics were regarded as good.

The failure to change clinical practice was echoed in the NICE ECT guidance document, which highlighted the marked discrepancy between researchers'/clinicians' view of ECT and consumers' (NICE, 2003, Modified 2009). *The ECT Handbook* (Scott, 2005) has been revised to account for much of the criticism raised (Waite and Easton, 2013) and the Royal College of Psychiatrists has released the *ECT Accreditation Service (ECTAS): Standards for the Administration of ECT*, to guide practice (Royal College of Psychiatrists, 2015).

Australia has also been proactive in addressing these criticisms, ensuring best practice, with many states and territories revising their Mental Health Acts and formulating minimum standard guidelines (Chief Psychiatrist of Western Australia, 2015; NSW Health, 2010; SA Health, 2014; Tasmanian Government, 2013; Victorian Government, 2014).

Minimum standards of ECT practice remains one of the most exciting and challenging areas vital to the future of this important treatment.

THE LIVED EXPERIENCE

Consumer recognition has been one of the major recent advances in ECT services following the marked discrepancy between clinicians' and consumers' views of ECT being highlighted by the NICE ECT guidance document (NICE, 2003, Modified 2009). It is now essential for clinicians and service providers to listen to the lived experience incorporating the view of consumers into ECT practice. Consumers potentially have a broad role, ranging from educating families, supporting patients who are currently undergoing ECT treatment, and challenging stigma and misinformation expressed in the media, through to sitting on ECT committees and advisory bodies within hospital services.

Having been diagnosed with clinical depression, I walk the road of the consumer and have observed the state of discomfort from both my family and friends, who didn't know what to do or say to support me during my hospitalizations or the months or recovery from my episodes.

(Kivler, 2016)

REFERENCES

Abrams, R. (2002a). *Electroconvulsive Therapy*, 4th edition. New York: Oxford University Press.

Abrams, R. (2002b). Stimulus titration and ECT dosing. *Journal of ECT*, 18(1), 3–9; discussion 14–15. Retrieved from www.ncbi.nlm.nih.gov/pubmed/11925511.

Abrams, R., Swartz, C.M., and Vedak, C. (1989). Antidepressant effects of right versus left lateral ECT and the lateralization theory of ECT action. *American Journal of Psychiatry*, 146, 1190–1192.

Abrams, R, Swartz, C.M., and Vedak, C. (1991). Antidepressant effects of high-dose right unilateral electroconvulsive therapy. *Archives of General Psychiatry*, 48(8), 746–748. Retrieved from www.ncbi.nlm.nih.gov/pubmed/1883258.

Abrams, R., and Fink, M. (1972). Clinical experiences with multiple electroconvulsive treatments. *Comprehensive Psychiatry, 13*(2), 115–121. Retrieved from www.ncbi.nlm.nih.gov/pubmed/5010591.

American Psychiatric Association. (1990). *The Practice of Electroconvulsive Therapy: Recommendations for Treatment, Training and Privileging: A Task Force Report.* Washington, DC: American Psychiatric Association.

American Psychiatric Association. (2001). *The practice of electroconvulsive therapy: Recommendations for treatment, training and privileging: A Task Force Report,* 2nd edition. Washington, DC: American Psychiatric Association.

Andrew, D.K., Coffey, C.E., Richard, D.W., and Tracey, H. (1998). Changes in seizure threshold over the course of electroconvulsive therapy affect therapeutic response and are detected by ictal EEG ratings. *The Journal of Neuropsychiatry and Clinical Neurosciences, 10*(2), 178–186. doi:10.1176/jnp.10.2.178 %M 9608406 %U. Retrieved from http://neuro.psychiatryonline.org/doi/abs/10.1176/jnp.10.2.178.

Bailine, S.H., Rifkin, A., Kayne, E., Selzer, J.A., Vital-Herne, J., Blieka, M., and Pollack, S. (2000). Comparison of bifrontal and bitemporal ECT for major depression. *American Journal of Psychiatry, 157*(1), 121–123. doi:10.1176/ajp.157.1.121.

Blachly, P.H. (1976). New developments in electroconvulsive therapy. *Diseases of the Nervous System, 37*(6), 356–358. Retrieved from www.ncbi.nlm.nih.gov/pubmed/1277986.

Boylan, L., Haskett, R.F., Mulsant, B.F., Greenberg, R.M., Prudic, J. Spicknall, K., . . . Sackeim, H.A. (2000). Determinants of seizure threshold in ECT: benzodiazepine use, anaesthetic dosage and other factors. *Journal of ECT, 16,* 3–16.

Carney, M.W., Rogan, P.A., Sebastian, J. and Sheffield, B. (1976). A controlled comparative trial of unilateral and bilateral sinusoidal and pulse ECT in endogenous depression. *Physicians Drug Mannual, 7,* 77–79.

Carney, S., and Geddes, J. (2003). Electroconvulsive therapy: Recent recommendations are likely to improve standards and uniformity of use. *British Medical Journal, 326*(7403), 1343–1344.

Cerletti, U. (1950). Old and new information about electro-shock. *American Journal of Psychiatry, 107,* 87–94.

Chief Psychiatrist of Western Australia. (2015). Chief Psychiatrist's practice standards for the administration of electroconvulsive therapy. Retrieved from www.chiefpsychiatrist.wa.gov.au/wp-content/uploads/2015/12/CP_ECT_Standards_2015.pdf.

Chittaranjan, A.N., Shah, P., Tharyan, M.S., Reddy, M., Thirunavukarasu, R.A., Kallivayalil, R., . . . Mohandas, E. (2012). Position statement and guidelines on unmodified electroconvulsive therapy. *Indian Journal of Psychiatry, 54*(2), 119–133. doi:10.4103/0019-5545.99530.

Christensen, P., Kragh-Sorensen, P., Sorensen, C., Thomsen, H.Y., Iversen, A.D., Christensen, K.S., . . . Tonnesen, E. (1986). EEG-monitored ECT: A comparison of seizure duration under anesthesia with etomidate and thiopentone. *Convulsive Therapy, 2*(3), 145–150. Retrieved from www.ncbi.nlm.nih.gov/pubmed/11940860.

Coffey, C.E., Lucke, J., Weiner, R.D., Krystal, A.D., and Aque, M. (1995). Seizure threshold in electroconvulsive therapy: I. Initial seizure threshold. *Biological Psychiatry, 37*(10), 713–720. doi:10.1016/0006-3223(95)00262-F.

d'Elia, G. (1970). Unilateral electroconvulsive therapy. *Acta Psychiatrica Scandinavica, Supplement 215,* 1–98.

d'Elia, G. (1976). Memory changes after unliateral electro-convulsive therapy with different electrode positions. *Cortex, 12*(3), 280–289.

Devanand, D.P., Lisanby, S.H., Nobler, M.S., and Sackeim, H.A. (1998). The relative efficiency of altering pulse frequency or train duration when determining seizure threshold. *Journal of ECT, 14,* 227–235. Retrieved from http://journals.lww.com/ectjournal/pages/articleviewer.aspx?year=1998andissue=12000andarticle=00002andtype=Abstract.

Duffett, R., and Lelliott, P. (1998). Auditing electroconvulsive therapy. The third cycle. *British Journal of Psychiatry, 172*(5), 401–405. Retrieved from www.ncbi.nlm.nih.gov/pubmed/9747401.

Dunn, R.A., and McLoughlin, D.M. (2013). ECT prescribing and practice. In Waite, J. and Easton, A. (Eds.), *The ECT Handbook,* 3rd edition. London: Royal College of Psychiatrists.

Dunne, R.A., and McLoughlin, D.M. (2012). Systematic review and meta-analysis of bifrontal electroconvulsive therapy versus bilateral and unilateral electroconvulsive therapy in depression. *The World Journal of Biological Psychiatry, 13*(4), 248–258. doi:10.3109/15622975.2011.615863.

Fink, M. (2009). *Electroconvulsive Therapy: A Guide for Professionals and Their Patients.* New York: Oxford University Press.

Fink, M., and Johnson, L. (1982). Monitoring the duration of electroconvulsive therapy seizures: "Cuff" and EEG methods compared. *Archives of General Psychiatry, 39*(10), 1189–1191. doi:10.1001/archpsyc.1982.04290100055009.

Folk, J.W., Kellner, C.H., Beale, M.D., Conray, J.M., and Duc, T.A. (2000). Anesthesia for electroconvulsive therapy: a review. *Journal of ECT, 16*(2), 157–170.

Folkerts, H.W. (1996). The ictal electroencephalogram as a marker for the efficacy of electroconvulsive therapy. *European Archives of Psychiatry and Clinical Neuroscience, 246*(3), 155–164.

Friedman, E., and Wilcox, P.H. (1942). Electro-stimulated convulsive dose in intact humans by means of unidirectional currents. *Journal of Nervous and Mental Disease, 96,* 56–63.

Galvez, V., Hadzi-Pavlovic, D., Smith, D., and Loo, C.K. (2015). Predictors of seizure threshold in right unilateral ultrabrief electroconvulsive therapy: role of concomitant medications and anaesthesia used. *Brain Stimulation, 8*(3), 486–492. doi:10.1016/j.brs.2014.12.012.

Galvez, V., McGuirk, L., and Loo, C.K. (2016). The use of ketamine in ECT anaesthesia: a systematic review and critical commentary on efficacy, cognitive, safety and seizure outcomes. *World Journal of Biological Psychiatry*, 1–21. doi:10.1080/15622975.2016.1252464.

Haeck, M., Gillmann, B., Janouschek, H., and Grözinger, M. (2011). Electroconvulsive therapy can benefit from controlled hyperventilation using a laryngeal mask. *European Archives of Psychiatry and Clinical Neuroscience, Nov* (261 Suppl 2), S173–176. doi:10.1007/s00406-011-0240-4.

Heikman, P., Tuunainen, A., and Kuoppasalmi, K. (1999). Value of the initial stimulus dose in right unilateral and bifrontal electroconvulsive therapy. *Psychological Medicine, 29*(6), 1417–1423.

Kellner, C.H., Knapp, R.G., Hausain, M.M., Rasmussen, K., Sampson, S., Cullum, M. . . . Petrides, G. (2010). Bifrontal, bitemporal and right unilateral electode placement in ECT: randomised trial. *British Journal of Psychiatry, 196*(3), 226–234. doi:10.1192/bjp.bp.109.066183.

Kellner, C.H., Husain, M.M., Knapp, R.G., McCall, W.V., Petrides, G., Rudorfer, M V., . . . Lisanby, S.H. (2016). Right unilateral ultrabrief pulse ECT in geriatric depression: phase 1 of the PRIDE study. *American Journal of Psychiatry, 173*(11), 1101–1109. doi:10.1176/appi.ajp.2016.15081101.

Kivler, C.A. (2016). The five B's for dealing with loved ones who are depressed. Retrieved from www.isen-ect.org/the-five-Bs-for-Dealing-with-Loved-Ones-Who-Are-Depressed.

Kolshus, E., Jelovac, A., and McLoughlin, D.M. (2017). Bitemporal v. high-dose right unilateral electroconvulsive therapy for depression: a systematic review and meta-analysis of randomized controlled trials. *Psychological Medicine, 47*(3), 518–530. doi:10.1017/S0033291716002737.

Krystal, A.D., Weiner, R.D., McCall, W.V., Shelp, F.E., Arias, R., and Smith, P. (1993). The effects of ECT stimulus dose and electrode placement on the Ictal electroencephalogram: An intraindividual crossover study. *Biological Psychiatry, 34*(11), 759–767. Retrieved from www.ncbi.nlm.nih.gov/pubmed/8292679.

Krystal, A.D., Coffey, C.E., Weiner, R.D., and Holsinger, T. (1998). Changes in seizure threshold over the course of electroconvulsive therapy affect therapeutic response and are detected by ictal EEG ratings. *The Journal of Neuropsychiatry and Clinical Neurosciences, 10*(2), 178–186. doi:10.1176/jnp.10.2.178.

Lancaster, N.P., Steinert, R.R., and Frost, I. (1958). Unilateral electro-convulsive therapy. *Journal of Mental Science, 104*, 221–227.

Lee, C. (2009). Goodbye suxamethonium! *Anaesthesia, 64 Suppl 1*, 73–81. doi:10.1111/j.1365-2044.2008.05873.x.

Letemendia, F.J.J., Delva, N.J., Rodenburg, M., Lawson, J.S., Inglis, J., Waldron, J.J., and Lywood, D.W. (1993). Therapeutic advantage of bifrontal electrode placement in ECT. *Psychological Medicine, 23*(2), 349–360. doi:10.1017/S0033291700028452.

Liberson, W.T. (1948). Brief stimulus therapy: Physiological and clinical observations. *American Journal of Psychiatry, 105*, 28–39.

Liberson, W.T., and Wilcox, P.H. (1945). Electro convulsive therapy: comparison of brief stimulation technique with Friedman–Wilcon–Reiter technique. *Digest of Neurology and Psychiatry, 13*, 292–302.

Little, J., Munday, J., Atkins, M.R., and Khalid, A. (2004). Does electrode placement predict time to rehospitalization? *Journal of ECT, 20*(4), 213–218. Retrieved from http://journals.lww.com/ectjournal/Fulltext/2004/12000/Does_Electrode_Placement_Predict_Time_to.5.aspx.

Loo, C., Simpson, B., and MacPherson, R. (2010). Augmentation strategies in electroconvulsive therapy. *Journal of ECT, 26*(3), 202–207. doi:10.1097/YCT.0b013e3181e48143.

Loo, C.K., Katalinic, N., Smith, D.J., Ingram, A., Dowling, N. Martin, D. . . . Schweitzer, I. (2014). A randomised controlled trial of brief and ultrabrief pulse right unilateral electroconvulsive therapy. *International Journal of Neuropsychopharmacology, 18*(1).

Luber, B., Nobler, M.S., Moeller, J.R., Katzman, G.P., Prudic, J., Devanand, D.P., . . . Sackeim, H.A. (2000). Quantitative EEG during seizures induced by electroconvulsive therapy: relations to treatment modality and clinical features. II. Topographic analyses. *Journal of ECT, 16*(3), 229–243. Retrieved from http://journals.lww.com/ectjournal/Fulltext/2000/09000/Quantitative_EEG_During_Seizures_Induced_by.3.aspx.

McAndrew, J., Berkley, B., and Matthews, C. (1967). The effect of dominant and nondominant unilateral ECT as compared to bilateral ECT. *American Journal of Psychiatry, 124*, 483–454.

Manley, D.T., and Swartz, C.M. (1994). Asymmetric bilateral right fronto-temporal left frontal stimulus electrode placement: comparisons with bifronto-temporal and unilateral placements. *Convulsive Therapy, 10*(4), 267–270. Retrieved from www.ncbi.nlm.nih.gov/pubmed/7850396.

Mayer, P. (2006). Ictal electroencephalgoraphic characteristics during electroconvulsive therapy: a review of determination and clinical relevance. *Journal of ECT, 22*(3), 213–217. Retrieved from http://journals.lww.com/ectjournal/Fulltext/2006/09000/Ictal_Electroencephalographic_Characteristics.11.aspx.

Mayer, P., Byth, K., and Harris, A. (2013). Acute antidepressant effects of right unilateral ultra-brief ECT: a double-blind randomised controlled trial. *Journal of Affective Disorders, 13*(149(1–3)), 426–429.

Mayur, P., Bray, A., Fernandes, J., Bythe, K., and Gilbett, D. (2010). Impact of hyperventilation on stimulus efficiency during the early phase of an electroconvulsive therapy course: a randomized double-blind study. *Journal of ECT, 26,* 91–94.

Metastasio, A., and Dodwell, D. (2013). A translation of "L'Elettroshock" by Cerletti and Bini, with an introduction. *The European Journal of Psychiatry, 27*(4). doi:10.4321/S0213-61632013000400001.

Muller, D.J. (1971). Unilateral ECT. (One year's experience at a city hospital). *Diseases of the Nervous System, 32*(6), 422–424. Retrieved from www.ncbi.nlm.nih.gov/pubmed/5570697.

NICE. (2003, Modified 2009). *Guidance on the Use of Electroconvulsive Therapy (Vol. Guidance Number 59).* London: National Institute for Health and Care Excellence; National Health Service.

Nobler, M.S., Luber, B., Moeller, J.R., Katzman, G.P., Prudic, J., Devanand, D.P., . . . Sackeim, H.A. (2000). Quantitative EEG during seizures induced by electroconvulsive therapy: relations to treatment modality and clinical features. I. Global analyses. *Journal of ECT, 16*(3), 211–228. Retrieved from http://journals.lww.com/ectjournal/Fulltext/2000/09000/Quantitative_EEG_During_Seizures_Induced_by.2.aspx.

NSW Health. (2010). ECT minimum standard of practice NSW. Retrieved from www.health.nsw.gov.au/policies/pd/2011/pdf/PD2011_003.pdf.

Peterchev, A.V., Rosa, M.A., Deng, Z.-D., Prudic, J., and Lisanby, S.H. (2010). ECT stimulus parameters: rethinking dosage. *Journal of ECT, 26*(3), 159–174. doi:10.1097/YCT.0b013e3181e48165.

Petrides, G., and Fink, M. (1996). The "half-age" stimulation strategy for ECT dosing. *Convulsive Therapy, 12*(3), 138–146. Retrieved from www.ncbi.nlm.nih.gov/pubmed/8872401.

Raghavendra, T. (2002). Neuromuscular blocking drugs: discovery and development. *Journal of the Royal Society of Medicine, 95*(7), 363–367. Retrieved from www.ncbi.nlm.nih.gov/pubmed/12091515.

Ranjkesh, F., Barekatain, M., and Akuchakian, S. (2005). Bifrontal versus right unilateral and bitemporal electroconvulsive therapy in major depressive disorder. *Journal of ECT, 21*(4), 207–210. Retrieved from www.ncbi.nlm.nih.gov/pubmed/16301878.

Royal Adelaide Hospital. (2015). Intravenous anaesthetics – RAH – intensive care unit. Retrieved from www.icuadelaide.com.au/files/primary/pharmacology/intravenous.pdf.

Royal College of Psychiatrists. (2015). *ECT Accreditation Service (ECTAS): Standards for the Administration of ECT,* 12th edition. London: Royal College of Psychiatrists.

SA Health. (2014). South Australian guidelines for electroconvulsive therapy. Retrieved from www.sahealth.sa.gov.au/wps/wcm/connect/0608270046ad5b01b89.

Sackeim, H.A., Decina, P., Kanzler, M., Kerr, B., and Malitz, S. (1987). Effects of electrode placement on the efficacy of titrated, low-dose ECT. *American Journal of Psychiatry, 144*(11), 1449–1455. Retrieved from www.ncbi.nlm.nih.gov/pubmed/3314538.

Sackeim, H.A., Decina, P., Prohovnik, I., and Malitz, S. (1987). Seizure threshold in electroconvulsive therapy: effects of sex, age, electrode placement, and number of treatments. *Archives of General Psychiatry, 44*(4), 355–360. doi:10.1001/archpsyc.1987.01800160067009.

Sackeim, H.A., Luber, B., Katzman, G.P., Moeller, J.R., Prudic, J., Devanand, D.P., and Nobler, M.S. (1996). The effects of electroconvulsive therapy on quantitative electroencephalograms. Relationship to clinical outcome. *Archives of General Psychiatry, 53*(9), 814–824. doi:10.1001/archpsyc.1996.01830090060009.

Sackeim, H.A., Prudic, J., Devanand, D.P., Kiersky, J.E., Fitzsimons, L., Moody, B.J., . . . Settembrino, J.M. (1993). Effects of stimulus intensity and electrode placement on the efficacy and cognitive effects of electroconvulsive therapy. *New England Journal of Medicine, 328*(12). Retrieved from www.nejm.org/doi/pdf/10.1056/NEJM199303253281204.

Sackeim, H.A., Prudic, J., Devanand, D.P., Nobler, M.S., Lisanby, S.H., Peyser, S., . . . Clark, J. (2000). A prospective, randomized, double-blind comparison of bilateral and right unilateral electroconvulsive therapy at different stimulus intensities. *Archives of General Psychiatry, 57*(5), 425–434. doi:10.1001/archpsyc.57.5.425.

Sackeim, H.A., Prudic, J., Fuller, R., Keilp, J., Lavori, P.W., and Olfson, M. (2007). The cognitive effects of electroconvulsive therapy in community settings. *Neuropsychopharmacology, 32*(1), 244–254. doi:10.1038/sj.npp.1301180.

Sackeim, H.A., Prudic, J., Nobler, M.S., Fitzsimons, L., Lisanby, S.H., Payne, N., . . . Devanand, D.P. (2008). Effects of pulse width and electrode placement on the efficacy and cognitive effects of electroconvulsive therapy. *Brain Stimulation, 1*(2), 71–83. doi:10.1016/j.brs.2008.03.001.

Scott, A.I.F. (2005). *The ECT Handbook,* 2nd edition. London: Royal College of Psychiatrists.

South Australian Medical Heritage Society. (2015). Electroconvulsive therapy (ECT): The South Australian experience. Retrieved from http://samhs.org.au/Virtual Museum/Medicine/drugs_nonsurg/ect/ect.html.

Spaans, H.-P., Verwijk, E., and Comijs, H.C. (2013). Efficacy and cognitive side effects after brief pulse and ultrabrief pulse right unilateral electroconvulsive therapy for major depression: a randomized, double-blind, controlled study. *Journal of Clinical Psychiatry, 2013*(74), 11.

Swartz, C.M. (1994). Asymmetric bilateral right fronto-temporal left frontal stimulus electrode placement. *Neuropsychobiology, 10*(4), 174–179.

Swartz, C.M. (1994). Optimizing the ECT stimulus. *Convulsive Therapy, 10*(2), 132–134; discussion 140–152. Retrieved from www.ncbi.nlm.nih.gov/pubmed/8069639.

Swartz, C.M. (2006). 4 ECT electrode options: Which is best for your patient? *Current Psychiatry, 5*(3), 114–115.

Swartz, C.M., and Evans, C.M. (1996). Beyond bitemporal and right unilateral electrode placements. *Psychiatric Annals, 26*, 705–708.

Swartz, C.M., and Larson, G. (1989). ECT stimulus duration and its efficacy. *Annals of Clinical Psychiatry, 1*, 147–152.

Swayama, E., Takahashi, M., and Inoue, A. (2008). Moderate hyperventilation prolongs electroencephalogram seizure duration of the first electroconvulsive therapy. *Journal of ECT, 24*, 195–198.

Tasmanian Government. (2013). Tasmania's Mental Health Act 2013: a guide for clinicians. Retrieved from www.dhhs.tas.gov.au/__data/assets/pdf_file/0017/152315/Clinicians Guide_CombinedAllChapters.pdf.

Tiller, J.W.G., and Lyndon, R.W. (2003). *Electroconvulsive Therapy: An Australian Guide*. Melbourne, Australia: Australian Post Graduate Medicine.

Tiller, J.W.G., and Ingram, N. (2006). Seizure threshold determination for electroconvulsive therapy: stimulus dose titration versus age-based estimations. *Australian and New Zealand Journal of Psychiatry, 40*(2), 188–192. doi:10.1080/j.1440-1614.2006.01773.x.

Tor, P.C., Bautovich, A., Wang, M.J., Martin, D., Harvey, S.B., and Loo, C. (2015). A systematic review and meta-analysis of brief versus ultrabrief right unilateral electroconvulsive therapy for depression. *Journal of Clinical Psychiatry, 10*(4088). doi:10.4088/JCP.14r09145.

Valentine, S.J., Keddie, K.M., and Dunne, D. (1968). A comparison of techniques in electroconvulsive therapy. *British Journal Psychiatry, 114*, 989–996.

Victorian Government. (2014). Mental Health Act 2014 handbook. Retrieved from www.health.vic.gov.au/mentalhealth/mhact2014.

Waite, J., and Easton, A. (2013). *The ECT Handbook*, 3rd edition. London: Royal College of Psychiatrists.

Walker, S.C., Bowley, C.J., and Walker, A.C. (2013). Anaesthesia for ECT. In Waite, J. and Easton, A. (Eds.), *The ECT Handbook*. London: Royal College of Psychiatrists.

Weaver, L.A., Ives, J.O., Williams, R., and Nies, A. (1977). A comparison of standard alternating current and low-energy briefpulse electrotherapy. *Biological Psychiatry, 12*, 525–543.

Weiner, R.D. (1980). ECT and seizure threshold: Effects of stimulus waveform and electrode placement. *Biological Psychiatry, 15*, 225–241.

Weiner, R.D. (1988). The first ECT devices. *Convulsive Therapy, 4*(1), 50–61.

Weiss, A.M., Hansen, S.M., Safranko, I., and Hughes, P. (2015). Effectiveness of left anterior right temporal electrode placement in electroconvulsive therapy: 3 case reports. *Journal of ECT, 31*(1), e1–3. doi:10.1097/YCT.0000000000000136.

Mechanism of action

After nearly 80 years of clinical practice, the precise mechanism of action for ECT remains unclear (Mankad, Beyer, Weiner and Krystal, 2010), though recent work suggests that changes in neuroplasticity may play an important role in clinical response (Pirnia et al., 2016). The absence of a clear understanding of how ECT works should not obscure the reality that it is the most effective treatment for severe mental disorders (Abrams, 2002), particularly depressive disorders with melancholia and psychosis (UK ECT Review Group, 2003).

It is apparent that the induction of a cerebral seizure that is generalised with grand mal quality and a high-intensity stimulus are essential to effective ECT (Anderson and Fergusson, 2013). These events cause therapeutic changes in the brain owing to multiple and varied effects that are long lasting throughout the central nervous system (Merkl, Heuser and Bajbouj, 2009). What is not known is how these macro changes produce micro alterations of brain function that are clearly observable at a clinical level. Neuroscience postulates that the efficacy of ECT may be related to changes in neural circuits of the brain that are related to the structure and function of neurons themselves; however, no precise mechanism has been identified (Scott, 2011).

Fink (2013) highlights four essential observations that are associated with effective ECT treatment. Repeated induction of a grand mal seizure is the central event in the treatment's efficacy, targeting and relieving specific behavioural patterns, like depressed mood, delusions, motor rigidity, mutism and suicidal thinking. Induced seizures are incremental and require repetition to produce the required behavioural and clinical effects of effective ECT treatment.

Not all seizures are effective and efficacy appears to be related to dose above threshold (Sackeim et al., 1993). Brain imaging studies may give some explanation to this observation. ECT-induced cerebral seizures are not truly generalised, even if they are associated with bilateral spike and wave rhythms on the EEG. Seizures propagate from the site of initiation and involve specific areas of the brain and spare others. Cerebral seizures differ with the type of ECT, being asymmetrical in right unilateral electrode placement with relative sparing of the left cortical and subcortical regions (Scott, 2011).

It is likely that a single mechanism of action for ECT is highly implausible since the treatment is effective in many disparate conditions, from mania and depression to Parkinson's disease (Lerer, 1998). Lerer (1998) states:

> ECT involves massive discharge over wide areas of the brain, activation of the peripheral autonomic nervous system, release of secretions of many endocrine glands. . . . All these activities cause so many changes in the chemical homeostasis of the body, that . . . the difficulty lies not in demonstrating such changes, but in differentiating . . . which of these changes may be related to the important antidepressant and amnestic effects and which are relevant to these.

PSYCHOLOGICAL HYPOTHESIS

Early on, a psychological explanation was put forward that ECT caused substantial delirium and memory impairment that supressed recollections of childhood trauma, resulting in patients being relieved of depressive, manic and psychotic symptoms after a course of treatment (Janis, 1950). This theory was popular for a period of time; however, practice changed, delirium was rare and the severity of cognitive deficits reduced bringing into question this hypothesis concerning ECT (Abrams, 2002).

ELECTROPHYSIOLOGICAL HYPOTHESIS

Fink and Kahn (1956) refuted the psychological explanation and suggested that ECT may work owing to the powerful electrophysiological effect that was demonstrated on the electroencephalogram (EEG). Many of the EEG features we now identify as being necessary for effective ECT like progressive slowing of frequencies, symmetry and increased amplitude (emerging delta and theta activity) were discredited, as many patients exhibiting these changes did not improve. This failure may have been due to the heterogeneity of the patients treated and the limitation of the EEG. It is now thought that EEG changes are necessary but not sufficient for sustained benefit from ECT (Fink, 2013).

NEUROENDOCRINE HYPOTHESIS

In the 1980s there was considerable interest in identifying ECT-induced changes in the neuroendocrine system, as it was noted that many of the vegetative functions disrupted by melancholic depression, like fatigue, tiredness, reduced appetite, weight loss, poor sleep, that are regulated by the hypothalamic–pituitary–adrenal (HPA) axis improve early during a course of ECT. Fink and Ottosson (1980) suggested a likely mode of action for ECT was via neuroendocrine pathways whereby the seizure stimulates a cascade of changes within the HPA axis. ECT has been shown to normalise the HPA axis, including restoring dexamethasone suppression of cortisol (Kunugi et al., 2005). One of the challenges in research into ECT-induced neurobiological effects is differentiating changes that may be related to the important depressive and amnesic effects from those changes that are irrelevant (Merkl et al., 2009).

ECT produces an acute surge in plasma catecholamines including growth hormone (Whalley et al., 1987), oxytocin (Devanand et al., 1998) and prolactin (Lisanby et al., 1998). The acute prolactin surge was reduced when right unilateral ECT was administered with an ineffective stimulus dose barely above seizure threshold, however the magnitude of the surge was unrelated to clinical outcome (Lisanby et al., 1998).

In summary, to date none of these neuroendocrine changes has been associated with the efficacy of ECT (Merkl et al., 2009; Scott, 2011).

NEUROCHEMICAL HYPOTHESES

Modigh (1976) suggested that changes in the concentrations of neurotransmitters like serotonin, noradrenaline, acetylcholine, dopamine and gamma-aminobutyric acid (GABA) might explain the efficacy of ECT. Further studies failed to find any consistent changes in neurotransmitter concentrations after electroconvulsive shock experiments in animals (Grahame-Smith, Green and Costain, 1978; Modigh, 1976). Related to this explanation was the hypothesis that the efficacy of ECT may be related to changes in neuroreceptor activity of neurons within the brain (Lehrer and Belmaker, 1982). Neither of these explanations gained credibility as supportive data was inconclusive (Merkl et al., 2009), highlighting a need to go beyond the monoamine hypothesis to explain the mode of action of ECT (Scott, 2011).

It is known that ECT is very effective in depressed patients who are resistant to antidepressant drugs and also those with psychotic symptoms, suggesting that either ECT has a mechanism that is different to that of antidepressants. ECT is more effective in eliciting biological responses that underlie common therapeutic action (Litchenberg and Lerer, 1989). Much work has been done examining ECT's effects on brain monoamine systems by considering the effects of electroconvulsive shock (ECS) in animal models. This work has shown that there are important differences in the effects of ECT and antidepressants on monoamine neurotransmitters, their receptors and post-receptor signal transducing mechanisms (Lerer, 1998; Nutt and Glue, 1993).

Mann (1998) noted that acute tryptophan depletion, which has been found to transiently reverse the antidepressant effect of selective serotonin reuptake inhibitors (SSRI), did not reverse the antidepressant effect of ECT, suggesting that increased levels of serotonin at postsynaptic receptors are not a critical part of the antidepressant effect of ECT. Further there was a correlation with the degree of catecholamine increase and clinical response to ECT (Mann, 1998).

In a small study of six patients with depression who had not taken any psychotropic drugs for 14 days before treatment, cerebrospinal fluid was obtained by lumbar puncture before and after eight unilateral ECT sessions. The concentration of homovanillic acid, the major metabolite of dopamine, increased significantly in all six patients (Nikisch and Mathe, 2008). There is evidence that lower dopaminergic activity may increase the risk of depression (Dunlop and Nemeroff, 2007; Merkl et al., 2009), supporting the finding that ECS changes the dopamine levels and dopamine receptors in the brain and this may be associated with treatment efficacy in ECT (Mann, 1998). This is in contrast to most other treatments for depression that do not directly increase dopamine function (Scott, 2011).

Other neurotransmitters have also been investigated, including glutamate concentrations in the dorsolateral prefrontal cortex and anterior cingulate cortex that increase into the normal range during a course of ECT and may predict treatment response (Kato, 2009; Merkl et al., 2011; Michael et al., 2003).

Remission from depression may be associated with the gradual modification of gene expression by antidepressant treatments (Scott, 2011). In a Finnish cohort of patients with treatment-resistant depression, two polymorphisms associated with dopamine metabolism affected the likelihood of remission with ECT (Huuhka et al., 2008). The greatest probability of remission was seen in patients with polymorphisms believed to lead to the lowest concentrations of dopamine in the prefrontal cortex of the brain, providing further evidence that supports the involvement of catecholamine metabolism in the mode of action of ECT (Huuhka et al., 2008).

In conclusion, the evidence suggests that there are important differences in the effects of ECT and antidepressant drugs on neurotransmitters, particularly dopamine function, providing an explanation of their differential therapeutic effects.

ANTICONVULSIVE HYPOTHESIS

An early model of the underlying pathophysiology of depression was an increased depletion of the neurotransmitter gamma-aminobutyric acid (GABA) in the cortical network of patients with depression. Sackeim, Decina, Prohovnik, Malitz and Resor (1983) proposed that it was a compensatory increase in the function of inhibitory neurotransmission in the brain circuit that was responsible for ECTs antidepressant and anticonvulsive properties. ECT had been used successfully in the treatment of epilepsy, suggesting that it had significant anticonvulsive properties owing to an increased level of GABA, resulting in a reduction of neuronal activity. Activation of GABA was thought to have potent antidepressant qualities (Sackeim et al., 1983). There has been more recent support for this hypothesis from a study of depressed patients that demonstrated a significant increase in occipital cortex-GABA concentrations, measured by proton magnetic resonance spectroscopy (MRS), in those that were successfully treated with ECT (Sanacora et al., 2003).

Further support for this mechanism of action for ECT comes from an analysis of the relationship between seizures and therapeutic effect in a large consecutive retrospective sample of 232 patients receiving ECT (Duthie, Perrin, Bennett, Currie and Reid, 2015). In this group, seizure threshold increased in 219 (94.4%) patients and stayed the same in 13 (5.6%). It did not decrease in any patients within the sample. There was a greater increase in seizure threshold in the responders compared to non-responders, highlighting that ECT is anticonvulsant. However, a rise in seizure threshold was not essential for a therapeutic effect but may represent an important maker of underlying neuroplasticity (Duthie et al., 2015).

NEUROGENESIS HYPOTHESIS

Neurogenesis has been proposed as a possible explanation of the mechanism of action of ECT. Its origin goes back to observations made by Ladislas Meduna in 1932. He found that concentrations of glia in post-mortem brains were low in patients who died of schizophrenia and high in those who died of epilepsy and schizophrenia. In addition, glia were rare in patients who had epilepsy. He hypothesised that an increase in glia cells may be the explanation that was protective of psychotic illness (Fink, 2013).

It was not until recently that new technologies enabled this theory to be tested. It is now known that electroshock in animal models causes widespread changes in gene expression, synaptic plasticity and neurogenesis. It is postulated that the clinical effects of ECT are exerted at least partly by reducing neuronal excitability and modifying synaptic plasticity (Kato, 2009), as well as increasing cell proliferation in the hippocampus, an area of the brain that is implicated in treatment with antidepressant medication (Madsen et al., 2000; Merkl et al., 2009). Recent work has shown that ECT leads to widespread neuroplasticity in neocortical, limbic and paralimbic regions and these changes may relate to the extent of antidepressant response. Variations in anterior cingulate cortex thickness discriminates between treatment responders and non-responders and may represent a biomarker of overall clinical response (Pirnia et al., 2016).

GENE EXPRESSION HYPOTHESIS

Racagni and Popoli (2008) propose that the antidepressant mechanism underlying the treatment of depression should be called the "hypothesis of neuroplasticity". Converging lines of evidence have shown that the antidepressant action may be due to changes in gene expression, synaptic transmission, plasticity and neurogenesis. Brain-derived neurotropic factor (BDNF) is a protein that encodes its own gene. The role of BDNF in the central nervous system (CNS) is to support the survival of existing neurons and encourage the growth and differentiation of new neurons. The restoration of ordinary concentrations of this growth factor may be one mechanism of the longer-term effect of antidepressant treatments (Racagni and Popoli, 2008). A preliminary report suggested that a course of ECT led to an increase in the serum concentrations of BDNF but several further studies have been inconsistent (Scott, 2011).

COGNITIVE EFFECTS OF ECT

Understanding the neurobiology of ECT-induced memory impairment is an important clinical concern and provides indirect understanding of the mechanism of action of ECT (Lerer, 1998). Much has been learned about the nature and persistence of ECT-induced cognitive deficits and how they can be diminished by modifications of treatment technique but little is know about the underlying neurochemical mechanisms except that there is no evidence for cell loss and the deficits are mostly transient (Lerer, 1998).

The complexity of this area is reflected in a study by Pigot, Andrade and Loo (2008), who reviewed the use of psychopharmacological agents in the attenuation of ECT-induced cognitive deficits, highlighting the implicated mechanisms of damage and identification of reported efficacy. The aim was to identify the possible molecular mechanism of the cognitive adverse effects of ECT and the efficacy of agents that may protect against these adverse effects. The review identified evidence that glutamatergic, cholinergic and glucocorticoid mechanisms are involved in the genesis of ECT-induced amnestic deficits while ketamine, celecoxib, mifepristone, donepezil, thyroid hormones, nitroprusside and other agents may have neuroprotective properties (Pigot et al., 2008). The study acknowledged the enormous complexity of this work as ECT influences almost every physiological system in the brain.

REFERENCES

Abrams, R. (2002). Does brief/pulse ECT cause persistent or permanent impairment? *Journal of ECT, 18*(2), 71–73.

Abrams, R. (2002). *Electroconvulsive therapy,* 4th edition. New York: Oxford University Press.

Anderson, I.M., and Fergusson, M. (2013). Mechanism of Action of ECT. In Waite, J. and Easton, A. (Eds.), *The ECT Handbook,* 3rd edition. London: Royal College of Psychiatrists.

Devanand, D.P., Lisanby, S., Lo, E.S., Fitzsimons, L., Cooper, T.B., Halbreich, U., and Sackeim, H.A. (1998). Effects of electroconvulsive therapy on plasma vasopressin and oxytocin. *Biological Psychiatry, 44*(7), 610–616. Retrieved from www.ncbi.nlm.nih.gov/pubmed/9787885.

Dunlop, B.W., and Nemeroff, C.B. (2007). The role of dopamine in the pathophysiology of depression. *Archives of General Psychiatry, 64*(3), 327–337. doi:10.1001/archpsyc.64.3.327.

Duthie, A.C., Perrin, J.S., Bennett, D.M., Currie, J., and Reid, I.C. (2015). Anticonvulsant mechanisms of electroconvulsive therapy and relation to therapeutic efficacy. *Journal of ECT, 31*(3), 173–178. doi:10.1097/YCT.0000000000 000210.

Fink, M. (2013). The mechanism of action of ECT. In Ghaziuddin, N. and Walter, G. (Eds.), *Electroconvulsive Therapy in Children and Adolescents* (pp. 18–28). New York: Oxford University Press.

Fink, M., and Kahn, R.I. (1956). Relation of EEG delta activity to behavioural responses in electroshock: quantitative serial studies. *Archives of Neurological Psychiatry (Chic.), 78,* 516–525.

Fink, M., and Ottosson, J.O. (1980). A theory of convulsive therapy in endogenous depression: significance of hypothalamic functions. *Psychiatry Research, 2*(1), 49–61. Retrieved from www.ncbi.nlm.nih.gov/pubmed/6106253.

Grahame-Smith, D.G., Green, A.R., and Costain, D.W. (1978). Mechanism of the antidepressant action of electroconvulsive therapy. *Lancet, 1*(8058), 254–257. Retrieved from www.ncbi.nlm.nih.gov/pubmed/74675.

Huuhka, K., Anttila, S., Huuhka, M., Hietala, J., Huhtala, H., Mononen, N., . . . Leinonen, E. (2008). Dopamine 2 receptor C957T and catechol-o-methyltransferase Val158Met polymorphisms are associated with treatment response in electroconvulsive therapy. *Neuroscience Letters, 448*(1), 79–83. doi:10.1016/j.neulet.2008.10.015.

Janis, I.L. (1950). Psychologic effects of electric convulsive treatments (post-treatment anmesias). *Journal of Mental Disorders, 111,* 359–382.

Kato, N. (2009). Neurophysiological mechanisms of electroconvulsive therapy for depression. *Neuroscience Research, 64*(1), 3–11. doi:10.1016/j.neures.2009.01.014.

Kunugi, H., Ida, I., Owashi, T., Kimura, M., Inoue, Y., Nakagawa, S., . . . Mikuni, M. (2005). Assessment of the dexamethasone/CRH test as a state-dependent marker for hypothalamic–pituitary–adrenal (HPA) axis abnormalities in major depressive episode: a Multicenter Study. *Neuropsychopharmacology*, *31*(1), 212–220. doi:10.1038/sj.npp.1300868.

Lehrer, B, and Belmaker, R.H. (1982). Mechanism of action of ECT. *Biological Psychiatry*, *17*, 497–511.

Lerer, B. (1998). The neurobiology of ECT: the road taken. *Journal of ECT*, *14*(3), 149–153.

Lisanby, S.H., Devanand, D., P, Prudic, J., Pierson, D., Nobler, M.S., Fitzsimons, L., and Sackeim, H.A. (1998). Prolactin resonse to electroconvulsive therapy: effects of electrode placement and stimulus dosage. *Biological Psychiatry*, *43*, 146–155. doi:10.1016/S0006-3223(97)00222-9.

Litchenberg, P., and Lerer, B. (1989). Implications of clinical spectrum for mechanisms of action: ECT and antidepressants reconsidered. *Journal of ECT*, *5*(3), 216–226.

Madsen, T.M., Treschow, A., Bengzon, J., Bolwig, T.G., Lindvall, O., and Tingstrom, A. (2000). Increased neurogenesis in a model of electroconvulsive therapy. *Biological Psychiatry*, *47*(12), 1043–1049. Retrieved from www.ncbi.nlm.nih.gov/pubmed/10862803.

Mankad, M.V., Beyer, J.L., Weiner, R.D., and Krystal, A. (2010). *Clinical Manual of Electroconvulsive Therapy*. Washington, DC: American Psychiatric Publishing.

Mann, J.J. (1998). Neurobiological correlates of the antidepressant action of electroconvulsive therapy. *Journal of ECT*, *14*(3), 172–180.

Merkl, A., Heuser, I., and Bajbouj, M. (2009). Antidepressant electroconvulsive therapy: mechanism of action, recent advances and limitations. *Experimental Neurology*, *219*(1), 20–26. doi:10.1016/j.expneurol.2009.04.027.

Merkl, A., Schubert, F., Quante, A., Luborzewski, A., Brakemeier, E.L., Grimm, S., . . . Bajbouj, M. (2011). Abnormal cingulate and prefrontal cortical neurochemistry in major depression after electroconvulsive therapy. *Biological Psychiatry*, *69*(8), 772–779. doi:10.1016/j.biopsych.2010.08.009.

Michael, N., Erfurth, A., Ohrmann, P., Arolt, V., Heindel, W., and Pfleiderer, B. (2003). Metabolic changes within the left dorsolateral prefreontal cortex occuring with electroconvulsive therapy in patients with treatment resistant unipolar depression. *Psychiological Medicine*, *33*, 1277–1284.

Modigh, K. (1976). Long-term effects of electroconvulsive shock therapy on synthesis turnover and uptake of brain monoamines. *Psychopharmacology*, *49*(2), 179–185. Retrieved from www.ncbi.nlm.nih.gov/pubmed/825905.

Nikisch, G., and Mathe, A.A. (2008). CSF monoamine metabolites and neuropeptides in depressed patients before and after electroconvulsive therapy. *European Psychiatry*, *23*, 356–359.

Nutt, D.J., and Glue, P. (1993). The Neurobiology of ECT: Animal Studies. In Coffey, E.C. (Ed.), *The Clinical Science of Electroconvulsive Therapy* (Vol. 38, pp. 213–234). Washington, DC, USA: American Psychiatric Press.

Pigot, M., Andrade, C., and Loo, C. (2008). Pharmacological attenuation of electroconvulsive therapy-induced cognitive deficits: theoretical background and clincial findings. *Journal of ECT*, *24*, 57–67.

Pirnia, T., Joshi, S.H., Leaver, A.M., Vasavada, M., Njau, S., Woods, R.P., . . . Narr, K.L. (2016). Electroconvulsive therapy and structural neuroplasticity in neocortical, limbic and paralimbic cortex. *Translational Psychiatry*, *6*(6), e832. doi:10.1038/tp.2016.102.

Racagni, G., and Popoli, M. (2008). Cellular and molecular mechanisms in the long-term action of antidepressants. *Dialogues in Clinical Neuroscience*, *10*(4), 385–400. Retrieved from www.ncbi.nlm.nih.gov/pubmed/19170396.

Sackeim, H.A., Decina, P., Prohovnik, I., Malitz, S., and Resor, S.R. (1983). Anticonvulsant and antidepressant properties of electroconvulsive therapy: a proposed mechanism of action. *Biological Psychiatry*, *18*(11), 1301–1310. Retrieved from www.ncbi.nlm.nih.gov/pubmed/6317065.

Sackeim, H.A., Prudic, J., Devanand, D.P., Kiersky, J.E., Fitzsimons, L., Moody, B.J., . . . Settembrino, J.M. (1993). Effects of Stimulus intensity and electrode placement on the efficacy and cognitive effects of electroconvulsive therapy. *New England Journal of Medicine*, *328*(12). Retrieved from www.nejm.org/doi/pdf/10.1056/NEJM199303253281204.

Sanacora, A., Mason, G.F., Rothman, D.L., Hyder, F., Ciarcia, J.J., Ostroff, R.B., . . . Krystal, J.H. (2003). Increased cortisol GABA concentrations in depressed patients recieving ECT. *American Journal of Psychiatry*, *160*, 577–579.

Scott, A.I.F. (2011). Mode of action of electroconvulsive therapy: an update. *Advances in Psychiatric Treatment*, *17*, 15–22.

UK ECT Review Group. (2003). Efficacy and safety of electroconvulsive therapy in depressive disorders: a systematic review and meta-analysis. *Lancet*, *361*, 799–808.

Whalley, L.J., Eagles. J.M., Bowler. G.M., Bennie, J.G., Dick, H.R., McGuire, R.J., and Fink, G. (1987). Selective effects of ECT on hypothalamic-pituitary activity. *Psychological Medicine*, *17*, 319–328.

Clinical indications for ECT: adults

ECT has been used to treat severe psychiatric illness since it was discovered in 1938. Owing to the benefits of the first treatment, it spread rapidly around the world, providing relief to many patients who were otherwise unresponsive to treatments at that time. ECT is particularly useful for depression. It also has a role in treating other illnesses such as schizophrenia, schizoaffective disorder, mania, catatonia, neuroleptic malignant syndrome, Parkinson's disease and postpartum psychosis (Abrams, 2002). Worldwide, the major indication for ECT is major depression (Lamprecht, Ferrier, Swann and Waite, 2013; NSW Health, 2010; Tiller and Lyndon, 2003).

MAJOR DEPRESSIVE DISORDER / UNIPOLAR DEPRESSION

ECT is a highly effective treatment for major depressive disorder with remission rates reported as being between 60% and 90% (Lamprecht et al., 2013; McCall, Dunn, Rosenquist and Hughes, 2002;

Sackeim et al., 2000; Sackeim et al., 1993). The best responses to ECT are patients who have a major depressive disorder with psychosis (Petrides et al., 2001).

Most randomised controlled trials comparing the efficacy of ECT to sham ECT in depressive illness conducted between 1963 and 1985 demonstrated that ECT was superior to anaesthesia alone (Brandon et al., 1984; Freeman, Basson and Crighton, 1978; Gregory, Shawcross and Gill, 1985; Johnstone et al., 1980; West, 1981; Wilson et al., 1963). In these studies, participants with depressive illness were randomised into two groups, one given anaesthesia and ECT and the other anaesthetic agents only without the induction of a seizure. One study failed to demonstrate the superiority of real compared simulated ECT (Lambourn and Gill, 1978) as the form of ECT administered in the study, low-dose brief-pulse right unilateral, has been shown to be clinically ineffective (Sackeim, Decina, Kanzler, Kerr and Malitz, 1987).

A number of meta-analyses have added weight to the superiority of real ECT compared to sham treatment in depressive illness (Kho, van Vreeswijk, Simpson and Zwinderman, 2003; Pagnin and de Queiroz, 2004; UK ECT Review Group, 2003).

Randomised controlled trials have compared ECT with tricyclic antidepressants (Gangadhar, Kapur and Kalyanasundaram, 1982; Greenblatt, Grosser and Wechsler, 1962; McDonald, Perkins and Marjerrison, 1966) and monoamine oxidase inhibitors (Davidson, McLeod, Law-Yone and Linnoila, 1978). A meta-analysis of this work demonstrated clear superiority for ECT compared to medication, 20% for tricyclic antidepressants and 45% for monoamine oxidase inhibitors (Janicak et al., 1985). Rifkin (1988) noted in a further review that the standards for adequate pharmacotherapy had changed over time and that few early studies used aggressive medication dosage or duration that may have caused a bias in favour of ECT.

There are few randomised control trials of ECT with modern antidepressant agents. Folkerts et al. (1997) compared ECT to paroxetine, a selective serotonin reuptake inhibitor (SSRI), and found that moderate-dose right unilateral electrode placement was more effective than medication. In a more recent meta-analysis, the UK ECT Review Group (2003) identified 18 randomised controlled trials that compared ECT to antidepressant medications; of these, 13 met strict selection criteria, with results again favouring ECT over medication. However, there were no trials comparing ECT to other SSRIs or newer dual-action agents like desvenlafaxine, duloxetine and mirtazapine.

Even though ECT has been shown to be more effective in treating depression, it is usually considered to be a second-line treatment. Exceptions are when there is a medical emergency and a rapid response is required (Porter and Ferrier, 1999). The recent revision by the British Association for Psychopharmacology of evidence-based guidelines for treating depressive disorders with antidepressants recommends that ECT should be considered as a first-line treatment for major depression in urgent and emergency situations, such as depressive stupor, high risk of suicide, extreme level of distress or poor fluid intake (Cleare et al., 2015). In all other situations, it should be considered when first-line strategies have failed or the patient expresses a clear choice (Cleare et al., 2015).

Responsiveness to ECT will vary on the subtype of depression that is being treated, medication resistance and the ECT technique that is being utilised (Fink et al., 2007; Mukherjee et al., 1994; Rasmussen et al., 2009; Sackeim et al., 2000; Sackeim et al., 1993; Sobin, Prudic, Devanand, Nobler and Sackeim, 1996). ECT has been shown to be particularly effective in treating psychotic depression (Parker, Roy, Hadzi-Pavlovic and Pedic, 1992; Petrides et al., 2001).

ECT is also effective in treating severe refractory depression with melancholic features (Hickie, Mason, Parker and Brodaty, 1996; Parker et al., 1999). Follow this early work by the Black Dog Institute Sydney, clinicians have generally believed that depression with melancholic features was more responsive to treatment with ECT than other forms of depression. This view has been challenged by a recent large study of 489 patients (Fink et al., 2007).

In this group, 311, or 63.6%, met DSM-IV criteria for depression with melancholic features. Melancholic features were a weak predictor of response to ECT, with 62.1% of patients with this diagnosis remitting compared to 78.7% for those with non-melancholic depression. The melancholic group also had a higher relapse rate when switched to continuation treatment with medication alone (Fink et al., 2007). It is possible that these findings may be explained on the basis that they are measuring different aspects of depression with the DSM-IV major depressive disorder specifier, "with melancholia" being a less sensitive tool than the sign-based rating system of psychomotor disturbance in patients with melancholia developed by Hickie et al. (1996).

There is some evidence to suggest that c-ECT plus long-term antidepressant treatment is effective in preventing recurrence in chronically depressed patients who have responded to an index course of treatment. Gagne, Furman, Carpenter and Price (2000), in a retrospective case-controlled study of 58 patients, where half received long-term antidepressant therapy alone after responding to an index course of ECT while the other group continued with medication and c-ECT, found that those who continued with ECT did significantly better. The cumulative survival probability without relapse or recurrence at two years was 93% for the combined group and 52% for medication alone. At five years, survival declined to 73% for the combination group and 18% for antidepressant treatment alone (Gagne et al., 2000). These findings have been ratified in the recently published PRIDE study, which demonstrated the superiority of c-ECT with medication over medication alone in depressed elderly patients who responded to an index course of ECT (Kellner et al., 2016).

Stek, van der Wurff, Hoogendijk and Beekman (2003) conducted the Cochrane Review of ECT for depression in elderly people. They highlighted the anecdotal evidence that antidepressant drugs can cause side effects in this group and ECT can be a useful alternative. Following a search of the literature for randomised studies that compared ECT to simulated ECT and antidepressants, the review concluded that it was not possible to draw firm conclusions on whether ECT was more effective than antidepressants or on the safety or side effects of ECT in the elderly. Only four studies were found, each of which has serious methodological problems (Stek et al., 2003).

Clinical practice guidelines (CPGs)

The evidence supporting the effectiveness of ECT in the treatment of unipolar depression has been exhaustively reviewed and summarised in the various clinical practice guidelines that are available around the world.

United Kingdom (UK)

UK ECT practitioners are governed by three significant guidelines: *Depression in Adults Recognition and Management*, published by the National Institute for Clinical Excellence (2016), The evidence-based guidelines for treating depressive disorders with antidepressants, a 2015 revision of the 2008 British Association for Psychopharmacology guidelines (Cleare et al., 2015) and *The ECT Handbook,* 3rd edition, published by the Royal College of Psychiatrists (Waite and Easton, 2013).

The NICE guidelines have an updated section covering the use of ECT in depression that replaces the relevant section in the guidance on the use of ECT document, reflecting a change in their recommendations (NICE, 2003, modified 2009). ECT should be considered for acute treatment of severe depression that is life-threatening, when a rapid response is required or when other treatments have failed. It should not be used routinely for moderate depression except in the face of treatment failure with multiple medications; should only be used in people who had a partial response to a previous course after an extensive risk–benefit analysis; and should be used with caution in the elderly. The choice of the type of ECT should balance efficacy against the risk of cognitive impairment, be given following fully informed consent, should not conflict with a valid advance care directive and the person's advocate or carer should have been informed (NICE, 2016).

Like other CPGs, the British Association for Psychopharmacology guidelines have four levels of evidence categories, which are followed by a rating of the strength recommendation from A to D, and S, standard of good practice (Cleare et al., 2015). There is strong evidence, category A, that there is high risk of relapse after the completion of an index course of ECT that is reduced through the use continuation pharmacotherapy. The use of ECT as a first-line treatment in emergency conditions is rated level C evidence, while the use of bilateral ECT in urgent circumstances is rated level B but carries a rating of level D in non-urgent cases. ECT is not recommended as a first-line treatment for major depression in non-urgent circumstances (Cleare et al., 2015).

The ECT Handbook, 3rd edition (Waite and Easton, 2013) is a comprehensive evidenced based work covering all aspects of ECT as it applies to the UK and a review is beyond the scope of *The ECT Workbook.*

Scotland

The Scottish Intercollegiate Guidelines Network does not have a CPG for pharmacological management of major depressive disorder in adults; however, it does have a CPG for non-pharmacological management of depression in adults (Scottish Intercollegiate Guidelines Network (SIGN), 2010) and perinatal mood disorders (Scottish Intercollegiate Guidelines Network (SIGN), 2012). In its treatment options for perinatal disorders, the CPG does discuss the role of ECT, highlighting that there is no good quality evidence on using ECT during pregnancy. The CPG concluded that ECT administered during pregnancy was effective and that the risk to the woman and child were low, based upon a comprehensive literature review that identified 339 case reports from 1941 to 2007, with partial remission reported in 78% of cases (Anderson and Reti, 2009). The CPG did not comment on the use of ECT in postpartum

depression or psychosis (Scottish Intercollegiate Guidelines Network (SIGN), 2012).

Spain

Spain has based their clinical practice guidelines on the management of depression in adults using the Scottish Intercollegiate Guidelines Network levels of evidence and grades of recommendations (Ministry of Health Social Services and Equity, 2014). The CPG considered the nature and safety of ECT, electrode placement and use in relapse prevention. The grade of recommendation for ECT was rated as A: at least one meta-analysis, systematic review or clinical trial rated as 1++ directly applicable to the target populate of the guide.

The CPG notes that ECT should be considered as a therapeutic option in patients with severe depression, mainly if there is a need for a rapid response due to high suicidal intent or severe physical damage or when other treatments have failed (Ministry of Health Social Services and Equity, 2014). Based upon good clinical practice, ECT should always be given by experienced professionals, following a physical and psychiatric assessment and in a hospital setting; informed consent is essential. The decision to use ECT should be made jointly with the patient and/or family after considering all of the alternatives and patient preference following provision of all of the necessary information, focusing on the purpose of the procedure, the side effects and a treatment plan (Ministry of Health Social Services and Equity, 2014).

World Federation of Societies of Biological Psychiatry (WFSBP)

The World Federation of Societies of Biological Psychiatry (WFSBP) provides two comprehensive reviews on the use of ECT in guidelines for the biological treatment of unipolar depressive disorders; Part 1, update 2013, on the acute and continuation treatment of unipolar depressive disorders, and Part 2 on the maintenance treatment of major depressive disorder – update 2015 (Bauer et al., 2013; Bauer et al., 2015).

These guidelines use six categories of evidence CE, from CE A (full evidence from controlled trials) to CE F (lack of evidence) and then make recommendations based upon the CE and additional aspects such as safety, tolerability and interaction potential labelled recommended grade (RG) 1 to 5. The evidence for use of ECT in the treatment of unipolar depressive disorder is CE C and RG 4 (Bauer et al., 2013).

Indications for using ECT as a first-line treatment include: severe major depression with psychosis or psychomotor retardation, "true" treatment-resistant major depression, refusal of food intake, rapid relief of overwhelming suicidal ideation, when medications are contraindicated like with pregnancy, where there has been previous response to ECT or patient preference (Bauer et al., 2013).

WFSBP rate the use of ECT during the maintenance phase of treatment as CE D, inconsistent results and RG 5. Periodic m-ECT has been recommended for patients who respond fully to ECT during the index course and continuation phase of treatment, especially for those who are not eligible or who do not respond to maintenance medication treatment (Bauer et al., 2015).

The WFSBP Guidelines on Brain Stimulation Treatments in Psychiatry section on ECT points the reader to key UK, US and German works on ECT that are regularly reviewed and does not offer any specific recommendations (Schlaepfer, George and Mayberg, 2010).

USA

The *Practice Guidelines for the Treatment of Patients With Major Depressive Disorder*, 3rd edition, published by the American Psychiatric Association in 2010, have three levels of endorsement supporting the recommendations made through the document; (1) recommended with substantial clinical confidence; (2) recommended with moderate clinical confidence; and (3) may be recommended on the basis of individual circumstances (Gelenberg et al., 2010).

The CPG gives a Level 1 rating for use of ECT as a treatment in the acute phase of severe major depressive disorder that has not responded to psychotherapeutic and/or pharmacological interventions, particularly in those who have had significant functional impairment or have not responded to numerous medication trials. It also recommends the use of ECT for individuals who have major depressive disorder with psychosis or catatonia and where there is an urgent need for response due to strong suicide intent or refusal to eat to drink with Level 1 confidence. A Level 2 recommendation is made for patient choice or those who have had a good response to ECT in the past (Gelenberg et al., 2010). The guideline concludes the section on ECT with a reference to the *Practice of Electroconvulsive Therapy: Recommendations for Treatment, Training and Privileging*, 2nd edition for more detailed information (American Psychiatric Association, 2001).

The Texas Medication Algorithm Project was a statewide quality assurance programme that developed and prospectively evaluated consensus-based medication algorithms for the treatment of individuals with severe and persistent mental illness with the aim of providing appropriate treatment recommendations to improve clinical outcomes (Crismon et al., 1999). The work is now extensive with algorithms covering major depressive disorder (Crismon et al., 1999), schizophrenia (Moore et al., 2007), bipolar disorder (Suppes et al., 2001), mania (Suppes et al., 2003) and mental illness in children (Pliszka et al., 2000). ECT is recommended as Stage 4 treatment of major depressive disorder if there has not been a response to medication trials and Stage 3 treatment for major depressive disorder with psychosis (Suehs, Bendele, Crismon, Madhukar, Trivedi and Kurian, 2008).

Canada

Canadian practitioners are guided by the Canadian Network for Mood and Anxiety Treatments (CANMAT) clinical guidelines for the management of major depressive disorder in adults (Kennedy, Lam, Parikh, Patten and Ravindran, 2009). Criteria for level of evidence used in the guideline ranges from Level 1 (at least 2 RCTs with adequate sample sizes, preferably placebo-controlled, and/or meta-analysis with narrow confidence interval) to Level 4 (expert opinion/consensus). The CPG then makes recommendations based upon the level of evidence ranging from first to third line. ECT has Level 1 evidence for acute efficacy, relapse prevention and safety and tolerability in the following conditions; acute suicidal ideation, major depression with psychosis and treatment-resistant depression. Repeated medication intolerance, catatonia, prior favourable response, rapidly deteriorating physical health and during pregnancy have Level 3 evidence, while patient choice is rated as Level 4 evidence (Kennedy et al., 2009).

Australia

In Australia, the Royal Australian and New Zealand College of Psychiatrists (RANZCP) published an updated clinical practice guideline (CPG) for mood disorders, the first CPG to address both depressive and bipolar disorders (Malhi et al., 2015). Like other CPGs it was based upon evidence-based recommendations (EBRs) graded from Level 1 to Level 4, evidence developed from articles and information obtained from a wide range of sources and then subjected to rigorous successive consultation and external review involving: expert and clinical advisors, the public, key stakeholders, professional bodies and specialist groups with an interest in mood disorders (Malhi et al., 2015).

The RANZCP CPG is extensive, covering a large number of disorders. Of these disorders, the ones that are relevant to *The ECT Workbook* include: unipolar depression/major depressive disorder, melancholia, psychotic depression, treatment-resistant depression and those covered in the next section: mania, ECT-induced mania, bipolar depression and rapid cycling bipolar disorder (Malhi et al., 2015).

The Australian CPG rates the use of ECT for unipolar depression as Level II evidence, Step 3 on the treatment algorithm when Steps 0 to 2 have been insufficient to bring about remission (Malhi et al., 2015). ECT is a safe and effective treatment for the more severe forms of depression, where its

antidepressant effect is found to be superior to medication strategies (Lisanby, 2007). Owing to the potential complications and logistic in administration it is usually administered after several failed trials of medication.

The CPG highlights that electrode placement and the dosage of ECT needs to be determined individually, weighing up the benefits and potential complications for each patient. It notes the wide variation in stimulus, dose above threshold, and electrode placement that renders comparative studies difficult to interpret owing to methodological inconsistencies (Malhi et al., 2015). Bitemporal ECT is more effective than unilateral ECT but has a great cognitive side effect burden, making individualisation of treatment important. Dosing 6 to 8 times above seizure threshold raises the efficacy of unilateral ECT, making it similar to bitemporal ECT with a higher cognitive burden that may be permanent (Carney and Geddes, 2003; Loo, Schweitzer and Pratt, 2006; Sackeim et al., 2007). Clinical experience suggests that bifrontal ECT can be associated with fewer cognitive side effects than bitemporal ECT and that there appears to be further cognitive advantage using ultrabrief unilateral ECT and query ultrabrief bifrontal ECT that may be a useful option for some patients (Malhi et al., 2015).

The CPG highlights that major depression with psychosis and melancholia as well as catatonia may have preferential response to ECT and that ECT may be the treatment of choice for this group of patients and can be invaluable as maintenance treatment for patients with treatment resistance depression (Malhi et al., 2015). Following recovery, adequate maintenance treatment should be continued for six to 12 months or longer, either as combination treatment with antidepressant and antipsychotic medications or as m-ECT, depending upon individual circumstances (Malhi et al., 2015).

In summary, most of the CPGs for treatment of depression provide similar basic principles of treatment, which include individualising a treatment plan, preparing a patient for potential long-term treatment, providing measurement-based care and treating to remission. Davidson (2010) reviewed the major American and European treatment guidelines for the treatment of depression and concluded that, while the guidelines were all evidence-based, certain factors can influence differences in specific recommendations, such as the consensus group's composition, underlying mandates and cultural attitudes. He noted that in all guidelines ECT was reserved for severe depression in combination with antidepressant and/or antipsychotic mediation (Davidson, 2010).

BIPOLAR DISORDER: MANIA, DEPRESSION AND MIXED STATE

Manic episodes are very responsive to ECT. Some of the earliest examples of response to ECT were in patients with mania. Mukherjee et al.'s (1994) review of the early studies in mania reported a response rate between 63% and 84%. Since that time there have only been a limited number of studies looking at the efficacy of ECT in mania. Versiani, Cheniaux and Landeira-Fernandez (2011) completed a systematic review and identified 28 studies where ECT had been used as a treatment for mania. In spite of methodological weakness in the studies reviewed, the review concluded that ECT was effective treatment for mania, especially in severe or treatment refractory cases. Effectiveness of ECT in treating acute mania was the conclusion reached in another literature review completed in the same year (Loo, Katalinic, Mitchell and Greenberg, 2011). They noted that ECT has clinically meaningful efficacy, especially in patients who have failed to respond to medication. However, there was insufficient evidence to support one electrode placement over another owing to methodological problems identified like inadequate dosing for unilateral ECT (Loo et al., 2011).

There have been three randomised control trials that have compared medication and ECT for the treatment of mania. Small et al. (1988) reported on 34 hospitalised patients and showed that ECT was more effective than lithium carbonate in acute mania in an eight-week trial.

Sikdar, Kulhara, Avasthi and Singh (1994) compared bitemporal ECT, chlorpromazine with simulated ECT and chlorpromazine in 30 patients with mania. There was a rapid response in the group that had real ECT and chlorpromazine with 12 patients achieving remission compared to only one patient in the control group. Those who received ECT had significantly shorter durations of illness.

Mukherjee et al. (1994) compared left unilateral, right unilateral and bitemporal ECT with a combination of lithium and haloperidol in 20 patients with mania who were difficult to treat with medication in the past. 59% of patients in the ECT groups responded compared to 0% in the medication group. There was no difference in the type of ECT used.

Recent work suggests that bifrontal ECT may be at least as efficacious as bitemporal ECT in severe mania and better tolerated (Grunze et al., 2009). Hiremani, Thirthalli, Tharayil and Gangadhar (2008) recruited 36 medication-free manic inpatients and randomised them into receiving either bifrontal or bitemporal ECT. Patients were assessed six times throughout the course of treatment. Manic patients treated with bifrontal ECT responded faster than those treated with bitemporal ECT, with no significant difference between the groups in performance on cognitive function tests (Hiremani et al., 2008). In another study of 28 inpatients, Barekatain, Jahangard, Haghighi and Ranjkesh (2008) showed that moderate-dose bifrontal ECT was as effective as bitemporal ECT, with fewer cognitive side effects in the treatment of patients with severe mania.

Karmacharya, England and Ongur (2008) highlighted the benefits in administering ECT to patients with delirious mania, characterised by sudden onset of symptoms including disorientation, incontinence, inappropriate toileting and taking clothes off. They noted consistent and significant benefits when treated with ECT and concluded that this was the definitive treatment for this severe psychiatric syndrome.

The lack of scientific evidence supporting the use of ECT in bipolar disorder depression, mania and mixed states is surprising and contrasts with the wealth of anecdotal clinical experience that suggests that ECT is an important tool in the treatment for this condition, owing in part to the high level of stigma that continues to be associated with ECT (Versiani et al., 2011).

Clinical practice guidelines (CPGs)

A review of clinical practice guidelines for bipolar disorder highlights the inconsistencies that exist in the role ECT has in treating bipolar depression, mania or mixed states.

United Kingdom (UK)

Despite the evidence cited above, ECT is no longer regularly considered in the UK for the treatment of mania (Whitehouse and Waite, 2013). The National Institute for Health and Clinical Excellence (2006) guideline on bipolar disorder did not mention ECT as an option to manage acute mania, in contrast to the 2003 acknowledgement in the NICE guidance on the use of ECT that it was effective in acute mania (NICE, 2003, modified 2009). The third edition of *The ECT Handbook* did not agree and concluded that ECT should be considered for the treatment of persistent or life-threatening symptoms in severe or prolonged manic episodes where this is an inadequate response to first-line treatments using mood-stabilising plus antipsychotic drugs (Waite and Easton, 2013). This inconsistency has now been rectified in the latest version of the NICE guide line for bipolar disorder where there is a brief statement that ECT can be used as a treatment for severe mania that has not responded to other interventions (NICE, 2014a).

USA

In the USA, the American Psychiatric Association (APA) clinical practice guidelines for bipolar disorder review the three prospective studies, noted above, that have assessed the clinical outcomes of treatment of acute mania with ECT, noting its benefit (Hirschfeld et al., 2010). The guideline concluded that, even though all of the studies had small sample sizes, the results were consistent with earlier retrospective comparisons on outcome in mania and with earlier naturalistic case series in bipolar depression and mixed states (Hirschfeld et al., 2010). The guidelines conclude by making reference to the APA Task Force report on ECT. This work highlights that ECT is an efficacious treatment for bipolar disorder mania, depression and mixed states, although it also acknowledges the paucity of evidence supporting the recommendations (American Psychiatric Association, 2001).

The Texas Medication Algorithm Project for bipolar disorder is more conservative and recommends the use of ECT as a Stage 4 treatment option where there has been only a partial response or no response to combination medication trials in bipolar depression and mania (Crismon, Argo, Bendele and Suppes, 2007).

World Federation of Societies of Biological Psychiatry (WFSBP)

The WFSBP provides comprehensive reviews on the use of ECT in three guidelines for the biological treatment of bipolar disorders: update 2009 on the treatment of acute mania, update 2010 on the treatment of acute bipolar depression, and update 2012 on the long-term treatment of bipolar disorder (Grunze et al., 2009; Grunze et al., 2010, 2013). All of the guidelines note that the category of evidence for the use of ECT in acute mania, acute bipolar depression and long-term treatment are limited to level C (evidence from uncontrolled studies: C1; case reports: C2; or expert opinion: C) or level D (inconsistent results; positive RCTs are outweighed by an approximately equal number of negative studies). They then note a recommended grade (RG) based upon the level of evidence.

WFSBP notes that RCTs have not been completed in mania and the evidence is, from numerous case reports, chart reviews, with several studies comparing ECT to pharmacological interventions, with only two prospective studies, already noted above, that the category of evidence is C1, with a recommended grade of 4, category C evidence (Grunze et al., 2009).

The same category of evidence and recommended grade is applied to treatment of acute bipolar depression, C1 and RG 4 (Grunze et al., 2010). The guideline states that, although controlled data is limited, ECT remains the most successful non-pharmacological treatment for bipolar depression (Grunze et al., 2010) This conclusion is based upon a comprehensive review of acute treatments for bipolar depression completed by Silverstone and Silverstone (2004) and case reports like the six patients who all responded to bitemporal ECT reported by Macedo-Soares, Moreno, Rigonatti and Lafer (2005).

In its update on the long-term treatments for bipolar disorder, WFSBP notes that there is a reasonable body of literature on open and comparator studies supporting the use of maintenance ECT (m-ECT) in bipolar depressed patients who have responded an acute index course of ECT (Grunze et al., 2013). The guideline refers to a comprehensive review of articles published in English, on continuation ECT (c-ECT) and m-ECT between 1998 to 2009, by Petrides, Tobias, Kellner and Rudorfer (2011). They identified 32 reports of which there were 24 case reports, six prospective naturalistic studies and two RCTs and concluded that c-ECT and m-ECT were valuable treatment modalities to prevent relapse and recurrence of mood disorder in patients who had responded to an index course of ECT (Petrides et al., 2011). This finding was replicated in a more recent review that stated that ECT is an effective treatment for acute mania, bipolar depression and mixed affective states and has useful efficacy in pharmacotherapy-resistant patients (Loo et al., 2011). In conclusion, WFSBP guidelines for long-term treatment of bipolar disorders rated the overall evidence for the use of m-ECT as RG 4, based on category C evidence (Grunze et al., 2013).

Scotland

The SIGN CPG for bipolar disorder has been withdrawn. It is over 10 years old, written in 2005, and its relevance to current practice is questionable.

Canada

The CANMAT guidelines for bipolar disorder algorithm for acute mania recommends that ECT should be considered as Step 4, "consider adding or switching to a second or third-line agent or ECT", if there has not been a response after completing medication and psychological options noted in the first three steps (Yatham et al., 2013). In the text, the guideline highlights that, although ECT can be an effective option, research studies have not been rigorous and therefore it continues to be recommended as second-line therapy (Level 3) (Yatham et al., 2013). For the treatment of bipolar depression, CANMAT guidelines algorithm recommends that ECT should be considered as Step 5, "consider ECT, third-line agents and novel or experimental options", after Steps 1 to 4 medication and psychological options have failed (Yatham et al., 2013). There is further clarification in the text that ECT should be used in patients who have psychotic bipolar depression, in those at high risk for suicide, and in those with a significant medical complications due to not eating and drinking (Yatham et al., 2013). In this CPG, the level of evidence supporting the use of ECT as maintenance treatment in bipolar disorder was four, based upon anecdotal report or expert opinion.

Australia

In Australia, the Royal Australian and New Zealand College of Psychiatrists (RANZCP) clinical practice guidelines for mood disorders notes that there is a limited but consistent evidence base supporting the use of ECT for acute mania (Malhi et al., 2015). It also acknowledges the paucity of studies and the methodological shortcomings in studies to date and the inability to recommend the best electrode placement due to problems with inadequate dosing for unilateral compared to bilateral ECT (Malhi et al., 2015). In the algorithm for bipolar depression, the RANZCP guidelines recommends using ECT as Step 3 when the first two steps using medication and psychological treatments were ineffective or not tolerated (Malhi et al., 2015). In the text, the guidelines identify the lack of studies evaluating the use of physical treatments like ECT in bipolar depression or mixed states, placing it at the same level as bright light therapy, vagus nerve stimulation and repetitive transcranial magnetic stimulation (Malhi et al., 2015). The CPG rates the use of ECT in the treatment of rapid cycle bipolar as Level 3 evidence based upon two literature reviews that found ECT to be efficacious in selected cases (Calabrese et al., 2001; Papadimitriou, Dikeos, Soldatos and Calabrese, 2007).

SCHIZOPHRENIA

The American Psychiatric Association (2001) highlighted that schizophrenia is the second most common indication for ECT use in the USA. Soon after its innovation, ECT was widely used to treat patients with schizophrenia. Following the advent of new antipsychotic medication in the 1960s, its use declined. Earlier results indicated that the benefits in this group were from 50% to 70% (American Psychiatric Association, 1990). Fink and Sackeim (1996) highlighted that patients with schizophrenia were most responsive if they had a rapid onset of symptoms and short durations of illness with affective and catatonic features. More recent evidence highlights that positive symptoms of schizophrenia respond better to ECT than negative symptoms (Chanpattana and Sackeim, 2010). It is therefore surprising that with this long history of response to ECT there are very few controlled trials examining the use of this treatment in schizophrenia (Fear, 2005).

Between 1995 and 1998, a number of literature reviews were published highlighting the clinical benefits of using ECT to treat patients with schizophrenia (Fink and Sackeim, 1996; Johns and Thompson, 1995; Krueger and Sackeim, 1995; Lehman et al., 1998).

A systematic review of ECT and schizophrenia was published as part of the Cochrane Collaboration by Tharyan and Adams (2005). They identified 24 randomised trials conducted over the previous 50 years. The review noted that many of the studies had significant methodological flaws, with inadequate sample sizes, trial durations and treatment regimes. They concluded that ECT, either alone or in combination with antipsychotic medication, resulted in increased rates of global improvement and faster rates of symptomatic improvement compared with sham or placebo ECT in the short-term treatment of schizophrenia. Similar to depression studies the advantage of ECT was lost within six to eight weeks of ceasing treatment despite ongoing use of antipsychotic medication (Tharyan and Adams, 2005).

Chanpattana et al. (1999) compared the efficacies of continuation ECT alone, flupenthixol alone, and continuation ECT with flupenthixol in a randomised controlled trial of 114 patients with treatment-resistant schizophrenia. They concluded that rates of relapse were much lower with the combination of ECT and antipsychotic medications compared to either alone (Chanpattana et al., 1999), supporting the use of ECT for those patients who respond to an acute course of ECT where medication alone has been ineffective or cannot be tolerated. This finding is supported by other open studies which show that adding ECT to antipsychotic drugs is a safe and potentially useful strategy for people with treatment-resistant schizophrenia (Braga and Petrides, 2005; Chanpattana and Sackeim, 2010).

A recent systematic review identified 31 articles on the use of ECT in schizophrenia (Pompili, 2013). The most common indication for using ECT in this condition was to augment pharmacotherapy, while the most common symptoms that were targeted was schizophrenia with catatonia, aggression and strong suicidal intent. The study found that the combinations of ECT risperidone and ECT with clozapine were the most effective in patients non-responsive to trials of mediation alone. The review concluded that ECT is recommended in treatment-resistant schizophrenia with catatonia, aggression or suicidal behaviour where a rapid global improvement and reduction of acute symptoms are required (Pompili, 2013).

There is little guidance in the literature to support the use of unilateral over bitemporal ECT. The systematic review conducted by Tharyan and Adams (2005) found no clear advantage for either placement. Phutane et al. (2013) conducted a double-blind randomised controlled trial where bifrontal electrode placement was compared to bitemporal ECT in 122 patients with schizophrenia. There was no control over prescribed medication or the total number of ECT sessions. After six treatment sessions 63% of patients treated with bifrontal ECT met response criteria, 40% experienced a reduction on the Brief Psychiatric Rating Scale (BPRS), compared to 13.2% treated with bitemporal ECT. The bifrontal group showed a significantly faster clinical response and greater improvement on all measures including causing less cognitive impairment (Phutane et al., 2013).

These finding need to be replicated and are in contrast to an earlier RCT where 62 patients with schizophrenia were administered bitemporal ECT at three different dosages: just above threshold and 2 times and 4 times above threshold (Chanpattana, Chakrabhand, Buppanharun and Sackeim, 2000). All groups were equivalent in the number of patients who met remitter criteria, with the low-dose group requiring more ECT treatments and more days to reach remitter status than the other two groups (Chanpattana et al., 2000).

These and other studies have challenged the anecdotal belief that people with schizophrenia require prolonged courses of ECT, up to 20 index treatments with most patients responding after eight to 12 treatments (Galletly et al., 2016). Caution needs to be exercised in prescribing prolonged courses of ECT owing to the known cognitive side effects, particularly bitemporal, which is associated with significantly more memory problems than bifrontal and unilateral treatment (Dunne and McLoughlin, 2012).

Clinical practice guidelines (CPGs)

The use of ECT is discussed in most recently published clinical practice guidelines for the treatment of psychosis and schizophrenia (Barnes and Schizophrenia Consensus Group of British Association for Psychopharmacology, 2011; Galletly et al., 2016; Hasan et al., 2012; Lehman et al., 2010; Moore et al., 2007; Scottish Intercollegiate Guidelines Network (SIGN), 2013). The exceptions are the clinical practice guidelines published by the Canadian Psychiatric Association (Addington et al., 2005) and the clinical guideline for psychosis and schizophrenia in adults (CG178) produced by NICE (NICE, 2014b). The Schizophrenia Consensus Group of British Association for Psychopharmacology acknowledged the inconclusive findings of the NICE guidance document for ECT (NICE, 2003, Modified 2009) but go on to discuss the available literature forming the same conclusions as the other guidelines (Barnes and Schizophrenia Consensus Group of British Association for Psychopharmacology, 2011).

In summary, most clinical practice guidelines for the treatment of psychosis and schizophrenia highlight that, although the level of evidence supporting the use of ECT in schizophrenia is limited to Levels 2 and 3, it may be of value when used in combination with antipsychotic medications in the treatment of acute schizophrenia and in treatment-resistant schizophrenia (Barnes and Schizophrenia Consensus Group of British Association for Psychopharmacology, 2011; Galletly et al., 2016; Hasan et al., 2012; Lehman et al., 2010; Moore et al., 2007; Scottish Intercollegiate Guidelines Network (SIGN), 2013).

ECT should be considered in the following circumstances:

- in those individuals where other approaches to treatment have failed,
- as an adjunct antipsychotic medications if there is a need for rapid improvement and reduction of symptoms,
- when there has been limited response to antipsychotic medication,
- to prevent relapse through the use of maintenance ECT combined with antipsychotic medication.

SCHIZOAFFECTIVE DISORDER

There is little evidence to guide the use of ECT in schizoaffective disorder. The Cochrane review on ECT identified only one study containing patients with schizoaffective that met the inclusion criterion but were then excused as they could not be separated from other patients who had affective disorders (Tharyan and Adams, 2005). On an anecdotal case report level, ECT appears to be effective in treating this condition, where other treatment options have failed and there is a high level of perplexity and affective symptoms.

Ries, Wilson, Bokan and Chiles (1981) reported a good response to in nine patients with schizoaffective disorder who had failed to respond to two different antipsychotic medication but commented that it is difficult to draw further conclusions about the use of ECT in this group owing to its heterogeneity. Another study also reported a good response in patients who had a schizoaffective disorder depressive episode (Lapense'e, 1992), with a further study demonstrating a favourable outcome when ECT was used as maintenance treatment in patients with this condition (Swoboda et al., 2001). A review of the maintenance ECT group within a local health district revealed that nearly two thirds of 20 patients had had a diagnosis of schizoaffective disorder.

CATATONIA

Practice wisdom suggests that ECT is the treatment of choice for catatonia. However, rather than being a clinical syndrome, it is heterogeneous condition spanning the divide between schizophrenia and affective disorders. This may explain why the evidence that does exist to support the use ECT in this group is conflicting, based upon case reports and not on randomised control trials (Hatta et al., 2007; Rohland, Carroll and Jacoby, 1993). Catatonia is a clinical syndrome that: may be caused by a medical condition rather than an independent disease entity (Gelenberg, 1976) and may be drug-induced (Lopez-Canino and A., 2004) or linked to neuroleptic malignant syndrome (NMS) (Vesperini, Papetti and Pringuey, 2010).

The treatment of choice for catatonia is benzodiazepines; antipsychotic medication demonstrates poor efficacy (Hawkins, Archer, Strakowski and Keck, 1995). Treatment should be based upon the underlying cause when it is identifiable. ECT should be considered when rapid resolution is necessary in malignant catatonia or when an initial trial of lorazepam has been ineffective (Hawkins et al., 1995). Those with schizophrenia respond less reliably, suggesting that the underlying processes causing the catatonia may be different in this group. Failure to treat the catatonia may increase the risk of drugs-induced neuroleptic malignant syndrome (Rosebush and Mazurek, 2010).

Certain catatonic signs are associated with antipsychotic medication, including akinesia and stupor, mutism, catalepsy and waxy flexibility (Lopez-Canino and A., 2004). Further, catatonia and NMS are both conditions that can compromise survival with successful treatment dependent upon early diagnosis (Philbrick and Rummans, 1994; Vesperini et al., 2010). Distinguishing clinically between the two conditions can be difficult with overlapping diagnostic criteria. The most commonly held belief is that they are two conditions on the same spectrum: NMS is a drug-induced form of malignant catatonia or a heterogeneous group that includes both catatonic and non-catatonic responses to antipsychotic medication (Philbrick and Rummans, 1994; Vesperini et al., 2010).

Hawkins et al. (1995), reviewed published articles spanning a nine-year period. Out of 178 patients there were 270 separate episodes of catatonia reported. The most common form of treatment was with benzodiazepines, which were effective in 70% of cases, with lorazepam used most frequently, resulting with a 79% remission rate. ECT was highly efficacious, resulting in a good outcome in 85%, particularly in cases of malignant catatonia (Hawkins et al., 1995).

Girish (2003) reported that ECT was superior to oral risperidone in patients with "non-organic, non-functional catatonia". Rosebush and Mazurek (2010) highlight that lorazepam is the treatment of choice for all types of catatonia. A course of ECT should be considered if the catatonia shows minimal or no response to the benzodiazepine treatment. ECT may be used more frequently in patients who have a primary diagnosis of schizophrenia with catatonia as they respond less reliably and robustly to benzodiazepines.

Malignant catatonia is a fatal condition that is characterised by psychomotor abnormalities, delirium and hyperpyrexia, resulting in exhaustion and dehydration (Baker, Suh and Prudic, 2008; Philbrick and Rummans, 1994; Vesperini et al., 2010). There are some case reports that recommend ECT as a first-line treatment for this lethal condition (Baker et al., 2008; Philbrick and Rummans, 1994). Most authors agree that ECT should be considered when there is no response to lorazepam (Fear, Dunne and McLoughlin, 2013; NSW Health, 2010).

A strong case for the use of ECT in catatonia is made in a recent case series of 13 patients who were treated with ultrabrief right unilateral (UB RUL) ECT (Kugler et al., 2015). In this report the authors highlighted that ECT should be seen as first line treatment for this condition and challenge the usual belief that the strongest form of ECT, bitemporal electrode placement, should be considered in these cases for its rapid speed of action and increased efficacy (Kugler et al., 2015). The study demonstrated that UB RUL was an effective treatment for patients with catatonia, as nine out of 10 patients responded rapidly to this treatment, with many showing symptom improvement after the first treatment (Kugler et al., 2015).

Clinical practice guidelines highlight that ECT can be effective in the treatment of catatonia but note that the level of evidence supporting their recommendations for its use in this condition is poor at the level of expert opinion (Gelenberg et al., 2010; Kennedy et al., 2009; Malhi et al., 2015).

NEUROLEPTIC MALIGNANT SYNDROME

Neuroleptic malignant syndrome is a medical emergency that can arise as a complication of using antipsychotic medications owing to abnormal dopaminergic activity in the brain. In 2001, a Task Force report of the American Psychiatric Association (American Psychiatric Association, 2001) identified the benefits of using ECT as treatment of this condition. ECT is often considered when medication strategies have failed. Davis, Janicak and Sakkas (1991) noted that those patients who did not receive active treatment had a higher mortality rate than those receiving ECT or medication: 21% compared to 10.3%. Strawn, Keck and Caroff (2007) suggested that, if neuroleptic malignant syndrome did not respond to withdrawal of antipsychotic medication, treatment with a dopamine agonist and muscle relaxant and supportive therapy then ECT should be considered. In a series of 45 case reports, with nine new cases of neuroleptic malignant syndrome treated with ECT, the authors highlighted that ECT is the preferred choice and can be a life-saving treatment in severe cases (Trollor and Sachdev, 1993). Such reports highlight the need for care in the administration of anaesthetic agents, particularly suxamethonium, owing to the high level of autonomic instability. This may result in a potential risk of a malignant hyperthermia a similarly worrying condition (Trimble and Krishnamoorthy, 2005).

PERINATAL DISORDERS

ECT can be safely administered to pregnant women. Lamprecht et al. (2013) note that there have been a large number of case reports demonstrating the efficacy of ECT in all trimesters of pregnancy, with very few complications. It may be the treatment of choice, particularly early in pregnancy where the exposure of the foetus to psychotropic may be contraindicated. Foetal monitoring in a hospital with obstetric support may be necessary if there are signs of foetal distress (Tiller and Lyndon, 2003). Consultations with the obstetrician are essential in this condition.

A literature review on the use of ECT in special populations agreed with the conclusion that ECT was safe and effective in treating depression in women during the perinatal period (Rabheru, 2001). ECT poses little risk to the breastfeeding mother and her feeding infant as anaesthetic agents administered during the treatment are rapidly excreted, unlike some psychotropic medication (Lee and Rubin, 1993).

Anderson and Reti (2009) completed a comprehensive literature review from 1941 to 2007, identifying 339 pregnant patients who were treated with ECT. ECT was safe and effective, resulting in partial to complete remission of symptoms in 84% of cases of women with depression. Among the 339 cases reviewed, there were 25 foetal or neonatal complications, but only 11 were likely related to ECT, with two deaths. The authors felt that only one of these events – a foetal death – was secondary to ECT after the mother developed status epilepticus. There were also 20 maternal complications reported with 18 likely related to ECT. The most common adverse event for the foetus was bradycardia and for the mother, uterine contractions and/or premature labour.

The American Psychiatric Association Task Force on ECT recommended that ECT can be administered safely in all three trimesters of pregnancy for severe postpartum illness (American Psychiatric Association, 2001).

Maxiner (2013) notes that as the pregnancy progresses the following factors may need to be considered:

1 intubation in late pregnancy to avoid aspiration by an expanding uterus causing upward pressure on the stomach;
2 elevation of the right hip to avoid aortocaval compression and hypotension;
3 close consultation with the obstetric team and non-invasive foetal heart monitoring after 14 weeks' gestational age.

Postpartum psychosis is a life-threatening and overwhelming condition that appears in women within the first three months after delivery as part of a manic/mixed episode. The condition is life-threatening as it often involves prominent suicidal and infanticidal ideation with plans. ECT is the treatment of choice owing to its ability to terminate the condition rapidly and effectively, allowing attachment and bonding to occur between mother and baby (Fink, 2009). Henshaw, Cox and Barton (2009) have completed a comprehensive analysis of the management of mental disorders in the perinatal period, providing recommendations that are clinically helpful when looking after pregnant women.

PARKINSON'S DISEASE

ECT works well in certain neurologic illnesses; what is surprising is that over the years many physicians have been unaware of the profound benefits of ECT (Kellner and Bernstein, 1993). Case reports indicate that ECT is beneficial in Parkinson's disease as it is known to enhance the dopaminergic function and increase GABA concentrations in both animals and humans (Faber and Trimble, 1991). Parkinson's disease is a neurodegenerative disorder characterised by tremor, rigidity, akinesia, gait and postural disturbances as well mood and cognitive changes. It is usually managed with medication; however, problematic complications can arise, like the "on–off" phenomena, where there are abrupt changes from excessive dyskinetic movements one moment to freezing instability the next as well as psychosis (Kellner and Bernstein, 1993).

There are ample reports spanning many years of the benefits of ECT in Parkinson's disease. Faber and Trimble (1991) reviewed the early literature and found 27 reports starting as early as 1959 that demonstrated the benefits of ECT in this condition, particularly when other treatments were unsatisfactory. Kennedy, Mittal and O'Jile (2003) reviewed 75 cases. They found that 58 of these patients who had ECT for motor symptoms improved but they were more vulnerable to cognitive impairment. Andersen et al. (1987) showed that ECT not only improved mood but was also effective in prolonging the duration of the "on" period in patients with severe "on–off" phenomena when compared to those patients who were given sham

ECT. There are a range of other studies that demonstrate improvement in mood and the motor symptoms of Parkinson's disease (Douyon, Serby, Klutchko et al., 1989; Moellentine et al., 1998). It has been suggested that these patients should commence treatment with brief-pulse right unilateral ECT to reduce the cognitive impairment (Kellner and Bernstein, 1993). Early reviews argued that maintenance ECT may have a role to play in treating both the mood and motor symptoms of this condition (Faber and Trimble, 1991; Krystal and Coffey, 1997). However, it is likely that the use of ECT in Parkinson's disease will be a thing of the past owing to the dramatic and profound impact that deep brain stimulation has in the treatment of this condition (Deep Brain Stimulation for Parkinson's Disease Study Group, 2001).

OTHER DIAGNOSES

ECT has been used to treat status epilepticus that has failed to respond to medication alone (Griesemer, Kellner, Beale and Smith, 1997). Other case reports identify the benefits of ECT in the treatment of post-stroke depression (Murray, Shea and Conn, 1989), in delirium (Krystal and Coffey, 1997), obsessive compulsive disorder (Maletzky, McFarland and Burt, 1994) and chronic pain (Rasmussen and Rummans, 2002). There have been growing reports on the use of ECT in treating self-injurious behaviour in patients with autistic spectrum disorders (ASD) and catatonia (Arora, Praharaj and Prakash, 2008; Black, Wilcox and M., 1985; Chung and Varghese, 2008; Cizadlo and Wheaton, 1995), with a recent review highlighting the benefits of using maintenance ECT and repetitive transcranial magnetic stimulation to suppress this severe disabling condition. There is a lack of evidence to support the use of ECT in these conditions. It is recommended that the ECT practitioner involve the patient and their families in gaining fully informed consent before proceeding with treatment. It may be useful to obtain a determination from the relevant mental health review tribunal to obtain independent advice, particularly if there are different opinions.

REFERENCES

Abrams, R. (2002). *Electroconvulsive Therapy*, 4th edition. New York: Oxford University Press.

Addington, D., Bouchard, R.-H., Goldberg, J., Honer, B., Malla, A., Norman, R., and Berzins, S. (2005). Clinical practice guidelines: treatment of schizophrenia. *Canadian Journal of Psychiatry*, *50* (Supplement 1). Retrieved from ww1.cpa-apc.org/Publications/Clinical_Guidelines/schizophrenia/november2005/cjp-cpg-suppl1-05_full_spread.pdf.

American Psychiatric Association. (1990). *The Practice of Electroconvulsive Therapy: Recommendations for Treatment, Training and Privileging: A Task Force Report*. Washington, DC: American Psychiatric Association.

American Psychiatric Association. (2001). *The Practice of Electroconvulsive Therapy: Recommendations for Treatment, Training and Privileging: A Task Force Report*, 2nd edition. Washington, DC: American Psychiatric Association.

Andersen, K., Balldin, J., Gottfries, C.G., Granérus A-K, Modigh, K., Svennerholm, L., and Wallin, A. (1987). A double-blind evaluation of electroconvulsive therapy in Parkinson's Disease with "on-off" phenomena. *Acta Neurologica Scandinavica*, *76*(3), 191–199.

Anderson, E.L., and Reti, I.M. (2009). ECT in pregnancy: a review of the literature from 1941 to 2007. *Psychosomatic Medicine*, *71*(2), 235–242. doi:10.1097/PSY.0b013e318190d7ca.

Arora, M., Praharaj, S.K., and Prakash, R. (2008). Electroconvulsive therapy for multiple major self-mutilations in bipolar psychotic depression. *Turk Psikiyatri Derg*, *19*(2), 209–212. Retrieved from www.ncbi.nlm.nih.gov/pubmed/18561053.

Baker, A.S., Suh, E., and Prudic, J. (2008). Malignant catatonia: role of right unilateral electroconvulsive therapy. *Journal of ECT*, *24*(2), 168–170. doi:10.1097/YCT.0b013e3181514144.

Baker, A.S., Suh, E., and Prudic, J. (2008). Malignant catatonia: role of right unilateral electroconvulsive therapy. *Journal of ECT*, *24*, 168–170.

Barekatain, M., Jahangard, L., Haghighi, M., and Ranjkesh, F. (2008). Bifrontal versus bitemporal electroconvulsive therapy in severe manic patients. *Journal of ECT*, *24*(3), 199–202. doi:10.1097/YCT.0b013e3181624b5d.

Barnes, T.R., and Schizophrenia Consensus Group of British Association for Pharmacology. (2011). Evidence-based guidelines for the pharmacological treatment of schizophrenia:

recommendations from the British Association for Psychopharmacology. *Journal of Psychopharmacology, 25*(5), 567–620. doi:10.1177/0269881110391123.

Bauer, M., Pfennig, A., Severus, E., Whybrow, P.C., Angst, J., Moller, H.J., and WFSBP Task Force on Unipolar Depressive Disorder. (2013). World Federation of Societies of Biological Psychiatry (WFSBP) guidelines for biological treatment of unipolar depressive disorders, part 1: update 2013 on the acute and continuation treatment of unipolar depressive disorders. *World Journal of Biological Psychiatry, 14*(5), 334–385. doi:10.3109/15622975.2013.804195.

Bauer, M., Severus, E., Kohler, S., Whybrow, P.C., Angst, J., Moller, H.J., and WFSBP Task Force on Treatment Guidelines for Unipolar Depressive Disorder. (2015). World Federation of Societies of Biological Psychiatry (WFSBP) guidelines for biological treatment of unipolar depressive disorders, part 2: maintenance treatment of major depressive disorder-update 2015. *World Journal of Biological Psychiatry, 16*(2), 76–95. doi:10.3109/15622975.2014.1001786.

Black, D.W., Wilcox, J.A., and Stewart, M. (1985). The use of ECT in children: case report. *Journal of Clinical Psychiatry, 46*, 98–99.

Braga, R.J., and Petrides, G. (2005). The combined use of electroconvulsive therapy and antipsychotics in patients with schizophrenia. *Journal of ECT, 21*. Retrieved from http://journals.lww.com/ectjournal/toc/2005/06000.

Brandon, S., Cowley, P., McDonald, C., Neville, P., Palmer, R. and Wellstood-Eason, S. (1984). Electroconvulsive therapy: results on depressive illness from the Leicestershire trial. *British Journal of Psychiatry, 146*, 177–183.

Calabrese, J.R., Shelton, M.D., Rapport, D.J., Kujawa, M., Kimmel, S.E., and Caban, S. (2001). Current research on rapid cycling bipolar disorder and its treatment. *Journal of Affective Disorders, 67*(1–3), 241–255. Retrieved from www.ncbi.nlm.nih.gov/pubmed/11869774.

Carney, S., and Geddes, J. (2003). Electroconvulsive therapy: recent recommendations are likely to improve standards and uniformity of use. *British Journal of Psychiatry, 326*, 1343–1344.

Chanpattana, W., Chakrabhand, M.L., Buppanharun, W., and Sackeim, H.A. (2000). Effects of stimulus intensity on the efficacy of bilateral ECT in schizophrenia: a preliminary study. *Biological Psychiatry, 48*(3), 222–228. Retrieved from www.ncbi.nlm.nih.gov/pubmed/10924665.

Chanpattana, W., Chakrabhand, M.L., Sackeim, H.A., Kitaroonchai, W., Kongsakon, R., Techakasem, P., . . . Kirdcharoen, N. (1999). Continuation ECT in treatment-resistant schizophrenia: a controlled study. *Journal of ECT, 15*(3), 178–192. Retrieved from www.ncbi.nlm.nih.gov/pubmed/10492856.

Chanpattana, W., and Sackeim, H.A. (2010). Electroconvulsive therapy in treatment-resistant schizophrenia: prediction of response and the nature of symptomatic improvement. *Journal of ECT, 26*(4), 289–298. doi:10.1097/YCT.0b013e3181cb5e0f.

Chung, A., and Varghese, J. (2008). Treatment of catatonia with electroconvulsive therapy in an 11-year-old girl. *Australian and New Zealand Journal of Psychiatry, 42*(3), 251–253. doi:10.1080/00048670701827317.

Cizadlo, B.C., and Wheaton, A. (1995). Case study: ECT treatment of a young girl with catatonia. *Journal of the American Academy of Child and Adolescent Psychiatry, 34*(3), 332–335. doi:10.1097/00004583-199503000-00019.

Cleare, A., Pariante, C.M., Young, A.H., Anderson, I.M., Christmas, D., Cowen, P.J., . . . Members of the Consensus Meeting. (2015). Evidence-based guidelines for treating depressive disorders with antidepressants: a revision of the 2008 British Association for Psychopharmacology guidelines. *Journal of Psychopharmacology, 29*(5), 459–525. doi:10.1177/0269881115581093.

Crismon, M.L., Argo, T.R., Bendele, S.D., and Suppes, T. (2007). Texas medication algorithm project: procedural manual bipolar disorders algorithms. Retrieved from www.jpshealthnet.org/sites/default/files/tmap_bipolar_2007.pdf.

Crismon, M.L., Trivedi, M., Pigott, T.A., Rush, A.J., Hirschfeld, R.M., Kahn, D.A., . . . Thase, M.E. (1999). The Texas Medication Algorithm Project: report of the Texas Consensus Conference Panel on Medication Treatment of Major Depressive Disorder. *Journal of Clinical Psychiatry, 60*(3), 142–156. Retrieved from www.ncbi.nlm.nih.gov/pubmed/10192589.

Davidson, J., McLeod, M., Law-Yone, B., and Linnoila, M. (1978). A comparison of electroconvulsive therapy and combined phenelzine-amitriptyline in refractory depression. *Archives of General Psychiatry, 35*(5), 639–642. Retrieved from www.ncbi.nlm.nih.gov/pubmed/727903.

Davidson, J.R. (2010). Major depressive disorder treatment guidelines in America and Europe. *Journal of Clinical Psychiatry, 71 Suppl E1*(suppl E1: e04), e04. doi:10.4088/JCP.9058se1c.04gry.

Davis, J.M., Janicak, P.G., and Sakkas, P. (1991). Electroconvulsive therapy in the treatment of the neuroleptic malignant syndrome. *Convulsive Therapy, 7*, 111–120.

Deep Brain Stimulation for Parkinson's Disease Study Group. (2001). Deep-brain stimulation of the subthalamic nucleus or the pars interna of the globus pallidus in Parkinson's disease. *New England Journal of Medicine, 345*(13), 956–963. doi:10.1056/NEJMoa000827.

Douyon, R., Serby, M., Klutchko, B., and Rotrosen, J. (1989). ECT and Parkinson's disease revisited: a 'naturalistic' study. *American Journal of Psychiatry, 146*, 1451–1455.

Dunne, R.A., and McLoughlin, D.M. (2012). Systematic review and meta-analysis of bifrontal electroconvulsive therapy versus bilateral and unilateral electroconvulsive therapy in depression. *The World Journal of Biological Psychiatry, 13*(4), 248–258. doi:10.3109/15622975.2011.615863.

Faber, R., and Trimble, M.R. (1991). Electroconvulsive therapy in Parkinson's disease and other movement disorders. *Movement Disorders, 6*(4), 293–303. doi:10.1002/mds. 870060405.

Fear, C.F. (2005). ECT in schizophrenia and catatonia. In Scott, A.I.F (Ed.), *The ECT Handbook,* 2nd edition. London: Royal College of Psychiatrists.

Fear, C.F., Dunne, R.A., and McLoughlin, D.M. (2013). The use of ECT in the treatment of schizophrenia and catatonia. In Waite, J., and Easton, A. (Eds.), *The ECT Handbook,* 3rd edition. London: Royal College of Psychiatrists.

Fink, M. (2009). *Electroconvulsive Therapy: A Guide for Professionals and Their Patients.* New York: Oxford University Press.

Fink, M, and Sackeim, H.A. (1996). Convulsive therapy in schizophrenia? *Schizophrenia Bulletin, 22,* 27–39.

Fink, M., Rush, A.J., Knapp, R., Rasmussen, K.G., Mueller, M., Rummans, T.A., . . . Kellner, C.H. (2007). DSM melancholic features are unreliable predictors of ECT response: a CORE publication. *Journal of ECT, 23,* 139–146.

Folkerts, H.W., Michael, N., Tolle, R., Schonauer, K., Muck, S., and Schulze-Monking, H. (1997). Electroconvulsive therapy vs. paroxetine in treatment-resistant depression – a randomized study. *Acta Psychiatrica Scandinavica, 96*(5), 334–342. Retrieved from www.ncbi.nlm.nih.gov/pubmed/ 9395150.

Freeman, C.P., Basson, J.V., and Crighton, A. (1978). Double-blind controlled trial of therapy (ECT) and simulated electro-convulsive therapy (ECT) in depressive illness. *Lancet, i,* 738–740.

Gagne, G.G., Jr, Furman, M.J., Carpenter, L.L., and Price, L.H. (2000). Efficacy of continuation ECT and antidepressant drugs compared to long-term antidepressants alone in depressed patients. *American Journal of Psychiatry, 157*(12), 1960–1965. doi:10.1176/appi.ajp.157.12.1960.

Galletly, C., Castle, D., Dark, F., Humberstone, V., Jablensky, A., Killackey, E., . . . Tran, N. (2016). Royal Australian and New Zealand College of Psychiatrists clinical practice guide-lines for the treatment of schizophrenia and related disorders. *Australian and New Zealand Journal of Psychiatry, 50*(5), 1–117. doi:10.1080/j.1440-1614.2005.01516.x.

Gangadhar, B.N., Kapur, R.L., and Kalyanasundaram, S. (1982). Comparison of electroconvulsive therapy with impipramine in endongenous depression: a double blind study. *British Journal of Psychiatry, 141,* 367–371.

Gelenberg, A.J. (1976). The catatonic syndrome. *Lancet, 1*(7973), 1339–1341. Retrieved from www.ncbi.nlm.nih.gov/ pubmed/58326.

Gelenberg, A.J., Freeman, M.P., Markowitz, J.C., Rosenbaum, J.F., Thase, M.E., Trivedi, M.H., and Van Rhoads, R.S. (2010). Practice guidelines for the treatment of patients with major depressive disorder, 3rd edition. *American Psychiatric Association.* Retrieved from www.psychiatryonline.com/ pracGuide/pracGuideTopic_7.aspx.

Girish, K.G.N.S. (2003). Electroconvulsive therapy and lorazepam in nonresponsive catatonia. *Indian Journal of Psychiatry, 45,* 21–25.

Greenblatt, M., Grosser, G.H., and Wechsler, H.A. (1962). A comparative study of selected antidepressant medications and ECT. *American Journal of Psychiatry, 119,* 114–153.

Gregory, S., Shawcross, C.R., and Gill, D. (1985). The Nottingham ECT Study. A double-blind comparison of bilateral, unilateral and simulated ECT in depressive illness. *British Journal of Psychiatry, 146,* 520–524.

Griesemer, D.A., Kellner, C.H., Beale, M.D., and Smith, G.M. (1997). Electroconvulsive therapy for treatment of intractable seizures. Initial findings in two children. *Neurology, 49*(5), 1389–1392. Retrieved from www.ncbi.nlm.nih.gov/pubmed/ 9371927.

Grunze, H., Vieta, E., Goodwin, G.M., Bowden, C., Licht, R.W., Moller, H.J., and Kasper, S. (2009). The World Federation of Societies of Biological Psychiatry (WFSBP) guidelines for the biological treatment of bipolar disorders: update 2009 on the treatment of acute mania. *World Journal of Biological Psychiatry, 10*(2), 85–116. doi:10.1080/15622970902 823202.

Grunze, H., Vieta, E., Goodwin, G.M., Bowden, C., Licht, R.W., Moller, H.J., . . . WFSBP Task Force on Treatment Guidelines for Bipolar Disorders (2010). The World Federation of Soci-eties of Biological Psychiatry (WFSBP) guidelines for the biological treatment of bipolar disorders: update 2010 on the treatment of acute bipolar depression. *World Journal of Biological Psychiatry, 11*(2), 81–109. doi:10.3109/ 15622970903555881.

Grunze, H., Vieta, E., Goodwin, G.M., Bowden, C., Licht, R.W., Moller, H.J., . . . WFSBP Task Force on Treatment Guidelines for Bipolar Disorders. (2013). The World Federation of Soci-eties of Biological Psychiatry (WFSBP) guidelines for the biological treatment of bipolar disorders: update 2012 on the long-term treatment of bipolar disorder. *World Journal of Biological Psychiatry, 14*(3), 154–219. doi:10.3109/ 15622975.2013.770551.

Hasan, A., Falkai, P., Wobrock, T., Lieberman, J., Glenthoj, B., Gattaz, W.F., . . . WFSBP Task Force on Treatment Guidelines for Schizophrenia. (2012). World Federation of Societies of Biological Psychiatry (WFSBP) guidelines for biological treatment of schizophrenia, part 1: update 2012 on the acute treatment of schizophrenia and the management of treatment resistance. *World Journal of Biological Psychiatry*, *13*(5), 318–378. doi:10.3109/15622975.2012.696143.

Hatta, K., Miyakawa, K., Ota, T., Usui, C., Nakamura, H., and Arai, H. (2007). Maximal response to electroconvulsive therapy for the treatment of catatonic symptoms. *Journal of ECT*, *23*(4), 233–235. doi:10.1097/yct.0b013e3181587949.

Hawkins, J.M., Archer, K.J., Strakowski, S.M., and Keck, P.E. (1995). Somatic treatment of catatonia. *International Journal of Psychiatry in Medicine*, *25*(4), 345–369. Retrieved from www.ncbi.nlm.nih.gov/pubmed/8822386.

Henshaw, C., Cox, J., and Barton, J. (2009). *Modern Management of Perinatal Psychiatric Disorders*. Glasgow, Scotland: Bell and Bain.

Hickie, I., Mason, C., Parker, G., and Brodaty, H. (1996). Prediction of ECT response: validation of a refined sign-based (CORE) system for defining melancholia. *British Journal of Psychiatry*, *169*(1), 68–74. Retrieved from www.ncbi.nlm.nih.gov/pubmed/8818371.

Hiremani, R.M., Thirthalli, J., Tharayil, B.S., and Gangadhar, B.N. (2008). Double-blind randomized controlled study comparing short-term efficacy of bifrontal and bitemporal electroconvulsive therapy in acute mania. *Bipolar Disorders*, *10*(6), 701–707. doi:10.1111/j.1399-5618.2008.00608.x.

Hirschfeld, R.M.A., Bowden, C.L., Gitlin, M.J., Keck, P.E., Suppes, T., Thase, M.E., . . . Perlis, R.H. (2010). Practice Guideline for the treatment of patients with bipolar disorder, 2nd edition. *American Psychiatric Association*. Retrieved from https://psychiatryonline.org/pb/assets/raw/sitewide/practice_guidelines/guidelines/bipolar.pdf.

Janicak, P.G., Davis, J.M., Gibbons, R.D., Ericksen, S., Chang, S., and Gallagher, P. (1985). Efficacy of ECT: a meta-analysis. *American Journal of Psychiatry*, *142*(3), 297–302. doi:10.1176/ajp.142.3.297.

Johns, C.A., and Thompson, J.W. (1995). Adjunctive treatments in schizophrenia: pharmacotherapies and electroconvulsive therapy. *Schizophrenia Bulletin*, *21*, 607–619.

Johnstone, E.C., Deakin, J.F., Lawler, P., Frith, C.D., Stevens, M., McPherson, K., and Crow, T.J. (1980). The Northwick Park electroconvulsive therapy trial. *Lancet*, *2*(8208–8209), 1317–1320. Retrieved from www.ncbi.nlm.nih.gov/pubmed/6109147.

Karmacharya, R., England, M.L., and Ongur, D. (2008). Delirious mania: clinical features and treatment response. *Journal of Affective Disorders*, *109*(3), 312–316. doi: 10.1016/j.jad.2007.12.001.

Kellner, C.H., and Bernstein, H.J. (1993). ECT as a treatment for neurologic illness. In Coffey, C.E. (Ed.), *The Clinical Science of Electroconvulsive Therapy*, 1st edition (Vol. 38, pp. 183–210). Washington, DC and London: American Psychiatric Association.

Kellner, C.H., Husain, M.M., Knapp, R.G., McCall, W.V., Petrides, G., Rudorfer, M.V., . . . Lisanby, S.H. (2016). A Novel Strategy for Continuation ECT in Geriatric Depression: Phase 2 of the PRIDE Study. *American Journal of Psychiatry*, *173*(11), 1110–1118. doi:10.1176/appi.ajp.2016.16010118.

Kennedy, R., Mittal, D., and O'Jile, J. (2003). Electroconvulsive therapy in movement disorders: an update. *Journal of Neuropsychiatry and Clinical Neuroscience*, *15*(4), 407–421. Retrieved from www.ncbi.nlm.nih.gov/pubmed/14627767.

Kennedy, S.H., Lam, R.W., Parikh, S.V., Patten, S.B., and Ravindran, A.V. (2009). Canadian Network for Mood and Anxiety Treatments (CANMAT) clinical guidelines for the management of major depressive disorder in adults. IV. Neurostimulation therapies. *Journal of Affective Disorders*, *117 Suppl 1*, S1–2. doi:10.1016/j.jad.2009.06.039.

Kho, K.H., van Vreeswijk, M.F., Simpson, S., and Zwinderman, A.H. (2003). A meta-analysis of electroconvulsive therapy efficacy in depression. *Journal of ECT*, *19*(3), 139–147. Retrieved from www.ncbi.nlm.nih.gov/pubmed/12972983.

Krueger, R.B., and Sackeim, H.A. (1995). *Electroconvulsive Therapy and Schizophrenia*. Oxford: Blackwell.

Krystal, A.D., and Coffey, C.E. (1997). Neuropsychiatric considerations in the use of electroconvulsive therapy. *Journal of Neuropsychiatry and Clinical Neurosciences*, *9*, 283–292.

Kugler, J.L., Hauptman, A.J., Collier, S.J., Walton, A.E., Murthy, S., Funderburg, L.G., and Garcia, K.S. (2015). Treatment of catatonia with ultrabrief right unilateral electroconvulsive therapy: a case series. *Journal of ECT*, *31*(3), 192–196. doi:10.1097/YCT.0000000000000185.

Lambourn, J., and Gill, D. (1978). A controlled comparison of simulated and real ECT. *British Journal of Psychiatry*, *133*, 514–519.

Lamprecht, H.C., Ferrier, N., Swann, A.G., and Waite, J. (2013). The use of ECT in the treatment of depression. In Waite, J., and Easton, A. (Eds.), *The ECT Handbook*, 3rd edition. London: Royal College of Psychiatrists.

Lapense'e, M.A. (1992). A reivew of schizoaffective disorder; II. Somatic Treatment. *Canadian Journal of Psychiatry*, *37*, 347–349.

Lee, J.J., and Rubin, A.P. (1993). Breast feeding and anesthesia. *Anesthesia*, *48*, 616–625.

Lehman, A.F., Steinwachs, D.M., and Dixon, L.B. (1998). Translating research into practice: the Schizophrenia Patient Outcomes Research Team (PORT) treatment recommendations. *Schizophrenia Bulletin*, *24*, 1–10.

Lehman, A.F., Lieberman, J.A., Dixon, L.B., McGlashan, T.H., Perkins, D.O., and Kreyenbuhl, J. (2010). *Practice Guidelines for the Treatment of Patients With Schizophrenia*, 2nd edition. American Psychiatric Association.

Lisanby, S.H. (2007). Electroconvulsive therapy for depression. *New England Journal of Medicine, 357*(19), 1939–1945. doi:10.1056/NEJMct075234.

Loo, C., Katalinic, N., Mitchell, P.B., and Greenberg, B. (2011). Physical treatments for bipolar disorder: a review of electroconvulsive therapy, stereotactic surgery and other brain stimulation techniques. *Journal of Affective Disorders, 132*(1–2), 1–13. doi:10.1016/j.jad.2010.08.017.

Loo, C.K., Schweitzer, I., and Pratt, C. (2006). Recent advances in optimizing electroconvulsive therapy. *Australian and New Zealand Journal of Psychiatry, 40*(8), 632–638. doi:10.1111/j.1440-1614.2006.01862.x.

Lopez-Canino, F.A., and Lopez-Canino, A. (2004). Drug-induced catatonia. In Caroff, S.N., Francis, A., and Fricchione, G.L. (Eds.), *Psychopathology to Neurobiology* (pp. 129–139). Washington, DC: American Psychiatric Press.

McCall, W.V, Dunn, A., Rosenquist, P.B, and Hughes, D. (2002). Markedly suprathreshold right unilateral ECT versus minimally suprathreshold bilateral ECT: antidepressant and memory effects. *Journal of ECT, 18*(3), 126–129. Retrieved from www.ncbi.nlm.nih.gov/pubmed/12394530.

McDonald, I.M., Perkins, M., and Marjerrison, G. (1966). A controlled comparison of amitriptyline and electroconvulsive therapy in the treatment of depression. *American Journal of Psychiatry, 122,* 1427–1431.

Macedo-Soares, M.B., Moreno, R.A., Rigonatti, S.P., and Lafer, B. (2005). Efficacy of electroconvulsive therapy in treatment-resistant bipolar disorder: a case series. *Journal of ECT, 21*(1), 31–34. Retrieved from www.ncbi.nlm.nih.gov/pubmed/15791175.

Maletzky, B., McFarland, B., and Burt, A. (1994). Refractory obsessive compulsive disorder and ECT. *Convulsive Therapy, 10*(1), 34–42. Retrieved from www.ncbi.nlm.nih.gov/pubmed/8055290.

Malhi, G.S., Bassett, D., Boyce, P., Bryant, R., Fitzgerald, P.B., Fritz, K., . . . Singh, A.B. (2015). Royal Australian and New Zealand College of Psychiatrists clinical practice guidelines for mood disorders. *Australian and New Zealand Journal of Psychiatry, 49*(12), 1–185. Retrieved from www.ranzcp.org/Files/Resources/Publications/CPG/Clinician/Mood-Disorders-CPG.aspx.

Maxiner, D.F. (2013). ECT in youth with comorbid medical and neurological disorders. In Ghaziuddin, N. and Walter, G. (Eds.), *Electroconvulsive Therapy in Children and Adolescents.* New York: Oxford University Press.

Ministry of Health Social Services and Equity. (2014). Clinical practice guideline on the management of depression in adults. Retrieved from www.guiasalud.es/contenidos/GPC/GPC_534_Depresion_Adulto_Avaliat_compl_en.pdf.

Moellentine, C., Rummnas, T., Ahlskog, J.E., Harmsen, W.S., Suman, V.J. O'Connor, M.K., . . . Pileggi, T. (1998). Effective-ness of ECT in patients with parkinsonism. *Journal of Neuropsychiatry and Clinical Neuroscience, 10,* 187–193.

Moore, T.A., Buchanan, R.W., Buckley, P.F., Chiles, J.A., Conley, R.R., Crismon, M.L., . . . Miller, A.L. (2007). The Texas Medication Algorithm Project antipsychotic algorithm for schizophrenia: 2006 update. *Journal of Clinical Psychiatry, 68*(11), 1751–1762. Retrieved from www.ncbi.nlm.nih.gov/pubmed/18052569.

Mukherjee, S., Sackeim, H.A., and Schnur, D.B. (1994). Electroconvulsive therapy of acute manic episodes: a review of 50 years' experience. *American Journal of Psychiatry, 151,* 169–176.

Murray, G., Shea, V., and Conn, D. (1989). Electroconvulsive therapy for post-stroke depression. *Journal of Clinical Psychiatry, 47,* 258–260.

NICE. (2003, modified 2009). *Guidance on the Use of Electroconvulsive Therapy (Vol. Guidance Number 59).* London: National Institute for Health and Care Excellence; National Health Service.

NICE. (2006). Bipolar disorder: the management of bipolar disorder in adults, children and adolescents, in primary and secondary care: clinical guideline [CG38]. Retrieved from www.nice.org.uk/guidance/cg38.

NSW Health. (2010). ECT minimum standard of practice NSW. Retrieved from www.health.nsw.gov.au/policies/pd/2011/pdf/PD2011_003.pdf.

NICE. (2014a). Bipolar disorder: assessment and management: clinical guideline [CG185]. Retrieved from www.nice.org.uk/guidance/cg185.

NICE. (2014b). Psychosis and schizophrenia in adults: prevention and management: clinical guideline [CG178]. Retrieved from www.nice.org.uk/guidance/cg178.

NICE. (2016). Depression in adults: recognition and management: clinical guideline [CG90]. Retrieved from www.nice.org.uk/guidance/cg90/chapter/1-Guidance-treatment-choice-based-on-depression-subtypes-and-personal-characteristics.

Pagnin, D., and de Queiroz, V. (2004). Efficacy of ECT in depression: a meta-analytic review. *Journal of ECT, 20,* 13–20.

Papadimitriou, G.N., Dikeos, D.G., Soldatos, C.R., and Calabrese, J.R. (2007). Non-pharmacological treatments in the management of rapid cycling bipolar disorder. *Journal of Affective Disorders, 98*(1–2), 1–10. doi:10.1016/j.jad.2006.05.036.

Parker, G., Mitchell, P., Wilhelm, K., Menkes, D., Snowden, J., Schweitzer, I., . . . Hadzi-Pavlovic, D. (1999). Are the newer antidepressant drugs as effective as established physical treatments? Results from an Australasian clinical panel review. *Australian and New Zealand Journal of Psychiatry, 33*(874–881).

Parker, G., Roy, K., Hadzi-Pavlovic, D., and Pedic, F. (1992). Psychotic (delusional) depression: a meta-analysis of physical treatments. *Journal of Affective Disorders, 24*(1), 17–24. Retrieved from www.ncbi.nlm.nih.gov/pubmed/1347545.

Petrides, G., Fink, M, Husain, M.M., Knapp, R.G., Rush, A.J., Mueller, M., . . . Kellner, C.H. (2001). ECT remission rates in psychotic versus nonpsychotic depressed patients: a report from CORE. *Journal of ECT, 17*(4), 244–253. Retrieved from www.ncbi.nlm.nih.gov/pubmed/11731725.

Petrides, G., Tobias, K.G., Kellner, C.H., and Rudorfer, M.V. (2011). Continuation and maintenance electroconvulsive therapy for mood disorders: review of the literature. *Neuropsychobiology, 64*(3), 129–140. doi:10.1159/000328943.

Philbrick, K.L., and Rummans, T.A. (1994). Malignant catatonia. *Journal of Neuropsychiatry and Clinical Neuroscience, 6*(1), 1–13. Retrieved from www.ncbi.nlm.nih.gov/pubmed/7908547.

Phutane, V.H., Thirthalli, J., Muralidharan, K., Naveen Kumar, C., Keshav Kumar, J., and Gangadhar, B.N. (2013). Double-blind randomized controlled study showing symptomatic and cognitive superiority of bifrontal over bitemporal electrode placement during electroconvulsive therapy for schizophrenia. *Brain Stimulation 6*(2), 210–217. doi:10.1016/j.brs.2012.04.002.

Pliszka, S.R., Greenhill, L.L., Crismon, M.L., Sedillo, A., Carlson, C., Conners, C.K., . . . Llana, M.E. (2000). The Texas Children's Medication Algorithm Project: report of the Texas Consensus Conference Panel on medication treatment of childhood attention-deficit/hyperactivity disorder. Part, I., *Journal of the American Academy of Child and Adolescent Psychiatry, 39*(7), 908–919.

Pompili, M.L.D., Dominici G., Lester, D., Longo, L., Marconi, G., Forte, A., . . . Girardi, P. (2013). Indications for electroconvulsive therapy in schizophrenia: a systematic review. *Schizophrenia Research, 146*, 1–9. doi:https://dx.doi.org/10.1016/j.schres.2013.02.005.

Porter, R., and Ferrier, N. (1999). Emergency treatment of depression. *Advances in Psychiatric Treatment, 5*, 3–10.

Rabheru, K. (2001). The use of electroconvulsive therapy in special patient populations. *Canadian Journal of Psychiatry, 46*(8), 710–719. doi:10.1177/070674370104600803.

Rasmussen, K.G., Mueller, M., Rummens, I., Hussain, M.M., Petrides, G., Knapp, R.G., . . . Kellner, C.H. (2009). Is baseline medication resistance associated with potential for relapse after successful remission of a depressive episode with ECT? Data from the Consortium for Research on Electroconvulsive Therapy (CORE). *Journal of Clinical Psychiatry, 70*, 232–237.

Rasmussen, K.G., and Rummans, T.A. (2002). Electroconvulsive therapy in the management of chronic pain. *Current Pain and Headache Report, 6*, 17–22.

Ries, R.K., Wilson, L., Bokan, J.A., and Chiles, J.A. (1981). ECT in medication resistant schizoaffective disorder. *Comprehensive Psychiatry, 22*(2), 167–173. Retrieved from www.ncbi.nlm.nih.gov/pubmed/7214880.

Rifkin, A. (1988). ECT versus tricylclic antidepressants in depression: a review of the evidence. *Journal of Clinical Psychiatry, 49*, 3–7.

Rohland, B.M., Carroll, B.T., and Jacoby, R.G. (1993). ECT in the treatment of the catatonic syndrome. *Journal of Affective Disorders, 29*(4), 255–261. Retrieved from www.ncbi.nlm.nih.gov/pubmed/8126312.

Rosebush, P.I., and Mazurek, M.F. (2010). Catatonia and its treatment. *Schizophrenia Bulletin, 36*(2), 239–242. doi:10.1093/schbul/sbp141.

Sackeim, H.A., Decina, P., Kanzler, M., Kerr, B., and Malitz, S. (1987). Effects of electrode placement on the efficacy of titrated, low-dose ECT. *American Journal of Psychiatry, 144*(11), 1449–1455. Retrieved from www.ncbi.nlm.nih.gov/pubmed/3314538.

Sackeim, H.A., Prudic, J., Devanand, D.P., Kiersky, J.E., Fitzsimons, L., Moody, B.J., . . . Settembrino, J.M. (1993). Effects of stimulus intensity and electrode placement on the efficacy and cognitive effects of electroconvulsive therapy. *New England Journal of Medicine, 328*(12), 839–846.

Sackeim, H.A., Prudic, J., Devanand, D.P., Nobler, M.S., Lisanby, S.H., Peyser, S., . . . Clark, J. (2000). A prospective, randomised, double blind comparison of bilateral and right unilateral electroconvulsive therapy at different stimulus intensities 57: 425–34. *Archives of General Psychiatry, 57*, 425–434.

Sackeim, H.A., Prudic, J., Fuller, R., Keilp, J., Lavori, P.W., and Olfson, M. (2007). The cognitive effects of electroconvulsive therapy in community settings. *Neuropsychopharmacology, 32*(1), 244–254. doi:10.1038/sj.npp.1301180.

Schlaepfer, T.E., George, M.S., and Mayberg, H. (2010). WFSBP Guidelines on brain stimulation treatments in psychiatry. *World Journal of Biological Psychiatry, 11*(1), 2–18. doi:10.3109/15622970903170835.

Scottish Intercollegiate Guidelines Network (SIGN). (2010). IGN non-pharmaceutical management of depression in adults. Edinburgh, UK: SIGN.

Scottish Intercollegiate Guidelines Network (SIGN). (2012). SIGN 127 • Management of perinatal mood disorders. Edinburgh, UK: SIGN.

Scottish Intercollegiate Guidelines Network (SIGN). (2013). *Management of schizophrenia: A National Clinical Guideline* (pp. 1–65). Edinburgh, UK: SIGN.

Sikdar, S., Kulhara, P., Avasthi, A., and Singh, H. (1994). Combined chlorpromazine and electroconvulsive therapy in mania. *British Journal of Psychiatry, 164*(6), 806–810. Retrieved from www.ncbi.nlm.nih.gov/pubmed/7952988.

Silverstone, P.H., and Silverstone, T. (2004). A review of acute treatments for bipolar depression. *International Clinical Psychopharmacology, 19*(3), 113–124. Retrieved from www.ncbi.nlm.nih.gov/pubmed/15107653.

Small, J.G, Klapper, M.H, Kellams, J.J, Miller, M.J, Milstein, V., Sharpley, P.H., and Small, I.F. (1988). Electroconvulsive treatment compared with lithium in the management of manic states. *Archives of General Psychiatry, 45*(8), 727–732. Retrieved from www.ncbi.nlm.nih.gov/pubmed/2899425.

Sobin, C., Prudic, J., Devanand, D.P., Nobler, M.S., and Sackeim, H.A. (1996). Who responds to electroconvulsive therapy? A comparison of effective and ineffective forms of treatment. *British Journal of Psychiatry, 169*(3), 322–328. Retrieved from www.ncbi.nlm.nih.gov/pubmed/8879718.

Stek, M., van der Wurff, F.F.B., Hoogendijk, W., and Beekman, A. (2003). Electroconvulsive therapy (ECT) for depression in elderly people. *Cochrane Database of Systematic Reviews*. Retrieved from www.cochrane.org/CD003593/DEPRESSN_electroconvulsive-therapy-ect-for-depression-in-elderly-people.

Strawn, J.R., Keck, J., P.E., and Caroff, S.N. (2007). Neuroleptic malignant syndrome. *American Journal of Psychiatry, 164,* 870–876.

Suehs, B., Bendele, S.D., Crismon, M.L., Madhukar, H., Trivedi, M.H., and Kurian, B. (2008). Texas medication algorithm project: procedural manual major depressive disorder algorithms. Retrieved from www.jpshealthnet.org/sites/default/files/tmap_depression_2010.pdf.

Suppes, T., Rush, A.J., Dennehy, E.B., Crismon, M.L., Kashner, T.M., Toprac, M.G., . . . Texas Medication Algorithm Project. (2003). Texas Medication Algorithm Project, phase 3 (TMAP-3): clinical results for patients with a history of mania. *Journal of Clinical Psychiatry, 64*(4), 370–382. doi:10.4088/JCP.v64n0403.

Suppes, T., Swann, A.C., Dennehy, E.B., Habermacher, E.D., Mason, M., Crismon, M.L., . . . Altshuler, K.Z. (2001). Texas Medication Algorithm Project: development and feasibility testing of a treatment algorithm for patients with bipolar disorder. *Journal of Clinical Psychiatry, 62*(6), 439–447. Retrieved from www.ncbi.nlm.nih.gov/pubmed/11465521.

Swoboda, E., Conca, A., Konig, P., Waanders, R., and Hansen, M. (2001). Maintenance electroconvulsive therapy in affective and schizoaffecitve disorder *Neuropsychobiology, 43,* 23–28.

Tharyan, P., and Adams, C.E. (2005). Electroconvulsive therapy for schizophrenia. *Cochrane Database of Systematic Reviews, 2*(CD000076).

Tiller, J.W.G., and Lyndon, R.W. (2003). *Electroconvulsive Therapy: An Australian Guide*. Melbourne, Australia: Australian Post Graduate Medicine.

Trimble, M.R., and Krishnamoorthy, E. (2005). The use of ECT in neuropsychiatric disorders. In Scott, A.I.F. (Ed.), *The ECT Handbook*, 2nd edition. London: Royal College of Psychiatrists.

Trollor, J.N., and Sachdev, P.S. (1993). Electroconvulsive treatment of neuroleptic malignant syndrome: a review and report of cases. *Australian New Zealand Journal of Psychiatry, 19*(33), 650–659.

UK ECT Review Group. (2003). Efficacy and safety of electroconvulsive therapy in depressive disorders: a systematic review and meta-analysis. *Lancet, 361,* 799–808.

Versiani, M., Cheniaux, E., and Landeira-Fernandez, J. (2011). Efficacy and safety of electroconvulsive therapy in the treatment of bipolar disorder: a systematic review. *Journal of ECT, 27*(2), 153–164. doi:10.1097/YCT.0b013e3181e6332e.

Vesperini, S., Papetti, F., and Pringuey, D. (2010). Are catatonia and neuroleptic malignant syndrome related conditions? *Encephale, 36*(2), 105–110. doi:10.1016/j.encep.2009.03.009.

Waite, J., and Easton, A. (2013). *The ECT Handbook*, 3rd edition London: Royal College of Psychiatrists.

West, E.D. (1981). Electric convulsion therapy in depression: a double blind controlled trial. *British Medical Journal, 282,* 355–357.

Whitehouse, A.M., and Waite, J. (2013). The use of ECT in the treatment of mania In Waite, J., and Easton, A. (Eds.), *The ECT Handbook*, 3rd edition. London: Royal College of Psychiatrists.

Wilson, I.C., Vernon, J.T., Guin, T., Sandifer, M.G. (1963). A controlled trial of treatments of depression. *Journal of Neuropsychiatry, 4,* 331–337.

Yatham, L.N., Kennedy, S.H., Parikh, S.V., Schaffer, A., Beaulieu, S., Alda, M., . . . Berk, M. (2013). Canadian Network for Mood and Anxiety Treatments (CANMAT) and International Society for Bipolar Disorders (ISBD) collaborative update of CANMAT guidelines for the management of patients with bipolar disorder: update 2013. *Bipolar Disorders, 15*(1), 1–44. doi:10.1111/bdi.12025.

Clinical indications: children and adolescents

HISTORY

Tiller and Lyndon (2003) noted that the first published account of ECT in minors was in 1942 in Paris, when two adolescents were successfully treated. Shorter (2013) goes on to say that the narrative surrounding the use of ECT in the child and adolescent population is similar to the adult population as it has been shown to be safe and effective and particularly useful in the treatment of melancholic major depression. Lauretta Bender, head of the children's ward in New York City, was

the first psychiatrist to introduce paediatric ECT into the USA in 1942, treating children between the ages of four and 12 years (Shorter, 2013).

As with adults, ECT was not rejected on scientific grounds in the 1960s and 1970s but because of media and other cultural prejudice. However, the lack of scientific evidence from randomised control trials did not help the cause. Shorter (2013) points out that the biggest concern early on was that age was not considered to be an important factor in its use, resulting in ECT being administered to a patient as young as three years after it was developed by Cerletti and Bini.

During the 1940s to 1960s there was considerable body of evidence that demonstrated that ECT was a safe and effective procedure in the paediatric population. But, as Shorter (2013) notes, the body of data was rejected owing to the widespread hysteria associated with the anti-psychiatry movement, which particularly targeted paediatric ECT as "putting electricity into the brains of helpless children".

There has been much opposition on the use of ECT in minors, with concern about the effect of seizures on the developing nervous system and cognitive development. Claims have been made that it may impair brain development, causing permanent damage, with the treatment being described as "deadly electroshock therapy" (Torpey, 2016).

In 1975, the anti-psychiatry movement in the USA was so strong that it resulted in a court decision that together with the advent of new psychopharmacological agents changed the use of paediatric ECT for good (Seneter, Winslade, Liston and Mills, 1984). This action resulted in a wave of laws and regulations in many states that resulted in extensive restrictions on the use of ECT in all ages, particularly those under the age of 18 years.

Over the years, this strong resistance to the use of ECT in paediatric and adolescent populations has mellowed. Ghaziuddin, Kutcher and Knapp (2004) endorsed ECT for the treatment of mood disorders in adolescents when more conservative treatments were unsuccessful. However, the challenges facing the use of ECT in paediatric populations remain ever-present with the new Western Australia mental health legislation banning the use of Electroconvulsive Therapy (ECT) on those under 14 (ABC, 2014; Gribbin, 2014).

(Walter and Rey, 1997b) completed a comprehensive review on the use of ECT in Australian young people between 1990 and 1996. They examined 60 reports and noted that although the overall the quality of studies were poor the effectiveness of ECT in adolescents across all diagnoses were the same as the adult population.

The Royal Australian and New Zealand College of Psychiatrists, the Royal College of Psychiatrists and the American Psychiatric Association ECT guidelines all have dedicated sections on the use of ECT in children and adolescents, providing direction concerning its use and group of patients (American Psychiatric Association, 2001; RANZCP, 2007, 2013; Waite and Easton, 2013). Under current legislation in Australia, the same rules apply to informed consent for ECT for young people under the age of 18 as for adults. A voluntary patient must be able to give informed consent. If consent is not possible, an application must be made to the relevant mental health review tribunal for a determination. Parents cannot consent to ECT being performed on their child.

It is good practice to actively involve families, carers and concerned relatives in the consent process. If there is disagreement then each of these groups should present their views to the relevant mental health review tribunal, which is able to make an independent determination.

CLINICAL CONCERNS

Clinical indications for ECT in children and adolescents are broadly similar to those noted for adults. Bloch, Levcovitch, Bloch, Mendlovic and Ratzoni (2001) compared the experience with ECT in two age groups in the same community psychiatric institution. Twenty-four consecutive adolescent patients were compared with 33 adult patients who commenced ECT on the same day, overcoming any difference in accepted protocols for diagnosis, treatment and application of ECT. ECT was equally effective for adolescents and adults, with 58% in each group gaining remission. The major difference was that, with the diagnosis, adolescents were referred within the psychotic spectrum compared to the majority of adults, who were referred within the affective spectrum of psychiatric illness (Bloch et al., 2001). This diagnostic difference suggests that the threshold for using ECT is much higher for adolescents, with more severe forms of illness, many of whom have failed multiple medication trials accompanied and had long courses of psychotherapy (Ghaziuddin, Gipson and Hodges, 2013). Adults were more likely to be referred for ECT because of the failure of conventional treatment, whereas adolescents were more likely to be referred owing to strong suicidal ideation and catatonia (Bloch, Levcovitch, Bloch, Mendlovic and Ratzoni, 2008).

There are a number of issues that arise in this age group that make the decision to use ECT more complex. There is substantial public apprehension about the use of ECT for the treatment of mental illness in young people as well as significant lack of information about the treatment among child and adolescent psychiatrists and psychologists. Surveys conducted across the USA and Australia in the 1990s highlighted that negative views held by psychiatrists and psychologist concerning the use of ECT in minors was directly proportional to the lack of adequate experience (Ghaziuddin, Ghazi, King, Walter and Rey, 2001; Rey and Walter, 1997). Education and experience was effective in demonstrating an improvement in the self rating scores obtained among a subgroup of the original Australian child and adolescent psychiatrists in a subsequent survey (Walter and Rey, 2003).

These concerns accentuate the importance of trying to balance the ethical principles of beneficence ("to do good"), non-maleficence ("to do no harm") and justice, to ensure that young people get access to the same treatments as adults and respect for patient autonomy (Roberson, Rey and Walter, 2013). If these principles are applied fairly and rationally decisions can be made that can lead to substantial clinical change in complex clinical situations with far-reaching consequences for patients and their families.

Ethical decision-making requires that the procedure is carefully explained to patients and their families to obtain fully informed consent with good documentation of this process, along with the diagnoses and other treatment strategies discussed.

Issues of development are important in this process. The younger the person, the less able they are to make autonomous and informed decisions about their health without the support of family and carers. Roberson et al. (2013) refer to this process as "assent". The American Academy of Child and Adolescent Psychiatry (AACAP) has formulated a system of values to help guide decision-making concerning mental health in young people. These include: remaining child and family focused, being culturally sensitive and integrated and providing timely, effective and evidence-based care in an integrated manner (Ghaziuddin et al., 2004).

As with adults, there is a range of factors that can facilitate appropriate referral for ECT and a successful outcome. Young patients respond well to ECT where there are clear and prominent psychiatric diagnoses with mood symptoms, like major depressive disorder with melancholia, bipolar depression (Ghaziuddin et al., 2013) or catatonia, which in adolescents is more often associated with mood disorders (Thakur, Jagadheesan, Dutta and Sinha, 2003). Comorbid diagnoses like anxiety and autistic spectrum disorders may make the response to ECT less robust and require a long-term management plan to ensure success (Ghaziuddin et al., 2013). Longer-term planning is also necessary when a young person having ECT has a complicated premorbid level of function or intellectual and other developmental disabilities. Complete remission is often only possible with ongoing supportive psychotherapy, social skills training and interventions to help them overcome the impact of the psychiatric disorder, which may have been present for many years (Ghaziuddin et al., 2013). In adults it is known that high levels of somatic symptoms predict a lower response rate to ECT (Rasmussen et al., 2004), a factor that appears to be evident in adolescents having ECT based upon extensive clinical experience (Ghaziuddin et al., 2013).

A further complexity in the use of ECT in young people is that young people are more likely to have lower seizure thresholds, and prolonged seizures are not uncommon during a course of ECT. In these cases, terminating a prolonged seizure is essential followed by a review of the induction agents utilised. In some ECT clinics it is common practice to reduce seizure threshold by adding a short-acting narcotic agent to the anticonvulsive induction agent. This practice is often not ideal in young people who have prolonged seizures and it is recommended that an induction agent with greater anticonvulsive properties should be considered.

As with adult ECT, principle-driven ethical practice in young people determines that treatment should commence with forms of ECT that have less cognitive impairment like ultrabrief ECT, with careful monitoring of clinical response. Stronger forms of ECT should be considered if there is a lack of clinical response bifrontal or bitemporal ECT.

In summary, ECT should be considered an important clinical tool that can be used very effectively in managing severe mental health problems in young people. As Roberson et al. (2013) notes, "it is an unavoidable conclusion that ECT in children and adolescents is a safe, effective and lifesaving treatment!"

CLINICAL INDICATIONS

Walter and Rey (1997b), reviewed published papers on the use of ECT in children and adolescents for the treatment of a range of conditions. They identified 60 studies, mostly case reports, involving 360 patients and concluded that ECT in adolescents was as effective as in adults and side effects were also not substantially different to adults. They did not find any deaths directly related to ECT. This finding has been replicated in a more recent study by Bloch et al. (2001). ECT is indicated in the following conditions.

MAJOR DEPRESSIVE DISORDER WITH MELANCHOLIA AND PSYCHOSIS

Major depressive disorder with psychosis has a varied response to medication, with a protracted time course of treatment resulting in high levels of distress and enduring symptoms. 63% showed improvement with ECT (Walter and Rey, 1997b).

The main criteria that should be used to consider ECT are severity of illness and associated imminent risk. The view that ECT should a treatment of last resort needs to be challenged as there may be occasions when it should be considered as first-line treatment (Ghaziuddin, 2013).

There are two systematic studies of treatment response in adolescent depression that highlight the need to consider the use of ECT owing to the poor response to medication. In the treatment of adolescent depression study (TADS) that examined 327 adolescents with a primary diagnosis of major depressive disorder who were given fluoxetine alone, CBT alone or combined fluoxetine and CBT. The results were that 71% responded in the combined group, 60.6% for fluoxetine alone and 43.2% in CBT alone (March et al., 2004). The extension study demonstrated that inadequate treatment duration was a risk factor for early decline (March et al., 2009).

The second large study of adolescents, Treatment of Resistant Adolescent Depression (TORDIA), involved 334 adolescents who had failed to respond to a prior trial of a selective serotonin inhibitor (SSRI). The participants were randomly assigned to either a different mediation (SSRI or venlafaxine) or medication switched with CBT (Asarnow et al., 2009). After 12 weeks the combined treatment group had a superior outcome to medication alone or psychotherapy alone. Response to treatment was more likely in adolescents with less severe depressive illness, less family conflict and an absence of self-injurious behaviour (Asarnow et al., 2009). The disturbing finding was that after six months the remission rate was only 38.9% in youth with lower depression severity, hopelessness and anxiety symptoms (Emslie et al., 2010).

Findings from these studies add weight to the need to consider ECT as a reasonable treatment option for severe depressive illness in young people as inadequate treatment duration and a past history of failure to respond to even one antidepressant appears to be associated with poor response to treatment and failure to gain remission (Ghaziuddin, 2013).

MAJOR DEPRESSIVE DISORDER WITH LETHAL SUICIDE ATTEMPTS/SEVERE SELF-INJURIOUS BEHAVIOUR (SIB)

Self-injurious behaviour is a unique diagnostic category associated with young people, particularly those with severe psychiatric disorder and intellectual disability or other forms of developmental delay that can have a robust response to ECT (Wachtel et al., 2009; Wachtel, Griffin and Reiti, 2010; Wachtel, Jaffe and Kellner, 2011; Wachtel, Kanahng, Dhossche, Cascella and Reti, 2008). SIBis defined as self-directed action that results in physical harm and may occur within a range of disorders including depression, anxiety, psychosis, personality disorders and intellectual disability. It is very common among individuals with intellectual disability, with estimates ranging from 10–50% (Wachtel and Dhossche, 2013). In this group, SIB is demarcated as occurring without specific suicidal ideation or intent. It takes the form of headbanging, hitting, slapping, punching, biting, kicking and scratching directed at one or more body surfaces, resulting in frank tissue injury (Furniss and Biswas, 2012).

SIB can pose a significant clinical challenge for many patients with psychiatric diagnoses as it involves repeated potentially lethal suicide attempts (usually three or more), a refusal to eat or drink, or threats to cause persistent and grave disability. It has been suggested that self-injury is an "unorthodox" symptom of psychiatric distress that usually has a poor response to psychotropic medication (Wachtel and Dhossche, 2013). It has been asserted that SIB may be an alternative sign of catatonia, as it is associated with irritability, odd gestures and mannerisms, stereotypies, pacing and odd repetitive behaviour that may explain the profound and global remission of symptom when treated with ECT (Black, Wilcox and Stewart, 1985; Carr, Dorrington, Schrader and Wale, 1983; Chung and Varghese, 2008; Cizadlo and Wheaton, 1995; Consoli et al., 2013; Siegel, Millligan, Robbins and Prentice, 2012).

Prior to commencing ECT, the clinical workup for these patients necessitates a complete multi-disciplinary assessment including pre-ECT medical evaluation as dictated by regulations of the ECT service and in concordance with the Practice Parameters for Use of Electroconvulsive Therapy with Adolescents guidelines (Ghaziuddin et al., 2004).

Issues of stigma can be challenging problem that can be improved through the education of clinicians (Walter and Rey, 2003). Education of the ECT clinic, theatre and recovery staff concerning safety, psychiatric disorder, nature of the SIB and/or intellectual disability can go along way to improve acceptance, enhancing respect, dignity and humanity of the patient undergoing ECT (Wachtel and Dhossche, 2013).

Further challenges to effective delivery of treatment are the lack of access to services that have sufficient skill in administering ECT to this challenging group of patients as well as the significant obstacles imposed by the relevant mental health legislation (Wachtel and Dhossche, 2013).

TREATMENT-RESISTANT DEPRESSION AND BIPOLAR DISORDER IN ADOLESCENTS

A common definition of treatment resistance in adults are those patients who have failed to respond to at least two or three psychotropic agents, in adequate dosages, for an adequate duration usually in combination with psychotherapy (Fava, 2003). Ghaziuddin (2013) notes that this has rarely, if ever, applied to adolescents. It is now no longer reasonably to insist that all medications at adequate doses and length be used in adolescents prior to ECT since the available armamentarium is large and the efficacy is very similar.

The incidence of treatment-resistant mood disorders that include treatment-resistant depression and bipolar disorder in adolescents is unknown. Estimates may be indirectly based upon the number of young people that are treated with ECT; however, this could can be misleading owing to the marked national and regional difference in

ECT practice (Ghaziuddin, 2013). Two surveys have demonstrated rates of 1.5% in patients under the age of 20 years (Thompson and Blaine, 1987) and 0.93% of patients under the age of 19 years treated with ECT during 1990–1996 (Walter and Rey, 1997a). Based upon the poor outcome in large multicentre medication trials, it is likely that TDM is a common disorder (Emslie et al., 2010; March et al., 2009).

It is likely that the condition has not been recognised for many years owing in part to the omission of mood disorder in young people as a category when adult psychiatry changed from using DSM-II (American Psychiatric Association, 1968) to DSM-III (American Psychiatric Association, 1980). Instead it was common for clinician to diagnoses adolescents with the less severe condition of adjustment disorder with depressed mood. Ghaziuddin (2013) asserts that these factors were significant in clinicians overlooking TRM, resulting in a lack of recognition that these disorders can be resistant to treatment during adolescence, reducing the opportunity for timely treatment to prevent prolonged morbidity or mortality.

CLINICAL WISDOM 2.6.1

Clinical experience suggests that ECT should be considered a reasonable alternative treatment in young people after two or three adequate trials of drugs from different classes of antidepressants like SSRIs and SNRIs. Tricyclic antidepressants generally do not work in children and adolescents and therefore should not be considered as a prerequisite before proceeding to ECT. As in adults, in some situations ECT may be the treatment of choice. However, in reality most child and adolescent psychiatrists do not consider ECT, even for the most severe forms of depression with strong suicidal ideation, psychosis or self-injurious behaviour, despite a failure to achieve an adequate response or remission using multiple medications and psychological treatments.

BIPOLAR DISORDER UNRESPONSIVE TO MOOD STABILISERS

In general, young people present with complex mood states and are often given a combination of medication as first-line treatment similar to adults. The most commonly prescribed drugs include lithium, valproate, lamotrigine or risperidone. This is driven by the lack of evidence in the use of mood stabiliser and/or antipsychotics in young people, with most clinicians treating adolescents based upon their experience in treating bipolar disorder in adults and influenced by the few randomised controlled trials that have been completed (Bramness, Groholt, Engeland and Furu, 2009; Geller et al., 2012). The risk of this practice is that these drugs may be associated with more side effects in younger people, sodium valproate commonly causing weight gain and polycystic ovarian syndrome in young women leading to infertility and second-generation antipsychotic drugs associated with significant weight gain leading to the metabolic syndrome (Riordan, Antonini and Murphy, 2011).

More recently, lamotrigine has been used as first-line treatment, particularly in bipolar disorder type two. Care is required in initiating treatment due to the potential for a severe body rash that can lead to significant morbidity and mortality (Lorberg, Youssef and Bhagwagar, 2009).

What is striking is that ECT is rarely listed as a treatment option in clinical practice guidelines for treating adolescent bipolar disorder; its absence is notable in the American Academy of Child and Adolescent Psychiatry Practice Parameters for the Assessment and Treatment of Children and Adolescents with Bipolar Disorder (McClellan and Werry, 1997). In other clinical practice guidelines it is listed as a treatment option with no age specification (Grunze et al., 2010; NICE, 2006).

SCHIZOPHRENIA SPECTRUM DISORDERS (SSD)

Schizophrenia spectrum disorders are conditions in which psychosis is the primary presenting symptom, including delusions, hallucinations, disorganised speech, thoughts and behaviour that are not better explained by a mood disorder, medical condition or substance use disorder (American Psychiatric Association, 2013).

Since the initial systematic review of all published cases of ECT in patients under the age of 18 years completed by Walter and Rey (1997b), there have been five other studies that have demonstrated that ECT is effective in this disorder. The original work identified 396 patients, of whom there was data on 205 patients. The rate of improvement in patients with SSD were considerably lower (42%) when compared to depression (63%) and 80% response for patients with mania and catatonia (Walter and Rey, 1997b).

As noted earlier in this chapter, Bloch et al. (2001) completed a chart review in which they compared 25 adolescent patients with 33 adult patients who commenced treatment on the same day. For all patients medication was continued during the course of ECT. All of the young patients were treated with bilateral ECT. What was striking in their results was the significant difference in diagnoses between the two groups: 19 of 25 adolescent patients fell within the schizophrenia spectrum, four with catatonic schizophrenia, 11 with non-catatonic schizophrenia and four with schizoaffective disorder. The outcome was better than in the previous study, with 58% improvement and 67% no readmission over the next 12 months (Bloch et al., 2001).

Stein et al. (2004) also conducted a chart review comparing 36 adolescent patients with 57 adults. In the group of adolescents, seven had catatonic schizophrenia and 12 non-catatonic schizophrenia and 33 out of the 37 were treated with bitemporal ECT, compared to 17 out of 57 adults with improvement in 58% and 68% no readmission rate over the subsequent year (Stein et al., 2004).

Baeza et al. (2009) reported three patents, all aged 13, one of whom had catatonia, the second increased positive psychotic symptoms and the third with disorganised behaviour and prominent agitation, who were treated with ECT. All had a favourable outcome with minimal adverse effects. In a further retrospective chart review of 13 adolescents diagnosed with SSD, all were treated with bitemporal electrode placement. Of the patients, 53.8% had a 20% reduction in measures of psychotic symptoms, with all having significant improvement on the clinical global impression. There was no deterioration after six months with seven patients having continuation ECT (Baeza et al., 2010).

In a longitudinal follow-up study that compared nine adolescents diagnosed with SSD (seven with schizophrenia and two with schizoaffective disorder) who were treated with ECT and antipsychotic medication and nine matched subjects who were treated with medication alone (de la Serna et al., 2011). There was no significant difference between the groups, with both showing significant improvement that was maintained at the two-year follow-up. There was no difference between the groups on clinical or neuropsychological measures (de la Serna et al., 2011).

In a large more recent case control prospective study, 112 patients aged between 13 and 20 years who presented with first-episode psychosis between 2004 to 2009 that was resistant to pharmacotherapy were matched for age and sex and then randomly assigned to a control or ECT group at a ratio of 1:2 (Zhang et al., 2012). They found that there was improvement in positive symptoms, insight and judgement at week two and week seven from baseline and there was improvement in sleep efficiency, rapid eye movement (REM) latency and density compared to controls with a greater report of adverse events in the ECT group notably transient headache and dizziness (Zhang et al., 2012).

Block, Stein and Walter (2013), in their review of the use of ECT in SSD, concluded that ECT was safe and tolerable intervention in adolescents with first-episode psychosis, and was more effective when combined with antipsychotic medication compared to mediation alone in the treatment-resistant SSD group. Psychosis in young people may be undifferentiated in acute settings and may take some years before the defining form of the disorder emerged. ECT should be considered as an emergency procedure when a young person presents with treatment-resistant psychosis that is characterised by internal extreme distress and agitation that is not rapidly relieved with medication. The extreme distress needs to reside within the patient and not simply with their carers or the treating team. Like adults with treatment-resistant schizophrenia, adolescents respond better to antipsychotic medication, including clozapine, than ECT (Block et al., 2013).

CATATONIA IN CHILDREN AND ADOLESCENTS

Catatonia was originally described by Kahlbaum in 1874 as a separate cyclic brain disorder, later incorporated into a type of dementia praecox, an early term for schizophrenia, and more recently as a syndrome of affective disorders in adults (Dhossche and Wachtel, 2013). Catatonia can be defined as a unique motor dysregulation syndrome characterised by specific signs: extreme negativism or muteness, stereotypies, odd voluntary movement, echolalia, echopraxia, immobility and at times alternating with excess movement and purposeless motor activity that is not influenced by external stimuli. It can be life-threatening particularly when it is aggravated by autonomic dysfunction and fever (Fink and Taylor, 2003).

Catatonia in young people is similar to adults in that it may be caused by multiple diagnoses, including organic brain disorders (Verhoeven and Tuinier, 2006), bipolar disorder (Wachtel et al., 2011), major depressive disorder (Wachtel et al., 2010), schizophrenia (Volkmar and Cohen, 1991), Down's syndrome (Ja and Ghaziuddin, 2011) and autism (Volkmar and Cohen, 1991). As with adult conditions, it is very responsive to treatment with high-dose benzodiazepines or ECT. Bush, Fink, Petrides, Dowling and Francis (1996) developed the "lorazepam test" to determine underlying catatonia. They administered 1 to 2 mg of lorazepam orally, intramuscularly or intravenously to 28 patients with catatonia to see if there was improvement in the catatonic symptoms. A positive response to an initial parenteral challenged predicted final lorazepam response, as did the length of catatonic symptoms prior to treatment. 76% of those who received a complete trial of lorazepam, had their catatonic symptoms resolved, with a further four patients responding to ECT (Bush et al., 1996). Young patients with catatonia can tolerate high doses of lorazepam (24 mg) without experiencing sedation, suggesting that they have high tolerance for benzodiazepines (Dhossche and Wachtel, 2013).

In summary, ECT can be beneficial for young people with catatonia when they do not respond to first-line treatment with lorazepam and there is ongoing significant impairment and distress.

TOLERABILITY OF ECT IN ADOLESCENTS

Studies dating back many years have demonstrated that the tolerability of ECT in young people is similar to adults (Cohen, Pallilère-Martinot and Basquin, 1997). The comprehensive literature review of some 60 studies including 396 patients on the use of ECT in adolescents conducted by Walter and Rey (1997b) concluded that ECT in adolescents seems to be as effective as in adults and side effects in this age group were also not substantially different to those in adults. Two separate comparative chart reviews that compared ECT treatment in in a total of 60 adolescents, with a total 90 adults, both concluded that ECT was equally effective for adolescent compared to adults and that it was generally well tolerated (Bloch et al., 2001; Stein et al., 2004), although one study did report that more adolescents prematurely ended treatment (Stein et al., 2004). It is possible that this that may reflect the difference in diagnostic referral between the groups, where ECT was more commonly used to treat severe schizophrenia spectrum disorders in the adolescent group compared to higher rates of affective disorders in adults (Bloch et al., 2001; Stein et al., 2004).

Another study of 42 young people below 18 years who received 49 treatment courses between

1990 and 1996 concluded that ECT was rapidly effective, with response noted within the first few treatments and that side effects were reported as being minor (Walter and Rey, 1997a).

Taieb et al. (2002) reported on 11 adolescents, six with depression and five with mania, matched with psychiatric controls that were treated with bilateral ECT. Both groups were followed for a mean duration of 5.2 years and the groups did not differ on social or school functioning. Twenty out of 22 had developed bipolar disorder at follow-up, with nearly two thirds of the group experiencing an additional episode of illness during this period (Taieb et al., 2002). It is of note that in this study the impact on school functioning was related to the severity of the mood disorder rather than ECT (Taieb et al., 2002).

Additional information concerning the tolerability of ECT in young people comes from one of the few case series where ECT was continued after the index course up to 81 weeks in six adolescents: two females and four males aged between 14 to 17 years who were diagnosed with a with severe treatment-resistant depression. Psychotropic medication was discontinued during the index course of bitemporal ECT and five out of six were hospitalised (Ghaziuddin, Dumas and Hodges, 2011). ECT was continued until remission or until minimal residual symptoms were evident during the ECT extension period. Four of the six cases achieved remission, with another case achieving 50% improvement. All achieved premorbid level of functioning and cognitive deficits were not evident. Neuropsychological testing was completed prior to and following ECT at two time points, four and 81 weeks. Results revealed that there was no decline in intellectual function, short-term memory or verbal memory, with a significant improvement in long-term delayed recall (Ghaziuddin et al., 2011).

In conclusion, ECT is safe and effective in treating severe psychiatric illness in young people aged 18 or younger, with cognitive and other side effects occurring at a rate similar to adults, and longer courses of treatment may achieve remission without resulting in adverse cognitive effects.

SPECIAL CONSIDERATIONS

Clinical decision-making when using ECT to treat young people should be guided by ethical considerations that are based upon sound principles. It is essential that physicians and allied mental health professionals have adequate training and experience to ensure the best outcome in the use of ECT in young people. If the patient is younger than 16 years of age it is recommended that an opinion be sought from two experienced child and adolescent psychiatrists. Application to the relevant mental health review tribunal is essential, particularly if there is disagreement or strong objections raised by the carers and family. If an adolescent is older than 16 years, only one opinion from a child and adolescent psychiatrist is required, with the other opinion being given by an adult psychiatrist. In this case, the older teenager is able to provide informed consent and/or refuse treatment. Informed consent is essential. It is recommended that guardians, parents and other caregivers be involved in the discussions concerned that risks and benefits of ECT for this person.

Prolonged seizures should be identified as being more likely in this group and appropriate strategies utilised to prevent them. Policies concerning ECT in minors should be compatible with the relevant jurisdiction: state and federal regulation governing ECT practice.

REFERENCES

ABC. (2014). Electroshock therapy on under-14s banned in WA after law passes Parliament [Press release]. Retrieved from www.abc.net.au/news/2014-10-17/mental-health-bill-passes-wa-parliament/5822874

American Psychiatric Association. (1968). *DSM II*. New York: American Psychiatric Association.

American Psychiatric Association. (1980). *DSM III*. New York: American Psychiatric Association.

American Psychiatric Association. (2001). *The Practice of Electroconvulsive Therapy: Recommendations for Treatment, Training and Privileging*, 2nd edition. Washington, DC: American Psychiatric Association.

American Psychiatric Association. (2013). *Desk Reference to the Diagnostic Criteria from DSM-5 and Statistical*

Manual of Mental Disorders, 5th edition. Arlington, VA: American Psychiatric Association.

Asarnow, J.R., Emslie, G., Clarke, G, Wagner, W.K.D., Spirito, A., Vitiello, B., . . . Brent, D. (2009). Treatment of selective serontonin reuptake inhibitor-resistant depression in adolescents: predictors and moderators of treatment response. *Journal of the American Academy of Child and Adolescent Psychiatry, 48*(3), 330–339.

Baeza, I., Flamarique, I., Garrido, J.M., Horga, G., Pons, A., Bernardo, M., . . . Castro-Fornieles, J. (2010). Clinical experience using electroconvulsve therapy in adolescents with schizophrenia spectrum disorders. *Journal of Child and Adolescent Psychopharmacology, 20*(3), 205–209.

Baeza, I., Pons, A., Guillermo Horga, G., Bernardo, M., Lázaro, M., and Castro-Fornieles, J. (2009). Electro-convulsive therapy in early adolescents with schizophrenia spectrum disorders. *Journal of ECT, 25*(4), 278–279.

Black, D., Wilcox, J., and Stewart, M. (1985). The use of ECT in children: case-report. *Journal of the American Academy of Child and Adolescent Psychiatry, 46,* 98–99.

Bloch, Y., Levcovitch, Y., Bloch, A.M., Mendlovic, S., and Ratzoni, G. (2001). Electroconvulsive therapy in adolescents: similarities to and differences from adults. *Journal of the American Academy of Child and Adolescent Psychiatry, 40*(11), 1332–1336. doi:10.1097/00004583-200111000-00014

Bloch, Y., Levcovitch, Y., Bloch, A.M., Mendlovic, S., and Ratzoni, G. (2008). Reasons for referral for electroconvulsive therapy: a comparison between adolescents and adults. *Australasian Psychiatry, 16*(3), 191–194.

Bloch, Y., Stein, D., and Walter, G. (2013). ECT in schizophrenia spectrum disorders. In Ghaziuddin, N. and Walter, G. (Eds.), *Electroconvulsive Therapy in Children and Adolescents.* New York: Oxford University Press.

Bramness, J.G., Groholt, B., Engeland, A., and Furu, K. (2009). The use of lithium, valproate or lamotrigine for psychiatric conditions in children and adolescents in Norway 2004–2007: a prescription database study. *Journal of Affective Disorders, 117*(3), 208–211.

Bush, G., Fink, M., Petrides, G., Dowling, F., and Francis, A. (1996). Catatonia. II. Treatment with lorazepam and electroconvulsive therapy. *Acta Psychiatrica Scandinavica, 93*(2), 137–143. Retrieved from www.ncbi.nlm.nih.gov/pubmed/8686484

Carr, V., Dorrington, C., Schrader, G., and Wale, J. (1983). The use of ECT for mania in childhood bipolar disorder. *British Journal of Psychiatry, 143,* 411–415.

Chung, A., and Varghese, J. (2008). Treatment of catatonia with electroconvulsive therapy in an 11-year-old girl. *Australian & New Zealand Journal of Psychiatry, 42*(3), 251–253. doi:10.1080/00048670701827317

Cizadlo, B., and Wheaton, A. (1995). Case study: ECT treatment of a young girl wtih catatonia. *Journal of the American Academy of Child and Adolescent Psychiatry, 34,* 332–335.

Cohen, D., Pallilère-Martinot M-L, and Basquin, M. (1997). Use of electroconvulsive therapy in adolescents. *Convulsive Therapy, 13*(1), 25–31.

Consoli, A., Cohen, J., Bodeau, N., Guinchat, V., Wachtel, L., and Cohen, D. (2013). Electroconvulsive therapy in adolescents with intelllectual disability and severe self-injurious behavior and agression. *European and Child Adolescent Psychiatry, 22*(1), 55–62.

de la Serna, E., Flamarique, I., Castro-Fornieles, J., Pons, A., Puig, O., Andres-Perpina, S., . . . Baeza, I. (2011). Two-year follow-up of cognitive functions in schizophrenia spectrum disorders of adolescent patients treated with electroconvulsive therapy. *Journal of Child and Adolescent Psychopharma-cology, 21*(6), 611–619. doi:10.1089/cap.2011.0012

Dhossche, D.M., and Wachtel, L.E. (2013). ECT for catatonia in autism. In Ghaziuddin, N. and Walter, G. (Eds.), *Electroconvulsive Therapy in Children and Adolescents* (pp. 217–246). New York: Oxford University Press.

Emslie, G. J., Mayes, T., Porta, G., Vitiello, B., Clarke, G., Wagner, K.D., . . . Brent, D. (2010). Treatment of Resistant Depression in Adolescents (TORDIA): week 24 outcomes. *American Journal of Psychiatry, 167*(7), 782–791. doi: 10.1176/appi.ajp.2010.09040552

Fava, M. (2003). Diagnosis and definition of treatment-resistant depression. *Biological Psychiatry, 53*(8), 649–659. Retrieved from www.ncbi.nlm.nih.gov/pubmed/12706951

Fink, M., and Taylor, M. (2003). *A Clinician's Guide to Diagnosis and Treatment.* Cambridge, UK: Cambridge University Press.

Furniss, F., and Biswas, A. (2012). Recent research on aetiology, development and phenomenology of self-injurious behavior in people with intellectual disabilities: a systematic review and implications for treatment. *Journal of Intellectual Disability Research, 56*(5), 453–475.

Geller, B., Luby, J.L., Joshi, P., Wagner, K.D., Emslie, G., Walkup, J.T., . . . Lavori, P. (2012). A randomised controlled trial of risperidone, lithium or divalproex sodium for initial treatment of bipolar I disorder, manic or mixed phase, in children and adolescents. *Archives of General Psychiatry, 69*(5), 515–528.

Ghaziuddin N. (2013). ECT in mood disorders. In Ghaziuddin, N. and Walter, G. (Eds.), *Electroconvulsive Therapy in Children and Adolescents* (pp. 161–190). New York: Oxford University Press.

Ghaziuddin, N., Dumas, S., and Hodges, E. (2011). Use of continuation or maintenance electroconvulsive therapy in adolescents with severe treatment resistant depression. *Journal of ECT, 27*(1), 168–174.

Ghaziuddin, N., Ghazi, N., King, C., Walter, G., and Rey, M.J. (2001). Electroconvulsive therapy for minors: experiences and attitudes of child psychiatrists and psychologists. *Journal of ECT, 17*(2), 109–117.

Ghaziuddin, N., Gipson, P., and Hodges, E. (2013). A practical guide to using ECT in minors. In Ghaziuddin, N. and Walter, G. (Eds.), *Electroconvulsive Therapy in Children and Adolescents* (pp. 78–103). New York: Oxford University Press.

Ghaziuddin, N., Kutcher, S., and Knapp, P. (2004). Practice parameter for the use of electroconvulsive therapy with adolescents. *Journal of the American Academy of Child and Adolescent Psychiatry, 43*, 1521–1539.

Gribbin C. (2014). Opinion divided over laws in WA that will allow some children to consent to electric shock treatment [Press release]. Retrieved from www.abc.net.au/news/2013-10-23/opinion-divided-over-children-electric-shock-laws/5041986

Grunze, H., Vieta, E., Goodwin, G.M., Bowden, C., Licht, R.W., Moller, H., ... WFSBP Task Force On Treatment Guidelines For Bipolar Disorders. (2010). The World Federation of Societies of Biological Psychiatry (WFSBP) guidelines for the biological treatment of bipolar disorders: update 2010 on the treatment of acute bipolar depression. *World Journal of Biological Psychiatry, 11*(2), 81–109. doi:10.3109/15622970903555881

Ja, S.N., and Ghaziuddin, N. (2011). Catatonia among adolescents with Down Syndrome: a review and 2 case reports. *Journal of ECT, 27*(4), 334–337.

Lorberg, B., Youssef, N.A., and Bhagwagar, S. (2009). Lamotrigine-associated rash: to rechallenge or not to rechallenge? *International Journal of Neuropsychopharmacology, 12*, 257–265.

McClellan, J., and Werry, J. (1997). Practice parameters for the assessment and treatment of children and adolescents with bipolar disorder. *Journal of the American Academy of Child and Adolescent Psychiatry, 36*(10 Suppl), 157S–176S.

March, J., Silva, S., Curry, J., Wells, K., Fairbank, J., Burns, B., ... Bartoi, M. (2009). The Treatment for Adolescents With Depression Study (TADS): outcomes over 1 year of naturalistic follow-up. *American Journal of Psychiatry, 166*(10), 1141–1149. doi:10.1176/appi.ajp.2009.0811 1620

March, J., Silva, S., Petrycki, S., Curry, J., Wells, K., Fairbank, J., ... Severe, J. (2004). Fluoxetine, cognitive-behaviour therapy, and their combination for adolescents with depression: Treatment for Adolescents with Depression Study (TADS) randomized controlled trial. *Journal of the American Medical Association, 292*(7), 807–820.

NICE. (2006). Bipolar disorder: the management of bipolar disorder in adults, children and adolescents, in primary and secondary care (clinical guideline CG38). *NICE.* Retrieved from www.nice.org.uk/guidance/cg38

RANZCP. (2007). Clinical memorandum #12 electroconvulsive therapy. Melbourne, Australia.

RANZCP. (2013). ECT position statement. Melbourne, Australia.

Rasmussen, K.G., Snyder, K.A., Knapp, R.G., Mueller, M., Yim, E., and Husain, M.M. (2004). Relationship between somatization and remission with ECT. *Psychiatric Research, 129*(3), 293–295.

Rey, J.M, and Walter, G. (1997). Half a century of ECT use in young people. *American Journal of Psychiatry, 154*, 595–602.

Riordan, H.J., Antonini, P., and Murphy, M.F. (2011). Atypical antipsychotics and metabolic syndrome in patients with schizophrenia: risk factors, monitoring, and healthcare implications. *American Health & Drug Benefits, 4*(5), 292–302. Retrieved from www.ncbi.nlm.nih.gov/pmc/articles/PMC4105724/

Roberson, M., Rey, J.M., and Walter, G. (2013). Ethical and consent aspects. In Ghaziuddin, N. and Walter, G. (Eds.), *Electroconvulsive Therapy in Children and Adolescents* (pp. 56–71). New York: Oxford University Press.

Seneter, N.W, Winslade, W.J, Liston, E.H, and Mills, M.J. (1984). Electroconvulsive therapy: the evolution of legal regulation. *American Journal Social Psychiatry, 4*, 11–15.

Shorter, E. (2013). The history of paediatric ECT. In Ghaziuddin, N. and Walter, G. (Eds.), *Electroconvulsive Therapy in Children and Adolescents* (Vol. 1, pp. 1–17). New York: Oxford University Press.

Siegel, M., Millligan, B., Robbins, D., and Prentice, G. (2012). Electroconvulsive therapy in an adolescent with autism and bipolar I disorder. *Journal of ECT, 28*(4), 252–255.

Stein, D., Kurtsman, L., Stier, S., Remnik, Y., Meged, S., and Weizman, A. (2004). Electroconvulsive therapy in adolescents and adult psychiatric inpatients: a retrospective chart design. *Journal of Affective Disorders, 82*(3), 335–342.

Taieb, O., Flament, M.F., Chevret, S., Jeammet, P., Allilaire, J.F., Mazet, P., and Cohen, D. (2002). Clinical relevance of electroconvulsive therapy (ECT) in adolescents with severe mood disorder: evidence from a follow-up study. *European Psychiatry, 17*(4), 206–212.

Thakur, A., Jagadheesan, K., Dutta, S., and Sinha, V.K. (2003). Incidence of catatonia in children and adolescents in a pediatric psychiatric clinic. *Australian and New Zealand Journal of Psychiatry, 37*(2), 200–203.

Thompson, J.W, and Blaine, J.D. (1987). Use of ECT in the United States in 1975 and 1980. *American Journal of Psychiatry, 144*(5), 557–562.

Tiller, J.W.G, and Lyndon, R.W. (2003). *Electroconvulsive Therapy: An Australian Guide.* Melbourne, Australia: Australian Post Graduate Medicine.

Torpey, N. (2016). Special Investigation: Shock Treatment: Alarming Spike in Risky Electroconvulsive Therapy on Children. *Sunday Mail (Brisbane).*

Verhoeven, W., and Tuinier, S. (2006). Prader-Willi syndrome: atypical psychoses and motor dysfunctions. *International Review of Neurobiology, 72,* 119–130.

Volkmar, F.R., and Cohen, D.J. (1991). Comorbid association of autism and schizophrenia. *American Journal of Psychiatry, 148*(12), 1705–1707. doi:10.1176/ajp.148.12.1705

Wachtel, L.E., Contrucci-Kuhn, S.A., Griffin, M., Thompson, A., Dhossche, D.M., and Reti, I.M. (2009). ECT for self-injury in an autistic boy. *European Child & Adolescent Psychiatry, 18*(7), 458–463. doi:10.1007/s00787-009-0754-8

Wachtel, L.E., and Dhossche, D.M. (2013). *Electroconvulsive Therapy for Children and Adolescents.* Oxford and New York: Oxford University Press.

Wachtel, L.E., Griffin, M., and Reiti, I. (2010). Electroconvulsive therapy in a man with autism experiencing severe depression, catatonia, and self-injury. *Journal of ECT, 20*(1), 70–73.

Wachtel, L.E., Jaffe, R., and Kellner, C.H. (2011). Electroconvulsive therapy for psychotropic-refractory bipolar affective disorder and severe self-injury and aggression in an 11 year-old autisitic boy. *European Child & Adolescent Psychiatry, 20*(3), 147–152.

Wachtel, L.E., Kanahng, S., Dhossche, D.M., Cascella, N., and Reti, I.M. (2008). Electroconvulsive therapy for catatonia in an autistic girl. *American Journal of Psychiatry, 165,* 329–333.

Waite J., and Easton A. (2013). *The ECT Handbook*, 3rd edition. London: Royal College of Psychiatrists.

Walter, G., and Rey, J.M. (1997a). An epidemiological study of the use of ECT in adolescents. *Journal of the American Academy of Child and Adolescent Psychiatry, 36,* 809–815.

Walter, G., and Rey, J.M. (1997b). Half a century of ECT use in young people. *American Journal of Psychiatry, 154*(5), 595–602.

Walter, G., and Rey, J.M. (2003). How Fixed Are Child Psychiatrists' Views About ECT in the Young? *Journal of ECT, 19*(2), 88–92.

Zhang, Z.J., Chen, Y.C., Wang, H.N., Wang, H.H., Xue, Y.Y., Feng, S.F., and Tan, Q. R. (2012). Electroconvulsive therapy improves antipsychotic and somnographic responses in adolescents with first-episode psychosis – a case-control study. *Schizophrenia Research, 137*(1–3), 97–103. doi: 10.1016/j.schres.2012.01.037

Clinical indications: older people

CLINICAL CONCERNS

ECT is a common treatment in the elderly, with an early British survey noting that 37% of index courses of ECT were administered to patients over the aged of 60 (Pippard and Ellam, 1981). This high rate of use in people aged 65 years or older was confirmed in another survey conducted by the Department of Health (1999), where 44% of women and 33% of men were in this age group, findings that have been replicated in Wales (Duffett, Siegert and Lelliott, 1999). Large surveys have also been conducted in the USA, where the use of ECT in people over the age of 65 is common (Olfson et al., 1998; Rosenbach, Hermann and Dorwart, 1997).

Glen and Scott (1999) note that in the 1990s there was a steady increase in the use of ECT in the elderly. Reasons for this increase may include an ageing population that develops more severe mental health problems, like major depression with melancholia, psychosis, refusal to eat and drink and episodes of depressive stupor, conditions that are more common with age that are particularly responsive to ECT (Benbow, 2005).

Depression in the elderly is often more likely to be medication-resistant (Prudic, Sackeim and Devannand, 1990). ECT is prescribed owing to poor tolerance of antidepressant medication as a result of increased sensitivity to side effects and complications due to the presence of comorbid medical conditions. However, the advent of newer antidepressant medication with increased tolerability may have begun to challenge this view (Olfson et al., 1998).

ECT is often prescribed when there is a need for a speedy response if the patient is severely compromised or at high risk, with research suggesting that older patients have a better outcome from ECT than younger patients (American Psychiatric Association, 2001; van der Wurff et al.,

2003). The elderly tolerate and respond to ECT very well and there appears to be a positive association between advancing age and the efficacy of ECT that may be related to clinical presentation of later-life depression (Flint and Gagnon, 2002).

Age is a reliable but modest predictor of seizure threshold. The oldest patients have the highest seizure threshold and need the greatest amount of energy to elicit suprathreshold seizures (Boylan et al., 2000; Mankad, Beyer, Weiner and Krystal, 2010; Sackeim, Decina, Prohovnik and Malitz, 1987). The impact of age has been considerably reduced with changes in anaesthetic protocols (Benbow, Shah and Crentsil, 2002) and the advent of ultrabrief ECT (Kellner et al., 2016).

Kiloh (1961) introduced the term pseudo-dementia to distinguish a dementia-like syndrome that may be a symptom of a depressive mood disorder rather a true dementia. The clinical manifestation is often indistinguishable from an irreversible brain disorder, with symptoms of memory deficits, slow illogical speech, social withdrawal and odd, erratic behaviour. Maintaining a highly level of clinical suspicion and taking a careful history are required to detect this condition. Fink (2009) notes that one of the distinguishing features of a pseudodementia compared to a true dementia is that it tends to have a more rapid onset appearing suddenly in an elderly adult. Once detected, ECT should be considered to prevent further decline and potential death.

CLINICAL INDICATIONS

ECT has been regarded as the treatment of choice for elderly people with depressive illness. Benbow (1991) conducted a survey of old-age psychiatrists in the early 1990s and found that ECT was the treatment of choice in older patients with depressive illness with psychotic symptoms, severe agitation and those who were at high risk of suicide. Other indications included depressive illness that has failed to respond to antidepressant medication, and those who had a better response to ECT in the past compared to pharmacotherapy (Benbow,

1991). It was also commonly used to treat schizo-affective disorder and depressive illness with dementia.

Recently, van Schaik et al. (2012) conducted a systematic review on the efficacy and safety of continuation ECT (c-ECT) and maintenance ECT (m-ECT) in depressed elderly patients that spanned the period from 1966 until 2010. The study was initiated as relapse and recurrence of geriatric depression after recovery is an important clinical issue that requires vigorous and safe treatment in the long term. They identified 22 studies that met search criteria including three randomised controlled trials, with seven studies exclusively in elderly patients (van Schaik et al., 2012). They noted that the available studies lacked rigorous methodology and failed to account for important geriatric issues such as level of cognitive function and comorbid medical conditions. Based upon the available studies, the group concluded that m-ECT is most likely as effective as continuation medication in severely depressed elderly patients who had a successful index course of treatment that was well tolerated (van Schaik et al., 2012).

TOLERABILITY OF ECT IN OLD AGE

The elderly are more likely to have comorbid medical conditions than young people. Coexisting medical and surgical conditions should be assessed and treated or stabilised before commencing ECT and often lead to an increase in complications. Burke, Rubin, Zorumski and Wetzel (1987) examined 136 patients aged between 40 and 60 years and showed that complications from ECT increase with age. The most common complications were severe confusion, falls and cardiorespiratory problems. Those taking a greater number of medications and a greater number of cardiovascular medications had significantly more complications during ECT; however, there was no relationship between complications and outcome or complications and laterality of treatments (Burke et al., 1987).

A prospective naturalistic study in older depressed patients showed that the number and severity of adverse events were not associated with increased age (Brodaty, Hickie and Mason, 2000), a finding that is at odds with most other reports. Damm et al. (2010) examined 4457 treatments in 380 patients to investigate the influence of age on ECT outcome, safety and adverse effects. They showed that there was a significant difference with an increased need for physical medications but not concomitant psychotropic medications in patients older than 65 years (Damm et al., 2010). These results are consistent with most other studies, where increasing age and medical co-morbidity increase the rate of complications with ECT (Benbow, 1987; Casey and Davies, 1996; Fraser and Glass, 1978, 1980; Gasper and Samarasinghe, 1982; Godber et al., 1987; Karlinsky and Shulman, 1984; Rubin, Kinscherf and Wehrman, 1991; Tomac, Rummans, Pileggi and Li, 1997).

Manly, Oakley Jr and Bloch (2000) completed a case control study where they examined the use of ECT in the very old, aged 75 or older, comparing the rate of falls, cardiovascular factors, confusion and gastrointestinal, pulmonary and metabolic side effects compared to patients treated with pharmacotherapy alone. Patients receiving ECT showed fewer cardiovascular and gastrointestinal side effects. Those who received ECT had longer lengths of stay in hospital with more favourable outcomes. Overall they concluded that there was a tendency for ECT to result in fewer side effects and better treatment outcomes and that it was relatively safe and more effective than medication, echoing the findings other studies in this age group (Casey and Davies, 1996; Damm et al., 2010; Tomac et al., 1997). This result was confirmed in a more recent literature review that concluded that ECT was safe an extremely effective in special populations, with the frail elderly being good candidates for this treatment because they are often unresponsive to or intolerant to psychotropic medications (Rabheru, 2001).

Reports generally agree that the elderly are more vulnerable to cognitive impairment during ECT and adverse effects persist longer after ECT (Burke et al., 1987; Sobin et al., 1995; Zervas et al., 1993). Patients who have pre-existing memory problems are at higher risk of developing cognitive impairment during treatment with ECT. Zervas et al. (1993) looked at the relationship between age and recovery of memory functions after a course of ECT in a group of patients aged between 20 and 65 years. Testing conducted 24 to 72 hours after the last treatment showed more severe cognitive deficits in older patients for verbal, visuospatial anterograde memory and retrograde memory, however the difference between younger and older patients changed over time, At follow-up, the difference was marginal in verbal anterograde memory after one month, a difference that was lost at the six-month review (Zervas et al., 1993).

Similar results were found in another study that assessed cognitive performance in depressed geriatric inpatients with or without pre-existing cognitive impairment that received their first course of ECT (Hausner, Damian, Sartorius and Frolich, 2011). 44 elderly inpatients with major depressive disorder were included in a prospective consecutive case series that was divided into three groups: no cognitive impairment (NCI), mild cognitive impairment (MCI) and those with dementia, who were assessed before ECT, after the sixth treatment, at six weeks and six months using the Mini Mental State Examination (Folstein, Folstein and McHugh, 1975). After an initial non-significant cognitive deterioration in all three groups, the NCI group showed cognitive improvement at six weeks and six months after ECT. The MCI group improved in cognition when assessed six months after ECT. There was a non-significant improvement over the course of the study for the dementia group; however, dementia patients who were taking anti-dementia mediation improved in cogitation to a clinically relevant extent after the sixth treatment whereas those without the anti-dementia treatment deteriorated (Hausner et al., 2011). After six months, one third of dementia patients continued to have a cognitive decline and pre-ECT cognitive deficits were the best predictor of MMSE decline at six weeks and six months. The study concluded that ECT was effective and well tolerated in geriatric depressed inpatients regardless of pre-existing cognitive impairment and cognitive defects were generally transient (Hausner et al., 2011).

MANAGEMENT SPECIAL CONSIDERATIONS

All elderly patients require a comprehensive psychiatric review with a complete diagnostic formulation. A complete physical review is essential before ECT to detect any medical or surgical conditions that require assessment and stabilisation by the relevant medical discipline. Regular assessment is required during the course of treatment to detect any changes in physical or mental state so that appropriate alterations in treatment can be initiated.

Elderly patients require a detailed assessment of their ability to give informed consent. If this is not possible, a determination by the relevant mental health review tribunal is essential.

It is important to ensure adequate efficacy of ECT in the elderly by reviewing all medications prescribed, eliminating benzodiazepines and anticonvulsant mood stabilisers at least 24 hours before ECT commences and choose an anaesthetic agent that has little impact on the seizure morphology to improve the quality of the seizure generated as elderly patients have higher seizure thresholds, particularly men. Careful monitoring is required if lithium is continued during ECT owing to the potential higher risk of postictal delirium in the recovery area.

Elderly patients are at increased risk of more severe memory deficits from ECT and due consideration should be given to electrode placement, stimulus intensity and treatment frequency to minimise adverse cognitive effects. Changing the frequency of ECT from thrice- to twice-weekly and considering the use of ultrabrief ECT may be indicated in this group and to reduce cognitive effects and improve the quality of the EEG morphology enhancing efficacy (Benbow, 2013).

In summary, age is not a contraindication to ECT and people should not be denied access, with the very elderly also having a favourable response and they have the right to be offered this important geriatric treatment to maintain a high quality of life.

REFERENCES

American Psychiatric Association. (2001). *The Practice of Electroconvulsive Therapy: Recommendations for Treatment, Training and Privileging: A Task Force Report*, 2nd edition. Washington, DC: American Psychiatric Association.

Benbow, S.M. (2005). The use of ECT for older adults. In Scott, A.I.F. (Ed.), *The ECT Handbook*, 2nd edition. London: Royal College of Psychiatrists.

Benbow, S.M. (2013). ECT for older adults. In Waite, J. and Easton, A. (Eds.), *The ECT Handbook*, 3rd edition. London: RCPsych Publishers.

Benbow, S.M. (1987). The use of electroconvulsive therapy in old age psychiatry. *International Journal Geriatric Psychiatry*, 2, 25–30.

Benbow, S.M. (1991). Old age psychiatrist's view on the use of ECT. *International Journal Geriatric Psychiatry*, 6, 317–322.

Benbow, S.M., Shah, P., and Crentsil, J. (2002). Anaesthesia for electroconvulsive therapy a role for etomidate. *Psychiatric Bulletin*, 26, 351–353.

Boylan, L., Haskett, R.F., Mulsant, B.F, Greenberg, R.M., Prudic, J., Spicknall, K., ... Sackeim, H.A. (2000). Determinants of seizure threshold in ECT: benzodiazepine use, anaesthetic dosage and other factors. *Journal of ECT*, 16, 3–16.

Brodaty, H., Hickie, I., and Mason, C. (2000). A prospective followup study of ECT outcome in older depressed patients. *Journal of Affective Disorders*, 60, 101–111.

Burke, W.J., Rubin, E.H., Zorumski, C.F., and Wetzel, R.D. (1987). The safety of ECT in geriatric psychiatry. *Journal of the American Geriatrics Society*, 35(6), 516–521. Retrieved from www.ncbi.nlm.nih.gov/pubmed/3571804.

Casey, D.A., and Davies, M.H. (1996). Electroconvulsive therapy in the very old. *General Hospital Psychiatry*, 18, 463–439.

Damm, J., Eser, D., Schule, C., Obermeier, M., Moller, H.J., Rupprecht, R., and Baghai, T.C. (2010). Influence of age on effectiveness and tolerability of electroconvulsive therapy. *Journal of ECT*, 26(4), 282–288. doi:10.1097/YCT.0b013e3181cadbf5.

Department of Health. (1999). *Electroconvulsive Therapy: Survey Covering the Period from January 1999 to March 1999, England (Statistical Bullletin)*. London: Department of Health.

Duffett, R., Siegert, D.R., and Lelliott, P. (1999). Electroconvulsive therapy in Wales. *Psychiatric Bulletin,* 23, 597–601.

Fink, M. (2009). *Electroconvulsive Therapy: A Guide for Professionals and Their Patients.* New York: Oxford University Press.

Flint, A.L., and Gagnon, I.B. (2002). Effective use of electroconvulsive therapy in late-life depression. *Canadian Journal of Psychiatry,* 47, 734–741.

Folstein, Folstein and McHugh, P.R. (1975). "Mini-mental state": a practical method for grading the cognitive state of patients for the clinician. *Journal of Psychiatric Research,* 12, 189–198.

Fraser, R.M., and Glass, I.B. (1978). Recovery from ECT in elderly patients. *British Journal of Psychiatry,* 133, 524–528.

Fraser, R.M., and Glass, I.B. (1980). Unilateral and bilateral ECT in elderly patients: a conmparative study. *Acta Psychiatrica Scandinavica,* 62, 13–31.

Gasper, D., and Samarasinghe, L.A. (1982). ECT in psychogeriatric practice – a study of risk factors, indications and outcome. *Comprehensive Psychiatry,* 23(170–175).

Glen, T., and Scott, A. (1999). Rates of electroconvulsive therapy use in Edinburgh 1992–1997. *Journal of Affective Disorders,* 54, 81–85.

Godber, C., Rosenvinge, H., Wilkinson, D., and Smithies, J. (1987). Depression in old age: prognosis after ECT. *International Journal Geriatric Psychiatry,* 2, 19–24.

Hausner, L., Damian, M., Sartorius, A., and Frolich, L. (2011). Efficacy and cognitive side effects of electroconvulsive therapy (ECT) in depressed elderly inpatients with coexisting mild cognitive impairment or dementia. *Journal of Clinical Psychiatry,* 72(1), 91–97. doi:10.4088/JCP.10m05973gry.

Karlinsky, H., and Shulman, K.T. (1984). The clinical use of electroconvulsive therapy in old age. *Journal of the American Geriatrics Society,* 32, 183–186.

Kellner, C.H., Husain, M.M., Knapp, R.G., McCall, W.V., Petrides, G., Rudorfer, M.V., . . . Lisanby, S.H. (2016). Right unilateral ultrabrief pulse ECT in geriatric depression: phase 1 of the PRIDE Study. *American Journal of Psychiatry,* 173(11), 1101–1109. doi:10.1176/appi.ajp.2016.15081101.

Kiloh, L.G. (1961). Pseudo-dementia. *Acta Psychiatrica Scandinavica,* 37, 336–351. Retrieved from www.ncbi.nlm.nih.gov/pubmed/14455934.

Mankad, Beyer, Weiner and Krystal, A. (2010). *Clinical Manual of Electroconvulsive Therapy.* Washington, DC: American Psychiatric Publishing.

Manly, D.T., Oakley, S.P., Jr, and Bloch, R.M. (2000). Electroconvulsive therapy in old-old patients. *The American Journal of Geriatric Psychiatry,* 8(3), 232–236. doi:10.1097/00019442-200008000-00009.

Olfson, M, Sackeim, H.A., Thompson, J., and Pincus, H.A. (1998). Use of ECT for the inpatient treatment of recurrent major depression. *American Journal of Psychiatry,* 155, 22–29.

Pippard, J., and Ellam, L. (1981). *Electroconvulsive Treatment in Great Britian in 1980.* London: Gaskell.

Prudic, J., Sackeim, H.A., and Devannand, D.P. (1990). Medication resistance and clinical response to electroconvulsive therapy. *Psychiatry Research,* 31(3), 287–296. Retrieved from www.ncbi.nlm.nih.gov/pubmed/1970656.

Rabheru, K. (2001). The use of electroconvulsive therapy in special patient populations. *Canadian Journal of Psychiatry,* 46(8), 710–719. doi:10.1177/070674370104600803.

Rosenbach, M.L., Hermann, R.C., and Dorwart, R.A. (1997). Use of electroconvulsive therapy in the Medicare population between 1987 and 1992. *Psychiatric Services,* 48, 1537–1542.

Rubin, E.H., Kinscherf, D.A., and Wehrman, S.A. (1991). Response to treatment of depression in the old and the very old. *Journal of Geriactric Psychiatry and Neurology,* 4, 65–70.

Sackeim, H.A., Decina, P., Prohovnik, I., and Malitz, S. (1987). Seizure threshold in electroconvulsive therapy: effects of sex, age, electrode placement, and number of treatments. *Archives of General Psychiatry,* 44(4), 355–360. doi:10.1001/archpsyc.1987.01800160067009.

Sobin, C., Sackeim, H.A., Prudic, J., Devanand, D.P., Moody, B.J., and McElhiney, M.C. (1995). Predictors of retrograde amnesia following ECT. *American Journal of Psychiatry,* 152(7), 995–1001. doi:10.1176/ajp.152.7.995.

Tomac, T.A., Rummans, T.A., Pileggi, T.S., and Li, H. (1997). Safety and efficacy of electroconvulsive therapy in patients over age 85. *American Journal of Geriatric Psychiatry,* 5(2), 126–130. Retrieved from www.ncbi.nlm.nih.gov/pubmed/9106376.

van der Wurff, F.B., Stek, M.L., Hoogendijk, W.J., and Beekman, A.T. (2003). The efficacy and safety of ECT in depressed older adults: a literature review. *International Journal Geriatric Psychiatry,* 18, 894–904.

van Schaik, A.M., Comijs, H.C., Sonnenberg, C.M., Beekman, A.T., Sienaert, P., and Stek, M.L. (2012). Efficacy and safety of continuation and maintenance electroconvulsive therapy in depressed elderly patients: a systematic review. *The American Journal of Geriatric Psychiatry,* 20(1), 5–17. doi:10.1097/JGP.0b013e31820dcbf9.

Zervas, I.M., Calev, A., Jandorf, L., Schwartz, J., Gaudino, E., Tubi, N., . . . Shapira, B. (1993). Age-dependent effects of electroconvulsive therapy on memory. *Convulsive Therapy,* 9(1), 39–42. Retrieved from www.ncbi.nlm.nih.gov/pubmed/11941190.

Efficacy of ECT

ECT is a highly effective treatment for severe psychiatric illness with efficacy estimated in the past at between 50% and 90% (Medical Research Council, 1975; Sackeim et al., 1993).

ECT is particularly useful for depression. It also has a role in treating other illnesses such as schizophrenia, schizoaffective disorder, mania, catatonia, neuroleptic malignant syndrome, Parkinson's disease and postpartum psychosis (Abrams, 2002). Worldwide, the major indication for ECT is depression, with recent estimates of remission rates ranging from 60% to as high as 90% (Lamprecht, Ferrier, Swann and Waite, 2013; McCall, Dunn, Rosenquist and Hughes, 2002). Patients who respond best to ECT are those with psychotic depression (Parker, Roy, Hadzi-Pavlovic and Pedic, 1992; Petrides et al., 2001). It has been shown to be effective in treating late-life depression (Flint and Rifat, 1998), mania (Loo, Katalinic, Mitchell and Greenberg, 2011; Versiani, Cheniaux and Landeira-Fernandez, 2011), schizophrenia (Fink and Sackeim, 1996), schizoaffective disorder (Ries, Wilson, Bokan and Chiles, 1981), catatonia (Kugler et al., 2015), neuroleptic malignant syndrome (Trollor and Sachdev, 1993) and postpartum depression and psychosis (Rabheru, 2001).

Despite multiple trials of new antidepressant medication, successful treatment of major depressive disorder has been estimated between 50% and 70% when used alone without psychotherapy (American Psychiatric Association, 2000). Results from a comprehensive meta-analysis that compared the efficacy and tolerability of 12 new-generation antidepressant medications demonstrated that, although some drugs were more effective and better tolerated than others, the overall response rate for the most effective remained similar to the rates noted above (Cipriani et al., 2009).

CLINICAL WISDOM 2.8.1

ECT is a highly effective treatment that can result in remission of severe mental illness with minimal side effects provided that careful scrutiny is given to diagnosis and technique. The most common reason for treatment failure is bad technique, medical complications occurring before, during or after treatment or severe cognitive impairment that results in termination of further ECT.

Response rates improve as illness severity increases with response rates as low as 40% when used in the treatment of mild to moderate depression (Pub Med Health, 2015). Overall there is some evidence that older drugs like tricyclic antidepressant are more effective in treating depression than the new-generation antidepressants (Barbui and Hotopf, 2001; Faravelli et al., 2003), although one meta-analysis failed to show a difference (Anderson, 2000). In all of these studies tolerability was a problem, reducing compliance and efficacy (Anderson, 2000; Barbui and Hotopf, 2001; Faravelli et al., 2003).

The high variability in reported remission rates for ECT may be predicted by a number of clinical variables, including the degree of medication resistance and more complex depressive subtypes being referred for ECT (Fink et al., 2007; Rasmussen et al., 2009; Sobin, Prudic, Devanand, Nobler and Sackeim, 1996). It may also be due to variations in treatment technique, particularly electrode placement and dose relative to seizure threshold (Sackeim et al., 2000; Sackeim et al., 1993).

In summary, ECT is very effective in treating a range of different disorders and may be more effective than antidepressant medication. This brings into question the recommendation that it should be used as a treatment of last resort and only when the condition is considered life-threatening, where a rapid response is required or where other treatments have failed (NICE, 2003, modified 2009).

REFERENCES

Abrams, R. (2002). *Electroconvulsive Therapy*, 4th edition. New York: Oxford University Press.

American Psychiatric Association. (2000). Practice Guidelines for the treatment of patients with major depressive disorder (revision). *American Journal of Psychiatry, 157*, 1–45.

Anderson, I.M. (2000). Selective serotonin reuptake inhibitors versus tricyclic antidepressants: a meta-analysis of efficacy and tolerability. *Journal of Affective Disorders, 58*, 19–36.

Barbui, C., and Hotopf, M. (2001). Amitriptyline v. the rest: still the leading antidepressant after 40 years of randomised controlled trials. *British Journal of Psychiatry, 178*, 129–144. Retrieved from www.ncbi.nlm.nih.gov/pubmed/11157426.

Cipriani, A., Furukawa, T.A., Salanti, G., Geddes, J.R., Higgins, J.P., Churchill, R., . . . Barbui, C. (2009). Comparative efficacy and acceptability of 12 new-generation antidepressants: a multiple-treatments meta-analysis. *Lancet, 373*(9665), 746–758. doi:10.1016/S0140-6736(09)60046-5.

Faravelli, C., Cosci, F., Ciampelli, M., Scarpato, M.A., Spiti, R., and Ricca, V. (2003). A self-controlled, naturalistic study of selective serotonin reuptake inhibitors versus tricyclic antidepressants. *Psychother Psychosom, 72*(2), 95–101. doi:68689.

Fink, M, and Sackeim, H.A. (1996). Convulsive therapy in schizophrenia? *Schizophrenia Bulletin, 22*, 27–39.

Fink, M., Rush, A.J., Knapp, R., Rasmussen, K.G., Mueller, M., Rummans, T.A., . . . Kellner, C.H. (2007). DSM melancholic features are unreliable predictors of ECT response: a CORE publication. *Journal of ECT, 23*, 139–146.

Flint, A.L., and Rifat, S.L. (1998). The treatment of psychotic depression in later life: a comparison of pharmacotherapy and ECT. *International Journal Geriatric Psychiatry, 13*, 23–28.

Kugler, J.L., Hauptman, A.J., Collier, S.J., Walton, A.E., Murthy, S., Funderburg, L.G., and Garcia, K.S. (2015). Treatment of catatonia with ultrabrief right unilateral electroconvulsive therapy: a case series. *Journal of ECT, 31*(3), 192–196. doi:10.1097/YCT.0000000000000185.

Lamprecht, H.C., Ferrier, N., Swann, A.G., and Waite, J. (2013). The use of ECT in the treatment of depression. In Waite, J. and Easton, A., (Eds.), *The ECT Handbook*, 3rd edition. London: Royal College of Psychiatrists.

Loo, C., Katalinic, N., Mitchell, P.B., and Greenberg, B. (2011). Physical treatments for bipolar disorder: a review of electroconvulsive therapy, stereotactic surgery and other brain stimulation techniques. *Journal of Affective Disorders, 132*(1–2), 1–13. doi:10.1016/j.jad.2010.08.017.

McCall, W.V., Dunn, A., Rosenquist, P.B., and Hughes, D. (2002). Markedly suprathreshold right unilateral ECT versus minimally suprathreshold bilateral ECT: antidepressant and memory effects. *Journal of ECT, 18*(3), 126–129. Retrieved from www.ncbi.nlm.nih.gov/pubmed/12394530.

Medical Research Council. (1975). Clinical trial of treatment for depressive illness. *British Medical Journal, 1*, 881–886.

NICE. (2003, modified 2009). *Guidance on the Use of Electroconvulsive Therapy (Vol. Guidance Number 59)*. London: National Institute for Health and Care Excellence; National Health Service.

Parker, G., Roy, K., Hadzi-Pavlovic, D., and Pedic, F. (1992). Psychotic (delusional) depression: a meta-analysis of physical treatments. *Journal of Affective Disorders, 24*(1), 17–24. Retrieved from www.ncbi.nlm.nih.gov/pubmed/1347545.

Petrides, G., Fink, M, Husain, M.M., Knapp, R.G., Rush, A.J., Mueller, M., . . . Kellner, C.H. (2001). ECT remission rates in psychotic versus nonpsychotic depressed patients: a report from CORE. *Journal of ECT, 17*(4), 244–253. Retrieved from www.ncbi.nlm.nih.gov/pubmed/11731725.

Pub Med Health. (2015). How effective are antidepressants? *Informed Health Online [Internet]*. Retrieved from www.ncbi.nlm.nih.gov/pubmedhealth/PMH0087089/.

Rabheru, K. (2001). The use of electroconvulsive therapy in special patient populations. *Canadian Journal of Psychiatry, 46*(8), 710–719. doi:10.1177/070674370104600803.

Rasmussen, K.G., Mueller, M., Rummans, T.A., Husain, M.M., Petrides, G., Knapp, R.G., . . . Kellner, C.H. (2009). Is baseline medication resistance associated with potential for relapse after successful remission of a depressive episode with ECT? Data from the Consortium for Research on Electroconvulsive Therapy (CORE). *Journal of Clinical Psychiatry, 70,* 232–237.

Ries, R.K., Wilson, L., Bokan, J.A., and Chiles, J.A. (1981). ECT in medication resistant schizoaffective disorder. *Comprehensive Psychiatry, 22*(2), 167–173. Retrieved from www.ncbi.nlm.nih.gov/pubmed/7214880.

Sackeim, H.A., Prudic, J., Devanand, D.P., Kiersky, J.E., Fitzsimons, L., Moody, B.J., . . . Settembrino, J.M. (1993). Effects of stimulus intensity and electrode placement on the efficacy and cognitive effects of electroconvulsive therapy. *New England Journal of Medicine, 328*(12), 839–846. doi:10.1056/NEJM199303253281204.

Sackeim, H.A., Prudic, J., Devanand, D.P., Nobler, M.S., Lisanby, S.H., Peyser, S., . . . Clark, J. (2000). A prospective, randomised, double blind comparison of bilateral and right unilateral electroconvulsive therapy at different stimulus intensities 57: 425–34. *Archives of General Psychiatry, 57,* 425–434.

Sobin, C., Prudic, J., Devanand, D.P., Nobler, M.S., and Sackeim, H.A. (1996). Who responds to electroconvulsive therapy? A comparison of effective and ineffective forms of treatment. *British Journal of Psychiatry, 169*(3), 322–328. Retrieved from www.ncbi.nlm.nih.gov/pubmed/8879718.

Trollor, J.N., and Sachdev, P., S. (1993). Electroconvulsive treatment of neuroleptic malignant syndrome: a review and report of cases. *Australian New Zealand Journal of Psychiatry, 19*(33), 650–659.

Versiani, M., Cheniaux, E., and Landeira-Fernandez, J. (2011). Efficacy and safety of electroconvulsive therapy in the treatment of bipolar disorder: a systematic review. *Journal of ECT, 27*(2), 153–164. doi:10.1097/YCT.0b013e3181e6332e.

Contraindications for ECT

ECT is a very safe treatment despite the invasive nature of the procedure (Mankad, Beyer, Weiner and Krystal, 2010). It is now widely accepted that the age of the patient is not a contraindication for using ECT, with the treatment being administered safely and effectively at each end of the age spectrum (Bloch, Levcovitch, Bloch, Mendlovic and Ratzoni, 2001; Manly, Oakley Jr and Bloch, 2000; Walter and Rey, 1997).

MORTALITY RATE

The overall mortality rate from ECT is very low and estimated at 2 to 10 per 100,000 (0.0001%), a rate similar to the rate for brief general anaesthesia (Shirwach, Reid and Carmody, 2001). Nutall et al. (2004) performed a retrospective review of all of the patients who were given ECT over a 13-year period; out of 2279 patients administered 17,394 treatments, there were no deaths, with 0.92% experiencing some complication at some time during the cause, usually cardiac arrhythmias that were transient and mild.

In one Australian state, there have been no deaths associated with ECT in the last 25 years after administering 200,000 ECT treatments (NSW Health, 2010). In Denmark there were no deaths attributed to ECT over a seven-year period following 99,728 treatments. Six patients did die on the day they had the treatment but the report concluded that ECT was conducted in a sufficiently careful and conscientious manner and the deaths were caused by severe medical complications (Ostergaard, Bolwig and Petrides, 2014).

It has been suggested that patients who receive ECT have a lower mortality rate due to non-psychiatric causes of death than do patients with psychiatric illness who do not receive ECT (Munk-Olsen et al., 2007).

COMPLEX COMORBIDITIES

The presence of a brain tumour and raised intracranial pressure has long been considered an absolute contraindication to ECT (American Psychiatric Association, 1990). Early case reports indicated that a high morbidity and mortality was common (Maltbie et al., 1980). In more recent years, the American Psychiatric Association Task Force Report questioned the absolute nature of this contraindication and recommended a detailed evaluation of the risk–benefit ratio for the individual patient (American Psychiatric Association, 2001), with some case reports demonstrating that ECT can be administered safely to patients with brain tumours, raised intracranial pressure (Patkar, Hill, Weinstein and Schwartz, 2000) and intracranial venous masses (Salaris, Szuba and Traber, 2000).

Mankad et al. (2010) identify other high risk disorders that require a careful risk–benefit analysis: space-occupying intracerebral lesions with the exception of small, slow-growing tumours without oedema or other mass effects; recent intracerebral haemorrhage; unstable vascular aneurysms or malformations; pheochromocytoma and high anaesthetic risks, namely the American Society of Anesthesiologists (Daabiss, 2011) ASA Class 4 or 5 (Mankad et al., 2010). In these situations, ECT should only be considered after a careful risk–benefit analysis has been completed including involvement of the relevant medical discipline.

The risk of ECT must be considered on an individual basis and weighed against the higher risks of untreated depression in the setting of serious medical illness. If the physician considers that the treatment is necessary as a life-saving procedure, the use of steroids, antihypertensive agents and hyperventilation may diminish the antecedent risks diminishing the rise in intracranial pressure (Weiner and Coffey, 1993).

CARDIOVASCULAR RISK

Applegate (1997) classed ECT as a low-risk procedure but highlighted the need to assess the degree of patient specific risk before commencing treatment owing to the potential cardiovascular complication. As noted above, most cardiovascular complications encountered during ECT are minor, however these complications are the main cause of mortality and serious morbidity with ECT (Weiner and Coffey, 1993; Zielinski, Roose and Devanand, 1998; Zielinski, Roose, Devanand, Woodring and Sackeim, 1993). Higher cardiac risks during ECT are similar to those encountered with surgical interventions. Of major concern are: recent myocardial infraction, severe valvular heart disease, clinically significant cardiac dysrhythmias, unstable angina, uncompensated congestive cardiac failure and some aneurysms (Zielinski et al., 1993).

It is generally recommended that if a patient has had a recent myocardial infarction, cerebral haemorrhage or cerebral infarction ECT should not proceed before three months (American Psychiatric Association, 2001; NSW Health, 2010; SA Health, 2014).

RISK OF UNTREATED PSYCHIATRIC ILLNESS

It is well known that untreated psychiatric conditions, like depression with melancholia, psychosis, agitation with high levels of anxiety and mania, carry an increased incidence of suicide and that ECT decreases this risk substantially (Fink, 2009). More than 50% of suicides occur during an episode of depression, with estimates of about 9% of successful suicide for those ever hospitalised and a lifetime risk of 2 5% to 4% for al person with depressive illness. Suicide is more frequent in persons over age 50, with more men being successful than women and greater than those with physical illness or substance use disorder (Fink, 2009).

In a large multisite collaborative study of 444 patients with unipolar depression referred for ECT, 131 (29.5%) reported suicidal thoughts or reported suicidal acts. With ECT, the thoughts of suicide were rapidly reduced, with 38.2% free of thoughts after one week, 61.1% after two weeks and 80.9% at the end of treatment (Kellner et al., 2005). This finding was replicated in an earlier study where ECT exerted a profound short-term effect on suicidal thinking (Prudic and Sackeim, 1999). Less is known about the capacity of ECT to reduce the long-term effects on the suicide rate (Prudic and Sackeim, 1999).

CHEMOTHERAPY

Occasionally the ECT practitioner will be confronted with the need to administer ECT to patients with severe mental illness who have a past history of cancer that has been successfully treated with chemotherapy. Bleomycin is a chemotherapeutic antibiotic isolated from the fungus *Streptomyces verticillus*. It is effective in the treatment of squamous cell and testicular cancers as well as lymphomas (Chemocare, 2017). Acute interstitial pneumonia and chronic pulmonary fibrosis are the principal therapy-limiting adverse effects of bleomycin. Hyperoxygenation is an important technique used in ECT to lower seizure threshold and reduce cardiovascular and cognitive abnormalities, which can be potentially lethal in patients who have been exposed to bleomycin as it can cause rapidly progressive severe pulmonary oxygen toxicity (Ingrassia, Ryu, Trastek and Rosenow, 1991; Toledo, Ross, Hood, and Block, 1982). In a retrospective series of five patients who received bleomycin six to 12 months prior to surgery all developed terminal adult respiratory distress syndrome three to five days post-operative. Autopsy revealed pulmonary changes consistent with pulmonary oxygen toxicity (Goldiner et al., 1978). Differences in patient risk factors may account for differential respiratory complications.

Current recommendations are that patients who have been exposed to bleomycin should be maintained on lowest fraction of inspired oxygen (FiO_2) to maintain peripheral capillary oxygen saturation (SpO_2) > 90% (Mathes, 1995).

Administering ECT in these anaesthetic conditions may place the patient at high risk of complications and extreme caution is required.

CONCLUSION

There is little evidence to guide clinical decision-making in these difficult clinical situations. Decisions need to be made on an individual basis with due consultation with all of the parties involved. The treating psychiatrist must assess the risks and benefits of ECT for each individual patient involving carers and other family members. When consent is not freely obtained, an application needs to be made to the relevant mental health tribunal.

Administering ECT in high-risk individuals can be a difficult clinical decision. It is recommended that treatment commence only after a comprehensive case review with the appropriate medical disciplines. Ideally in these situations ECT should be administered in a theatre complex with close proximity to appropriate life support and/or cardiac intensive care unit. Pharmacological management of potential risks factors is essential to ensure the best outcome.

REFERENCES

American Psychiatric Association. (1990). *The Practice of Electroconvulsive Therapy: Recommendations for Treatment, Training and Privileging: A Task Force Report*. Washington, DC: American Psychiatric Association.

American Psychiatric Association. (2001). *The Practice of Electroconvulsive Therapy: Recommendations for Treatment, Training and Privileging: A Task Force Report*, 2nd edition. Washington, DC: American Psychiatric Association.

Applegate, R.J. (1997). Diagnosis and management of ischemic heart disease in the patient scheduled to undergo electroconvulsive therapy. *Journal of ECT*, 13(3), 128–144. Retrieved from http://journals.lww.com/ectjournal/Fulltext/1997/09000/Diagnosis_and_Management_of_Ischemic_Heart_Disease.4.aspx.

Bloch, Y., Levcovitch, Y., Bloch, A.M., Mendlovic, S., and Ratzoni, G. (2001). Electroconvulsive therapy in adolescents: similarities to and differences from adults. *Journal of the American Academy of Child and Adolescent Psychiatry*, 40(11), 1332–1336. doi:10.1097/00004583-200111000-00014.

Chemocare. (2017). Bleomycin – drug information –Chemocare. Retrieved from http://chemocare.com/chemotherapy/drug-info/bleomycin.aspx.

Daabiss, M. (2011). American Society of Anaesthesiologists physical status classification. *Indian Journal of Anaesthesia, 55*(2), 111–115. doi:10.4103/0019-5049.79879.

Fink, M. (2009). Electroconvulsive *Therapy: A Guide for Professionals and Their Patients.* New York: Oxford University Press.

Goldiner, P.L., Carlon, G.C., Cvotkovic, E., Schweizer, O., and Hawlands, W.S. (1978). Factors influencing postoperative mobidity and mortality in patients treated with bleomycin. *British Medical Journal, 1,* 1664–1667.

Ingrassia, T.S., Ryu, J.H., Trastek, V.F., and Rosenow, E.C. (1991). *Oxygen-exacerbated Bleomycin Pulmonary Toxicity.* Paper presented at the Mayo Clinic Proceedings.

Kellner, C.H., Fink, M., Knapp, R., Petrides, G., Husain, M., Rummans, T., . . . Malur, C. (2005). Relief of expressed suicidal intent by ECT: a consortium for research in ECT study. *American Journal of Psychiatry, 162*(5), 977–982. doi:10.1176/appi.ajp.162.5.977.

Maltbie, A.A., Wingfield, M.S., Volow, M.R., Weiner, R.D., Sullivan, J.L., and Cavenar, J.O., Jr, (1980). Electroconvulsive therapy in the presence of brain tumor – case reports and an evaluation of risk. *Journal of Nervous and Mental Disease, 168,* 400–405.

Mankad, M.V., Beyer, J.L., Weiner, R.D., and Krystal, A. (2010). *Clinical manual of electroconvulsive therapy.* Washington, DC: American Psychiatric Publishing.

Manly, D.T., Oakley, S.P., Jr, and Bloch, R.M. (2000). Electroconvulsive therapy in old-old patients. *The American Journal of Geriatric Psychiatry, 8*(3), 232–236. doi:10.1097/00019442-200008000-00009.

Mathes, D.D. (1995). Supplemental oxygen and hyperoxia exposure in the operating room. *Anesthesia & Analgesia, 81,* 624–629.

Munk-Olsen, T., Laursen, T.M., Videbech, P., Mortensen, P.B., and Rosenberg, R. (2007). All-cause mortality among recipients of electroconvulsive therapy. *British Journal of Psychiatry, 190,* 435–439.

NSW Health. (2010). ECT minimum standard of practice NSW. Retrieved from www.health.nsw.gov.au/policies/pd/2011/pdf/PD2011_003.pdf.

Nutall, G.A., Bowersox, M.R., Douglass, S.B., McDonald, J., Rasmussen, L.J., Decker, P.A., . . . Rasmussen, K.G. (2004).

Morbidity and mortality in the use of electroconvulsive therapy. *Journal of ECT, 20*(4), 237–241.

Ostergaard, S.D., Bolwig, M.D., and Petrides, G. (2014). No causal association between electroconvulsive therapy and death. *Journal of ECT, 30*(4), 264–264.

Patkar, A.A., Hill, K.P., Weinstein, S.P., and Schwartz, S.L. (2000). ECT in the presence of brain tumor and increased intracranial pressure: evaluation and reduction of risk. *Journal of ECT, 16*(2), 189–197. Retrieved from www.ncbi.nlm.nih.gov/pubmed/10868329.

Prudic, J., and Sackeim, H.A. (1999). Electroconvulsive therapy and suicide risk. *Journal of Clinical Psychiatry, 60 Suppl 2,* 104–110; discussion 111–106. Retrieved from www.ncbi.nlm.nih.gov/pubmed/10073397.

SA Health. (2014). South Australian guidelines for electroconvulsive therapy. Retrieved from www.sahealth.sa.gov.au/wps/wcm/connect/0608270046ad5b01b89.

Salaris, S., Szuba, M.P., and Traber, K. (2000). ECT and intracranial vascular masses. *Journal of ECT, 16*(2), 198–203. Retrieved from www.ncbi.nlm.nih.gov/pubmed/10868330.

Shirwach, R.S., Reid, W.H., and Carmody, T.J. (2001). An analysis of reported deaths following electroconvulsive therapy in Texas, 1993–1998. *Psychiatric Services, 52,* 1095–1097.

Toledo, C.H., Ross, W.E., Hood, C.I., and Block, E.R. (1982). Potentiation of bleomycin toxicity by oxygen. *Cancer Treatment Report, 66*(2), 359–362. Retrieved from www.ncbi.nlm.nih.gov/pubmed/6173124.

Walter, G., and Rey, J.M. (1997). Half a century of ECT use in young people. *American Journal of Psychiatry, 154*(5), 595–602.

Weiner, R.D., and Coffey, C.E. (1993). Electroconvulsive therapy in the medial and neurologic patient. In Stroudemire, A., Fogel, B.S., and Greenberg, D. (Eds.), *Psychiatric Care of the Medical Patient,* 2nd edition (pp. 419–428). New York: Oxford University Press.

Zielinski, R.J., Roose, S.P., and Devanand, D.P. (1998). Cardiovascular complications of ECT in depressed patients with cardiac disease. *American Journal of Psychiatry, 150,* 904–909.

Zielinski, R.J., Roose, S.P., Devanand, D.P., Woodring, S., and Sackeim, H.A. (1993). Cardiovascular complications of ECT in depressed patients with cardiac disease. *American Journal of Psychiatry, 150*(6), 904–909. Retrieved from www.ncbi.nlm.nih.gov/pubmed/8494067.

Brain stimulation: new directions

In recent years there has been a rapid expansion of new technologies exploring novel ways to treat depression and other conditions as an alternative or adjuvant therapy to existing pharmacological, physical and psychological treatments. The enormous expansion of studies in this area is reflected in the exponential increase in articles submitted to the journal *Brain Stimulation* over the last five years, with many new and novel strategies being examined (Valis-Sole, 2017). This section reviews some of these treatments and modalities.

DEFINITION

Neuromodulation involves novel techniques aimed at stimulating focal regions of the cortex and subcortical structures directly or indirectly, externally or internally, altering selective brain areas that produce a change in neuronal function (Lisanby, 2004). Most techniques apply a brief electrical stimulus via a precisely placed electrode inside the body or one that is located externally to focal regions of the brain and subcortical structures to bring about a therapeutic response, collectively known as brain stimulation (Lisanby, 2004).

During the decade of the brain (1990–2000), research become increasingly sophisticated with the aid of powerful imaging techniques like computer tomography (CT) and magnetic resonance imaging (MRI), which have led to novel brain stimulation techniques. Data rapidly accumulated demonstrating that the things we do and experiences we have create changes to the brain structure and function (neuroplasticity) (Halett, 2007). Memory involves the formation of new synapses with dendritic sprouting. Rather than being a static organ that has a limited number of neurons, the brain is dynamic and has the capacity to regenerate and adapt to stimuli (Lisanby, 2004).

Stress has been shown to reduce the dendritic spines, length and complexity of apical dendrites, resulting in generalised atrophy. Induced electrical currents are sufficient to depolarise neurons at the site of stimulation and to exert trans-synaptic effects to connected regions (Lisanby, 2004). Neuro-

stimulation uses change in neurotransmitter activity to alter the structure and function of the brain resulting in neurogenesis (Halett, 2007).

ADVANTAGES OF BRAIN STIMULATION TECHNIQUES

There are a number of advantages of brain stimulation strategies. The treatment is directed at specific brain sites. Different and specific effects at different sites can be achieved either with increased or decreased levels of activity. Stimulus parameters can be adjusted by fine-tuning the treatments to individual differences minimising any potential side effects. The treatments can be specific in units of time, given as either a constant flow of energy or intermittent bursts of stimulus that deliver discrete bundles over a period of time (Loo, 2015). These neuromodulation techniques confer therapeutic benefit by regulating functional irregularities in targeted disturbed neural circuits by excitation or inhibition of either the same or different areas of the brain in varying patterns (Janicak, Dowd, Rado and Welch, 2010). The impact on the brain is different to pharmacotherapy, being episodic in nature, mitigating adaptation to the therapy's beneficial effects and avoiding systemic adverse effects (Janicak et al., 2010).

Brain stimulation can be categorised into three major areas of physical treatments, the convulsive therapies, the non-convulsive therapies and surgically invasive techniques (Loo, 2015). The first convulsive therapy was ECT. Other newer techniques include magnetic seizure therapy (MST) and focal electrical assisted seizure therapy (FEAST). Non-convulsive cortical stimulation techniques include: repetitive transcranial magnetic stimulation (TMS), deep transcranial magnetic stimulation (dTMS), transcranial direct current stimulation (tDCS) and caloric vestibular stimulation (CVS). There are a number of surgically invasive techniques that stimulate deep vein structures, including deep brain stimulation (DBS), vagus nerve stimulation (VNS) and direct cortical stimulation (DCS).

CONVULSIVE STIMULATION TECHNIQUES

Magnetic seizure therapy (MST)

Magnetic seizure therapy is the use of a repetitive transcranial magnetic stimulation, generated by a high-powered magnetic stimulator to trigger a seizure originating in the superficial frontal cortex of the brain (Lisanby et al., 2001). MST has the goal of improving the tolerability of ECT through better control over the site of seizure onset and patterns of seizure spread, factors thought to be major contributors to the efficacy and side effects of ECT

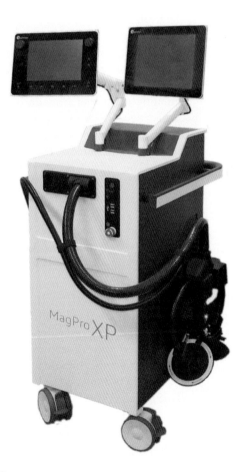

Photo 2.10.1 *MST Magpro XP device*

Source: Magventure Versatility in Magnetic Stimulation, 2015

(Lisanby, 2004). An MST device replaced the ECT device to administer treatment under the same conditions and following the same protocols as ECT (Lisanby, 2002). The stimulus generated by MST is a spike rather than a square wave, adminis-tered at 2 tesla, 100 Hz, and delivered over six seconds, given three times a week (Photo 2.10.1) (Lisanby, 2004).

Following successful trials in primates (Lisanby et al., 2003), the first trial of MST in humans was undertaken in 2001 (Lisanby et al., 2001). Following this successful test of concept study, other trials have followed, demonstrating: improvement in mood in refractory major depression (Kayser et al., 2011; Kosel, Frick, Lisanby, Fisch and Schlaepfer, 2003), quicker recovery of orientation after MST compared to ECT (Kirov et al., 2008; White et al., 2006), less cognitive impairment (Lisanby, 2002) and the need for lower doses of muscle relaxants compared to ECT (White et al., 2006). A recent literature review identified 74 studies to date, with eight meeting eligibility criteria. It concluded that MST was effective in improving depressive symptoms in patients with unipolar depression, with a reduction in cognitive side effects and a quicker time to recovery (Cretaz, Brunoni and Lafer, 2015). Further research is required to develop the technique further and to study its effectiveness in bipolar depression (Cretaz et al., 2015).

MST is similar to ECT in that it requires an anaesthetic including use of a muscle relaxant. The amount of muscle relaxant used in MST is considerably lower than ECT as there is less direct stimulation to the facial muscles and the motor cortex owing to better focusing of the stimulus (Lisanby, 2002). It is known that in ECT the skull deflects at least 90% of the applied electrical current, whereas it is entirely transparent to a magnetic field that passes through the tissue unimpeded. In this way, it is possible to focus the stimulus more precisely on the desired cortical site and control the extent of stimulation (Lisanby, 2004), identifying that it may be useful to reduce the current used in ECT and that altering the pulse amplitude may compensate for anatomical variability, leading to more consistent clinical outcomes (Deng, Lisanby and Peterchev, 2009).

The precise anatomical site for the regulation of mood in the brain is unknown. Research has focused on the dorsolateral, prefrontal cortex and the cingulate gyrus, areas that have been shown to be deficit in a range of psychiatric disorders (Lisanby, 2004).

Various electrode placements used in MST have been studied. Extrapolating from the efficacy in ECT, bitemporal electrode placement has been the most common treatment modality investigated (Lisanby, 2004). The only Australian trial to date used bilateral 100 Hz MST (Fitzgerald et al., 2013). Five out of 13 patients with major depression had a response. There was an overall group reduction in depressive severity with no evidence of any cognitive decline (Fitzgerald et al., 2013)

The early devices were cumbersome and could only be utilised in research settings. With the advance in research and technology commercial devices are now available (Magventure Versatility in Magnetic Stimulation, 2015; Neurolite Advanced Medical Solutions, 2015).

More research is required to characterise the unique characteristics of MST, highlighting the strengths and weakness compared to ECT. Results to date are promising, offering a new, better-tolerated technique that can immediately replace ECT, administered under the same conditions, reducing the stigma that continues to plague ECT.

Focal electrically assisted seizure therapy (FEAST)

Focal electrically assisted seizure therapy is a technique that has been developed by Harold Sackeim along with magnetic seizure therapy in an attempt to reduce the adverse events associated with conventional ECT (Berman, Truesdale, Luber, Schroeder and Lisanby, 2005). FEAST utilises a unidirectional stimulus with asymmetrical electrodes, small triangular anode and larger cathodes with a ratio of greater than 5:1 surface area, compared to ECT, where a bidirectional stimulus

is applied through large 5 cm diameter electrodes (Berman et al., 2005).

The variability of ECT in efficacy and cognitive side effects is thought to be secondary to anatomical variations that determine intracerebral current paths and current density of the ECT stimulus preventing spatial targeting (Berman et al., 2005). Attempts to address these factors in traditional ECT have been limited to altering the location of the electrodes and stimulus dose above threshold. FEAST aims to evaluate the role of other key electrical parameters such as current directionality, polarity and electrode configuration (Spellman, Peterchev and Lisanby, 2009).

Preliminary results using animal models are promising. FEAST was shown to successfully and reliably induce seizures, with lower seizure thresholds using lower levels of energy, with a mean of less than 3 mC compared to a mean of 6 mC with 0.3 ms pulse-width ECT. A variety of seizure types was elicited by varying the stimulus intensity ranging from fully generalised motor seizures, unilateral seizures to focal unilateral EEG seizures without motor involvement (Berman et al., 2005).

Seizure threshold was lower using a unidirectional stimulus than with a bidirectional stimulus in FEAST, with both stimuli having lower seizure thresholds compared to the ECT (Spellman et al., 2009). Ictal and postictal expression were shown to be polarity-dependent using the FEAST paradigm. Ictal power was greater in the posterior-anode unidirectional FEAST, with postictal suppression being strongest in the anterior anode set-up. EEG power was higher in the stimulated hemisphere in posterior-anode FEAST, which is consistent with the anode being the site of strongest activation. FEAST demonstrates that the direction of the current, polarity and electrode configuration influences the efficacy and potential cognitive side effects of seizure induction in ECT (Spellman et al., 2009).

The benefits of FEAST over conventional ECT have been highlighted in a recent open-label trial involving 20 depressed adults (Sahlem et al., 2016). Clinical and cognitive assessments were obtained at baseline and at the end of treatment course. Time to reorientation was assessed after each treatment for all participants. Results highlighted that FEAST was well tolerated with no dropouts. Five patients failed to progress and were switched to conven-tional ECT, 65% of patients met response criteria, while 55% met remission criteria, an outcome that was similar to conventional ECT. What was notable was the time to reorientation appeared quicker and there was no deterioration in neuropsychological measures (Sahlem et al., 2016).

FEAST is part of a growing interest in different neuromodulation techniques that aim to maximise the efficacy of ECT but minimise the adverse events (Janicak et al., 2010; Loo, Schweitzer and Pratt, 2006).

NON-CONVULSIVE STIMULATION TECHNIQUES

Repetitive transcranial magnetic stimulation (rTMS)

Repetitive transcranial magnetic stimulation (TMS) involves rapidly alternating magnetic fields emanating from a handheld coil placed directly over the targeted area on the scalp that alter the function of small cortical areas (Schlaepfer and Kosel, 2004). The magnetic field passes unimpeded through the scalp and skull. Single, paired or repetitive magnetic impulses are applied via the coil to induce small

electrical currents that flow in the opposite direction, in the underlying superficial cortical structures depolarising the neurons, as illustrated in Photo 2.10.2.

The device consists of two parts, a stimulator that generates brief pulses of strong electrical currents whose frequency and intensity can be varied and a stimulation coil connected directly to the stimulator (Schlaepfer and Kosel, 2004)

Magnetic induction via a coil is inefficient and a powerful impulse is required. Electrical energy is stored in high-capacity condensers until the time of the stimulation, when it is discharged in a fraction of a second directly into the coil, generating a magnetic field usually in the range of 1 to 2 tesla. Magnetic fields are different to electrical fields as they pass through tissue unimpeded. Coils vary in type from circular or doughnut-shaped coils but he most common is a figure of eight. The stimuli penetrate the cortex to about 1 centimetre with a maximum current density of 19 mA/cm^2 (Schlaepfer and Kosel, 2004).

Since its inception, TMS has quickly found a place in neuroscience, used alone or combined with other methods such as electroencephalography and neuroimaging, showing promise for testing functional connectivity, neuroplasticity, information processing, indirect and direct motor control and application in targeting mood and psychotic symptoms (Schlaepfer and Kosel, 2004). There are

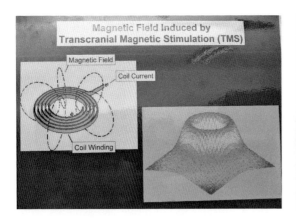

Photo 2.10.2 *rTMS magnetic field*

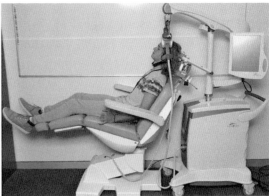
Photo 2.10.3 *Neurostar rTMS device*

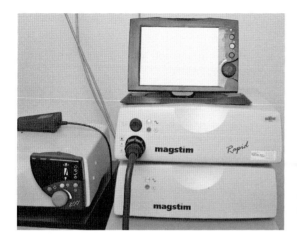

Photo 2.10.4 *Magstim rTMS device*

a number of different rTMS devices commercially available worldwide. Each device claims to have different specifications but all perform equally well in the clinical setting. Four rTMS devices are shown in Photos 2.10.3, 2.10.4, 2.10.5 and 2.10.7.

History of rTMS

Knowledge that a magnetic field that varies over time can induce a current in a nearby conductor has been known since the observations made by Faraday in 1831 (Schlaepfer and Kosel, 2004). Geddes (1991) notes that it was first applied to humans in 1896 by a French scientist, d'Arsonval, who placed a subject's head into a large electromagnetic coil that induced flickering-light sensations not elicited by visual perception (phosphenes), vertigo and syncope. In 1959, Kolin first demonstrated that an alternating stimulus could stimulate the sciatic nerve of a frog, causing contraction of the gastrocnemius muscle. Six years later, Bickford induced muscles twitching in humans by applying a pulsed magnetic field to the ulnar, peroneal and sciatic nerves (Geddes, 1991).

The invention of TMS is attributed to Barker, Jalinous and Freeston (1985), who used a 10-cm circular diameter coil to induce muscle twitching when placed on the scalp over the motor cortex, using a brief pulse of 110 microseconds with a peak current of 4000 amperes and pulsed at a maximal

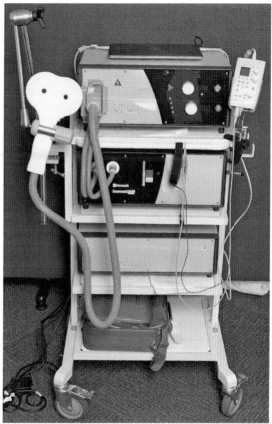

Photo 2.10.5 *Neurosoft Neuro-MS/D rTMS device*

rate of 0.33 Hz. It was extended to neuropsychiatry by Bickford, Guidi and Fortesque (1987), who demonstrated that a single-pulse to the motor cortex of healthy volunteers had transient mood elevations. This led to preliminary open trials of rTMS in the early 1990s using a circular coil to the vertex that showed some improvement in patients with major depression (Loo, Galvez, Martin, Alonzo and Nikolin, 2015).

Figure of eight coils replaced the circular coil and the dorsolateral prefrontal cortex (DLPFC) was the new anatomical site of interest in treating depression. Randomised controlled trial were conducted that demonstrated improvement in patients with major depression (Pascual-Leone, Rubio, Pallardó and Catalá, 1996). Over the next few years there were a growing number of randomised controlled trials and meta-analyses that showed consistent statistical significance for the superiority of rTMS over a sham control in the treatment of depression (Loo and Mitchell, 2005), with the first trial completed in Australia in 1999 (Loo et al., 1999).

Following a large industry-funded trial by Neurostar, the device shown in Photo 2.10.3 (O'Reardon et al., 2007), rTMS gained FDA approval in 2008 for use in depression. In 2009, safety and treatment guidelines were published as part of a consensus conference that was held in Certosa di Pontignano Siena (Italy) (Rossi, Hallett, Rossini and Pascual-Leone, 2009), the Canadian Network for Mood and Anxiety accepted rTMS as an evidence-based treatment for depression (Kennedy et al., 2009). In the same year it was ratified by the Australian Therapeutic Goods Administration and accepted by the Royal Australian and New Zealand College Psychiatrists, which released the rTMS Position Statement 79, which has now been revised (RANZCP, 2013).

In 2010, the World Federation of Societies of Biological Psychiatry issued rTMS treatment guidelines (Schlaepfer and George, 2010) and it was accepted as evidence-based treatment for depression by the American Psychiatric Association (2010). In 2015, the Interventional Procedures Advisory Committee of the National Institute for Health and Care Excellence (NICE) in the United Kingdom published a consultation document outlining recommendations for rTMS (NICE, 2015). Three devices have been cleared by the Food and Drug Administration (FDA) for use in treating depression (Galletly, Clarke, Carnell and Gill, 2015) All of these guidelines are comprehensive, covering areas such as efficacy, adverse effects, patient selection, prescription and treatment, as well as governance, credentialing and training.

A group of European experts has recently issued the most comprehensive evidence-based treatment guideline covering rTMS use in a broad range of conditions including depression (Lefaucheur et al., 2014). They report:

- Level A evidence (definite efficacy)
  - Antidepressant effect of high-frequency rTMS to the left dorsolateral prefrontal cortex (DLPFC).
  - Analgesic effect of high-frequency rTMS to the primary motor cortex (M1) on the side contralateral to the pain.
- Level B evidence (probable efficacy)
  - Antidepressant effect of low-frequency rTMS to the right DLPFC.
  - Improvement of negative symptoms of schizophrenia with high-frequency rTMS left DLPFC.
- Level C evidence (possible efficacy)
  - Improvement in tinnitus and auditory hallucinations with low-frequency rTMS to the left temporoparietal cortex.

Resting motor threshold

The stimulus dose used in rTMS is determined by establishing the resting motor threshold (RMT). The representation of the primary motor cortex is large, making it possible to isolate the first dorsal interosseous muscle (FDI). Motor evoked potentials are measured by electromyography (EMG), with electrodes placed on the "snuff box" and the index finger of the right hand, as illustrated in Photo 2.10.6. Single pulses of TMS are delivered over a predetermined site beginning 5 cm to the left of the vertex.

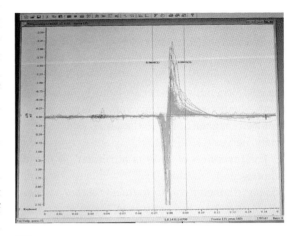

Photo 2.10.6 *Resting motor threshold*

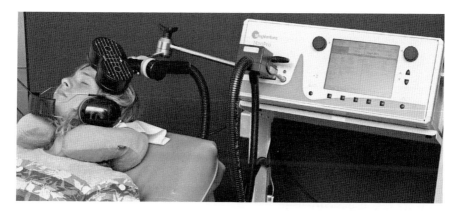

Photo 2.10.7 *Treatment set-up and Magpro rTMS device*

The coil is moved in an anterior–posterior direction, looking for the strongest twitch, and then in a lateral–medial direction to localise the twitch the FDI. The RMT is determined by reducing TMS intensity until activation occurs 50% of the time, with three out of six pulses being above threshold (see Photo 2.10.7). Treatment is then administered to the DLPFC at a site 1 cm anterio-lateral to position F3/F4 (Loo et al., 2015).

Patient set-up

After determination of the RMT, the patient is made comfortable in a reclining chair. The chair can be purpose-built and come as a complete package like the package offered by Neurostar, as shown in Photo 2.10.3. Other manufacturers offer a chair but their high price encourages most TMS services to

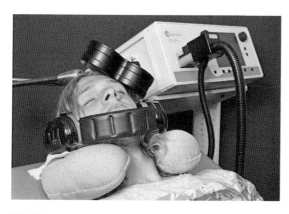

Photo 2.10.8 *rTMS patient set-up*

purchase a standard reclining chair from a retail store.

After the patient reclines in the chair, a travel pillow supports the neck and earplugs are inserted to protect the ears. The figure of eight coil is fixed securely into place by adjusting the coil arm (Photo 2.10.8). The device is turned on and treatment is begun, usually below the predetermined treatment parameters. The frequency is slowly increased as tolerated by the patient to the predetermined stimulus parameters. The patient is asked to remain very still throughout the 20- to 30-minute session.

Safety

rTMS is a non-invasive treatment that has a very good safety profile. The most common side effects are:

- Headache: 5–20% of subjects experience localised pain resulting from direct stimulation of muscles under the coil and stimulation of facial and scalp nerves. The procedure is more painful at higher intensities and frequencies (Schlaepfer and Kosel, 2004).
- Facial twitching from the stimulation of scalp muscles.
- Changes in auditory performance due to the noise generated by the coil by the passing electrical current. Ear protection is mandatory (Loo et al., 2015; Schlaepfer and Kosel, 2004).

- Syncopal episodes, which are common and thought to be due to vasovagal mechanisms rather than caused directly by TMS (Rossi et al., 2009).
- A low risk of manic switching in patients with bipolar illness with minimal risk of ophthalmological complications (Rossi et al., 2009).
- No significant changes in cognition after rTMS course in patients with depression (Loo et al., 2015).
- Seizures, which are the most severe side effect, though they are rare using current treatment guidelines, with an incidence of 0.1% to 0.6%, comparable to antidepressant medication (Rossi et al., 2009).

rTMS stimulus parameters

The stimulus involves:

- the impulse resembles a spike rather than a square wave used in ECT;
- frequency – pulses per second (hertz);
- train duration – between two and four seconds;
- intensity – amplitude of the spike;
- inter-train duration – often 25 to 26 seconds;
- percentage above the motor threshold – slowly increased with time to 120% above the motor threshold (Loo et al., 2015).

In studies of rTMS administered to the motor cortex, monitored by EMG recording of twitching in peripheral muscles, high-frequency rTMS (10 hertz) has been shown to increase excitability, while low-frequency rTMS (1 hertz) reduces excitability (Chen et al., 1997; Loo et al., 2015; Schlaepfer and Kosel, 2004).

Over the years, stimulus parameters have increased in intensity, with early rTMS studies using 20 hertz, 20 by 2-second trains producing 800 stimuli in a session with a total of only 8000 stimuli delivered over the whole course of 10 sessions, delivering 8000 stimuli over a course of treatment. Recent studies use 10 hertz, 75 by 4-second trains producing 3000 stimuli per session and a resultant 90,000 stimuli being delivered over

30 session course. The Nuerostar trial that was used to gain FDA approval used 10 hertz, 75 by 4-second trains with 26-second inter-train intervals at a dose of 120% above the motor threshold, delivering 3000 stimuli (Loo et al., 2015).

Factors that affect efficacy of rTMS

One of the challenges with rTMS, like with many brain stimulation techniques, is the large number of factors that impact on the effectiveness of the treatment. Some of these variables include:

- patient factors, like type of depression and medications;
- site of stimulation: DLPFC, parietal, temporal or deep areas,;
- stimulus parameters: intensity, frequency (hertz), waveform, train duration and inter-train duration;
- frequency of treatment sessions: three times a week, five times a week or two sessions on the same day;
- changing coil technology;
- adjunctive treatments, like medications and psychological interventions;
- priming (Loo et al., 2015).

rTMS in depression

rTMS is a very effective treatment for all types of depression (Kedzior, Azorina and Reitz, 2014). Low-frequency rTMS inhibits neuron activity and suppresses cerebral blood flow in the brain, whereas high-frequency rTMS has been shown to activate neuronal activity and increase cerebral blood flow.

There is now significant data that demonstrates that left-sided, high-frequency rTMS (20 Hz) to the DLPFC (Carpenter et al., 2012; Fitzgerald et al., 2006; Lisanby et al., 2008; O'Reardon et al., 2007) and right-sided, low-frequency rTMS (1 Hz) to the DLPFC (Brunelin et al., 2014; Fitzgerald et al., 2003) have significantly greater antidepressant effects then sham treatment.

Over the years there have been an increasingly large number of studies and trials of rTMS in depression. In 2008 24 RCTs were included in the meta-analysis 2008 (Lam, Chan, Wilkins-Ho and Yatham, 2008). Results from this study were inconclusive. Even though rTMS was shown to provide significant benefits in the short term, the low response and remission rates and the short durations of treatment meant that it could not be recommended as monotherapy in treatment-resistant depression (Lam et al., 2008). By 2010 the number of randomised controlled trials comparing rTMS to sham had grown to 34, with a further six studies comparing rTMS to ECT (Slotema, Blom, Hoek and Sommer, 2010). Results from this study were positive: the mean weighted effect size of rTMS versus sham for depression was 0.55 (P < .001). Monotherapy with rTMS was more effective than rTMS as adjunctive to antidepressant medication. ECT was superior to rTMS in the treatment of depression (mean weighted effect size –0.47, P = .004) (Slotema et al., 2010).

The largest meta-analysis was published in 2014 (Kedzior et al., 2014). The initial study identified 14 randomised controlled trials involving 659 patents from 2008–2013 and reported a significant reduction in depression scores following rTMS compared to sham treatment (Kedzior et al., 2014). Data was then pooled with a previous meta-analysis that involved 40 randomised controlled trials covering the period 1997–2008, increasing the power of the study, which was now based upon 54 studies. Results indicated that left-sided, high-frequency rTMS, right-sided, low-frequency rTMS and bi-lateral or sequential rTMS were significantly better in reducing depression than sham studies, independent of concurrent antidepressant use (Kedzior et al., 2014). All forms of depression responded, including unipolar and bipolar, treatment-resistant, medication-free or those patients commenced on medication during treatment. Further, they noted that rTMS was more effective in studies that had a greater proportion of females and had less stimuli per treatment session (Kedzior et al., 2014).

rTMS in schizophrenia
There has been some evidence that rTMS may be beneficial in treating schizophrenia, with the first study published in 2003 (Hoffman et al., 2003). Since that time, work has progressed with the publication of a meta-analysis reviewing all published studies completed between 1966 and 2012, with 17 randomised controlled trials eligible for analysis (Slotema, Aleman, Daskalakis and Sommer, 2012). This study demonstrated a moderate mean weighted effect size in favour of high-frequency rTMS of 0.44 (95% confidence interval of 0.19–0.68) when rTMS was directed to the left temporoparietal area in the treatment of auditory hallucinations in schizophrenia, with other target areas of the brain having a less impressive mean weighted effect size of 0.33 (95% confidence interval of 0.17–0.50) (Slotema et al., 2012). The effect of rTMS was no longer significant at one-month follow-up. Side effects were low with little difference in dropout rates between real and sham rTMS (Slotema et al., 2012).

Research in this area is robust. Two years later an updated meta-analysis was published including an additional eight randomised controlled trials where the severity of auditory verbal hallucinations was used as the outcome measure (Slotema, Blom, van Lutterveld, Hoek and Sommer, 2014). This meta-analysis replicated the mean weight effect size of the previous study in favour of active high-frequency rTMS over sham treatment but there was no significant mean weight effect size for the severity of psychosis (Slotema et al., 2014). The other paradigm that was shown to be effective in treating auditory verbal hallucinations and medication-resistant auditory verbal hallucinations was low-frequency (1 hertz) rTMS when applied to the left temporoparietal, whereas it was not superior to sham treatment when applied to the right temporoparietal area (Slotema et al., 2014).

rTMS as a clinical treatment option
The data reviewed above provides very strong evidence that rTMS is an effective treatment for depression and a range of other conditions. The challenge facing Australia and many other nations is how to establish this treatment in a clinical setting (Galletly et al., 2015). The Australian government

is concerned that the allocation of a Medicare item number for rTMS will result in high initial and recurrent costs, as patients demand this safe and effective treatment. Galletly et al. (2015) notes that, although there have been very few economic studies involving rTMS, the reports that have appeared show that rTMS is cost-effective treatment when initiated early compared to antidepressant medication, which involves ongoing switching between antidepressants (Simpson, Welch, Kozel, Demitrack and Nahas, 2009). Early studies demonstrated that rTMS had economic advantages over ECT (Kozel, George and Simpson, 2004) but recently these advantages have been lost, favouring ECT (Vallejo-Torres et al., 2015).

Naturalistic studies that highlight the effectiveness of rTMS as a treatment option for depression in routine clinical practice are beginning to appear in the literature (Galletly et al., 2015). Naturalistic studies are not subject to the rigours of research settings, with flexible selection criteria and more medical and psychiatric comorbidities, making them a useful avenue to translate research findings into clinical practice (Carpenter et al., 2012). In a study of 307 patients who were treated across 42 different community clinical settings, the patient-reported response rate was 41.5%, with a remission rate of 26.5% (Carpenter et al., 2012). Similar results were reported in an Australian naturalistic study that reviewed the first six years of rTMS in a private hospital setting, with a remission rate of 28%, while a further 12% had a response to the treatment (Galletly et al., 2015). This study highlighted the challenges faced in translating a safe and effective treatment with a growing evidence base into clinical practice.

RANZCP Position Statement 79: rTMS (RANZCP, 2013)

In 2008, the Royal Australian and New Zealand College of Psychiatrists accepted rTMS as a legitimate form of therapy for treatment-resistant depression based in a hospital setting with trained staff. The revision of this document in 2013 expanded its use to schizophrenia following the growing evidence that it can facilitate improvement and remission for this condition (RANZCP, 2013). The document reviews the safety data for rTMS, highlighting that it is a safe and well-tolerated treatment that can be administered to alert patients who have given informed consent without an anaesthetic. rTMS can be administered alone or in combination with psychological therapies and / or pharmacotherapy (RANZCP, 2013).

The position statement reviews the evidence supporting efficacy in depression and schizophrenia and recommends the clinical indications for its use. It identifies how patients should be selected, noting that there is little supporting evidence for its use in pregnant women or children and adolescents recommending that it should only be used as a treatment for patients over 16 years of age. The document highlights the need for fully informed consent, that it needs to be prescribed by a psychiatrist and that the treatment should be administered by highly trained staff that follow the formal policies and procedures that govern the prescription of rTMS in the institution where it is administered (RANZCP, 2013).

Deep repetitive transcranial magnetic stimulation (dTMS)

Research into TMS continues to progress with studies appearing using a new H-coil that stimulates deeper neuronal pathways compared to rTMS. This technique is known as deep transcranial magnetic stimulation (dTMS). dTMS relies on a new style of coil known as H-coils. H-coils achieve effective three-dimensional stimulation of deep neuronal regions without inducing unbearable fields at a cortical level (Roth, Amir, Levkovitz and Zangen, 2007). Field distributions of two different H-coils have been tested against conventional figure of eight coils, using a head model filled with physiologic saline solution. Three-dimensional distributions maps were generated using a stimulator output of 120% hand motor threshold (Roth et al., 2007).

The H1-coil generated suprathreshold fields at the lateral and medial frontal regions at depths of up to 4–5 cm. The H2-coil generated suprathreshold fields at the medial prefrontal regions at depths of 2–3 cm and at lateral frontal regions at depths of 5–6 cm compared to the figure of eight coil, which generated a suprathreshold field focally under the coil's central segment at a depths up to 1.5 cm (Roth et al., 2007). Adjusting the stimulator output and varying the distance between the coil and the skull can control the depth of stimulation. Deep stimulation results in the H-coils being less focal, delivering a wider electrical field distribution to the brain enabling stimulation of several brain regions simultaneously (Roth et al., 2007).

dTMS safety data

Thirty-two healthy volunteers were enrolled in a study to assess the health risks and cognitive and emotional effects of two H-coils designed to stimulated deep portions of the prefrontal cortex using different stimulation frequencies (Levkovitz et al., 2007). Subjects were randomly assigned to four groups, the two H-coils, a figure of eight coil and a sham control group. Results showed that the novel H-coils were well tolerated, with no adverse physical or neurological outcomes (Levkovitz et al., 2007). There was no deterioration in cognitive function. The H1-coil resulted in a transient short-term effect on spatial recognition memory on the first day of treatment only and reports of "detachment", while the H2-coil transiently improved spatial working memory (Levkovitz et al., 2007).

New work has examined the safety and characterisation of a novel multi-channel TS stimulator for which the stimulus parameters of each channel can be independently controlled (Roth, Levkovitz, Pell, Ankry and Zangen, 2014). The study demonstrated significant improvements in stimulation efficiency and a 70% reduction of energy dissipated as heat for a four-channel coil in comparison to a standard single-element figure of eight coil.

dTMS in psychiatric conditions

Early trials of dTMS are showing promising results. In a small trial, seven patients with major depression were treated using the H1-coil with stimulation parameters set at 120% intensity of the motor threshold and a frequency of 20 Hz with a total of 1680 pulses per session. Five patients completed the study, with one attaining remission and three others achieving a response of greater than 50% reduction in rating scores, while the other person had a partial response (Rosenberg, Shoenfeld, Zangen, Kotler and Dannon, 2010). The same group of patients who had relapsed 12 months after the initial course of treatment were offered a second course of dTMS. Response rates were similar to the first course but the magnitude of response to the second course was smaller compared to the initial treatment, suggesting a tolerance effect with repeated stimulation (Rosenberg et al., 2011).

In a larger trial, 64 patients who had failed to respond to medication and were medication-free were randomly assigned to different treatment configurations including high- and low-intensity, right- or left-sided stimulation for four weeks to the prefrontal cortex (Levkovitz et al., 2009). A significant improvement was found when high- but not low-frequency stimulation was used. There were no adverse effects and a number of cognitive scores improved during the course of treatment (Levkovitz et al., 2009).

There is some suggestion that dTMS may be effective in patients who did not respond to a course of ECT (Rosenberg, Zangen, Stryjer, Kotler and Dannon, 2010) and it may be an effective add-on treatment in schizophrenia, with one trial of high-frequency dTMS demonstrating improvement in cognition and negative symptoms that was maintained two weeks post-treatment (Levkovitz, Rabany, Harel and Zangen, 2011).

A large multicentre trial of dTMS involving 212 patients demonstrated that dTMS was a novel intervention in patients with major depressive disorder that had not responded to one to four antidepressant trials (Levkovitz et al., 2015). Response and remission rates were higher in the active compared to sham groups: 38.4% compared to 21.4% had a response and 32.6% compared to 14.6% were in remission. This trial led to USA FDA approval of the Brainsway Deep TMS device.

dTMS in other conditions

dTMS targeting different cortical areas has been trialled in a range of other conditions including:

- improved lower limb function for extended periods in patients who have had a cerebro-vascular accident during the chronic post-stroke period using high-frequency dTMS to the lower limb motor cortex over 11 daily sessions under sham conditions (Chieffo et al., 2014; Chieffo et al., 2015);
- improvements in social relating impairment and socially related anxiety in patients with autistic spectrum disorder using low-frequency dTMS to bilateral dorsomedial prefrontal cortex over 10 daily sessions under sham conditions (Enticott et al., 2014; Enticott, Kennedy, Zangen and Fitzgerald, 2011);
- changing well subjects' self-reported empathy ratings when used to examine the role of the medial prefrontal cortex in cognitive theory of mind studies following administration of low-frequency dTMS to bilateral medial prefrontal cortex (Krause, Enticott, Zangen and Fitzgerald, 2012);
- a reduction in cigarette consumption and nicotine dependence using high- but not low-frequency dTMS to the prefrontal cortex and the insula bilaterally over 13 daily sessions under sham conditions (Dinur-Klein et al., 2014).

Transcranial direct current stimulation (tDCS)

Transcranial direct current stimulation is a novel form of brain stimulation that has been extensively investigated over the last decade (Shiozawa et al., 2014). It was originally developed in the early nineteenth century and was first described as an effective treatment for major depression in the

Photo 2.10.9 *tDCS vertex determination 1*

Photo 2.10.10 *tDCS vertex determination 2*

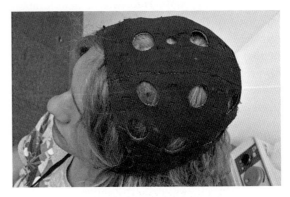

Photo 2.10.11 *tDCS cap and electrode positions*

1960s (Nitsche, Boggio, Fregni and Pascual-Leone, 2009; Nitsche et al., 2008). tDCS is different to rTMS in that it is less focal and involves low-energy stimulation that results in polarisation of membranes but not to the extent of inducing an action potential or discharging neurons.

Patient set-up

The patient is asked to sit comfortably in a chair. The vertex is determined by measuring the intersection between the line drawn from the nasion to inion and a line from the left to the right tragus of the ear, as shown in Photos 2.10.9 and 2.10.10. A permanent pen marks the spot and a rubber cap positioned into place using the vertex mark as a guide (Photo 2.10.11). The cap has holes located in the correct electrode positions that are marked before the cap is taken off. The treating electrodes are soaked in saline (Photo 2.10.12) and held into

correct position by the patient (Photo 2.10.13) before a plastic rubber support is tied around the head to support them (Photo 2.10.14).

This non-invasive technique involves stimulating the brain with low-dose electrical current via an anode and a cathode placed at different sites

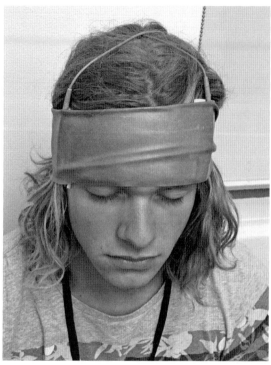

Photo 2.10.14 *tDCS electrodes in correct position*

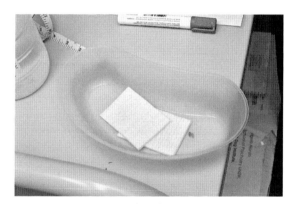

Photo 2.10.12 *tDCS electrodes soaked in saline*

Photo 2.10.13 *tDCS correct electrode positions*

Photo 2.10.15 *tDCS neurocom stimulator*

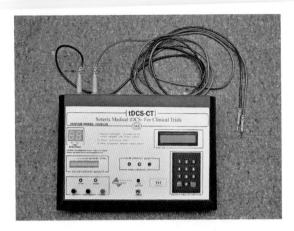

Photo 2.10.16 *tDCS Soterix Medical for clinical trials*

on the scalp, producing neuronal excitation or inhibition. The power utilised in tDCS is 1–2 mA, compared to the 800–900 mA utilised in ECT (Loo et al., 2015). Devices are illustrated in Photos 2.10.15 and 2.10.16.

Other forms of transcranial electrical stimulation

There are various other forms of transcranial electrical stimulation (Loo et al., 2015):

- transcranial random noise stimulation (tRNS)
- transcranial alternating current stimulation (tACS)
- transcranial pulsed current stimulation (tPCS).

Evidence base for tDCS

The technique that has the largest evidence base is tDCS (Been, Ngo, Miller and Fitzgerald, 2007). Contemporary protocols involve the application of two surface electrodes, one serving as the anode and the other as the cathode. A 1 mA or 2 mA direct current is applied for up to 20 minutes between two 35 cm2 (5 cm × 7 cm) placed on the scalp. The current flows from the anode to the cathode, with some being diverted through the scalp and some moving through the brain. Current flow causes an increase or decrease in cortical excitability dependent upon the direction and intensity of the

current. Neural imaging has demonstrated that the application of a low current results in many changes in the brain's function, particularly in the motor cortex, the visual cortex and the frontal cortex. It has been shown that the effects of a single stimulation session can last for up to an hour post-treatment without any other intervention (Been et al., 2007).

Anodal tDCS has an excitatory effect on the local cerebral cortex by depolarising neurons, while the opposite applies under the cathode through a process of hyperpolarisation. Increasing the size of the reference electrode and reducing the size of the stimulation electrode allows for more focal treatment effects (Been et al., 2007). The mechanisms of action are complex, with evidence suggesting that cathodal hyperpolarisation stabilises membranes through calcium and sodium channel blockade while the anodal depolarisation is thought to act at the synaptic level, enhancing D cysloserine, reducing L-dopa and antagonising NMDA and dopamine, to name a few (Loo et al., 2015).

tDCS is considered to be a safe and well-tolerated treatment, with most adverse events being mild: skin redness and tingling, with no evidence of cognitive decline (Loo et al., 2015). tDCS has been shown to have an impact on a wide variety of brain functions including enhanced motor learning and neuroplasticity (Kuo et al., 2008), increase and decrease in moving and stationary phosphine thresholds in the visual cortex (Been et al., 2007), bimodal effects of anodal and cathodal tDCS on the somatosensory cortex (Been et al., 2007), and enhancing cognitive performance (Martin et al., 2013).

Early work suggested that tDCS was effective in treating severe treatment-resistant depression, with recommendations for it to be considered as an adjuvant treatment for hospitalised treatment-resistant patients (Ferrucci et al., 2009). There have now been seven randomised control trials of tDCS in treating unipolar or bipolar depression, with or without concurrent medication, using various protocols involving 1 or 2 mA for 20 minutes during five to 15 sessions over a 1.5-week to three-week period (Blumberger, Tran, Fitzgerald, Hoy and Daskalakis, 2012; Boggio et al., 2008; Brunoni et al., 2013; Fregni et al., 2006; Loo et al., 2012; Loo et al., 2010; Palm et al., 2011). Results are variable, with two studies showing non-significant results (Loo et al., 2010; Palm et al., 2011), four studies showing significant response rates (Blumberger et al., 2012; Boggio et al., 2008; Fregni et al., 2006; Loo et al., 2012) and one study that had significant response and remission rates that persisted for a one-month period (Brunoni et al., 2013).

The initial meta-analysis of six randomised controlled trials commented that the sample size was small and tDCS was used as monotherapy or as an add-on therapy (Berlim, Van den Eynde and Daskalakis, 2013). The results were inconclusive, with no significant differences between active and sham tDCS in terms of response and remission rates. However, the researchers did conclude that there was a significant difference when tDCS was used as monotherapy compared to participants where it was used as add-on therapy. They

recommended that a larger and more extensive trial was needed (Berlim et al., 2013).

In an attempt to clarify these conflicting results the data was re-examined in a further meta-analysis that aimed to assess the efficacy of tDCS in the treatment of major depression based on seven randomised controlled trials with a total of 259 subjects (Shiozawa et al., 2014). As noted previously, most studies had small sample sizes ranging from 10 (Fregni et al., 2006) to 64 participants (Loo et al., 2012). In this analysis, active versus sham tDCS was significantly superior as a treatment for acute depression on all outcome measures as well as response and remission rates. They did not identify any predictors of response owing to the low statistical power of the studies included.

The recommendation in this analysis for a larger study to assess tDCS beyond the acute depressive episode has been established. In 2015, a multicentre monotherapy trial involving 120 active and sham participants with unipolar and bipolar depression was established. The study used a purpose-built device that utilised a triple-blinded protocol. Each participant was assessed with a detailed neuro-psychological test battery. The study incorporated improved stimulus parameters, using a current of 2.5 mA over a 30 minute period for 20 sessions over a four-week period followed by a taper phase (Loo et al., 2015). The results of this study are pending.

There is growing evidence that tDCS may be helpful in treating refractory hallucinations in schizophrenia and negative symptoms, with a high level of response with and effect size of 1.58 for refractory hallucinations and 1.0 effect size for negative symptoms (Brunelin et al., 2012). Caution is required in interpreting these robust results owing to the small sample size: 15 patients who received 10 tDCS treatments compared to 15 patients in the sham group. Robust results from early trials using rTMS techniques in treating hallucinations changed considerably when larger negative studies appeared in the literature, reducing the mean effect size of the response over sham treatments (Sommer, Aleman, Slotema and Schutter, 2012).

CLINICAL WISDOM 2.10.1

Results from tDCS clinical trials are encouraging highlighting the potential benefits of evidence-based, low-cost, safe neurostimulation treatments that can be accessed by a large number of patients who may not respond to conventional treatments, who may be ineligible for ECT or who may lack sufficient medical resources in their local area. These treatment approaches will develop to a point where they will become first-line before ECT is considered. However, owing to their simplicity and low cost they are open to a dangerous and misinformed "do it yourself" approach to treatment, with information on how to build your own device or alternatively other models, like the Neurogadget, readily available for purchase on the Internet (Neurogadget, 2017).

Neurogadget. (2017). News about brain-computer interfaces (BCI), mind-controlled gadgets & biofeedback. Retrieved from www.facebook.com/neurogadget.

Vestibular stimulation

The vestibular system within the inner ear forms a major component of the balance, spatial orientation and movement systems within the body. It provides information about head position, movement, coordination, eye control and some aspects of language development. It is known that about 20% of visual neurons respond to vestibular stimulation (SPD Australia, 2016). Vestibular stimulation is the technique of sending specific messages to the balance area of the ear by using temperature change (caloric vestibular stimulation) to stimulate the three semicircular canals, or electrical energy that stimulates both the semicircular canals and the two otolith organs: the utricle and the saccule (galvanic vestibular stimulation).

Caloric vestibular stimulation (CVS)

Caloric vestibular stimulation involves the installation of cold or warm water into the external ear canal. This elicits convention currents in the fluid within the semicircular canal fluid that in turn activate the afferent vestibular nerve signals to the vestibular nuclei and activation of the contralateral cortical and subcortical structures. After 20 seconds or so, subjects demonstrate slow phase nystagmus eye movements towards the stimulated ear, eliciting sensations of virtual body rotations and vertigo (Gabriella Bottini, Gandola, Sedda and Ferrè, 2013; Miller and Ngo, 2007). For many years this technique has been limited to routine diagnostic assessment in neurological investigation. In recent years it has been applied in a wide range of contexts with dramatic results (Miller and Ngo, 2007), like increased somatosensory perceptual sensitivity immediately after CVS on both the ipsilateral and contralateral sides of the body (Ferrè, Bottini, and Haggard, 2011). These findings have generated considerable interest in the potential clinical applications of CVS (Been et al., 2007).

When the auditory canal is irrigated with cold water there is activation in the contralateral cortical and subcortical brain regions shown in functional brain imaging studies (Bottini et al., 1994; Ferrè, Bottini and Haggard, 2012). It is thought that spatial and bodily representations are multisensory processes that form the somatosensory system, which overlaps with vestibular information from the balance organs in the inner ear (Bottini et al., 2013). CVS has been shown to have effects on a wide range of visual and cognitive phenomena as well as post-stroke conditions, mania and chronic pain states (Been et al., 2007). Left-cold CVS has been shown to affect the perception of distinct somatosensory modalities, with increased sensitivity to touch and reduced sensitivity to pain on both the ipsilateral and contralateral hands (Bottini et al., 2013).

CVS has been shown to modulate deficits like personal neglect, anosognosia (denial of the presence of hemiparesis) (Ronchi et al., 2013), somatoparaphrenia (denial of ownership of a limb or the entire side of the body) and hemianaesthesia (loss of tactile sensations on one side of the body) (Bottini et al., 2013; Bottini et al., 2005). High-level brain activation by unilateral caloric vestibular stimulation shifts the predominance of perceived coherent visual images, where each eye is presented with images that are perceptually regrouped into rivalling coherent groups, but not half-field images as would be expected with eye rivalry, suggesting that each process is controlled by separate neural mechanisms (Ngo, Liu, Tilley, Pettigrew and Miller, 2007).

In recent work, 32 participants were asked to respond to targets or withhold responses when shown either positive or negative pictures from the international affective picture system (Preuss, Hasler and Mast, 2014). Each subject was exposed to cold (20°C) left or right-ear CVS or sham stimulation (37°C). Results demonstrated improvement in affective control during right-ear CVS when viewing positive stimuli but decreased during left-ear CVS when compared to sham stimulation. Positive mood ratings decreased during left-ear CVS when compared to sham stimulation but there was no effect after right-ear CVS (Preuss et al., 2014). The result support earlier work in which three patients, one with mania and two with schizophrenia demonstrating delusions and of insight, were challenged with left- versus right-ear ice water (4°C) at baseline, immediately after CVS treatment and then at three other times over the next 24 hours (Levine et al., 2012). All three patients showed a difference favouring left- rather than right-ear CVS, which was maintained for 20 minutes and diminished over a 60-minute period (Levine et al., 2012).

Galvanic vestibular stimulation (GVS)

The galvanic vestibular stimulation (GVS) technique is very simple, with various electrode placements studied. The most common is bilateral bipolar GVS in which a controlled current of ~1 mA is delivered to anodal electrode placed on the mastoid process behind one ear and a cathodal electrode behind the other ear. Other configurations include bilateral monopolar GVS (with electrodes of the same polarity at both ears and a distant reference electrode) and unilateral monopolar GVS (stimulating electrode at just one ear). GVS has been used for nearly 200 years to investigate the vestibular system (Lobel, Kleine, Bihan, Leroy-Willig and Berthoz, 1998). The strength of GVS as a tool to probe vestibular function and the balance system is that it can be controlled precisely delivering a pure disturbance at a receptor level uncomplicated by inputs from other sensory channels, mediating its effects via stimulation of the semicircular canals and the otolith afferent pathways equally, (Fitzpatrick and Day, 2004; Lobel et al., 1998).

In healthy male subjects, GVS was shown to induce clear perceptions of body movement and moderate cutaneous sensations at the electrode sites. fMRI scanning did not interfere with the stimulus and showed that the activation was in the region of the temporoparietal junction, the central sulcus, the interior intraparietal sulcus and the premotor regions of the frontal lobe (Lobel et al., 1998; Lobel et al., 1999). In another study healthy subjects were asked to detect faint tactile stimuli to the fingertips of the left and right hand with or without GVS. They found that left anodal and right cathodal

GVS significantly enhanced sensitivity to mild shocks on either hand without affecting response bias. There was no such response using either right anodal and left cathodal GVS or sham stimulation (Ferrè, Day, Bottini and Haggard, 2013).

In a study of 255 GVS sessions delivered to 55 patients, GVS was shown to be safe, with only minor side effects reported: itching (10.2%) and tingling (10.7%) under the electrodes. Healthy individuals and patients who had a stroke did not differ in the incidence or rated intensity of adverse events with vertigo, seizures or nausea observed in neither group (Utz et al., 2011). The literature suggests that GVS along with tDCS are exciting and easily applicable tools for neuropsychological as well as clinical therapeutic investigations (Utz, Dimova, Oppenländer and Kerkhoff, 2010).

Evoked potentials (EP)

Evoked potentials measure the electrophysiological response of the nervous system to a variety of stimuli and can be either sensory or motor in origin (Evans, 2014).

Sensory evoked potentials

Although all sensory modalities can potentially be tested, only a few are used routinely in clinical practice. Sensory evoked potentials can be generated by visual, auditory and somatosensory stimuli and are commonly used for clinical evoked potential studies or intraoperative monitoring (Leggatt, 2014). With the advent of MRI scanning, the use of sensory evoked potentials in a clinical/diagnostic setting has reduced but their role in surgery has expanded (Leggatt, 2014).

Visual evoked potentials (VEPs)

VEPs are used to test the function of the visual pathway from the retina to the occipital cortex by measuring the conduction of the visual pathways from the optic nerve, optic chiasm, and optic rations to the occipital cortex. They can be either flash or checkerboard types of stimuli (Evans, 2014).

Short-latency brainstem auditory evoked potentials (BAEPs)

The brainstem auditory evoked potential (BAEP) measures the functioning of the auditory nerve and auditory pathways in the brainstem. The test is performed with the patient under sedation or under general anaesthesia. A standard broadband monaural click stimulation is used on the ear tested while a masking noise 30 – 40 dB lower in intensity is used on the contralateral ear. The intensity of the click is 65–70 dB above the click perception threshold and click repeated at a rate of about 10 Hz. BEAPS are used in aiding the assessment of hearing loss (Evans, 2014).

Somatosensory evoked potentials (SEPs)

Somatosensory evoked potentials are a series of waves that reflect sequential activation of neural structures along the somatosensory pathways usually elicited by electrical stimulation of peripheral nerves (Leggatt, 2014). Common sites for electrical stimulation are the posterior tibial nerve at the ankle, the median nerve at the wrist or the peroneal nerve at the knee, with recording electrodes placed on the scalp, over the spine, and over peripheral nerves proximal to the stimulation site. The actual SEP is the result of summated effects of action potentials and synaptic potentials in a volume conductor. The signal generated is subjected to a high level of electrical noise and must be averaged to make the results useful by improving the signal to noise ratio (Evans, 2014).

SEPs are used for clinical diagnosis in patients with neurological diseases, to evaluate patients with sensory symptoms and for intraoperative monitoring during surgery that place parts of the somatosensory pathways at risk. For example, SEPs are generated to monitor cortical ischaemia during procedures like carotid endarterectomy and for mapping the sensory areas of the brain during surgery. Experience in using SEP spinal cord monitoring reduced neurological deficits per 100 cases to less than half when used by spinal orthopaedic surgeons for thoracic and lumbar surgery (Nuwer, Dawson, Carlson, Kanim and Sherman,

1995). By contrast, in cervical surgery SEP monitoring was inferior to motor evoked potentials (MEPs) (Hilibrand, Schwartz, Sethuraman, Vaccaro and Albert, 2004).

Motor evoked potentials

Motor evoked potentials can be generated magnetically (see navigated rTMS) and electrically. Magnetic stimulation is used clinically, whereas electrically generated stimuli are painful and are used during neurosurgical procedures to monitor the functional integrity of the pyramidal tract.

Transcranial electrical motor evoked potential monitoring (TCeMEP)

TCeMEP involves administering electrical stimuli to the scalp that produces an electric current within the brain. These stimuli activate motor pathways within the pyramidal tracts that are recorded by receivers located on the spinal cord, peripheral nerves or muscles (MacDonald, 2006). The technique is used to ensure that functionality of the motor pathways is not compromised during spinal cord procedures that place these structure at risk (Zentner, 1989). Different monitoring procedures may be better for different types of surgery (MacDonald, 2006).

Direct cortical stimulation remains the "gold standard" for intraoperative neurophysiological assessment to minimise neurological deficits that complicate surgical procedures. Newer technologies will gradually challenge this position as further refinements are made to their methodology (MacDonald, 2006).

SURGICALLY INVASIVE TECHNIQUES

Deep brain stimulation (DBS)

Deep brain stimulation is a surgical technique in which stimulation electrodes are surgically implanted into precise anatomical areas, altering electrical activity that changes brain function (Greenberg, 2004). DBS relies on modern stereotypic techniques to implant bilateral electrodes with millimetre accuracy into specific brain targets. Bilateral leads 1.27 millimetres in diameter are attached on one end to four platinum/iridium micro-electrodes and on the other end a pulse generator is usually placed in the chest wall. The device is sometimes referred to as a "brain pacemaker" (Greenberg, 2004). X-rays are used to show the location of the implanted electrodes.

Stereotactic techniques are complex combining multiple imaging modalities, physiological mapping and high-speed surgical navigation computers to target the precise intracranial nuclei like the subthalamic nucleus and the globus pallidus internal segment for Parkinson's disease (Greenberg, 2004).

Once the patient has recovered from surgery, the stimulator is turned on and then programmed using a portable device that communicates with the implanted generator by telemetry. Various stimulation parameters, including voltage, pulse width and frequency, are adjusted to achieve optimal response of symptoms (Fitzgerald and Segrave, 2015). Chronic stimulation can be unipolar, bipolar or multipolar as each of these electrodes can be used as an anode or cathode to provide a variety of electrical field patterns (Greenberg, 2004).

A major advantage of DBS compared with conventional ablative neurosurgery is that DBS is reversible and the device can be removed. The exact mechanism of action is not well understood. It is thought that brain stimulation exerts its effects through a number of different but interrelated rhythms: the site of stimulation, the disease being treated and the stimulation parameters that are being used. High-frequency stimulation is thought to inhibit transmission, resulting in a functional lesion rather than just disrupting one limited brain region (Fitzgerald and Segrave, 2015; Greenberg, 2004).

DBS and Parkinson's disease

The United States Food and Drug Administration (FDA) approved the first device, Medtronic's Activa Deep Brain Stimulation Therapy System, for tremors associated with essential tremor and Parkinson's

disease in 1997 (FDA News Release, 2015). In 2002, the indication was expanded to include the symptoms of Parkinson's disease. In 2015 the FDA announced that it had approved a second neurostimulation system developed by Brio (FDA News Release, 2015).

Approval was based upon mounting evidence that stimulation of the subthalamic nucleus and the pars interna of the globus pallidus was associated with significant improvement in motor function in patients with Parkinson's disease whose condition could not be helped further by pharmacotherapy (Bejjani et al., 1999; Deep Brain Stimulation for Parkinson's Disease Study Group, 2001). Bilateral high-frequency DBS was performed in 96 patients where the electrodes were implanted in the subthalamic nucleus, and 38 patients where the electrodes were implanted in the globus pallidus. Three months after the procedures were performed, double-blinded, crossover evaluations were completed demonstrating that stimulation of the both regions resulted in improvement of the mean motor score compared to no stimulation (Deep Brain Stimulation for Parkinson's Disease Study Group, 2001).

There was also improvement in the percentage of time during the day that patients had good mobility without involuntary movements: 27% for no stimulation to 74% ($P < 0.001$) with subthalamic stimulation and from 28% to 64% ($P < 0.001$) with pallidal stimulation (Deep Brain Stimulation for Parkinson's Disease Study Group, 2001). These findings have been replicated, with more recent studies demonstrating a significant, substantial and sustained clinically therapeutic benefit over three to four years with longer trials and longer periods of follow-up (Rodriguez-Oroz et al., 2005) and specific treatment protocols developed (Kern and Kumar, 2007). Even though DBS is extremely effective in the treatment of Parkinson's disease, the mechanism of action remains elusive (Albert, Cook, Prato and Thomas, 2009; Breit, Schulz and Benabid, 2004; Greenberg, 2004).

Adverse events included intracranial haemorrhage in seven patients and infection necessitating removal of the lead in two (Deep Brain Stimulation for Parkinson's Disease Study Group, 2001). Other adverse events reported include cognitive decline, speech difficulty, instability, gait disorders and depression, which was more common in patients treated with DBS of the STN (Rodriguez-Oroz et al., 2005).

DBS and depression

There has been growing enthusiasm that DBS may be a useful treatment for treatment-resistant depression following early observations that major depressive symptoms could be induced with stimulation and then reversed when it was turned off (Bejjani et al., 1999). In a study of 20 patients who were implanted with bilateral DBS stimulators into the subthalamic area for intractable Parkinson's disease, it was observed that one woman had transient acute depression when high frequency was delivered to the left substantia nigra 2 mm below the site where stimulation alleviated the signs of the primary disease (Bejjani et al., 1999).

Since that time a precise definition of treatment-resistant depression has been developed to aid interventional studies along with the rationale behind using DBS to treat this condition (Hauptman, DeSalles, Espinoza, Sedrak and Ishida, 2008). Potential anatomical targets have been identified guiding human studies: inferior thalamic peduncle (Jiménez et al., 2005), anterior cingulate cortex (area 24a) (Sakas and Panourias, 2006) and lateral habenula (Henn, 2012).

Four sites have become operative targets of depressed patients who have undergone DBS for mood disorders (Mosley, Marsh and Carter, 2015):

- The anterior limb of the internal capsule (ALIC) or ventral striatum/ventral capsule (VC/VS) (Holtzheimer et al., 2012; Malone Jr et al., 2009);
- nucleus accumbens (NAcc) (Bewernick, Kayser, Sturm and Schlaepfer, 2012; Millet et al., 2014);
- sucbcallosal cingulate gyrus (Lozano et al., 2008) or subgenual cingulate gyrus (area 25) (Mayberg et al., 2005);

- superolateral branch of the medial forebrain bundle (s1MFB) (Schlaepfer, Bewernick, Kayser, Mädler and Coenen, 2013).

To date there have been eight open-label studies using DBS in treatment-resistant depression, with all published trials showing promising and positive results (Mosley et al., 2015). These results have not been sustained in two double-blind placebo-controlled randomised controlled trials (RCT), where there was no difference between the active and sham groups (Dougherty et al., 2015) and one study failed to complete owing to poor results (Mosley et al., 2015).

An alarming outcome from the majority of DBS studies has been the high rate of completed or attempted suicide in seven out of eight open trials (Mosley et al., 2015). There were five reports of suicidal ideation, four suicide attempts and one successful suicide in the only published RCT (Dougherty et al., 2015). It has been suggested that the suicidal aspects observed in these individuals' post-DBS were not associated with acute alteration in stimulation parameters and are thought to be unrelated to the treatment itself but rather a consequence of severe treatment-resistant psychiatric disease that did not respond to a treatment considered to be of last resort (Fitzgerald and Segrave, 2015).

The failure of these trials and the high suicide rates have generated a robust discussion in the literature, highlighting some of the potential reasons for treatment failure (Fitzgerald and Segrave, 2015; Mosley et al., 2015). These include:

- placebo effect;
- the pattern of network activation;
- surgical suitability (including patient characteristics and level of treatment resistance);
- study design;
- implantation site; and
- stimulus programming and stimulation parameters.

Fitzgerald (2016) raises the complex scientific, legislative and ethical considerations that need to be resolved to progress this area of research. It has been suggested that the failure of recent multisite DBS studies to demonstrate clinical efficacy is more a demonstration of failed trials than of failed treatment (Schlaepfer, 2015).

DBS and obsessive compulsive disorder (OCD)

There is a growing literature that indicates that DBS may be an effective treatment for intractable obsessive compulsive disorder (Fitzgerald and Segrave, 2015). It has been proposed that OCD is a neurobiological condition that has dysfunctional involvement of a series of cortical and subcortical brain regions particularly of the cortico–striatal–thalamo–cortical circuitry, with abnormal, increased metabolic activity in the orbitofrontal cortex (OFC), the anterior cingulate cortex (ACC), medical prefrontal cortex and the caudate nucleus, particularly the ventral division. Symptom severity is directly correlated with hyperactivity in the OFC and caudate nucleus changes that normalise with treatment (Fitzgerald and Segrave, 2015). The neuroanatomical sites that form the targets used for DBS in the treatment of OCD are somewhat different to those used for treatment-resistant depression.

These targets have been established by the following methods (Fitzgerald and Segrave, 2015):

- neuroimaging;
- lesional psychosurgery procedures;
- observations of response to surgery for other conditions like Parkinson's disease;
- gradual target refinement following ongoing evaluation of clinical outcomes in relation to lead location.

Target sites that have been used in OCD include (Fitzgerald and Segrave, 2015):

- anterior limb of the internal capsule (ALIC): one open study and two blinded;
- ventral capsule/ventral striatum (VC/VS): four open studies and one blinded;

- nucleus accumbens (NA): two open studies and two blinded;
- subthalamic nucleus (STN): three open studies and one blinded;
- inferior thalamic peduncle: one study;
- combined ALIC and VC/VS: one study.

The 12 open-label case reports and case series noted above show a high level of response to DBS, whereas the results from six studies with a blinded component had less robust results, reflecting the same trend that was noted in the results of the randomised control trials of DBS in treatment-resistant depression (Fitzgerald and Segrave, 2015).

The area continues to develop rapidly, with an increased number of studies appearing highlighting Greenberg's (2004) comments that as DBS becomes more refined and available it would open up new avenues for research and possible treatments of severe and treatment refractory neuropsychiatric disorders. In 2004 there was only a single case report in the literature on DBS being used for intractable OCD.

DBS has become an important evidence-based treatment for intractable Parkinson's disease throughout the world, giving sustained and significant therapeutic benefit that persists for at least three to four years (Rodriguez-Oroz et al., 2005). Ongoing work is required to transform DBS from a promising treatment restricted to research studies into a viable clinical alternative for a range of treatment-resistant psychiatric disorders. To date DBS cannot be recommended in the clinical management of any psychiatric disorder (Fitzgerald and Segrave, 2015; Mosley et al., 2015).

Vagus nerve stimulation (VNS)

Vagus nerve stimulation is an neurosurgical brain stimulation technique that modulates the neurochemistry and activity of the brain by stimulating the vagus nerve (Albert et al., 2009). The vagus nerve is the 10th cranial nerve. It is functionally diverse nerve, with many different actions including sensory, motor and parasympathetic that innervate the head and face. It is a complex nerve that has innervations of large and widely distributed brain regions.

A neurocybernetic prosthesis system (NCP) is implanted in a subcutaneous pocket in the chest just below the clavicle, similar to a pacemaker placement (Terry, Tarver and Zabara, 1991). The prosthesis delivers a constant-current electrical signals to the left cervical vagus nerve via a lead connected to an electrode that is a multi-turn silicone helix with a platinum band on the inner turn of one helix that is wrapped around the nerve (Terry et al., 1991). The device is turned on two weeks after the day the surgical procedure is performed by a neurosurgeon. Stimulator settings are programmed to deliver intermittent stimulation with a current of 0.25–3.0 mA, a frequency of 20–50 Hz and a pulse width of 500 nanoseconds for 30 to 90 seconds every five to 10 minutes (Mohr, Rodriguez, Slavíčková and Hanka, 2011).

Once inserted, the parameters are set by telemetry initiated by a "magic" wand attached to a computer. It is usual for a stimulation to be continuous. The stimulator is one for 30 seconds followed by a five-minute rest. Treatment then continues indefinitely 24 hours a day.

VNS and intractable epilepsy

VNS has been available for the treatment of intractable and severe epilepsy since the 1990s (Mohr et al., 2011). It has been shown that VNS suppresses seizure activity by stimulating the locus coeruleus causing the release of noradrenaline, a neuromodulator that has anticonvulsant effects (Krahl, Clark, Smith and Browning, 1998). Controlled trials show that VNS has a strong antiepileptic property when administered at high stimulus intensity (Lisanby, 2004; Marangell, Martinez, Jurdi and Zboyan, 2007). The safety of VNS has been extensively examined: a cohort of 791 patients was followed for 1335 person-years from implantation to determine the rates of all-cause mortality and sudden, unexpected, unexplained deaths in epilepsy (Annegers et al., 1998). They concluded that the mortality rates and

standardised mortality ratios were comparable with studies of young adults with intractable epilepsy who were not treated with the NCP system, with rates similar to medication studies. Its use in epilepsy varies considerably across institutions and neurologists within the USA.

VNS and treatment-resistant depression

The technique has now been substantially tested in patients with treatment-resistant depression, gaining regulatory approval in some areas of Europe and Canada in 2001 (Mohr et al., 2011), from KEMA European Union in June 2005 (KEMA European Union, 2015) and the Food and Drug Administration (FDA), USA, in July 2005 (FDA, 2005), the first non-pharmacological, somatic therapy for depression to be approved by the FDA since ECT (Lisanby, 2004).

The precise antidepressant mechanism of action is not known with hypotheses based on the neurobiology of the vagus nerve, a mixed nerve that is composed of 80% afferent fibres (Mohr et al., 2011). Antidepressant effects are attributed to the projections of afferent fibres to the nucleus tractus solitarius, which relays incoming sensory information to the brain through an automatic feedback loop, direct projections to the reticular formation in the medulla, ascending projections to the forebrain and the locus coeruleus (Mohr et al., 2011). Noradrenergic fibres from the locus coeruleus connect to the amygdala, hypothalamus, insula, thalamus, orbitofrontal cortex and other limbic regions responsible for mood and anxiety regulation (Mohr et al., 2011).

All studies have allowed concurrent treatment with antidepressants, mood stabilisers or other psychotropic drugs (Mohr et al., 2011). Hypotheses that depression may respond arose following observations in two studies where VNS was being used to treat epilepsy, where improvements in mood were noted as well as seizure control (Elger, Hoppe, Falkai, Rush and Elger, 2000; Harden et al., 2000). Early trials showed response rates between 40% and 50% depending upon the measures used, with substantial functional improvement that was sustained over a long period (Rush et al., 2000).

These results were replicated in a larger open trial of 60 patients, who had failed at least two different antidepressants during the current episode with non-psychotic depression, where there was a response rate of 39% (Sackeim et al., 2001). What was striking in this study was the variability in response relative to treatment resistance. A history of treatment resistance was predictive of VNS response. Patients who had never received ECT (lifetime) were 3.9 times more likely to respond than those who had received ECT. The treatment was ineffective in 13 patients who had received more than seven adequate antidepressant trials, suggesting that it may be most effective in patients with low to moderate, but not extreme, treatment resistance (Sackeim et al., 2001).

Most VNS studies have been open naturalistic trials with the primary result from the only randomised controlled trial, where VNS was compared to sham intervention, were inconclusive, with no evidence of short-term efficacy (Rush et al., 2005). The one-year follow-up study had a lower response and remission rate of 27.2% and 15.8%, respectively, raising the question of how much of this improvement can be attributed to VNS (Rush et al., 2005).

Improvement has been shown to continue with sustained use. After one year of stimulation there was a sustained response rate, 40% to 46%, with a significant increase in the remission rate from 17% to 29% (Marangell et al., 2002) and a sustained improvement at two-year follow-up to 42% and a slight reduction in the remission rate to 22% (Nahas et al., 2005). The two-year follow-up study showed that VNS was well tolerated, with only four out of 59 withdrawing (Nahas et al., 2005).

Similar results were obtained in an equivalent European open uncontrolled multicentred study of VNS therapy in 74 patients who had treatment-resistant depression. Response rates at three months were 37%, increasing to 53% after one year, with remission rates increasing from 17% to 33% after one year (Schlaepfer et al., 2008). After two years

the response rate remained constant at 53.1%, while the remission rate increased to 38.9% (Bajbouj et al., 2010). Like the US study, VNS had a comparatively benign adverse effect profile.

These results were replicated by George et al. (2005), in a study of patients with treatment-resistant depression. VNS plus treatment as usual was given to 205 patients, who were compared with 124 patients who had treatment as usual over a 12-month period. VNS plus treatment as usual group was associated with greater improvement per month across 12 months, where the response rate was 27% compared to 13%.

There was no difference in the side effects whether VNS was used in patients with treatment-resistant depression or intractable epilepsy. These side effects included: voice alteration, coughing, neck pain and dyspnoea; however, tolerance developed rapidly to these side effects, making long-term use possible (Lisanby, 2004; Mohr et al., 2011). There were no serious cognitive effects (Sackeim et al., 2001), with preliminary evidence suggesting improvement in sleep architecture (Armitage, Husain, Hoffmann and Rush, 2003).

VNS is safe, well tolerated and had no long-term side effects. It has a slow onset of antidepressant action, suggesting that VNS is not suitable for acute treatment of treatment-resistant depression, with the full benefits being realised as late as two years in patients with low to moderate but not extreme depressive illness (Mohr et al., 2011). Further work is needed to help explain why the only randomised controlled trial failed to demonstrate any significant improvement compared to sham VNS (Rush et al., 2005).

Transcutaneous vagus nerve stimulation (t-VNS)

VNS is an invasive intervention that limits it use. A new form of treatment known as transcutaneous vagus nerve stimulation (t-VNS) is an novel approach that involves electrodes clipped to the patient's ear, based upon the idea that there are afferent and efferent vagus nerve distribution on the surface of the ear (Fang et al., 2016). It is safe and well tolerated by patients (Kreuzer et al., 2012) and is being trialled in intractable epilepsy chronic pain and depression (Ellrich, 2011).

In a study of 34 patients with mild to moderate major depressive disorder there was a significant improvement in scores using the 24 Hamilton Depression Rating Scale in the group who received t-VNS compared to patients who were given sham treatment (Fang et al., 2016). Functional neuroimaging scans taken before and after the treatment course showed increased functional connectivity between the default mode network and precuneus and orbital prefrontal cortex in patients having active treatment (Fang et al., 2016).

Transcutaneous vagus nerve stimulation is novel, non-invasive, safe and low-cost treatment modality that can significantly reduce the severity of depression in patients, offering promise for the future (Fang et al., 2016).

Direct cortical stimulation (DCS)

Direct cortical stimulation is the gold standard neurosurgical technique that surgeons utilise during craniotomies for epilepsy and brain tumour resections to directly map areas of the brain immediately prior to the surgical procedure (Silverstein, 2012). Cortical mapping either can guide the intraoperative surgical team concerning the layout of important anatomical structures and their function, like the motor and language areas, to prevent post-operative deficits. Methods include sensorimotor localisation recorded directly from the surface of the brain when stimulated from a peripheral nerve or direct cortical stimulation of the motor cortex to elicit a distal muscle response either with a 60-Hz stimulation or using a train-of-five technique (Silverstein, 2012). The latter technique involves consecutive pulses, with an inter-stimulus interval of 4 ms and individual pulse width of 0.5 ms and 40 mA (Szelényi, Joksimovic and Seifert, 2007).

DCS is invasive and may result in intraoperative stimulation associated seizures (Silverstein, 2012).

Other perioperative non-invasive methods are showing promise in providing an alternative method of cortical mapping.

Navigated repetitive TMS (nTMS)

Navigated repetitive transcranial magnetic stimulation is a technique that may allow for the lesion-based interrogation of motor and language pathways noninvasively (Tarapore et al., 2013; Tarapore et al., 2012). nTMS maps were generated using a repetitive TMS protocol to deliver trains of stimulations during picture-naming and other tasks. Strong correlations have been found for positive and negative maps when compared with the maps generated intraoperatively using DCS (Tarapore et al., 2013; Tarapore et al., 2012). Further work is being undertaken to develop stimulus parameters to make the technique more refined, increasing specificity and sensitivity (Krieg et al., 2014)

In a study of 32 patients with left-sided peri-sylvian tumours, 20 had onset TMS, where the patients received rTMS pulse trains, starting at the picture presentation onset, compared to 12 patients who underwent rTMS pulse trains, starting at 300 ms after picture presentation onset (delayed TMS), and the result compared to DCS. Around the Broca's area there was no difference sensitivity and positive predictive value but onset TMS had greater specificity. This was in contrast to other posterior language regions, where there was greater specificity for early pulse onset rTMS (Krieg et al., 2014).

In summary nTMS is an innovative non-invasive procedure that has considerable potential to challenge direct cortical stimulation as a useful intraoperative cortical mapping tool.

Pre-surgical functional magnetic resonance imaging (fMRI) for language assessment

fMRI has been used as a pre-surgical test for patients with intractable temporal lobe epilepsy who require surgery. In some centres it has replaced the Wada test, in which the patient is given a unilateral injection of sodium amobarbital into the internal carotid artery that temporally anaesthetises the hemisphere ipsilateral to the injection site, enabling hemispheric dominance for language and memory to be determined by testing contralateral side (Wang, Peters, de Ribaupierre and Mirsattari, 2012). fMRI provides a safer, less invasive technique that is better tolerated.

Language fMRI involves the blood oxygenation level-dependent (BOLD) contrast mechanism as an indirect measure of underlying neuronal activity (Wang et al., 2012). It is known that when certain functional areas in the brain are activated there is an increase in local metabolism and oxygen consumption. Changes in brain metabolism and cerebral blood flow are linked by neurovascular coupling, causing activated local areas in the brain to experience a decrease in oxyhaemoglobin and an increase in deoxyhaemoglobin in the postcapillary vascular bed (Wang et al., 2012). Haemoglobin has different magnetic properties depending on its state of oxygenation, being dia-magnetic when oxygenated and paramagnetic when deoxygenated. These oxygen-related changes to the blood lead to local changes to the magnetic field that result in detectable changes in the mag-netic resonance signal, which is measured by the MRI scanner. These changes are measured while the patient is asked to do complex language tasks that have been carefully designed to activate language areas with equal activation of other brain areas (Wang et al., 2012).

Language fMRI is less invasive but results from studies that have compared it to DCS in patients with gliomas have demonstrated contradictory results to date and further work is required for this promising brain mapping technique can be used routinely prior to neurosurgery (Giussani et al., 2010).

Magnetoencephalography (MEG)

Magnetoencephalography (MEG) is fast, non-invasive, patient-friendly functional neuroimaging technique for mapping brain activity. It is reputed to be the most modern imaging tool available to radiologists (Braeutigam, 2013). Magnetic fields that are produced naturally by electrical currents within the brain are detected by very sensitive magnetometers. There are two types: supercon-ducting quantum interference devices (SQUIDs), which are the most common, and spin exchange relation-free (SERF) magnetometers (Braeutigam, 2013).

MEG can be used to detect local brain regions affected by pathology before surgical intervention, detecting perceptual and cognitive processes and localising the regions of the brain from which epileptic seizures originate. Owing to the extreme sensitivity of the technique, a patient is required to sit in a purpose-built, magnetically shielded room that eliminates all of the external magnetic signals including the Earth's magnetic field (Braeutigam, 2013).

MEG is different to an EEG in that MEG fields are less distorted than electrical fields by the skull and scalp, resulting in better spatial resolution, detecting activity that originates from the sulci rather than at the top of the cortical gyri (Cohen and Cuffin, 1983). An EEG detects activity in more brain regions than MEG but the latter has greater capacity to localise the activity (Braeutigam, 2013).

Along with navigated TMS, MEG is showing promise preoperatively in mapping the motor cortex with results having a high correlation with intraoperative maps generated by DCS (Tarapore et al., 2012).

CONCLUSION

Brain stimulation is an exciting and rapidly expanding area of research that is providing relief for thousands of patients with psychiatric and neurological disorders who have failed to respond to traditional treatment approaches. Very few of these new treatments have the response and remission rate of ECT, which continues to be a leader in its field 80 years later.

REFERENCES

Albert, G.C., Cook, C.M., Prato, F.S., and Thomas, A.W. (2009). Deep brain stimulation, vagal nerve stimulation and transcranial stimulation: an overview of stimulation parameters and neurotransmitter release. *Neuroscience and Biobehavioral Reviews, 33*(7), 1042–1060. doi:10.1016/j.neubiorev.2009.04.006.

American Psychiatric Association. (2010). *Practice Guideline for the Treatment of Patients with Major Depressive Disorder,* 3rd edition. Retrieved from www.psychiatryonline.com/pracGuide/pracGuideTopic7.aspx

Annegers, J.F., Coan, S.P., Hauser, W.A., Leestma, J., Duffell, W., and Tarver, B. (1998). Epilepsy, vagal nerve stimulation by the NCP system, mortality, and sudden, unexpected, unexplained death. *Epilepsia, 39*(2), 206–212.

Armitage, R., Husain, M., Hoffmann, R., and Rush, A.J. (2003). The effects of vagus nerve stimulation on sleep EEG in depression: a preliminary report. *Journal of Psychosomatic Research, 54,* 475–482.

Bajbouj, M., Merkl, A., Schlaepfer, T.E., Frick, C., Zobel, A., Maier, W., . . . Heuser, I. (2010). Two-year outcome of vagus nerve stimulation in treatment-resistant depression. *Journal of Clinical Psychopharmacology, 30*(3), 273–281. doi:10.1097/JCP.0b013e3181db8831.

Barker, A.T., Jalinous, R., and Freeston, I.L. (1985). Non-invasive magnetic stimulation of human motor cortex. *Lancet, 2,* 1106–1107.

Been, G., Ngo, T.T., Miller, S.M., and Fitzgerald, P.B. (2007). The use of tDCS and CVS as methods of non-invasive brain stimulation. *Brain Research Reviews, 56*(2), 346–361. doi:10.1016/j.brainresrev.2007.08.001.

Bejjani, B.-P., Damier, P., Arnulf, I., Thivard, L., Bonnet, A.-M., Dormont, D., . . . Agid, Y. (1999). Transient acute depression induced by high-frequency deep-brain stimulation. *New England Journal of Medicine, 340*(19), 1476–1480. doi:10.1056/NEJM199905133401905.

Berlim, M.T., Van den Eynde, F., and Daskalakis, Z.J. (2013). Clinical utility of transcranial direct current stimulation (tDCS) for treating major depression: A systematic review and meta-analysis of randomized, double-blind and sham-controlled trials. *Journal of Psychiatric Research, 47*(1), 1–7. doi:10.1016/j.jpsychires.2012.09.025.

Berman, R.M., Truesdale, S.H.A., Luber, B., Schroeder, C., and Lisanby, S., H. (2005). Focal Electrically-administered Seizure Therapy (FEAST): nonhuman primate studies of a novel form of focal brain stimulation. *Journal of ECT, 21*(1), 57. Retrieved from http://journals.lww.com/ectjournal/Fulltext/2005/03000/Focal_Electrically_administered_Seizure_Therapy.31.aspx.

Bewernick, B.H., Kayser, S., Sturm, V., and Schlaepfer, T.E. (2012). Long-term effects of nucleus accumbens deep brain stimulation in treatment-resistant depression: evidence for sustained efficacy. *Neuropsychopharmacology, 37*(9), 1975–1985. doi:10.1038/npp.2012.44.

Bickford, R.G., Guidi, M., and Fortesque, P. (1987). Magnetic stimulation of human peripheral nerve and brain: response enhancement by combined magnetoelectrical technique. *Neurosurgery, 20,* 110–116.

Blumberger, D.M., Tran, L.C., Fitzgerald, P.B., Hoy, K.E., and Daskalakis, Z.J. (2012). A randomized double-blind sham-controlled study of transcranial direct current stimulation for treatment-resistant major depression. *Frontiers in Psychiatry, 3*(74). doi:10.3389%2Ffpsyt.2012.00074.

Boggio, P.S., Rigonatti, S.P., Ribeiro, R.B., Myczkowski, M.L., Nitsche, M.A., Pascual-Leone, A., and Fregni, F. (2008). A randomized, double-blind clinical trial on the efficacy of cortical direct current stimulation for the treatment of major depression. *International Journal of Neuropsychopharmacology, 11*(2), 249–254. doi:10.1017/S1461145707007833.

Bottini, G., Gandola, M., Sedda, A., and Ferrè, E.R. (2013). Caloric vestibular stimulation: interaction between somatosensory system and vestibular apparatus. *Frontiers in Integrative Neuroscience, 7,* 66. doi:10.3389/fnint.2013.00066.

Bottini, G., Paulesu, E., Gandola, M., Loffredo, S., Scarpa, P., Sterzi, R., . . . Vallar, G. (2005). Left caloric vestibular stimulation ameliorates right hemianesthesia. *Neurology, 65*(8), 1278–1283. doi:10.1212/01.wnl.0000182398.14088.e8.

Bottini, G., Sterzi, R., Paulesu, E., Vallar, G., Cappa, S.F., Erminio, F., . . . Frackowiak, R.S. (1994). Identification of the central vestibular projections in man: a positron emission tomography activation study. *Experimental Brain Research, 99*(1), 164–169. doi:10.1007/BF00241421.

Braeutigam, S. (2013). Magnetoencephalography: fundamentals and established and emerging clinical applications in radiology. *ISRN Radiology, 2013*(Article ID 529463), 529463. doi:10.5402/2013/529463.

Breit, S., Schulz, J.B., and Benabid, A.L. (2004). Deep brain stimulation. *Cell and Tissue Research, 318*(1), 275–288. doi:10.1007/s00441-004-0936-0.

Brunelin, J., Jalenques, I., Trojak, B., Attal, J., Szekely, D., Gay, A., . . . Poulet, E. (2014). The efficacy and safety of low frequency repetitive transcranial magnetic stimulation for treatment-resistant depression: the results from a large multicenter French RCT. *Brain Stimulation, 7*(6), 855–863. doi:10.1016/j.brs.2014.07.040.

Brunelin, J., Mondino, M., Gassab, L., Haesebaert, F., Gaha, L., Suaud-Chagny, M.F., . . . Poulet, E. (2012). Examining transcranial direct-current stimulation (tDCS) as a treatment for hallucinations in schizophrenia. *American Journal of Psychiatry, 169,* 719–724.

Brunoni, A.R., Ferrucci, R., Bortolomasi, M., Scelzo, E., Boggio, P.S., Fregni, F., . . . Priori, A. (2013). Interactions between transcranial direct current stimulation (tDCS) and pharmacological interventions in the Major Depressive Episode: findings from a naturalistic study. *European Psychiatry*, *28*(6), 356–361. doi:10.1016/j.eurpsy.2012. 09.001.

Carpenter, L.L., Janicak, P.G., Aaronson, S.T., Boyadjis, T., Brock, D.G., Cook, I.A., . . . Demitrack, M.A. (2012). Transcranial magnetic stimulation (TMS) for major depression: a multisite, naturalistic, observational study of acute treatment outcomes in clinical practice. *Depression and Anxiety*, *29*(7), 587–596. doi:10.1002/da.21969.

Chen, R., Classen, J., Gerloff, C., Celnik, P., Wassermann, E.M., Hallett, M., and Cohen, L.G. (1997). Depression of motor cortex excitability by low_frequency transcranial magnetic stimulation. *Neurology*, *48*(5), 1398–1403. doi:10.1212/wnl.48.5.1398.

Chieffo, R., De Prezzo, S., Houdayer, E., Nuara, A., Di Maggio, G., Coppi, E., . . . Leocani, L. (2014). Deep Repetitive Transcranial Magnetic Stimulation With H-coil on Lower Limb Motor Function in Chronic Stroke: A Pilot Study. *Archives of Physical Medicine and Rehabilitation*, *95*(6), 1141–1147. doi:10.1016/j.apmr.2014.02.019.

Cohen, D, and Cuffin, B.N. (1983). Demonstration of useful differences between the magnetoencephalogram and electro-encephalogram. *Electroencephalogry and Clinical Neurophysiology*, *56*, 38–51.

Cretaz, E., Brunoni, A.R., and Lafer, B. (2015). Magnetic seizure therapy for unipolar and bipolar depression: a systematic review. *Neural Plasticity*, *2015*, 521398. doi:10.1155/2015/521398.

Deep Brain Stimulation for Parkinson's Disease Study Group. (2001). Deep-brain stimulation of the subthalamic nucleus or the pars interna of the globus pallidus in Parkinson's disease. *New England Journal of Medicine*, *345*(13), 956–963. doi:10.1056/NEJMoa000827.

Deng, Z.-D., Lisanby, S.H., and Peterchev, A.V. (2009). *Effect of Anatomical Variability on Neural Stimulation Strength and Focality in Electroconvulsive Therapy (ECT) and Magnetic Seizure Therapy (MST)*. Paper presented at the Annual International Conference of the IEEE, Minneapolis MN. http://ieeexplore.ieee.org/xpl/login.jsp?tp=andarnumber=5334 091andurl=http%3A%2F%2Fieeexplore.ieee.org%2Fxpls %2Fabs_all.jsp%3Farnumber%3D5334091.

Dinur-Klein, L., Dannon, P., Hadar, A., Rosenberg, O., Roth, Y., Kotler, M., and Zangen, A. (2014). Smoking cessation induced by deep repetitive transcranial magnetic stimulation of the prefrontal and insular cortices: a prospective, randomized controlled trial. *Biological Psychiatry*, *76*(9), 742–749. doi:10.1016/j.biopsych.2014.05.020.

Dougherty, D.D., Rezai, A.R., Carpenter, L.L., Howland, R.H., Bhati, M.T., O'Reardon, J.P., . . . Malone, D.A., Jr (2015). A randomized sham-controlled trial of deep brain stimulation of the ventral capsule/ventral striatum for chronic treatment-resistant depression. *Biological Psychiatry*, *78*(4), 240–248. doi:10.1016/j.biopsych.2014.11.023.

Elger, G., Hoppe, C., Falkai, P., Rush, A.J., and Elger, C.E. (2000). Vagus nerve stimulation is associated with mood improvements in epilepsy patients. *Epilepsy Research*, *42*(2–3), 203–210.

Ellrich, J. (2011). Transcutaneous vagus nerve stimulation. *European Neurological Review*, *6*(4), 254–256. doi:10.17925/ enr.2011.06.04.254.

Enticott, P.G., Fitzgibbon, B.M., Kennedy, H.A., Arnold, S.L., Elliot, D., Peachey, A., . . . Fitzgerald, P.B. (2014). A double-blind, randomized trial of deep repetitive transcranial magnetic stimulation (rTMS) for autism spectrum disorder. *Brain Stimulation*, *7*(2), 206–211. doi:10.1016/j.brs.2013.10.004.

Enticott, P.G., Kennedy, H.A., Zangen, A., and Fitzgerald, P.B. (2011). Deep repetitive transcranial magnetic stimulation associated with improved social functioning in a young woman with an autism spectrum disorder. *Journal of ECT*, *27*(1), 41–43. doi:10.1097/YCT.0b013e3181f07948.

Evans, A.B. (2014). Clinical utility of evoked potentials. Retrieved from http://emedicine.medscape.com/article/ 1137451-overview-a2.

Fang, J., Rong, P., Hong, Y., Fan, Y., Liu, J., Wang, H., . . . Kong, J. (2016). Transcutaneous vagus nerve stimulation modulates default mode network in major depressive disorder. *Biological Psychiatry*, *79*(4), 266–273. doi:10.1016/j.biopsych.2015. 03.025.

FDA. (2005). VNS therapy system – P970003s05. Retrieved from www.fda.gov/MedicalDevices/ProductsandMedical Procedures/DeviceApprovalsandClearances/RecentlyApproved Devices/ucm078532.htm.

FDA News Release. (2015). FDA approves brain implant to help reduce Parkinson's disease and essential tremor symptoms. Retrieved from www.fda.gov/NewsEvents/Newsroom/ PressAnnouncements/ucm451152.htm.

Ferrè, E., Bottini, G., and Haggard, P. (2012). Vestibular inputs modulate somatosensory cortical processing. *Brain Structure and Function*, *217*(4), 859–864. doi:10.1007/ s00429-012-0404-7.

Ferrè, E.R., Bottini, G., and Haggard, P. (2011). Vestibular modulation of somatosensory perception. *European Journal of Neuroscience*, *34*(8), 1337–1344. doi:10.1111/j.1460-9568.2011.07859.x.

Ferrè, E.R., Day, B.L., Bottini, G., and Haggard, P. (2013). How the vestibular system interacts with somatosensory perception: a sham-controlled study with galvanic vestibular stimulation. *Neuroscience Letters, 550,* 35–40. doi:10.1016/j.neulet.2013.06.046.

Ferrucci, R., Bortolomasi, M., Vergari, M., Tadini, L., Salvoro, B., Giacopuzzi, M., . . . Priori, A. (2009). Transcranial direct current stimulation in severe, drug-resistant major depression. *Journal of Affective Disorders, 118*(1–3), 215–219. doi:10.1016/j.jad.2009.02.015.

Fitzgerald, P.B. (2016). Deep brain stimulation in depression. *Australian and New Zealand Journal of Psychiatry, 50*(1), 94–95. doi:10.1177/0004867415611755.

Fitzgerald, P.B., Benitez, J., Castella, A. d., Daskalakis, Z.J., Brown, T.L., and Kulkarni, J. (2006). A randomized, controlled trial of sequential bilateral repetitive transcranial magnetic stimulation for treatment-resistant depression. *American Journal of Psychiatry, 163*(1), 88–94. doi:10.1176/appi.ajp.163.1.88.

Fitzgerald, P.B., Brown, T.L., Marston, N.U., Daskalakis, Z., de Castella, A., and Kulkarni, J. (2003). Transcranial magnetic stimulation in the treatment of depression: a double-blind, placebo-controlled trial. *Archives of General Psychiatry, 60*(10). doi:10.1001/archpsyc.60.9.1002.

Fitzgerald, P.B., Hoy, K.E., Herring, S.E., Clinton, A.M., Downey, G., and Daskalakis, Z.J. (2013). Pilot study of the clinical and cognitive effects of high-frequency magnetic seizure therapy in major depressive disorder. *Depression and Anxiety, 30*(2), 129–136. doi:10.1002/da.22005.

Fitzgerald, P.B., and Segrave, R.A. (2015). Deep brain stimulation in mental health: review of evidence for clinical efficacy. *Australian and New Zealand Journal of Psychiatry, 49*(11), 979–993. doi:10.1177/0004867415598011.

Fitzpatrick, R.C., and Day, B.L. (2004). Probing the human vestibular system with galvanic stimulation. *Journal of Applied Physiology, 96*(4), 2301–2316. doi:10.1152/japplphysiol.00008.2004.

Fregni, F., Boggio, P.S., Nitsche, M.A., Marcolin, M.A., Rigonatti, S.P., and Pascual-Leone, A. (2006). Treatment of major depression with transcranial direct current stimulation. *Bipolar Disorders, 8*(2), 203–204. doi:10.1111/j.1399-5618.2006.00291.x.

Galletly, C., Clarke, P., Carnell, B.L., and Gill, S. (2015). A clinical repetitive transcranial magnetic stimulation service in Australia: 6 years on. *Australian and New Zealand Journal of Psychiatry, 49*(11), 1040–1046.

Geddes, L.A. (1991). History of Magnetic Stimulation of the Nervous System. *Journal of Clinical Neurophysiology, 8*(1), 3–9. Retrieved from www.ncbi.nlm.nih.gov/pubmed/2019649.

George, M.S., Rush, A.J., Marangell, L.B., Sackeim, H.A., Brannan, S.K., Davis, S.M., . . . Goodnick, P. (2005). A one-year comparison of vagus nerve stimulation with treatment as usual for treatment-resistant depression. *Biological Psychiatry, 58*(5), 364–373. doi:10.1016/j.biopsych.2005.07.028.

Giussani, C., Roux, F.-E., Ojemann, J., Sganzerla, E.P., Pirillo, D., and Papagno, C. (2010). Is preoperative functional magnetic resonance imaging reliable for language areas mapping in brain tumor surgery? Review of language functional magnetic resonance imaging and direct cortical stimulation correlation studies. *Neurosurgery, 66*(1), 113–120. doi:10.1227/01.neu.0000360392.15450.c9.

Greenberg, B.D. (2004). Deep brain stimulation in psychiatry. In Lisanby, S.H. (Ed.), *Brain Stimulation in Psychiatric Treatment* (Vol. 1, pp. 53–65). Washington, DC: American Psychiatric Publishing.

Halett, M. (2007). Transcranial magnetic stimulation: a primer. *Neuron, 55*(2), 187–199.

Harden, C.L., Pulver, M.C., Ravdin, L.D., Nikolov, B., Halper, J.P., and Labar, D.R. (2000). A pilot study of mood in epilepsy patients treated with vagus nerve stimulation. *Epilepsy & Behaviour, 1*(2), 93–99. doi:10.1006/ebeh.2000.0046.

Hauptman, J.S., DeSalles, A.A., Espinoza, R., Sedrak, M., and Ishida, W. (2008). Potential surgical targets for deep brain stimulation in treatment-resistant depression. *Neurosurg Focus, 25*(1), E3. doi:10.3171/foc/2008/25/7/e3.

Henn, F.A. (2012). Circuits, cells, and synapses: toward a new target for deep brain stimulation in depression. *Neuropsychopharmacology, 37*(1), 307–308. doi:10.1038/npp.2011.193.

Hilibrand, A.S., Schwartz, D.M., Sethuraman, V., Vaccaro, A.R., and Albert, T.J. (2004). Comparison of transcranial electric motor and somatosensory evoked potential monitoring during cervical spine surgery. *The Journal of Bone and Joint Surgery, 86*(6), 1248–1253. Retrieved from http://jbjs.org/jbjsam/86/6/1248.full.pdf.

Hoffman, R.E., Hawkins, K.A., Gueorguieva, R., Boutros, N.N., Rachid, F., Carroll, K., and Krystal, J.H. (2003). Transcranial magnetic stimulation of left temporoparietal cortex and medication-resistant auditory hallucinations. *Archives of General Psychiatry, 60*(1), 49–56. doi:10.1001/archpsyc.60.1.49.

Holtzheimer, P.E., Kelley, M.E., Gross, R.E., et al. (2012). Subcallosal cingulate deep brain stimulation for treatment-resistant unipolar and bipolar depression. *Archives of General Psychiatry, 69*(2), 150–158. doi:10.1001/archgenpsychiatry.2011.1456.

Janicak, P.G., Dowd, S.M., Rado, J.T., and Welch, M.J. (2010). The re-emerging role of therapeutic neuromodulation: recent developments have revived interest in for difficult-to-treat patients. *Current Psychiatry, 9*(11), 68–74.

Jiménez, F., Velasco, F., Salin-Pascual, R., Hernández, J.A., Velasco, M., Criales, J.L., and Nicolini, H. (2005). A patient with a resistant major depression disorder treated with deep brain stimulation in the inferior thalamic peduncle. *Neurosurgery, 57*(3), 585–593. doi:10.1227/01.neu.0000170434.44335.19.

Kayser, S., Bewernick, B.H., Grubert, C., Hadrysiewicz, B.L., Axmacher, N., and Schlaepfer, T.E. (2011). Antidepressant effects, of magnetic seizure therapy and electroconvulsive therapy, in treatment-resistant depression. *Journal of Psychiatric Research, 45*(5), 569–576. doi:10.1016/j.jpsychires.2010.09.008.

Kedzior, K.K., Azorina, V., and Reitz, S.K. (2014). More female patients and fewer stimuli per session are associated with the short-term antidepressant properties of repetitive transcranial magnetic stimulation (rTMS): a meta-analysis of 54 sham-controlled studies published between 1997–2013. *Neuropsychiatric Disease and Treatment, 10*, 727–756. doi:10.2147/NDT.S58405.

KEMA European Union. (2015). Cyberonics receives KEMA European Union approval for next generation VNS therapy generators and for in-house hydrogen peroxide sterilization process. Retrieved from www.prnewswire.com/news-releases/cyberonics-receives-kema-european-union-approval-for-next-generation-vns-therapy-generators-and-for-in-house-hydrogen-peroxide-sterilization-process-54443292.html.

Kennedy, S.H., Milev, R., Giacobbe, P., Ramascubba, R., Lam, R.W., Parikh, S.V., . . . Ravindran, A.V. (2009). Canadian Network for Mood and Anxiety Treatments (CANMAT) clinical guidelines for the management of major depressive disorder in adults: IV. Neurostimulation therapies. *Journal of Affective Disorders, 117*, S44-S53.

Kern, D.S., and Kumar, R. (2007). Deep brain stimulation. *The Neurologist, 13*(5), 237–252. doi:10.1097/NRL.0b013e3181492c48.

Kirov, G., Ebmeier, K.P., Scott, A.I., Atkins, M., Khalid, N., Carrick, L., . . . Lisanby, S.H. (2008). Quick recovery of orientation after magnetic seizure therapy for major depressive disorder. *British Journal of Psychiatry, 193*(2), 152–155. doi:10.1192/bjp.bp.107.044362.

Kosel, M., Frick, C., Lisanby, S.H., Fisch, H.U., and Schlaepfer, T.E. (2003). Magnetic seizure therapy improves mood in refractory major depression. *Neuropsychopharmacology, 28*(11), 2045–2048. doi:10.1038/sj.npp.1300293.

Kozel, F.A., George, M.S., and Simpson, K.N. (2004). Decision analysis of the cost-effectiveness of repetitive transcranial magnetic stimulation versus electroconvulsive therapy for treatment of nonpsychotic severe depression. *CNS Spectrums, 9*(6), 476–482. Retrieved from www.ncbi.nlm.nih.gov/pubmed/15162090.

Krahl, S.E., Clark, K.B., Smith, D.C., and Browning, R.A. (1998). Locus coeruleus lesions suppress the seizure-attenuating effects of vagus nerve stimulation. *Epilepsia, 39*(7), 709–714. Retrieved from http://onlinelibrary.wiley.

com/store/10.1111/j.1528–1157.1998.tb01155.x/asset/j.1528–1157.1998.tb01155.x.pdf?v=1andt=iifktavwands=04d3d93e9f6494d1200081f54dfbbc54a01355e6.

Krause, L., Enticott, P.G., Zangen, A., and Fitzgerald, P.B. (2012). The role of medial prefrontal cortex in theory of mind: A deep rTMS study. *Behavioural Brain Research, 228*(1), 87–90. doi:10.1016/j.bbr.2011.11.037.

Kreuzer, P.M., Landgrebe, M., Husser, O., Resch, M., Schecklmann, M., Geisreiter, F., . . . Langguth, B. (2012). Transcutaneous vagus nerve stimulation: retrospective assessment of cardiac safety in a pilot study. *Frontiers in Psychiatry, 3*, 70. doi:10.3389/fpsyt.2012.00070.

Krieg, S.M., Tarapore, P.E., Picht, T., Tanigawa, N., Houde, J., Sollmann, N., . . . Nagarajan, S. (2014). Optimal timing of pulse onset for language mapping with navigated repetitive transcranial magnetic stimulation. *Neuroimage, 100*, 219–236. doi:10.1016/j.neuroimage.2014.06.016.

Kuo, M.-F., Unger, M., Liebetanz, D., Lang, N., Tergau, F., Paulus, W., and Nitsche, M.A. (2008). Limited impact of homeostatic plasticity on motor learning in humans. *Neuropsychologia, 46*(8), 2122–2128. doi:10.1016/j.neuropsychologia.2008.02.023.

Lam, R.W., Chan, P., Wilkins-Ho, M., and Yatham, L.N. (2008). Repetitive transcranial magnetic stimulation for treatment-resistant depression: a systematic review and meta-analysis. *Canadian Journal of Psychiatry, 53*(9), 621–631.

Lefaucheur, J.-P., André-Obadia, N., Antal, A., Ayache, S.S., Baeken, C., Benninger, D.H., . . . Garcia-Larrea, L. (2014). Evidence-based guidelines on the therapeutic use of repetitive transcranial magnetic stimulation (rTMS). *Clinical Neurophysiology, 125*(11), 2150–2206. doi:10.1016/j.clinph.2014.05.021.

Leggatt, A.D. (2014). General principles of somatosensory evoked potentials. Retrieved from http://emedicine.medscape.com/article/1139906-overview.

Levine, J., Toder, D., Geller, V., Kraus, M., Gauchman, T., Puterman, M., and Grisaru, N. (2012). Beneficial effects of caloric vestibular stimulation on denial of illness and manic delusions in schizoaffective disorder: a case report. *Brain Stimulation: Basic, Translational, and Clinical Research in Neuromodulation, 5*(3), 267–273. doi:10.1016/j.brs.2011.03.004.

Levkovitz, Y., Harel, E.V., Roth, Y., Braw, Y., Most, D., Katz, L.N., . . . Zangen, A. (2009). Deep transcranial magnetic stimulation over the prefrontal cortex: evaluation of anti-depressant and cognitive effects in depressive patients. *Brain Stimulation, 2*(4), 188–200. doi:10.1016/j.brs.2009.08.002.

Levkovitz, Y., Isserles, M., Padberg, F., Lisanby, S.H., Bystritsky, A., Xia, G., . . . Zangen, A. (2015). Efficacy and safety of deep transcranial magnetic stimulation for major depression:

a prospective multicenter randomized controlled trial. *World Psychiatry, 14*(1), 64–73. doi:10.1002/wps.20199.

Levkovitz, Y., Rabany, L., Harel, E.V., and Zangen, A. (2011). Deep transcranial magnetic stimulation add-on for treatment of negative symptoms and cognitive deficits of schizophrenia: a feasibility study. *International Journal of Neuropsychopharmacology, 14*(7), 991–996. doi:10.1017/s1461145711000642.

Levkovitz, Y., Roth, Y., Harel, E.V., Braw, Y., Sheer, A., and Zangen, A. (2007). A randomized controlled feasibility and safety study of deep transcranial magnetic stimulation. *Clinical Neurophysiology, 118*(12), 2730–2744. doi:10.1016/j.clinph.2007.09.061.

Lisanby, S.H. (2002). Update on magnetic seizure therapy: a novel form of convulsive therapy. *Journal of ECT, 18*(4), 182–188. Retrieved from www.ncbi.nlm.nih.gov/pubmed/12468992.

Lisanby, S.H. (2004). *Brain Stimulation in Psychiatric Treatment* (Vol. 23). Arlington, VA: American Psychiatric Publishing.

Lisanby, S.H., Husain, M.M., Rosenquist, P.B., Maixner, D., Gutierrez, R., Krystal, A., . . . George, M.S. (2008). Daily left prefrontal repetitive transcranial magnetic stimulation in the acute treatment of major depression: clinical predictors of outcome in a multisite, randomized controlled clinical trial. *Neuropsychopharmacology, 34*(2), 522–534. doi:10.1038/npp.2008.118.

Lisanby, S.H., Luber, B., Finck, A.D., Schroeder, C., and Sackheim, H.A. (2001). Deliberate seizure induction with repetitive transcranial magnetic stimulation. *Archives of General Psychiatry, 58*, 199–200.

Lisanby, S.H., Moscrip, T., Morales, O., Luber, B., Schroeder, C., and Sackeim, H.A. (2003). Neurophysiological characterization of magnetic seizure therapy (MST) in non-human primates. *Supplements to Clinical Neurophysiology, 56*, 81–99. Retrieved from www.ncbi.nlm.nih.gov/pubmed/14677385.

Lobel, E., Kleine, J.F., Bihan, D.L., Leroy-Willig, A., and Berthoz, A. (1998). Functional MRI of galvanic vestibular stimulation. *Journal of Neurophysiology, 80*(5), 2699–2709. Retrieved from http://jn.physiology.org/jn/80/5/2699.full.pdf.

Lobel, E., Kleine, J.F., Leroy-Willig, A., Van De Moortele, P.-F., Bihan, D.L., Grüsser, O.-J., and Berthoz, A. (1999). Cortical areas activated by bilateral galvanic vestibular stimulation. *Annals of the New York Academy of Sciences, 871*(1), 313–323. doi:10.1111/j.1749-6632.1999.tb09194.x.

Loo, C. (2015). *Brain Stimulation: A New Tool in Psychiatry.* Paper presented at the Principals and Practice of TMS, Black Dog Institute, Sydney, Australia.

Loo, C., Mitchell, P., Sachdev, P., McDarmont, B., Parker, G., and Gandevia, S. (1999). Double-blind controlled investigation of transcranial magnetic stimulation for the treatment of

resistant major depression. *American Journal of Psychiatry, 156*(6), 946–948. doi:10.1176/ajp.156.6.946.

Loo, C.H., Galvez, V., Martin, D., Alonzo, A., and Nikolin, S. (2015). *Brain Stimulation: A New Tool in Psychiatry.* Paper presented at the Principles and Practice of TMS, Black Dog Institute, Sydney, Australia.

Loo, C.K., Alonzo, A., Martin, D., Mitchell, P.B., Galvez, V., and Sachdev, P. (2012). Transcranial direct current stimulation for depression: 3-week, randomised, sham-controlled trial. *British Journal of Psychiatry, 200*(1), 52–59. doi:10.1192/bjp.bp.111.097634.

Loo, C.K., and Mitchell, P.B. (2005). A review of the efficacy of transcranial magnetic stimulation (TMS) treatment for depression, and current and future strategies to optimize efficacy. *Journal of Affective Disorders, 88*(3), 255–267. doi:10.1016/j.jad.2005.08.001.

Loo, C.K., Sachdev, P., Martin, D., Pigot, M., Alonzo, A., Malhi, G.S., . . . Mitchell, P. (2010). A double-blind, sham-controlled trial of transcranial direct current stimulation for the treatment of depression. *International Journal of Neuropsychopharmacology, 13*(1), 61–69. doi:10.1017/S1461145709990411.

Loo, C.K., Schweitzer, I., and Pratt, C. (2006). Recent advances in optimizing electroconvulsive therapy. *Australian and New Zealand Journal of Psychiatry, 40*(8), 632–638. doi:10.1111/j.1440-1614.2006.01862.x.

Lozano, A.M., Mayberg, H.S., Giacobbe, P., Hamani, C., Craddock, R.C., and Kennedy, S.H. (2008). Subcallosal cingulate gyrus deep brain stimulation for treatment-resistant depression. *Biological Psychiatry, 64*(6), 461–467. doi:10.1016/j.biopsych.2008.05.034.

MacDonald, D. (2006). Intraoperative motor evoked potential monitoring: overview and update. *Journal of Clinical Monitoring and Computing, 20*(5), 347–377. doi:10.1007/s10877-006-9033-0.

Magventure Versatility in Magnetic Stimulation. (2015). MagPro MST. Retrieved from www.magventure.com/en-gb/the-magnetic-alternative-to-ECT.

Malone, D.A., Jr, Dougherty, D.D., Rezai, A.R., Carpenter, L.L., Friehs, G.M., Eskandar, E.N., . . . Greenberg, B.D. (2009). Deep brain stimulation of the ventral capsule/ventral striatum for treatment-resistant depression. *Biological Psychiatry, 65*(4), 267–275. doi:10.1016/j.biopsych.2008.08.029.

Marangell, L.B., Martinez, M., Jurdi, R.A., and Zboyan, H. (2007). Neurostimulation therapies in depression: a review of new modalities. *Acta Psychiatrica Scandinavica, 116*(3), 174–181. doi:10.1111/j.1600-0447.2007.01033.x.

Marangell, L.B., Rush, A.J., George, M.S., Sackeim, H.A., Johnson, C.R., Husain, M.M., . . . Lisanby, S.H. (2002). Vagus nerve stimulation (VNS) for major depressive episodes: one year outcomes. *Biological Psychiatry*, *51*(4), 280–287. doi:10.1016/S0006–3223(01)01343–9.

Martin, D.M., Liu, R., Alonzo, A., Green, M., Player, M.J., Sachdev, P., and Loo, C.K. (2013). Can transcranial direct current stimulation enhance outcomes from cognitive training? A randomized controlled trial in healthy participants. *International Journal of Neuropsychopharmacology*, *16*(9), 1927–1936. doi:10.1017/s1461145713000539.

Mayberg, H.S., Lozano, A.M., Voon, V., McNeely, H.E., Seminowicz, D., Hamani, C., . . . Kennedy, S.H. (2005). Deep brain stimulation for treatment-resistant depression. *Neuron*, *45*(5), 651–660. doi:10.1016/j.neuron.2005.02.014.

Miller, S.M., and Ngo, T.T. (2007). Studies of caloric vestibular stimulation: implications for the cognitive neurosciences, the clinical neurosciences and neurophilosophy. *Acta Neuropsychiatrica*, *19*(3), 183–203. doi:10.1111/j.1601-5215.2007.00208.x.

Millet, B., Jaafari, N., Polosan, M., Baup, N., Giordana, B., Haegelen, C., . . . Reymann, J.M. (2014). Limbic versus cognitive target for deep brain stimulation in treatment-resistant depression: accumbens more promising than caudate. *European Neuropsychopharmacology*, *24*(8), 1229–1239. doi:10.1016/j.euroneuro.2014.05.006.

Mohr, P., Rodriguez, M., Slavíčková, A., and Hanka, J. (2011). The application of vagus nerve stimulation and deep brain stimulation in depression. *Neuropsychobiology*, *64*(3), 170–181. Retrieved from www.karger.com/DOI/10.1159/000325225.

Mosley, P.E., Marsh, R., and Carter, A. (2015). Deep brain stimulation for depression: scientific issues and future directions. *Australian and New Zealand Journal of Psychiatry*, *49*(11), 967–978. doi:10.1177/0004867415599845.

Nahas, Z., Marangell, L.B., Husain, M.M., Rush, A.J., Sackeim, H.A., Lisanby, S.H., . . . George, M.S. (2005). Two-year outcome of vagus nerve stimulation (VNS) for treatment of major depressive episodes. *Journal of Clinical Psychiatry*, *66*(9), 1097–1104. Retrieved from www.ncbi.nlm.nih.gov/pubmed/16187765.

Neurolite Advanced Medical Solutions. (2015). *MagPro MST.* Retrieved from www.neurolite.ch/?q=en/node/171.

NICE. (2015). Interventional procedure consultation document: repetitive transcranial magnetic stimulation for depression. Retrieved from www.nice.org.uk/guidance/ipg542/resources/repetitive-transcranial-magnetic-stimulation-for-depression-1899871923433669.

Nitsche, M.A., Boggio, P.S., Fregni, F., and Pascual-Leone, A. (2009). Treatment of depression with transcranial direct current stimulation (tDCS): a review. *Experimental Neurology*, *219*(1), 14–19. doi:10.1016/j.expneurol.2009.03.038.

Nitsche, M.A., Cohen, L.G., Wassermann, E.M., Priori, A., Lang, N., Antal, A., . . . Pascual-Leone, A. (2008). Transcranial direct current stimulation: State of the art 2008. *Brain Stimulation: Basic, Translational, and Clinical Research in Neuromodulation*, *1*(3), 206–223. doi:10.1016/j.brs.2008.06.004.

Nuwer, M.R., Dawson, E.G., Carlson, L.G., Kanim, L.E.A., and Sherman, J.E. (1995). Somatosensory evoked potential spinal cord monitoring reduces neurologic deficits after scoliosis surgery: results of a large multicenter survey. *Electroencephalography and Clinical Neurophysiology/Evoked Potentials Section*, *96*(1), 6–11. doi:10.1016/0013-4694(94)00235-D.

O'Reardon, J.P., Solvason, H.B., Janicak, P.G., Sampson, S., Isenberg, K.E., Nahas, Z., . . . Sackeim, H.A. (2007). Efficacy and safety of transcranial magnetic stimulation in the acute treatment of major depression: a multisite randomized controlled trial. *Biological Psychiatry*, *62*(11), 1208–1216. doi:10.1016/j.biopsych.2007.01.018.

Palm, U., Schiller, C., Fintescu, Z., Obermeier, M., Keeser, D., Reisinger, E., . . . Padberg, F. (2011). Transcranial direct current stimulation in treatment resistant depression: a randomized double-blind, placebo-controlled study. *Brain Stimulation: Basic, Translational, and Clinical Research in Neuromodulation*, *5*(3), 242–251. doi:10.1016/j.brs.2011.08.005.

Pascual-Leone, A., Rubio, B., Pallardó, F., and Catalá, M.D. (1996). Rapid-rate transcranial magnetic stimulation of left dorsolateral prefrontal cortex in drug-resistant depression. *The Lancet*, *348*(9022), 233–237. doi:10.1016/S0140-6736(96)01219-6.

Preuss, N., Hasler, G., and Mast, F.W. (2014). Caloric vestibular stimulation modulates affective control and mood. *Brain Stimulation*, *7*(1), 133–140. doi:10.1016/j.brs.2013.09.003.

Raffaella Chieffo, Fabio Giatsidis, Elise Houdayer, Mario Fichera, Arturo Nuara, Elisabetta Coppi, . . . Letizia Leocani. (2015). Deep repetitive transcranial magnetic stimulation and cycling improve lower limb function in chronic stroke: a randomized, placebo-controlled, crossover study. *Neurology*, *84*(14 Supplement S5.002). Retrieved from www.neurology.org/content/84/14_Supplement/S5.002.

RANZCP. (2013). Position Statement 79: Repetitive transcranial magnetic stimulation. Retrieved from www.wpanet.org/uploads/News-Zonal-Representatives/wpa-policy-papers-from-zone-18/ZONE 18-RANZCP.PS-79-PPC-Repetitive-Transcranial-Magnetic-Stimula.pdf.

Rodriguez-Oroz, M.C., Obeso, J.A., Lang, A.E., Houeto, J.-L., Pollak, P., Rehncrona, S., . . . Van Blercom, N. (2005). Bilateral deep brain stimulation in Parkinson's disease: a multicentre study with 4 years follow-up. *Brain*, *128*(10), 2240–2249. doi:10.1093/brain/awh571.

Ronchi, R., Rode, G., Cotton, F., Farne, A., Rossetti, Y., and Jacquin-Courtois, S. (2013). Remission of anosognosia for right hemiplegia and neglect after caloric vestibular stimulation. *Restorative Neurology and Neuroscience, 31*(1), 19–24. doi:10.3233/RNN-120236.

Rosenberg, O., Isserles, M., Levkovitz, Y., Kotler, M., Zangen, A., and Dannon, P.N. (2011). Effectiveness of a second deep TMS in depression: a brief report. *Progress in Neuro-Psychopharmacology and Biological Psychiatry, 35*(4), 1041–1044. doi:10.1016/j.pnpbp.2011.02.015.

Rosenberg, O., Shoenfeld, N., Zangen, A., Kotler, M., and Dannon, P.N. (2010). Deep TMS in a resistant major depressive disorder: a brief report. *Depression and Anxiety, 27*(5), 465–469. doi:10.1002/da.20689.

Rosenberg, O., Zangen, A., Stryjer, R., Kotler, M., and Dannon, P.N. (2010). Response to deep TMS in depressive patients with previous electroconvulsive treatment. *Brain Stimulation, 3*(4), 211–217. doi:10.1016/j.brs.2009.12.001.

Rossi, S., Hallett, M., Rossini, P.M., and Pascual-Leone, A. (2009). Safety, ethical considerations, and application guidelines for the use of transcranial magnetic stimulation in clinical practice and research. *Clinical Neurophysiology, 120*(12), 2008–2039. doi:10.1016/j.clinph.2009.08.016.

Roth, Y., Amir, A., Levkovitz, Y., and Zangen, A. (2007). Three-dimensional distribution of the electric field induced in the brain by transcranial magnetic stimulation using figure-8 and deep H-coils. *Journal of Clinical Neurophysiology, 24*(1), 31–38. doi:10.1097/WNP.0b013e31802fa393.

Roth, Y., Levkovitz, Y., Pell, G.S., Ankry, M., and Zangen, A. (2014). Safety and characterizatin of a novel muti-channe TMS stimulator. *Brain Simulation, 7*, 194–205.

Rush, A.J., George, M.S., Sackeim, H.A., Marangell, L.B., Husain, M.M., Giller, C., . . . Goodman, R. (2000). Vagus nerve stimulation (VNS) for treatment-resistant depressions: a multicenter study. *Biological Psychiatry, 47*(4), 276–286. doi:10.1016/S0006-3223(99)00304-2.

Rush, A.J., Marangell, L.B., Sackeim, H.A., George, M.S., Brannan, S.K., Davis, S.M., . . . Cooke, R.G. (2005). Vagus nerve stimulation for treatment-resistant depression: a randomized, controlled acute phase trial. *Biological Psychiatry, 58*(5), 347–354. doi:10.1016/j.biopsych.2005.05.025.

Rush, A.J., Sackeim, H.A., Marangell, L.B., George, M.S., Brannan, S.K., Davis, S.M., . . . Barry, J.J. (2005). Effects of 12 months of vagus nerve stimulation in treatment-resistant depression: a naturalistic study. *Biological Psychiatry, 58*(5), 355–363. doi:10.1016/j.biopsych.2005.05.024.

Sackeim, H.A., Keilp, J.G., Rush, A.J., George, M.S., Marangell, L.B., Dormer, J.S., . . . Zboyan, H. (2001). The effects of vagus nerve stimulation on cognitive performance in patients with treatment-resistant depression. *Neuropsychiatry, Neuropsychology, and Behavioral Neurology, 14*(1), 53–62.

Sackeim, H.A., Rush, A.J., George, M.S., Marangell, L.B., Husain, M.M., Nahas, Z., . . . Goodman, R.R. (2001). Vagus

nerve stimulation (VNS) for treatment-resistant depression: efficacy, side effects, and predictors of outcome. *Neuropsychopharmacology, 25*(5), 713–728. doi:10.1016/S0893-133X (01)00271-8.

Sahlem, G.L., Short, E.B., Kerns, S., Snipes, J., DeVries, W., Fox, J.B., . . . Sackeim, H.A. (2016). Expanded safety and efficacy data for a new method of performing electro-convulsive therapy: focal electrically administered seizure therapy. *Journal of ECT, 32*(3), 197–203. doi:10.1097/yct. 0000000000000328.

Sakas, D.E., and Panourias, I.G. (2006). Rostral cingulate gyrus: a putative target for deep brain stimulation in treatment-refractory depression. *Medical Hypotheses, 66*(3), 491–494. doi:10.1016/j.mehy.2005.07.036.

Schlaepfer, T.E. (2015). Deep brain stimulation for major depression-steps on a long and winding road. *Biological Psychiatry, 78*(4), 218–219. doi:10.1016/j.biopsych.2015. 06.020.

Schlaepfer, T.E., Bewernick, B.H., Kayser, S., Mädler, B., and Coenen, V.A. (2013). Rapid effects of deep brain stimulation for treatment-resistant major depression. *Biological Psychiatry, 73*(12), 1204–1212. doi:10.1016/j.biopsych. 2013.01.034.

Schlaepfer, T.E., Frick, C., Zobel, A., Maier, W., Heuser, I., Bajbouj, M., . . . Hasdemir, M. (2008). Vagus nerve stimulation for depression: efficacy and safety in a European study. *Psychological Medicine, 38*(5), 651–661. doi:10.1017/ s0033291707001924.

Schlaepfer, T.E., and George, M.S. (2010). WFSBP Guidelines on brain stimulation treatments in psychiatry. *The World Journal of Biological Psychiatry, 11*(1), 2–18. doi:10.3109/ 15622970903170835.

Schlaepfer, T.E., and Kosel, M.K. (2004). Transcranial magnetic stimulation in depression. In Lisanby, S.H. (Ed.), *Brain Stimulation in Psychiatric Treatment* (Vol. 1). Washington, DC: American Psychiatric Publishing.

Shiozawa, P., Fregni, F., Benseñor, I.M., Lotufo, P.A., Berlim, M.T., Daskalakis, J.Z., . . . Brunoni, A.R. (2014). Transcranial direct current stimulation for major depression: an updated systematic review and meta-analysis. *International Journal of Neuropsychopharmacology, 17*(9), 1443–1452. doi:10. 1017/s1461145714000418.

Silverstein, J. (2012). Mapping the motor and sensory cortices: a historical look and a current case study in sensorimotor localization and direct cortical motor stimulation. *Neurodiagnostic Journal, 52*(1), 54–68. Retrieved from www.ncbi.nlm.nih.gov/pubmed/22558647.

Simpson, K.N., Welch, M.J., Kozel, F.A., Demitrack, M.A., and Nahas, Z. (2009). Cost-effectiveness of transcranial magnetic stimulation in the treatment of major depression: a health economics analysis. *Advances in Therapy, 26*(3), 346–368. doi:10.1007/s12325-009-0013-x.

Slotema, C.W., Aleman, A., Daskalakis, Z.J., and Sommer, I.E. (2012). Meta-analysis of repetitive transcranial magnetic stimulation in the treatment of auditory verbal hallucinations: update and effects after one month. *Schizophrenia Research, 142*(1–3), 40–45. doi:10.1016/j.schres.2012.08.025.

Slotema, C.W., Blom, J.D., Hoek, H.W., and Sommer, I.E.C. (2010). Should we expand the toolbox of psychiatric treatment methods to include repetitive transcranial magnetic stimulation (rTMS)? A meta-analysis of the efficacy of rTMS in psychiatric disorders. *Journal of Clinical Psychiatry, 71*(7), 873–874. Retrieved from www.sydneytms.com.au/wp-content/uploads/2015/03/TMS_Meta_Analysis.pdf.

Slotema, C.W., Blom, J.D., van Lutterveld, R., Hoek, H.W., and Sommer, I.E.C. (2014). Review of the efficacy of transcranial magnetic stimulation for auditory verbal hallucinations. *Biological Psychiatry, 76*(2), 101–110. doi:10.1016/j.biopsych.2013.09.038.

Sommer, I.E., Aleman, A., Slotema, C.W., and Schutter, D.J. (2012). Transcranial stimulation for psychosis: the relationship between effect size and published findings. *American Journal of Psychiatry, 169*(11), 1211. doi:10.1176/appi.ajp.2012.12060741.

SPD Australia. (2016). Supporting and advocating people with sensory processing disorders Retrieved from www.spdaustralia.com.au.

Spellman, T., Peterchev, A.V., and Lisanby, S.H. (2009). Focal electrically administered seizure therapy: a novel form of ECT illustrates the roles of current directionality, polarity, and electrode configuration in seizure induction. *Neuro-psychopharmacology, 34*(8), 2002–2010. doi:10.1038/npp.2009.12.

Szelényi, A., Joksimovic, B., and Seifert, V. (2007). Intraoperative risk of seizures associated with transient direct cortical stimulation in patients with symptomatic epilepsy. *Journal of Clinical Neurophysiology, 24*(1), 39–43. doi:10.1097/01.wnp.0000237073.70314.f7.

Tarapore, P.E., Findlay, A.M., Honma, S.M., Mizuiri, D., Houde, J.F., Berger, M.S., and Nagarajan, S.S. (2013). Language mapping with navigated repetitive TMS: proof of technique and validation. *Neuroimage, 82*, 260–272. doi:10.1016/j.neuroimage.2013.05.018.

Tarapore, P.E., Tate, M.C., Findlay, A.M., Honma, S.M., Mizuiri, D., Berger, M.S., and Nagarajan, S.S. (2012). Preoperative multimodal motor mapping: a comparison of magnetoencephalography imaging, navigated transcranial magnetic stimulation, and direct cortical stimulation. *Journal of Neurosurgery, 117*(2), 354–362. doi:10.3171/2012.5.jns112124.

Terry, R.S., Tarver, W.B., and Zabara, J. (1991). The implantable neurocybernetic prosthesis system. *Pacing and Clinical Electrophysiology, 14*(1), 86–93.

Utz, K.S., Dimova, V., Oppenländer, K., and Kerkhoff, G. (2010). Electrified minds: Transcranial direct current stimulation (tDCS) and Galvanic Vestibular Stimulation (GVS) as methods of non-invasive brain stimulation in neuropsychology – a review of current data and future implications. *Neuropsychologia, 48*(10), 2789–2810. doi:10.1016/j.neuropsychologia.2010.06.002.

Utz, K.S., Korluss, K., Schmidt, L., Rosenthal, A., Oppenlander, K., Keller, I., and Kerkhoff, G. (2011). Minor adverse effects of galvanic vestibular stimulation in persons with stroke and healthy individuals. *Brain Injury, 25*(11), 1058–1069. doi:10.3109/02699052.2011.607789.

Valis-Sole, J. (2017). *Novel Forms of Stimulation Therapy for Neurological Disorders*. Paper presented at the 2nd International Brain Stimulation Conference, Barcelona, Spain.

Vallejo-Torres, L., Castilla, I., Gonzalez, N.I., Hunter, R., Serrano-Pérez, P., and Perestela-Pérez, L. (2015). Cost-effectiveness of electroconvulsive therapy compared to repetitive transcranial magnetic stimulation for treament-resistant severe depression: a decision model. *Psychological Medicine, 45*, 1459–1470.

Wang, A., Peters, T.M., de Ribaupierre, S., and Mirsattari, S.M. (2012). Functional magnetic resonance imaging for language mapping in temporal lobe epilepsy. *Epilepsy Research and Treatment, 2012*, 8. doi:10.1155/2012/198183.

White, P.F., Amos, Q., Zhang, Y., Stool, L., Husain, M.M., Thornton, L., . . . Lisanby, S.H. (2006). Anesthetic considerations for magnetic seizure therapy: a novel therapy for severe depression. *Anesthesia & Analgesia, 103*(1), 76–80, table of contents. doi:10.1213/01.ane.0000221182.71648.a3.

Zentner, J. (1989). Noninvasive motor evoked potential monitoring during neurosurgical operations on the spinal cord. *Neurosurgery, 24*(5), 709–712. Retrieved from http://journals.lww.com/neurosurgery/Fulltext/1989/05000/Noninvasive_Motor_Evoked_Potential_Monitoring.8.aspx.

CHAPTER 3

Organisational/ administrative skills

Setting up an ECT service/clinical governance

There is limited literature about establishing an ECT service. Many reviews are critical about the lack of audit and procedures that govern ECT practice. In 1981, the *Lancet* reported that ECT was "a shameful state of affairs": "If ever ECT is legislated against or falls into disuse, it will not be because it is ineffective or a dangerous treatment; it will be because Psychiatrists have failed to supervise and monitor its use adequately" (Editorial, 1981).

Unfortunately, little has changed in ECT practice in 36 years. Leiknes, Jarosh-von Schweder and Høie (2012) reviewed the contemporary use of ECT worldwide. They identified 70 studies, seven from Australia and New Zealand, 33 from Europe, 15 from Asia, three from Africa and 12 from North and Latin America. Worldwide there was enormous difference in ECT practice; the average number of ECT treatments administered per patients was eight; unmodified ECT – treatment administered without anaesthesia – was widely used in over 90% of Asian countries as well as in Africa, Latin America, Russia, Turkey and Spain (Leiknes et al., 2012). Worldwide, the preferred electrode placement was bilateral, with the exception of Europe, Australia and New Zealand, where unilateral placement was preferred. The mainstream practice was with a brief-pulse stimulus, however sine wave devices were still in use. An interesting difference was that the majority of treatments in the Western world were on older women with depression, compared to younger men with schizophrenia in Asian countries. Mandatory reporting and overall country ECT register data was sparse, with some countries using ECT as an acute first-line option while others enabled other professions, such as geriatricians and nurses, to administer treatment. Overall there was inadequate training, a limited number of sites in some countries administering treatment, and clinical treatment guidelines were not followed (Leiknes et al., 2012).

The high level of worldwide variability and inability to follow clinical treatment guidelines is in part related to the many challenges that exist in setting up a new ECT service. One of the primary long-standing obstacles that interfere with the smooth delivery of ECT within a service is stigma. ECT is often portrayed as being barbaric and risky (Torpey, 2016). ECT has low priority with hospital administrators, who have limited budgets and scarce resources allocating monies to other "more essential lifesaving procedures". This leaves the ECT service with limited resources, making it difficult to comply with minimum standards guidelines, implement quality measures and complete audits, making measurement-based ECT practice impossible to achieve (Leiknes et al., 2012; Trivedi, 2009).

Setting up an ECT service within a general hospital encounters further problems. ECT administered in hospital theatres is challenged by "urgent surgical cases", with the implication that ECT is not a life-saving treatment, resulting in delay or cancellation of treatment. One of the common contentions that result in ad hoc service delivery is the inability to ensure that the "list; defined as four hours with eight patients" is always full to capacity. ECT lists are highly variable, with a marked fluctuation in referral rates that challenges resource allocation.

In all negotiations with hospital administrators concerning an ECT service, it is very important to remain patient-focused, an emphasis that will facilitate change in the organisation avoiding being sidelined by politics or stigma.

APPROACH TO SERVICE DELIVERY

There are two major perspectives in establishing an ECT service. The first involves a dimensional approach through the adaptation of tools used for clinical audit. Audit tools have extensive checklists that can be implemented in a sequential manner. This approach can be cumbersome and somewhat overwhelming (Little, Munday and Atkins, 2005). The national audits of ECT programmes in Scotland and England provide a model for this approach (Royal College of Psychiatrists, 2015; SEAN, 2015), with Scotland well ahead of the UK.

A categorical/dimensional approach has been proposed as a second model by Little et al. (2005). This approach identifies three important principles. The first is to gain agreement on the need for an ECT service. The evidence for this approach is that ECT is the single most effective treatment for severe depression (UK ECT Review Group, 2003). This finding was confirmed by the Consortium for Research in ECT (CORE), which identified an 87% response rate for unipolar depression if ECT was administered correctly (Husain et al., 2004). ECT is capable of reducing the length and cost of a hospital stay, as well as reducing the readmission rate (Lalitanatpong, 2005). These facts alone are often not adequate to establish agreement between ECT clinicians and managers and must be set in the context of best practice patient outcomes.

The second guiding principle is for the ECT service to develop a vision to drive the service (Little et al., 2005). The guiding principle behind the vision is to remain patient-focused so that cooperation can be achieved at all levels within the service. The ECT team requires adequate knowledge of ECT with recent clinical experience, have a high level of enthusiasm and understand the evidence base that underpins ECT practice. They must be sensitive to referring psychiatrists, balancing clinical autonomy with safe evidence-based treatment.

The third principle is to identify key concepts that provide governance and credibility to the service allowing it to develop over time. A young service will adopt a clinical approach based upon clinical experience and a standardised treatment approach. The ECT service goes through a phase of formulisation whereby it expands to offer a range of different interventions, techniques and training experiences. A mature service with a high level of credibility and skill is able to offer education and training to a broad range of staff, develop a research focus and provide a measurement-based service (Little et al., 2005). This will improve the respect for patients having ECT owing to increased support and understand from general hospital staff that has grown in their understanding of the power of this highly effective treatment.

The establishment of a new service will involve a review of current practices within the hospital without criticism. It needs to incorporate practitioners who are currently practising ECT with an aim of respecting their clinical autonomy in the context of education about best practice. Credibility is best established by using "a bottom up approach". Gaining the support of "staff at the front line" is vital in implementing minimum standards and change.

Further, it is necessary to encourage cohesiveness among staff involved in the service by inviting key players to join the team. It is important to listen to what others have to say incorporating their views into the overall plan. It is useful to increase the visibility of psychiatric services by becoming involved in hospital-wide forums, like participating in grand round activities and presenting at the continuing medical education meetings run by the anaesthetists. It is very important to wait and not expect change overnight. Complex hospital systems have their own inertia, which requires considerable effort and time to change.

ECT SERVICE GOALS

Communication

Open and free dialogue with various groups within the hospital service is essential. A "go to them, don't expect them to come to you" approach is recommended. Regular meetings with staff are essential. These would include representatives from the hospital and mental health administrators, medical staff council, inpatient units, recovery area, theatres and the department of anaesthetics. Throughout this process, respect for clinical autonomy and toleration of different views is essential.

ECT committee

An important component of any ECT service is having a structure that incorporates an ECT committee. This committee may be specific to a local hospital or may have a regional focus. The later has become possible with the development of video or telephone conferencing facilities. It should have a broad membership to consolidate communication and clear terms of reference.

The terms of reference should include clinical governance, accountability, training, education, implementation of audit activities and overseeing research projects as a service evolves.

The committee should meet regularly and have a clear structure, particularly in how it reports to senior management. An agenda should be prepared and minutes should be taken and circulated to the group prior to the next meeting. If the committee is region-based, each site should be represented and given time to discuss local issues that can be pursued and followed up further by the committee or directly by the service. A further strength of a regionally based committee is that it improves communication between sites, enhancing networking and support.

ECT clinical guidelines

An important task for the ECT committee is to develop a local ECT clinical guideline (protocol) that is meaningful and relevant to the local setting. This document can be time-consuming to prepare. If the health district is large, with many sites doing only small numbers of treatments, it may be more practical to have an area-based clinical guideline that can be adapted to highlight specific hospital needs as appropriate. The ECT guideline should provide a clear clinical framework that is a reference point to prevent confusion and errors about technique and process, enabling open discussion to create an atmosphere of cooperation.

Reference should be made to clinical practice guidelines covering depression, bipolar disorder and schizophrenia developed by national colleges and associations (Gelenberg et al., 2010; Goodwin et al., 2016; Grunze et al., 2010; Kennedy, Lam, Parikh, Patten and Ravindran, 2009; Malhi et al., 2015; Ministry of Health Social Services and Equity, 2014; Suehs, Bendele, Crismon, Trivedi and Kurian, 2008). Many regions have developed minimum standards of ECT practice documents that provide specific evidence-based recommendations concerning all aspects of ECT (American Psychiatric Association, 2001; Chief Psychiatrist of Western Australia, 2015; NSW Health, 2010; Queensland Mental Health Review Tribunal, 2000; SA Health, 2014; Waite and Easton, 2013). This information can be made site-specific to enhance the credibility of the local service.

Database

A vital component of any ECT service is a database that stores clinical information in a format that provides easy clinical reference and the capacity for audit and research. The database should include a range of clinical outcomes, including number of treatments, type of ECT, titration method, change in type of ECT if failure to progress, measures of cognition and treatment outcome, remission or relapse and side effects, to list a few. Ideally, a mature database should be a computer-based system that has the potential for benchmarking with other services.

ECT team

An important goal for any service is to establish an effective and specialised ECT team. This team should include all those practitioners involved on a day-to-day basis in the delivery of ECT. The establishment of the ECT team reduces the stigma associated with the treatment and enhances credibility. It provides consistency of treatment and improves the standard of care by strengthening the "art" as well as the "science" of ECT practice.

The team should focus on the ECT journey, acknowledging the total experience for the patient during an index course of treatment that contributes to the "lived experience" from consent to completion (Rose, Fleischmann and Wykes, 2009).

Team members

Clinical director of ECT services

The clinical director of ECT services should be a senior psychiatrist who has an interest in ECT. This appointment is essential to facilitate change through support, leadership, governance, audit and research initiatives. Essential requirements include: recent ECT experience, regular credentialing and training to maintain skills, membership of relevant peak bodies like the International Society for ECT and Neurostimulation (ISEN) and regional colleges or societies, faculties, sections and special interest groups that promote high standards of clinical practice, training and research pertaining to ECT and neurostimulation (ISEN, 2017; SEN, 2017).

The director of ECT should have a high level of clinical acumen with a vision for the service that drives negotiations with senior anaesthetists, hospital management, providing support at all levels within the service, enhancing the cohesion of the team.

Psychiatry registrars/trainees

The ECT teams should have provision for psychiatric registrars to have opportunities for training at a basic or advanced level with the opportunity to come back regularly for refresher courses. Following credentialing, psychiatric trainees should be actively involved in administering ECT with supervision and support from the clinical director.

ECT coordinator/nurse specialist

The ECT coordinator is "the powerhouse of the ECT team", providing coordination and oversight of all aspects of the service within the hospital sharing the vision of the ECT clinical director. The aim of the coordinator is to manage the total experience of the patient having ECT, by supporting other staff with open communication and leadership, ensuring records are accurate and legislative requirements are met to ensure best practice. The coordinator should have dedicated hours allocated, determined by the level of activity of ECT service within the hospital. A minimum requirement would be four hours, two or three times a week, with extra hours to complete administrative tasks (Chief Psychiatrist of Western Australia, 2015; NSW Health, 2010; SA Health, 2014; Tiller and Lyndon, 2003; Waite and Easton, 2013).

Other team members

Other team members include: anaesthetists, anaesthetic technicians, recovery staff, other perioperative staff and nurse managers. The exact team would depend upon the unique needs of the hospital itself. In many settings it would be important to involve psychiatry registrars to promote specialist training and teaching.

Legislative framework

The ECT service must comply with the relevant mental health legislation that governs the region in which the treatment is administered (Chief Psychiatrist of Western Australia, 2006; Dunne, Kavanagh and McLoughlin, 2009; Leiknes et al., 2012; NSW Health, 2010; Queensland Mental Health Review Tribunal, 2000; SA Health, 2014; The Minister of Health, 2004; Winslade, Liston, Ross and Weber, 1984; Yuzda, Parker, Parker, Geagea and Goldbloom, 2002). Most Mental Health Acts have stringent requirements governing the administration of ECT in an authorised hospital, particularly for patients who are in hospital on an involuntary basis. In most Australian states the director general of health must approve the location for the administration of ECT.

In most regions worldwide a medical officer with psychiatric experience administers ECT, although in some parts of the world other professions, like geriatricians and nurses, can give the treatment (Leiknes et al., 2012). In Australia it is a requirement that two doctors must be present, one of whom is trained in the administration of ECT and the other trained in anaesthetic techniques.

Different procedures will apply whether the ECT is given within a general hospital theatre or whether it is administered in a stand-alone ECT suite.

Consent

Particular attention is required to ensure that patients provide fully informed consent. Most legislation identifies the specific requirements that must be met to comply with administering ECT within a certain region.

The process of consent should not be done defensively but rather with an open and honest approach, addressing issues of stigma, highlighting that modern ECT is very different to past practice. Honest answers should be given in relation to the potential cognitive effects from ECT, acknowledging recent work by Sackeim et al. (2007) that clearly demonstrates that there may be a risk of more permanent memory loss if high-dose bitemporal ECT is administered.

Consent has been described as a process rather than an event as sufficient time should be given for adequate discussion about ECT, the potential benefits and shortcomings with different forms of information provided to patients and their carers (Waite et al., 2013).

If patients are not able to give voluntary consent for ECT, an application needs to be made to the relevant regional mental health tribunal for determination. All staff need to ensure that orders issued by the tribunal are within the limits specified by the involuntary schedule.

Consent for ECT in patients with special needs, for example developmental delay and autistic spectrum disorders, should be determined by the relevant mental health tribunal.

There are large global variations in the process of consent for ECT for voluntary and involuntary patients (Leiknes et al., 2012). In some jurisdictions, like United Kingdom, consent for voluntary patients is obtained by the treating psychiatrist, with another opinion from a second opinion-appointed doctor (SOAD), reserved for involuntary patients (Waite et al., 2013), whereas in other places a second opinion is required for all voluntary patients (NSW Health, 2010) or only where there is doubt about capacity (SA Health, 2014). In most states and territories in Australia and New Zealand, ECT may only be administered to involuntary patients after a mental health tribunal has made an ECT determination (Chief Psychiatrist of Western Australia, 2015; NSW Health, 2010; NZ Minister of Health, 2004; SA Health, 2014; Victorian Government, 2014a).

In the USA there is a high level of variability between states in the law surrounding consent for ECT (Winslade et al., 1984). In many states there is serious boundary and role confusion owing to progressive intrusion of state authority into areas that were traditionally in the domain of medical judgement and clinical care, resulting in overregulation by legislatures and courts and causing serious delays or denials of service and often failure to resolve critical issues involving competence and consent (Winslade et al., 1984).

Special provisions are required to administer ECT to people under the age of 18. Worldwide, policy, procedures and legislation vary widely from country to country and from different jurisdictions in the same country, with use and consent procedures becoming increasingly more restrictive (Roberson, Rey and Walter, 2013). In countries like the USA, UK, Canada and Australia the use of ECT is strictly regulated, while in other regions like Scandinavia it is quite liberal (Gazdag, Takács, Ungvari and Sienaert, 2012).

Some countries like India, Spain, Nigeria, Japan and Romania continue to administer unmodified ECT to all age groups (Chanpattana, Kunigiri, Kramer and Gangadhar, 2005). A recent review of unmodified ECT recommended that the practice should be banned except under exceptional circumstances (Chittaranjan et al., 2012), while the World Health Organization has called for it to be banned completely (Freeman and Pathare, 2005). In Slovenia and Luxembourg ECT is not available for anyone and patients need to travel to neighbouring countries to receive the treatment (Gazdag et al., 2012). In India, the revised draft mental health legislation prohibits the use of ECT in minors (Balhara and Mathur, 2012).

Recent legislation in Victoria, Australia, specifies that everyone below the age of 18 must be presented to the mental health tribunal before ECT can proceed (Victorian Government, 2014b), while other states of Australia (NSW Health, 2010; SA Health, 2014) and the UK only have this requirement when a minor is incapable of providing consent (Waite et al., 2013).

As with adults, the use of ECT for patients under the age of 18 within the USA is complex and onerous with vast difference between states. Legislation ranges from a requirement to obtain opinions from three qualified child and adolescent psychiatrists in the state of Michigan to authorisation by a court order in the neighbouring state of Illinois (Roberson et al., 2013). Such complexities have resulted in significant clinical and ethical dilemmas for the ECT clinician in an environment where there is a growing expectation to receive effective treatment with ECT (Leong and Eth, 1991).

The decision to proceed with ECT should be based upon documented assessment of the potential risks and benefits of the treatment. The risks associated with ECT may be enhanced during pregnancy and in older people and young people. Valid consent should be obtained in all cases where the individual has the ability to grant or refuse their consent. In situations where consent is not possible, advance care directives should be taken fully into account and the individual's advocate should be consulted.

Clinical status should be assessed following each ECT session. Treatment should be tapered after an initial response to enable complete remission reducing the potential for adverse effects. Cognitive function should be monitored regularly throughout the course of treatment.

Equipment

It is very important that an ECT service continues to update its ECT device to bring it into line with evidence-based medicine. A criticism of audits in the past has been that ECT sites have failed to comply with this requirement, often administering ECT with old and outdated equipment (Duffett and Lelliott, 1998; Sackeim et al., 1993; Sackeim et al., 2007).

The minimum requirement for an ECT device is that it meets the regulatory standards for the country in which it is being used. The machine should: deliver a brief pulse at constant-current stimulus, have electroencephalogram (EEG) monitoring, have a wide-range output, with capacity to administer ultrabrief ECT, and be capable of providing stimuli according the stimulus dosing protocol discussed in Section 5.3. It is useful for the device to have four-channel recording including right and left EEG, electrocardiogram (ECG) and electromyogram (EMG) and there should be an appropriate backup device available in the event of malfunction (American Psychiatric Association, 2001; RANZCP, 2007; Waite and Easton, 2013).

The anaesthetist should ensure that each patient has a new face mask for ventilation with 100%

CLINICAL WISDOM 3.1.1

Stigma is the most damaging factor, making setting up a new ECT service or improving an existing one challenging. It undermines credibility, making it difficult to achieve parity with other surgical procedures. Factors that contribute to stigma can be very subtle often incorporated into every day clinical practice. ECT services are under scrutiny, from administrators who run the regional health services to the eyes and ears of junior and senior medical, nursing, allied health, cleaning and catering staff who interact with the service directly or the patient having the treatment.

    10 tips to reduce stigma in a general hospital ECT service!

1 Develop an ECT team and committee that work in a cohesive and consistent manner following a protocol that all members of the department adhere to that reports directly to the hospital management.
2 Remain patient-focused with careful attention to the needs of families and carers, who often want to be involved in all components of the treatment.
3 Move ECT treatment from behind a curtain in the recovery area to a fully equipped procedure room or theatre, thereby giving ECT the same status as other short surgical lists.
4 Remove ECT from the end of an emergency list, where the treatment is often not considered to be life-saving and cancellations are common.
5 Aim for a regular morning ECT list twice or three times a week.
6 Transfer patients to and from the treatment area in the same manner as other patients using the service.
7 Replace handheld or metal disc electrodes with disposable electrodes to remove the fear in observers that can reinforce negative images of ECT portrayed in the media. Remind staff that students or other observers are in the treatment room for the first time.
8 Work in close collaboration with perioperative staff, making them feel part of the ECT service.
9 Encourage the anaesthetist and anaesthetic staff to be part of the ECT team, preventing the divide and tension that can often be present in the treatment room. Ensure that the team remains patient-focused through involvement in discussion about clinical progress, quality of the EEG and the potential impact of anaesthetic agents.
10 Develop a protocol with the anaesthetist concerning best practice for high-acuity patients who need ECT.

oxygen before and during the treatment. Oxygen should be delivered by intermittent positive pressure ventilation via a self-inflating bag from either a cylinder with a reserve or an anaesthetic machine that has appropriate circuits for scavenging and supply.

Other equipment should include: a pulse oximeter that determines oxygen saturation, an electrocardiograph (ECG) that monitors cardiac rhythm, a capnograph (ETC02) that monitors end-tidal carbon dioxide levels, a blood pressure (BP) cuff that regularly monitors BP, a second BP cuff that is used to isolate the right foot after suxamethonium has been administered, and a tendon hammer, used to ensure complete relaxation has been achieved.

Oxygen and a pulse oximeter are required during transfer from the treatment room to the recovery area. The recovery area should have: an oxygen source, suction equipment, BP and pulse oximeter monitoring, access to emergency drugs and equipment, access to the medical record and the capacity to provide the patient with a light meal and drinks before they return to the ward or home.

Emergency equipment and drugs need to be readily available in the ECT suite or theatre area for resuscitation. Equipment should include: a cardiac defibrillator, a laryngoscope laryngeal mask airways, endotracheal tubes with appropriate connectors, a stethoscope, a thermometer, intravenous infusion sets with fluids, stands and intravenous catheters and an emergency drug box that complies with local protocols. These aspects of care are easily met when ECT is administered within a theatre setting; however, special attention needs to be given when ECT is administered in the stand-alone site.

Environment

General hospital

In a general hospital, ECT is best administered within a day-only procedure room or theatre that is fully equipped. Inpatients and outpatients require access to admissions and a waiting area prior to going into the theatre and a fully equipped recovery area before discharge back to the ward or home.

Local protocols should be followed for patient transfers between different areas during treatment. ECT staff should follow the local theatre protocols concerning dress and attire. Dedicated theatre time and a dedicated team ensure reliable and efficient treatment maximising the patient's journey through ECT. In smaller centres, this may not be possible owing to the low patient volume and treatment is often administered before or after a general surgical list. Due diligence is required to prioritise ECT to prevent patients being "bumped or cancelled", with priority being given to "acute emergency cases".

In some cases it may be necessary to compromise by accepting a less than ideal schedule for ECT until stigma dissipates and goodwill established by preoperative staff.

Stand-alone ECT suite

When ECT is conducted in a stand-alone setting it should meet local mental health and anaesthetic protocols. The facility should comprise four areas: a quiet admissions waiting area, a treatment room that is fully equipped to theatre standards, a recovery area that is fully equipped to meet the requirements specified above and a transition room where patients can be given light meals and drinks prior to transfer to the ward or home (American Psychiatric Association, 2001; Freeman and Fergusson, 2013; NSW Health, 2010; SA Health, 2014; Victorian Government, 2014a).

Initial assessment

Careful attention needs to be given to conducting a comprehensive history, mental state examination and physical workup prior to a patient being administered ECT. Decisions need to be made as to who is the primary person responsible to coordinate this assessment. In a public hospital setting, it is usually the psychiatric registrar under the supervision of the psychiatrist, whereas in a private hospital setting it is the treating psychiatrist.

The ECT team needs to develop an ECT clinical guideline that specifies the referral process including the requirements for physical assessment. The referring psychiatric team usually conducts the initial assessment with a further review by the anaesthetist. There should be clear pathways for routine and urgent medial problems, specifying how requests for consultation from other disciplines like cardiology should proceed.

The physical assessment should include: a complete medical and surgical history that highlights current and past medications, previous anaesthetics and surgical interventions as well as previous courses of ECT. Allergies need to be clearly identified and a physical examination needs to be completed and documented in the medical record. The guidelines should include recommendations concerning appropriate investigations that need to be completed as part of the pre-anaesthetic assessment. Patients deemed to be high risk should have more intensive investigations and need to be reviewed by the appropriate discipline prior to undertaking ECT.

Careful attention needs to be given to medications that can interfere with seizure threshold and EEG morphology. Benzodiazepines should ideally be ceased owing to their potential to raise the seizure threshold and reduce the efficacy of ECT (Jha and Stein, 1996). Acute clinical distress should be managed by high-dose atypical antipsychotic medication. Anticonvulsant medication used as mood stabilisers should be ceased if possible or withheld the night before as they reduce seizure length and a higher stimulus may be required to achieve a good response, particularly when unilateral ECT is administered (Zarate, Tohen and Baraibar, 1997). Sienaert and Peuskens (2007) concluded that, although specific drugs like carbamazepine and valproate may have an impact on seizure threshold, ECT can be administered safely and effectively in patients who are treated with a range of anticonvulsants. When used as primary agents in bipolar disorder there may be some benefit in withholding the dose 12 to 24 hours before ECT is administered. They should be withdrawn if there is a lack of clinical response to ECT.

The ECT guideline should specify a protocol to govern the use of lithium, owing to conflicting reports about its use with ECT. There is some evidence that it may increase the incidence of adverse effects associated with ECT, including postictal delirium, delayed time to recovery and other neurological abnormalities (Sartorius, Wolf and Henn, 2005). Others report that it is safe to continue lithium during a course of ECT (Dolenc and Rasmussen, 2005). The ECT team should make a recommendation concerning the use of lithium during ECT, with the final decision left to the treating psychiatrist. If lithium is maintained during treatment, it is recommended that the serum level be at the lower end of the therapeutic range owing to some reports that time to recovery after ECT may be related to serum lithium levels (Tirthalli, Harish and Gangadhar, 2011).

ECT technique

It is important that the ECT service has a protocol that governs the technique used to deliver ECT. Issues to consider include:

Dosing strategy. Strategies range from stimulus dose titration to age-based or half-age fixed dosing techniques (Fink, 2009; Petrides and Fink, 1996). There is growing evidence that using a stimulus dose titration method (Sackeim et al., 1993) is more sensitive, enabling individualised treatment owing to the marked variation in patients' seizure threshold during a course of ECT (Galvez, Hadzi-Pavlovic, Smith and Loo, 2015).

Electrode placement. There is growing evidence that ultrabrief right unilateral electrode placement ECT should be the first-line treatment (Kellner et al., 2016; Tor et al., 2015), with recommendations to change to a stronger form of ECT if there is no clinical response after Treatment 6 or when clinical acuity is high.

Electroencephalogram (EEG). Review of the EEG should become part of routine clinical practice. The team needs to develop a high level of skill in reading an EEG within the clinical context, engaging the treating team in dialogue about response to ECT. The EEG Parameter Rating Scale is a useful tool that can assist with training and clinical decisions that are based upon the EEG (Edwards, Koopowitz and Harvey, 2003). Further information concerning this topic can be found in a review article by Mayur (2006).

Electrode delivery system. The ECT team needs to decide how the stimulus will be applied. Many centres continue to use handheld electrodes, with some device manufacturers only offering this system (ECRON Limited, 2016; MECTA Corporation, 2015). Disposable electrodes can also be applied while the patient is awake, providing a fresh look and bringing ECT into line with modern surgical practice (Somatics L.L.C., 1989). Disposable electrodes can reduce stigma for those observing the treatment and potentially improve the accuracy of delivery. If the disposable pads are used, adherence to a strict protocol of site preparation is required to minimise impedance and maximise adherence. The rubber band technique involves inserting metal discs at the correct anatomical site that are held in place by the band. The band needs to be tightened firmly making it difficult to apply when the patient is awake and locating the correct anatomical site may be harder to achieve. This technique has been used to portray ECT as a frightening and barbaric treatment and may be best abandoned (De Brito, 2004).

Anaesthetic technique

In conjunction with the department of anaesthetics an anaesthetic protocol needs to be organised. Issues to consider include:

- **Pre-oxygenation.** Administering 100% oxygen for three or four minutes prior to induction to minimise memory impairment, reduce seizure threshold and minimise any potential cardio-vascular complications.
- **Induction agents.** Choice of induction agents and the doses administered are important as they have an impact on seizure quality and potential efficacy. When combination induction

agents are administered, careful attention must be given to ensure a patient is unconscious avoiding "awareness". Awareness is a highly distressing state in which the patient is aware of what is happening during the procedure when paralysed after they have been induced with an insufficient dose of the induction agent (Sandin, Enlund, Samuelsson and Lennmarken, 2000). The isolated limb technique may be helpful in not only motoring the motor fit but also enabling voluntary response to command when induction is too shallow.

- **Muscle relaxants.** Suxamethonium is the most commonly used muscle relaxant owing to its rapid onset and offset. Discussion concerning dosage is important to ensure complete paralysis as well as how to manage suxamethonium-induced myalgia and other common unwanted effects of treatment. A deep tendon reflex may be elicited as a guide to paralysis.
- **Essential medication.** It is common practice to administer antihypertensive medications with a sip of water the morning prior to ECT to stabilise the haemodynamic effects of ECT.
- **Bite blocks.** The type of bite block / mouth guard utilised is important, with of options including reusable sterilised bite blocks or disposable bite blocks.
- **Recovery.** Attention to the recovery phase is important. The length of time a patient remains in the treatment area will depend upon whether it has been administered within a theatre area or a stand-alone ECT suite. It is recommended that a patient recovery tool be utilised to provide objective measures, highlighting when it is appropriate for a patient to be discharged from the recovery area back to the inpatient unit or home.

Anaesthetic agents

There is growing evidence highlighting the impact that standard anaesthetic agents have on the quality and length of the seizure elicited with ECT (Galvez et al., 2015; MacPherson and Loo, 2008). A technique that has become popular is to reduce the dose of the primary induction agent through the addition of an ultrabrief opioid like remifentanil, potentially improving the quality and length of the seizure (Recart, Rawal, White, Byerly and Thornton, 2003; Vishne, Aronov, Amiaz, Etchin and Grunhaus, 2005).

Continuation and maintenance ECT

It is mandatory that the ECT clinical guidelines include how a patient will be managed when they require ongoing ECT.

Continuation ECT (c-ECT) is defined as treatments that are given beyond the index episode up to six months, while maintenance ECT (m-ECT) is defined as ECT administered after a six-month period, which is used as the primary technique to maintain wellness (Frederikse, Petrides and Kellner, 2006). It is recommended that during this period the patient be offered trials of different medications

to find a new combination that may reduce the need for ECT.

m-ECT is usually considered in patients who have had a poor response or cannot tolerate pharmacotherapy. There is good evidence that m-ECT is safe and effective, prevents relapse and reduces the readmission rate to hospital (Kellner et al., 2006); however, it is underutilised in clinical practice (Abraham, Milev, Delva and Zaheer, 2006).

Audit

A new ECT service should incorporate a system of measuring outcomes, to track what they do and how they do it, highlighting strengths and weakness in order to achieve a high level of evidenced base practice. Implementation of measures to track clinical response and cognitive changes are the first step in achieving a more comprehensive audit-based process. Once established, it enables benchmarking with other hospitals. There are a number of evidence-based audit models available that can aid practice (Hodge and Buley, 2015; SEAN, 2015).

The lived experience

One of the major advances in ECT practice that has arisen since the NICE guidance document on ECT (NICE, 2003, modified 2009) is the recognition that consumer experiences are vital and must be integrated into a modern ECT service (Rose et al., 2009). Despite the many advances in the evidence base underpinning modern ECT, the voice of the anti-ECT lobby is growing in strength, exacerbating the stigma and misinformation about this life-saving treatment (Fink, 1997). International bodies like the International Society for ECT and Neurostimulation (ISEN, 2016) and bi-national bodies like the Royal Australian and New Zealand College of Psychiatrists (RANZCP), Section for ECT and Neurostimulation (SEN, 2017), recognise that administrators, legislative bodies and the media are most attentive to consumers with a lived experience. Both groups have active consumer networks that advocate the benefits of ECT at all levels.

CLINICAL WISDOM 3.1.2

Setting up an ECT service is a challenging and at times frustrating process. There is often enormous resistance within a hospital service for change. Introducing a procedure like ECT that is surrounded by controversy and stigma requires considerable dedication and persistence. Open dialogue, respect for clinical autonomy, patient focus and a vision are vital to achieve success in this task. Further, it is essential for the hospital administration to recognise the importance of the technique and to allocate resources appropriately. These resources are needed to fund a modern ECT device, appropriate staff and environment for the treatment to be administered safely and effectively. Attention must be given to fully informed consent and the strength of the lived experience in overcoming stigma and misinformation. Perseverance will bring about change slowly, ensuring that this highly successful treatment remains available to consumers in the long term.

REFERENCES

Abraham, G., Milev, R., Delva, N., and Zaheer, J. (2006). Clinical outcome and memory function with maintenance electroconvulsive therapy: a retrospective study. *Journal of ECT, 22*(1), 43–45.

American Psychiatric Association. (2001). *The Practice of Electroconvulsive Therapy: Recommendations for Treatment, Training and Privileging: A Task Force Report*, 2nd edition. Washington, DC: American Psychiatric Association.

Balhara, Y.P.S., and Mathur, S. (2012). Prohibition for children and adolescents in mental health care act of India: a step in the right direction? *Journal of ECT, 28*, 1–2.

Chanpattana, W., Kunigiri, G., Kramer, B.A., and Gangadhar, B.N. (2005). Survey of the practice of electroconvulsive therapy in teaching hospitals in India. *Journal of ECT, 39*, 54–60.

Chief Psychiatrist of Western Australia. (2006). *The Chief Psychiatist's guidelines for the use of electroconvulsive therapy in Western Australia 2006*. Retrieved from www.chiefpsychiatrist.health.wa.gov.au/docs/guides/ECT_Guide.pdf.

Chief Psychiatrist of Western Australia. (2015). Chief Psychiatrist's practice standards for the administration of electroconvulsive therapy. Retrieved from www.chiefpsychiatrist.wa.gov.au/wp-content/uploads/2015/12/CP_ECT_Standards_2015.pdf.

Chittaranjan, A.N., Shah, P., Tharyan, M.S., Reddy, M., Thirunavukarasu, R.A., Kallivayalil, R., . . . Mohandas, E. (2012). Position statement and guidelines on unmodified electroconvulsive therapy. *Indian Journal of Psychiatry, 54*(2), 119–133. doi:10.4103/0019-5545.99530.

De Brito, K. (2004). It has a brutal history. We don't know if it works. So why are we still using electric shock therapy? Australian Report, *Marie Clare Magazine*.

Dolenc, T.J., and Rasmussen, K.G. (2005). The safety of electroconvulsive therapy and lithium in combination: a case series and review of the literature. *Journal of ECT, 21*(3), 165–170.

Duffett, R., and Lelliott, P. (1998). Auditing electroconvulsive therapy. The third cycle. *British Journal of Psychiatry, 172*(5), 401–405. Retrieved from www.ncbi.nlm.nih.gov/pubmed/9747401.

Dunne, R., Kavanagh, A., and McLoughlin, D.M. (2009). Editorial: Electroconvulsve therapy, capacity and the law in Ireland. *Irish Journal of Psychological Medicine, 26*(1), 3–5. Retrieved from www.tara.tcd.ie/xmlui/bitstream/handle/2262/40657/Editorial.pdf?sequence=1andisAllowed=y.

ECRON Limited. (2016). Ectonustim Series 6+.

Editorial. (1981). ECT in britain, a shameful state of affairs. *Lancet*, 1207–1208.

Edwards, M., Koopowitz, L., and Harvey, E. (2003). A naturalistic study of the measurement of seizure adequacy in electroconvulsive therapy. *Australian and New Zealand Journal of Psychiatry, 37*(3), 312–318. Retrieved from www.ncbi.nlm.nih.gov/pubmed/12780470.

Fink, M. (1997). Prejudice against ECT: competition with psychological philosophies as a contribution to its stigma. *Convulsive Therapy, 13*(4), 253–265.

Fink, M. (2009). *Electroconvulsive Therapy: A Guide for Professionals and Their Patients*. New York: Oxford University Press.

Frederikse, M., Petrides, G., and Kellner, C. (2006). Continuation and maintenance electroconvulsive therapy for the treatment of depressive illness: a response to the National Institute for Clinical Excellence report. *Journal of ECT, 22*(1), 13–17.

Freeman, C.P., and Fergusson, M.G. (2013). The ECT suite. In Waite, J., and Eaton, W.W. (Eds.), *The ECT Handbook*, 3rd edition (pp. 8–13). London: Royal College of Psychiatrists.

Freeman, M., and Pathare, S. (2005). *WHO Resource Book on Mental Health, Human Rights and Legislation*. Geneva, Switzerland: World Health Organization (WHO).

Galvez, V., Hadzi-Pavlovic, D., Smith, D., and Loo, C.K. (2015). Predictors of seizure threshold in right unilateral ultrabrief electroconvulsive therapy: role of concomitant medications and anaesthesia used. *Brain Stimulation, 8*(3), 486–492. doi:10.1016/j.brs.2014.12.012.

Gazdag, G., Takács, R., Ungvari, G., and Sienaert, P. (2012). The practice of consenting to electroconvulsive therapy in the European Union. *Journal of ECT, 28*, 4–6.

Gelenberg, A.J., Freeman, M.P., Markowitz, J.C., Rosenbaum, J.F., Thase, M.E., Trivedi, M.H., and Van Rhoads, R.S. (2010). Practice guidelines for the treatment of patients with major depressive disorder, 3rd edition. *American Psychiatric Association*. Retrieved from www.psychiatryonline.com/pracGuide/pracGuideTopic_7.aspx.

Goodwin, G.M., Haddad, P.M., Ferrier, I.N., Aronson, J.K., Barnes, T., Cipriani, A., . . . Young, A.H. (2016). Evidence-based guidelines for treating bipolar disorder: revised third edition recommendations from the British Association for Psychopharmacology. *Journal of Psychopharmacology, 30*(6), 495–553. doi:10.1177/0269881116636545.

Grunze, H., Vieta, E., Goodwin, G.M., Bowden, C., Licht, R.W., Moller, H.J., . . . WFSBP Task Force on Treatment Guidelines for Bipolar Disorders. (2010). The World Federation of Societies of Biological Psychiatry (WFSBP) guidelines for the biological treatment of bipolar disorders: update 2010 on the treatment of acute bipolar depression. *World Journal of Biological Psychiatry, 11*(2), 81–109. doi:10.3109/15622970903555881.

Hodge, S., and Buley, N. (2015). *ECT Accreditation Service (ECTAS) Standards for the administration of ECT*, 12th edition. London: Royal College of Psychiatrists' Centre for Quality Improvement.

Husain, M.M., Rush, A.J., Fink, M, Knapp, R., Petrides, G., Rummans, T., . . . Kellner, C.H. (2004). Speed of response and remission in major depressive disorder with acute electroconvulsive therapy (ECT): a Consortium for Research in ECT (CORE) report. *Journal of Clinical Psychiatry, 65*(4), 485–491. Retrieved from www.ncbi.nlm.nih.gov/pubmed/15119910.

ISEN. (2016). Resources for patients. Retrieved from www.isen-ect.org/educational-content.

ISEN. (2017). International Society for ECT and Neurostimulation. Retrieved from www.isen-ect.org.

Jha, R., and Stein, G. (1996). Decreased efficacy of combined benzodiazepines and unilateral ECT in treatment of depression. *Acta Psychiatrica Scandinavica, 94*(2), 101–104.

Kellner, C.H., Knapp, R.G., Petrides, G., Rummans, T.A., Husain, M.M., Rasmussen, K., . . . M., F. (2006). Continuation electroconvulsive therapy vs pharmacotherapy for relapse prevention in major depression: a multisite study from the Consortium for Research in Electroconvulsive Therapy (CORE). *Archives of General Psychiatry, 63*(12), 1337–1344.

Kellner, C.H., Husain, M.M., Knapp, R.G., McCall, W.V., Petrides, G., Rudorfer, M.V., . . . Lisanby, S.H. (2016). Right unilateral ultrabrief pulse ECT in geriatric depression: phase 1 of the PRIDE study. *American Journal of Psychiatry, 173*(11), 1101–1109. doi:10.1176/appi.ajp.2016.15081101.

Kennedy, S.H., Lam, R.W., Parikh, S.V., Patten, S.B., and Ravindran, A.V. (2009). Canadian Network for Mood and Anxiety Treatments (CANMAT) clinical guidelines for the management of major depressive disorder in adults. IV. Neurostimulation therapies. *Journal of Affective Disorders, 117 Suppl 1*, S1–2. doi:10.1016/j.jad.2009.06.039.

Lalitanatpong, D. (2005). The use of electroconvulsive therapy and the length of stay of psychiatric inpatients at King Chulalongkorn Memorial Hospital, Thai Red Cross Society. *Journal of the Medical Association of Thailand, 88 Suppl 4*, S142–148.

Leiknes, K.A., Jarosh-von Schweder, L., and Høie, B. (2012). Contemporary use and practice of electroconvulsive therapy worldwide. *Brain and Behavior, 2*(3), 283–344. doi:10.1002/brb3.37.

Leong, G.B., and Eth, S. (1991). Legal and ethical issues in electroconvulsive therapy. *Psychiatric Clinics of North America, 14*(4), 1007–1020. Retrieved from www.ncbi.nlm.nih.gov/pubmed/1771147.

Little, J., Munday, J., and Atkins, M. (2005). Building an ECT service: an outcomes-equivalent approach. *Australasian Psychiatry, 13*(2), 140–147. doi:10.1111/j.1440-1665.2005.02177.x.

MacPherson, R., and Loo, C. (2008). Cognitive impairment following electroconvulsive therapy – does the choice of anaesthetic agent make a difference? *Journal of ECT, 24*(1), 52–56.

Malhi, G.S., Bassett, D., Boyce, P., Bryant, R., Fitzgerald, P.B., Fritz, K., . . . Singh, A.B. (2015). Royal Australian and New Zealand College of Psychiatrists clinical practice guidelines for mood disorders. *Australian and New Zealand Journal of Psychiatry, 49*(12), 1–185. Retrieved from www.ranzcp.org/Files/Resources/Publications/CPG/Clinician/Mood-Disorders-CPG.aspx.

Mayur, P. (2006). Ictal electro-encephalographic characteristics during electroconvulsive therapy: a review of determination and clinical relevance. *Journal of ECT, 22*(3), 213–217.

MECTA Corporation. (2015). spECTrum 5000Q – MECTA Corp. Retrieved from www.mectacorp.com/spectrum-5000Q.html.

Ministry of Health Social Services and Equity. (2014). Clinical practice guideline on the management of depression in adults. Retrieved from www.guiasalud.es/contenidos/GPC/GPC_534_Depresion_Adulto_Avaliat_compl_en.pdf.

NICE. (2003, modified 2009). *Guidance on the Use of Electroconvulsive Therapy (Vol. Guidance Number 59)*. London: National Institute for Health and Care Excellence; National Health Service.

NSW Health. (2010). ECT minimum standard of practice NSW. Retrieved from www.health.nsw.gov.au/policies/pd/2011/pdf/PD2011_003.pdf.

NZ Minister of Health. (2004). Use of electroconvulsive therapy (ECT) in New Zealand: a review of efficacy, safety, and regulatory controls (2004). Retrieved from www.supportingfamilies.org.nz/Libraries/Documents/Use_of_Electroconvulsive_Therapy_ECT_in_New_Zealand.sflb.ashx.

Petrides, G., and Fink, M. (1996). The "half-age" stimulation strategy for ECT dosing. *Convulsive Therapy, 12*(3), 138–146. Retrieved from www.ncbi.nlm.nih.gov/pubmed/8872401.

Queensland Mental Health Review Tribunal. (2000). Electroconvulsive Therapy Guideline V2.0. Retrieved from http://mhrt.qld.gov.au/wp-content/uploads/2010/04/Electroconvulsive-Therapy-Guideline-V2.0–150211.pdf.

RANZCP. (2007). Clinical memorandum #12 electroconvulsive therapy. Melbourne, Australia.

Recart, A., Rawal, S., White, P.F., Byerly, S., and Thornton, L. (2003). The effect of remifentanil on seizure duration and acute hemodynamic responses to electroconvulsive therapy. *Anesthesia & Analgesia, 96*(4), 1047–1050. Retrieved from www.ncbi.nlm.nih.gov/pubmed/12651657.

Roberson, M., Rey, J.M., and Walter, G. (2013). Ethical and consent aspects. In Ghaziuddin, N. and Walter, G. (Eds.),

Electroconvulsive Therapy in Children and Adolescents (pp. 56–71). New York: Oxford University Press.

Rose, D.S., Fleischmann. P, and Wykes, T.H. (2009). Consumers' views of electroconvulsive therapy: a qualitative analysis. *Journal of Mental Health, 13*(3), 285–293. doi: 10.1080/09638230410001700916.

Royal College of Psychiatrists. (2015). *ECT Accreditation Service (ECTAS): Standards for the Administration of ECT,* 12th edition. London: Royal College of Psychiatrists.

SA Health. (2014). South Australian guidelines for electro-convulsive therapy. Retrieved from www.sahealth.sa.gov.au/wps/wcm/connect/0608270046ad5b01b89.

Sackeim, H.A., Prudic, J., Devanand, D.P., Kiersky, J.E., Fitzsimons, L., Moody, B.J., . . . Settembrino, J.M. (1993). Effects of stimulus intensity and electrode placement on the efficacy and cognitive effects of electroconvulsive therapy. *New England Journal of Medicine, 328*(12), 839–846. doi:10.1056/NEJM199303253281204.

Sackeim, H.A., Prudic, J., Fuller, R., Keilp, J., Lavori, P.W., and Olfson, M. (2007). The cognitive effects of electroconvulsive therapy in community settings. *Neuropsychopharmacology, 32*(1), 244–254. doi:10.1038/sj.npp.1301180.

Sandin, R.H., Enlund, G., Samuelsson, P., and Lennmarken, C. (2000). Awareness during anaesthesia: a prospective case study. *Lancet, 355*(9205), 707–711. doi:10.1016/S0140-6736(99)11010-9.

Sartorius, A., Wolf, J., and Henn, F.A. (2005). Lithium and ECT – concurrent use still demands attention: three case reports. *World Journal of Bioloigical Psychiatry, 6*, 121–124.

SEAN. (2015). Scottish ECT Audit Network. Retrieved from www.sean.org.uk/.

SEN. (2017). RANZCP: Section for ECT and Neuro-stimulation. Retrieved from www.ranzcp.org/Membership/Faculties-sections/Electroconvulsive-Therapy-and-Neurostimulation.aspx.

Sienaert, P., and Peuskens, J. (2007). Anticonvulsants during electroconvulsive therapy: review and recommendations. *Journal of ECT, 23*(2), 120–123. doi:10.1097/YCT.0b013e3180330059.

Somatics, L.L.C. (1989). Thymapad. Retrieved from www.thymatron.com/catalog_accessory.asp?C=6andI=3.

Suehs, B., Bendele, S.D., Crismon, M.L., Madhukar, H., Trivedi, M.H., and Kurian, B. (2008). Texas medication algorithm project: procedural manual major depressive disorder algorithms. Retrieved from www.jpshealthnet.org/sites/default/files/tmap_depression_2010.pdf.

The Minister of Health. (2004). Use of electroconvulsive therapy (ECT) in New Zealand: a review of efficacy, safety, and regulatory controls. Auckland, New Zealand.

Tiller, J.W.G., and Lyndon, R.W. (2003). *Electroconvulsive Therapy: An Australian Guide.* Melbourne, Australia: Australian Post Graduate Medicine.

Tirthalli, J., Harish, T., and Gangadhar, B.N. (2011). A prospective comparative study of interaction between lithium and modified electroconvulsive therapy. *World Journal of Bioloigical Psychiatry, 12*, 149–155.

Tor, P.C., Bautovich, A., Wang, M.J., Martin, D., Harvey, S.B., and Loo, C. (2015). A systematic review and meta-analysis of brief versus ultrabrief right unilateral electroconvulsive therapy for depression. *Journal of Clinical Psychiatry, 10*(4088). doi:10.4088/JCP.14r09145.

Torpey, N. (2016). Special Investigation: Shock Treatment: Alarming Spike in Risky Electroconvulsive Therapy on Children *Sunday Mail (Brisbane, Australia`).*

Trivedi, M.H. (2009). Tools and strategies for ongoing assessment of depression: a measurement-based approach to remission. *Journal of Clinical Psychiatry, 70 Suppl 6*(suppl 6), 26–31. doi:10.4088/JCP.8133su1c.04.

UK ECT Review Group. (2003). Efficacy and safety of electroconvulsive therapy in depressive disorders: a systematic review and meta-analysis. *Lancet, 361*, 799–808.

Victorian Government. (2014a). Mental Health Act 2014 handbook. Retrieved from www.health.vic.gov.au/mentalhealth/mhact2014/.

Victorian Government. (2014b). Victoria's Mental Health Act 2014 (the Act). Retrieved from www.health.vic.gov.au/mentalhealth/mhactreform/.

Vishne, T., Aronov, S., Amiaz, R., Etchin, A., and Grunhaus, L. (2005). Remifentanil supplementation of propofol during electroconvulsive therapy: effect on seizure duration and cardiovascular stability. *Journal of ECT, 21*(3), 235–238.

Waite, J., Barnes, R.D., Bennett, D.M., Lyons, D., McLoughlin, D.M., and Series, H. (2013). Consent, capacity and the law. In Waite, J., and Easton, A. (Eds.), *The ECT Handbook,* 3rd edition. London: Royal College of Psychiatrists.

Waite, J., and Easton, A. (2013). *The ECT Handbook,* 3rd edition. London: Royal College of Psychiatrists.

Winslade, W.J., Liston, E.H., Ross, J.W., and Weber, K.D. (1984). Medical, judicial, and statutory regulation of ECT in the United States. *American Journal of Psychiatry, 141*(11), 1349–1355. doi:10.1176/ajp.141.11.1349.

Yuzda, E., Parker, K., Parker, V., Geagea, J., and Goldbloom, D. (2002). Electroconvulsive therapy training in Canada: a call for greater regulation. *Canadian Journal of Psychiatry, 47*(10), 938–944.

Zarate, C.A., Jr, Tohen, M., and Baraibar, G. (1997). Combined valproate or carbamazepine and electroconvulsive therapy. *Annals of Clinical Psychiatry, 9*(1), 19–25. Retrieved from www.ncbi.nlm.nih.gov/pubmed/9167833.

CHAPTER 4

Clinical skills

The sequence of ECT

REFERRAL

The sequence of ECT commences in most services after a medical officer (hospital inpatient team, community team or a private psychiatrist) completes an ECT referral and forwards it to the ECT coordinator. The ECT coordinator then organises a pre-anaesthetic consultation with the anaesthetist prior to the commencement of ECT. This consultation may occur a few days before ECT commences or immediately before treatment is given. If the anaesthetist is concerned about the patient's physical condition treatment will be delayed until they have been assessed and treated by the relevant medical specialist.

If patients are unable to consent for treatment, the options available to the medical officer will depend upon legislation that governs ECT in their region (discussed elsewhere). In many jurisdictions the officer must apply to the relevant mental health tribunal for a hearing to make a determination that ECT is reasonable and proper treatment, necessary and desirable for the safety or welfare of the patient (NSW Health, 2010; SA Health, 2014; Victorian Government, 2014). In other countries, like the United Kingdom, the treating team must appoint a second opinion-appointed doctor (SOAD), who may authorise a course of ECT on behalf of the Care Quality Commission, if it is appropriate for the treatment to be given taking into account the nature and degree of the mental disorder and an only relevant circumstances (Waite et al., 2013).

This process can occur concurrently with the referral to the ECT coordinator, alerting them to place the patient on the ECT list as soon as the order has been ratified.

EMERGENCY ECT

Emergency ECT is defined as treatment that is given urgently to save life or prevent serious deterioration in the patient's condition. The treating doctor must follow the legislative provisions that govern ECT in their region. In the United Kingdom, treatment can proceed in this situation as long as the treatment does not have unfavourable physical or psychological consequences that cannot be reversed (Waite et al., 2013), whereas legislation in the USA is very complicated and state-dependent (Winslade, Liston, Ross and Weber, 1984). Since 2014, most states and territories within Australia require the treating doctor to apply for an urgent hearing with the relevant mental health tribunal before proceeding with ECT.

THE ECT JOURNEY

After the patient has been referred they will be allocated the next available place on the ECT list. In some centres the first treatment is called the "titration session", where the seizure threshold and stimulus dose are determined (Galvez, Hadzi-Pavlovic, Smith and Loo, 2015), whereas others services will estimate the dose required and commence treatment (Petrides and Fink, 1996). Practice-based experience supports the benefits of empirical titration to accurately determine seizure threshold minimising unwanted side effects.

Recovery can be a complicated process. It is not uncommon for patients to experience a postictal delirium as they wake up. When severe the delirium can be challenging and difficult to manage. It is common for a patient to go through this experience each time they wake from the anaesthetic. Careful monitoring is required with prophylactic medication, like midazolam, administered after the treatment before they are transferred to the recovery area. Cognitive testing during the recovery period is important owing to evidence that a delayed time to recovery predicts retrograde memory loss (autobiographical) during a course of treatment (Martin et al., 2013; Porter, Douglas and Knight, 2008). After the patient has regained consciousness they are often given a drink and a light meal before returning to the ward or home. In some regions there is a legal requirement that a responsible adult accompany ambulatory patients for 24 hours after the treatment, with a further provision that they do not drive during this period.

In most centres within the USA, Australia and New Zealand ECT is administered three times a week, whereas in the United Kingdom, Ireland and several other European countries it is given twice a week. There is evidence that ECT can be as effective if given twice a week (Lerer et al., 1995; McAllister, Perri, Jordan, Rauscher and Sattin, 1987; Shapira et al., 1998). One advantage of twice-weekly ECT is that it is associated with less cognitive impairment and useful for elderly patients. However, it does result in an increased length of stay (Lerer et al., 1995).

The referring doctor must review a patient regularly during a course of ECT to evaluate clinical improvement and identify any side effects experienced by the patient. These findings should be clearly documented in the patient's medical record. Any complications identified should be brought to the attention of the ECT coordinator, who can raise these issues with the anaesthetist and the ECT practitioner at the next treatment.

It is important to alleviate side effects or complications experienced by the patient after each treatment to make their journey during ECT more comfortable, administrating appropriate intervention immediately prior to, during or after the treatment has been administered. If cognitive impairment is detected or there are other physical difficulties encountered in the treatment, particularly for the elderly, the frequency of ECT can be reduced without reducing the efficacy of treatment (Lerer et al., 1995; NSW Health, 2010).

The frequency of evaluation will depend upon the clinical situation. It is recommended for an index course of treatment that this clinical assessment should occur at least twice per week and monthly for maintenance treatment (NSW Health, 2010; SA Health, 2014).

MEASUREMENT DURING ECT

All units delivering ECT should determine appropriate measures that can be administered before ECT commences, after the sixth treatment and the end of treatment. Objective measures assist evaluation by identifying clinical improvement as well as cognitive changes that arise during ECT allowing treatment to be changed. If there is no clinical response the clinician can alter the stimulus dose or electrode placement or reduce the frequency in the event of cognitive impairment. Continuation and maintenance patients also require frequent assessment and monitoring.

There is no argument that ECT is a very effective treatment that can be associated with cognitive impairment. What is debated are the exact magnitude and extend of the deficits (Loo 2008). Finding the right evaluation tools can be challenging. Assessment of clinical improvement is more straightforward with a range of validated questionnaires that can be utilised; however, some are associated with a per patient cost to administer (Hamilton, 1960). In clinical practice, open access tools are necessary so that they become part of the daily routine, allowing data to be utilised for clinical and audit purposes.

Finding the correct tool that can be utilised to assess cognitive impairment can be more challenging owing to the enormous complexities and individual variations that occur across the spectrum of memory and cognition (Fraser, O'Carroll and Ebmeier, 2008; Gardner and O'Connor, 2008; Ingram, Saling and Schweitzer, 2008). Little objective evidence supports the benefits of many approaches (Rasmussen, 2016).

Evaluation tools that have been recommended include:

- Montreal Cognitive Assessment (MoCA) (Nasreddine et al., 2005);

- Clinical Global Impression Scale (CGI-S) (Busner and Targum, 2007);
- Audio Recorded Cognitive Screen (ARCS) (Schofield, 2012);
- Montgomery and Asberg Depression Rating Scale (MADRS) (Montgomery and Asberg, 1979);
- Brief Psychiatric Rating Scale (BPRS) (Overall and Gorham, 1962);
- Young Mania Rating Scale (YMRS) (Young, Biggs, Ziegler and Meyer, 1978);
- Autobiographical Memory Interview – Short Form, Version 3 (McElhiney, Moody and Sackeim 2001);
- Brief ECT Cognitive Screen (BECS) (Martin et al., 2013).

Incorporating psychometric assessment into routine clinical practice has the potential to improve the quality and safety of ECT delivered within a service by providing objective evidence that a patient is improving as well as early identification of any cognitive impairment so that alterations can be made to treatment parameters and schedule (Rasmussen, 2016). The relevant local district administration and ECT committee should authorise evaluation tools before implementation.

MEMORY

As noted earlier, one of the most challenging areas is the impact that ECT has on cognition. Assessment of memory is complex owing to the patchy and inconsistent losses and the absence of a "gold standard" test to aid clinical reviews (Rasmussen, 2016). Asking the patient "how is your memory?" and talking with the patient's family or carers after they return from leave can be useful but the benefits are limited.

It has been proposed that regular assessment of cognitive function is important, at least weekly using objective and self-report tests, to detect unwanted side effects, guiding treatment parameters and selection of the optimal inter-ECT interval (Porter, Heenan and Reeves, 2008; Rasmussen,

2016). Unfortunately, there are no known tools that have been developed that enable a patient to identify and manage the memory changes that occur during a course of ECT.

In the 1990s, based upon the premise that memory was an active and dynamic process, a group of nurses in Western Australia encouraged patients to keep a diary while they underwent a course of ECT to manage any memory problems that arose. The initiative came from a local brain injury unit, which was retraining memory in patients with acquired brain injuries.

The author adapted the concept and developed the ECT Memory Control Diary. The utility of the diary has not been tested formally. Anecdotal evidence, based upon the opinion of many clinicians involved in the care and management of patients referred for ECT, indicated that the diary provided patients with a simple tool, completed on a daily basis, that helped them overcome the embarrassment and frustration that can result from memory impairment secondary to ECT.

A proof of concept study is currently being conducted to determine the validity of the diary in patients having ECT. The aim is to determine whether the diary provides subjective benefits to patients who use it compared to normal controls. Patients having ECT usually experience depression and apathy, and since the memory diary is undertaken without clinician supervision, it is possible that patients do not give their full effort and the results might therefore not truly reflect their current cognitive capacity. Nursing staff allocated to a patient having ECT on each shift will remind the patients using the diary to refresh their memory of the previous days events by reading entries made and completing new entries at the beginning and end of each day. The diary jogs patient's memories of events that occurred previously and a current record.

Anecdotal evidence suggests that the ECT Memory Control Diary may have utility when used in a group setting. The strength of a group is that it can provide patients with support and encouragement to complete the diary, raising general aware-ness about the dynamic aspects of memory and how ECT can affect it. Group members are able to discuss their use of the diary, identifying any memory difficulties that they may be experiencing gaining encouragement and support to continue with ECT.

AUDIT

Implementation of psychometric and cognitive assessment is the first step in achieving a more comprehensive audit to ensure best practice of ECT within a local health district. Scotland has pioneered service audits over many years with the development of the Scottish ECT Accreditation Network (SEAN, 2015). This body has taken a central role in ensuring that clinical audit and monitoring is undertaken at all ECT sites within Scotland. Their website has a comprehensive reference list of guidelines, audits tools and rating scales that have been developed or applied throughout the world.

A process of implementation is essential once an ECT service audit has been completed. The United Kingdom ran three audits of ECT practice in 1991, 1992 and 1996 (Duffett and Lelliott, 1998). After each audit, new guidelines were written and training in ECT was offered by the Royal College of Psychiatrists.

The 1996 audit highlighted that previous attempts to change clinical practice had failed, with only 33% of clinics meeting the guideline standards and 41% using outdated equipment. The responsible consultant attended their weekly ECT treatment session in only 16% of cases and only one third had clear policies to guide and train junior doctors to administer ECT effectively. The audit concluded that only 33% of clinics were regarded as good.

These findings failed to have any significant impact on how ECT was administered within the country, contributing to the restrictive recommendations made by the National Institute for Health and Clinical Excellence (NICE, 2003). Based upon two meta-analyses one completed by clinicians

(UK ECT Review Group, 2003) and the other by consumers (Rose, Fleischmann, Wykes, Leese and Bindman, 2003), NICE concluded that ECT should only be used to achieve rapid and short-term improvement of severe symptoms after adequate trials of other treatment options were ineffective or when the condition was potentially life-threatening.

The NICE ECT guidance document was controversial and met with significant resistance from clinicians in the United Kingdom and elsewhere in the world owing to the restrictive nature of the recommendations concerning ECT and failure to comply with usual clinical practice (McCall, Dunn and Rosenquist, 2004).

The recommendations were at odds with *The ECT Handbook*, 2nd edition (Scott, 2005), which that was also released around the same time. This discrepancy has now been resolved following revisions of both the NICE guidance (2003, modified 2009) and *The ECT Handbook*, 3rd edition (Waite and Easton, 2013).

In response to the criticism, the Royal College of Psychiatrists followed Scotland's lead and released the twelfth edition of the ECT Accreditation Service (Hodge and Buley, 2015). The document is comprehensive and covers nine topics:

- the ECT clinic and facilities
- staff and training
- assessment and preparation
- consent
- anaesthetic practice
- the administration of ECT
- recovery, monitoring and follow-up
- special precautions
- protocols.

For each topic there is a detailed list of standards that a service must meet based upon three criteria:

- Type 1: failure to meet these standards would result in a significant threat to patient safety or dignity and/or would breach the law.
- Type 2: standards that an accredited clinic would be expected to meet.

- Type 3: standards that an excellent clinic should meet.

The tool recommends a three-year audit cycle including seven random case reviews each year and an internal annual audit of the ECT service by staff and hospital management, followed by a comprehensive review (checklist based) by externally appointed auditors at the end of the three-year period. Since the implementation of these audits there has been a substantial improvement in the standards of ECT services within the United Kingdom (Freeman, Cresswell, Fergusson and Cullen, 2013).

It is recommended that the ECT committee within the local region develop an audit process based upon these tools that suits the needs of the district. High-volume users will need to comply with more stringent standards (Types 2 and 3 criteria) compared to low-volume, occasional users, which would need to meet the minimum standards (Type 1 criteria).

ECT TAPERING/STEP-DOWN

ECT has undergone major innovations and changes over the last 80 years. These changes have been not only in the technical areas of stimulus dose titration and EEG monitoring but also in the area of clinical application. In the past, ECT was approached as a static treatment, "one size fits all". Most modern ECT practitioners manage ECT as a "dynamic" treatment that can be individualised to ensure remission while minimising complications. There are many components that can be changed and varied to suit the needs of an individual patient to ensure a good outcome.

It is no longer acceptable practice to prescribe "six treatments of ECT using bilateral electrode placement aiming for a motor fit greater than 25 seconds". This static view of ECT was very entrenched for many years and continues to be incorporated in legislation worldwide. It is now recommended that the treating team prescribe "a course of ECT ranging from 6 to 12 treatments".

The course has a number of variables that can be altered: the stimulus, the number of treatments, electrode placement, whether the treatment is administered twice or three times a week, over a three- or four-weekly period, as an inpatient or outpatient. Factors that determine the frequency and course of treatment include clinical response, complications and side effects, particularly cognitive impairment.

ECT tapering can be defined as stepping down the frequency of ECT treatments towards the end of the treatment course once remission has been achieved to prevent relapse during the period of disengagement or discharge from hospital until a good outcome has been achieved with medication (Sackeim et al., 1994) and psychosocial intervention. The exact number and frequency of treatments will be determined on an individual basis and may range from twice a week to weekly for one month, a protocol used in phase two of the PRIDE study (Kellner et al., 2016).

ECT RECORD

A suitable recording system needs to be developed by the ECT committee to record each ECT treatment in a manner that provides easy retrieval. It is recommended that high-volume units consider installing a computer-based system (NSW Health, 2010).

An ECT medical record should include:

- informed consent documents;
- legal documentation for involuntary patients;
- results of a comprehensive physical examination and investigations completed by the treating team, anaesthetist and/or other physician;
- type of ECT administered including: pulse width, energy administered, and the quality of the EEG;
- adverse reactions that occur before, during or after treatment;
- results from clinical and cognitive testing used to assess efficacy and memory;
- number of treatments;
- the reason why ECT was ceased.

REFERENCES

Busner, J., and Targum, S.D. (2007). The clinical global impressions scale: applying a research tool in clinical practice. *Psychiatry (Edgmont)*, 4(7), 28–37.

Duffett, R., and Lelliott, P. (1998). Auditing electroconvulsive therapy. The third cycle. *British Journal of Psychiatry*, 172(5), 401–405. Retrieved from www.ncbi.nlm.nih.gov/pubmed/9747401.

Fraser, L.M., O'Carroll, R.E., and Ebmeier, K.P. (2008). The effect of electroconvulsive therapy on autobiographical memory: a systematic review. *Journal of ECT*, 24(1), 10–17.

Freeman, C.P., Cresswell, J., Fergusson, G.M., and Cullen, L. (2013). Inspection of ECT clinics. In Waite, J., and Eaton, W.W. (Eds.), *The ECT Handbook*, 3rd edition (pp. 109–112). London: Royal College of Psychiatrists.

Galvez, V., Hadzi-Pavlovic, D., Smith, D., and Loo, C.K. (2015). Predictors of seizure threshold in right unilateral ultrabrief electroconvulsive therapy: role of concomitant medications and anaesthesia used. *Brain Stimulation* 8(3), 486–492. doi:10.1016/j.brs.2014.12.012.

Gardner, B.K., and O'Connor, D.W. (2008). A review of the cognitive effects of electroconvulsive therapy in older adults. *Journal of ECT*, 24(1), 68–80.

Hamilton, M. (1960). A rating scale for depression. *Journal of Neurology, Neurosurgery, and Psychiatry*, 23, 56–62. Retrieved from www.ncbi.nlm.nih.gov/pubmed/14399272.

Hodge, S., and Buley, N. (2015). *ECT Accreditation Service (ECTAS) Standards for the administration of ECT*, 12th edition. London: Royal College of Psychiatrists' Centre for Quality Improvement.

Ingram, A., Saling, M.M., and Schweitzer, I. (2008). Cognitive side effects of brief pulse ECT: a review. *Journal of ECT*, 24(1), 3–9.

Kellner, C.H., Husain, M.M., Knapp, R.G., McCall, W.V., Petrides, G., Rudorfer, M.V., . . . Lisanby, S.H. (2016). A novel strategy for continuation ECT in geriatric depression: phase 2 of the PRIDE study. *American Journal of Psychiatry*, 173(11), 1110–1118. doi:10.1176/appi.ajp.2016.16010118.

Lerer, B., Shapira, B., Calev, A., Tubi, N., Drexler, H., Kindler, S., . . . Schwartz, J.E. (1995). Antidepressant and cognitive effects of twice- versus three-times-weekly ECT. *American Journal of Psychiatry*, 152(4), 564–575.

Loo, C. (2008). Cognitive outcomes in electroconvulsive therapy: optimizing current clinical practice and researching future strategies. *Journal of ECT*, 24(1), 1–2.

McAllister, D.A., Perri, M.G., Jordan, R.C., Rauscher, F.P., and Sattin, A. (1987). Effects of ECT given two vs. three times weekly. *Psychiatry Research*, 21(1), 63–69. Retrieved from www.ncbi.nlm.nih.gov/pubmed/3602221.

McCall, W.V., Dunn, A., and Rosenquist, P.B. (2004). Quality of life and function after electroconvulsive therapy. *British Journal of Psychiatry, 185*(5), 405–409. doi:10.1192/bjp.185.5.405.

McElhiney, M.C., Moody, B.J., and Sackeim, H.A. (2001). *Manual for Administration and Scoring the Columbia University Autobiographical Memory Interview – Short Form, Version 3.* New York: Psychiatric Institute.

Martin, D.M., Katalinic, N., Ingram, A., Schweitzer, I., Smith, D.J., Hadzi-Pavlovic, D., and Loo, C.K. (2013). A new early cognitive screening measure to detect cognitive side-effects of electroconvulsive therapy? *Journal of Psychiatric Research, 47*(12), 1967–1974. doi:10.1016/j.jpsychires.2013.08.021.

Montgomery, S.A., and Asberg, M. (1979). A new depression scale designed to be sensitive to change. *British Journal of Psychiatry, 134*(4), 382–389. doi:10.1192/bjp.134.4.382.

Nasreddine, Z.S., Phillips, N.A., Bedirian, V., Charbonneau, S., Whitehead, V., Collin, I., . . . Chertkow, H. (2005). The Montreal Cognitive Assessment, MoCA: a brief screening tool for mild cognitive impairment. *Journal of the American Geriatrics Society, 53*(4), 695–699. doi:10.1111/j.1532-5415.2005.53221.x.

NICE. (2003, modified 2009). *Guidance on the Use of Electroconvulsive Therapy (Vol. Guidance Number 59).* London: National Institute for Health and Care Excellence; National Health Service.

NSW Health. (2010). ECT minimum standard of practice NSW. Retrieved from www.health.nsw.gov.au/policies/pd/2011/pdf/PD2011_003.pdf.

Overall, J.E., and Gorham, D.R. (1962). The brief psychiatric rating scale. *Psychological Reports, 10*, 799–812. doi:10.2466/pr0.1962.10.3.799.

Petrides, G., and Fink, M. (1996). The "half-age" stimulation strategy for ECT dosing. *Convulsive Therapy, 12*(3), 138–146. Retrieved from www.ncbi.nlm.nih.gov/pubmed/8872401.

Porter, R., Heenan, H., and Reeves, J. (2008). Early effects of electroconvulsive therapy on cognitive function. *Journal of ECT, 24*(1), 35–39. doi:10.1097/YCT.0b013e31816207f0.

Porter, R.J., Douglas, K., and Knight, R.G. (2008). Monitoring of cognitive effects during a course of electroconvulsive therapy: recommendations for clinical practice. *Journal of ECT, 24*(1), 25–34. doi:10.1097/YCT.0b013e31815d9627.

Rasmussen, K.G. (2016). What type of cognitive testing should be part of routine electroconvulsive therapy practice? *Journal of ECT, 32*(1), 7–12. doi:10.1097/yct.0000000000000257.

Rose, D.S., Fleischmann. P, Wykes. T, Leese. M, and Bindman. J. (2003). Patients' perspectives on electroconvulsive therapy: systematic review. *British Medical Journal, 326*(7403), 1363. Retrieved from www.bmj.com/content/326/7403/1363.abstract.

SA Health. (2014). South Australian guidelines for electroconvulsive therapy. Retrieved from www.sahealth.sa.gov.au/wps/wcm/connect/0608270046ad5b01b89.

Sackeim, H.A., Long, J., Luber, B., Moeller, J.R., Prohovnik, I., Devanand, D.P., and Nobler, M.S. (1994). Physical properties and quantification of the ECT stimulus: 1 basic principles. *Convulsive Therapy, 10*, 93–123.

Schofield, P.W. (2012). Audio Recorded Cognitive Screen (ARCS). Retrieved from www.cognitionhealth.com/.

Scott, A.I.F. (2005). *The ECT Handbook,* 2nd edition. London: Royal College of Psychiatrists.

SEAN. (2015). Scottish ECT Audit Network. Retrieved from www.sean.org.uk/.

Shapira, B., Tubi, N., Drexler, H., Lidsky, D., Calev, A., and Lerer, B. (1998). Cost and benefit in the choice of ECT schedule. Twice versus three times weekly ECT. *British Journal of Psychiatry, Jan*(172), 44–48.

UK ECT Review Group. (2003). Efficacy and safety of electroconvulsive therapy in depressive disorders: a systematic review and meta-analysis. *Lancet, 361*, 799–808.

Victorian Government. (2014). Mental Health Act 2014 handbook. Retrieved from www.health.vic.gov.au/mentalhealth/mhact2014/.

Waite, J., Barnes, R.D., Bennett, D.M., Lyons, D., McLoughlin, D.M., and Series, H. (2013). Consent, capacity and the law. In Waite, J., and Easton, A. (Eds.), *The ECT handbook,* 3rd edition. London: Royal College of Psychiatrists.

Waite, J., and Easton, A. (2013). *The ECT Handbook,* 3rd edition. London: Royal College of Psychiatrists.

Winslade, W.J., Liston, E.H., Ross, J.W., and Weber, K.D. (1984). Medical, judicial, and statutory regulation of ECT in the United States. *American Journal of Psychiatry, 141*(11), 1349–1355. doi:10.1176/ajp.141.11.1349.

Young, R.C., Biggs, J.T., Ziegler, V.E., and Meyer, D.A. (1978). A rating scale for mania: reliability, validity and sensitivity. *British Journal of Psychiatry, 133*(5), 429–435. doi:10.1192/bjp.133.5.429.

Adverse events of ECT

ECT adverse events can be divided into complications that occur during the treatment, immediately post-treatment or after the course has been completed.

ADVERSE EVENTS DURING ECT

Adverse events can occur during ECT treatment from either the seizure or anaesthetic agents administered.

Cardiovascular events

It is known that there is a profound physiological effect on the body after the stimulus has been delivered in ECT (Abrams, 2002). Immediately after stimulation there is a marked parasympathetic vagal outflow that can induce bradycardia, hypotension and an electrocardiac pause. It is followed by an intense sympathetic surge during the seizure that results in tachycardia, hypertension and increased myocardial oxygen consumption. Once the seizure has terminated there a rapid drop in heart rate and blood pressure (Abrams, 2002). Careful monitoring by the anaesthetist is required to ensure cardio-respiratory stability during this period. It is not uncommon for the anaesthetist to use anticho-linergic agents like glycopyrrolate or atropine or a beta blocker like labetalol or esmolol pre-ECT to minimise this response.

It is known that patients with pre-existing hyper-tension have a more pronounced blood pressure (BP) elevation than those who are normotensive and can be adversely affected by the physiological response of ECT (Prudic et al., 1987).

A patient with known cardiovascular disease can be given ECT safely if they take their usual medication before treatment and are carefully monitored through observation of pulse, BP and oximetry once the treatment has commenced (Zielinski, Roose, Devanand, Woodring and Sackeim, 1993). See Section 4.3 for further discussion of this topic.

Asystole / electrocardiac pause

The absence of heart rate for a period of time is known as asystole or electrocardiac pause. It is a well-known acute cardiac event occurring during ECT that is a direct consequence of the electrical stimulation used to initiate the seizure. The stimulus triggers a profound period of bradycardia due to the unopposed stimulation from the parasym-pathetic nervous system, causing an electrocardiac pause recorded on the ECG (Coughlin et al., 2012) illustrated in EEG 4.2.1. Cardiovascular changes including bradycardia and asystole are particularly common when subconvulsive stimuli are admin-istered but have little clinical significance (McCall, Reid and Ford, 1994). In a study of 38 geriatric patients, 65.8% experienced cardiac pause at some time during the course of ECT, with 40.1% lasting for greater than five seconds, which was associated with a younger age, higher dose of suxamethonium and absence of cardiac rhythm disturbances pre-ECT (Burd and Kettl, 1998). In another report,

involving 50 patients, asystole of greater than two seconds was observed in 48.7% of treatments administered with a return to normal function without incident (Hase et al., 2005).

Concern has been raised that using ultrabrief ECT may result in a more profound period of parasympathetic surge resulting in longer and more troublesome electrocardiac pauses owing to maximal stimulus dose being delivered over an eight-second period compared to four seconds with standard pulse width (Coughlin et al., 2012). In a retrospective analysis of 58 patients undergoing ECT with right unilateral electrode placement, it was shown that pulse width was not associated with any clinically significant electrocardiac pause at maximal stimulus dose (Coughlin et al., 2012). The only significant finding of the study was a statistical significant difference in electrocardiac pause between pulse stimuli of two-second and four-second duration but this was not clinically significant (Coughlin et al., 2012).

Stewart, Loo, MacPherson, and Hadzi-Pavlovic (2011) investigated the incidence of bradycardia, any slowing of heart rate and asystole, an absence of heart rate greater than five seconds, using different forms of ECT in 476 ECT treatments in 114 patients. Bradycardia and asystole were relatively common side effects during the ECT stimulus in all forms of ECT. Bifrontal ECT was associated with less severe bradycardia and asystole than bitemporal or right unilateral (RUL) ECT. Ultrabrief pulse width stimulation resulted in less bradycardia and asystole than standard pulse-width stimulation for RUL ECT (Stewart et al., 2011).

These findings suggest that bradycardia and asystole alone do not necessitate suspension of further ECT treatment, as they are relatively common transient phenomena that carry little clinical risk. An electrocardiac pause that lasts longer than 10 seconds has been defined as the cut off point differentiating inconsequential with a clinically significant pause (Tang and Ungvari, 2001).

Risks associated with electrocardiac pause include:

- use of a beta blocker to control hypertension;
- subconvulsive stimuli used during a stimulus dose titration session to determine seizure threshold;
- bilateral electrode placement due to greater cholinergic surge;
- use of thiopentone as an induction agent and high doses of suxamethonium (Tang and Ungvari, 2001).

In this setting, the anaesthetist should consider pre-medication with an intravenous anticholinergic agent like atropine or glycopyrrolate, reduce the dose of thiopentone by augmenting with an ultra-

brief narcotic agent and avoid excessive doses of suxamethonium. The psychiatrist should consider administering bifrontal rather than a bitemporal or RUL ECT when a patient is at risk of arrhythmias and prolonged asystole during ECT (Stewart et al., 2011). The benefits of switching from bitemporal to bifrontal electrode placement is illustrated in EEG 4.2.2. Such a decision needs to be balanced with the potential for greater cognitive impairment and consideration given to administering RUL ultrabrief rather than standard pulse-width ECT as it also has a lower incidence of acute cardiac effects (Stewart et al., 2011).

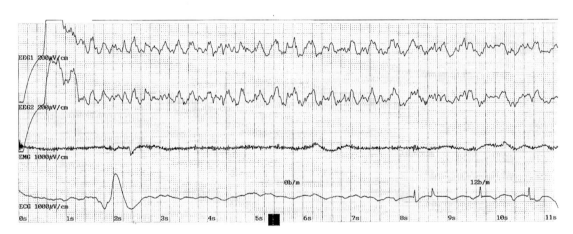

EEG 4.2.1 *Electrocardiac pause: illustrated in channel 4 at the bottom of the trace*

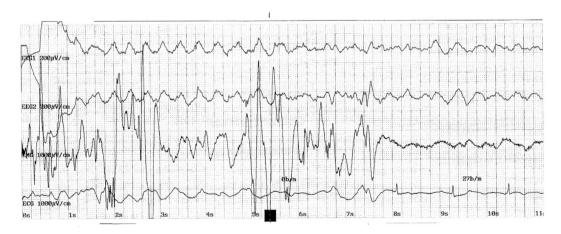

EEG 4.2.2 *Reduced electrocardiac pause: illustrated in channel 4 at the bottom of the trace*

CLINICAL WISDOM 4.2.1

EEG 4.2.1 is an example of a clinically significant electrocardiac pause with duration of eight seconds that was closely monitored by the anaesthetist but did not stop treatment continuing. Bitemporal electrode placement was initiated in this patient owing to the severity of her symptoms. She was treated with a combination of thiopentone and remifentanil as the induction agents, with sufficient suxamethonium to induce complete paralysis. The patient also developed troublesome cognitive impairment and the decision was made to change to bifrontal ECT after Treatment 7. Bifrontal ECT maintained clinical improvement, reduced the severity of cognitive impairment with a significant reduction in the length of the electrocardiac pause on subsequent treatments as shown in EEG 4.2.2. The patient gained remission.

Oral and dental trauma

Trauma to the tongue and oral cavity are the most common complications associated with ECT (Watts, Groft, Bagian and Mills, 2011), with injury to the teeth another established risk (Beli and Bentham, 1998). These complications arise directly from the vigorous clenching of the jaw following direct stimulation of the muscles of mastication, particularly the masseter, temporalis and pterygoid, that is only partially modified by the muscle relaxant suxamethonium. It has been estimated that the jaw muscles are stimulated to 60–70% of their maximal contractive force as the stimulus is delivered (Martin, 2013).

Poor oral hygiene is common in patients with psychiatric illness (Stevens et al., 2010). It has been estimated that tongue and lip trauma occur in 20% of cases and damage to teeth and other hard tissues occur in 1–2% of patients receiving ECT (Beli and Bentham, 1998). Patients with poor oral hygiene may have badly maintained teeth that have the potential for fracture and serious risk of aspiration.

Routine check of the oral cavity is important before ECT commences. If teeth are chipped or loose, the patient may need to be referred to a dentist.

Martin (2013) highlights that there has been recent technological advances in dentistry with dental implants and modern ceramics, allowing the development of complex restorations with excellent aesthetics, replacing the need for dentures. These innovations have occurred in the setting of increased awareness of patients' rights and their capacity to seek compensation in the setting of serious injury.

Malpractice with ECT has a low liability as it is a very safe and effective treatment that usually results in a functional and much improved patent who is able to go home to a relieved family (Slawson, 1989). In a review of claims made against the American Psychiatric Association professional liability insurance programme between 1972 and 1983, 17 were related to electroconvulsive therapy, with nine settling in favour of the psychiatrist and one being determined by a jury. Patients won the other seven cases.

Malpractice suites create a hostile climate that destroys the trust on which effective treatment of all patients must be based. The author concluded that malpractice losses were not a significant factor in ECT and had minimal impact on clinical practice (Slawson, 1985).

It is important for the anaesthetist to correctly insert a soft mouthguard prior to the stimulus and manually support the chin during the administration of the stimuli to minimise trauma. If an ET tube or laryngeal mask is used it is important to stop the front teeth taking the force of the muscle contraction during the stimulus. Either a disposable bite block halved or rolled green gauze can be inserted on each side of the mouth, facilitating the bite force to be absorbed through the back molar teeth rather than the easier-to-damage front teeth.

Psychiatrists as well as anaesthetists need to be aware of potential oral and dental complications and minimise the risk by developing a risk management strategy that involves careful assessment, identification and prospective management (Beli and Bentham, 1998; Morris, Roche, Bentham and Wright, 2002).

Fractures

In the past, fractures of thoracic vertebrae and dislocation of the jaw were relatively common events when ECT was delivered in an unmodified fashion. The advent of modern anaesthetic agents and routine use of muscle relaxants make these complications extremely rare.

Unmodified ECT continues to be used in a number of countries around the world (Chanpattana, Kunigiri, Kramer and Gangadhar, 2005). Recent data suggests that in these countries the musculo-skeletal risks are not as large as historically portrayed, most likely due to seizure modification using parenteral benzodiazepines (Chittaranjan et al., 2012). A set of guidelines has been developed that makes recommendations to guide practice when unmodified ECT is administered in exceptional circumstances (Chittaranjan et al., 2012).

Complications secondary to medication

A rare complication that can occur is prolonged apnoea owing to homozygous pseudocholine-sterase deficiency complicating the administration of the muscle relaxant suxamethonium. The clinical expression of this deficiency is variable, with paralysis ranging from 15 minutes through to a few hours. A true homozygous patient will have a prolonged recovery period, whereas a heterozygote carrier may be affected for much shorter periods of time (Dorkins, 1982; Ding and White, 2002).

The treatment for this condition may involve prolonged airway maintenance until the patients are able to spontaneously maintain their own respiration. It may be necessary to continue a level of induction during this period to prevent the patient from being aware that they are paralysed and cannot breathe spontaneously minimising this potentially frightening experience (Ding and White, 2002).

It is reported in the anaesthetic literature that suxamethonium may cause malignant hyperthermia (Ding and White, 2002). Malignant hyperthermia is a manifestation of exposure to susceptible individuals to triggering drugs. Without exposure it is not possible to identify susceptible patients (Hopkins, 2000). There is no clinical feature that is specific to malignant hyperthermia. The predominant symptom is progressive pyrexia, which usually leads to death. Other symptoms include: masseter spasm, hypermetabolism and muscle rigidity and breakdown (rhabdomyolysis) (Glahn et al., 2010).

Dantrolene is a hydantoin derivative that directly interferes with muscle contraction by inhibiting calcium ion release from the sarcoplasmic reticulum possible by binding to ryanodine receptor type 1 (RYR-1). The initial dose is 2.5 mg/kg, repeated every five minutes until reversal of the reaction occurs or a total dose of 10 to 20 mg/kg is reached (Chapin, 2016). All theatres or stand-alone ECT suites should have access to dantrolene, which can be administered rapidly to prevent this medical emergency.

Prolonged seizures

There is general agreement that if a seizure is not terminated within three to five minutes patients are more at risk of confusion and memory impairment. However, there is little agreement or evidence base on how long is too long. Some argue that a prolonged seizure should be defined as greater than 120 seconds (Abrams, 2002; Whitehouse and Scott, 2005), whereas others have been more lenient, defining it as any seizure greater than 180 seconds (American Psychiatric Association, 2001; NSW Health, 2010; SA Health, 2014).

Prolonged seizures are most commonly observed at the first treatment (Fink, 2009; Sackeim, Devanand and Prudic, 1991). It is generally thought that prolonged seizures are more common in patients under the age of 18 years than adults owing to young people having a lower seizure threshold (Consoli, DeCarvalho and Cohen 2013). Case reports vary from those supporting this view (Guttmacher and Cretella, 1988; Moise and Petrides, 1996), to others that fail to confirm this observation (Schneekloth, Rummans and Logan, 1993). Walter and Rey (2003), in their epidemiology review, found that prolonged seizures were very uncommon, with a rate of only 0.4% in all ECT sessions examined in the study.

Other causes of prolonged seizures are in patients who take medications that lower seizure threshold (Abrams, 2002) and those with pre-existing medical conditions that lower seizure threshold like electrolyte imbalance (Finlayson, Vieweg, Wilkey and Cooper, 1989).

There is general consensus that EEG monitoring is mandatory to detect prolonged seizures and flag the appropriate intervention (Abrams, 2002; Mankad, Beyer, Weiner and Krystal, 2010; NSW Health, 2010; RANZCP, 2007; SA Health, 2014; Tiller and Lyndon, 2003; Waite and Easton, 2013). There have been reports of non-convulsive status epilepticus after ECT causing sudden onset of delirium, agitation and lack of responsiveness to command (Grogan, Wagner, Sullivan and Labar, 1995; Solomons, Holliday and Illing, 1998). EEG monitoring is invaluable in these situations as the motor fit often terminates well before the cerebral activity. Assisted ventilation with oxygen is essential as prolonged seizures can cause an increase in cognitive impairment and confusion during the recovery period (Tiller and Lyndon, 2003).

ECT can be effective in terminating a prolonged seizure. Administration of a further stimulus that is at least two levels above the previous dose is effective owing to the anticonvulsant properties of ECT, which cause an increase in seizure threshold during the course of treatment (Griesemer, Kellner, Beale and Smith, 1997; Krystal and Coffey, 1997).

A prolonged seizure should be aborted once detected. In most instances the seizure is terminated pharmacologically with the administration of an anaesthetic agent with anticonvulsive properties like thiopentone or propofol, or a benzodiazepine like midazolam (American Psychiatric Association, 2001; Whitehouse and Scott, 2005).

Most anaesthetists prefer using another dose of the induction agent as benzodiazepines like midazolam can cause prolonged sedation, extending recovery time and, additionally, it may not be readily available in the treatment room (Tiller and Lyndon, 2003). In patients under the age of 18 there may be some benefit in using propofol, an induction agent that has a higher seizure threshold compared to thiopentone (Galvez, Hadzi-Pavlovic, Smith and Loo, 2015), as the preferred drug to prevent prolonged seizures (Walter and Rey, 1997).

CLINICAL WISDOM 4.2.3

Prolonged seizures may indicate a rise in threshold and consideration should be given to increasing the energy used to stimulate at the next treatment session. They are also very common in patients under the aged of 20 years. In this age group it may be necessary to manage recurrent prolonged seizures by using a single induction agent (thiopentone or propofol) and avoiding a combination anaesthetic regimen like thiopentone plus remifentanil, which may contribute to improved seizure propagation. Prolonged seizures are usually terminated by a further dose of thiopentone or midazolam if available. It is possible to terminate a prolonged seizure by restimulating the patient at a dose at least two levels above the previous dose.

ADVERSE EVENTS IMMEDIATELY POST-ECT TREATMENT

Transient postictal delirium

Transient postictal delirium or excitability can occur in a minority of patients after one or more ECT treatments and is characterised by motor agitation, disorientation and poor response to verbal commands (Davanand, Briscoe and Sackeim, 1989). Disorientation can last for variable periods of time from five to 45 minutes. Postictal delirium can result in physical injury to the patient, as they thrash around the bed, hitting hard objects, and injury to the staff looking after them in the recovery area.

Treatment is dependent upon the severity of the disturbance. Mild to moderate episodes can be managed by supportive care given by the recovery staff through gentle reassurance that the patient is in a safe place.

More severe episode are managed with intravenous medication administered by the anaesthetist after spontaneous respirations return before the patient is transferred to the recovery area. Drug choices include: another dose of either, the same or a different induction agent, a benzodiazepine, like midazolam, or an antipsychotic drug like droperidol with the occasional use of clonidine. Prophylaxis should be initiated when the postictal delirium is thought to be recurrent, a decision that is made by the ECT team.

Staff can make adjustments to the electric bed that was used to transport the patient from the treatment area, "trapping" the disorientated patient in a V shape. The head and foot of the bed are both tilted upwards and the height of the bed reduced to the lowest setting to prevent injury and falls. Staff should exercise caution, remaining aware of their own and the patient's safety at all times. If the patient fails to settle, other staff may need to be engaged to contain them while the anaesthetist administers further pharmacological agents to achieve restraint.

It has been suggested that using an increased anaesthetic dose prior to ECT may prevent postictal

CLINICAL WISDOM 4.2.4

The practice of administering a higher dose of induction agent prior to the stimulus to control postictal excitement is inadvisable. It is likely to have a deleterious effect on the treatment owing to the need for a higher stimulus dose to achieve a suprathreshold seizure that can cause more cognitive impairment and may result in a slower time to recovery.

excitement (Davanand and Sackeim, 1992) Caution is required if the bolus is given too closely to the treatment as it may require the use of a stronger stimulus, potentially increasing cognitive impairment.

What is striking is the variable nature of the condition. It can occur only once at different times with different patients during the treatment cycle or in susceptible patients after each ECT session.

MacPherson and Loo (2008) note that disorientation that lasts for longer than 20 minutes has been shown to be associated with more severe retrograde memory disturbance. Early detection is critical and may be facilitated by the application of the Brief ECT Cognitive Screen (BECS) (Martin et al., 2013).

Headaches

The incidence of postictal headaches varies and has been estimated at between 20% and 30% of patients (Abrams, 2002) or as high as 45% during and shortly after the recovery period, and may last for several hours (Devanand, Fitzsimons, Prudic and Sackeim, 1995; Tubi et al., 1993; Weiner, Ward and Ravaris, 1994). Younger patients are more prone to headaches than older people (Devanand et al., 1995; Walter and Rey, 1997). The headache is typically a throbbing pain located over the frontal area of the head and in most patients mild in nature responding to conservative measures or simple analgesics (Sackeim, Ross, Hopkins, Calev and Devanand, 1987).

Severe post-treatment headache are more common in patients with a history of incapacitating headache, those who are younger than 45 years of age and those who had seizures of longer duration, although the precise aetiology is unknown (Dinwiddie, Dezheng Huo and Gottlieb, 2010).

Post-ECT-related headache does not appear to be related to therapeutic response (Devanand et al., 1995; Sackeim et al., 1987), stimulus dosage (Devanand et al., 1995) or electrode placement (Devanand et al., 1995; Tubi et al., 1993).

Treatment of post-ECT headache is symptomatic, with the majority responding to intravenous fluids, prophylactic analgesics, paracetamol, aspirin or non-steroidal anti-inflammatory drugs given immediately before or after each treatment. In severe cases of refractory post-ECT headache may respond

---

CLINICAL WISDOM 4.2.5

For more persistent post-ECT headaches, analgesia can be administered pre- and peri-ECT treatment to maximise the effectiveness. In some cases it may be necessary to consult with the anaesthetist to discuss alternative oral or intravenous treatments. Options include the administration of:

- oral analgesia with a sip of water one hour before the treatment session;
- intravenous non-steroidal anti-inflammatory drugs, like ibuprofen;
- intravenous local anaesthetic, like lignocaine, after the seizure;
- intravenous fluids administered during the treatment session;
- intravenous or intramuscular opioid. Caution is required when giving patients codeine products after ECT, as they can produce nausea, reduce respiratory effort and delay recovery.

A medical consultation should be considered if severe headaches persist post-ECT and are not responsive to the interventions noted above.

---

to prophylaxis, with subcutaneous or intranasal sumatriptan given several minutes before ECT (DeBattista and Mueller, 1995). Some anaesthetists have recommended the use of intravenous lignocaine administered immediately after the seizure has terminated. Caution is required, as lignocaine may block seizure initiation completely if given before the stimulus (Devanand and Sackeim, 1988).

Myalgia

Severe post-ECT deep muscle pain in all areas of the body is a common complication that may be present in 9% of patients after their first ECT (Scottish ECT Accreditation Network, 2011). It may be transient or occur after each treatment. It is thought that, following administration of suxamethonium, depolarisation of the muscle spindles results in contraction of muscle fibres, producing pain before relaxation is achieved. Myalgia arising from the administration of suxamethonium is not inevitable and the severity was not predicted by degree of fasciculation or motor activity but was worse in patients younger than 45 years (Dinwiddie et al., 2010).

Treatment involves use of minor analgesics, such as paracetamol and non-steroidal anti-inflammatory drugs that can give some relief of symptoms. If recurrent, a patient may benefit from the administration of a non-depolarising muscle relaxant, like mivacurium or rocuronium, before the induction agents and suxamethonium are given, blocking the depolarisation. These agents need to be given early owing to their slow onset of action.

Nausea and vomiting

It is estimated that post-operative nausea and vomiting occurs in 6% of patients (Scottish ECT Accreditation Network, 2011). The true incidence is difficult to quantify as nausea and vomiting may be secondary to headache and can be a side effect to analgesics and anaesthetic agents. If mild the symptoms often respond to dopamine-blocking agents like prochlorperazine or metoclopramide.

CLINICAL WISDOM 4.2.6

ECT practitioners recognise that suxamethonium-induced myalgia is a relatively common side effect after the first ECT and may occur following subsequent treatments. If persistent, it can make a patient's journey through ECT challenging. Prophylactic treatment may involve pre-treatment with a small dose of a non-depolarising muscle relaxant, like mivacurium or rocuronium, before suxamethonium is administered or intravenous administration of paracetamol or a non-steroidal anti-inflammatory drugs immediately after the seizure has ceased. Eliminating this disabling side effect is essential to prevent a patient withdrawing their consent for further ECT.

Time between administration of a non-depolarising medication and the induction agents is important. If delayed, the patient may be aware that they are paralysed, creating high levels of distress when they recover. Non-depolarising muscle relaxants are rarely used as primary induction agents as they have a slow onset and offset of action, increasing the length of the procedure.

If these agents are ineffective or cause side effects, nausea usually responds to serotonin 5-HT$_3$ receptor antagonists like ondansetron, administered orally (GSK, 2014; White et al., 2002) or as a single intravenous dose, 4 mg to 8 mg, before or after the seizure. Routine use of these agents is not recommended owing to their cost.

ADVERSE EFFECTS AFTER THE COURSE OF ECT TREATMENT

Cognitive disturbance

One of the most challenging areas to manage in administering ECT is the potential risk of cognitive disturbance, which may get worse over the course of ECT (Loo 2008), an area that has been extensively investigated with a number recent systematic reviews and meta-analyses (Fraser, O'Carroll and Ebmeier, 2008; Gardner and O'Connor, 2008; Ingram, Saling and Schweitzer, 2008; Semkovska, Keane, Babalola and McLoughlin, 2011; Semkovska and McLoughlin, 2010).

Opponents of ECT focus on this complication as a reason for the treatment to be minimised or eliminated completely (Donahue, 2000; Dukakis and Tye, 2006). Those that have had the treatment support it use as a life-saving treatment but highlight the need for more collaborative research to tease out why some consumers experience disabling cognitive side effects and others have improvement in memory (Rose, 2003).

Donahue (2000) gives a very moving account of the very high cost she had to pay to gain the benefit from ECT. She acknowledges that the 33 treatments she was given, a combination of right unilateral and bitemporal "may have saved not just my mental health but my life. If I had the same decision to make over again I would choose ECT over a life condemned to psychic agony, and possible suicide." However, over the next six to 12 months she began to experience very significant gaps in her memory: "my long term memory deficits far exceed anything my doctors anticipated".

This finding has been supported by a systematic review of patients' perspectives on ECT, with at least one third of patients reporting persistent memory loss (Rose, Fleischmann, Wykes, Leese and Bindman, 2003), and other work showing that nearly half of the consumers in the study reported that they had not received sufficient information about ECT and common side effects, while others stated that they felt like they had not adequately consented for the treatment (Rose, Wykes, Bindman and Fleischmann, 2005). Adequate preparation of the patient and their families to the predictable, expected and rare cognitive effects as experienced by consumers is vital to informed consent and can make the patient's journey through a course of ECT easier to manage (Kellner, 1996).

Most clinical practice guidelines and minimum standard documents highlight that many conditions, like melancholic depression, mania and schizophrenia, that are commonly treated with ECT can cause significant cognitive impairment (Addington et al., 2005; Bauer et al., 2013; Cleare et al., 2015; Davidson, 2010; Galletly et al., 2016; Gelenberg et al., 2010; Malhi et al., 2015; NSW Health, 2010; Porter, Douglas and Knight, 2008; SA Health, 2014). Clinicians working in the area of ECT frequently observe improvement in consumer's memory and cognitive function as the symptoms of depression and psychosis remit. This is in marked contrast to the data presented by opponents of ECT (Benbow, 2005; Coleman et al., 1996; Prudic, Peyser and Sackeim, 2000). These differences in part reflect the significant contribution that ECT technique has on cognitive function, resulting in more permanent impairment (Sackeim et al., 2007). As discussed in Section 5.2, unilateral ultrabrief ECT is associated with reduced cognitive side effects.

These data highlight the need to be honest and comprehensive about the benefits and potential cognitive side effects that can occur during a course of ECT.

Acute effects

Postictal delirium, general disorientation and confusion immediately after ECT are common phenomena (Benbow, 2005). They have been found to correlate with age, electrode placement and stimulus dosing (Kellner et al., 2010; Sobin et al., 1995). Acute effects are more severe if the patient is administered a bitemporal ECT electrode placement, a broader pulse width and a sine wave stimulus (Daniel and Crovitz, 1982; Sackeim et al., 1993).

Patients recover at different rates, regaining orientation to time, place and person differently in their own way (Daniel and Crovitz, 1982; Semkovska et al., 2011). Deficits are generally short-lived, with patients gaining clarity within minutes to hours (Rasmussen, 2016). There are a number of studies that have shown that time to reorientation is correlated with retrograde amnesia (Martin et al., 2013; Sobin et al., 1995). This topic is discussed in more details in a previous section.

Retrograde amnesia

Retrograde memory deficits are characterised by difficulties in recalling material learned prior to ECT (Benbow, 2005) and relates to frequency of treatment, type of electrode placement and stimulus parameters (Sackeim, 2014).

One important component of retrograde memory is autobiographical memory, the recollection of specific personal events. Autobiographical memory is a multifaceted higher-order cognitive process that has both episodic and semantic memory components (Willoughby, Desrocher, Levine and Rovet, 2012). *Episodic autobiographical memory* refers to remembering past events that are specific in time and place that typically involve the recollection of vivid sensory, perceptual and emotional details (Tulving, 2002; Willoughby et al., 2012). Examples include my last birthday or my graduation. An important critical component of episodic autobiographical memory that differentiates it from other forms of declarative memory is the requirement for the ability to travel back in time mentally in order to re-experience the event at the time of recollection (Tulving, 2002; Wheeler, Stuss and Tulving, 1997).

In contrast, *semantic autobiographical memory* refers to the recollection of personal facts, traits and general self-knowledge that are independent of time, place and any sense of re-experiencing a past event (Conway and Pleydell-Pearce, 2000; Tulving, 2002). Examples include "I am a male who is 30 years old".

These two forms of autobiographical memory are highly interconnected, especially during the early stages of retrieval, when personal semantic knowledge can aid memory search and retrieval operations (Conway and Pleydell-Pearce, 2000; Willoughby et al., 2012). There is now evidence that suggests that episodic and semantic autobiographical memory can be differentiated further. Episodic autobiographical memory retrieval has been associated with greater activity in the hippocampus (Addis, Moscovitch and McAndrews, 2007; Hoscheidt, Nadel, Payne and Ryan, 2010), as well as a later and more gradual developmental trajectory compared to semantic memory retrieval (Piolino et al., 2007).

Retrograde amnesia is the most persistent cognitive deficit from ECT and is greater for impersonal than for personal memory and may persist beyond two months (Lisanby, Maddox, Prudic, Devanand and Sackeim, 2000). It has been reported that loss of these memories are more distressing owing to the personal nature of their content (Lisanby et al., 2000).

Retrograde amnesia generally improves over weeks to months after the index course of treatment has been completed (Porter, Heenan and Reeves, 2008), however it has been shown that persistent deficits can occur, particularly in patients receiving high-dose bitemporal ECT with antiquated equipment using sine wave technology (Sackeim et al., 2007). It has been shown that time to recovery is a strong predictor of the magnitude of retrograde amnesia for autobiographic information (Sobin et al., 1995). A new clinical tool, the Brief ECT Cognitive Screen (BECS), may identify at-risk patients early in their treatment course, enabling clinicians to change treatment options that may minimise these effects (Martin et al., 2013).

Recent studies have shown a clear difference between objective measures of memory function (UK ECT Review Group, 2003) and those recording subjective findings. Studies lead by consumers highlight more severe and enduring memory problems in a third to a half of consumers involved in the analysis (Philpot et al., 2004; Rose et al., 2003).

A recent systematic review of autobiographical memory studies for the period 1980 to 2007 concluded that autobiographical memory impairment does occur as a result of ECT, with objective measures showing memory loss was for less than six months while subjective reports were longer than six months after ECT (Fraser et al., 2008). ECT predominately affects the memory of prior personal events that are within six months of treatment. The loss was reduced when brief-pulse stimulation was used, unilateral ECT administered and the electrical current titrated relative to the patient's own seizure threshold (Fraser et al., 2008).

Current debate: evaluating autobiographical memory

There has been considerable debate concerning effective tools that can evaluate retrograde amnesia for autobiographical information. Semkovska and McLoughlin (2010) conducted a large meta-analysis of 84 objective cognitive performance studies, using 24 different cognitive variables, but did not include autobiographical amnesia among the domains examined because of their contention that standardised retrograde amnestic tests lacked reliability and validity.

In a further review of retrograde autobiographical memory (AM) (Semkovska and McLoughlin, 2013), the authors extend their criticism of research in this area, stating that normative data and validation studies in healthy volunteers have not been published supporting the use of the semistructured autobiographical memory (AM) questionnaire (Squire, Slater and Miller, 1981), or the personal memory questionnaire (Weiner, Rogers, Davidson and Squire, 1986), making the results invalid. The same criticism has been levelled at the two most frequently used measures of AM in contemporary ECT literature, the Columbia University Autobiographical Memory Interview (CUAMI) (McElhiney et al., 1995) and the Columbia University Autobiographical Memory Interview – Short Form (CUAMI-SF) (McElhiney, Moody and Sackeim 2001).

In his response, Sackeim (2014) identified that retrograde amnesia for AM was the most critical adverse effect from ECT, with most modern research demonstrating long-term autobiographical amnesia after ECT has used the CUAMI or the short form of this scale, CUAMI-SF. After a review of the substantial studies supporting the reliability and validity of the scales, Sackeim goes onto highlight that results obtained have consistently converged, with patient self-evaluation of ECT's effect on memory clearly demonstrating long-term differences in the magnitude of autobiographical amnesia as a function of ECT technique (Sackeim, 2014).

One of the greatest contentions raised against the scales has been equating loss of autobiographical memory consistency to retrograde amnesia and that what the CUAMI has been capturing after an ECT course is an indistinguishable mix of loss of consistency; due to the effect of time, lack of specificity; due to the effect of depression, and retrograde amnesia; and due to the effect of ECT, with a need for formal reliability and validation studies of the scales (Semkovska and McLoughlin, 2014).

The final rebuttal challenges the contention that there has been a lack of clarity concerning the nature, extent and duration of retrograde amnesia attributable to ECT. In reality, there is a lack of dispute over any of the multitude of facts learned about AM after ECT using the CUAMI and CUAMI-SF. Rather, there appears to be an acceptance that in randomised and observational studies long-term deficits on these instruments have repeatedly shown that patients who receive bilateral ECT, wider pulse stimulation and larger number of treatments had worse amnesia scores two and six months after treatment than patients treated with right unilateral ECT, ultrabrief stimulation or fewer sessions (Sackeim, 2014).

Academic debate can be healthy and necessary but the complete lack of agreement and rigidity of the criticism levelled against the CUAMI and CUAMI-SF undermines the harsh reality that after ECT many patients report persistent memory loss for events that occurred during the ECT course and the weeks and months before the course (Sackeim, 2014).

In a self-report study that evaluated memory problems prospectively in depressed patients receiving bilateral and unilateral ECT compared to depressed patients receiving other treatments other than ECT, depressed patients who did not have ECT denied poor memory at seven months after hospitalisation. Compared to bilateral ECT, right unilateral ECT was associated with only mild memory complaints (Squire and Slater, 1983). At three years after treatment approximately one third of the consumers who received bilateral ECT reported poor memory. Reports were influenced by three factors: recurrence or persistence of conditions that were present before ECT; the experience of amnesia initially associated with ECT; and a subsequent tendency to question if memory had ever recovered and impaired memory for events that had occurred up to six months before treatment and up to two months afterwards (Squire and Slater, 1983).

These findings have been replicated in a more recent systematic review where at least one third of patients reported persistent memory loss well after the course of ECT (Rose et al., 2003). As noted previously, some patients report a dense retrograde amnesia with gaps in memory of personal auto-biographical event, like recent holidays, illnesses and weddings, that can extend back several years (Donahue, 2000).

Conclusion

Evaluation of retrograde autobiographical memory is complex, generating considerable debate. Different forms of ECT are associated with different cognitive outcomes, which may result in consumers reporting persistent cognitive impairment. It is prudent for the ECT practitioner to regularly revisit informed consent for ECT during a course of treatment when: the electrode placement is changed, the stimulus is altered from ultrabrief to brief-pulse ECT, adverse events are detected, there are changes in health status, the specified number of treatments has been exceeded or the treatment changes from continuation to maintenance ECT to ensure a high level of consumer satisfaction (Mankad, 2015).

In summary, retrograde amnesia can involve both autobiographical and impersonal memory domains, with the loss improving substantially and quickly after the completion of ECT. The severity is greater and more persistent following bilateral ECT using high dose or older devices with sine wave or broad pulse-width technology. The extent of loss is not correlated with the degree of clinical improvement but clinical improvement does appear to impact on the amount of retrograde memory loss following self-report (Weiner, Coffey and Krystal, 2000).

Anterograde amnesia

Anterograde memory deficits refer to the difficulty a person has in acquiring and retaining new verbal and non-verbal material after a single treatment or course of ECT (Abrams, 2002). Disturbance of this area of cognition is commonly observed during and after a course of ECT (Ingram et al., 2008; Vamos, 2008) and is related to stimulus parameters (Sackeim et al., 2008). It is known that deficits in retention are more frequent and often slower to recover than those in skills to acquire information. Return to baseline measures is usually rapid, with most studies showing a return to baseline after a few weeks (Gangadhar, Kapur and Kalyanasundaram, 1982; Sackeim et al., 1993; Weeks, Freeman and Kendell, 1980; Weiner et al., 1986).

A recent meta-analysis of 84 cognitive performance studies highlighted that: over 70% of studies had shown a significant decrease in cognitive performance at day three and after the last treatment; improvement occurred between days four and 15 post-ECT with no measurable negative effects on cognitive function after that time; and in 60% of cases test results showed improvement compared to baseline tests (Semkovska and McLoughlin, 2010). A further review identified that bitemporal ECT was associated with more deficits in verbal and visual episodic memory, with brief pulse causing less impairment on visual memory than sine wave ECT. There was no correlation between mean electrical dosage, age or total number of treatments and cognitive change (Semkovska and McLoughlin, 2010).

If anterograde amnesia is severe, the person may have limited capacity to return to work, make important financial or personal decisions or drive a car until the cognitive impairment resolves. Careful monitoring is required to guide clinical decisions to minimise the impact of the treatment on the consumers' quality of life (Prudic, 2008).

Subjective memory deficits

As noted in a previous section, subjective reports of cognitive function show a poor correlation with objective neuropsychological measurement (Coleman et al., 1996; Vamos, 2008). Those patients who report the greatest symptomatic improvement from ECT also report the greatest improvement in subjective memory functioning. It is possible that those patients who report the most impairment of memory are those who feel invalidated, have significant disruption to daily routine and have low self-esteem. The discrepancy between measured cognitive function and subjectively experienced impairment requires that both perspectives are considered rather than only relying on one or the other (Vamos, 2008).

Many patients have a positive experience and are happy with their ECT treatment. It has been estimated that up to 80% of patients would reconsent for a further course of treatment if required (Pettinati et al., 1994). In a recent study, 405 patients with unipolar and bipolar major depressive episodes were administered a quality of life questionnaire. There was a significant improvement in quality of life after the course of ECT, with age, ECT treatment parameters and baseline quality

CLINICAL WISDOM 4.2.7

Apprehension to ECT is not limited to patients but also to carers and relatives. They should be given as much opportunity as necessary to discuss the treatment with their loved one and the ECT treatment team. Fears are usually due to limited or wrong information or memories of an experience that happened to a relative maybe years earlier using old techniques. Information sheets should be provided and any videos of the procedure to allay fears. Carers and relatives must be notified in writing in some regions that the patient will appear before the next mental health tribunal, where an application will be made for a determination concerning involuntary ECT. Carers and relatives should be encouraged to attend and express their views to the tribunal, which can provide an objective, independent and un-emotive review of the case that can be reassuring to the family.

of life scores significant predictors of change in a patient's subjective life experience (Waite et al., 2016).

Fear of ECT

It has been suggested that patients' apprehensions and negative subjective reactions to the experience of having ECT should be viewed as an adverse side effect (Sackeim 1992). The literature concerning fear and ECT is limited featuring in some editorials and case reports, with a recent literature review presented at an international conference (Obbels, Verwijk, Bouckaert and Sienaert, 2017). In this review the prevalence of ECT-related anxiety from 22 identified studies were broad ranging from 14% to 75% of cases. There was a wide range of subjects included in the studies, with the most commonly reported fear associated with memory loss and brain damage (Obbels et al., 2017).

Intense fear concerning ECT is not new, being identified first by Gallineck (1956). He noted that there was a second level, "pathological fear" that was in addition to the usual fear people had undergoing any surgical procedure. It commences before the treatment and if unchecked may get worse as the treatment progresses creating an obstacle to compliance. It can interfere with consent for any further treatment in the future even if the patient had a good response to ECT (Fox, 1993).

Fox (1993) noted that fear and objection to ECT had been part of the treatment since inception even though there have been substantial changes to technique and the consent process, illustrating the impact of this condition in three case reports. It has been postulated that this fear may be due to the sense of disconnectedness, loss of control and disorientation experienced by some patients upon wakening from the treatment (Gallineck, 1956).

There are many reasons why patients dislike treatment with ECT. There is the repeated burden on family and friends who have to accompany the patient to the hospital for treatment, not to mention the inconvenience of having to forgo a whole day on a regular basis. There is the displeasure that comes with the long wait for treatment, the typical

apprehension about needing a general anaesthetic, the unpleasant recovery period, which can involve periods of confusion, and the troublesome cognitive burden that must endured (Fox, 2009). Those patients who do not develop pathological fear recognise the potential life-saving aspect of ECT (Kivler 2010).

Fear is found not only in the person about to have ECT but also their family and carers (McCall, 2007). Intense fear may be related to the negative depictions of ECT in the popular media that extend back over many years, to the fear that they may become paralysed while still awake or owing to the experience of a family member that had a course of treatment in the past. Complications encountered early in the course of treatment can be a common reason for the patient and their families to cease a course of ECT prematurely. However, the majority of patients are able to overcome their fear of ECT by saying "you win", conceding to the experience of the ECT practitioner and going on to have a successful course of treatment (McCall, 2008).

Fear is common in involuntary consumers who have been retained in hospital by a treatment order and have been ordered to have ECT by a mental health tribunal against their will. This decision may be exacerbated by lack of insight, severity of the symptoms experienced and strong resistance by carers. Such patients can be very apprehensive, frightened and aggressive during the first few ECT treatment sessions. Recovery and repetition usually brings passive cooperation and acceptance of the treatment in most but not all patients. It is remarkable that this group does not seem to represent a high risk for future bitter ECT complaint (Rasmussen, 2015). The ECT practitioner may be on solid legal ground to pursue ECT over the wishes of the family, particularly if the patient is in a potentially life-threatening condition, however there may be a difference between what legally can be done versus what should be done (McCall, 2007).

In summary, many patients do not like ECT and are often the last to appreciate the benefits of ECT (McCall, 2007). Involvement of family and carers should be a fundamental component of the consent process, with some proponents suggesting that this process should involve written consent from both the patient and the family (Rajkumar, Saravanan and Jacob, 2006) and others going further and suggesting that the family routinely be present during each ECT session (Evans and Staudenmier, 2005).

Other strategies to minimise fear and anxiety such as music and an aquarium in the waiting room, as well as emotional support, were not helpful; however, talking-through techniques, information leaflets and animal-assisted therapy may have some merit (Obbels et al., 2017).

Other cognitive deficits

Other areas of cognition that can be affected by ECT include visual episodic memories, frontal lobe and executive functioning, attention, concentration and information processing. Losses in these areas can be extremely distressing for consumers. To date, there has been little investigation into these domains

CLINICAL WISDOM 4.2.8

More concerted efforts should be made to conduct research that can better explain the discrepancy between measured cognitive function and subjective cognitive impairment to reduce the gap in clinical knowledge. Academic debate has a place in progressing knowledge provided that solutions can be found that lead to more sensitive scales to detect deficits early. Improvement in assessment tools must be combined with listening to the lived experience to create increased consensus between consumers and clinicians about the benefits and risks associated with ECT, improving the information that is discussed, and aiding informed consent. It has been noted that:

> human memory is one of the most precious aspects of our personality . . . determining . . . who we are and how we see ourselves and others. The memories of our past give us an understanding of where we fit in the world.
> (Donahue, 2000)

(Ingram et al., 2008). The type and severity of cognitive deficits change rapidly with time following each ECT treatment and will vary with the time of assessment relative to the last treatment and the number of treatments administered. The type of ECT is highly significant to the cognitive outcome.

More intense treatment with bitemporal electrode placement, wider pulse widths, sine wave ECT, increased frequency of treatments, high stimulus dose above threshold, high dose of anaesthetic induction agents and lack of titration of the electrical current relative to the patient's own seizure threshold are factors associated with more severe cognitive impairment (Sackeim, 2014). The advent of ultrabrief ECT has had a significant impact in minimising the impact of technique on cognitive outcomes (Loo et al., 2014; Sackeim et al., 2008; Tor et al., 2015).

Patient variables are another dimension that must be considered in assessing the cognitive side effects of ECT. Age, attitudes, underlying neurological and other medical disorders, prescribed and non-prescribed medications and educational achievements can contribute to how ECT is experienced.

Finally, there has been some work looking at the neurobiological correlates associated with ECT-induced cognitive dysfunction (Nobler and Sackeim, 2008). It has been postulated for many years, supported by recent work, that the medial temporal lobes especially the hippocampus mediate anterograde and possibly retrograde amnesia. They note that recent functional neuroimaging studies in normal volunteers have demonstrated that frontal cortical regions are also involved in human memory processes. They conclude both medial temporal and frontal regions as being most associated with cognitive dysfunction during ECT treatment (Nobler and Sackeim, 2008).

Detection of cognitive deficits

One of the biggest criticisms of ECT over many years is the impact the treatment has on cognition

(Abrams, 2002; Swartz, 2009). There is growing evidence that the treatment can have long-term effects on various cognitive domains (Sackeim, 2014).

A close therapeutic alliance enables discussion about potential memory problems from ECT to be dealt with in a way that eases rather than heightens apprehensions. For many years ECT practitioners have recognised the need for a battery of instruments that can be administered over a 20-minute period to assess cognitive and clinical change before, during and shortly after a course of treatment (Kellner, 1996). This battery should in a timely manner, enable the clinician to modify their ECT technique thereby minimising cognitive decline (Porter et al., 2008; Prudic, 2008). Twenty years on, a simple battery of instruments with a sound evidence base remains elusive, with many high-quality sources of information on ECT failing to provide specific suggestions (Rasmussen, 2016).

Keith G. Rasmussen (2016) highlights five reasons why cognitive testing should be completed routinely:

- to guide clinical care
- to advice patients on activity restrictions
- as a therapeutic tools
- to plan cognitive rehabilitation strategies
- medical legal purposes.

The ECT committee should be responsible for: deciding on the reasons for undertaking cognitive testing, what type of questions should be answered and with what tool, who will be responsible for administering the tests and whether the data collected can contribute to audit, research and knowledge (Rasmussen, 2016).

The test battery must be cost-effective and easily incorporated into routine clinical care. Research trials have provided dense and details data sets about the cognitive impact of different types of ECT (Sackeim, 2014), but these studies do not easily translate into routine clinical care (Rasmussen, 2016). Testing memory is a complex process and little objective evidence supports the benefits of

many approaches (Rasmussen, 2016). The need to monitor cognitive function has become increasingly necessary due to the potential medico-legal implications of enduring cognitive impairment (Porter et al., 2008; Sackeim, 2014).

Porter et al. (2008) have proposed a battery of five tests that are simple and easy to administer at baseline and after the third and sixth treatment, and that can be incorporated into routine clinical practice:

- The Modified Mini Mental State (3MSE) examination (Teng and Chui, 1987);
- Hopkins Verbal Learning Test (Brandt, 1991);
- Autobiographical memory interview (AMI) – short form (Kopelman, Wilson and Baddeley, 1990);
- Digit–symbol substitution task (Wechsler, 1997);
- Reorientation (Porter et al., 2008).

The previous discussion in this chapter highlights the current debate about available instruments to assess retrograde autobiographical memory. The reader may opt to utilise the CUAMI-SF (McElhiney, Moody and Sackeim 2001) rather than the AMI recommended by Porter et al. (2008), as it has been developed specifically for memory loss associated with ECT.

It has been suggested that testing be conducted at least 48 hours after the last treatment and repeated two to three months after the index course (Porter et al., 2008). A criticism of this battery is the time taken to collect the data, the need for dedicated staff to administer the tests and how the data is utilised once collected (Rasmussen, 2016).

Freeman (2013) reviewed the test battery proposed by Robertson and Pryor (2006), but acknowledged that it is very comprehensive, covering non-verbal and visuospatial memory, working memory and executive function, so even a subset of the tests would take 30 to 40 minutes to administer, making it impractical for routine clinical practice.

Porter et al. (2008) identified that changes in cognition can be detected as early as after the third treatment, supporting more recent data that early detection is possible and may guide clinical treatment decisions to optimise the efficacy and cognitive outcomes of ECT (Martin et al., 2013).

The Black Dog Institute has established a recent initiative, the Clinical Alliance and Research in ECT (CARE) Network, to assist hospitals administering ECT to measure practice outcomes. The initial aims were to develop a set of standardised measures with recording forms that were simple to use as clinical and audit tools with potential for collaborative research. The group has been successful in recruiting a growing number of hospitals in the Australasian region and beyond.

Audio Recorded Cognitive Screen (ARCS)

A new tool that is easy to administer in a clinical setting is the Audio Recorded Cognitive Screen (ARCS), which now has its own website (Schofield, 2012). This instrument assesses cognition over five domains: executive functioning/attention, memory, language, verbal fluency and visuospatial functioning (Schofield et al., 2010). The patient completes the test in a quiet room after being handed headphones and a CD that guides them through the cognitive battery over the next 30 minutes. The instrument has been well validated in other conditions such as multiple sclerosis (Lechner-Scott et al., 2010) and psychosis (Loughland et al., 2010).

The utility of the ARCS for assessment of individuals undergoing ECT has recently been validated in 30 patients with unipolar or bipolar depression, demonstrating that it is a cost-effective, simple tool that is easily completed by consenting patients of all ages that can be incorporated into routine clinical practice.

Strategies to improve efficacy and minimise cognitive impairment

There are a number of techniques that can be considered to improve efficacy and minimising cognitive impairment:

- routine use of ultrabrief ECT (Tor et al., 2015);
- when brief-pulse ECT is considered, commence with low-stimulus intensity in relation to individual seizure threshold, moderate dose (3 times) rather than high dose (5–8 times) (McCall, Reboussin, Weiner and Sackeim, 2000);
- ceasing drug treatments that are known to exacerbate memory, like lithium (Dolenc and Rasmussen, 2005; Sartorius, Wolf and Henn, 2005);
- cease drug treatments that have the capacity to raise seizure threshold, like anticonvulsant mood stabilisers (Sienaert and Peuskens, 2007);
- choose an anaesthetic induction agent that has less effect on seizure threshold, like thiopentone (Galvez et al., 2015), etomidate or ketamine (Datto, Rai, Ilivicky and Caroff, 2002);
- consider hyperventilation (Datto et al., 2002);
- ensure adequate hydration (Datto et al., 2002);
- consider induction augmentation through the addition of an ultrabrief narcotic to markedly reduce the dose of the primary anaesthetic agent, thereby potentially reducing the anticonvulsant effect and enhancing seizure quality (Datto et al., 2002);
- consider augmentation with methylxanthines like caffeine (Calev, Fink, Petrides, Francis and Fochtmann, 1993; Coffey, Figiel, Weiner and Saunders, 1990);
- reduce the frequency of treatment to increase tolerability (Prudic, 2008);
- taper further treatments once a clinical response has been achieved (Prudic, 2008);
- consider a second opinion from an ECT specialist;
- consider a break in treatment if there is a failure to progress to enable a comprehensive review of diagnosis and management, including the use of other agents that may be contributing to a high seizure threshold.

REFERENCES

Abrams, R. (2002). *Electroconvulsive Therapy*, 4th edition. New York: Oxford University Press.

Addington, D., Bouchard, R.-H., Goldberg, J., Honer, B., Malla, A., Norman, R., and Berzins, S. (2005). Clinical practice guidelines: treatment of schizophrenia. *Canadian Journal of Psychiatry, 50*(Supplement 1). Retrieved from ww1.cpa-apc.org/Publications/Clinical_Guidelines/schizophrenia/november2005/cjp-cpg-suppl1–05_full_spread.pdf.

Addis, D.R., Moscovitch, M., and McAndrews, M.P. (2007). Consequences of hippocampal damage across the autobiographical memory network in left temporal lobe epilepsy. *Brain, 130*(Pt 9), 2327–2342. doi:10.1093/brain/awm166.

American Psychiatric Association. (2001). *The Practice of Electroconvulsive Therapy: Recommendations for Treatment, Training and Privileging: A Task Force Report*, 2nd edition. Washington, DC: American Psychiatric Association.

Bauer, M., Pfennig, A., Severus, E., Whybrow, P.C., Angst, J., Moller, H.J., and WFSBP Task Force on Unipolar Depressive Disorder. (2013). World Federation of Societies of Biological Psychiatry (WFSBP) guidelines for biological treatment of unipolar depressive disorders, part 1: update 2013 on the acute and continuation treatment of unipolar depressive disorders. *World Journal of Biological Psychiatry, 14*(5), 334–385. doi:10.3109/15622975.2013.804195.

Beli, N., and Bentham, B. (1998). Nature and extent of dental pathology and complications arising in patients recieving ECT. *Psychiatric Bulletin, 22*, 562–565.

Benbow, S.M. (2005). Adverse effects of ECT. In Scott, A.I.F. (Ed.), *The ECT Handbook*, 2nd edition. London: Royal College of Psychiatrists.

Brandt, J. (1991). The Hopkins Verbal Learning Test: development of a new memory test with six equivalent forms. *Clinical Neurpsychology, 5*, 125–142.

Burd, J., and Kettl, P. (1998). Incidence of asystole in electroconvulsive therapy in elderly patients. *American Journal of Geriatric Psychiatry, 6*(3), 203–211. Retrieved from www.ncbi.nlm.nih.gov/pubmed/9659953.

Calev, A., Fink, M., Petrides, G., Francis, A., and Fochtmann, L.J. (1993). Caffeine pretreatment enhances clinical efficacy and reduces cognitive effects of electroconvulsive therapy. *Convulsive Therapy, 9*(2), 95–100.

Chanpattana, W., Kunigiri, G., Kramer, B.A., and Gangadhar, B.N. (2005). Survey of the practice of electroconvulsive therapy in teaching hospitals in India. *Journal of ECT, 39*, 54–60.

Chapin, J.W. (2016). Malignant hyperthermia treatment and management. *Drugs and Diseases, Critical Care*.

Chittaranjan, A.N., Shah, P., Tharyan, M.S., Reddy, M., Thirunavukarasu, R.A., Kallivayalil, R., . . . Mohandas, E. (2012). Position statement and guidelines on unmodified electroconvulsive therapy. *Indian Journal of Psychiatry, 54*(2), 119–133. doi:10.4103/0019-5545.99530.

Cleare, A., Pariante, C.M., Young, A.H., Anderson, I.M., Christmas, D., Cowen, P.J., . . . Members of the Consensus Meeting. (2015). Evidence-based guidelines for treating depressive disorders with antidepressants: A revision of the 2008 British Association for Psychopharmacology guidelines. *Journal of Psychopharmacology, 29*(5), 459–525. doi:10.1177/0269881115581093.

Coffey, C.E., Figiel, G.S., Weiner, R.D., and Saunders, W.B. (1990). Caffeine augmentation of ECT. *American Journal of Psychiatry, 147*(5), 579–585. doi:10.1176/ajp.147.5.579.

Coleman, E.A., Sackeim, H.A., Prudic, J., Devanand, D.P., McElhiney, M.C., and Moody, B.J. (1996). Subjective memory complaints before and after electro-convulsive therapy. *Biological Psychiatry, 39*, 346–356.

Consoli, A., DeCarvalho, W., and Cohen, D. (2013). Side effects of ECT. In Waite, J., and Easton, A. (Eds.), *Electroconvulsive Therapy in Children and Adolescents* (pp. 140–160). New York: Oxford University Press.

Conway, M.A., and Pleydell-Pearce, C.W. (2000). The construction of autobiographical memories in the self-memory system. *Psychological Review, 107*(2), 261–288. Retrieved from www.ncbi.nlm.nih.gov/pubmed/10789197.

Coughlin, J.M., Rodenbach, K., Lee, P.-H., Hayat, M.J., Griffin, M.M., Mirski, M.A., and Reti, I.M. (2012). Asystole in ultrabrief pulse electroconvulsive therapy. *Journal of ECT, 28*(3), 165–169. doi:10.1097/YCT.0b013e31825003f9.

Daniel, W.F., and Crovitz, H.F. (1982). Recovery of orientation after electroconvulsive therapy. *Acta Psychiatrica Scandinavica, 66*(6), 421–428. Retrieved from www.ncbi.nlm.nih.gov/pubmed/7180562.

Datto, C., Rai, A., Ilivicky, H.J., and Caroff, S.N. (2002). Augmentation of seizure induction in electroconvulsive therapy: a clinical reappraisal. *Journal of ECT, 18*(3), 118–125.

Davanand, D.P., Briscoe, K.M., and Sackeim, H.A. (1989). Clincal features and predictors of postictal excitement. *Convulsive Therapy, 5*(2), 140–146.

Davanand, D.P., and Sackeim, H.A. (1992). Use of increased anaesthetic dose prior to electroconvulsive therapy to prevent postictal excitement. *General Hospital Psychiatry, 14*, 345–349.

Davidson, J.R. (2010). Major depressive disorder treatment guidelines in America and Europe. *Journal of Clinical Psychiatry, 71 Suppl E1*(suppl E1: e04), e04. doi:10.4088/JCP.9058se1c.04gry.

DeBattista, C., and Mueller, K. (1995). Sumatriptan prophylaxis for post electroconvulsive therapy headaches. *Headache, 35*, 502–503.

Devanand, D.P., and Sackeim, H.A. (1988). Seizure elicitation blocked by pretreatment with lidocaine. *Convulsive Therapy, 4*(3), 225–229.

Devanand, D.P., Fitzsimons, L., Prudic, J., and Sackeim, H.A. (1995). Subjective side effects during electroconvulsive therapy. *Convulsive Therapy, 11*(4), 232–240. Retrieved from www.ncbi.nlm.nih.gov/pubmed/8919573.

Ding, Z., and White, P.F. (2002). Anesthesia for electroconvulsive therapy. *Anesthesia and Analgesia, 94*(5), 1351–1364. doi:10.1097/00000539-200205000-00057.

Dinwiddie, S.H., Dezheng Huo, D., and Gottlieb, O. (2010). The course of myalgia and headache after electroconvulsive therapy. *Journal of ECT, 26*(2), 160–120.

Dolenc, T.J., and Rasmussen, K.G. (2005). The safety of electroconvulsive therapy and lithium in combination: a case series and review of the literature. *Journal of ECT, 21*(3), 165–170.

Donahue, A.B. (2000). Electroconvulsive therapy and memory loss: a personal journey. *Journal of ECT, 16*(2), 133–143.

Dorkins, H.R. (1982). Suxamethonium: the development of a modern drug from 1906 to the present day. *Medical History, 26*(2), 145–168.

Dukakis, K., and Tye, L. (2006). *Shock: The Healing Power of Electroconvulsive Therapy*. New York: Penguin.

Evans, G., and Staudenmier, J.J. (2005). Family member presence during electroconvulsive therapy: patient rights versus medical culture. *Journal of ECT, 21*(1), 48–50. Retrieved from www.ncbi.nlm.nih.gov/pubmed/15791179.

Fink, M. (2009). *Electroconvulsive Therapy: A Guide for Professionals and Their Patients*. New York: Oxford University Press.

Finlayson, A.J., Vieweg, W.V., Wilkey, W.D., and Cooper, A.J. (1989). Hyponatremic seizure following ECT. *Canadian Journal of Psychiatry, 34*(5), 463–464. Retrieved from www.ncbi.nlm.nih.gov/pubmed/2504479.

Fox, H.A. (1993). Patients' fear of and objection to electroconvulsive therapy. *Hosp Community Psychiatry, 44*(4), 357–360. Retrieved from www.ncbi.nlm.nih.gov/pubmed/8462942.

Fox, H.A. (2009). Patients' objections to electroconvulsive therapy. *Journal of ECT, 25*(4), 288. doi:10.1097/YCT.0b013e31819fe012.

Fraser, L.M., O'Carroll, R.E., and Ebmeier, K.P. (2008). The effect of electroconvulsive therapy on autobiographical memory: a systematic review. *Journal of ECT, 24*(1), 10–17.

Freeman, C.P. (2013). Cognitive adverse effects of ECT. In Waite, J., and Easton, A. (Eds.), *The ECT Handbook*, 3rd edition. London: Royal College of Psychiatrists.

Galletly, C., Castle, D., Dark, F., Humberstone, V., Jablensky, A., Killackey, E., . . . Tran, N. (2016). Royal Australian and New Zealand College of Psychiatrists clinical practice guidelines for the treatment of schizophrenia and related disorders. *Australian and New Zealand Journal of Psychiatry, 50*(5), 1–117. doi:10.1080/j.1440-1614.2005.01516.x.

Gallineck, A. (1956). Fear and anxiety in the course of electroshock therapy. *American Journal of Psychiatry, 113*, 428–434.

Galvez, V., Hadzi-Pavlovic, D., Smith, D., and Loo, C.K. (2015). Predictors of seizure threshold in right unilateral ultrabrief electroconvulsive therapy: role of concomitant medications and anaesthesia used. *Brain Stimulation 8*(3), 486–492. doi:10.1016/j.brs.2014.12.012.

Gangadhar, B.N., Kapur, R.L., and Kalyanasundaram, S. (1982). Comparison of electroconvulsive therapy with impipramine in endongenous depression: a double blind study. *British Journal of Psychiatry, 141*, 367–371.

Gardner, B.K., and O'Connor, D.W. (2008). A review of the cognitive effects of electroconvulsive therapy in older adults. *Journal of ECT, 24*(1), 68–80.

Gelenberg, A.J., Freeman, M.P., Markowitz, J.C., Rosenbaum, J.F., Thase, M.E., Trivedi, M.H., and Van Rhoads, R.S. (2010). Practice guidelines for the treatment of patients with major depressive disorder, 3rd edition. *American Psychiatric Association*. Retrieved from www.psychiatryonline.com/pracGuide/pracGuideTopic_7.aspx.

Glahn, K.P., Ellis, F.R., Halsall, P.J., Muller, C.R., Snoeck, M.M., Urwyler, A., . . . European Malignant Hyperthermia, G. (2010). Recognizing and managing a malignant hyperthermia crisis: guidelines from the European Malignant Hyperthermia Group. *British Journal of Anaesthesia, 105*(4), 417–420. doi:10.1093/bja/aeq243.

Griesemer, D.A., Kellner, C.H., Beale, M.D., and Smith, G.M. (1997). Electroconvulsive therapy for treatment of intractable seizures. Initial findings in two children. *Neurology, 49*(5), 1389–1392. Retrieved from www.ncbi.nlm.nih.gov/pubmed/9371927.

Grogan, R., Wagner, D.R., Sullivan, T., and Labar, D. (1995). Generalized nonconvulsive status epilepticus after electroconvulsive therapy. *Convulsive Therapy, 11*(1), 51–56. Retrieved from www.ncbi.nlm.nih.gov/pubmed/7796069.

GSK. (2014). Zofran: product information. Retrieved from www.pharma.us.novartis.com/product/pi/pdf/zofran.pdf.

Guttmacher, L.B., and Cretella, H. (1988). Electroconvulsive therapy in one child and three adolescents. *Journal of Clinical Psychiatry, 49*(1), 20–23. Retrieved from www.ncbi.nlm.nih.gov/pubmed/3422073.

Hase, K., Yoshioka, H., Nakamura, T., Kamei, T., Isse, K., and Nakamura, M. (2005). Asystole during electroconvulsive therapy. *Masui, 54*(11), 1268–1272.

Hopkins, P.M. (2000). Malignant hyperthermia: advances in clinical management and diagnosis. *British Journal of Anaesthesia, 85*(1), 118–128. Retrieved from www.ncbi.nlm.nih.gov/pubmed/10928000.

Hoscheidt, S.M., Nadel, L., Payne, J., and Ryan, L. (2010). Hippocampal activation during retrieval of spatial context from episodic and semantic memory. *Behavioural Brain Research, 212*(2), 121–132. doi:10.1016/j.bbr.2010.04.010.

Ingram, A., Saling, M.M., and Schweitzer, I. (2008). Cognitive side effects of brief pulse ECT: a review. *Journal of ECT, 24*(1), 3–9.

Kellner, C.H., Knapp, R.G., Hausain, M.M., Rasmussen, K., Sampson, S., Cullum, M., . . . Petrides, G. (2010). Bifrontal, bitemporal and right unilateral electode placement in ECT: randomised trial. *British Journal of Psychiatry, 196*(3), 226–234. doi:10.1192/bjp.bp.109.066183.

Kellner, C.H. (1996). The cognitive effects of ECT: bridging the gap between research and clincial practice. *Convulsive Therapy, 12*, 133–134.

Kivler, C.A. (2010). *Will I Ever Be the Same Again? Transforming the Face of ECT (Shock Therapy).* New York: Three Gem/Kivler.

Kopelman, M., Wilson, B., and Baddeley, A. (1990). *The Autobiographical Memory Interview.* Suffolk, UK: Thames Valley Test.

Krystal, A.D., and Coffey, C.E. (1997). Neuropsychiatric considerations in the use of electroconvulsive therapy. *Journal of Neuropsychiatry and Clinical Neurosciences, 9*, 283–292.

Lechner-Scott, J., Kerr, T., Spencer, B., Agland, S., Lydon, A., and Schofield, P.W. (2010). The Audio Recorded Cognitive Screen (ARCS) in patients with multiple sclerosis: a practical tool for multiple sclerosis clinics. *Multiple Sclerosis, 16*(9), 1126–1133. doi:10.1177/1352458510374743.

Lisanby, S.H., Maddox, J.H., Prudic, J., Devanand, D.P., and Sackeim, H.A. (2000). The effects of electroconvulsive therapy on memory of autobiographical and public events. *Archives of General Psychiatry, 57*(6), 581–590. Retrieved from www.ncbi.nlm.nih.gov/pubmed/10839336.

Loo, C. (2008). Cognitive outcomes in electroconvulsive therapy: optimizing current clinical practice and researching future strategies. *Journal of ECT, 24*(1), 1–2.

Loo, C.K., Katalinic, N., Smith, D.J., Ingram, A., Dowling, N., Martin, D., . . . Schweitzer, I. (2014). A randomised controlled trial of brief and ultrabrief pulse right unilateral electroconvulsive therapy. *International Journal of Neuropsychopharmacology, 18*(1).

Loughland, C.M., Allen, J., Gianacas, Schofield, P.W., Lewin, T.J., Hunter, M., and Carr, V.J. (2010). Brief neuropsychological profiles in psychosis: a pilot study using the Audio Recorded Cognitive Screen (ARCS). *Acta Neuropsychiatrica, 22*(5), 243–252. doi:10.1111/j.1601-5215.2010.00492.x.

McCall, W.V. (2007). Electroconvulsive therapy: all in the family. *Journal of ECT, 23*(4), 213–214.

McCall, W.V. (2008). You win. *Journal of ECT, 24*(4), 243.

McCall, W.V., Reboussin, D.M., Weiner, R.D., and Sackeim, H.A. (2000). Titrated moderately suprathreshold vs fixed high-dose right unilateral electroconvulsive therapy. *Archives of General Psychiatry, 57*(5), 438. doi:10.1001/archpsyc.57.5.438.

McCall, W.V., Reid, S., and Ford, M. (1994). Electrocardiographic and cardiovascular effects of sub-convulsive stimulation during titrated right unilateral ECT. *Convulsive Therapy, 10*(1), 25–33. Retrieved from www.ncbi.nlm.nih.gov/pubmed/8055289.

McElhiney, M.C., Moody, B.J., and Sackeim, H.A. (2001). *Manual for Administration and Scoring the Columbia University Autobiographical Memory Interview – Short Form, Version 3.* New York: Psychiatric Institute.

McElhiney, M.C., Moody, B.J., Steif, B.L., Prudic, J., Devanand, D.P., Nobler, M.S., and Sackeim, H.A. (1995). Autobiographical memory and mood: effects of electro-convulsive therapy. *Neuropsychology Review, 9*, 501–517.

MacPherson, R., and Loo, C. (2008). Cognitive impairment following electroconvulsive therapy – does the choice of anaesthetic agent make a difference? *Journal of ECT, 24*(1), 52–56.

Malhi, G.S., Bassett, D., Boyce, P., Bryant, R., Fitzgerald, P.B., Fritz, K., . . . Singh, A.B. (2015). Royal Australian and New Zealand College of Psychiatrists clinical practice guidelines for mood disorders. *Australian and New Zealand Journal of Psychiatry, 49*(12), 1–185. Retrieved from www.ranzcp.org/Files/Resources/Publications/CPG/Clinician/Mood-Disorders-CPG.aspx.

Mankad, M. (2015). Informed consent for electroconvulsive therapy – finding balance. *Journal of ECT, 31*(3), 143–146. doi:10.1097/YCT.0000000000000241.

Mankad, M.V., Beyer, J.L., Weiner, R.D., and Krystal, A. (2010). *Clinical Manual of Electroconvulsive Therapy.* Washington, DC: American Psychiatric Publishing.

Martin, D. (2013). Dental issues related to ECT. In Waite, J., and Easton, A. (Eds.), *The ECT Handbook*, 3rd edition. London: Royal College of Psychiatrists.

Martin, D.M., Katalinic, N., Ingram, A., Schweitzer, I., Smith, D.J., Hadzi-Pavlovic, D., and Loo, C.K. (2013). A new early cognitive screening measure to detect cognitive side-effects of electroconvulsive therapy? *Journal of Psychiatric Research, 47*(12), 1967–1974. doi:10.1016/j.jpsychires.2013.08.021.

Moise, F.N., and Petrides, G. (1996). Case study: electroconvulsive therapy in adolescents. *Journal of the American Academy of Child and Adolescent Psychiatry, 35*(3), 312–318. doi:10.1097/00004583-199603000-00012.

Morris, A.J., Roche, S.A., Bentham, P., and Wright, J. (2002). A dental risk management protocol for electroconvulsive therapy. *Journal of ECT, 18*(2), 84–89.

Nobler, M.S., and Sackeim, H.A. (2008). Neurobiological correlates of the cognitive side effects of electro-convulsive therapy. *Journal of ECT, 24*(1), 40–45.

NSW Health. (2010). ECT minimum standard of practice NSW. Retrieved from www.health.nsw.gov.au/policies/pd/2011/pdf/PD2011_003.pdf.

Obbels, J., Verwijk, E., Bouckaert, F., and Sienaert, P. (2017). ECT-related fear: what have we (not) learned? *Brain Stimulation, 10*(2), 325–326.

Pettinati, H.M., Tamburello, T.A., Ruetsch, C.R., and Kaplan, F.N. (1994). Patient attitudes towards electroconvulsive therapy. *Psychopharmacology Bulletin, 30*, 471–475.

Philpot, M., Collins, C., Trivedi, P., Treloar, A., Gallacher, S., and Rose, D. (2004). Eliciting user views of ECT in two mental health trusts with a user-designed questionaire. *Journal of Mental Health, 13*, 403–413.

Piolino, P., Hisland, M., Ruffeveille, I., Matuszewski, V., Jambaqué, I., and Eustache, F. (2007). Do school-age children remember or know the personal past? *Consciousness and Cognition, 16*, 84–101.

Porter, R., Heenan, H., and Reeves, J. (2008). Early effects of electroconvulsive therapy on cognitive function. *Journal of ECT, 24*(1), 35–39. doi:10.1097/YCT.0b013e31816207f0.

Porter, R.J., Douglas, K., and Knight, R.G. (2008). Monitoring of cognitive effects during a course of electroconvulsive therapy: recommendations for clinical practice. *Journal of ECT, 24*(1), 25–34. doi:10.1097/YCT.0b013e31815d9627.

Prudic, J. (2008). Strategies to minimize cognitive side effects with ECT: aspects of ECT technique. *Journal of ECT, 24*(1), 46–51.

Prudic, J., Peyser, S., and Sackeim, H.A. (2000). Subjective memory complaints: a review of patient self-assessment of memory after electroconvulsive therapy. *Journal of ECT, 16*(2), 121–132. Retrieved from www.ncbi.nlm.nih.gov/pubmed/10868322.

Prudic, J., Sackeim, H.A., Decina, P., Hopkins, N., Ross, F.R., and Malitz, S. (1987). Acute effects of ECT on cardiovascular functioning: relations to patient and treatment variables. *Acta Psychiatrica Scandinavica, 75*(4), 344–351.

Rajkumar, A.P., Saravanan, B., and Jacob, K.S. (2006). Perspectives of patients and relatives about electroconvulsive therapy: a qualitative study from Vellore, India. *Journal of ECT, 22*(4), 253–258.

RANZCP. (2007). Clinical memorandum #12 electroconvulsive therapy. Melbourne, Australia.

Rasmussen, K.G. (2015). Rage against the (ECT) machine. *Journal of ECT, 31*(1), 1–2. doi:10.1097/YCT.00000000000 00171.

Rasmussen, K.G. (2016). What type of cognitive testing should be part of routine electroconvulsive therapy practice? *Journal of ECT, 32*(1), 7–12. doi:10.1097/yct.0000000000000257.

Robertson, H., and Pryor, R. (2006). Memory and cognitive effects of ECT: informing and assessing patients. *Advances in Psychiatric Treatment., 12*, 228–238.

Rose, D. (2003). Collaborative research between users and professionals: peaks and pitfalls. *The Psychiatrist, 27*(11), 404–406. Retrieved from http://pb.rcpsych.org/content/27/11/404.abstract.

Rose, D.S., Fleischmann. P, Wykes. T, Leese. M, and Bindman. J. (2003). Patients' perspectives on electroconvulsive therapy: systematic review. *Bristish Medical Journal, 326*(7403), 1363. Retrieved from www.bmj.com/content/326/7403/1363.abstract.

Rose, D.S., Wykes, T.H., Bindman, J.P., and Fleischmann, P.S. (2005). Information, consent and perceived coercion: patients' perspectives on electroconvulsive therapy. *The British Journal of Psychiatry, 186*(1), 54–59. Retrieved from http://bjp.rcpsych.org/content/186/1/54.abstract.

SA Health. (2014). South Australian Guidelines for Electro-convulsive Therapy. Retrieved from www.sahealth.sa.gov.au/wps/wcm/connect/060827004bad5b01b89.

Sackeim, H.A. (1992). The cognitive effects of electro-convulsive therapy. In Moos, W.H., Ganzu, E.R., and Thal, L.J. (Eds.), *Cognitive Disorders: Pathophysiology and Treatment.* (pp. 183–228). New York: Marcel Dekker.

Sackeim, H.A. (2014). Autobiographical memory and electro-convulsive therapy: do not throw out the baby. *Journal of ECT, 30*(3), 177–186. doi:10.1097/yct.0000000000000117.

Sackeim, H.A. (2014). Autobiographical memory and electro-convulsive therapy: final thoughts on the bathwater. *Journal of ECT, 30*(3), 189–190.

Sackeim, H.A., Decina, P., Prohovnik, I., and Malitz, S. (1987). Seizure threshold in electroconvulsive therapy: effects of sex, age, electrode placement and the number of treatments. *Archives of General Psychiatry, 44*, 355–360.

Sackeim, H.A., Devanand, D.P., and Prudic, J. (1991). Stimulus intensity, seizure threshold, and seizure duration: impact on the efficacy and safety of electroconvulsive therapy. *Psychiatric Clinics of North America, 14*(4), 803–843.

Sackeim, H.A., Prudic, J., Devanand, D.P., Kiersky, J.E., Fitzsimons, L., Moody, B. J., . . . Settembrino, J.M. (1993). Effects of Stimulus intensity and electrode placement on the efficacy and cognitive effects of electroconvulsive therapy. *New England Journal of Medicine, 328*(12). Retrieved from www.nejm.org/doi/pdf/10.1056/NEJM199303253281204.

Sackeim, H.A., Prudic, J., Fuller, R., Keilp, J., Lavori, P.W., and Olfson, M. (2007). The cognitive effects of electroconvulsive therapy in community settings. *Neuropsychopharmacology*, *32*(1), 244–254. doi:10.1038/sj.npp. 1301180.

Sackeim, H.A., Prudic, J., Nobler, M.S., Fitzsimons, L., Lisanby, S.H., Payne, N., . . . Devanand, D.P. (2008). Effects of pulse width and electrode placement on the efficacy and cognitive effects of electroconvulsive therapy. *Brain Stimulation 1*(2), 71–83. doi:10.1016/j.brs.2008.03.001.

Sackeim, H.A., Ross, R., Hopkins, N., Calev, L., and Devanand, D.P. (1987). Subjective side effects acutely following ECT: associations with treatment modality and clinical response. *Journal of ECT*, *3*(2), 100–110.

Sartorius, A., Wolf, J., and Henn, F.A. (2005). Lithium and ECT – concurrent use still demands attention: three case reports. *World Journal of Bioloigical Psychiatry*, *6*, 121–124.

Schneekloth, M.D., Rummans, T.D., and Logan, M.D. (1993). Electroconvulsive therapy in adolescents. *Convulsive Therapy*, *9*(3), 158–166.

Schofield, P.W. (2012). Audio Recorded Cognitive Screen (ARCS). Retrieved from www.cognitionhealth.com/.

Schofield, P.W., Lee, S.J., Lewin, T.J., Lyall, G., Moyle, J., Attia, J., and McEvoy, M. (2010). The Audio Recorded Cognitive Screen (ARCS): a flexible hybrid cognitive test instrument. *Journal of Neurology, Neurosurgery, and Psychiatry*, *Jun 81*(6), 602–607. doi:10.1136/jnnp.2009. 188003.

Scottish ECT Accreditation Network. (2011). *Annual Report 2011: A summary of ECT in Scotland for 2010*. Scotland: NHS National Services.

Semkovska, M., Keane, D., Babalola, O., and McLoughlin, D.M. (2011). Unilateral brief-pulse electroconvulsive therapy and cognition: effects of electrode placement, stimulus dosage and time. *Journal of Psychiatric Research*, *45*(6), 770–780. doi:10.1016/j.jpsychires.2010.11.001.

Semkovska, M., and McLoughlin, D.M. (2010). Objective cognitive performance associated with electroconvulsive therapy for depression: a systematic review and meta-analysis. *Biological Psychiatry*, *68*, 568–577.

Semkovska, M., and McLoughlin, D.M. (2013). Measuring retrograde autobiographical amnesia following electroconvulsive therapy: historical perspective and current issues. *Journal of ECT*, *29*(2), 127–133.

Semkovska, M., and McLoughlin, D.M. (2014). Retrograde autobiographical amnesia after electroconvulsive therapy: on the difficulty of finding the baby and clearing murky bathwater. *Journal of ECT*, *30*(3), 187–188.

Sienaert, P., and Peuskens, J. (2007). Anticonvulsants during electroconvulsive therapy: review and recommendations. *Journal of ECT*, *23*(2), 120–123. doi:10.1097/YCT.0b013e 3180330059.

Slawson, P. (1985). Psychiatric malpractice: the electroconvulsive therapy experience. *Journal of ECT*, *1*(3), 190–203.

Slawson, P. (1989). Psychiatric malpractice and ECT: a review of national loss experience. *Journal of ECT*, *5*(2), 126–130.

Sobin, C., Sackeim, H.A., Prudic, J., Devanand, D.P., Moody, B.J., and McElhiney, M.C. (1995). Predictors of retrograde amnesia following ECT. *American Journal of Psychiatry*, *152*(7), 995–1001. Retrieved from www.ncbi.nlm.nih.gov/ pubmed/7793470.

Solomons, K., Holliday, S., and Illing, M. (1998). Nonconvulsive status epilepticus complicating electroconvulsive therapy. *International Journal Geriatric Psychiatry*, *13*, 731–734.

Squire, L.R., and Slater, P.C. (1983). Electroconvulsive therapy and complaints of memory dysfunction: a prospective three-year follow-up study. *British Journal of Psychiatry*, *142*, 1–8. Retrieved from www.ncbi.nlm.nih.gov/pubmed/6831121.

Squire, L.R., Slater, P.C., and Miller, P.L. (1981). Retrograde amnesia and bilateral electroconvulsive therapy. Long-term follow-up. *Archives of General Psychiatry*, *38*(1), 89–95. Retrieved from www.ncbi.nlm.nih.gov/pubmed/7458573.

Stevens, T., Spoors, J., Hale, R., and Bembridge, H. (2010). Percieved oral health needs in psychiatric inpatients: impact of a dedicated dental clinic. *The Psychiatrist*, *34*, 518–521.

Stewart, P.T., Loo, C.K., MacPherson, R., and Hadzi-Pavlovic, D. (2011). The effect of electrode placement and pulsewidth on asystole and bradycardia during the electroconvulsive therapy stimulus. *International Journal of Neuropsychopharmacology*, *14*(5), 585–594. doi:10.1017/S1461145 710001458.

Swartz, C.M. (2009). *Electroconvulsive and Neuromodulation Therapies*. New York: Cambridge University Press.

Tang, W.-K., and Ungvari, G.S. (2001). Asystole during electroconvulsive therapy: a case report. *Australian and New Zealand Journal of Psychiatry*, *35*(3), 382–385. doi:10.1046/ j.1440-1614.2001.00892.x.

Teng, E.L., and Chui, H.C. (1987). The Modified Mini-Mental State (3MS) examination. *Journal of Clinical Psychiatry*, *48*(8), 314–318. Retrieved from www.ncbi.nlm.nih.gov/ pubmed/3611032.

Tiller, J.W.G., and Lyndon, R.W. (2003). *Electroconvulsive Therapy: An Australian Guide*. Melbourne, Australia: Australian Post Graduate Medicine.

Tor, P.C., Bautovich, A., Wang, M.J., Martin, D., Harvey, S.B., and Loo, C. (2015). A systematic review and meta-analysis of brief versus ultrabrief right unilateral electroconvulsive therapy for depression. *Journal of Clinical Psychiatry*, *10*(4088). doi:10.4088/JCP.14r09145.

Tubi, N., Calev, A., and Higal, D. (1993). Subjective symptoms in depression and during the course of electroconvulsive therapy. *Neuropsychiatry, Neuropsychology, and Behavioral Neurology, 6*, 187–192.

Tulving, E. (2002). Episodic memory: from mind to brain. *Annual Review of Psychology, 53*, 1–25. doi:10.1146/annurev. psych.53.100901.135114.

UK ECT Review Group. (2003). Efficacy and safety of electroconvulsive therapy in depressive disorders: a systematic review and meta-analysis. *Lancet, 361*, 799–808.

Vamos, M. (2008). The cognitive side effects of modern ECT: patient experience or objective measurement? *Journal of ECT, 24*(1), 18–24. doi:10.1097/YCT.0b013e31815d9611.

Waite, J., and Easton, A. (2013). *The ECT Handbook*, 3rd edition. London: Royal College of Psychiatrists.

Waite, S., Galvez, V., Li, A., Oxley, C., Kumar, D., De Felice, C.N., . . . Loo, C. (2016). *Patient-Rated Quality of Life (QOL) After Electroconvulsive Therapy: A Multisite Naturalistic Australian Study*. Paper presented at the Regional Challenges Worldwide Influence 2016 International RANZCP Congress of Psychiatry, Hong Kong.

Walter, G., and Rey, J.M. (1997). An epidemiological study of the use of ECT in adolescents. *Journal of the American Academy of Child and Adolescent Psychiatry, 36*, 809–815.

Walter, G., and Rey, J.M. (2003). Has the practice and outcome of ECT in adolescents changed? Findings from a whole-population study. *Journal of ECT, 19*(2), 84–87.

Watts, B.V., Groft, A., Bagian, J.P., and Mills, P.D. (2011). An examination of mortality and other adverse events related to electroconvulsive therapy using a national adverse event report system. *Journal of ECT, 27*(2), 105–108.

Wechsler, D. (1997). *The Wechsler Adult Intelligence Scale-III*. San Antonio, TX: The Psychological Corporation.

Weeks, D., Freeman, C.P., and Kendell, R.E. (1980). ECT: III: enduring cognitive deficits? *British Journal of Psychiatry, 137*, 26–37. Retrieved from www.ncbi.nlm.nih.gov/pubmed/7459537.

Weiner, R.D., Ward, T., and Ravaris, C.L. (1994). Headache and electroconvulsive therapy. *Headache, 34*, 155–159.

Weiner, R.D., Coffey, C.E., and Krystal, A.D. (2000). Electroconvulsive therapy in the medical and neurologic patient. In Stoudemire, A., Fogel, B.S., and Grenberg, D. (Eds.), *Psychiatric Care of the Medical Patient*, 2nd edition (pp. 419–428). New York: Oxford University Press.

Weiner, R.D., Rogers, H.J., Davidson, J.R., and Squire, L.R. (1986). Effects of stimulus parameters on cognitive side effects. *Annals of the New York Academy of Science, 462*, 315–325. Retrieved from www.ncbi.nlm.nih.gov/pubmed/3458412.

Wheeler, M.A., Stuss, D.T., and Tulving, E. (1997). Toward a theory of episodic memory: the frontal lobes and autonoetic consciousness. *Psychological Bulletin, 121*(3), 331–354. Retrieved from www.ncbi.nlm.nih.gov/pubmed/9136640.

White, P.F., Issioui, T., Hu, J., Jones, S.B., Coleman, J.E., Waddle, J.P., . . . Ing, C.H.. (2002). Comparative efficacy of acustimulation (ReliefBand) versus ondansetron (Zofran) in combination with droperidol for preventing nausea and vomiting. *Anesthesiology, 97*, 1075–1081.

Whitehouse, A.M., and Scott, A.F. (2005). Monitoring seizure activity. In Scott, A.F. (Ed.), *The ECT Handbook*, 2nd edition. London: Royal College of Psychiatrists.

Willoughby, K.A., Desrocher, M., Levine, B., and Rovet, J.F. (2012). Episodic and semantic autobiographical memory and everyday memory during late childhood and early adolescence. *Frontiers in Psychology, 3*(53), 53. doi:10.3389/fpsyg.2012.00053.

Zielinski, R.J., Roose, S.P., Devanand, D.P., Woodring, S., and Sackeim, H.A. (1993). Cardiovascular complications of ECT in depressed patients with cardiac disease. *American Journal of Psychiatry, 150*(6), 904–909. Retrieved from www.ncbi.nlm.nih.gov/pubmed/8494067.

Medical risks and management

ECT is a safe treatment that is rated as a low-risk procedure with a low mortality rate. The American Psychiatric Association (2001) has estimated that the rate of ECT mortality is 1 per 10,000 patients or 1 per 80,000 treatments, similar to the rate for other minor surgery (Badrinath and Guttmacher, 1984; Brand et al., 1994; Hal, Kozak and Gilum, 1997; McCabe, 1985; Warner, Shields and Chute, 1993) or childbirth (Salanave et al., 1999). The morbidity and mortality rate is thought to be lower with ECT than antidepressant medication (Sackeim, 1998), with the mortality rate decreasing in recent years even though it is frequently used in the elderly (Weiner, Coffey and Krystal, 2000) and in medically compromised patients (Weiner and Coffey, 1993).

In Australia, NSW Health (2010) noted that during the last 25 years there have been no deaths associated with ECT following more than 200,000 ECT treatments in that state. In the USA, a large retrospective review covering 13 years and 2279 patients who were given 17,394 treatments failed to identify any deaths associated with ECT (Nuttall et al., 2004).

Watts, Groft, Bagian and Mills (2011) completed an audit in Veterans Affairs hospitals in the USA between 1999–2010 and found no deaths associated with ECT, allowing them to estimate a mortality rate of 1 in 73,440 treatments.

With the exception of raised intracranial pressure, there is no absolute contraindication for ECT (Beyer, Weiner and Glenn, 1998). The pros and cons of administering ECT in high-risk patients should be considered on an individual basis following close consultation with the treating medical teams. If treatment with ECT becomes life-saving in the setting of a significant medical condition, the antecedent risks can generally be minimised pharmacologically (Weiner and Coffey, 1993).

It is essential that all patients have appropriate medical and anaesthetic consultation prior to commencing ECT. A routine physical examination and appropriate investigations need to be organised by the treating team. Following the initial work up by the treating team, the anaesthetists will assess the suitability of the patient to receive an anaesthetic and thus fit for ECT. It is not uncommon for this review to occur immediately before ECT if the patient is relatively healthy. If the patient has pre-existing medically complications a review should be organised a few days prior to treatment so that any compromises to the patient's health can be resolved.

CARDIOVASCULAR COMPLICATIONS

Pathophysiology

Patients with serious cardiac complications can be safely and confidently administered ECT (Bankhead, Torrens and Harris, 2006). Changes in the cardiovascular system during a course of ECT are predictable and pronounced with an immediate and intense increase in parasympathetic efferent activity with sinus arrest, sinus bradycardia, hypotension and brief periods of asystole (Applegate, 1997). After the transient vagal discharge, sympathoadrenal stimulation results in tachycardia and hypertension resulting in a two- to fourfold increase in myocardial oxygen demand (Applegate, 1997) and cardiac work peaking during the clonic phase of seizure activity (Partridge, Weinger and Hauger, 1991). The sympathetic outflow typically lasts a few minutes and quickly diminishes as the seizure subsides (Rayburn, 1997). The sympathetic response is mediated by neurohormones, with levels of adrenaline and noradrenaline increasing dramatically to levels between threefold and 15-fold higher than baseline, respectively (Weinger et al., 1991). It is believed that these cardiac changes represent the primary cause of mortality and morbidity in ECT but the risk is small (McCall, 1993). It has been observed that with repeated treatment the magnitude of the sympathetic response diminishes, suggesting that the initial session of ECT is likely to produce the most significant perturbations in the haemodynamic response (Rayburn, 1997).

Other common cardiovascular changes noted during a course of ECT include:

- increased blood pressure and heart rate on arrival to the ECT suite due to the patient feeling very anxious about having the treatment (Fox, 1993);
- reduction in blood pressure with compensatory increase in heart rate following induction of anaesthetic agents (Rayburn, 1997);
- increased incidence of ventricular ectopic beats with a spontaneous reduction immediately after a seizure has terminated (Applegate, 1997);
- marked increases in cerebral blood flow, intracranial and intraocular pressure (Husum, Vester-Andersen, Buchmann and Bolwig, 1983);
- the most serious cardiac complications occur during the postictal period (Hirachan and Maskey, 2016).

Clinical application

A retrospective review that examined 17,394 ECT treatments found that only 0.92% of patients experienced a complication at some time during the first series of ECT treatments. Of these complications, the majority were arrhythmias that did not cause permanent injury or morbidity (Nuttall et al., 2004). In another study of 40 patients with major depressive disorder with significant cardiovascular disease, left ventricular impairment, ventricular arrhythmias and/or conduction defects that had ECT were matched to 40 depressive patients without cardiac disease who were given ECT. A direct comparison was also possible in 21 patients with cardiovascular disease, who were treated with a tricyclic antidepressant before progressing to ECT owing to medication failure (Zielinski, Roose, Devanand, Woodring and Sackeim, 1993). The patients with cardiac disease had a significantly higher rate of cardiac complications during ECT than did the comparison group without cardiac disease. The type of pre-existing cardiac abnormality strongly predicted the type of cardiac complication that occurred during treatment. Most of the complications were transitory and did not prevent the completion of ECT. Of the 21 patients with cardiac disease who had received tricyclic

trials before ECT, 11 had been forced to discontinue drug treatment because of substantial cardiovascular side effects, whereas 38 out of 40 cardiac patients completed the course of ECT (Zielinski et al., 1993).

High-risk cardiovascular conditions

There are a number of cardiovascular conditions that present a higher risk during ECT:

- uncompensated congestive cardiac failure (Rayburn, 1997);
- aortic aneurysms (Mueller, Albin, Barnes and Rasmussen, 2009);
- left ventricular aneurysms (Gardner, Kellner, Hood and Hendrix, 1997);
- recent myocardial infarction (Magid, Lapid, Sampson and Mueller, 2005);
- severe valvular heart disease (Mueller, Barnes, Varghese, Nishimura and Rasmussen, 2007; Rayburn, 1997);
- unstable angina (Applegate, 1997);
- patients on warfarin (Mehta, Mueller, Gonzalez-Arriaza, Pankratz and Rummans, 2004; Petrides and Fink, 1996);
- uncontrolled or poorly controlled hypertension (Rayburn, 1997);
- clinically significant cardiac dysrhythmias (Applegate, 1997);
- implanted cardiac pacemakers (Dolenc, Barnes, Hayes and Rasmussen, 2004; MacPherson, Loo and Barrett, 2006);
- automated implantable cardioverter defibrillators. A cardiology technician should be present in the ECT suite to inactivate the device prior to ECT and restart once the treatment is complete (Davis et al., 2009; Dolenc et al., 2004; Lapid, Rummans, Hofmann and Olney, 2001).

Management of the haemodynamic risk

It is essential that careful screening for cardiac problems be undertaken using a comprehensive history, completing a full physical examination, and performing an ECG and a stress test if indicated. Relevant blood tests like electrolytes are essential prior to commencing ECT. It is recommended. that a cardiologist consultation be undertaken to comment on the degree of risk and means to diminish it, if abnormalities are detected (Applegate, 1997). It is important to discuss the degree of increased risk with the patient and family during the informed consent process.

It is essential that all patients having ECT be given their usual antihypertensive medications immediately prior to the commencement of ECT (American Psychiatric Association, 2001). As noted above, it is now routine practice for anaesthetists to use adjuvants to intervene where relevant. These include beta blockers like esmolol or labetalol, vasodilators like calcium channel blockers and atropine-like drugs. However, there are some concerns that some of these agents like labetalol and esmolol may shorten seizure duration and attenuate morphology (Hart, 2013; Kovac et al., 1991; Weinger et al., 1991).

McCall (1993), in his review of the cardiovascular effects of ECT, noted that over-zealous control of blood pressure and heart rate might compromise the patient's safety. The under treatment of cardiovascular effects is preferable to over-treatment as this relies on the body's natural homeostatic mechanism.

Allowances should be made for patients to develop hypertension as a consequence of severe anxiety or panic attacks prior to ECT. Careful discussion needs to be had with the anaesthetist and the treating teams to ensure that the patient is normotensive at other times prior to the treatment. If this is the case, ECT should proceed (Fox, 1993).

The routine use of glycopyrrolate (100–600 micrograms) or atropine (300–600 micrograms) to minimise bradycardia or sinus pause when subconvulsive stimuli are applied during titration is no longer recommended owing to improvements in anaesthetic technique (Hart, 2013). Glycopyrrolate is the preferred agent, as it does not cross the blood–brain barrier (Proakis and Harris, 1978).

If sinus bradycardia secondary to suxamethonium is severe it may be best to avoid it completely and use a non-depolarising muscle relaxant alone (Birkenhäger, Pluijms, Groenland and van den Broek, 2010).

Myocardial infarction (MI) and unstable angina

The risk with ECT is greatest during the first 10 days and persists for at least three months after a myocardial infarction, with arrhythmia and less commonly myocardial rupture possible consequences (Aloysi, Maloutas, Gomes and Kellner, 2011). Clinical decision-making in this area is guided by case reports. The closer ECT is administered to the event the more likely there will be a negative outcome. There is a need to ensure that the ECT clinic develops appropriate protocols and processes to identify individuals who present as high risk and ensure that they are carefully assessed and treated to minimise the risks of ECT (Tess and Smetana, 2009).

There have been two recent case reports of ECT being administered safely in patients who have had recently myocardial infarctions despite the known physiological burden on the cardiovascular system. ECT was given to an elderly man who was severely depressed with catatonia 10 days after he had an acute MI. This was safely achieved using appropriate cardiac management and monitoring (Magid et al., 2005). In another case, careful cardiac management enabled ECT to safely resume 19 days after an elderly patient suffered a non-ST segment elevation MI after her first treatment (Aloysi et al., 2011). ECT has also been administered safely in patients with severe aortic stenosis (Mueller et al., 2007; Rasmussen, 1997; Rayburn, 1997).

Caution should be used when a patient has unstable angina or poorly compensated congestive cardiac failure due to increased physiological stress increasing the risk of a myocardial infarct (Applegate, 1997). A review by a cardiologist is recommended.

Cardiac pacemakers

In the past there were concerns about using ECT in patients who had pacemakers inserted. However, modern technology has meant that there is little impact on their functioning during a course of ECT (Dolenc et al., 2004). A recent case review identified 10 patients who had cardiac pacemakers in situ and underwent a total of 147 ECT treatments. In all but one treatment the anaesthesia proceeded uneventfully, with the pacemaker having a potential protective effect (MacPherson et al., 2006). For high-risk patients it may be useful to have a cardiac technician present at the first ECT session to ensure that there are no irregularities.

ECT has been administered safely in patients with automatic internal cardioverter defibrillators (AICD) (Davis et al., 2009; Dolenc et al., 2004; Lapid et al., 2001). In these patients the AICD was deactivated during each ECT treatment and reactivated immediately upon completion of each treatment. The presence of a cardiac technician is essential in this setting. In all of these cases consultation with a cardiologist is recommended.

Aneurysms

An aneurysm is defined as a localised blood-filled balloon that causes a bulge in the wall of a blood vessel. The most common aneurisms occur in the aortic, abdominal vessels and on the circle of Willis that are known as berry aneurisms. Consultation with a vascular or neurosurgeon is required before commencing ECT.

There is a lack of Level 1 and Level 2 evidence on the use of ECT in patients with aneurisms with the clinical decision guided by case reports only. A case series of 10 patients suggested that ECT can be safely administered in patients with untreated abdominal aortic aneurism (Mueller et al., 2009). There are a number of cases that report successful administration of ECT in patients with intracranial aneurysms (Bader, Silk, Dequardo and Tandon, 1995; Drop, Viguera and Welch, 2000; Hunt and Kaplan, 1998; Husum et al., 1983; Najjar and Guttmacher, 1998; Viguera et al., 1998).

Antihypertensive agents like beta blockers in conjunction with intravenous nitroprusside may be necessary to reduce treatment-induced hypertension that occurs during the seizure (Weinger et al., 1991). A thorough evaluation is required prior to proceeding with ECT in consultation with the appropriate surgeon.

NEUROLOGICAL DISORDERS

Cerebral infarction and haemorrhage

Depression associated with cerebral infarction or haemorrhage is common and thought to be a direct consequence of brain injury and may respond to ECT (Murray, Shea and Conn, 1989; NSW Health, 2010; SA Health, 2014). It is generally considered that ECT given one month after a cerebral vascular accident does not present a major risk. However, unless it is a medical emergency, most treatment teams would not administer ECT until the damage is fully resolved after three months. In the early stage the brain is susceptible to the acute hypertensive surge following the administration of ECT with a potential for another event. If the risk is great enough this can be blunted pharmacologically after discussion with the treating medical team.

In a study that reviewed 193 patients with depression and recent stoke, 14 went on to have ECT with 12 showing substantial improvement, none deteriorated and cognition improved in five out of six patients who were reported to have cognitive decline (Murray et al., 1989).

Caution should be exercised in patients with cerebral ischaemic small vessel disease, as there can be an increased likelihood of ECT-induced delirium, particularly if the structural abnormalities are located in the basal ganglia and subcortical white matter (Figiel, Coffey, Djang, Hoffman and Doraiswamy, 1990). This is in contrast to another prospective study of 51 patients referred for ECT who were over 60 years of age and had subcortical white matter hyperintensity on magnetic resonance scans, where there was an excellent response to ECT (Coffey, Figiel, Djang, Saunders and Weiner, 1989).

Intracranial pathology

There are case reports that ECT has been used safely and effectively in the presence of a variety of intracranial lesions including: intracranial aneurisms, multiple sclerosis, cerebral lupus, traumatic brain injury, myasthenia gravis, muscular dystrophy and tumours not associated with raised intracranial pressure (Kellner and Bernstein, 1993; Krystal and Coffey, 1997; Weiner and Coffey, 2000). Patients with organic brain lesions are likely to be more susceptible to cognitive side effects of ECT and appropriate cautions are recommended. The primary risk of increasing intracranial pressure following the use of ECT is coning. Potential complications can be diminished with the use of steroids, diuretics, antihypertensive agents and hyperventilation but an appropriate risk–benefit analysis should be conducted by the whole team before ECT is commenced (Krystal and Coffey, 1997).

Epilepsy

Epilepsy does not represent a significant risk factor for ECT if well diagnosed and treated, as early studies that demonstrated the anticonvulsant properties of ECT (Sackeim, Decina, Portnoy, Neeley and Malitz, 1987; Sackeim, Decina, Prohovnik and Malitz, 1987). Neurologists are generally conservative and often recommend minimal changes in anticonvulsant therapy in epileptic patients undergoing ECT. Anticonvulsant medication during ECT has little impact on efficacy but they can make the treatment less effective by raising seizure threshold and attenuating seizure morphology, thus higher stimulus doses are required (Sienaert and Peuskens, 2007; Zarate, Tohen and Baraibar, 1997). Others have expressed concerns that seizures with long duration but weak expression may have minimal therapeutic properties (Nobler et al., 1993; Sackeim et al., 1993; Sackeim et al., 2000). Simplifying the number of drugs, reducing the dose of medication to minimise this effect and use of a titration method to determine treatment stimulus are recommended.

In clinical practice, withholding anticonvulsant medication 24 hours or even the night before ECT is seen as a useful strategy when stopping them may not be possible, to minimise the impact on the seizure generated, but there is little evidence to support this practice (American Psychiatric Association, 2001).

As the course of treatment progresses, patients with epilepsy are less likely to have spontaneous seizures when medications are reduced owing to a rise in seizure threshold that is common during a course of ECT treatment (Sackeim, 2004).

Multiple sclerosis

Multiple sclerosis, also known as disseminated sclerosis, is an inflammatory disease in which the insulating covers of nerve cells in the brain and spinal cord are damaged. This damage disrupts the ability of parts of the nervous system to communicate, resulting in a wide range of signs and symptoms, including physical, mental and at times psychiatric problems. ECT is generally well tolerated in this group (Coffey, Weiner, McCall and Heinz, 1987). There are report that suggest that patients with active cerebral demyelisation may experience further deterioration in neurological functioning during the course of treatment (Mattingly, Baker and Zorumski, 1992) It is recommended that the patient's neurologist is involved in the decision to proceed with ECT.

Rasmussen and Keegan (2007) report on three patients with MS who received safe and effective ECT without evidence of acute neurological deterioration. They reinforce the importance of ensuring that patients have a though neurological review and fully informed consent about the possibility of neurological decline before commencing ECT.

Myasthenia gravis

Myasthenia gravis is an autoimmune neuromuscular disease that results in fluctuating muscle weakness and fatigue caused by circulating antibodies that block acetylcholine receptors at the postsynaptic neuromuscular junction. This inhibits the excitatory effect of the neurotransmitter acetylcholine on nicotinic receptors at the neuromuscular junction.

Patients with myasthenia gravis have an increased sensitivity to suxamethonium, resulting in an increased resistance and a slower recovery from depolarising agents (Wainwright and Brodrick, 1987). It is recommended that the anaesthetist should reduce the dose of suxamethonium or consider a non-depolarising muscle relaxant to reduce the period of time for airway management (Pande and Grunhause, 1990). However, this may not be straightforward as patients with myasthenia gravis may have an increased sensitivity to non-depolarising muscle relaxants (Eisenkraft, Brook and S.M., 1988)

Gitlin, Jahr, Margolis and J. (1993) report on the successful use of mivacurium, a non-depolarising agent, in five cases, one of whom had myasthenia gravis. The successful outcome of the cases reported are difficult to interpret as the patients were not given a single ECT treatment under the anaesthetic (current technique), rather they used multiple modified ECT (MMECT), a technique in which two or more stimulations were administered over a 30-minute period.

In a recent case report, ECT was successfully administered to a patient with myasthenia gravis who developed a steroid-induced major depressive episode with psychotic features (Calarge and Crowe, 2004).

It is evident that patients who have myasthenia gravis undergoing ECT require extra time to allow for the slow onset and offset of the muscle relaxants.

Skull defects and intracranial metal objects

The ECT practitioner is left without guidance on the use of ECT in the presence of skull defects and intracranial metal objects due to the scarce literature (Mortier, Sienaert and Bouckaert, 2013). The presence of intracranial space-occupying lesions is considered to be a relative contraindication for ECT owing to an increase of intracranial pressure that would cause either bleeding or herniation (American Psychiatric Association, 2001).

Clinicians have to weigh up the possible benefits of ECT against theoretical risks in the absence of any guidelines, recommendations of the manufacturers and systematic literature (Gahr, Connemann, Freudenmann and Schonfeldt-Lecuona, 2014). Head injury and metallic plate implantation with subsequent severe depression is a challenging clinical problem, and a high suicide risk makes effective treatment imperative (Amanullah, Delva, McRae, Campbell and Cole, 2012).

Clinical problems range from patients who have intracranial masses or mass effects (Rasmussen, Perry, Sutor and Moore, 2007) to those with extra- or intracranial metallic objects (cMO) (Gahr et al., 2014). Cranial metal objects include: aneurysm clipping systems, coils used for endovascular embolisation of intracranial aneurysms, or head implants like osteosynthesis material, cochlear implants, deep brain stimulation devices or metallic foreign bodies (Gahr et al., 2014).

The theoretical concerns of cMO are:

- The electrical conductivity of cMO are better than brain tissue, representing low-impedance paths for the ECT current that may significantly alter the induced electric field distribution in the brain regarding field strength and focality.
- There is a risk of vascular complications, especially bleeding, at the application site of the metal object, like an aneurysm clip as ECT is associated with a hyper-dynamic state characterised by arterial hypertension, tachycardia, increased cerebral blood flow rate and velocity.
- There is a risk of developing a prolonged seizure and potential status epilepticus during ECT as a consequence of a pre-existing device-induced symptomatic epilepsy (Gahr et al., 2014).

Case report highlight that ECT can be performed safely and successfully in the following situations:

- skull deficits following a craniotomy (Crow, Meller, Christenson et al., 1996; Hsiao and Evans, 1984; Roccaforte and Burke, 1989);
- surgical skull defects (Amanullah et al., 2012; Everman et al., 1999);
- gunshot wound to the head with a persisting skull defect and intracranial metallic particles (Crow et al., 1996; Mortier et al., 2013) and intracranial shrapnel (Hartmann and Saldivia, 1990);
- large titanium mesh cranial base reconstruction (190 × 120 × 70 mm, 0.8 mm in thickness) following removal of a meningioma that covered almost all of the right hemisphere (Shiwaku, Masaki, Yasugi and Narushima, 2015);
- stainless steel skull plate (Madan and Anderson, 2001);
- extra- or intracranial metal objects (Amanullah et al., 2012; Mortier et al., 2013);
- deep brain stimulating electrodes (Ducharme, Flaherty, Seiner, Dougherty and Morales, 2011; Moscarillo and Annunziata, 2000);
- intracranial masses (K. G. Rasmussen et al., 2007);
- presence of a brain tumour and increased intracranial pressure (Patkar, Hill, Weinstein and Schwartz, 2000);
- intracranial venous masses (Salaris, Szuba and Traber, 2000).

Amanullah et al. (2012) provide sound advice to clinicians who are faced with the challenge of treating patients with these conditions:

- complete a thorough history and examination;
- take fully informed consent or use a mental health tribunal;
- CT scan to confirm and map the lesion or implant;
- carefully mark the planned electrode sites on the patient's head;
- use ultrabrief stimuli and unilateral electrode placement; a low-stimulus dose should be applied to avoid excessive local current density through the defect;

- discuss with the anaesthetist the possibility of restimulation if there are subconvulsive seizures;
- baseline psychometric assessment if possible;
- place electrodes as far away from the metallic implant as possible;
- hyperventilate with 100% oxygen.

NEUROPSYCHIATRIC DISORDERS

Dementia

Comorbid depression is common in patients with dementia, affecting a quarter to three quarters of patients. ECT can be a useful treatment as brain deterioration often makes these patients resistant to psychotropic medication. Treating patients with dementia requires the ECT practitioner to be aware of the special needs and potential complications that can arise (Weiner and Coffey, 2000).

The differential diagnosis between depression and dementia is complicated as patients with dementia are often unable to express the usual subjective depressive symptoms of low mood and anhedonia. The existence of the reversible pseudodementia of depression may make it difficult to ascertain whether one is dealing with episodic affective illness, dementing illness or a combination of both (Kellner and Bernstein, 1993) Potential cognitive impairment from ECT is one of the greatest challenges confronting the clinician when treating patients with dementia. ECT-induced cognitive impairment in patients with dementia is relatively uncommon. In addition, there is little evidence to suggest that ECT will worsen dementia in the long term (Price and McAllister, 1989).

Price and McAllister (1989) reviewed the results of ECT in 135 depressive patients: 56 with cortical dementia, 57 with subcortical leukoencephalopathy dementia and 22 with depressive dementia. Overall, 86% had a positive therapeutic response to ECT, 73% in those with dementia. Significant cognitive or memory side effects were found in 21% of cases, virtually all of which were transient and reversible with a worse outcome for bilateral ECT. Patients had a mean age of 66.7 years; women were twice as likely to have ECT as men; the average number of treatments was 8.4, a number similar to non-demented depressed patients; and nearly half of the patients with cognitive or memory dysfunction prior to ECT showed an improvement, rather than a decrement following ECT owing to improvement in attention and concentration (Price and McAllister, 1989). Other case reports have demonstrated similar outcomes (Benbow, 1987, 1988; Greenwald et al., 1989; Liang, Lam and Ancill, 1988). Patients with subcortical dementias (Huntington's, chorea or Parkinson's disease) with depression are more likely to respond to ECT than those with a cortical dementia (e.g. Alzheimer's disease or Pick's disease). There is some evidence to suggest that elderly patients who have white matter lesions (hyperintensity) on magnetic resonance scans with a probably vascular cause showed an excellent response to ECT (Coffey, Figiel, Djang and Weiner, 1989).

Kellner and Bernstein (1993) recommend a therapeutic trial of ECT for patients with this set of comorbidities who do not fulfil the classic symptoms of melancholic depression. To minimise the cognitive side effects of ECT it is recommended that ECT be administered: using an ultrabrief or brief-pulse stimulus, unilateral electrode placement; avoiding excessively high stimulus dosage; and administering the treatment twice a week or less frequently once there has been a clinical response (Price and McAllister, 1989).

With careful diagnosis, appropriate medical and neurological evaluation and stabilisation, ECT can be highly effective in relieving depressive symptoms in patients with dementia, with some suggestion that ECT may improve cognitive and memory dysfunction.

Pseudodementia/depressive dementia

Severe depressive illness can be associated with profound cognitive dysfunction (Kellner and Bernstein, 1993). In the past this phenomenon was known as pseudodementia and referred to the cognitive disturbance that occurred in the context of a significant behavioural disturbances caricatured by functional psychiatric disorders (Wells, 1979). A more recent review challenged the idea that this term described a homogenous group, rather it referred to at least two groups and that cognitive impairment associated with depressive illness is more appropriately viewed as a depression-induced organic mental disorder (McAllister, 1983). More focused study of the context in which this problem occurred led Folstein and McHugh (1978) to suggest that the cognitive impairment associated with major depressive illness was in fact a truly reversible dementia recommending that it be called "depressive dementia" or "dementia syndrome of depression".

Neuroleptic malignant syndrome (NMS)

Neuroleptic malignant syndrome (NMS) is a life-threatening neurological disorder commonly caused by an adverse reaction to neuroleptic/antipsychotic medication. Common presenting symptoms include muscle rigidity, fever, autonomic instability and cognitive changes such as delirium (Bond, 1983; Caroff and Mann, 1993; Casey, 1987). It is often associated with a range of laboratory abnormalities including: an elevated level of plasma creatine phosphokinase aldolase, transaminases and lactic acid dehydrogenase concentrations from rhabdomyolysis, metabolic acidosis, hypoxia, decreased serum iron concentrations, elevated catecholamines, and leucocytosis with or without left shift (Strawn, Keck and Caroff, 2007).

NMS is often difficult to distinguish from more common extrapyramidal side effects of antipsychotic medication (Strawn et al., 2007). Differentiating it from malignant catatonia can be difficult and there are some who think that NMS and malignant catatonia are two entities on the same spectrum of illness (Vesperini, Papetti and Pringuey, 2010).

Acute treatment of NMS involves ceasing the antipsychotic medication and urgent referral to a physician for medical management. Medical intervention consists of: supportive therapy, keeping the patient warm, aggressive volume resuscitation, correction of electrolyte abnormalities, loading with alkalinised fluid to prevent renal failure, administering dopaminergic agents like bromocriptine and dantrolene to reduce muscle rigidity and using benzodiazepines to control the agitation (Rosenberg and Green, 1989; Scheftner and Shulman, 1992; Strawn et al., 2007).

If these interventions are not successful or the patient fails to improve ECT has been used with favourable results in this condition even late in the course of NMS (Addonizio and Susman, 1987; Casey, 1987; Davis, Janicak and P., 1991; Lazarus, 1986; Ozer et al., 2005; Strawn et al., 2007; Trollor and Sachdev, 1993). Trollor and Sachdev (1993) competed a review of the use of ECT in the treatment of NMS. They reported that ECT was consistently effective even after failed pharmacotherapy and that clinical response often occurred over the course of the first few treatments, with bitemporal ECT recommended. Treatment response to ECT was not predicted by age, sex, psychiatric condition or any specific features of NMS (Trollor and Sachdev, 1993).

Caution needs to be used in administering suxamethonium in the presence of extensive muscular rigidity as it may result in an increased risk of hyperkalemia. In these cases a non-depolarising muscle relaxant should be considered (Price and McAllister, 1989). Close observation is necessary to exclude metabolic and/or cardiovascular instability during the treatment (Addonizio and Susman, 1987).

Parkinson's disease (PD)

Parkinson's disease is a neurodegenerative disorder of the central nervous system resulting from the death of dopamine-generating cells in the substantia nigra, a region in the mid-brain. Classically it has a triad of symptoms: tremor, rigidity and slowness of movement with difficulties in walking. Medical treatment is complicated by the "on–off" syndrome and very severe psychotic symptoms such as delusions and hallucinations (Kellner and Bernstein,

1993). Dementia and cognitive decline may also occur, as well as depressive illness. ECT has been shown to be beneficial in treating not only the major depressive symptoms but also can result in improvement in tremor, rigidity and movement (Trimble and Krishnamoorthy, 2005). There have also been successful trials in using ECT as an antiparkinsonian agent to treat the "on–off" phenomena via mediating a change in dopamine responsiveness (Andersen et al., 1987).

In their review, Trimble and Krishnamoorthy (2005) noted that there was an absence of well-designed clinical trials concerning the use of ECT in PD and that the literature consisted of single or multiple case reports. The vast majority of case reports demonstrated improvement in mood as well as physical symptoms resulting in the development of clinical recommendations to guide the use of ECT in this condition (Kellner and Bernstein, 1993; Rasmussen and Abrams, 1991; Zervas and Fink, 1991):

- ECT should be used in patients refractory to drug treatment with severe disability.
- Fully informed consent is essential.
- Commence with brief-pulse (now best to consider ultrabrief) right unilateral electrode placement to reduce cognitive side effects that are more common with this condition.
- Reduce the dose of L-dopa by half, and discontinue adjunctive treatment to prevent emergent dyskinesia and postictal delirium.
- Use a high electrical dosage to induce a suprathreshold seizure with robust features on the EEG.
- Cease when maximum improvement is noted, when the patient maintains improvement between the last two treatments.
- If treating PD without mood symptoms, improvement always starts after the third treatment; cease if no improvement after the sixth treatment.
- Reinstate optimal PD medication, L-dopa and adjunctive drugs as soon as ECT is ceased.

- If cognitive impairment is severe, the frequency of treatment should be reduced.
- Consider continuation/maintenance ECT to prevent or delay the return of physical and psychiatric symptoms.

ECT for this condition may be limited in some regions owing to restrictions placed upon the treatment by mental health legislation.

Worldwide, the use of ECT for PD has reduced owing to the growing evidence that bilateral deep brain stimulation (DBS) is associated with significant improvement in motor function and quality of life in patients with severe disease after six to 12 months of treatment with minimal morbidity (Breit, Schulz and Benabid, 2004). Rodriguez-Oroz et al. (2005) report the positive long-term results of a multicentre study involving 69 patients who were treated with DBS over a four-year period. They highlight that the treatment is safe and results in substantial clinical improvement.

Muscular skeletal disorders

ECT can be safely administered to depressed patients who have severe joint or bone disease. The dose of suxamethonium (0.5–2.3 mg/kg) should be high to ensure complete muscular relaxation (Dighe-Deo and Shah, 1998; Hanretta and Malek-Ahmadi, 1995; Kellner, Tolhurst and Burns, 1991). Clinical observations including loss of the deep tendon knee reflex, time between administration of suxamethonium and treatment (90–120 seconds) and cessation of muscle fasciculations can be augmented by the use of a nerve stimulator placed over the ulnar nerve, with treatment proceeding only after suppression of the twitch response, ensuring complete paralysis (Baker, 1986; Beale et al., 1994).

There are case reports of ECT being successfully administered in the following conditions:

- severe cervical spine disease (Kellner et al., 1991);
- wrist fracture (Baethge and Bschor, 2003);

- Harrington rods (Hanretta and Malek-Ahmadi, 1995; Milstein, Small and French, 1992);
- severe osteoporosis (Baker, 1986);
- osetogenesis imperfecta (Coffey, Weiner, Kalayjian and Christison, 1986);
- long bone fractures (Dighe-Deo and Shah, 1998)
- joint contracture (Mashimo, Kanaya and Yamauchi, 1995; Mashimo, Sato and Yamauchi, 1996);
- multiple bone fractures and generalised plasmocytoma (Weller and Kornhuber, 1992);
- bilateral petrous bone and femoral neck fractures (Weller and Kornhuber, 1992) in the setting of other complex medical conditions (Regestein and Reich, 1985).

ENDOCRINE

Osteoporosis

Osteoporosis is a disease that is characterised by a progressive reduction in bone mass and mineral density which can lead to pathological fractures. This weakness in bone increases the risk of fracture in ECT. Using modern anaesthetic technique bony fractures are rare, but without careful screening and excellent ECT technique, fracture can still occur during treatment (Nott and Watts, 1999). It is recommended that higher doses of suxamethonium are used to eliminate the motor seizure completely (Mirzakhani, Welch, Eikermann and Nozari, 2012). The use of isolated limb/cuff monitoring technique should be avoided if the condition is severe to prevent a potential crush injury (Baethge and Bschor, 2003).

Diabetes mellitus

Changes in the management of insulin and oral hypoglycaemic medication may be necessary prior to ECT as insulin requirements fluctuate during the course of treatment (Finestone and Weiner, 1984).

Rasmussen and Ryan (2005) studied the effect of ECT on the blood sugars levels of 33 non-diabetic patients before and 20 minutes after ECT treatment. They showed that there was a 9% (98 mg/dl) increase in blood sugar levels 20 minutes after treatment possibly due to pulses of cortisol or catecholamines during the treatment but these changes were not clinically significant. This finding was in line with the results of a retrospective study completed by Rasmussen, Ryan and Mueller (2006), who examined the records of 18 Type 2 diabetic patients who underwent ECT and found an increase in blood sugar levels of 9% (12.7 mg/dl) 20 minutes post-ECT. They recommended careful monitoring of blood sugar levels in diabetic patients during a course of ECT.

The frequency and nature of routine blood glucose monitoring should be consistent with the protocols utilised in the hospital in which ECT is being administered. There have been reports that hyperglycaemia might occur in patients who do not have diabetes and careful monitoring is required (Rasmussen and Ryan, 2005) and that ECT may result in complete remission of diabetic symptoms in recent onset non-insulin dependent diabetic patients (Fakhri, Fadhli and el Rawi, 1980). These findings have not been replicated in other work, which showed no significant changes in acute glycaemic control associated with ECT, suggesting that this treatment is safe and efficacious in depressed patients with diabetes (Netzel et al., 2002).

Some practitioners withhold insulin and hypoglycaemic medications until after treatment but it is recommended that half the dose of the long-acting insulin be administered before the treatment, with the other half given after it has been completed (Weiner and Sibert, 1996). This practice is common in many regions around the world. It is usual practice to place patients with diabetes first on the list to reduce the monitoring required during long periods of fasting. It is important to monitor blood glucose one hour before and after each treatment to ensure appropriate management of hypoglycaemic states.

Hypothalamic–pituitary–thyroid axis

There is some evidence that the hypothalamic–pituitary–thyroid axis is affected by treatment with ECT. Esel et al. (2002) examined the changes that occurred in thyroid hormones in 18 patients with unipolar or bipolar depression. They took blood samples immediately before ECT, then 30 and 60 minutes after ECT during the first and last (seventh) ECT treatments to examine serum levels of thyroid-stimulating hormone (TSH), free thyroiodothyronine (fT3) and free thyroxine (fT4). In both the first and seventh ECTs, there was a significant increase in TSH levels 30 min after ECT compared to the pre-ECT values and a significant decrease 30 minutes after treatment seven in fT4. There were no differences between the type of depression treated or males and females. Although the results were significantly different, it was not possible to determine if the neuroendocrine change were related to the therapeutic effects of ECT.

Hyperthyroidism

Overactivity of the thyroid gland can result in thyrotoxicosis. There have been mixed reports concerning the use of ECT in these patients with warnings ranging from there being a substantial risk of a thyroid storm at the time of ECT (Farah and McCall, 1995) through to the safe use of this treatment in Grave's disease following partial treatment in by propylithiouracil (Farah and McCall, 1995). Appropriate consultation with a specialist endocrinologist is recommended. Some of the common symptoms that may be exacerbated by ECT can be controlled if a beta blocker is administered at the time of treatment.

Hypothyroidism

Hypothyroidism is a state in which the thyroid gland is underactive, commonly caused by Hashimoto's disease, an autoimmune disorder. If untreated it may cause treatment-resistant depression, a condition that often leads to ECT. Limited evidence suggests that ECT is safe and effective if the hypothyroid condition has been stabilised prior to the course of treatment (Garrett, 1985).

Chronic adrenal insufficiency (Addison's disease)

Chronic adrenal insufficiency is a rare endocrine disorder in which the adrenal glands do not produce sufficient steroid hormones. It is recommended that consultation with an endocrinologist be undertaken before embarking on a course of ECT. Little is known about the impact of ECT on this condition with one case report, suggesting that these patients may require and a dose of cortisone before each treatment to improve the outcome of treatment due to the transient adrenocortical stimulation that occurs during treatment (Cumming and Kort, 1956) and another that demonstrated a successful outcome (Craddock and Zeller, 1952).

Other endocrine conditions

ECT has been administered safely with a good outcome in:

- hyperparathyroidism (Cunningham and Anderson, 1995);
- hypoparathyroidism (Casamassima et al., 2009);
- Cushing's disease (Ries and Bokan, 1979);
- pseudohypoparathyroidism (McCall, Coffey and Maltbie, 1989);
- pheochromocytoma, which has been identified as a condition where ECT may be contraindicated owing to hypertension or other episodic symptoms (Carr and Woods, 1985), whereas others have suggested that although the condition represents challenges, the risks can be minimised by using beta blockers, alpha blockers or blockers of tyrosine hydroxylase (Weiner et al., 2000).

METABOLIC DISORDERS

These conditions need to be corrected before ECT commences.

Hyperkalemia

Hyperkalemia is a condition in which there is an elevation of potassium concentrations within the body. Suxamethonium is a common muscle relaxant used in ECT that can cause small rises in the extracacellular potassium in the order of 0.5–1 mEq/l, which under normal circumstances has little clinical significance (Hudcova and Schumann, 2006). In the presence of hyperkalemia, exposure to suxamethonium during ECT may result in severe cardiac abnormalities because of this transient rise in serum potassium (Bali, 1975).

Hudcova and Schumann (2006) report a case of a seriously obese patient immobilised by catatonia, treated with ECT, who developed a life-threatening ventricular tachycardia following exposure to suxamethonium. Immobilisation caused changes at the neuromuscular junction, believed to be up-regulation of nicotinic cholinergic receptors and subsequent serious hyperkalemia following succinylcholine administration.

Efforts should be made to return the serum potassium level to the normal range before commencing ECT to ensure that suxamethonium does not have any serious cardio-toxic effects. If this cannot be achieved a switch to a non-depolarising muscle relaxant should be made.

Hypokalaemia

Hypokalaemia is a condition in which there is a decrease in potassium concentrations within the body. The normal range is between 3.5 and 5 mmol/L. Replacing potassium before ECT is administered is essential to minimise the risk of cardiovascular complications, prolonged paralysis and apnoea, which could seriously compromise the treatment.

Hyponatremia

Hyponatremia is an electrolyte disturbance in which the sodium iron concentration is lower than the normal range, 135 to 145 millemoles per litre (mmol/L) and may be caused by psychotropic medications although the mechanism is unknown (Madhusoodanan et al., 2002).

Symptoms of hyponatremia can mimic depression, psychosis, confusion, agitation and lethargy. Early recognition of this state is important and periodic monitoring of serum electrolytes is necessary. Treatment involves stopping the medication and assuring normal extracellular fluid volume. Infrequently, intravenous infusion of hypertonic saline is required (Madhusoodanan et al., 2002; Sharma and Pompei, 1996).

Hyponatremia needs to be corrected prior to commencing ECT, as it can lower seizure threshold, leading to an increased risk of spontaneous seizures (Finlayson, Vieweg, Wilkey and Cooper, 1989), prolonged seizures or a severe postictal delirium (Greer and Stewart, 1993).

Hypernatremia

Hypernatremia is an electrolyte disturbance that results in an elevated level of sodium within the bloodstream. It is commonly associated with dehydration along with hyperkalemia (Mashimo et al., 1996). It needs to be corrected prior to commencing ECT to reduce complications. Unlike infants, adults often have few symptoms until their serum sodium concentration exceeds 160 mmol/L. Symptoms typically include intense thirst, muscle weakness, confusion insomnia and potential coma (Adrogue and Madias, 2000).

Renal dialysis

Renal dialysis involves mechanical removal of toxic substances from the blood in the setting of chronic renal failure. Administration of ECT to patients maintained on chronic haemodialysis present potential management problems, fluctuating volume loads, altered serum pH (metabolic acidosis), cardio

toxicity from serum potassium elevation with suxamethonium, increased fracture susceptibility due to hyperparathyroidism with renal osteodystrophy and hypertension (Williams and Ostroff, 2005).

ECT treatment should be scheduled on the day after dialysis has been completed to ensure that potassium elevations with suxamethonium are not deleterious. Patients with significant osteodystrophy require complete muscle paralysis before the treatment is administered (Pearlman, 1988). Alternatively, if the risk of hyperkalemia is high a lower dose of suxamethonium should be used. Sustained hypertension can be a complicating factor and drugs like esmolol should be used prophylactically to control BP during subsequent treatments (Williams and Ostroff, 2005).

OTHER MEDICAL ILLNESSES

Eye pathology

The impact of ECT on intraocular pressure (IOP) has been of interest for many years (Lincoff et al., 1955; Manning and Hollander, 1954; Mc, Mills and Markson, 1950; Ottosson and Rendahl, 1963). There has been one report, after multiple cardioversion shocks, of disruption to the iris pigment epithelium that was deposited on the anterior lens surface, iris stroma, corneal endothelium and trabecular meshwork with similar findings in three patients who had more than 10 ECT treatments (Berger, 1978).

It is now well known that there is a small reduction in IOP after the administration of most anaesthetic induction agents, with an increase in IOP of up to 2.5 mmHg after suxamethonium is administered (Cunningham and Barry, 1986; Van Den Berg and Honjol, 1998). There is a further statistically significant surge in pressure following the application of the stimulus, with a mean change from baseline 14.1 mmHg to 27.4 mmHg. The maximum individual IOP observed during ECT-induced seizure was 39 mmHg, with all pressures returning to baseline 90 seconds after completion of seizure activity. The cause of the increase in IOP following seizure induction is unknown (Edwards, Stoudemire and Vela, 1990).

It is recommended that ophthalmological advice be sought in patients who have advanced glaucoma before commencing ECT (Abrams, 2002; Edwards et al., 1990). It is good practice to administer anti-glaucoma drops before each ECT treatment for patients who take them routinely. Caution should be utilised when using long-acting anticholinesterase ophthalmic drops like echothiophate (Messer et al., 1992) as they can greatly prolong the suxamethonium-induced apnoea and alternatives need to be found (Packman, Meyer and Verdun, 1978).

ECT has been administered safely in the following eye conditions:

- glaucoma (Good, Dolenc and Rasmussen, 2004; Nathan, Dowling, Peters and Kreps, 1986);
- glaucoma surgery as a protective measure to blunt the IOP spikes (Song, Lee, Weiner and Challa, 2004);
- post-eye surgery (Saad, Black, Krahn and Rummans, 2000);
- retinal detachment (Karliner, 1982);
- traumatic eye injury (Wachtel, Jaffe and Kellner, 2011).

It is highly recommended that there is close consultation with the treating ophthalmologist in all cases before commencing ECT.

Obesity

Obesity is not a contraindication for ECT that can be administered successfully on all occasions (Kadar et al., 2002). Patients who are morbidly obese do present an anaesthetic risk, making repeated venous access difficult, potentially complicated airway management and increasing the likelihood of oesophageal reflux (Weiner and Coffey, 2000). Special bariatric surgical beds should be used in all cases. In m-ECT patients, consideration should be given to inserting a permanent venous line like a "Port-a-cath" to avoid the persistent trauma that can be caused by multiple attempts to access veins that have become thrombosed.

Oesophageal reflux with or without a hiatus hernia presents a risk of increased aspiration during procedures involving anaesthesia like ECT and treatment to reduce gastric acidity may be considered in the high-risk patient (Weiner and Coffey, 2000). In high-risk patients who frequently desaturate after the seizure or where there is a risk of aspiration an endotracheal tube or laryngeal mask may be beneficial (Nishihara, Ohkawa, Hiraoka, Yuki and Saito, 2003).

Dentition

It is very important during ECT to ensure protection of the teeth and routine examination should be undertaken (Minneman, 1995; Weiner and McCall, 1992). Dental injuries are the most common complications of ECT (Watts et al., 2011). Mental health patients commonly have poor dental health owing to dental negligence, where decayed teeth and periodontal disease dominate the clinical picture (Stevens et al., 2010).

A rigid Guedel airway is commonly used to administer 100% oxygen during ventilation once induction has been completed. This should be removed and an appropriate soft rubber or foam mouthguard be inserted to protect the teeth against the strong contraction of the masseter muscle. Special care needs to be given if dentition is poor or if there are few teeth remaining and dental consultation should be considered. Denture and other appliances should routinely be removed after the patient has been anaesthetised to prevent damage or obstruction to the airway. Each mental health facility that administers ECT should develop an appropriate dental risk management protocol (Morris, Roche, Bentham and Wright, 2002).

Chronic obstructive pulmonary disease and asthma

Chronic obstructive pulmonary disease (COAD) and asthma are common chronic respiratory conditions that may complicate ECT. Before ECT commences care must be taken to screen for significant pulmonary dysfunction (Schak, Mueller, Barnes and Rasmussen, 2008). Although not common, an exacerbation of a patient's underlying asthma may occur sequentially during the treatment course in susceptible patients (Mueller, Schak, Barnes and Rasmussen, 2006). It is recommended that the conditions be stabilised and that patients are pre-treated with bronchodilators and careful pre-oxygenation before each treatment (Schak et al., 2008; Wingate and Hansen-Flaschen, 1997). Careful assessment and management of patients with COPD and asthma enable them to complete a course of ECT safely (Mueller et al., 2006).

In the past, theophylline was a common drug used to treat chronic respiratory disease. Initiating a course of ECT in patients taking this drug was associated with status epilepticus and consequent brain damage or even death (Rasmussen and Zorumski, 1993). Safety of ECT was ensured by reducing the dose or ceasing theophylline prior to commencement of ECT (Rasmussen and Zorumski, 1993). Worldwide, the use of theophylline in controlling COPD is less common, with the advent of new agents making these concerns less relevant in modern ECT practice.

Theophylline continues to be listed as a method of reducing seizure threshold in patients who have short or minimal seizure expression, even when a high-energy stimulus is administered (Fink and Sackeim, 1998; Loo, Simpson and MacPherson, 2010).

Gastro-oesophageal reflux disease (GORD)

Gastro-oesophageal reflux disease is a condition of chronic mucosal damage caused by stomach acid regurgitating from the stomach into the oesophagus. This condition is associated with an increased risk of aspiration during a general anaesthetic (Weiner et al., 2000). It is common in patients with morbid obesity and pregnant patients. As a result, anaesthetists recommend pre-treatment with the appropriate anti-reflux medication with a sip of water prior to commencing ECT.

Urinary retention

ECT should not be administered to patients with acute urinary retention owing to the possibility of bladder rupture as a result of powerful abdominal muscle contractions. In one reported case of bladder rupture the risk was considerably increased owing to a combination of factors, including a failure to void before treatment, the anticholinergic effect of a high-dose tricyclic antidepressant (amitriptyline) and a lack of adequate suxamethonium to modify the seizure to reduce the intensity of muscle contractions (O'Brien and Morgan, 1991). All patients should void close to each ECT treatment and in severe cases catheterisation should be considered prior to treatment.

Anticoagulation

Warfarin is considered safe in surgical procedures if the international normalised ratio (INR) is between 1.5 and 2.5 (Petrides and Fink, 1996).

In one case warfarin was changed to heparin before ECT commenced. The patient developed a deep vein thrombosis after the second ECT treatment. ECT was ceased and he was recommenced on warfarin. Warfarin was continued 12 months later when the depression returned and he had a second successful course of ECT without complication (Hay, 1987). This was in contrast to another case series where ECT was successful administered to three patients who were maintained on heparin (Loo, Cuche and Benkelfat, 1985). Tancer and Evans (1989) report the successful administration of ECT in three depressed geriatric patients who received oral anticoagulant warfarin for cardiovascular disease.

In a retrospective study of 35 consecutively hospitalised patients who were administered 300 ECT treatments and received long-term warfarin therapy, the only complication reported was ventricular tachycardia that resulted in temporary transfer to a cardiology for sustained monitoring, with no other serious complications noted despite increase in blood pressure and pulse during ECT treatment. The study concluded that ECT was safe when patients were maintained on long-term anticoagulation therapy provided the INR was monitored regularly and maintain at a safe level (Mehta et al., 2004).

Pseudocholinestase deficiency

Pseudocholinesterase deficiency is an inherited blood plasma enzyme abnormality that makes patients sensitive to the administration of the suxamethonium, resulting in prolonged recovery times. Pseudocholinestase deficiency can be a problem for patients having ECT but it is a rare condition (Fredman et al., 1994).

The predominant drug used for total body relaxation during each ECT treatment is suxamethonium, which is metabolised by the pseudocholinestase enzyme. Absence or depletion of this enzyme results in prolonged periods of paralysis, up to hours, requiring airway management by the anaesthetist until the suxamethonium is slowly metabolised by other pathways in the body. It has been shown to have a higher incidence in certain Indian, Persian, Iraqi and Jewish communities. Investigation for this condition is based upon cholinesterase genotyping (Lehman and Liddell, 1969).

The investigation measures the level of butyrylcholinestase, which has a reference range between 6.0 and 14.00 kU/l. Any value below 6.0 kU/l can be problematic, however exceptions occur. The presence of a variation in the pseudocholinestase gene cannot necessarily be excluded when a result falls within the reference range and a number of patients whose results fall below the reference range may have no genetic variation (Pathologynorth, 2015).

In one case series, ECT was administered to three patients using a non-depolarising muscle relaxant atracurium (0.3–0.5 mg/kg) with a good outcome in each case. One patient had pseudocholinesterase deficiency, another had potential cholinesterase inhibition due to chronic use of echothiopate iodide solution for glaucoma and the third had severe

multiple sclerosis where there was a risk of hyperkalemia and excessive muscle weakness with exposure to succinylcholine (Hicks, 1987).

Mivacurium (0.08–0.2 mg/kg) and rocuronium (0.3–0.6 mg/kg) are alternate non-depolarising agents that could be used in these cases. These agents are expensive increasing the cost of treatment and all have an extended duration of action, making the recovery time longer. It is recommended that a nerve stimulator be used to monitor the onset and offset of action with these agents (Fredman et al., 1994).

PREGNANCY

Pregnancy does not convey protection against mental illness. Medications used to treat this illness are associated with a range of potential adverse effects on the foetus, making ECT a useful alternative treatment (Anderson and Reti, 2009). ECT is a relatively safe and effective treatment during pregnancy (American Psychiatric Association, 2001; Lamprecht, Ferrier and Swann, 2005). A number of large case series have reported the safety of ECT for the treatment of severe mental illness during pregnancy.

Miller (1994) conducted a review of 300 women who had ECT during pregnancy and identified a complication rate of 9.3%, with many of these complications not being directly linked the treatment.

Anderson and Reti (2009) reviewed the literature from 1941 to 2007 and identified 339 cases of women treated with ECT. They showed that the average number of treatments administered (10.7 sessions) were similar to non-pregnant women; 84% of women with depression had a partial response, with a lower rate of 61% when used to treat schizophrenia. There were 25 foetal or neonatal complications, with 11 being related to ECT, and 20 maternal complications, with 18 related to ECT. Common adverse events included confusion, memory loss, muscle soreness and headache; these were noted to be worse in pregnant women. Foetal bradyarrhythmias occurred at a rate of 2.7% and the induction of premature labour occurring at a rate of 3.5%. The study concluded that ECT was an effective treatment for severe mental illness during pregnancy and the risks to mother and foetus were low (Anderson and Reti, 2009).

The safe use of ECT during pregnancy has been demonstrated in other case reports (Levi, Austin and Halliday, 2012; Nayak, Kulkarni, Kedare and Kaushal, 2015; O'Reardon, Cristancho, von Andreae, Cristancho and Weiss, 2011; Ozdemir, Poyraz, Erten, Cirakoglu and Tomruk, 2016; Saatcioglu and Tomruk, 2011) and may be the treatment of choice for postpartum psychosis (Focht and Kellner, 2012).

These findings have been challenged by two recent systematic reviews that demonstrate a higher complication rate than those reported above (Calaway, Coshal, Jones, Coverdaleand Livingston, 2016; Leiknes, Cooke, Jarosch-von Schweder, Harboeand Hoie, 2015) and a recent case report (Pinette, Santarpio, Wax and Blackstone, 2007), highlighting the need for caution when administering ECT to pregnant women.

Leiknes et al. (2015) conducted a systematic review identifying 169 women who were treated with ECT. The mean number of treatments was 9.4 sessions, with most women receiving treatment during the second trimester and many were primiparous. Both unilateral and bilateral ECT was administered and thiopentone were the main anaesthetic agent used. Adverse events were reported in 29% of cases and including: foetal heart rate reduction, uterine contractions and premature labour with delivery occurring between 29 and 37 weeks gestation with foetal death in 7.1% of cases. They concluded that ECT should only be used as a last resort under very stringent diagnostic and clinical indications. It is of note that this systematic review used very stringent inclusion criteria, eliminating many case reports from their analysis.

Caution in the use of ECT in pregnancy was supported by another systematic review that examined the safety of ECT during the first trimester of pregnancy from 1943 to 2015. Thirty-two women were identified, ranging in age from 24 to 39 years; the gestation of the foetus at the initiation of ECT ranged between two weeks to three months with the type of treatment administered rarely identified. Psychiatric conditions included depression, schizophrenia and bipolar and panic disorders. It was noted that 15.2% of first-trimester pregnancies incurred an adverse outcome after ECT, including vaginal bleeding, self-limited abdominal pain and foetal spasms. The rate of miscarriage in this study was 3.13%, significantly lower than the rate of spontaneous loss reported in the general population, which has been estimated as 25% to 50% of all pregnancies less than 14 weeks' gestation (Allison, Sherwood and Schust, 2011).

Based upon the limited available data, there is a low risk and high efficacy in the use of ECT to manage severe major depressive and bipolar disorders during pregnancy. A number of factors need to be taken into account when making this decision.

Early detection of perinatal psychiatric illness is crucial for the welfare of women and their offspring so that evidence-based psychological therapies can be offered early, preventing the need for more invasive treatments (Cooper, Murray, Wilson and Romaniuk, 2003; O'Hara and Wisner, 2014). If these interventions fail, biological methods have to be considered.

Medications are complex to administer, particularly during the first trimester, with many carrying high risks to mother and foetus and with congenital anomalies identified for benzodiazepines, antipsychotic drugs, lithium and other mood stabilisers (Altshuler et al., 1996; Cohen et al., 2010; Kuller et al., 1996; McElhatton, 1994; Nurnberg, 1989; Oates, 1986; Sadock, Sadock and Ruiz, 2009). Fortunately, tricyclic antidepressants, some of the newer antidepressant medications and a number of antipsychotic drugs can be safely used during the perinatal period (Cohen et al., 2010; Oates, 1986).

If these options fail or there has been a marked deterioration in the clinical state ECT should be considered. It is important to identify any complications of the pregnancy that may increase the risk of ECT or the anaesthetic that is administered during the treatment.

Withholding ECT carries its own risk as severe depression can undermine women's decision-making capacity about the management of the pregnancy. ECT has the potential to align a patient's decision-making capacity with their long-held values, avoiding premature termination of pregnancy (Coverdale, Chervenak, McCullough and Bayer, 1996). The rapidity and success of treatment are crucial to returning mothers with depression to a state where informed decisions can be made about the future of their pregnancies, especially with regard to the decision of whether or not to continue the pregnancy to term (Calaway et al., 2016).

Gastro-oesophageal reflux is common in pregnant women presenting an increased risk of aspiration during treatment and should be discussed during the consent process for ECT. Other rare adverse events should also be discussed such as spontaneous abortion, pre-term labour, abruption and utero-placental insufficiency (Lamprecht et al., 2005; Pinette et al., 2007; Saatcioglu and Tomruk, 2011).

In all cases, an obstetrician should be consulted before ECT commences to clarify the risk to the patient and foetus and make treatment modifications as required. Treatment should be undertaken in facilities that have resources available to deal with obstetric and neonatal emergencies (Miller, 1994).

Anaesthetic considerations

A pre-anaesthetic consult prior to ECT is necessary to prevent complications arising during the treatment with appropriate discussion with the treating obstetrician or other appropriate discipline (Katz and Castell, 1998; Rowe, 1997). Gastro-oesophageal reflux is common in pregnancy and should be managed aggressively with lifestyle modification and dietary changes prior to commencing treatment. If this is not adequate, antacids, antacid/alginic acid combinations or sucralfate are the first-line medial therapy, with H2-receptor antagonists used as second-line therapy. Except for omeprazole, all proton-pump inhibitors are considered safe to use during pregnancy and are classified as category B drugs by the US Food and Drug Administration (FDA) (Gerson, 2012).

If ECT is administered in women beyond 24 weeks, the risk of aspiration increases with advanced pregnancy, and intubation with a soft laryngeal mask airway is recommended for each treatment (Verghese and Brimacombe, 1996; Walker and Swartz, 1994). The soft laryngeal mask airway is designed to protect dentition and does not have

---

CLINICAL WISDOM 4.3.1

Managing women before, during or after pregnancy can be a rewarding but challenging task for psychiatrists. Pregnancy increases the risk of injury associated with mental illness and requires active management with frequent review of the clinical state with or without hospitalisation. ECT can be used successfully in this group of patients, bringing about rapid remission of symptoms allowing the mother to bond with her baby. Depression interrupts the process of attachment between the mother and her new born. Failure of the mother and at times the father to form a close bond with the new baby can have long-term and permanent serious consequences for all members of the family, particularly the newborn infant, who can often be treated differently to other siblings. The ECT practitioner is in a unique position to dramatically alter this potential problem by honestly discussing many of the issues noted above leading to fully informed consent. Failure to mention ECT as a treatment option owing to personal stigma or other reasons can be seen as a serious breach in the duty of care for these patients. Involvement of the family and other carers in this process is essential to ensure the best possible outcome for the mother and her new baby.

to be removed before the stimulus is delivered (Bosson, 2016).

The Collaborative Perinatal Project in the USA does not suggest any increase in teratogenesis for common agents used in short anaesthetic procedures (Klebanoff, 2009). Suxamethonium has a low ratio of placental transfer and presents no major impact on the foetus (Guay, Grenier and Varin, 1998). Methohexital and thiopentone are thought to have a low teratogenic risk, although this has not been formally studied. Glycopyrrolate is preferred to atropine as it has a more limited placental transfer rate (Abboud et al., 1983; Ferrill, Kehoe and Jacisin, 1992; Proakis and Harris, 1978). Anticholinergic agents decrease the tone of the lower oesophageal sphincter muscle and may increase the risk of regurgitation if not intubated (Klebanoff, 2009).

Procedural modifications

Care should be taken to well oxygenate the patient to maximise delivery of oxygen to the foetus to avoid hypoxia. Hyperventilation to lower seizure threshold should be avoided in pregnancy as respiratory alkalosis can hinder oxygen uploading from maternal to foetal haemoglobin (Anderson and Reti, 2009).

After 20 weeks' gestation a wedge should be placed under the patient's right hip to displace the uterus from the aorta and venae cava avoiding compression to improve placental perfusion and minimise the risk of hypoxia to the foetus (Walker and Swartz, 1994).

ECT must be administered in a hospital equipped with full obstetric facilities. It is recommended that tocohynamometry be used during ECT administration to monitor uterine activity. If detected it can be terminated by tocolysis with a beta2-adrenergic agonist like ritodrine (Matijevic, Grgic and Vasilj, 2006).

It is also recommended that intravenous hydration with a non-glucose-containing solution be given before each treatment due to the potential volume depletion and its risks to the cardiovas-

cular system (American Psychiatric Association, 2001).

When gestational age is greater than 14 weeks, foetal heart rate should be measured before and after each treatment (Miller, 1994). In pregnancies where there are foetal heart rate abnormalities it is suggested that a non-stress test with a tocometer be completed before and after each treatment. The aim is for foetal heart rate to be between 30 and 60 beats per minute (Walker and Swartz, 1994). It is very important to have appropriate resources available to deal with any obstetric and neonatal emergencies (Bhatia, Baldwin and Bhatia, 1999; Miller, 1994).

Postnatal considerations

Postpartum is defined as the period of time after the delivery of the placenta and extends for about eight weeks. Investigators frequently use the term "postnatal psychosis" to denote severe postpartum mental illness in general (Sadock et al., 2009), a condition that responds extremely well to ECT (Focht and Kellner, 2012).

There is evidence that depression during this period may respond better to ECT than in other circumstances, with a more rapid and complete remission of mood and psychotic symptoms (Reed et al., 1999). Severe postnatal disorders may respond rapidly to ultrabrief-pulse ECT causing minimal clinically observable side effects, assisting mothers to resume care of their infants more quickly (Levy, Austin and Halliday, 2012).

It is reported that 85% of women can experience some mood disturbance post-delivery, with up to 15% having clinically significant problems (Focht and Kellner, 2012). Between 30% and 50% of women experience symptoms in subsequent pregnancies. If a patient has a postpartum psychosis, there is an high risk of recurrence in up to 70% of women (Cohen et al., 2010) and ECT may be the treatment of choice (Focht and Kellner, 2012).

Further compelling evidence that supports the use of ECT during this period is the damage to attachment that can occur owing to maternal mental illness. Levi et al. (2012) highlight the detrimental effects of maternal depression on maternal bonding, infant attachment and development. It is known that 5% of women affected by severe depressive illness may suicide and 5% may commit infanticide (Levi et al., 2012).

Breastfeeding

Breastfeeding is promoted internationally as the preferred method of feeding and should be actively encouraged as it provides short-term and long-term health, economic and environmental advantages to children, women and society (Rollins et al., 2016; Scott and Binns, 1999). Despite its established benefits, breastfeeding is no longer a norm in many communities owing to multifactorial determinants (Rollins et al., 2016). Physicians should encourage new mother to persist with breastfeeding during the first six months of life. Women are vulnerable postpartum to psychiatric disorders and frequently face the need to decide whether to take psychotropic medication while breastfeeding and are confronted with the worry that virtually all psychotropic medications enter breast milk (Burt et al., 2001; Chaudron and Jefferson, 2000; Fortinguerra, Clavenna and Donati, 2009; Llewellyn and Stowe, 1998; Ward et al., 2001). There is a lack of safety information concerning the use of medication in lactation and breastfeeding (Worsley, Gilbert, Gavrilidis, Naughton and Kulkarni, 2013). Pharmacokinetics of drugs screened in breast milk is complex. Neonatal metabolism availability is dependent upon immature liver and kidney and blood barrier (Fortinguerra et al., 2009). Intense fear concerning the safety of psychotropic drugs during breastfeeding resulted in a tragic outcome for one family, where the mother killed both of her children after stopping her treatment for postnatal depression because she feared it would harm her baby (Worsley et al., 2013).

There is a clear advantage of ECT during this period, although there is no published data on the effects of this treatment on breast milk (Lamprecht, Ferrier, Swann and Waite, 2013). ECT can result in rapid improvement of symptoms, often around three or four treatments (Forray and Ostroff, 2007).

There is no evidence that medications used in ECT are detrimental to a breastfeeding infant and the level of information on the excretion of drugs into breast milk has improved (Cobb, Liu, Valentine and Onuoha, 2015; Dalal, Bosak and Berlin, 2014; Lee and Rubin, 1993).

Common anaesthetic agents used during ECT:

- methohexital: infant exposure from breast milk is reported to be less than 1% of the maternal dose (Borgatta et al., 1997);
- thiopentone: infant exposure from breast milk is reported to be negligible following exposure of the infant to a thiopentone dose of 3.8–7.0 mg/kg (Andersen, Qvist, Hertz and Mogensen, 1987), with a slow decline over a nine-hour period (Esener, Sarihasan, Guven and Ustun, 1992);
- etomidate: mean plasma concentrations declined rapidly and were undetectable after a two-hour period (Cobb et al., 2015; Esener et al., 1992);
- propofol: analysis revealed low levels in the breast milk that were cleared rapidly from the neonatal circulation, resulting in minimal effects on the suckling infant and is an ideal induction agent in obstetric patients (Cobb et al., 2015; Daillet al., 1989);
- ketamine: there are currently no human studies evaluating the transfer into breast milk (Cobb et al., 2015);
- neuromuscular blocking agents: there are no studies to date to evaluate the transfer of these drugs to breast milk. It is presumed that they do not cross the blood–milk barrier as they are relatively large in size, have low lipid solubility and are polarised in nature (Cobb et al., 2015);
- suxamethonium, infant exposure is minimal as absorption from the GIT is poor (Lee and Rubin, 1993);
- narcotic drugs: fentanyl crosses into the colostrum but was rapidly metabolised and can be used safely in breastfeeding women (Leuschen, Wolf and Rayburn, 1990; Steer, Biddle, Marley, Lantz and Sulik, 1992).

REFERENCES

Abboud, T., Raya, J., Sadri, S., Grobler, N., Stine, L., and Miller, F. (1983). Fetal and maternal cardiovascular effects of atropine and glycopyrrolate. *Anesthesia & Analgesia, 62*(4), 426–430. Retrieved from www.ncbi.nlm.nih.gov/pubmed/6829946.

Abrams, R. (2002). *Electroconvulsive Therapy*, 4th edition. New York Oxford University Press.

Addonizio, G., and Susman, V.L. (1987). ECT as a treatment alternative for patients with symptoms of neuroleptic malignant syndrome. *Journal of Clinical Psychiatry, 48*, 102–105.

Adrogue, H.J., and Madias, N.E. (2000). Hypernatremia. *New England Journal of Medicine, 342*(20), 1493–1499. doi:10.1056/NEJM200005183422006.

Allison, J.L., Sherwood, R.S., and Schust, D.J. (2011). Management of first trimester pregnancy loss can be safely moved into the office. *Review of Obstetric Gynecology., 4*, 5–14.

Aloysi, A.S., Maloutas, E., Gomes, A., and Kellner, C.H. (2011). Safe resumption of electroconvulusve therapy after non-ST segment elevation myocardial infaction. *Journal of ECT, 27*(1), e39–41.

Altshuler, L.L., Cohen, L., Szuba, M.P., Burt, V.K., Gitlin, M., and Mintz, J. (1996). Pharmacologic management of psychiatric illness during pregnancy: dilemmas and guidelines. *American Journal of Psychiatry, 153*(5), 592–606. doi:10.1176/ajp.153.5.592.

Amanullah, S., Delva, N., McRae, H., Campbell, L.A., and Cole, J. (2012). Electroconvulsive therapy in patients with skull defects or metallic implants: a review of the literature and case report. *Primary Care Companion CNS Disorders, 14*(2). doi:10.4088/PCC.11r01228.

American Psychiatric Association. (2001). *The Practice of Electroconvulsive Therapy: Recommendations for Treatment, Training and Privileging: A Task Force Report*, 2nd edition. Washington, DC: American Psychiatric Association.

Andersen, K., Balldin, J., Gottfries, C.G., Granérus A-K, Modigh, K., Svennerholm, L., and Wallin, A. (1987). A double-blind evaluation of electroconvulsive therapy in Parkinson's Disease with "on-off" phenomena. *Acta Neurologica Scandinavica, 76*(3), 191–199.

Andersen, L.W., Qvist, T., Hertz, J., and Mogensen, F. (1987). Concentrations of thiopentone in mature breast milk and colostrum following an induction dose. *Acta Anaesthesiologica Scandinavica, 31*(1), 30–32. Retrieved from www.ncbi.nlm.nih.gov/pubmed/3825473.

Anderson, E.L., and Reti, I.M. (2009). ECT in pregnancy: a review of the literature from 1941 to 2007. *Psychosomatic Medicine, 71*(2), 235–242. doi:10.1097/PSY.0b013e318190d7ca.

Applegate, R.J. (1997). Diagnosis and management of ischemic heart disease in the patient scheduled to undergo electroconvulsive therapy. *Journal of ECT, 13*(3), 128–144. Retrieved from http://journals.lww.com/ectjournal/Fulltext/1997/09000/Diagnosis_and_Management_of_Ischemic_Heart_Disease.4.aspx.

Bader, G.M., Silk, K.R., Dequardo, J.R., and Tandon, R. (1995). Electroconvulsive therapy and intracranial aneurysm. *Journal of ECT, 11*(2), 139–143.

Badrinath, S.S., and Guttmacher, L.B. (1984). Epidemiologic considerations in electroconvulsive therapy. *Archives of General Psychiatry, 41*, 246–253.

Baethge, C., and Bschor, T. (2003). Wrist fracture in a patient undergoing electroconvulsive treatment monitored using the "cuff" method. *European Archives of Psychiatry and Clinical Neuroscience, 253*(3), 160–162.

Baker, N.J. (1986). Electroconvulsive therapy and severe osteoporosis: use of a nerve stimulator to assess paralysis. *Convulsive Therapy, 2*(4), 285–288. Retrieved from www.ncbi.nlm.nih.gov/pubmed/11940878.

Bali, I.M. (1975). The effect of modified electroconvulsive therapy on plasma potassium concentration. *British Journal of Anaesthesia, 47*, 398–401.

Bankhead, A.J., Torrens, J.K., and Harris, T.H. (2006). The anticipation and prevention of cardiac complications in electroconvulsive therapy: a clinical and electrocardiographic study. *American Journal of Psychiatry, 106*(12), 911–917. doi:10.1176/ajp.106.12.911.

Beale, M.D., Kellner, C.H., Lemert, R., Pritchett, J.T., Bernstein, H.J., Burns, C.M., . . . Roy, R. (1994). Skeletal muscle relaxation in patients undergoing electroconvulsive therapy (letter). *Anesthesiology, 80*, 957.

Benbow, S.M. (1987). The use of electroconvulsive therapy in old age psychiatry. *International Journal Geriatric Psychiatry, 2*, 25–30.

Benbow, S.M. (1988). ECT for depression in dementia (letter). *British Journal of Psychiatry, 152*, 859.

Berger, R.O. (1978). Ocular complications of electroconvulsive therapy. *Annals of Ophthalmology, 10*(6), 737–743. Retrieved from www.ncbi.nlm.nih.gov/pubmed/677654.

Beyer, J.L., Weiner, R.D., and Glenn, M.D. (1998). *Electroconvulsive Therapy: A Programmed Text*, 2nd edition. Washington, DC: American Psychiatric Press.

Bhatia, S.C., Baldwin, S.A., and Bhatia, S.K. (1999). Electroconvulsive therapy during the third trimester of pregnancy. *Journal of ECT, 15*, 270–274.

Birkenhäger, T.K., Pluijms, E.M., Groenland, T.H., and van den Broek, W.W. (2010). Severe bradycardia after anesthesia before electroconvulsive therapy. *Journal of ECT, 26*(1), 53–54.

Bond, W.S. (1983). Detection and management of the neuroleptic malignant syndrome. *Clinical Pharmacy, 3*(3), 302–307.

Borgatta, L., Jenny, R.W., Gruss, L., Ong, C., and Barad, D. (1997). Clinical significance of methohexital, meperidine and dizepam in breast milk. *Journal of Clinical Pharmacology, 37,* 186–192.

Bosson, N. (2016). Laryngeal mask airway. *Medscape.* Retrieved from http://emedicine.medscape.com/article/82527-overview.

Brand, N., Clarke, Q., Eather, L., Garbutt, M., Leedow, M., Perry, J., . . . Spillane, P. (1994). Surgical morbidity in the North Coast Health Region. *Journal of Quality in Clinical Practice, 14*(2), 103–110. Retrieved from www.ncbi.nlm.nih.gov/pubmed/8049853.

Breit, S., Schulz, J.B., and Benabid, A.L. (2004). Deep brain stimulation. *Cell and Tissue Research, 318*(1), 275–288. doi:10.1007/s00441-004-0936-0.

Burt, V.K., Suri, R., Altshuler, L., Stowe, Z., Hendrick, V.C., and Muntean, E. (2001). The use of psychotropic medications during breast-feeding. *American Journal of Psychiatry, 158*(7), 1001–1009.

Calarge, C.A., and Crowe, R.R. (2004). Electroconvulsive therapy in myasthenia gravis. *Annals of Clinical Psychiatry, 16*(4), 225–227. doi:10.3109/10401230490522052.

Calaway, K., Coshal, S., Jones, K., Coverdale, J., and Livingston, R. (2016). A systematic review of the safety of electroconvulsive therapy use during the first trimester of pregnancy. *Journal of ECT, 32*(4), 230–235. doi:10.1097/YCT.0000000000000330.

Caroff, S.N., and Mann, S.C. (1993). Neuroleptic malignant syndrome. *Medical Clinics of North America, 77*(1), 185–202.

Carr, M.E., Jr, and Woods, J.W. (1985). Electroconvulsive therapy in a patient with unsuspected pheochromocytoma. *Southern Medical Journal, 78*(5), 613–615. Retrieved from www.ncbi.nlm.nih.gov/pubmed/3992309.

Casamassima, F., Lattanzi, L., Perlis, R.H., Fratta, S., Litta, A., Longobardi, A., . . . Cassano, G.B. (2009). Efficacy of electroconvulsive therapy in Fahr disease associated with bipolar psychotic disorder: a case report. *Journal of ECT, 25*(3), 213–215. doi:10.1097/YCT.0b013e3181914d28.

Casey, D.A. (1987). Electroconvulsive therapy in the neuroleptic malignant syndrome. *Convulsive Therapy, 3*(4), 278–283. Retrieved from www.ncbi.nlm.nih.gov/pubmed/11940929.

Chaudron, L.H., and Jefferson, J.W. (2000). Mood stabilizers during breastfeeding: a review. *Journal of Clinical Psychiatry, 61*(2), 79–90. Retrieved from www.ncbi.nlm.nih.gov/pubmed/10732654.

Cobb, B., Liu, R., Valentine, E., and Onuoha, O. (2015). Breastfeeding after anesthesia: a review for anesthesia providers regarding the transfer of medications into breast milk. *Translational Perioperative and Pain Medicine, 1*(2), 1–7.

Coffey, C.E., Figiel, G.S., Djang, W.T., Saunders, W.B., and Weiner, R.D. (1989). White matter hyperintensity on magnetic resonance imaging: clinical and neuroanatomic correlates in the depressed elderly. *Journal of Neuropsychiatry and Clinical Neuroscience, 1*(2), 135–144. doi:10.1176/jnp.1.2.135.

Coffey, C.E., Weiner, R.D., Kalayjian, R., and Christison, C. (1986). Electroconvulsive therapy in osteogenesis imperfecta: issues of muscular relaxation. *Convulsive Therapy, 2*(3), 207–211. Retrieved from www.ncbi.nlm.nih.gov/pubmed/11940868.

Coffey, C.E., Weiner, R.D., McCall, W.V., and Heinz, E.R. (1987). Electroconvulsive therapy in multiple sclerosis: a magnetic resonance imaging study of the brain. *Convulsive Therapy, 3*(2), 137–144. Retrieved from www.ncbi.nlm.nih.gov/pubmed/11940906.

Cohen, L.S., Wang, B., Nonacs, R., Viguera, A.C., Lemon, E.L., and Freeman, M.P. (2010). Treatment of mood disorders during pregnancy and postpartum. *Psychiatric Clinics of North America, 33*(2), 273–293. doi:10.1016/j.psc.2010.02.001.

Cooper, P.J., Murray, L., Wilson, A., and Romaniuk, H. (2003). Controlled trial of the short- and long-term effect of psychological treatment of post-partum depression. I. Impact on maternal mood. *British Journal of Psychiatry, 182*(5), 412–419. doi:10.1192/bjp.182.5.412.

Coverdale, J.H., Chervenak, F.A., McCullough, L.B., and Bayer, T. (1996). Ethically justified clinically comprehensive guidelines for the management of the depressed pregnant patient. *American Journal of Obstetrics and Gynecology, 174*(1 Pt 1), 169–173. Retrieved from www.ncbi.nlm.nih.gov/pubmed/8572002.

Craddock, W.L., and Zeller, N.H. (1952). Use of electroconvulsive therapy in a case of Addison's disease. *AMA Archives of Internal Medicine, 90*(3), 392–394.

Crow, S., Meller, W., Christenson, G., and Mackenzie, T. (1996). Use of ECT after brain injury. *Convulsive Therapy, 12,* 113–116. Retrieved from http://journals.lww.com/ectjournal/toc/1996/06000.

Cumming, J., and Kort, K. (1956). Apparent reversal by cortisone of an electro-convulsive refractory state in a psychotic patient with Addison's disease. *Canadian Medical Association Journal, 74*(4), 291–292. Retrieved from www.ncbi.nlm.nih.gov/pmc/articles/PMC1824078/.

Cunningham, A.J., and Barry, P. (1986). Intraocular pressure–physiology and implications for anaesthetic management. *Canadian Anaesthetists Society Journal, 33*(2), 195–208. Retrieved from www.ncbi.nlm.nih.gov/pubmed/3516335.

Cunningham, S.J., and Anderson, D.N. (1995). Delusional depression, hyperparathyroidism, and ECT. *Convulsive Therapy, 11*(2), 129–133. Retrieved from www.ncbi.nlm.nih.gov/pubmed/7552053.

Dailland, P., Cockshott, I.D., Lirzin, J.D., Jacquinot, P., Jorrot, J.C., Devery, J., . . . Conseiller, C. (1989). Intravenous propofol during cesarean section: placental transfer, concentrations in breast milk, and neonatal effects. A preliminary study. *Anesthesiology, 71*(6), 827–834.

Dalal, P.G., Bosak, J., and Berlin, C. (2014). Safety of the breast-feeding infant after maternal anesthesia. *Pediatric Anesthesia, 24*(4), 359–371. doi:10.1111/pan.12331.

Davis, A., Marc Zisselman, M., Simmons, T., Vaughn McCall, W.V., McCafferty, J., and Rosenquist, P.B. (2009). Electroconvulsive therapy in the setting of implantable cardioverter-defibrillators. *Journal of ECT, 25*(3), 198–201.

Davis, J.M., Janicak, P.G., and P., S. (1991). Electroconvulsive therapy in the treatment of the nueuroleptic malignant syndrome. *Convulsive Therapy, 7,* 111–120.

Dighe-Deo, D., and Shah, A. (1998). Electroconvulsive therapy in patients with long bone fractures. *Journal of ECT, 14*(2), 115–119. Retrieved from www.ncbi.nlm.nih.gov/pubmed/9641808.

Dolenc, T.J., Barnes, R.D., Hayes, R.L., and Rasmussen, K.G. (2004). Electroconvulsive therapy in patients with cardiac pacemakers and implantable cardioverter defibrillators. *Pacing and Clinical Electrophysiology, 27*(9), 1257–1263.

Drop, I.J., Viguera, A., and Welch, C.A. (2000). ECT in patients with intracranial aneurysm. *Journal of ECT, 16*(1), 71–72.

Ducharme, S., Flaherty, A.W., Seiner, S.J., Dougherty, D.D., and Morales, O.G. (2011). Temporary interruption of deep brain stimulation for Parkinson's disease during outpatient electroconvulsive therapy for major depression: a novel treatment strategy. *Journal of Neuropsychiatry and Clinical Neuroscience, 23*(2), 194–197. doi:10.1176/appi.neuropsych.23.2.194.10.1176/jnp.23.2.jnp194.

Edwards, R.M., Stoudemire, A., and Vela, M.A. (1990). Intraoccular pressure changes in nonglaucomatous patients undergoing electroconvulsive therapy. *Convulsive Therapy, 6,* 209–213.

Eisenkraft, J.B., Brook, W.J., and Mann, S.M. (1988). Resistance to succinylincholine in myasthenia gravis *Anesthesiology, 69,* 760–763.

Esel, E.,1, Turan, T., Kula, M., Reyhancan, M., Gonul, A., Basturk, M., and Sofuoglu, S. (2002). Effects of electroconvulsive therapy on hypothalamic–pituitary–thyroid axis activity in depressed patients. *Prog Neuropsychopharmacol Biological Psychiatry., October 26*(6), 1171–1175.

Esener, Z., Sarihasan, B., Guven, H., and Ustun, E. (1992). Thiopentone and etomidate concentrations in maternal and umbilical plasma, and in colostrum. *British Journal of Anaesthesia, 69*(6), 586–588.

Everman, P.D., Kellner, C.H., Beale, M.D., and Burns, C. (1999). Modified electrode placement in patients with neurosurgical skull defects [Letter]. *Journal of ECT, 15,* 237–239.

Fakhri, O., Fadhli, A.A., and el Rawi, R.M. (1980). Effect of electroconvulsive therapy on diabetes mellitus. *Lancet, 2*(8198), 775–777. Retrieved from www.ncbi.nlm.nih.gov/pubmed/6107455.

Farah, A., and McCall, W.V. (1995). ECT administration to a hyperthyroid patient. *Convulsive Therapy, 11*(2), 126–128. Retrieved from www.ncbi.nlm.nih.gov/pubmed/7552052.

Ferrill, M.J., Kehoe, W.A., and Jacisin, J.J. (1992). ECT during pregnancy: physiologic and pharmacologic considerations. *Convulsive Therapy, 8*(3), 186–200. Retrieved from www.ncbi.nlm.nih.gov/pubmed/11941169.

Figiel, G.S., Coffey, C.E., Djang, W.T., Hoffman, G., Jr, and Doraiswamy, P.M. (1990). Brain magnetic resonance imaging findings in ECT-induced delirium. *Journal of Neuropsychiatry and Clinical Neuroscience, 2*(1), 53–58. doi:10.1176/jnp.2.1.53.

Finestone, D.H., and Weiner, R.D. (1984). Effects of ECT on diabetes mellitus: an attempt to account for conflicting data. *Acta Psychiatrica Scandinavica, 70,* 321–326.

Fink, M., and Sackeim, H.A. (1998). Theophylline and ECT. *Journal of ECT, 14*(4), 286–290. Retrieved from www.ncbi.nlm.nih.gov/pubmed/9871854.

Finlayson, A.J., Vieweg, W.V., Wilkey, W.D., and Cooper, A.J. (1989). Hyponatremic seizure following ECT. *Canadian Journal of Psychiatry, 34*(5), 463–464. Retrieved from www.ncbi.nlm.nih.gov/pubmed/2504479.

Focht, A., and Kellner, C.H. (2012). Electroconvulsive therapy (ECT) in the treatment of postpartum psychosis. *Journal of ECT, 28*(1), 31–33. doi:10.1097/YCT.0b013e3182315aa8.

Folstein, S.E., and McHugh, P.R. (1978). Dementia syndrome of depression. In Katzman, R., Terry, R.D. and Bick, K.L. (Eds.), *Alzheimer's Disease: Senile Dementia and Related Disorders.* New York: Raven Press.

Forray, A., and Ostroff, R.B. (2007). Use of electroconvulsive therapy in the treatment of postpartum affective disorders. 2007; 23 (3): 188–193. *Journal of ECT, 23*(3), 188–193.

Fortinguerra, F., Clavenna, A., and Donati, M. (2009). Psychotropic drug use during breastfeeding: a review of the evidence. *Paediatrics, 124*(4), 547–556.

Fox, H.A. (1993). Patients' fear of and objection to electroconvulsive therapy. *Hospital Community Psychiatry, 44*(4), 357–360. Retrieved from www.ncbi.nlm.nih.gov/pubmed/8462942.

Fredman, B., d'Etienne, J., Smith, I., and White, P.F. (1994). Use of muscle relaxants for electroconvulsive therapy: how much is enough? *Anesthesia and Analgesia:, 78,* 195–196.

Gahr, M., Connemann, B.J., Freudenmann, R.W., and Schonfeldt-Lecuona, C. (2014). Safety of electroconvulsive therapy in the presence of cranial metallic objects. *Journal of ECT, 30*(1), 62–68. doi:10.1097/YCT.0b013e318295e30f.

Gardner, M.W., Kellner, C.H., Hood, D.E., and Hendrix, G.H. (1997). Safe administration of ECT in a patient with a cardiac aneurysm and multiple cardiac risk factors. *Convulsive Therapy, 13*(3), 200–203.

Garrett, M.D. (1985). Use of ECT in a depressed hypothyroid patient. *Journal of Clinical Psychiatry, 46,* 64–66.

Gerson, L.B. (2012). Treatment of gastroesophageal reflux disease during pregnancy. *Gastroenterology Hepatology (NY), 8*(11), 763–764. Retrieved from www.ncbi.nlm.nih.gov/pubmed/24672414.

Gitlin, M.C., Jahr, J.S., Margolis, M.A., and McCain, J. (1993). Is mivacurium chloride effective in electroconvulsive therapy? A report of four cases, including a patient with myasthenia gravis. *Anesthesia and Analgesia, 77*(2), 392–394.

Good, M.S., Dolenc, T.J., and Rasmussen, K.G. (2004). Electroconvulsive therapy in a patient with glaucoma. *Journal of ECT, 20*(1), 48–49. Retrieved from www.ncbi.nlm.nih.gov/pubmed/15087998.

Greenwald, B., Kramer-Ginsberg, E., Martin, D., Laitman, L.B., Hermann, C.K., Mohs, R.C., and Davis, K.L. (1989). Dementia with conexistent major depression. *American Journal of Psychiatry, 146,* 1472–1478.

Greer, R.A., and Stewart, R.B. (1993). Hyponatremia and ECT. *American Journal of Psychiatry, 150*(8), 1272. doi:10.1176/ajp.150.8.1272.

Guay, J., Grenier, Y., and Varin, F. (1998). Clinical pharmacokinetics of neuromuscular relaxants in Pregnancy. *Clinical Pharmacokinetics, 34,* 483–496.

Hal, M.J., Kozak, L.J., and Gilum, B.S. (1997). National survey of ambulatory surgery. *Statistical Bulletin of the Metropolitan Insurance Company, 78,* 18–27.

Hanretta, A.T., and Malek-Ahmadi, P. (1995). Use of ECT in a patient with a Harrington rod implant. *Convulsive Therapy, 11*(4), 266–270.

Hart, A. (2013). *ECT in Anaesthesia.* Paper presented at the ECT: a misunderstood treatment: a conference for ECT clinical staff. Newcastle, Australia.

Hartmann, S.J., and Saldivia, A. (1990). ECT in an elderly patient with skull defects and shrapnel. *Convulsive Therapy, 6*(2), 165–171. Retrieved from www.ncbi.nlm.nih.gov/pubmed/11941059.

Hay, D.P. (1987). Anticoagulants and ECT. *Convulsive Therapy, 3*(3), 236–237. Retrieved from www.ncbi.nlm.nih.gov/pubmed/11940924.

Hicks, F.G. (1987). ECT modified by atracurium. *Convulsive Therapy, 3*(1), 54–59. Retrieved from www.ncbi.nlm.nih.gov/pubmed/11940891.

Hirachan, A., and Maskey, A. (2016). Acute myocardial infarction following electroconvulsive therapy in a schizophrenic patient. *The Egyptian Heart Journal.* doi:10.1016/j.ehj.2016.05.002.

Hsiao, J.K., and Evans, D.L. (1984). ECT in a depressed patient after craniotomy. *American Journal of Psychiatry, 141*(3), 442–444. doi:10.1176/ajp.141.3.442.

Hudcova, J., and Schumann, R. (2006). Electroconvulsive therapy complicated by life-threatening hyperkalemia in a catatonic patient. *General Hospital Psychiatry, 28*(5), 440–442. doi:10.1016/j.genhosppsych.2006.07.003.

Hunt, S.A., and Kaplan, E. (1998). ECT in the presence of cerebral aneurysm. *Journal of ECT, 14*(2), 123–124.

Husum, B., Vester-Andersen, T., Buchmann, G., and Bolwig, T.G. (1983). Electroconvulsive therapy and intracranial aneurysm. Prevention of blood pressure elevation in a normotensive patient by hydralazine and propranolol. *Anaesthesia, 38*(12), 1205–1207. Retrieved from www.ncbi.nlm.nih.gov/pubmed/6660461.

Kadar, A.G., Ing, C.H., White, P.F., Wakefield, C.A., Kramer, B.A., and Clark, K. (2002). Anesthesia for electroconvulsive therapy in obese patients. *Anesthesia & Analgesia, 94*(2), 360–361, table of contents. Retrieved from www.ncbi.nlm.nih.gov/pubmed/11812699.

Karliner, W. (1982). Electroshock therapy in the presence of retinal detachment. *Diseases of the Nervous System, 19,* 401.

Katz, P.O., and Castell, D.O. (1998). Gastroesophageal reflux disease during pregnancy. *Gastroenterology Clinics of North America, 27*(1), 153–167. Retrieved from www.ncbi.nlm.nih.gov/pubmed/9546088.

Kellner, C.H., and Bernstein, H.J. (1993). ECT as a treatment for neurologic illness. In Coffey, C.E. (Ed.), *The Clinical Science of Electroconvulsive Therapy,* 1st edition (Vol. 38, pp. 183–210). Washington, DC and London: American Psychiatric Association.

Kellner, C.H., and Bernstein, H.J. (1993). ECT as a treament for neurologic illness. In Coffey, C.E. (Ed.), *The Clinical Science of Electroconvulsive Therapy.* Washington, DC: American Psychiatric Press.

Kellner, C.H., Tolhurst, J.E., and Burns, C.M. (1991). ECT in the presence of severe cervical spine disease. *Convulsive Therapy, 7*(1), 52–55. Retrieved from www.ncbi.nlm.nih.gov/pubmed/11941098.

Klebanoff, M.A. (2009). The collaborative perinatal project: a fifty year retrospective. *Paediatric Perinatal Epidemiology, January 23*(1), 2–8.

Kovac, A.L., Goto, H., Pardo, M.P., and Arakawa, K. (1991). Comparison of two esmolol bolus doses on the haemodynamic response and seizure duration during electroconvulsive therapy. *Canadian Journal of Anaesthesia, 38,* 204–209.

Krystal, A.D., and Coffey, C.E. (1997). Neuropsychiatric considerations in the use of electroconvulsive therapy. *Journal of Neuropsychiatry and Clinical Neurosciences, 9,* 283–292.

Kuller, J.A., Katz, V.L., McMahon, M.J., Wells, S.R., and Bashford, R.A. (1996). Pharmacologic treatment of psychiatric disease in pregnancy and lactation: fetal and nenatal effects. *Obstetrics and Gynecology, 87,* 789–794.

Lamprecht, H.C., Ferrier, N., and Swann, A.G. (2005). *The Use of ECT in Depressive Illness.* London: Royal College of Psychiatrists.

Lamprecht, H.C., Ferrier, N., Swann, A.G., and Waite, J. (2013). The use of ECT in the treatment of depression. In Waite, J., and Easton, A. (Eds.), *The ECT Handbook,* 3rd edition. London: Royal College of Psychiatrists.

Lapid, M., Rummans, T.A., Hofmann, V.E., and Olney, B.A. (2001). ECT and automatic internal cardioverter–defibrillator. *Journal of ECT, 17*(2), 146–148.

Lazarus, A. (1986). Treatment of neuroleptic malignant syndrome with electroconvulsive therapy. *Journal of Nervous and Mental Disease, 174,* 47–49.

Lee, J.J., and Rubin, A.P. (1993). Breast feeding and anesthesia. *Anesthesia, 48,* 616–625.

Lehman, H., and Liddell, J. (1969). Human cholinesterase (pseudocolinesterase): genetic varients and their recognition *British Journal of Anaesthesiaesiology, 41,* 235–244.

Leiknes, K.A., Cooke, M.J., Jarosch-von Schweder, L., Harboe, I., and Hoie, B. (2015). Electroconvulsive therapy during pregnancy: a systematic review of case studies. *Archives of Womens Mental Health, 18*(1), 1–39. doi:10.1007/s00737-013-0389-0.

Leuschen, M.P., Wolf, L.J., and Rayburn, W.F. (1990). Fentanyl excretion in breast milk. *Journal of Clinical Pharmacology, 9*(5), 336–337. Retrieved from www.ncbi.nlm.nih.gov/pubmed/2350936.

Levi, Y., Austin, M.N., and Halliday, G. (2012). Use of ultra brief pulse electroconvulsive therapy to treat severe postnatal mood disorder. *Australasian Psychiatry, 20*(5), 429–432. Retrieved from http://journals.sagepub.com/doi/pdf/10.1177/1039856212458979.

Levy, Y., Austin, M.-P., and Halliday, G. (2012). Use of ultra-brief pulse electroconvulsive therapy to treat severe postnatal mood disorder. *Australasian Psychiatry, 20*(5), 429–432.

Liang, R.A., Lam, R.W., and Ancill, R.J. (1988). ECT in the treatment of mixed depression and dementia. *British Journal of Psychiatry, 152,* 281–284. Retrieved from www.ncbi.nlm.nih.gov/pubmed/3167352.

Lincoff, H.A., Ellis, C.H., Devoe, A.G., Debeer, E.J., Impastato, D.J., Berg, S., . . . Magda, H. (1955). The effect of succinylcholine on intraocular pressure. *American Journal of Ophthalmology, 40*(4), 501–510. Retrieved from www.ncbi.nlm.nih.gov/pubmed/13258731.

Llewellyn, A., and Stowe, Z.N. (1998). Psychtrophic medications in lactation. *Journal of Clinical Psychiatry, 59(suppl 2),* 41–52.

Loo, C., Simpson, B., and MacPherson, R. (2010). Augmentation strategies in electroconvulsive therapy. *Journal of ECT, 26*(3), 202–207. doi:10.1097/YCT.0b013e3181e48143.

Loo, H., Cuche, H., and Benkelfat, C. (1985). Electroconvulsive therapy during anticoagulant therapy. *Convulsive Therapy, 1*(4), 258–262. Retrieved from www.ncbi.nlm.nih.gov/pubmed/11940831.

McAllister, T.W. (1983). Overview: pseudodementia. *American Journal of Psychiatry, 140*(5), 528–533. doi:10.1176/ajp.140.5.528.

McCabe, P. (1985). Morbidity and mortality rates for peripheral vascular surgery. *Infection Control, 6*(3), 94–95. Retrieved from www.ncbi.nlm.nih.gov/pubmed/3845068.

McCall, W.V. (1993). Antihypertensive medications and ECT. *Convulsive Therapy, 9*(4), 317–325. Retrieved from www.ncbi.nlm.nih.gov/pubmed/11941227.

McCall, W.V., Coffey, C.E., and Maltbie, A.A. (1989). Successful electroconvulsive therapy in a depressed patient with pseudohypoparathyroidism. *Convulsive Therapy, 5*(1), 114–117.

McClellan, J.W., Mills, M., Jr, and Markson, J.W. (1950). Measurement of intra-ocular tension in insulin and electroconvulsive therapy. *Bulletin of the Menninger Clinic, 14*(6), 220–225. Retrieved from www.ncbi.nlm.nih.gov/pubmed/24538642.

McElhatton, P.R. (1994). The use of pheonthiazines during pregnancy and lactation. *Reproductive Toxicology, 6,* 461–475.

MacPherson, R.D., Loo, C.K., and Barrett, N. (2006). Electroconvulsive therapy in patients with cardiac pacemakers. *Anaesthesia and Intensive Care Journal, 34*(4), 470–474. Retrieved from www.ncbi.nlm.nih.gov/pubmed/16913344.

Madan, S., and Anderson, K. (2001). ECT for a patient with a metallic skull plate. *Journal of ECT, 17*(4), 289–291. Retrieved from www.ncbi.nlm.nih.gov/pubmed/11731732.

Madhusoodanan, S., Bogunovic, O.J., Moise, D., Brenner, R., Markowitz, S., and Sotelo, J. (2002). Hyponatraemia associated with psychotropic medications. *Adverse Drug*

Reactions and Toxicological Reviews, 21(1–2), 17–29. doi:10.1007/BF03256181.

Magid, M., Lapid, M.L., Sampson, S.M., and Mueller, P.S. (2005). Use of electroconvulsive therapy in a patient 10 days after myocardial infarction. *Journal of ECT, 21*(3), 182–185.

Manning, E.L., and Hollander, W.M. (1954). Glaucoma and electroshock therapy. *American Journal of Ophthalmology, 37*(6), 857–859. Retrieved from www.ncbi.nlm.nih.gov/pubmed/13158478.

Mashimo, K., Kanaya, M., and Yamauchi, T. (1995). Electroconvulsive therapy for a schizophrenic patient in catatonic stupor with joint contracture. *Convulsive Therapy, 11*(3), 216–219. Retrieved from www.ncbi.nlm.nih.gov/pubmed/8528667.

Mashimo, K., Sato, Y., and Yamauchi, T. (1996). Effective electroconvulsive therapy for stupor in the high risk patient: a report of two cases. *Psychiatry and Clinical Neuroscience, 50*(3), 129–131. Retrieved from www.ncbi.nlm.nih.gov/pubmed/9201758.

Matijevic, R., Grgic, O., and Vasilj, O. (2006). Ritodrine in oral maintenance of tocolysis after active preterm labor: randomized controlled trial. *Croatian Medical Journal, 47*(1), 25–31. Retrieved from www.ncbi.nlm.nih.gov/pubmed/16489694.

Mattingly, G., Baker, K., and Zorumski, C.F. (1992). Multiple Sclerosis and ECT: possible value of gadolinimum-enhanced magneti resonance scans for identifying high-risk patients. *Journal of Neuropsychiatry and Clinical Neurosciences, 4*, 145–151.

Mehta, V., Mueller, P.S., Gonzalez-Arriaza, H.L., Pankratz, V.S., and Rummans, T.A. (2004). Safety of electroconvulsive therapy in patients receiving long-term warfarin therapy. *Mayo Clinic Proceedings, 79*(11), 1396–1401. doi:10.4065/79.11.1396.

Messer, G.J., Stoudemire, A., Knos, G., and Johnson, G.C. (1992). Electroconvulsive therapy and the chronic use of pseudocholinesterase-inhibitor (echothiophate iodide) eye drops for glaucoma: a case report. *General Hospital Psychiatry, 14*, 56–60.

Miller, L.J. (1994). Use of electroconvulsive therapy during pregnancy. *Community Psychiatry, 45*, 444–450.

Milstein, V., Small, I.F., and French, R.N. (1992). ECT in a patient with Harrington rods. *Convulsive Therapy, 8*(2), 137–140. Retrieved from www.ncbi.nlm.nih.gov/pubmed/11941160.

Minneman, S.A. (1995). A history of oral protection for the ECT patient: past, present, and future. *Convulsive Therapy, 11*, 94–103.

Mirzakhani, H., Welch, C.A., Eikermann, M., and Nozari, A. (2012). Neuromuscular blocking agents for electroconvulsive therapy: a systematic review. *Acta Anaesthesiologica Scandinavica, 56*(1), 3–16. doi:10.1111/j.1399-6576.2011.02520.x.

Morris, A.J., Roche, S.A., Bentham, P., and Wright, J. (2002). A dental risk management protocol for electroconvulsive therapy. *Journal of ECT, 18*(2), 84–89.

Mortier, P., Sienaert, P., and Bouckaert, F. (2013). Is electroconvulsive therapy safe in the presence of an intracranial metallic object? Case report and review of the literature. *Journal of ECT, 29*(3). Retrieved from http://journals.lww.com/ectjournal/toc/2013/09000.

Moscarillo, F.M., and Annunziata, C.M. (2000). ECT in a patient with a deep brain-stimulating electrode in place. *Journal of ECT, 16*(3), 287–290. Retrieved from www.ncbi.nlm.nih.gov/pubmed/11005051.

Mueller, P.S., Albin, S.M., Barnes, R.D., and Rasmussen, K.G. (2009). Safety of electroconvulsive therapy in patients with unrepaired abdominal aortic aneurysm: report of 8 patients. *Journal of ECT, 25*(3), 165–169.

Mueller, P.S., Barnes, R.D., Varghese, R., Nishimura, R.A., and Rasmussen, K.G. (2007). The safety of electroconvulsive therapy in patients with severe aortic stenosis. *Mayo Clinic Proceedings, 82*(11), 1360–1303.

Mueller, P.S., Schak, K.M., Barnes, R.D., and Rasmussen, K.G. (2006). Safety of electroconvulsive therapy in patients with asthma. *Netherlands Journal of Medicine, 64*(11), 417–421. Retrieved from www.ncbi.nlm.nih.gov/pubmed/17179572.

Murray, G., Shea, V., and Conn, D. (1989). Electroconvulsive therapy for post-stroke depression. *Journal of Clinical Psychiatry, 47*, 258–260.

Najjar, F., and Guttmacher, L.B. (1998). ECT in the presence of intracranial aneurysm *Journal of ECT, 14*(4), 266–271.

Nathan, R.S., Dowling, R., Peters, J.L., and Kreps, A. (1986). ECT and glaucoma. *Convulsive Therapy, 2*(2), 132–133. Retrieved from www.ncbi.nlm.nih.gov/pubmed/11940857.

Nayak, A., Kulkarni, P., Kedare, J., and Kaushal, P. (2015). Safety of modified electroconvulsive therapy (ECT) in the third trimester of pregnancy. *Indian Journal of Mental Health, 2*(3), 338–341.

Netzel, P.J., Mueller, P.S., Rummans, T.A., Rasmussen, K.G., Pankratz, V.S., and Lohse, C.M. (2002). Safety, efficacy, and effects on glycemic control of electroconvulsive therapy in insulin-requiring type 2 diabetic patients. *Journal of ECT, 18*(1), 16–21. Retrieved from www.ncbi.nlm.nih.gov/pubmed/11925516.

Nishihara, F., Ohkawa, M., Hiraoka, H., Yuki, N., and Saito, S. (2003). Benefits of the laryngeal mask for airway management during electroconvulsive therapy. *Journal of ECT, 19*(4), 211–216. Retrieved from www.ncbi.nlm.nih.gov/pubmed/14657773.

Nobler, M.S., Sackeim, H.A., Solomoub, M., Luberb, B., Devanand, D.P., and Prudic, J. (1993). EEG manifestations during ECT: effects of electrode placement and stimulus intensity. *Biological Psychiatry, 34*(5), 321–330. doi:10.1016/0006-3223(93)90089-V.

Nott, M.R., and Watts, J.S. (1999). A fractured hip during electro-convulsive therapy. *European Journal of Anaesthesiology, 16*(4), 265–267. Retrieved from www.ncbi.nlm.nih.gov/pubmed/10234499.

NSW Health. (2010). ECT minimum standard of practice NSW. Retrieved from www.health.nsw.gov.au/policies/pd/2011/pdf/PD2011_003.pdf.

Nurnberg, H.G. (1989). An overview of somatic treatment of psychosis during pregnancy and postpartum. *General Hospital Psychiatry, 11*(328–338).

Nuttall, G.A., Bowersox, M.R., Douglass, S.B., McDonald, J., Rasmussen, L.J., Decker, P.A., . . . Rasmussen, K.G. (2004). Morbidity and mortality in the use of electroconvulsive therapy. *Journal of ECT, 20*(4), 237–241. Retrieved from http://journals.lww.com/ectjournal/Fulltext/2004/12000/Morbidity_and_Mortality_in_the_Use_of.9.aspx.

O'Brien, P.D., and Morgan, D.H. (1991). Bladder rupture during ECT. *Convulsive Therapy, 7*(1), 56–59. Retrieved from www.ncbi.nlm.nih.gov/pubmed/11941099.

O'Hara, M.W., and Wisner, K.L. (2014). Perinatal mental illness: definition, description and aetiology. *Best Practice and Research: Clinical Obstetrics and Gynaecology, 28*(1), 3–12. doi:10.1016/j.bpobgyn.2013.09.002.

O'Reardon, J.P., Cristancho, M.A., von Andreae, C.V., Cristancho, P., and Weiss, D. (2011). Acute and maintenance electroconvulsive therapy for treatment of severe major depression during the second and third trimesters of pregnancy with infant follow-up to 18 months: case report and review of the literature. *Journal of ECT, 27*(1), e23–26. doi:10.1097/YCT.0b013e3181e63160.

Oates, M.R. (1986). The treatment of psychiatric disorders in pregnancy and the puerperium. *Clinical Obstetrics and Gynaecology, 13*(2), 385–395. Retrieved from www.ncbi.nlm.nih.gov/pubmed/3089667.

Ottosson, J.O., and Rendahl, I. (1963). Effect of trimethaphan on intraocular pressure in electroconvulsive therapy. *Archives of Ophthalmology, 70*(4), 466–470. Retrieved from www.ncbi.nlm.nih.gov/pubmed/14078867.

Ozdemir, A., Poyraz, C.A., Erten, E., Cirakoglu, E., and Tomruk, N. (2016). Electroconvulsive therapy in women: a retrospective study from a mental health hospital in Turkey. *Psychiatric Quarterly, 87*(4), 769–779. doi:10.1007/s11126-016-9425-3.

Ozer, F., Meral, H., Aydin, B., Hanoglu, L., Aydemir, T., and Oral, T. (2005). Electroconvulsive therapy in drug-induced psychiatric states and neuroleptic malignant syndrome. *Journal of ECT, 21*(2), 125–127. Retrieved from www.ncbi.nlm.nih.gov/pubmed/15905757.

Packman, P.M., Meyer, D.A., and Verdun, R.M. (1978). Hazards of succcinylcholine administration during electrotherapy. *Archives of General Psychiatry, 35*, 1137–1141.

Pande, A.C., and Grunhause, L.J. (1990). ECT for depression in the presence of myathenia gravis. *Convulsive Therapy, 6*, 172–175.

Partridge, B.L., Weinger, M.B., and Hauger, R. (1991). Is the cardiovascular response to electroconvulsive therapy due to the electricity or the subsequent convulsion? *Anesthesia Analgesia, 72*, 706–709.

Pathologynorth. (2015). Butyrylcholinestase: pathology test. Retrieved from www.pathologynorth.com.au/home.aspx.

Patkar, A.A., Hill, K.P., Weinstein, S.P., and Schwartz, S.L. (2000). ECT in the presence of brain tumor and increased intracranial pressure: evaluation and reduction of risk. *Journal of ECT, 16*(2), 189–197. Retrieved from www.ncbi.nlm.nih.gov/pubmed/10868329.

Pearlman, C.A. (1988). Hemodialysis, chronic renal failure, and ECT. *Convulsive Therapy, 4*, 332–333.

Petrides, G., and Fink, M. (1996). Atrial fibrillation, anticoagulation, and electroconvulsive therapy. *Convulsive Therapy, 12*, 91–98.

Pinette, M.G., Santarpio, C., Wax, J.R., and Blackstone, J. (2007). Electroconvulsive therapy in pregnancy. *Obstetrics and Gynecology, 110*(2 Pt 2), 465–466. doi:10.1097/01.AOG.0000265588.79929.98.

Price, T.R.P., and McAllister, T.W. (1989). Safety and efficacy of ECT in depressed patients with dementia: a review of clinical experience. *Convulsive Therapy, 5*, 61–74.

Proakis, A.G., and Harris, G.B. (1978). Comparative penetration of glycopyrrolate and atropine across the blood – brain and placental barriers in anesthetized dogs. *Anesthesiology, 48*(5), 339–344.

Rasmussen, K., and Abrams, R. (1991). Treatment of Parkinson's disease with ECT. *Psychiatric Clinics of North America, 14*, 925–933.

Rasmussen, K.G., and Ryan, D.A. (2005). The effect of electroconvulsive therapy treatments on blood sugar in nondiabetic patients. *Journal of ECT, 21*(4), 232–233.

Rasmussen, K.G., Ryan, D.A., and Mueller, P.S. (2006). Blood glucose before and after ECT treatments in type 2 diabetic patients. *Journal of ECT, 22*(2), 124–126.

Rasmussen, K.G. (1997). Electroconvulsive therapy in patients with aortic stenosis. *Convulsive Therapy, 13*(3), 196–199. Retrieved from www.ncbi.nlm.nih.gov/pubmed/9342136.

Rasmussen, K.G., and Keegan, B.M. (2007). Electroconvulsive therapy in patients with multiple sclerosis. *Journal of ECT, 23*(3), 179–180. doi:10.1097/YCT.0b013e31806548c6.

Rasmussen, K.G., Perry, C.L., Sutor, B., and Moore, K.M. (2007). ECT in patients with intracranial masses. *Journal of Neuropsychiatry and Clinical Neuroscience, 19*(2), 191–193. doi:10.1176/jnp.2007.19.2.191.

Rasmussen, K.G., and Zorumski, C.F. (1993). Electroconvulsive therapy in patients taking theophylline. *Journal of Clinical Psychiatry, 54*(11), 427–431. Retrieved from www.ncbi.nlm.nih.gov/pubmed/8270586.

Rayburn, B.K. (1997). Electroconvulsive therapy in patients with heart failure or valvular heart disease. *Convulsive Therapy, 13*, 145–156.

Reed, P., Sermin, N., Appleby, L., and Faragher, B. (1999). A comparison of clinical response to electroconvulsive therapy in puerperal and non-puerperal psychoses *Journal of Affective Disorders, 54*, 255–260.

Regestein, Q.R., and Reich, P. (1985). Electroconvulsive therapy in patients at high risk for physical complications. *Journal of ECT, 1*(2), 101–114.

Ries, R., and Bokan, J. (1979). Electroconvulsive therapy following pituitary surgery. *Journal of Nervous and Mental Disease, 167*(12), 767–768. Retrieved from www.ncbi.nlm.nih.gov/pubmed/41885.

Roccaforte, W.H., and Burke, W.J. (1989). ECT following craniotomy. *Psychosomatics, 30*(1), 99–101. doi:10.1016/S0033-3182(89)72324-0.

Rodriguez-Oroz, M.C., Obeso, J.A., Lang, A.E., Houeto, J.-L, Pollak, P., Rehncrona, S., . . . Van Blercom, N. (2005). Bilateral deep brain stimulation in Parkinson's disease: a multicentre study with 4 years follow-up. *128*(10), 2240–2249. doi:10.1093/brain/awh571.

Rollins, N.C., Bhandari, N., Hajeebhoy, N., Horton, S., Lutter, C.K., Martines, J.C., . . . Victora, C.G. (2016). Why invest, and what it will take to improve breastfeeding practices? *The Lancet, 387*(10017), 491–504.

Rosenberg, M.R., and Green, M. (1989). Neuroleptic malignant syndrome. Review of response to therapy. *Archives of Internal Medicine, 149*(9), 1927–1931. Retrieved from www.ncbi.nlm.nih.gov/pubmed/2673115.

Rowe, T.F. (1997). Acute gastric aspiration: prevention and treatment. *Semin Perinatol, 21*, 313–319.

SA Health. (2014). South Australian guidelines for electroconvulsive therapy. Retrieved from www.sahealth.sa.gov.au/wps/wcm/connect/0608270046ad5b01b89.

Saad, D.A., Black, J.L., 3rd, Krahn, L.E., and Rummans, T.A. (2000). ECT post eye surgery: two cases and a review of the literature. *Journal of ECT, 16*(4), 409–414. Retrieved from www.ncbi.nlm.nih.gov/pubmed/11314879.

Saatcioglu, O., and Tomruk, N. (2011). The use of electroconvulsive therapy in pregnancy: a review. *The Israel Journal of Psychiatry and Related Sciences, 48*, 6–11.

Sackeim, H.A. (1998). The use of electroconvulsive therapy in late-life depression. In Salzman, C. (Ed.), *Geriatric Psychopharmacology,* 3rd edition (pp. 262–309). Philadelphia, PA: Williams and Wilkins.

Sackeim, H.A. (2004). Convulsant and anticonvulsant properties of electroconvulsive therapy: towards a focal form of brain stimulation. *Clinical Neuroscience Research,* 39–57.

Sackeim, H.A., Decina, P., Portnoy, S., Neeley, P., and Malitz, S. (1987). Studies of dosage, seizure threshold, and seizure duration in ECT. *Biological Psychiatry, 22*(3), 249–268. doi:10.1016/0006-3223(87)90144-2.

Sackeim, H.A., Decina, P., Prohovnik, I., and Malitz, S. (1987). Seizure threshold in electroconvulsive therapy: effects of sex, age, electrode placement, and number of treatments. *Archives of General Psychiatry, 44*(4), 355–360. doi:10.1001/archpsyc.1987.01800160067009.

Sackeim, H.A., Prudic, J., Devanand, D.P., Kiersky, J.E., Fitzsimons, L., Moody, B.J., . . . Settembrino, J.M. (1993). Effects of Stimulus intensity and electrode placement on the efficacy and cognitive effects of electroconvulsive therapy. *New England Journal of Medicine, 328*(12). Retrieved from www.nejm.org/doi/pdf/10.1056/NEJM199303253281204.

Sackeim, H.A., Prudic, J., Devanand, D.P., Nobler, M.S., Lisanby, S.H., Peyser, S., . . . Clark, J. (2000). A prospective, randomized, double-blind comparison of bilateral and right unilateral electroconvulsive therapy at different stimulus intensities. *Archives of General Psychiatry, 57*(5), 425–434. doi:10.1001/archpsyc.57.5.425.

Sadock, B.J., Sadock, V.A., and Ruiz, P. (2009). *Caplan and Sadock's Comprehensive Textbook of Psychiatry,* 9th edition. Philadelphia PA: Lippincott, Williams and Wilkins.

Salanave, B., Bouvier-Colle, M.H., Varnoux, N., Alexander, S., and Macfarlane, A. (1999). Classification differences and maternal mortality: a European study. MOMS Group. Mother mortality and severe morbidity. *International Journal of Epidemiology, 28*, 64–69.

Salaris, S., Szuba, M.P., and Traber, K. (2000). ECT and intracranial vascular masses. *Journal of ECT, 16*(2), 198–203. Retrieved from www.ncbi.nlm.nih.gov/pubmed/10868330.

Schak, K.M., Mueller, P.S., Barnes, R.D., and Rasmussen, K.G. (2008). The safety of ECT in patients with chronic obstructive pulmonary disease. *Psychosomatics, 49*(3), 208–211. doi:10.1176/appi.psy.49.3.208.

Scheftner, W.A., and Shulman, R.B. (1992). Treatment choice in neuroleptic malignant syndrome. *Convulsive Therapy, 8*(4), 267–279. Retrieved from www.ncbi.nlm.nih.gov/pubmed/11941178.

Scott, J.A., and Binns, C.W. (1999). Factors associated with the initiation and duration of breastfeeding: a review of the literature. *Breastfeeding Review, 7*(1), 5–16. Retrieved from www.ncbi.nlm.nih.gov/pubmed/10197366.

Sharma, H., and Pompei, P. (1996). Antidepressant-induced hyponatraemia in the aged. Avoidance and management strategies. *Drugs & Aging, 8*(6), 430–435. Retrieved from www.ncbi.nlm.nih.gov/pubmed/8736626.

Shiwaku, H., Masaki, H., Yasugi, D., and Narushima, K. (2015). A case of a depressed patient with major titanium cranial base reconstruction successfully treated by ECT. *American Journal of Psychiatry, 172*(10), 1024–1025.

Sienaert, P., and Peuskens, J. (2007). Anticonvulsants during electroconvulsive therapy: review and recommendations. *Journal of ECT, 23*(2), 120–123. doi:10.1097/YCT.0b013e 3180330059.

Song, J., Lee, P.P., Weiner, R., and Challa, P. (2004). The effect of surgery on intraocular pressure fluctuations with electroconvulsive therapy in a patient with severe glaucoma. *Journal of ECT, 20*(4), 264–266. Retrieved from www.ncbi. nlm.nih.gov/pubmed/15591863.

Steer, P.L., Biddle, C.J., Marley, W.S., Lantz, R.K., and Sulik, P.L. (1992). Concentration of fentanyl in colostrum after an analgesic dose. *Canadian Journal of Anaesthetics, 39*(3), 231–235. doi:10.1007/bf03008782.

Stevens, T., Spoors, J., Hale, R., and Bembridge, H. (2010). Percieved oral health needs in psychiatric inpatients: impact of a dedicated dental clinic. *The Psychiatrist, 34*, 518–521.

Strawn, J.R., Keck, J., P.E., and Caroff, S.N. (2007). Neuroleptic malignant syndrome. *American Journal of Psychiatry, 164*, 870–876.

Tancer, M.E., and Evans, D.L. (1989). Electroconvulsive therapy in geriatric patients undergoing anticoagulation therapy. *Convulsive Therapy, 5*(1), 102–109. Retrieved from www.ncbi.nlm.nih.gov/pubmed/11940999.

Tess, A.V., and Smetana, G.W. (2009). Medical evaluation of patients undergoing electroconvulsive therapy. *New England Journal of Medicine, 360*, 1437–1444.

Trimble, M.R., and Krishnamoorthy, E.S. (2005). The use of ECT in neuropsychiatric disorders. In Scott, A.I.F. (Ed.), *The ECT Handbook*, 2nd edition. London: Royal College of Psychiatrists.

Trollor, J.N., and Sachdev, P., S. (1993). Electroconvulsive treatment of neuroleptic malignant syndrome: a review and report of cases. *Australian New Zealand Journal of Psychiatry, 19*(33), 650–659.

Van Den Berg, A.A., and Honjol, N.M. (1998). Electroconvulsive therapy and intraocular pressure. *Middle East Journal of Anaesthesiology, 14*(4), 249–258. Retrieved from www.ncbi.nlm.nih.gov/pubmed/9557912.

Verghese, C., and Brimacombe, J.R. (1996). Survey of laryngeal mask airway usage in 11,910 patients: safety and efficacy for conventional and nonconventional usage. *Anesthesia and Analgesia, 82*(1), 129–133. Retrieved from http://journals.lww.com/anesthesia-analgesia/Fulltext/1996/01000/Survey_of_Laryngeal_Mask_Airway_Usage_in_11,910.23.aspx.

Vesperini, S., Papetti, F., and Pringuey, D. (2010). Are catatonia and neuroleptic malignant syndrome related conditions? *Encephale, 36*(2), 105–110. doi:10.1016/j.encep.2009.03.009.

Viguera, A., Rordorf, G., Schouten, R., Welch, C. and Drop, L. (1998). Intracranial haemodynamics during attenuated responses to electrconvulsive therapy in the presence of an intracranial aneurysm. *Journal of Neurology, Neurosurgery, and Psychiatry, 64*, 802–805.

Wachtel, L.E., Jaffe, R., and Kellner, C.H. (2011). Electroconvulsive therapy for psychotropic-refractory bipolar affective disorder and severe self-injury and aggression in an 11-year-old autistic boy. *European Journal of Child and Adolescent Psychiatry, 20*(3), 147–152. doi:10.1007/s00787-010-0155-z.

Wainwright, A.P., and Brodrick, P.M. (1987). Suxamethonium in myasthenia gravis. *Anaesthesia, 42*(9), 950–957. Retrieved from www.ncbi.nlm.nih.gov/pubmed/3674355.

Walker, R., and Swartz, C.M. (1994). Electroconvulsive therapy during high-risk pregnancy. *General Hospital Psychiatry, 16*, 348–353.

Walker, R., and Swartz, C.M. (1994). Electroconvulsive therapy during high-risk pregnancy. *General Hospital Psychiatry, 16*(5), 348–353. Retrieved from www.ncbi.nlm.nih.gov/pubmed/7995506.

Ward, R.M., Bates, B.A., Benitz, W.E., Burchfield, D.J., Ring, J.C., Walls, R.P., and Walson, P.D. (2001). The transfer of drugs and other chemicals into human milk. *Pediatrics, 108*(3), 776–789.

Warner, M.A., Shields, S.E., and Chute, C.G. (1993). Major morbidity and mortality within 1 month of ambulatory surgery and anesthesia. *Journal of the American Medical Association, 270*, 1437–1441.

Watts, B.V., Groft, A., Bagian, J.P., and Mills, P.D. (2011). An examination of mortality and other adverse events related to electroconvulsive therapy using a national adverse event report system. *Journal of ECT, 27*(2), 105–108.

Weiner, R.D., and Coffey, C.E. (1993). Electroconvulsive therapy in the medial and neurologic patient. In Stroudemire, A., Fogel, B.S., and Greenberg, D. (Eds.), *Psychiatric Care of the Medical Patient*, 2nd edition (pp. 419–428). New York: Oxford University Press.

Weiner, R.D., Coffey, C.E., and Krystal, A.D. (2000). Electroconvulsive therapy in the medical and neurologic patient. In Stoudemire, A., Fogel, B.S., and Grenberg, D. (Eds.),

Psychiatric Care of the Medical Patient, 2nd edition (pp. 419–428). New York: Oxford University Press.

Weiner, R.D., and Mccall, W.V. (1992). Dental examination for ECT. *Convulsive Therapy, 8,* 146–147.

Weiner, R.D., and Sibert, T.E. (1996). Use of ECT in treatment of depression in patients with diabetes mellitus. *Journal of Clinical Psychiatry, 57,* 138.

Weinger, M.B., Partridge, B.L., Hauger, R., Hauger, R., Mirow, A., and Brown, M. (1991). Prevention of the cardiovascular and neuroendocrine response to electroconvulsive therapy: II effects of pretreatment regimens on catecholamines, ACTH, vasopressin and cortisol. *Anesthesia & Analgesia., 73,* 563–569.

Weller, M., and Kornhuber, J. (1992). Electroconvulsive therapy in a geriatric patient with multiple bone fractures and generalized plasmocytoma. *Pharmacopsychiatry, 25*(6), 278–280. Retrieved from www.ncbi.nlm.nih.gov/pubmed/1494595.

Wells, C.E. (1979). Pseudodementia. *American Journal of Psychiatry, 136*(7), 895–900. doi:10.1176/ajp.136.7.895.

Williams, S., and Ostroff, R. (2005). Chronic renal failure, hemodialysis, and electroconvulsive therapy: a case report. *Journal of ECT, 21*(1), 41–42. Retrieved from www.ncbi.nlm.nih.gov/pubmed/15791177.

Wingate, B.J., and Hansen-Flaschen, J. (1997). Anxiety and depression in advanced lung disease. *Clinical Chest Medicine, 18,* 495–505.

Worsley, R., Gilbert, H., Gavrilidis, E., Naughton, B., and Kulkarni, J. (2013). Breastfeeding and psychotropic medications. *Lancet, 381*(9870), 905. doi:10.1016/S0140-6736(13)60671-6.

Zarate, C.A., Jr, Tohen, M., and Baraibar, G. (1997). Combined valproate or carbamazepine and electroconvulsive therapy. *Annals of Clinical Psychiatry, 9*(1), 19–25. Retrieved from www.ncbi.nlm.nih.gov/pubmed/9167833.

Zervas, L., and Fink, M. (1991). ECT for refractory Parkinson's disease. *Convulsive Therapy, 7*(3), 222–223.

Zielinski, R.J., Roose, S.P., Devanand, D.P., Woodring, S., and Sackeim, H.A. (1993). Cardiovascular complications of ECT in depressed patients with cardiac disease. *American Journal of Psychiatry, 150*(6), 904–909. Retrieved from www.ncbi.nlm.nih.gov/pubmed/8494067.

Drug interactions

Medications taken by a patient should be reviewed before a course of ECT commences to prevent potential adverse effects, interactions with the seizure and seizure threshold and prolonged recovery. Systematic reviews of the data available concerning the use of drugs during a course of ECT for depressive illness (McIntosh and Lawrie, 2005) and the use of continuation pharmacotherapy after ECT for depressive illness (Mcintosh and Lawrie, 2005) highlight the lack of large trials and common outcome measures used between the studies to guide clinical practice, a finding upheld in a more recent review by the same group (Dixon and Santiago, 2013).

Available evidence suggests that the therapeutic response to ECT may be augmented by antidepressants and psychotropic medication without any major risk to patients and that maintenance treatment with medication after a course of ECT significantly prevents relapse.

There are a number of guiding principles that should be adhered to when reviewing a patient's

CLINICAL WISDOM 4.4.1

Clinical experience suggests that anticonvulsant mood-stabilising drugs do attenuate the seizure by increasing the seizure threshold, resulting in reduced seizure potentiation and generalisation and attenuation of seizure length and postictal suppression, reducing the clinical efficacy of the treatment. The risk of lithium-induced delirium after ECT is uncommon if clinically indicated continuing lithium during a course of treatment may be a viable option with close monitoring of cognitive function.

medication regime. It is usual practice to continue medications that have been prescribed for medical conditions during the course of ECT treatment, however the timing and dosage may require adjustment. Patients should have essential medication, such as antihypertensive, anti-reflux and cardiac medications on the morning before ECT to prevent complications, with a sip of water guided by regional protocols concerning water and medication only before a surgical procedure.

- ECT provides an opportunity to change antidepressant medication. The relapse rate after a course of ECT is very high, making it essential to commence a new combination of pharmacotherapy to ensure remission is maintained over the next six months after the index course of ECT has been completed (Lauritzen, Odgaard and Clemmesen, 1996; Sackeim et al., 2001).
- Other medication, like mood stabilisers, may need to be discontinued, withheld the night before or changed owing to their potential to interfere with the therapeutic action of ECT by raising seizure threshold or increasing the adverse effects of the treatment.

ANTIDEPRESSANTS

The recommendation that antidepressants should be discontinued during the course of ECT had

its origins in studies completed during the 1960s and 1970s in patients who were not treatment-resistant, where there were mixed treatment outcomes (Sackeim et al., 2009). Benefits were few and potential confusion and increased risk of memory difficulties were common and the combination were discouraged (Abrams, 2002; Fink, 2009). Clinical practice guidelines supported these recommendations owing to a paucity of finding demonstrating efficacy (American Psychiatric Association, 2001; Scott, 2005). Recent work refutes this conclusion, demonstrating treatment with a tricyclic antidepressant, like nortriptyline, may enhance the efficacy of ECT and reduce the cognitive adverse effects, with a weaker result for venlafaxine (Sackeim et al., 2009). The variability in findings suggest that other factors like ECT technique may have an impact on patients response (Sackeim et al., 2007), highlighting the need to choose forms of ECT that minimise cognitive impairment (Tor et al., 2015).

Lauritzen et al. (1996) conducted a randomised controlled trial of 87 patients with depression and cardiac disease who had ECT during the acute phase of treatment, with 74 patients progressing to the six-month follow-up phase. Thirty-five subjects who had ECG abnormalities were randomised to paroxetine and placebo during ECT and 52 without ECG abnormalities were randomised to either imipramine or paroxetine and ECT. In the ECG abnormal group there was no difference between those that had paroxetine or placebo with ECT after course of treatment. This was in contrast to the normal ECG group, who were treated concurrently with imipramine, which had a superior outcome to the paroxetine comparison group at the end of the index course. At three months, the cardiac group that received paroxetine were significantly more likely to remain well than those receiving placebo treatment but this effect was lost after six months. In the group with normal ECGs, those who received paroxetine were more likely to remain well at three and six months compared to those who received imipramine owing to problematic side effects of the latter group.

These results are in keeping with an earlier retrospective study of 84 patients with major depression who were given high- and low-dose imipramine with suprathreshold right unilateral ECT or ECT alone (Nelson and Benjamin, 1989). Subjects were matched for age, gender and rate of psychotic depression. Records were blindly rated for rate of improvement, cognitive side effects and cardiac events. Subjects who received a combination of imipramine and ECT had a superior clinical outcome compared to placebo group. The imipramine group required fewer ECT treatments with no increase in cardiac complications or postictal confusion compared to controls.

In a more recent study, Bernardo et al. (2000) randomised patients with major depression into those that received venlafaxine and ECT and another who were given either clomipramine. There was no difference in the number of treatments, cardiovascular changes or mean seizure duration.

Sackeim et al. (2009) conducted a prospective, randomised, double-blind, placebo-controlled trial of 319 patients with unipolar depression from three university-based hospitals that were randomly assigned to treatment with nortriptyline or venlafaxine and ECT or placebo and ECT. Similar to the results above, those subjects treated with the tricyclic antidepressant nortriptyline had enhanced efficacy and reduced levels of cognitive adverse effects compared to placebo, whereas the venlafaxine group had a weaker degree of improvement and tended to have worse cognitive adverse effects. In this study, high-dose right unilateral ECT had a similar efficacy to bitemporal ECT, with less severe amnesia.

The safety of psychotropic medication with ECT is reflected in the changes that have been made with each edition of the Australian psychotropic guidelines, *Recommendations for Drugs and ECT* (Psychotropic Expert Group, 2013). Early editions had detailed tables highlighting the potential difficulties in using psychotropic medication with ECT. The latest edition has omitted the table completely, reflecting current evidence that highlights the need to use antidepressant augmentation to improve clinical outcomes, reducing the high rate of relapse after completion of ECT (Sackeim, 2000; Sackeim et al., 1990).

It is well recognised that maintaining a patient on an antidepressant that has failed prior to ECT will be ineffective after the treatment has been completed (Sackeim et al., 1990). It is advisable to commence a different class of medication or combination that has not failed in the past to prevent the risk of treatment failure (American Psychiatric Association, 2001; Tiller and Lyndon, 2003).

Tricyclic antidepressants (TCA)

Tricyclic antidepressants are known to prolong the cardiac QTc interval on the ECG. These drugs are generally considered safe when combined with ECT and may offer a therapeutic advantage (Nelson and Benjamin, 1989; Sackeim et al., 2009).

Tricyclic antidepressants are associated with potential adverse events including:

- blocking alpha-receptors, causing postural hypertension;
- causing anticholinergic side effects, leading to confusion and slower time to recovery;
- targeting histamine receptors, resulting in sedation and lengthen time to recovery.

These factors should be monitored if these medications are continued or initiated during a course of ECT.

If a tricyclic antidepressant is initiated during ECT, a moderate dose should be utilised increasing the dose towards the end of the course of treatment to prevent relapse. If a patient has failed to respond to a tricyclic antidepressant prior to the course of ECT it should be withdrawn and a different tricyclic or class of antidepressant medication should be considered to prevent relapse (NSW Health, 2010).

Selective serotonin/noradrenaline reuptake inhibitors (SSRI and SNRI)

There has only been one case report that suggests that fluoxetine may be associated with a prolonged seizure (Caracci and Decina, 1991), with 15 other reported cases (Gutierrez-Esteinou and Pope, 1989; Harsch and Haddox, 1990; Kellner and Bruno, 1989) highlighting that there is no reason for concern with some suggestion that fluoxetine may shorten seizures (Gutierrez-Esteinou and Pope, 1989).

In Lauritzen et al.'s (1996) study of 46 patients with major depression who were treated with paroxetine and ECT there was no increase in adverse events in the paroxetine group compared to placebo. Masdrakis et al. (2008) presented three female cases with major depression that had ECT while being treated with escitalopram. They concluded that the combination was well tolerated, with only minimal side efforts reported.

Venlafaxine is an antidepressant that is serotonergic at low doses, recruiting noradrenaline pathways at higher doses. There have been a number of case reports on its use with ECT and two randomised controlled trials. Bernardo, Navarro, Salva, Arrufat and Baeza (2000) randomised 18 patients into bilateral ECT with a tricyclic antidepressant (imipramine 150 mg to 300 mg a day or clomipramine 150 mg to 250 mg a day) or bilateral ECT with venlafaxine 150 mg a day. No patients had prolonged or spontaneous seizures outside of the treatment session and there were no statistically significant differences in mean seizure length, blood pressure or electrocardiogram. These findings were in contrast to another study, where higher doses of venlafaxine were used ranging from 150 mg to 375 mg, which reported increased episodes of asystole and hypotension (Gonzalez et al., 2002). Similar concerns were raised in a large, prospective randomised placebo-controlled trial of 319 patients randomised into RUL or BT ECT alone, with nortriptyline achieving therapeutic blood levels of 100–120 ng/ml or with venlafaxine up to 225 mg a day (Sackeim et al., 2009). Neither group demonstrated any difference in the number of adverse events or serious adverse events. The nortriptyline group showed improvement on all measures of cognitive adverse events except auto-biographical memory, while the venlafaxine group measures were basically unchanged or worse.

It is recommended that the risk and benefits of combinations of medications with ECT should be considered and discussed with the patient and the anaesthetist. Most concerns are minor and can be managed in the treatment room.

Noradrenaline reuptake inhibitors

Reboxetine has its primary action on noradrenaline reuptake inhibition. Little is known about the safety of reboxetine and the use of ECT as there have been no published case reports.

Agomelatine

Agomelatine is an antidepressant that has its primary action on melatonin. Little is known about the safety of agomelatine and ECT, as there have been no published case reports. Owing to its novel mechanism of action, it is unlikely to have an impact on seizure threshold or recovery.

Trazodone

Trazodone is an antidepressant that is no longer available in many countries around the world owing to reports of toxicity. Caution is required in its use with ECT owing to reports of cardiac problems and prolonged seizures (Jarvis, Goewert and Zorumski, 1992).

Monoamine oxidase inhibitors (MAOI)

MAOI antidepressant drugs eliminate the action of the enzyme monoamine oxidase in a permanent or reversible manner, leading to a secondary increase in neurotransmitters serotonin and noradrenaline. Without this enzyme, patients are at serious risk of hypertensive crises or serotonergic syndrome when taking certain medications (indirect sympathomimetic agents like ephedrine or direct acting sympathomimetic drugs like adrenaline or noradrenaline) or eating certain food rich in tyramine and postural hypotension. Once ceased normal enzyme function may take anywhere from 14 to 20 days. This is not the case for reversible agents like moclobemide.

In the past it was considered that the combination of ECT and irreversible monoamine oxidase inhibitors may not be safe owing to reports of hypertension, hypotension and hyperreflexia with the combination due to the potential interaction with suxamethonium (Abrams, 2002). It was routine practice to wean people off these medications for at least two weeks prior to starting a course of ECT (American Psychiatric Association, 2001). Current treatment no longer requires this level of caution as the combination can be used safely. It is recommended that the anaesthetist be informed that that patient is taking a MAOI (Dixon and Santiago, 2013). Reversible inhibitors of monoamine oxidase A (RIMA) like moclobemide can also be used safely with ECT, although their clinical benefit is questionable.

Bupropion (Zyban)

The safety of bupropion in ECT is unclear. There are some reports that bupropion may increase the rate of spontaneous seizures in susceptible patients on higher doses and it may result in prolonged seizures with ECT (Davidson, 1989). However, other case reports are inconclusive (Kellner, Pritchett and Jackson, 1994). Caution is recommended with dose reduction or withdrawal prior to commencing ECT.

BENZODIAZEPINES

The concurrent use of benzodiazepines and ECT may result in treatment failure and should be avoided (Abrams, 2002; American Psychiatric Association, 2001; NSW Health, 2010; SA Health, 2014; Scott, 2005; Tiller and Lyndon, 2003). This advice comes after significant debate in the late

1980s and 1990s about whether ECT could be effective if patients remained on benzodiazepines that were being used extensively to treat anxiety (Cohen and Lawton, 1992; Standish-Barry, Deacon and Snaith, 1985).

In the 1970s it had been reported that benzodiazepines may reduce the antidepressant efficacy of ECT but this early study did not evaluate the effect on seizure propagation or seizure threshold (Kay, Fahy and Garside, 1970). Studies began to appear that benzodiazepines could interfere with the action of ECT (Cohen and Lawton, 1992).

Pettinati et al. (1990) demonstrated that the clinical outcome was inferior in patients with major depression who received right unilateral ECT and continued receiving benzodiazepines, compared to matched controls, as it inhibited the propagation of the seizure reducing the effectiveness of the treatment.

In another study, Jha and Stein (1996) reported a retrospective analysis of 124 patients who received benzodiazepines and ECT. They found that patients having right unilateral ECT showed significantly poorer responses and longer stays in hospital than the group who received benzodiazepines and bilateral ECT. They concluded that the prescription of benzodiazepines with ECT compromised the therapeutic benefit of unilateral ECT for depression strengthening existing data that RUL ECT is a weaker form of treatment if it is not dosed at a suprathreshold level (Sackeim et al., 1993).

During this period, flumazenil a newly marketed short-acting benzodiazepine-competitive antagonist was shown to be effective in reversing the detrimental effects of benzodiazepines on ECT (Bailine, Safferman, Vital-Herne and Bernstein, 1994).

Krystal et al. (1998) explored the dosing, safety and efficacy of pre-ECT administration of flumazenil in 35 patients who were taking benzodiazepines with 49 patients who received ECT without these drugs. There was no difference in efficacy, seizure duration or adverse events as a function of flumazenil, highlighting that flumazenil may be a safe and effective method of administering effective ECT to patients who are maintained on benzodiazepines. If flumazenil is used before ECT, it is recommended that a short-acting benzodiazepine like midazolam be administered intravenously soon after the seizure to avoid discontinuation symptoms during the recovery period (Bailine et al., 1994).

The use of flumazenil is unusual in modern ECT practice owing to increased awareness of safety issues concerning benzodiazepines with tolerance and dependence significant problems for this class of medication and the need to find alternative treatments for severe anxiety disorders (Pollack, Stein, Davidson and Ginsberg, 2004).

The most comprehensive review on the impact of benzodiazepines with ECT was conducted by Greenberg and Pettinati (1993), who highlighted the lack of adequate trials with many contradictory findings and design flaws. They highlight that benzodiazepines possess anticonvulsant properties that may potentially elevate seizure threshold, inhibit seizure propagation and alter some of the neurobehavioral effects or electroconvulsive shock (ECS) in animal models. The limited data reviewed enabled them to conclude that these drugs have the potential to shorten seizure duration and decrease treatment efficacy, particularly with unilateral ECT.

Benzodiazepines with longer half-lives can be more problematic, resulting in decreased seizure quality and length, heightening the risk of cognitive impairment and reducing the overall efficacy of ECT.

It is recommended that all benzodiazepines, whether being used as tranquilisers or hypnotics, be ceased at least 24 hours before commencing ECT. Significant challenges exist in ceasing benzodiazepines quickly owing to issues of tolerance and withdrawal seizures if they are ceased too quickly. Programmes to withdrawal these drugs are usually completed over weeks. It is known that seizure threshold increases during a course of ECT, minimising any discontinuation phenomena and enabling withdrawal of these drugs at a quicker rate (Sackeim, 2004).

It is of note that studies examining the effect of benzodiazepine on seizure threshold failed to demonstrate any meaningful clinical impact. In the CORE study, administering a benzodiazepine within 24 hours of ECT did not predict seizure threshold (Petrides et al., 2009).

In summary, it is recommended that benzodiazepines be weaned whenever possible 24 hours before ECT commences. Long-acting benzodiazepines are more troublesome than short-acting drugs. The use of flumazenil pre-ECT should be considered as an effective last resort if withdrawing the benzodiazepines it is not possible.

CLINICAL WISDOM 4.4.2

Combining benzodiazepines with ECT should be done very cautiously and only if there are no other options owing to the impact on seizure generation and propagation. If utilised, the benzodiazepine should be removed early in the course of treatment. Rising seizure threshold as ECT progresses prevents discontinuation phenomena, enabling the drugs to be removed at a quicker rate. If the benzodiazepines are being used to contain high levels of agitation or anxiety in a patient before ECT, administering high doses of sedating atypical antipsychotic medications, like quetiapine, may be an alternative as this class of drug has minimal effect on seizure threshold.

ANTIPSYCHOTIC MEDICATION

It is usual practice to use sedative antipsychotic medication as an alternative for night-time sedation and agitation during the course of ECT. Current evidence supports early studies (Gujavarty, Greenberg and Fink, 1987) that the combination of antipsychotic medications with ECT is safe and efficacious treatment strategy for patients with schizophrenia, especially those refractory to conventional treatments (Braga and Petrides, 2005;

Greenhalgh, Knight, Hind, Beverley and Walters, 2005). This is particularly the case for patients who fail to respond to clozapine, for whom ECT may provide a substantial benefit in treatment-resistant schizophrenia (Tharyan and Adams, 2005), with economic modelling suggesting that it is more cost-effective to the comparative treatment with haloperidol and chlorpromazine (Greenhalgh et al., 2005).

In a systematic review of the combined use of ECT and antipsychotic medication, Braga and Petrides (2005) identified 42 reports including 1371 patients, with the majority of studies focused on typical antipsychotic mediation. Results from open studies showed that the combination was very safe and useful but these findings were not confirmed in the eight double-blind trials owing to a low number of patients included in the trials, ethical concerns submitting patients to long sham conditions and the use of short course of ECT, six to 11 sessions. Most studies preferred bitemporal ECT. Typical antipsychotic drugs studies were chlorpromazine, haloperidol, tifluoperazine, perphenazine, loxapine, flupenthixol, fluphenazine and thiothixene.

Penothiazines have been implicated in causing cardiac irregularities, like the prolongation of a QTc interval and inducing postural hypertension. If these drugs are used in combination with ECT, it was recommended that an ECG be completed prior to commencing the course of treatment. If an abnormality is detected then the drug should be ceased prior to commencing ECT.

There have been some case reports that highlight ECT can be used safely with aripiprazole alone or in combination with other psychotropic medication like venlafaxine, quetiapine, haloperidol, levomepromazine and clozapine (Lopez-Garccia, Chiclana and Gonzalez, 2009; Masdrakis et al., 2008).

There is one case report where ECT was administered safely and successful in a patient who was taking a combination of olanzapine and duloxetine (Hanretta and Malek-Ahmadi, 2006).

Clozapine

Concerns have been raised about combining clozapine with ECT owing to the increased risk of prolonged seizures and concomitant states of confusion due to this drug's ability to markedly lower seizure threshold (Bloch, Pollack and Mor, 1996). In clinical practice this appears to be very rare. It is recommended that the dose of clozapine be reviewed during the course of ECT to ensure patients safety (Bloch et al., 1996).

In an early study of 12 patients with schizophrenia, ECT was safely administered while they continued to take clozapine in doses as high as 550 mg a day. Three gained remission, one had a moderate response, four others had a partial response to treatment and four patients failed to respond to the combination of clozapine and ECT (Frankenburg, Suppes and McLean, 1993).

Kho et al. (2004) report on 11 patients with schizophrenia who were non-responders to clozapine. Eight had remission with a combination of clozapine and ECT. Five patients relapsed following remission and ceased ECT; three of these patients gained a second remission of symptoms when ECT was recommenced and remained well with maintenance ECT. They did not report any adverse effects.

In another study (Kupchik et al., 2000), of 36 schizophrenic patients who failed to respond to clozapine, typical antipsychotic drugs or ECT alone, 67% gained benefit from the combined treatment. Adverse reactions were experienced by 16.6% of patients, including: a single case of prolonged ECT-induced seizures, a single case of supraventricular tachycardia and three others with sinus tachycardia and blood pressure elevation. The researchers concluded that combining ECT and clozapine is a safe option for treatment-resistant patients with schizophrenia.

Havaki-Kontaxaki, Ferentinos, Kontaxakis, Paplos and Soldatos (2006) conducted a systematic review regarding the safety and efficacy of concurrent administration of clozapine and ECT in patients who were resistant to clozapine. They identified one open-label trial and six case studies comprising 21 patients with schizophrenia and one with schizoaffective disorder. The duration of clozapine monotherapy before ECT was 12 weeks in 10 patients (45.4%) and the average plasma clozapine level was 350 mg/ml; seven patients (31.8%) reported higher levels, with doses ranging from 200 to 900 mg per day. Seven patients were administered unilateral ECT, 10 patients received bilateral ECT and the remainder were given both electrode placements. 72.7% (16 patients) of the group showed marked improvement, whereas six patients (27.3%) had moderate, minimal or no response. It was not possible to determine predictors of outcome and side effects were minor, reported in five patients (22.7%), with 10 patients (5.4%) relapsing during the follow-up period. Substantial improvement persisted beyond four months in only five patients (22.7%), a finding that is consistent with other groups of patients, where resistance to medication is a strong predictor of relapse following an initial response to ECT (Sackeim et al., 1990).

MOOD STABILISERS

Anticonvulsant medication

Anticonvulsant mood stabilisers are effective in treating epilepsy. Their mechanism of action varies, with carbamazepine and lamotrigine modulating ion channels, benzodiazepines potentiating gamma-amino butyric acid (GABA) and drugs like sodium valproate, gabapentin and topiramate having multiple modes of action (Deshmukh, Thakur and Dewangan, 2011). All of these drugs have the capacity to impair seizure morphology by reducing the amplitude, concordance, postictal suppression that may result in reduced therapeutic efficacy of ECT. However, there is conflicting data concerning their use in this treatment.

The data to date has been based predominantly on case reports or case series. Zarate, Tohen and Baraiba (1997), compared the charts of seven patients receiving ECT and either sodium valproate or carbamazepine with ECT alone. Three patients

responded well to treatment, two had a moderate response, one had a partial response and the final patient did not respond. They concluded that anticonvulsants might be safely used in conjunction with ECT when prophylaxis with an anticonvulsant drug is planned. However, they noted that these drugs attenuated seizure morphology, reduced seizure length and required higher stimulus energy compared to ECT alone, particularly when unilateral treatment was utilised.

Sienaert and Peuskens (2007) completed a literature review on the concurrent use of ECT and anticonvulsant drugs. Drugs included in their review were carbamazepine, sodium valproate, lamotrigine, gabapentin and topiramate. They noted that there were no prospective, randomised trials examining the outcome and safety of this combination. Existing data was from case reports of patients treated with ECT and anticonvulsants for epilepsy or psychiatric conditions or where the conditions are comorbid. They conclude that there were no severe adverse effect or complication reported apart from the occasional difficulty in eliciting seizures and there was no evidence that the combining the two modalities augmented therapeutic efficacy of ECT.

Lamotrigine

The combination of lamotrigine and ECT has been described in several case series involving 52 patients. Layne, Young, Votolato, Miller and Martin (2005) reported on 14 patients who were given ECT concurrent with lamotrigine in doses ranging from 25 to 500 mg. All patients had seizures of adequate duration, with some requiring an increase in the dose of energy during the course of ECT.

Penland and Ostroff (2006) examined nine patients with bipolar disorder, where lamotrigine was slowly titrated during an index course of ECT. All patients achieved remission with clinically adequate seizures. There was no increase in adverse events, rashes or severe cognitive impairment. The conclusion in this study that lamotrigine was safe and did not interfere with routine ECT clinical practice has been criticised on the basis that there methodology was flawed owing to the low doses of lamotrigine involved – only five patients achieved a dose of 100 mg – and the rapid progression to continuation ECT treatment (Freeman, 2007). It is not uncommon for doses of lamotrigine to exceed 250 mg a day in routine treatment of bipolar disorder (Marangell et al., 2004) and progression to continuation ECT is uncommon.

Sienaert et al. (2006) completed a retrospective study in nine patients who had ECT treatments both with and without lamotrigine. One hundred and forty-four ECT sessions with lamotrigine, with doses from 25 mg to 400 mg per day, were compared to 96 ECT sessions without this medication. Clinically adequate seizures were obtained in each patient, with the duration of the motor seizure longer in two patients during treatments with lamotrigine.

In more recent work, the same group examined 19 patients who underwent 289 treatment sessions with 11 patients who had ECT alone or were given lamotrigine for part of their treatment. They concluded that there was no difference in seizure adequacy or duration and the combination was well tolerated. There was a higher incidence of missed seizures in the group that received lamotrigine and ECT. The study concluded that therapeutic doses of lamotrigine did not have a clinically significant effect on the length of the ECT-induced seizure or on the stimulus dose required (Sienaert et al., 2011).

Anticonvulsants and epilepsy

Using anticonvulsant medication in patients with a history of epilepsy is more complicated. It is recommended that a consultation with the treating neurologist be undertaken prior to commencing ECT. Current recommendation is that these drugs should be administered at a minimum effective dose during the course of ECT (Sienaert and Peuskens, 2007). There are some reports that epileptic patients who have ECT are at higher risk of having prolonged seizures (Hsiao, Messenheimer

and Evans, 1987). If the dose of medication is reduced, it should be done cautiously to prevent the occurrence of inter-treatment seizures (Lunde, Lee and Rasmussen, 2006).

Lithium

Twenty-five years since the original systematic literature review, there continues to be a debate about the risks and benefits associated with using lithium during a course of ECT. Mukherjee (1993) noted that there had been a marked reduction in serious adverse effects associated with ECT–lithium combination and that these events may be less related to lithium neurotoxicity and more to the change from high-dose sine wave ECT to cognitive sparing square wave techniques.

Clear guidance concerning the use of lithium during a course of ECT remains elusive. Old and more recent case reports highlight the increased risk of delirium, neurotoxicity and prolonged seizures (Ahmed and Stein, 1987; Sartorius, Wolf and Henn, 2005; Small and Milstein, 1990; Weiner et al., 1980), while others report the safe use of lithium during a course of ECT (Dolenc and Rasmussen, 2005; Lippman and El-Mallakh, 1994). There is some evidence that high serum levels of lithium may be correlated with the a slower time to recovery after ECT treatment (Thirthalli, Harish and Gangadhar, 2011). This risk is rapidly reduced when the dose is reduced or complete withdrawn (American Psychiatric Association, 2001).

Lithium can potentiate the neuromuscular blockade of suxamethonium, delaying post-ECT recovery, and it may reduce the pressor effects of noradrenaline (Naguib and Koorn, 2002).

The decision concerning the use of lithium for patients proposed for ECT needs to be considered on its own merits, particularly if a patient has bipolar disorder. Withholding lithium during ECT may place the patient at risk of having a manic episode, increasing the course of ECT. Goodwin (2003) has identified that lithium should be continued for at least two years for the benefit of prophylaxis to outweigh the risk of relapse if discontinued, preventing it from becoming ineffective.

Many guidelines recommend that the risk of neurotoxicity can be reduced by omitting the night-time dose prior to ECT and delaying the administration of the morning dose until after full recovery has been achieved (NSW Health, 2010; SA Health, 2014; Waite and Easton, 2013), while others are more conservative, highlighting that lithium should be discontinued 48 hours prior to ECT. If lithium is to be continued, it should be maintained at a low level in the bottom of the reference range (Dixon and Santiago, 2013). The PRIDE study has demonstrated that lithium can be safely and effectively used in geriatric patients during continuation ECT when lithium is maintained at the lower end of the dose range (Kellner et al., 2016).

Rasmussen (2015) reviewed the literature concerning the use of lithium for post-ECT relapse prevention and concluded that in the main there is strong evidence that lithium can prevent relapse in the first six months after index ECT if patients are able to comply with all aspects of lithium usage. It goes on to highlight eight important clinical questions about post-ECT lithium usage that remain unanswered that would benefit from further research aiding the ECT practitioner.

Dolenc and Rasmussen (2005) provide some clinical guidance after reviewing the literature and presenting 12 patients who completed a course of ECT while taking lithium without complication:

- For patients already taking lithium without clear benefit, it is best to stop lithium before commencing ECT but a washout period is usually not necessary.
- If there have been clear benefits from ongoing use of lithium, particularly in bipolar mania, it is best to continue it during the index course of ECT at the lowest blood level to be effective and to monitor carefully for unwanted side effects.
- Alternatively, the lithium could be discontinued when ECT is being used to treat bipolar

depression and substituted with an atypical antipsychotic medication to prevent switching into mania.

- The proven benefits of lithium in preventing the high relapse rate post-ECT highlights that it should be commenced immediately after the index course of treatment has been completed (Sackeim et al., 2001).
- If there have been proven benefits of lithium treating manic symptoms and ECT being used for depression in bipolar disorder, lithium should be continued during maintenance ECT with appropriate monitoring after each treatment.

OTHER DRUGS

Caffeine

Caffeine is a naturally occurring xanthine alkaloid that acts by antagonising the adenosine receptor in the body. It has been demonstrated that it can prolong seizure duration when administered prior to ECT without affecting the seizure threshold (Dixon and Santiago, 2013). It has been noted that caffeine can increase mean seizure duration by 127% (Coffey et al., 1987; Sawynok, 1995).

In a further study, Coffey, Figel, Weiner and Saunders (1990) evaluated the use of caffeine and ECT in 40 depressed patients. They randomised the patients to caffeine-augmented ECT or increased stimulus dose to maintain duration greater than 30 seconds. The stimulus dose group had a 49% increase in absolute dose, whereas the caffeine group had minimal change in stimulus dose. There was an increase in anxiety and blood pressure post-seizure in the caffeine group.

There is compelling evidence that caffeine can increase seizure length (Datto, Rai, Ilivicky and Caroff, 2002) but has little impact on seizure threshold, challenging the view that caffeine has a direct impact on clinical improvement (McCall, Reid, Rosenquist, Foreman and Kiesow-Webb, 1993; Nobler and Sackeim, 1993). However, there are reports of increased levels of anxiety, agitation, cardiac arrhythmias and prolonged seizures, making its routine use in clinical practice uncommon (Datto et al., 2002).

More recent studies confirm the evidence that caffeine can prolong the duration of ECT seizures but it has not been clearly shown in controlled trials to increase efficacy and caution is required when used as it may be associated with significant adverse effects (Loo, Simpson and MacPherson, 2010). Caffeine should only be used to prolong seizure duration during ECT when all other options, like concurrent antidepressant treatment, frequency of ECT treatments, hyperventilation and augmentation of the induction agent with remifentanil, have been exhausted (Dixon and Santiago, 2013; Loo, Kaill, Paton and Simpson, 2010).

Theophylline

Another strategy to increase seizure duration with ECT in the past was to administer intravenous theophylline at the time of ECT or give it as a single oral dose the night before treatment. It has been proposed that this may be an alternative strategy to caffeine (Schwartz and Lewis, 1991). However, like caffeine it does not decrease seizure threshold and provides little advantage to patients who have had repeated missed seizures (McCall et al., 1993). It has been associated with a high incidence of status epilepticus even when the plasma levels are in the therapeutic range. Its use is largely abandoned (Abrams, 2002; American Psychiatric Association, 2001).

Antihypertensive agents

Cardiovascular complications are the most common cause of medical morbidity and mortality with ECT (Dolinski and Zvara, 1997; Zielinski et al., 1993) but most are mild and self-limiting, making the administration of ECT safe in the setting of cardiovascular disease if routine medication is maintained during the course of treatment (Bankhead, Torrens and Harris, 2006; Takada et al., 2005).

Anaesthetists need to give special consideration to patients with known cardiovascular disease (Dolinski and Zvara, 1997). Routine administration of antihypertensive agents the morning before ECT is common practice to prevent excessive cardiovascular instability during the treatment (Bankhead et al., 2006; NSW Health, 2010; Rice, Sombrotto, Markowitz and Leon, 1994; SA Health, 2014).

Digoxin

There have been reports of arrhythmias when digoxin is used with suxamethonium in surgery. However, there do not appear to be any instances of these complications occurring during ECT. It is speculated that this phenomena is due to the lower dose of suxamethonium used in ECT compared to surgery. Digoxin is very safe if the plasma levels are within the normal range and potassium levels are also maintained within the normal range (Applegate, 1997).

Diabetic medication

It is recommended that consultation with an endocrinologist prior to a course of ECT is best practice. Long-acting insulin may be safely given to patients before a course of ECT. However, it is recommend that oral hypoglycaemic medication should be withheld until after the treatment (American Psychiatric Association, 2001; NSW Health, 2010; SA Health, 2014; Tiller and Lyndon, 2003; Walker, Bowley and Walker, 2013). It is usual practice to place patients with diabetes first on the list so they can return to the ward as soon as practicable to have breakfast and their diabetic medications.

Acetylcholinesterase inhibitors

Acetylcholinesterase inhibitors are being used more commonly in patients with early onset dementia, a group of patients who are presenting more commonly for ECT (Manjola, 2015). Concerns have been expressed about the potential effect that these drugs might have during a course of ECT due to the synergistic enhancement of neuro-muscular blockade with suxamethonium causing brady-cardia, cardiac arrhythmias and the potential for these drugs reduce seizure threshold when used with ECT (Bowman, 2002).

In contrast, the evidence suggests that these drugs are safe to use during ECT and that they may have beneficial effects in reducing cognitive impairment, especially new learning (Matthews et al., 2008), improving time to recovery (Prakash, Kotwal and Prabhu, 2006) and reducing cognitive impairment caused by maintenance ECT (Rao, Palaniyappan, Chandur, Venkatasubramanian and Gangadhar, 2009).

AUSTRALIAN PSYCHOTROPIC THERAPEUTIC GUIDELINES

There have been many changes to the advice given concerning psychotropic drugs and ECT in the quick-reference Psychotropic Therapeutic Guidelines over the last 10 years (Psychotropic Expert Group, 2013). These changes are reflected in the drug interaction and ECT tables listed in the various volumes. In 2008 Version 6, the table was omitted completely. This followed more recent information that medications and ECT were safe and tricyclic antidepressants may improve cognitive outcomes (Sackeim et al., 2009; Sackeim et al., 2001).

The 2011 Psychotropic Therapeutic Guidelines make the following recommendations:

- Taper then cease all benzodiazepines before ECT as they raise the seizure threshold.
- Where there is a risk of postictal delirium, lithium should be ceased.
- For antiepileptic mood-stabilising drugs, leave the decision to the individual treating team as maintaining, reducing or ceasing are all common practice. A recent review article supports this view (Sienaert and Peuskens, 2007), concluding that there is no evidence that combining ECT and anticonvulsant therapy augments the thera-peutic effect of this treatment.

- Antipsychotics generally can be continued. Caution should be exercised when combining with clozapine owing to its potential to lower seizure threshold and cause myocarditis.
- Antidepressant medication should be changed during the course of ECT to increase the effec-tiveness of the treatment. There is a high level of relapse when ECT is ceased (Sackeim et al., 2001), requiring aggressive medication manage-ment after the index course has been completed (Rasmussen, 2015).

REFERENCES

Abrams, R. (2002a). *Electroconvulsive Therapy*, 4th edition. New York: Oxford University Press.

Ahmed, S.K., and Stein, G.S. (1987). Negative interaction between lithium and ECT. *British Journal of Psychiatry, 151*, 419–420.

American Psychiatric Association. (2001). *The Practice of Electroconvulsive Therapy: Recommendations for Treatment, Training and Privileging: A Task Force Report*, 2nd edition. Washington, DC: American Psychiatric Association.

Applegate, R.J. (1997). Diagnosis and management of ischemic heart disease in the patient scheduled to undergo electro-convulsive therapy. *Journal of ECT, 13*(3), 128–144. Retrieved from http://journals.lww.com/ectjournal/Fulltext/1997/09000/Diagnosis_and_Management_of_Ischemic_Heart_Disease.4.aspx.

Bailine, S.H., Safferman, A., Vital-Herne, J., and Bernstein, S. (1994). Flumazenil reversal of benzodiazepine-induced sedation for a patient with severe pre-ECT anxiety. *Convulsive Therapy, 10*(1), 65–68. Retrieved from www.ncbi.nlm.nih.gov/pubmed/7914463.

Bankhead, A.J., Torrens, J.K., and Harris, T.H. (2006). The anticipation and prevention of cardiac complications in electroconvulsive therapy: a clinical and electrocardiographic study. *American Journal of Psychiatry, 106*(12), 911–917. doi:10.1176/ajp.106.12.911.

Bernardo, M., Navarro, V., Salva, J., Arrufat, F.J., and Baeza, I. (2000). Seizure activity and safety in combined treatment with venlafaxine and ECT: a pilot study. *Journal of ECT, 16*(1), 38–42. Retrieved from www.ncbi.nlm.nih.gov/pubmed/10735330.

Bloch, Y., Pollack, M., and Mor, I. (1996). Should the admin-istration of ECT during clozapine therapy be contraindicated? *British Journal Psychiatry 169*, 253–254.

Bowman, B. (2002). Concurrent use of ECT and cholinesterase inhibitor medications. *Australian and New Zealand Journal of Psychiatry., 6*, 816–816.

Braga, R.J., and Petrides, G. (2005). The combined use of electroconvulsive therapy and antipsychotics in patients with schizophrenia. *Journal of ECT, 21.* Retrieved from http://journals.lww.com/ectjournal/toc/2005/06000.

Caracci, G., and Decina, P. (1991). Fluoxetine and Prolonged Seizure. *Convulsive Therapy, 7*(2), 145–147. Retrieved from www.ncbi.nlm.nih.gov/pubmed/11941116.

Coffey, C.E., Figel, G.S., Weiner, R.D., and Saunders, W.B. (1990). Caffeine augmentation of ECT. *American Journal of Psychiatry, 147*(5), 579–585. Retrieved from www.ncbi.nlm.nih.gov/pubmed/2183632.

Coffey, C.E., Weiner, R.D., Hinkle, P.E., Cress, N., Daughtry, G., and Wilson, W.H. (1987). Augmentation of ECT seizures with caffeine. *Biological Psychiatry, 22*(5), 637–649. Retrieved from www.ncbi.nlm.nih.gov/pubmed/3580438.

Cohen, S.I., and Lawton, C. (1992). Do benzodiazepines interfere with the action of electroconvulsive therapy? *British Journal of Psychiatry, 160*(4), 545–546.

Datto, C., Rai, A.K., Ilivicky, H.J., and Caroff, S.N. (2002). Augmentation of seizure induction in electroconvulsive therapy: a clinical reappraisal. *Journal of ECT, 18*(3), 118–125.

Davidson, J. (1989). Seizures and bupropion: a review. *Journal of Clinical Psychiatry, 50*(7), 256–261. Retrieved from www.ncbi.nlm.nih.gov/pubmed/2500425.

Deshmukh, R., Thakur, A.S., and Dewangan, D. (2011). Mechanism of action of anticonvulsant drugs: a review. *International Journal of Pharmaceutical Sciences and Research, 2*(2), 225.

Dixon, M., and Santiago, A. (2013). Psychotropic drug treatment during and after ECT. In Waite, J., and Easton, A. (Eds.), *The ECT Handbook,* 3rd edition (pp. 45–59). London: Royal College of Psychiatrists.

Dolenc, T., and Rasmussen, K. (2005). The safety of electroconvulsive therapy and lithium in combination: a case series and reveiw of the literature. *Journal of ECT, 21,* 165–170.

Dolinski, S.Y., and Zvara, D.A. (1997). Anesthetic considerations of cardiovascular risk during electroconvulsive therapy. *Convulsive Therapy, 13*(3), 157–164. Retrieved from www.ncbi.nlm.nih.gov/pubmed/9342131.

Fink, M. (2009). *Electroconvulsive Therapy: A Guide for Professionals and Their Patients.* New York: Oxford University Press.

Frankenburg, F.R., Suppes, T., and McLean, P.E. (1993). Combined clozapine and electroconvulsive therapy. *Journal of ECT, 9*(3), 176–180. Retrieved from http://journals.lww.com/ectjournal/Fulltext/1993/09000/Combined_Clozapine_and_Electroconvulsive_Therapy_.4.aspx.

Freeman, S.A. (2007). The effect of lamotrigine on electroconvulsive therapy outcomes. *Journal of ECT, 23*(1), 38. doi:10.1097/01.yct.0000264341.34695.e9.

Gonzalez, Pinto, A., Gutierrez, M., Tonzalez, N., Elizagarate, E., Perez, D.E., . . . Micro, J.A. (2002). Efficacy and safety of venlafaxine–ECT combination and treatment resistant depression *Journal of Neuropsychiatry & Clinical Neuroscience, 14*(2), 206–209.

Goodwin, G.M. (2003). Evidence-based guidelines for treating bipolar disorder. *Journal of Psychopharmacology, 17,* 149–173.

Greenberg, R.M., and Pettinati, H.M. (1993). Benzodiazepines and electroconvulsive therapy. *Convulsive Therapy, 9*(4), 262–273. Retrieved from www.ncbi.nlm.nih.gov/pubmed/11941222.

Greenhalgh, J., Knight, C., Hind, D., Beverley, C., and Walters, S. (2005). Clinical and cost-effectiveness of electroconvulsive therapy for depressive illness, schizophrenia, catatonia and mania: systematic reviews and economic modelling studies. *Health Technology Assessment, 9*(9), 1–156, iii–iv. Retrieved from www.ncbi.nlm.nih.gov/pubmed/15774232.

Gujavarty, K., Greenberg, L.B., and Fink, M. (1987). Electroconvulsive therapy and neuroleptic medication in therapy-resistant positive-symptom psychosis. *Convulsive Therapy, 3*(3), 185–195. Retrieved from www.ncbi.nlm.nih.gov/pubmed/11940915.

Gutierrez-Esteinou, R., and Pope, H.G. (1989). Does fluoxetine prolong electrically induced seizures? *Convulsive Therapy, 5*(4), 344–348.

Hanretta, A.T., and Malek-Ahmadi, P. (2006). Combined use of ECT with duloxetine and olanzapine: a case report. *Journal of ECT, 22*(2), 139–141.

Harsch, H.H., and Haddox, J.D. (1990). Electroconvulsive therapy and fluoxetine. *Convulsive Therapy, 6*(3), 250–251. Retrieved from www.ncbi.nlm.nih.gov/pubmed/11941076.

Havaki-Kontaxaki, B.J., Ferentinos, P.P., Kontaxakis, V.P., Paplos, K.G., and Soldatos, C.R. (2006). Concurrent administration of clozapine and electroconvulsive therapy in clozapine-resistant schizophrenia. *Clinical Neuropharmacology, 29*(1), 52–56. Retrieved from http://journals.lww.com/clinicalneuropharm/Fulltext/2006/01000/Concurrent_Administration_of_Clozapine_and.12.aspx.

Hsiao, J.K., Messenheimer, J.A., and Evans, D.L. (1987). ECT and neurological disorders. *Convulsive Therapy, 3*(2), 121–136. Retrieved from www.ncbi.nlm.nih.gov/pubmed/11940905.

Jarvis, M., Goewert, A., and Zorumski, C. (1992). Novel antidepressants and maintenance electroconvulsive therapy: a review. *Annals of Clinical Psychiatry, 4,* 275–284.

Jha, R., and Stein, G. (1996). Decreased efficacy of combined benzodiazepines and unilateral ECT in treatment of depression. *Acta Psychiatrica Scandinavica, 94*(2), 101–104.

Kay, D.W., Fahy, T., and Garside, R.F. (1970). A seven-month double-blind trial of amitripyline and dizepam in ECT-treated depressed patients. *British Journal of Psychiatry, 117,* 667–671.

Kellner, C.H., Pritchett, J.T., and Jackson, C.W. (1994). Buproprion coadministration with electroconvulsive therapy: two case reports. *Journal of Clinical Psychopharmacology, 14*, 215–216.

Kellner, C.H., and Bruno, R.M. (1989). Fluoxetine and ECT. *Convulsive Therapy, 5*(4), 367–368. Retrieved from www.ncbi.nlm.nih.gov/pubmed/11941039.

Kellner, C.H., Husain, M.M., Knapp, R.G., McCall, W.V., Petrides, G., Rudorfer, M.V., . . . Lisanby, S.H. (2016). A novel strategy for continuation ECT in geriatric depression: phase 2 of the PRIDE study. *American Journal of Psychiatry, 173*(11), 1110–1118. doi:10.1176/appi.ajp.2016.16010118.

Kho, K.H., Blansjaar, B.A., de Vries, S., Babuskova, D., Zwinderman, A.H., and Linszen, D.H. (2004). Electroconvulsive therapy for the treatment of clozapine nonresponders suffering from schizophrenia. *European Archives of Psychiatry and Clinical Neuroscience, 254*(6), 372–379. doi:10.1007/s00406-004-0517-y.

Krystal, A.D., Watts, B.V., Weiner, R.D., Moore, S., Steffens, D., and Lindahl, V.L. (1998). The use of flumazenil in the anxious and benzodiazepine-dependent ECT patient. *Journal of ECT, 14*(1), 5–14.

Kupchik, M., Spivak, B., Mester, R., Reznik, I., Gonen, N., Weizman, A., and Kotler, M. (2000). Combined electroconvulsive–clozapine therapy. *Clinical Neuropharmacology, 23*(1), 14–16. Retrieved from http://journals.lww.com/clinical neuropharm/Fulltext/2000/01000/Combined_Electroconvulsive_ Clozapine_Therapy.3.aspx.

Lauritzen, L., Odgaard, K., and Clemmesen, L. (1996). Relapse prevention by means of paroxetine in ECT-treated patients with major depression: a comparison with imipramine and placebo in medium-term continuation therapy. *Acta Psychiatrica Scandinavica, 94*, 241–251.

Layne, E., Young, J.A., Votolato, N.A., Miller, K.M., and Martin, B.S. (2005). Effect of concurrent lamotrigine in patients receiving electroconvulsive therapy. *Journal of ECT, 21*(1), 60. Retrieved from http://journals.lww.com/ectjournal/ Fulltext/2005/03000/Effect_of_Concurrent_Lamotrigine_in_ Patients.39.aspx.

Lippman, S.B., and El-Mallakh, R. (1994). Can electroconvulsive therapy be given during lithium treatment? *Lithium, 5*, 205–209.

Loo, C., Simpson, B., and MacPherson, R. (2010). Augmentation strategies in electroconvulsive therapy. *Journal of ECT, 26*(3), 202–207. doi:10.1097/YCT.0b013e3181e48143.

Loo, C.K., Kaill, A., Paton, P., and Simpson, B. (2010). The difficult-to-treat electroconvulsive therapy patient – Strategies for augmenting outcomes. *Journal of Affective Disorders, 124*(3), 219–227. doi:10.1016/j.jad.2009.07.011.

Lopez-Garccia, P.L., Chiclana, C., and Gonzalez, R. (2009). Combined use of ECT with aripiprazole. *World Journal of Biological Psychiatry, 10*, 942–943.

Lunde, M.E., Lee, E.K., and Rasmussen, K.G. (2006). Electroconvulsive therapy in patients with epilepsy. *Epilepsy Behaviour, 9*, 355–359.

McCall, W.V., Reid, S., Rosenquist, P., Foreman, A., and Kiesow-Webb, N. (1993). A reappraisal of the role of caffeine in ECT. *American Journal of Psychiatry, 150*(10), 1543–1545. Retrieved from www.ncbi.nlm.nih.gov/pubmed/ 8379563.

Mcintosh, A.M., and Lawrie, S.M. (2005). Systematic review: continuation pharmacotherapy after ECT for depressive illness. In Scott, A.I. (Ed.), *The ECT Handbook*, 2nd edition. (pp. 99–108). London: Royal College of Psychiatrists.

McIntosh, A.M., and Lawrie, S.M. (2005). Systematic review of psychotropic medication given during a course of ECT for depressive illness: therapeutic and adverse consequences. In Scott, A.I. (Ed.), *The ECT Handbook*, 2nd edition (pp. 85–98). London: Royal College of Psychiatrists.

Manjola, U. (2015). Dementia, agitation, and aggression: the role of electroconvulsive therapy. Special report. *Psychiatric Times.*

Marangell, L.B., Martinez, J.M., Ketter, T.A., Bowden, C.L., Goldberg, J.F., Calabrese, J.R., . . . Thase, M.E. (2004). Lamotrigine treatment of bipolar disorder: data from the first 500 patients in STEP_BD. *Bipolar Disorder, 6*, 139–143.

Masdrakis, V.G., Oulis, P., Florakis, A., Valamoutopoulos, T., Markatou, M., and Papadimitriou, G.N. (2008). The safety of the electroconvulsive therapy-escitalopram combination. *Journal of ECT, 24*(4), 289–291. doi:10.1097/YCT.0b013e 31816ba99d.

Masdrakis, V.G., Oulis, P., Zervas, I.M., Karakatsanis, N.A., Kouzoupis, A.V., Karapoulios, E., and Soldatos, C.R. (2008). The safety of the electroconvulsive therapy-aripiprazole combination: four case reports. *Journal of ECT, 24*(3), 236–238. doi:10.1097/YCT.0b013e3181571c0e.

Matthews, J.D., Blais, M., Park, L., Welch, C., Baity, M., Murakami, J., . . . Fava, M. (2008). The impact of galantamine on cognition and mood during electroconvulsive therapy: a pilot study. *Journal of Psychiatric Research, 42*(7), 526–531. doi:10.1016/j.jpsychires.2007.06.002.

Mukherjee, S. (1993). Combined ECT and lithium therapy. *Convulsive Therapy, 9*(4), 274–282.

Naguib, M., and Koorn, R. (2002). Interactions betwen psychotropics, anaesthetics and electroconvulsive therapy. Implications for drug choice and patient management. *CNS Drugs, 16*, 229–247.

Nelson, J.P., and Benjamin, L. (1989). Efficacy and safety of combined ECT and tricycic antidepressant therapy in the treatment of depressed geriatric patients. *Convulsive Therapy, 5*, 321–329. Retrieved from http://journals.lww.com/ ectjournal/toc/1989/12000.

Nobler, M.S., and Sackeim, H.A. (1993). Augmentation strategies in electroconvulsive therapy: a synthesis. *Convulsive Therapy, 9*(4), 331–351. Retrieved from www.ncbi.nlm.nih.gov/pubmed/11941229.

NSW Health. (2010). ECT minimum standard of practice NSW. Retrieved from www.health.nsw.gov.au/policies/pd/2011/pdf/PD2011_003.pdf.

Penland, H.R., and Ostroff, R.B. (2006). Combined use of lamotrigine and electroconvulsive therapy in bipolar depression: a case series. *Journal of ECT, 22*(2), 142–147. Retrieved from http://journals.lww.com/ectjournal/Fulltext/2006/06000/Combined_Use_of_Lamotrigine_and_Electroconvulsive.13.aspx.

Petrides, G., Braga, R.J., Fink, M., Mueller, M., Knapp, R., Husain, M., . . . Kellner, C. (2009). Seizure threshold in a large sample: implications for stimulus dosing strategies and bilateral ECTs. A report from Core. *Journal of ECT, 25*(4), 232–237.

Pettinati, H.M., Stephens, S.M., Willis, K.M., and Robin, S.E. (1990). Evidence for less improvement in depression in patients taking benzodiazepines during unilateral ECT. 147: 1029–1035. *American Journal of Psychiatry, 147*, 1029–1035.

Pollack, M.H., Stein, M.B., Davidson, J.R., and Ginsberg, D.L. (2004). New challenges for anxiety disorders: where treatment, resilience, and economic priority converge. *CNS Spectrums, 9*(04), 1–4.

Prakash, J., Kotwal, A., and Prabhu, H. (2006). Therapeutic and prophylactic utility of the memory-enhancing drug donepezil hydrochloride on cognition of patients undergoing electroconvulsive therapy: a randomized controlled trial. *Journal of ECT, 22*(3), 163–168. doi:10.1097/01.yct.0000230365.81368.2d.

Psychotropic Expert Group. (2013). *Therapeutic Guidelines: Psychotropic*, 7th edition. Melbourne, Australia: Therapeutic Guidelines.

Rao, N.P., Palaniyappan, P., Chandur, J., Venkatasubramanian, G., and Gangadhar, B.N. (2009). Successful use of donepezil in treatment of cognitive impairment caused by maintenance electroconvulsive therapy: a case report. *Journal of ECT, 25*(3), 216–218.

Rasmussen, K.G. (2015). Lithium for post-electroconvulsive therapy depressive relapse prevention: a consideration of the evidence. *Journal of ECT, 31*, 87–90.

Rice, E.H., Sombrotto, L.B., Markowitz, J.C., and Leon, A.C. (1994). Cardiovascular morbidity in high-risk patients during ECT. *American Journal of Psychiatry, 151*(11), 1637–1641. doi:10.1176/ajp.151.11.1637.

SA Health. (2014). South Australian guidelines for electroconvulsive therapy. Retrieved from www.sahealth.sa.gov.au/wps/wcm/connect/0608270046ad5b01b89.

Sackeim, H.A. (2000). Memory and ECT: from polarization to reconciliation. *Journal of ECT, 16*(2), 87–96. Retrieved from www.ncbi.nlm.nih.gov/pubmed/10868319.

Sackeim, H.A. (2004). Convulsant and anticonvulsant properties of electroconvulsive therapy: towards a focal form of brain stimulation. *Clinical Neuroscience Research*, 39–57.

Sackeim, H.A., Dillingham, E.M., Prudic, J., Cooper, T., McCall, W.V., Rosenquist, P., . . . Haskett, R.F. (2009). Effect of concomitant pharmacotherapy on electroconvulsive therapy outcomes: short-term efficacy and adverse effects. *Archives of General Psychiatry, 66*(7), 729–737. doi:10.1001/archgenpsychiatry.2009.75.

Sackeim, H.A., Haskett, R.F., Mulsant, B.H., Thase, M.E., Mann, J.J., Pettinati, H.M., . . . Prudic, J. (2001). Continuation pharmacotherapy in the prevention of relapse following electroconvulsive therapy: a randomized controlled trial. *Journal of the American Medical Association, 285*(10), 1299–1307. Retrieved from www.ncbi.nlm.nih.gov/pubmed/11255384.

Sackeim, H.A., Prudic, J., Devanand, D.P., Decina, P., Kerr, B., and Malitz, S. (1990). The impact of medication resistance and continuation pharmacotherapy on relapse following response to electroconvulsive therapy in major depression. *Journal of Clinical Psychopharmacology, 10*(2), 96–104. Retrieved from http://journals.lww.com/psychopharmacology/Fulltext/1990/04000/The_Impact_of_Medication_Resistance_and.4.aspx.

Sackeim, H.A., Prudic, J., Devanand, D.P., Kiersky, J.E., Fitzsimons, L., Moody, B.J., . . . Settembrino, J.M. (1993). Effects of stimulus intensity and electrode placement on the efficacy and cognitive effects of electroconvulsive therapy. *New England Journal of Medicine, 328*(12), 839–846.

Sackeim, H.A., Prudic, J., Fuller, R., Keilp, J., Lavori, P.W., and Olfson, M. (2007). The cognitive effects of electroconvulsive therapy in community settings. *Neuropsychopharmacology, 32*(1), 244–254. doi:10.1038/sj.npp.1301180.

Sartorius, A., Wolf, J., and Henn, F.A. (2005). Lithium and ECT – concurrent use still demands attention: three case reports. *World Journal of Bioloigical Psychiatry, 6*, 121–124.

Sawynok, J. (1995). Pharmacological rationale for the clinical use of caffeine. *Drugs, 49*, 37–50.

Schwartz, C.M., and Lewis, R.K. (1991). Theophylline reversal electroconvulsive therapy (ECT seizure inhibition). *Psychosomatics, 32*(1), 47–51.

Scott, A.I.F. (2005). *The ECT Handbook*, 2nd edition. London: Royal College of Psychiatrists.

Sienaert, P., Demunter, H., Vansteelandt, K., and Peuskens, J. (2006). Effect of lamotrigine on concurrent electroconvulsive therapy. *European Neuropsychopharmacology, 16(suppl 4)*, S348.

Sienaert, P., and Peuskens, J. (2007). Anticonvulsants during electroconvulsive therapy: review and recommendations. *Journal of ECT, 23*(2), 120–123. doi:10.1097/YCT.0b013 e3180330059.

Sienaert, P.,1, Roelens, Y., Demunter, H., Vansteelandt, K., Peuskens, J., and Van Heeringen, C. (2011). Concurrent use of lamotrigine and electroconvulsive therapy. *Journal of ECT, 27*(2), 48052. Retrieved from www.ncbi.nlm.nih.gov/pubmed/20562637.

Small, J.G., and Milstein, V. (1990). Lithium interactions: lithium and electroconvulsive therapy. *Journal of Clinical Psychopharmacology, 10*(5), 346–350. Retrieved from www.ncbi.nlm.nih.gov/pubmed/2258451.

Standish-Barry, H.M., Deacon, V., and Snaith, R.P. (1985). The relationship of concurrent benzodiazepine administration to seizure duration in ECT. *Acta Psychiatrica Scandinavica, 71*(3), 269–271. Retrieved from www.ncbi.nlm.nih.gov/pubmed/3984767.

Takada, J.Y., Solimene, M.C., da Luz, P.L., Grupi, C.J., Giorgi, D.M.A., Rigonatti, S.P., . . . Ramires, J.A.F. (2005). Assessment of the cardiovascular effects of electroconvulsive therapy in individuals older than 50 years. *Brazilian Journal of Medical and Biological Research, 38*, 1349–1357. Retrieved from www.scielo.br/scielo.php?script=sci_arttextandpid=S0100–879X2005000900009andnrm=iso.

Tharyan, P., and Adams, C.E. (2005). Electroconvulsive therapy for schizophrenia. *Cochrane Database of Systematic Reviews, 2*(CD000076).

Thirthalli, J., Harish, T., and Gangadhar, B.N. (2011). A prospective comparative study of interaction between lithium and modified electroconvulsive therapy. *World Journal of Bioloigical Psychiatry, 12*, 149–155.

Tiller, J.W.G., and Lyndon, R.W. (2003). *Electroconvulsive Therapy: An Australian Guide*. Melbourne, Australia: Australian Post Graduate Medicine.

Tor, P.C., Bautovich, A., Wang, M.J., Martin, D., Harvey, S.B., and Loo, C. (2015). A systematic review and meta-analysis of brief versus ultrabrief right unilateral electroconvulsive therapy for depression. *Journal of Clinical Psychiatry, 10*(4088). doi:10.4088/JCP.14r09145.

Waite, J., and Easton, A. (2013). *The ECT Handbook*, 3rd edition. London: Royal College of Psychiatrists.

Walker, S.C., Bowley, C.J., and Walker, A.C. (2013). Anaesthesia for ECT. In Waite, J., and Easton, A. (Eds.), *The ECT Handbook*. London: Royal College of Psychiatrists.

Weiner, R.D., Whanger, A.D., Erwin, C.W., and Wilson, W.P. (1980). Prolonged confusional state and EEG seizure activity following concurrent ECT and lithium use. *American Journal of Psychiatry, 137*, 1452–1453.

Zarate, C.A., Tohen, M., and Baraiba, R.G. (1997). Combined valproate or carbamazepine electroconvulsive therapy. *Annals of Clinical Psychiatry, 9*(1), 19–25. Retrieved from www.ncbi.nlm.nih.gov/pubmed/9167833.

Zielinski, R.J., Roose, S.P., Devanand, D.P., Woodring, S., and Sackeim, H.A. (1993). Cardiovascular complcications of ECT in depressed patients with cardiac disease. *American Journal of Psychiatry, 150*, 904–909.

Tips for clinical practice

One of the biggest challenges facing an ECT practitioner contemplating setting up a new ECT service or modernising an existing one is confronting the question "to do or not to do?" based upon the evidence, clinical guidelines and what is learned by clinical experience.

Evidence-based practice remains the gold standard; however, the practitioner quickly confronts the clinical reality that the evidence base is limited and there are many areas where there is marked variation in clinical practice. In order to develop a successful ECT service, the evidence base must be guided by practice-based experience to develop techniques that are appropriate for a local health region. The discussion that follows is based upon years of clinical wisdom.

BACKGROUND

Nearly 40 years ago the criticism was made that medical education had become very sophisticated in conveying scientific knowledge and technical skills about the body yet at the same time failed to give corresponding attention to the scientific understanding of human behaviour, psychological or social aspects of illness and patient care, with communication going in one direction, from the doctor, who was regarded as the expert, to the patient, who passively accepted the advice (Engel, 1978).

Engel (1989) argued that there was need for a new paradigm, the biopsychosocial model, that was holistic in its approach. The biopsychosocial model was both a philosophy of clinical care, providing an understanding of how suffering, disease and illness are affected by multiple levels of organisation and a practical clinical guide providing a way of understanding the patient's subjective experience as an essential contributor to accurate diagnosis, health outcomes and humane care (Borrell-Carrio, Suchman and Epstein, 2004).

It is the author's assertion that the advent of evidence-based medicine has changed the focus away from the biopsychosocial model, which was fundamental to psychiatry training. The biopsychosocial model emphasised self-awareness, active cultivation of trust, an emotional style characterised by empathic curiosity, self-calibration as a way to reduce bias, education of the emotions to assist with diagnosis, and forming therapeutic relationships, using informed intuition and communicating clinical evidence to foster dialogue and open communication with patients (Borrell-Carrio et al., 2004).

In contrast, evidence-based medicine focuses on the conscientious, explicit, judicious and reasonable use of modern best evidence to make decisions about the care of individual patients (Swanson, Schmitz and Chung, 2010). The intent of evidence-based medicine was to integrate high-quality clinical research into clinical practice that in turn demanded better evidence than was traditionally available, resulting in the development of systematic reviews and meta-analyses (Masic, Miokovic and Muhamedagic, 2008).

In practice, the authoritative aura given to the collection of the information, the restricted quality and scope of what was collected as "best available evidence" packaged as systematic reviews and meta-analyses conveyed little meaning to issues involving aetiology, diagnosis, prognosis or clinical decisions that depend on pathophysiological changes, psychosocial factors, support, personal preferences of patients, and strategies to provide comfort and reassurance (Feinstein and Horwitz, 1997). There are now concerns that evidence-based practice with an emphasis on experimental evidence has devalued basic sciences and the tacit knowledge that accumulates with clinical experience by forsaking tradition, anecdote and theoretical reasoning (Greenhalgh, Howick and Maskrey, 2014).

It is not surprising that in this environment there has been growing criticism that medicine, psychiatry and ECT practice in particular, is out of touch with consumers, leading to the highly critical National Institute for Clinical Excellence (2003, modified 2009) guidance on the use of electroconvulsive therapy, which was based upon two meta-analyses, one by experts (UK ECT Review Group, 2003) and the other led by consumers (Rose, Fleischmann, Wykes, Leese and Bindman, 2003). Consumers emphasised that ECT practitioners were out of touch, with recent studies suggesting that nearly half of patients reported that they did not receive sufficient information about ECT and its side effects (Rose, Wykes, Bindman and Fleischmann, 2005). Further qualitative research suggests that consumer views about ECT are complex, with twice as many testimonies expressing negative views about the treatment as were positive (Rose, Fleischmann and Wykes, 2009).

It is imperative that ECT practitioners have a sound understanding of the evidence base that underpins ECT but it is also important for them to have the capacity to integrate this knowledge into their own clinical practice. In this way they will develop a rich and varied consumer-focused, practice-based experience that will guide their delivery of ECT treatment.

STIGMA OR NO STIGMA?

One of the first challenges an ECT practitioner has to deal with is recognising the life-saving benefits of ECT, which are markedly different to the stigma and misinformation that remains prevalent in the community (Torpey, 2016). As a junior consultant involved with ECT, it can take some time to recognise how deeply these fears are ingrained and how easily they can be projected onto patients who are consenting for the treatment. Even the best treatments will not be good enough with patients who hoped for a cure becoming disappointed, afraid and angry. Some patients have confusing expectations.

Rationally, we know that being ill or having poor relationships and no work is unpleasant but it is hard to escape the burden of our own motivations, needs and desires that play out in the relationship that is fundamental in medicine the therapeutic alliance (Hughes and Keer, 2000). The therapeutic alliance is a rational, implicit contract between doctor and patient than can be straightforward with mutual cooperation or complicated by covert agendas that may be unconscious and unspoken from both parties (Hughes and Keer, 2000)

Recognising the complex interplay between transference and counter-transference that underpins the therapeutic alliance is fundamental in being a good psychiatrist and crucial to an ECT practitioner who has a high level of practice-based experience. Once the practitioner has identified the feelings evoked in them by the patient's projections and the origins of their own feelings concerning the treatment, they are in a strong position to provide sound evidence-based clinical advice that helps the patient overcome their fears, enabling free and fully informed consent.

TO TALK OR NOT TO TALK?

One of the core features of a successful ECT service is the multidisciplinary team that has open and clear communication. Talking between team members is important to disseminate clinical information about the patient being treated, bringing together the patient's current mental state and physical comorbidities with the relevant anaesthetic issues. Communication ensures that all legal documentation is up to date, that the set-up is accurate prior to ECT and that all details are recorded after the treatment has been administered.

Introducing the patient to team members when they come in for treatment and involving them in relevant discussion if well enough creates a happy and relaxed environment that can minimise the their anxiety.

Open communication minimises mistakes being made during the delivery of ECT. Wrong electrode placement, pulse width, stimulus energy and doses of anaesthetic agents can be easily overlooked if there is tension within the treatment room or if there are poor protocols to guide the treatment.

An essential requirement that should be built into an ECT protocol is a "time out" procedure that is compatible with regional day surgical requirements. Timing the period after suxamethonium has been administered enables the ECT team to agree that the muscle fasciculations have ceased and treatment should commence, often between 90 to 120 seconds.

There are times during ECT when talking is not helpful. Remaining patient-focused can be challenging when the list is "long and routine". It is not uncommon for the team to engage in "idle chit-chat" that is completely unrelated to the patient but very common in a surgical environment. Avoiding this practice increases the speed of the procedure, reduces patient anxiety if awake, reduces the distraction during the procedure, and minimises errors, particularly when there are potential complications.

OPERATING THEATRE OR STAND-ALONE SUITE?

In the past it was not uncommon for ECT to be routinely administered in the recovery area of a theatre block. Theatre staff recognised that for all other procedures this practice was completely unacceptable but somehow made the exception

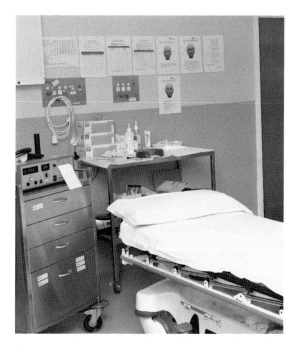

Photo 4.5.1 *ECT stand-alone suite*

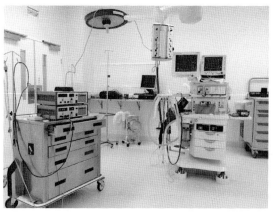

Photo 4.5.2 *ECT operating theatre*

for ECT, suggesting that it is not a "legitimate treatment". There are few other treatments in medicine that are given this level of disrespect by eliminating privacy, increasing stigma and making ECT different to every other day-only surgical procedure that is undertaken within the hospital. Changing this practice normalises ECT, ranking it at the same level as any other surgical procedure.

The ECT practitioner must negotiate with theatre managers and staff to change this practice by highlighting the issues noted above so that ECT can be moved into a theatre or day-only theatre area, illustrated in Photo 4.5.2, or develop a stand-alone ECT suite, illustrated in Photo 4.5.1.

The ECT suite should have a comfortable area where patients can wait, a treatment room and a recovery area that has enough space to accommodate trolleys and associated monitoring equipment for all patients who are regaining consciousness as specified in minimum standard documents (American Psychiatric Association, 2001; Freeman and Fergusson, 2013; NSW Health, 2010; RANZCP, 2007; SA Health, 2014).

Stand-alone ECT suites have the advantage of being located close to the inpatient mental health facility and staffed by a dedicated ECT team, including an anaesthetist who is under the direct control of the mental health service. However, the suite can only deal with routine cases owing to limited equipment. Complex patients with high-acuity need to be referred to another hospital with more intensive facilities.

There are a number of advantages in administering ECT in a fully equipped theatre. Treatment can be given to patients with higher levels of comorbidities and other complexities that would not be possible in a less intense area. Theatres are equipped with emergency trolleys and staff who can assist in the event of a medical emergency.

The availability of volatile induction agents like sevoflurane allows the containment of aggressive behaviour in involuntary patients, providing safety to the patient and staff and humanly gaining intravenous access and allowing the set-up for ECT to relaxed and careful to prevent errors.

Volatile agents also have a place for patients who have severe needle phobias, when multiple attempts are required for successful placement of the intravenous catheter and patients with distressing side effects to intravenous induction agents (Rasmussen, Spackman and Hooten, 2005).

There have reports of sevoflurane being used successfully during a course of ECT in women during the third trimester of pregnancy as it stabilises contractions (Walker, Bowley and Walker, 2013; Ding and White, 2002).

If a volatile gas is used, the ECT practitioner should be aware that these agents are more anti-convulsant than the injectable barbiturates; drugs attenuating seizure length, increasing time to recovery and higher stimulus doses may be required (Rasmussen et al., 2005).

One strategy to minimise the effect of the volatile induction agent on seizure expression is to turn it off, allow a suitable washout period so that the mini-mum alveolar concentration (MAC) returns to zero, and administer an injectable anaesthetic agent and suxamethonium before the treatment commences.

One of the problems in administering treatment in a theatre complex is the lack of priority allocated to ECT. ECT is often put on the end of the emergency list, making the start time inconsistent or causing the list to be cancelled for more "urgent" cases if the surgical demand is high. These parameters have a negative impact on patients who have been fasting from midnight and are often already agitated and distressed.

TO TITRATE OR NOT TO TITRATE?

A common question that arises in clinical prac-tice is whether stimulus dose titration should be incorporated during the initial ECT treatment. The concept of stimulus dose titration arose during the 1980s, when it was shown that there were large differences in seizure thresholds between patients and not all seizures were effective (Sackeim et al., 1993; Sackeim, Decina, Kanzler, Kerr and Malitz, 1987; Sackeim, Decina, Portnoy, Neeley and Malitz, 1987). Multiple factors affect the seizure threshold, including electrode placement, advanced age, male sex, greater burden of medial illness, weight, duration of mood disorder, history of previous ECT and anaesthetic agents (Boylan et al., 2000). Titrating the stimulus dose meant that the energy administered was specific to that patient, reducing cognitive impairment.

Others have argued that this technique is a crude arbitrary measure that provides little clinical

advantage, lengthening the overall course of treat-ment and exposing the patient to unnecessary anaesthesia (Swartz, 2001). Alternative methods may be more complex, like the benchmark Method (Swartz, 2002), or result in excessive stimulus energy, like the age-based dosing method (Abrams, 2002). A compromise technique, half-age-based dosing, may overcome this problem (Petrides and Fink, 1996).

Clinical wisdom would suggest that stimulus dose titration is advantageous in ensuring the lowest stimulus possible for each individual patient minimising cognitive impairment.

TO CLEAN OR NOT TO CLEAN?

Many junior doctors often query why there is so much attention given to electrode site preparation. The amount of cleaning will depend upon the type of electrode used. The discussion below is particu-larly important when using disposable electrodes.

Ohm's law determines the relationship between voltage, current and resistance or impedance when applied to a biological system. Impedance is a measure of the obstacles that need to be over-come in order for the current to flow. The lower the impedance, the less push or voltage is needed for a fixed flow of electrons, ensuring the delivery of a more efficient stimulus with less shunting through the scalp and skull (Beyer, Weiner and Glenn, 1998).

Cleaning the scalp and skin with normal saline by vigorous rotating movements removes grime, excessive skin follicles and oils and minimises the impact of a low hairline, ensuring better adhesion of the disposable electrodes and conductivity and resulting in a more efficient stimulus.

Application of an alcohol swab eliminates the moisture left behind by normal saline and further aids cleaning.

Abrasive gels may add an advantage in lowering the impedance but care needs to be exercised to prevent excessive abrasion and damage to the skin, particularly in the older person. A useful clinical sign that can flag when to cease scrubbing the skin is if a light red skin flare appears at the preparation site.

DISPOSABLE OR HANDHELD ELECTRODES?

Which electrodes to choose can pose a serious challenge to the new ECT practitioner? Device manufactures offer a range of options, including:

- handheld solid electrodes;

Photo 4.5.3 *Thymatron handheld electrode*

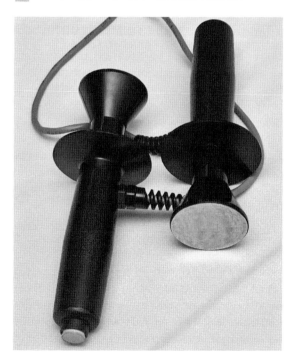

Photo 4.5.4 *MECTA handheld electrodes*

- solid metal discs that are placed under a tight rubber band placed around the forehead of the patient;

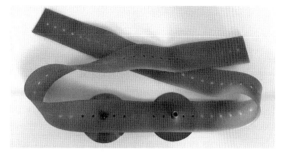

Photo 4.5.5 *Rubber band and metal discs*

- disposable electrode pads, like the Thymapad (Somatics L.L.C., 1989);

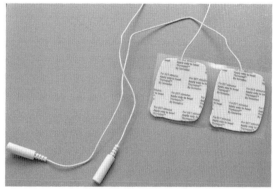

Photo 4.5.6 *Disposable electrodes (Thymapad)*

- options that can be used alone or supported by a handheld dummy electrode.

Photo 4.5.7 *Dummy electrodes*

Factors that need to be considered include: minimising impedance, ease of use, stigma or personal preference.

Clinical wisdom highlights the importance of stigma and anatomical accuracy in the choice of the electrodes as much as the ease and speed of the procedure. The choice of the electrodes is particularly important if the ECT service is involved in training and teaching, where medical staff, nursing staff and students freely rotate through the treatment area. Use of the disposable pad in these circumstances is preferable as it portrays ECT as a modern treatment that fits into the disposable, infection control culture of a theatre complex. If the surface has been well prepared, preferably with an impedance-enhancing agent, and well secured, the disposable pads have a larger surface area and disperse the currently more effectively across the skin. Another advantage is that single-use design prevents contamination and cross-infection and there are no exposed metal surfaces to give accidental shocks to the operator.

Placing firm pressure from the centre of the hand over the pad during the set-up period enhances adhesion resulting in a significant reduction in impedance at the time of treatment, often up to 300–400 ohms.

If the hairline is low or the hair remains thick under the pad then it can be supported by a dummy electrode handle. Disposable electrodes are difficult to use in the vertex position for unilateral electrode placement owing to the thickness of the hair and a solid electrode is preferred. The exception occurs in men who are bald, where the disposable electrode can be very effective.

Disadvantages of the disposable system are the increased cost per treatment session, and careful cleaning and application technique is required to ensure consistent low impedance for each treatment.

Use of the metal discs with the rubber band is less common due to stigma and patient discomfort. The band has to be tightly secured usually after the patient is anaesthetised.

Solid handheld electrodes continue to be put forward as the preferred way to administer ECT not only by manufacturers (MECTA Corporation, 2015) but also in photos published on page 31 of the latest edition of the Royal College of Psychiatrists's *The ECT Handbook* (Waite and Easton, 2013).

A disadvantage of handheld electrodes are that they move easily away from the correct anatomical landmark when the head is moved by the anaesthetist prior to treatment, particularly when bifrontal or left frontal right temporal ECT is administered. Final adjustments are essential before treatment is administered.

Caution is needed when using the handheld electrodes so that the treatment button located at the top of the handle, as shown in Photo 4.5.4, is not pushed accidentally. The rationale for locating the switch in this position is that it enables the ECT practitioner to administer the stimulus rather than relying on a second operator to push the button located on the front of the device.

TO MONITOR OR NOT TO MONITOR?

Considerable clinical variation exists as to what constitutes appropriate monitoring during ECT treatment. All devices offer the potential for at least four monitoring channels. How these are determined is dependent upon the service. Many services feel that minimum is best, one or two EEG channels only, to allow for a rapid turnover of patients. This may be appropriate for patients who do not have comorbid illness or when a single induction agent is utilised.

A more comprehensive approach to monitoring during ECT is to utilise at least four channels, left and right EEG, electrocardiogram (ECG) and electromyogram (EMG) or optical motion sensor (OMS). Dual EEG recording ensures that there is seizure concordance between left and right hemispheres of the brain. This can aid interpretation for more complex EEG traces and determination of the seizure end point, improving the information available to the clinician.

Electromyogram (EMG)

Many argue that setting up an EMG with the aid of cuff monitoring is time-consuming and unnecessary except during a titration session as the length of the motor fit does not correlate with the clinical efficacy of the treatment and may carry an increased risk of deep vein thrombosis (NSW Health, 2010; Scott and Waite, 2013). This argument has validity for routine treatments, particularly if a single anaesthetic induction agent is utilised.

The technique is particularly useful in determining whether a seizure has occurred or not following stimulation in a titration session. Highly attenuated EEG activity is inconclusive as this type of activity is common with a threshold seizure, whereas the absence of a motor fit indicates that a subconvulsive stimulus has been administered and a subsequent stimulus should be applied.

Cuff monitoring

As noted in Section 5.5, cuff monitoring using the isolated limb technique can be particularly useful and necessary when attempts are made to minimise the dose of the induction agent, like thiopentone, methohexital or propofol alone, or when using an augmentation technique by adding a short-acting narcotic agent like remifentanil to lower the dose of the induction agent to prevent awareness.

Cuff monitoring is usually performed on the right lower leg as illustrated in Photo 5.1.1. In some cases, like severe oedema of the lower legs, the cuff can be placed on the wrist with a "stress ball" placed in the hand for protection, as illustrated in Photo 5.1.2.

Awareness

Awareness is a highly distressing situation in which the patient has not been fully anaesthetised, resulting in them being conscious during the administration of the muscle relaxant and the surgical procedure, resulting in immense distress (Hardman and Aitkenhead, 2005; Myles, Leslie,

McNeil, Forbes and Chan, 2004). Anaesthetists are highly sensitive to this phenomena, often erring on the side of caution by administering larger doses of anaesthetic agents than necessary.

Educating anaesthetists that they are part of a different therapeutic paradigm and their actions can have a profound impact on the treatment outcome is essential. Open communication prevents the administration of unnecessarily high doses of induction agents, reducing the strength of the stimulus and cognitive impairment.

Electrocardiogram (ECG)

ECG monitoring can vary from service to service. Those that do not monitor separately highlight that ECT is a safe treatment, that induced cardiovascular changes rarely result in serious complications and that the technique simply increases set-up and turnaround time.

Some clinicians would agree that adding an ECG is useful for the anaesthetist to carefully monitor the cardiovascular response to ECT. Incorporating ECG monitoring into the Thymatron or MECTA record during ECT provides a hard copy in the event of an abnormality being detected. A common finding is cardiac asystole immediately after the stimulus has been applied, illustrated in EEG 4.2.1, a feature that is more prominent in younger patients (Burd and Kettl, 1998) and less likely with bifrontal ECT; an electrode placement should be considered for patients deemed to be at risk (Stewart, Loo, MacPherson and Hadzi-Pavlovic, 2011).

ECG monitoring can be useful for teaching and training purposes as it demonstrates the cardiovascular changes that occur following the stimulus: bradycardia, tachycardia before returning to baseline activity.

Deep tendon knee reflex

Eliciting a deep tendon knee reflex is an objective method used to determine that maximum paralysis has been achieved following the administration of suxamethonium, as illustrated in Photo 4.5.8.

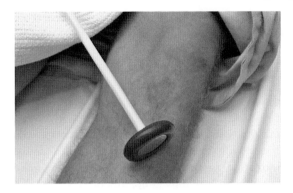

Photo 4.5.8 *Deep tendon knee reflex*

It is usually best to elicit the reflex soon after induction of the patient to demonstrate the strength of the response, providing a baseline to determine that it has ceased. Advantages include lessening stigma and fear in observers (students and others) by reducing the risk of an unmodified seizure.

Some ECT services suggest that a timed approach is better: time zero immediately after the dose of suxamethonium has been administered, with full relaxation occurring between 90 and 120 seconds. Age and sex are factors that can either extend or reduce this time.

Clinical wisdom suggests that both techniques are useful and easy to complete, utilising minimal extra time and ensure full paralysis of the patient prior to treatment.

Nerve stimulator

Some anaesthetists have suggested the use of a nerve stimulator as the best technique to provide objective evidence of full paralysis once the suxamethonium has been administered. However, in clinical practice setting up a nerve stimulator adds to the complexity of the procedure and it can be painful if it is turned on while the patient is awake.

TO MEASURE OR NOT TO MEASURE?

The anatomical locations of the treatment electrodes are clearly illustrated in Figures 5.2.2 to 5.2.6.

The location of each electrode placement appears very straightforward and easily identified in these figures; however, it is more difficult in real life owing to the significant variation of human anatomy and movement that occurs before ECT is administered. Precise location of the treating electrode is important to provide consistency in treatment outcome, reducing postictal confusion and minimising cognitive impairment over a course of ECT.

Measurement of the correct site can be achieved by using a ruler or set square from the tragus of the ear to the outer canthus of the eye and marker 2.5 cm above for RUL ECT, BT ECT and triangulating 90 degrees from this line to a mark 5 cm posterior, as illustrated in Photos 5.2.1, 5.2.2, 5.2.7, 5.2.8, 5.2.9 and 5.2.10 to 5.2.14.

Photo 5.2.6 demonstrates the technique to accurately find the vertex position for right unilateral ECT: the index fingers are placed over the ear canals on both sides and joined behind the head in the coronal plan, joining an imaginary line from the nasion to the inion with adjustments made for the pillow used and extension of the neck by the anaesthetist.

Measurement complies with "best practice" by ensuring the correct location all of the time independent of the experience of the operator. It adds little extra time to the set-up once the practitioner is familiar with the technique. The use of disposable electrodes have an advantage over handheld electrodes as the correct location will not be disrupted by any movements made by the anaesthetist once they are placed into position, whereas with handheld electrodes enormous variations are possible.

ULTRABRIEF OR NOT ULTRABRIEF?

A common dilemma that has challenged the ECT practitioner for many years is what type of ECT should be administered. Issues to consider include speed of recovery, cognitive impairment, severity of illness, voluntary or involuntary consent, age and patient preference.

Twenty-five years ago ECT was a simple procedure involving two options: should the patient be given right unilateral or bitemporal ECT? At that time, most regions around the world had locally manufactured ECT devices. In the USA, MECTA manufactured the initial device, with the Thymatron DGx coming later. Devices manufactured by ECRON dominated the UK market, with many other manufacturers providing devices made across Europe.

In Australia, the market was dominated by Kabtronics, a Brisbane manufacturer that used hardware produced by Clipsal, an electrical components manufacturer. The Kabtronics device was ahead of its time, with the capacity to individually alter the four components of the stimulus, duration, pulse width, voltage and amplitude similar to the modern MECTA spECTrum Q device. However, the innovations were lost as the treating doctor was instructed during a "see one, do one, teach one" ECT training session never to alter the parameters that were written about each switch, which often varied between sites. For example, all patients in that hospital were administered the same brief-pulse stimulus with a duration of 4.0 seconds, pulse width of 1.5 milliseconds, 1 pulse per second, and a current of 1 amps, equivalent to delivering 60% (405 mC) on a modern ECT device.

What was confusing and disturbing in hindsight was that different services often had different preset amounts and there was no clear governance structure to ensure minimum standards.

Twenty-five years later, ECT has become a complex procedure, with nine or more treatment options available, requiring the ECT practitioner to make a large number of clinical decisions about the treatment administered.

One of the recent advances in ECT practice is the advent of ultrabrief ECT. The evidence base underpinning ultrabrief ECT has grown to the level that an increasing number of ECT practitioners would consider this as the first line of treatment (Galletly, Paterson and Burton, 2012; Harrison, 2015; Loo, Katalinic, Martin and Schweitzer, 2012; Loo et al., 2014; Tor et al., 2015).

The effectiveness of ultrabrief ECT and its marked reduction in cognitive impairment has begun to challenge the traditional view that patients who were involuntary, had high acuity or were elderly should be given bitemporal ECT.

ECT services around the world continue to administer bitemporal ECT to all patients but the growing body of data supporting ultrabrief ECT, with its significant cognitive advantage, is getting harder to ignore. Recent studies have challenged the work by Sackeim et al. (2008) refuting the finding that ultrabrief bitemporal ECT was ineffective, with more studies required (Niemantsverdriet, Birkenhager and van den Broek, 2011).

Most experienced ECT practitioners use bitemporal ECT as a last resort. Even the United Kingdom, which for many years has been a strong advocate for bitemporal ECT, has softened its position, as recorded in the recent publication *The ECT Handbook* (Waite and Easton, 2013): "the choice of electrode placement and stimulus dose should balance efficacy against the risk of cognitive impairment". Units that predominantly treat complex, high-acuity patients with psychotic depression, mania or schizophrenia may decide to continue administering a stronger form of ECT. The cognitive advantages of high-dose right unilateral ECT over bitemporal ECT has been validated in a recent meta-analysis (Kolshus, Jelovac and McLoughlin, 2017).

WHAT NEXT AFTER ULTRABRIEF?

The question that most units administering ultrabrief ECT are struggling with is what do I do if the patient fails to respond after Treatment 6? Once again the evidence base is limited, with little to guide the physician.

Clinical wisdom suggests that a stronger form of treatment is required to bring about recovery. Options include: brief-pulse (0.5–1.0 ms) unilateral electrode placement, brief-pulse or standard pulse-width bifrontal or bitemporal ECT. Individual ECT services need to determine their own protocols using practice-based experience by pooling the wealth of shared clinical experience of the practitioners administering the ECT.

A useful "rule of thumb" that has guided physicians in this situation for many years has been changing from a unilateral electrode placement to a bilateral position. Brief-pulse (0.5–1.0 ms) bifrontal ECT is the preferred position owing to the growing awareness of the worsening and sometimes permanent cognitive impairment from high-dose, standard pulse-width ECT (1.5 ms), particularly when administering bilateral ECT (Sackeim, 2014).

TWICE A WEEK OR THREE TIMES A WEEK?

There is a fundamental difference between the USA and most of Europe, on the one hand, and the UK, on the other, in that the former give ECT three times a week while the UK has always preferred to administer treatment twice a week. As reviewed in another section of this *Workbook*, Australia has followed the lead of the USA in administering treatment three times a week. For some time the evidence has suggested that both protocols are effective (Lerer et al., 1995; McAllister, Perri, Jordan, Rauscher and Sattin, 1987; Shapira et al., 1998).

The skilled ECT practitioner will vary the frequency dependent upon:

- age: twice a week is preferred for older persons to reduce cognitive impairment and allow time for physical recovery from the anaesthetic;
- high acuity: the rate of recovery is greater with three times a week ECT;
- cognitive impairment: twice a week is preferred to reduce the impact of treatment;
- response rate: three times a week is preferred as it has a quicker onset of action;
- reduced length of stay: three times a week is preferred;
- reduced severity of side effects: twice a week is preferred;
- over numbers on the ECT list in the public system: twice a week is preferred;

- outpatient ECT: twice a week is preferred to reduce the demand on the family to transport the patient to the ECT facility.

TO RESTRAIN OR NOT TO RESTRAIN?

Before ECT

A common dilemma confronting the ECT practitioner, particularly in a large public hospital, is how to manage agitated or aggressive patients where ECT has been determined as the appropriate treatment by the relevant mental health tribunal.

Practitioners in a private hospital rarely treat these patients as they are not able to give informed consent, are a danger to themselves and/or others and are scheduled under an involuntary treatment order to the local public mental health facility.

Many of these patients have severe psychiatric disorders, including bipolar or unipolar depression with lethal suicide intent, bipolar mania, or schizophrenia with lethal delusions to self-harm or hurt other people. They are not able to function in the community owing to the high risk to themselves and others. Should such patients be pharmacologically or physically restrained with shackles, transported to the treatment area by a large contingent of strong nurses/security guards or all of the above?

This dilemma can be very challenging when ECT is administered within a theatre complex of a general hospital and there are large distances between the mental health wards and theatres.

Clinical wisdom suggests that all of the methods listed above are useful in handling agitated and aggressive patients who need ECT. Each mental health service should develop a set of ECT guidelines based upon the Prevention and Management of Violence and Aggression (PMVA) guidelines. These guidelines aid the clinician, ensuring individually focused, safe, evidence-based, best practice to bring about remission in the least restrictive environment.

After ECT

Questions concerning the use of patient restraints also arise during the recovery phase after ECT treatment. Patients with a postictal delirium that are difficult to manage and are not responsive to verbal commands frequently confront nurses who work in recovery.

There is a range of interventions that should be considered:

- administering intravenous medications (under the supervision of the anaesthetist);
- electric bed positioning (using a V or poorly formed W position);
- request for more staff to supervise each limb and the head until the patient regains consciousness or is safe;
- involvement of family or carers.

Guidance for these techniques should be included in the ECT practice guidelines for each service.

TO TIME OR NOT TO TIME?

All patients vary in their response to ECT. It is a common observation that the same patient can have the same anaesthetic drugs and the same ECT parameters but have a different outcome after the treatment, with a slow return to baseline of vital signs and time to recovery. This has significant implication for the recovery of the patient in the recovery area.

There are two different methods used to determine fitness of the patient to return to the ward: time-based recovery and protocol-based recovery. Time-based recovery requires the patient to wait for two hours after the treatment, moving from the bed to a reclining chair with light refreshments, before leaving the recovery area. Protocol-based recovery scores the patient's recovery on a post-anaesthetic discharge scoring system whereby the patient is allowed to return to the ward or home when alert and orientated.

Clinical wisdom suggests that both have their benefits, with time-based recovery preferred for day patients having ECT, while the protocol-based recovery is better for inpatients, allowing more rapid flow through recovery area. Individual local health districts need to comply with the procedures specified by the theatre complex in which they are based. For a new ECT service, ongoing negotiation with the perioperative team is necessary to allow for more than one protocol. In this regard, stand-alone ECT suites are preferred as the recovery process is determined solely by mental health services.

To time or not to time has become an important consideration after the administration of suxamethonium before the delivery of the stimulus to ensure full muscle relaxation and minimise the impact of the induction agent on the induced seizure. In some centres timers are used routinely to eliminate guesswork.

TO TREAT OR NOT TO TREAT?

A fundamental dilemma that all ECT practitioners struggle with is the ethics in administering ECT to involuntary patients who flatly refuse to comply with treatment.

This dilemma is particularly troublesome:

- for the junior psychiatric register who has come into psychiatry with a high degree of altruism and have to confront the mental health tribunal for the first time as the primary spokesperson for the mental health team. In many regions the tribunal is the sole body that determines whether ECT is indicated if the patient is involuntary, operating as a quasi-court utilising an adversarial model whereby the patient is entitled to legal representation;
- for the doctor administering ECT in a theatre complex when the patient loudly protests against having the treatment, that they may be killed if the treatment proceeds or the reverse when the patient believes the stigma "ECT is a treatment that kills people", loudly stating that ECT will fulfil their wish for suicide;

- for the ECT practitioner who voluntarily consents the patient for ECT but the carers and families are strongly opposed to the treatment proceeding.

These scenarios raise many ethical questions that are associated with ECT:

- Are the rights of families and carers more important than the individual?
- Is ECT a humane treatment when the community and factional interests have very strong feelings to the contrary?
- When does a patient have the right to refuse ECT?
- Should clinical care directives be mandatory for all mental health patients, particularly those who require ECT?
- Should ECT proceed when the patient requests it, with sufficient grounds, but the treating team consider that another avenue of treatment should be pursued instead?
- Does a patient admitted to hospital on a voluntary basis have the right to refuse treatment even when pharmacotherapy has failed to work?
- Should they become an involuntary patient, if there are sufficient determinants, and be given ECT even though they have refused consent?

One of the challenges that ECT practitioners are currently facing worldwide is proposed restriction on ECT clinical practice by the US Food and Drug Administration (FDA) as part of their reclassification of the ECT device. The FDA has proposed to reclassify ECT devices from class III to:

> class II (special controls) for severe major depressive episode (MDE) associated with Major Depressive Disorder (MDD) or Bipolar Disorder (BPD) in patients 18 years of age and older who are treatment-resistant or who require a rapid response due to the severity of their psychiatric or medical condition.
>
> (US FDA, 2015)

This raises a range of ethical dilemmas including:

- Should ECT be used in patients under the age of 18?
- Should it only be reserved for treatment-resistant patients?
- Can voluntary patients request the treatment even if they have not been classified as treatment-resistant?
- Does a governmental statutory body like the US FDA have the right to make determinations about clinical matters that form the fundamentals of informed consent in patients having ECT without strong evidence supporting their recommendations?

This matter was hotly debated following a similar determination made in the United Kingdom by the National Institute for Health and Clinical Excellence (NICE) that provided guidance that markedly restricted clinical practice owing to the significant difference in opinion between ECT practitioners and consumers (NICE, 2003, modified 2009).

A significant outcome from the debate surrounding the NICE guidance document was the emergence of more effective audit procedures like the recent United Kingdom ECT Accreditation Service (Royal College of Psychiatrists, 2015) and the validation of the lived experience (Kivler, 2010).

Data from consumers highlighted the marked discrepancies, with nearly 50% of patients complaining that they had not received sufficient information about the treatment and its side effects and a further third of patients feeling that did not freely consent for the procedure (Rose et al., 2003; Rose et al., 2005).

At every level incorporating the lived ECT experience into clinical practice is essential. For consumers it is a fundamental right, for ECT practitioners it has become part of the minimum standards and for ECT associations it is the only way for this very effective treatment to survive criticism and challenge.

TO CONTINUE OR NOT TO CONTINUE?

A common question that confronts the ECT practitioner is when an index course of treatment should cease.

There is no evidence base to guide treatment. This decision must be made on an individual basis within the clinical context of the patient being treated. Some patients have a robust response early in the treatment course, while others make a slow but steady recovery. The decision to stop treatment is relatively straightforward in patients who gain remission after seven to nine treatments but it is a more challenging decision in patients who have a partial response to treatment but plateau in improvement during the course of treatment.

In this situation the psychiatrist should conduct a comprehensive review of the case to ensure that psychological, social, family and cultural issues are also addressed. It is not uncommon for patients to go through an emotionally distressing period as the biological symptoms respond to treatment, leaving the patient vulnerable to negative cognitions that may result in self-harm. Treatment should continue during this period associated with close monitoring of the patient. However, a point is reached when further ECT will not resolve the patient's distress but may exacerbate it owing to the impact of cognitive impairment.

In this circumstance ECT should be ceased, psychotropic medication strengthened to prevent relapse and the patient engage in more appropriate treatments like psychotherapy or family therapy to relieve the underlying distress.

Clinical wisdom suggests that the preferred option is for the patient to have a second opinion after Treatment 12 from an experienced ECT practitioner who is not known to the patient before the next treatment. Occasionally treatment may progress two or three sessions beyond 12; however, longer courses of treatment are not common, suggesting a need to review the diagnosis and treatment parameters. Excessive treatments can lead to significant memory loss that may be permanent, subjecting ECT to criticism and stigma.

WHICH DEVICE: MECTA OR THYMATRON?

Which ECT device should I purchase is a common question asked when setting up a new ECT service or replacing an old device in an existing service.

Historically, the Thymatron device became the predominant model used in Australia, replacing the Kabtronics device, illustrated in Photos 1.3.4, 1.3.7 and 1.3.8, in the late 1990s.

In 1995, the first Australian ECT conference was held at the Taronga Park Zoo in Sydney. Keynote speakers at the meeting were Professors Harold Sackeim and Richard Weiner, who pioneered many of the modern techniques used in current ECT practice, including the use of an EEG to aid treatment decisions and stimulus dose titration.

Manufacturers of ECT devices were invited to sponsor the conference and exhibit modern machines that incorporated EEG technology. Somatics L.L.C. (Somatics L.L.C., 2015) was the only company to accept the invitation; MECTA was absent.

The meeting had a large audience of Australian and New Zealand ECT practitioners who rapidly embraced the new EEG technology and purchased devices from the company they met at the conference.

Both devices have merits and problems. In recent years, MECTA devices have become more popular owing to progressive design, incorporating a touch screen and more sophisticated electronic data acquisition software and offering a range of different devices with different features.

Somatics L.L.C. only offers one device, Thymatron System IV, which looks identical to when it was first released in early 2000. Internal changes have been made, with the incorporation of new computer software to keep up to date with modern ultrabrief technology, but the electronic data capture technology remains limited.

One interesting feature of the Thymatron IV is that it has an audible warble that changes tone during the seizure. It can be useful to alert if the recording electrodes are not attached properly and it enables the operator to determine the end of the seizure if the paper trace runs out of paper. The Thymatron IV has a useful feature called the Postictal Suppression Index (PSI), an objective measure of the quality of the electrical silence at the end of the seizure.

MECTA offers a range models that have different recording capacities. There are two top-of-the-range models, spECTrum 5000Q and 5000M (MECTA Corporation, 2015). The spECTrum 5000Q offers four switches, giving precise control over stimulus parameters, whereas the spECTrum 5000M is like the Thymatron System IV and uses a single dial that automatically alters the different parameters when the stimulus energy is altered.

A group of Australian expert psychiatrists recently discussed the question "which ECT device should I purchase?". There was a wide and varied response. The group felt that the more complex MECTA spECTrum 5000Q would appeal to those with more detailed knowledge of ECT and research interests, providing a deeper level of understanding of the stimulus administered and enabling flexibility for research purposes. This device has a more comprehensive EEG electronic data capture program, which may eventually eliminate the recorded paper trace.

The group agreed that a more complex device might cause confusion for general psychiatrists doing ECT occasionally, particularly in regional areas, or if ECT was administered by a large number of practitioners with different levels of experience increasing the risk of errors. The simplicity of the single-dial devices would appeal to these services.

The cost of both devices is similar and both can be used with handheld or disposable electrodes. There are fundamental differences in the set-up of each device, making it necessary to retrain staff if a service changes from one device to the other (see Section 5.7). A major limitation of the MECTA device is that it only comes with hand held electrodes, illustrated in Photo 4.5.4. As noted earlier, it is essential for services to consider disposable electrodes, Photo 4.5.6, as the preferred option to reduce the high level of stigma associated with bulky hand held electrodes.

CONCLUSION

ECT is a very effective treatment for severe mental illness. There is a lack of a sufficient evidence base to guide many clinical decisions in the delivery of ECT treatment, with a heavy reliance upon practice-based experience. Poor technique can have a significant impact on the efficacy and side effects of the treatment, further tarnishing the ECT brand (Sackeim et al., 2007).

Clinical teams need to make decisions in many areas to ensure consistency of treatment and best practice. Patient outcome is enhanced if there is widespread agreement about the ECT techniques utilised by the service and early involvement of consumers who can share their lived experience.

Increased awareness and understanding of clinical practice techniques minimises complications and maximises best practice outcomes. Open communication between the ECT service, the referring psychiatrist and the anaesthetist is essential to ensure best practice. Every ECT service must develop a comprehensive clinical guideline that provides governance, ensuring best patient-focused clinical care.

REFERENCES

Abrams, R. (2002). *Electroconvulsive Therapy*, 4th edition. New York: Oxford University Press.

American Psychiatric Association. (2001). *The Practice of Electroconvulsive Therapy: Recommendations for Treatment, Training and Privileging: A Task Force Report*, 2nd edition. Washington, DC: American Psychiatric Association.

Beyer, J.L., Weiner, R.D., and Glenn, M.D. (1998). *Electroconvulsive Therapy: A Programmed Text*, 2nd edition. Washington, DC: American Psychiatric Press.

Borrell-Carrio, F., Suchman, A.L., and Epstein, R.M. (2004). The biopsychosocial model 25 years later: principles, practice, and scientific inquiry. *Annals of Family Medicine*, 2(6), 576–582. doi:10.1370/afm.245.

Boylan, L., Haskett, R.F., Mulsant, B.F., Greenberg, R.M., Prudic, J., Spicknall, K., . . . Sackeim, H.A. (2000). Determinants of seizure threshold in ECT: benzodiazepine use, anaesthetic dosage and other factors. *Journal of ECT*, 16, 3–16.

Burd, J., and Kettl, P. (1998). Incidence of asystole in electroconvulsive therapy in elderly patients. *American Journal of Geriatric Psychiatry, 6*(3), 203–211. Retrieved from www.ncbi.nlm.nih.gov/pubmed/9659953.

Ding, Z., and White, P.F. (2002). Anesthesia for electroconvulsive therapy. *Anesthesia and Analgesia, 94*(5), 1351–1364. doi:10.1097/00000539-200205000-00057.

Engel, G.L. (1978). The biopsychosocial model and the education of health professionals. *Annals of the New York Academy of Sciences, 310*(1), 169–181. doi:10.1111/j.1749-6632.1978.tb22070.x.

Engel, G.L. (1989). The need for a new medical model: a challenge for biomedicine. *Holistic Medicine, 4*(1), 37–53. doi:10.3109/13561828909043606.

Feinstein, A.R., and Horwitz, R.I. (1997). Problems in the "evidence" of "evidence-based medicine". *American Journal of Medicine, 103*(6), 529–535. Retrieved from www.ncbi.nlm.nih.gov/pubmed/9428837.

Freeman, C.P., and Fergusson, M.G. (2013). The ECT suite. In Waite, J., and Eaton, A. (Eds.), *The ECT Handbook*, 3rd edition (pp. 8–13). London: Royal College of Psychiatrists.

Galletly, C., Paterson, T., and Burton, C. (2012). A report on the introduction of ultrabrief pulse width ECT in a private psychiatric hospital. *Journal of ECT, 28*(1), 59. doi:10.1097/YCT.0b013e318221b42e.

Greenhalgh, T., Howick, J., and Maskrey, N. (2014). Evidence based medicine: a movement in crisis? *British Medical Journal, 348*(30), g3725. doi:10.1136/bmj.g3725.

Hardman, J.G., and Aitkenhead, A.R. (2005). Awareness during anaesthesia. *Continuing Education in Anaesthesia, Critical Care and Pain, 5*(6), 183–186. doi:10.1093/bjaceaccp/mki049.

Harrison, P. (2015). *PRIDE Continues to Support ECT in Depressed Elderly*. Paper presented at the 28th European College of Neuropsychopharmacology (ECNP) Congress. Amsterdam, The Netherlands.

Hughes, P., and Keer, I. (2000). Transference and countertransference in communication between doctor and patient. *Advances in Psychiatric Treatment, 6*, 57–64.

Kivler, C.A. (2010). *Will I Ever Be the Same Again? Transforming the Face of ECT (Shock Therapy)*. New York: Three Gem/Kivler.

Kolshus, E., Jelovac, A., and McLoughlin, D.M. (2017). Bitemporal v. high-dose right unilateral electroconvulsive therapy for depression: a systematic review and meta-analysis of randomized controlled trials. *Psychological Medicine, 47*(3), 518–530. doi:10.1017/S0033291716002737.

Lerer, B., Shapira, B., Calev, A., Tubi, N., Drexler, H., Kindler, S., . . . Schwartz, J.E. (1995). Antidepressant and cognitive

effects of twice- versus three-times-weekly ECT. *American Journal of Psychiatry, 152*(4), 564–575.

Loo, C.K., Katalinic, N., Martin, D., and Schweitzer, I. (2012). A review of ultrabrief pulse width electroconvulsive therapy. *Therapeutic Advances in Chronic Disease, 3*(2), 69–85. doi:10.1177/2040622311432493.

Loo, C.K., Katalinic, N., Smith, D.J., Ingram, A., Dowling, N., Martin, D., . . . Schweitzer, I. (2014). A randomised controlled trial of brief and ultrabrief pulse right unilateral electroconvulsive therapy. *International Journal of Neuropsychopharmacology, 18*(1).

McAllister, D.A., Perri, M.G., Jordan, R.C., Rauscher, F.P., and Sattin, A. (1987). Effects of ECT given two vs. three times weekly. *Psychiatry Research, 21*(1), 63–69. Retrieved from www.ncbi.nlm.nih.gov/pubmed/3602221.

Masic, I., Miokovic, M., and Muhamedagic, B. (2008). Evidence based medicine – new approaches and challenges. *Acta Informatica Medica, 16*(4), 219–225. doi:10.5455/aim.2008.16.219-225.

MECTA Corporation. (2015). spECTrum 5000Q – MECTA Corp. Retrieved from www.mectacorp.com/spectrum-5000Q.html.

Myles, P.S., Leslie, K., McNeil, J., Forbes, A., and Chan, M.T.V. (2004). Bispectral index monitoring to prevent awareness during anaesthesia: the B-Aware randomised controlled trial. *The Lancet, 363*(9423), 1757–1763. doi:10.1016/S0140–6736(04)16300–9.

NICE. (2003, modified 2009). *Guidance on the Use of Electroconvulsive Therapy (Vol. Guidance Number 59)*. London: National Institute for Health and Care Excellence; National Health Service.

Niemantsverdriet, L., Birkenhager, T.K., and van den Broek, W.W. (2011). The efficacy of ultrabrief-pulse (0.25 millisecond) versus brief-pulse (0.50 millisecond) bilateral electroconvulsive therapy in major depression. *Journal of ECT, 27*(1), 55–58. doi:10.1097/YCT.0b013e3181da8412.

NSW Health. (2010). ECT minimum standard of practice NSW. Retrieved from www.health.nsw.gov.au/policies/pd/2011/pdf/PD2011_003.pdf.

Petrides, G., and Fink, M. (1996). The "half-age" stimulation strategy for ECT dosing. *Convulsive Therapy, 12*(3), 138–146. Retrieved from www.ncbi.nlm.nih.gov/pubmed/8872401.

RANZCP. (2007). Clinical memorandum #12 electroconvulsive therapy. Melbourne, Australia.

Rasmussen, K.G., Spackman, T.N., and Hooten, W.M. (2005). The clinical utility of inhalational anesthesia with sevoflurane in electroconvulsive therapy. *Journal of ECT, 21*(4), 239–242.

Rose, D.S., Fleischmann, P., and Wykes, T.H. (2009). Consumers' views of electroconvulsive therapy: a qualitative analysis.

Journal of Mental Health, 13(3), 285–293. doi:10.1080/09638230410001700916.

Rose, D.S., Fleischmann. P, Wykes. T, Leese. M, and Bindman. J. (2003). Patients' perspectives on electroconvulsive therapy: systematic review. *British Medical Journal, 326*(7403), 1363. Retrieved from www.bmj.com/content/326/7403/1363.abstract.

Rose, D.S., Wykes, T.H., Bindman, J.P., and Fleischmann, P.S. (2005). Information, consent and perceived coercion: patients' perspectives on electroconvulsive therapy. *British Journal of Psychiatry, 186*(1), 54–59. Retrieved from http://bjp.rcpsych.org/content/186/1/54.abstract.

Royal College of Psychiatrists. (2015). *ECT Accreditation Service (ECTAS): Standards for the Administration of ECT,* 12th edition. London: Royal College of Psychiatrists.

SA Health. (2014). South Australian guidelines for electroconvulsive therapy. Retrieved from www.sahealth.sa.gov.au/wps/wcm/connect/060827004bad5b01b89.

Sackeim, H.A., Prudic, J., Devanand, D.P., Kiersky, J.E., Fitzsimons, L., Moody, B.J., . . . Settembrino, J.M. (1993). Effects of stimulus intensity and electrode placement on the efficacy and cognitive effects of electroconvulsive therapy. *New England Journal of Medicine, 328*(12), 839–846. doi:10.1056/NEJM199303253281204.

Sackeim, H.A., Prudic, J., Nobler, M.S., Fitzsimons, L., Lisanby, S.H., Payne, N., . . . Devanand, D.P. (2008). Effects of pulse width and electrode placement on the efficacy and cognitive effects of electroconvulsive therapy. *Brain Stimulation 1*(2), 71–83. doi:10.1016/j.brs.2008.03.001.

Sackeim, H.A. (2014). Autobiographical memory and electroconvulsive therapy: do not throw out the baby. *Journal of ECT, 30*(3), 177–186. doi:10.1097/yct.0000000000000117.

Sackeim, H.A., Decina, P., Kanzler, M., Kerr, B., and Malitz, S. (1987). Effects of electrode placement on the efficacy of titrated, low-dose ECT. *American Journal of Psychiatry, 144*(11), 1449–1455. Retrieved from www.ncbi.nlm.nih.gov/pubmed/3314538.

Sackeim, H.A., Decina, P., Portnoy, S., Neeley, P., and Malitz, S. (1987). Studies of dosage, seizure threshold, and seizure duration in ECT. *Biological Psychiatry, 22*(3), 249–268. doi:10.1016/0006-3223(87)90144-2.

Sackeim, H.A., Prudic, J., Fuller, R., Keilp, J., Lavori, P.W., and Olfson, M. (2007). The cognitive effects of electroconvulsive therapy in community settings. *Neuropsychopharmacology, 32*(1), 244–254. doi:10.1038/sj.npp.1301180.

Scott, A.I., and Waite, J. (2013). Monitoring a course of ECT. In Waite, J. (Ed.), *The ECT Handbook,* 3rd edition (pp. 60–70). London: Royal College of Psychiatrists.

Shapira, B., Tubi, N., Drexler, H., Lidsky, D., Calev, A., and Lerer, B. (1998). Cost and benefit in the choice of ECT schedule. Twice versus three times weekly ECT. *British Journal of Psychiatry, Jan*(172), 44–48.

Somatics, L.L.C. (1989). Thymapad. Retrieved from www.thymatron.com/catalog_accessory.asp?C=6andI=3.

Somatics, L.L.C. (2015). Somatics, LLC – manufacturer of the Thymatron ECT machine. Retrieved from www.thymatron.com/main_home.asp.

Stewart, P.T., Loo, C.K., MacPherson, R., and Hadzi-Pavlovic, D. (2011). The effect of electrode placement and pulsewidth on asystole and bradycardia during the electroconvulsive therapy stimulus. *International Journal of Neuropsychopharmacology, 14*(5), 585–594. doi:10.1017/S1461145710001458.

Swanson, J.A., Schmitz, D., and Chung, K.C. (2010). How to practice evidence-based medicine. *Plastic and Reconstructive Surgery, 126*(1), 286–294. doi:10.1097/PRS.0b013e3181dc54ee.

Swartz, C.M. (2001). Stimulus dosing in electroconvulsive therapy and the threshold multiple method. Editorial *Journal of ECT, 17,* 87–90.

Swartz, C.M. (2002). ECT dosing by the benchmark method. *German Journal of Psychiatry, 5,* 1–4. Retrieved from www.gjpsy.uni-goettingen.de.

Tor, P.C., Bautovich, A., Wang, M.J., Martin, D., Harvey, S.B., and Loo, C. (2015). A systematic review and meta-analysis of brief versus ultrabrief right unilateral electroconvulsive therapy for depression. *Journal of Clinical Psychiatry, 10*(4088). doi:10.4088/JCP.14r09145.

Torpey, N. (2016). Special investigation: shock treatment: alarming spike in risky electroconvulsive therapy on children. *Sunday Mail* (Brisbane, Australia).

UK ECT Review Group. (2003). Efficacy and safety of electroconvulsive therapy in depressive disorders: a systematic review and meta-analysis. *Lancet, 361,* 799–808.

US Center for Devices and Radiological Health (2016). *Electroconvulsive Therapy (ECT) Devices for Class II Intended Uses: Draft Guidance for Industry, Clinicians and Food and Drug Administration Staff.*

Waite, J., and Easton, A. (2013). *The ECT Handbook,* 3rd edition. London: Royal College of Psychiatrists.

Walker, S.C., Bowley, C.J., and Walker, A.C. (2013). Anaesthesia for ECT. In Waite, J., and Easton, A. (Eds.), *The ECT Handbook.* London: Royal College of Psychiatrists.

CHAPTER 5

Technical skills

ECT technique

BASIC STEPS

The early preparation and set-up of the patient is listed below using a Thymatron System IV device with some detail not applicable to MECTA users.

- Prepare equipment as per protocol and use the "EctoBrain" if using a Thymatron System IV as an external check that the device is ready for use, as illustrated in Photo 5.7.2.
- Both the Thymatron and MECTA devices do an internal check to ensure that they are ready for use.

- Welcome the patient and ensure they have fasted from midnight.
- Introduce them to the ECT team. Ask the patient to make themselves comfortable on the bed.
- Cover the patient with a warm blanket as theatres can be very cold places.
- Complete the first "time out" procedure.
- A dedicated doughnut-shaped ECT pillow is inserted under the patient's head to allow good access for electrode placement, particularly when using a unilateral position, as illustrated in Photo 5.1.3.

- Ventilation with 100% oxygenation administered through a mask should commence while monitoring equipment is established, as illustrated in Photo 5.1.19. Some patients are frightened of the mask as it can make them anxious and agitated. Some prefer to hold it in place themselves or put the "tube" into their mouth. If this process creates too much distress or the patient is too agitated, oxygenation can be administered after they are unconscious to minimise distress.

ISOLATED LIMB TECHNIQUE (ILT)

Isolating the right foot prior to the administration of the neuromuscular blocking agent was one of the early techniques used to determine the presence and length of the motor seizure, as illustrated in Figure 5.1.1 and Photo 5.1.1. The right limb was routinely used for RUL ECT, with the stimulus applied on the same side as the blood pressure cuff to demonstrate ipsilateral seizure generalisation. The upper limb should be considered as an alternative in patients with comorbid medical condition, leading to peripheral oedema, as shown in Photo 5.1.2.

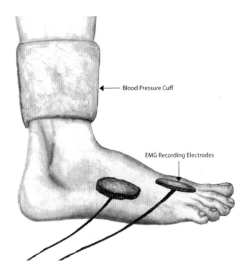

Figure 5.1.1 *Isolated limb technique right lower limb*

Source: Adapted from Beyer et al., 1998

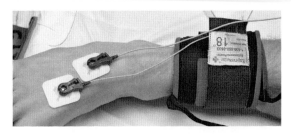

Photo 5.1.1 *Isolated limb technique ankle*

Photo 5.1.2 *Isolated limb technique wrist*

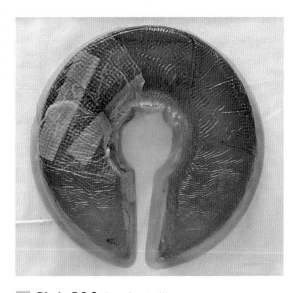

Photo 5.1.3 *Doughnut pillow*

Initially (Fink and Johnson, 1982; Hamilton, 1987), work comparing motor seizures measured by cuff monitoring, with the seizures recorded on the EEG, highlighted that prolonged seizures were often missed if cuff monitoring were used alone, with EEG monitoring shown to be superior

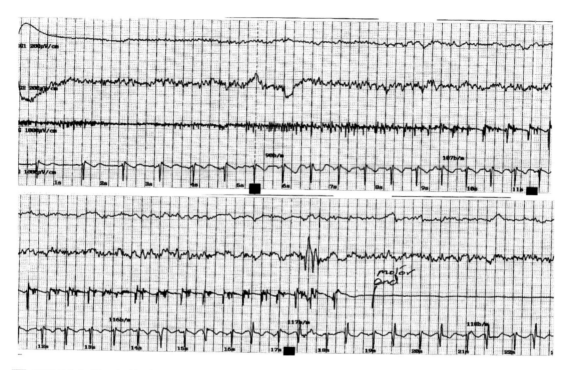

EEG 5.1.1 *Threshold seizure*

(Greenberg, 1985; Jayaprakash, Gangadhar, Janakiramaiah and Subbakrishna, 1998; Wise et al., 2000).

In modern ECT the ILT is used during a titration session. Appearance of the motor fit demonstrates that threshold has been reached and a seizure has occurred. Reliance on the EEG is unpredictable, as illustrated in EEG 5.1.1. Isolating the limb from suxamethonium enables the patient to withdraw their foot after the cuff has been inflated to 220–240 mmHg in response to pain if induction has not been complete when attempts are made to administer the lowest possible dose of induction agent to minimise the impact on seizure expression. The patient responds to the command "move your right

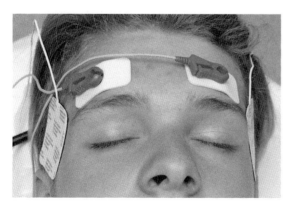

Photo 5.1.4 *RUL and BT frontal monitoring leads*

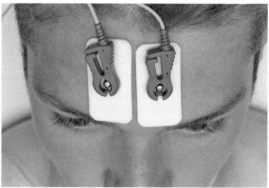

Photo 5.1.5 *BF frontal monitoring leads*

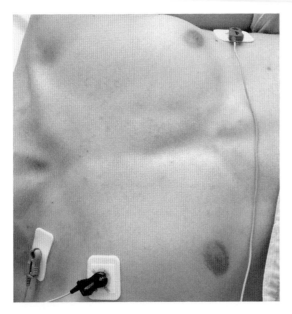

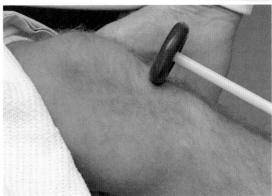

Photo 5.1.7 *Deep tendon knee reflex*

Photo 5.1.6 *Earth and ECG monitoring electrodes*

foot", indicating that they are still awake and aware of the events that are taking place within the treatment room. Another dose is administered before the treatment proceeds.

TREATMENT STEPS

- Systematically connect the leads from the yoke to the disposable EEG, ECG and EMG (or OMS if using a MECTA) electrodes and place on the correct anatomical site. Frontal recording electrodes are illustrated in Photo 5.1.4 for bilateral and unilateral placement and Photo 5.1.5 for bifrontal placement. The set-up for the earth electrode and the ECG electrodes are illustrated in Photo 5.1.6. The EMG monitoring electrodes are shown in Photos 5.1.1 and 5.1.2.
- Connect disposable or handheld treatment electrodes to the device electrode cable and apply to the correct anatomical site dependent upon the type of ECT being administered (for details refer to Section 5.2).
- Position the handheld electrode into the correct anatomical site and apply pressure.

- Applying firm pressure to the surface of the disposable treatment electrodes using the palm of the hand and handheld treatment electrode, from set-up to the administration of the treatment, can substantially reduce to the impedance to less than 1500 ohms.
- Activate the recording device to obtain baseline measurements, ensuring that all electrodes are attached.
- Complete the second "time out" procedure.
- Once set-up is complete, administer induction agents.
- Inflate cuff to isolated limb.
- Administer suxamethonium.
- Watch for muscle fasciculation, indicating the polarising action of suxamethonium.

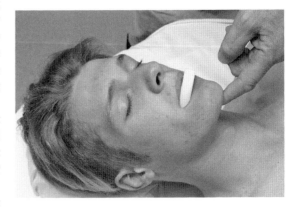

Photo 5.1.8 *Disposable bite block with jaw support*

- Commence timer, treatment is administered once fasciculations have ceased after 90 to 120 seconds and the deep tendon knee reflex is absent. It is useful to elicit the knee deep tendon reflex early on to demonstrate that it has been eliminated after the suxamethonium has been administered, as illustrated in Photo 5.1.7.
- Insert bite block correctly to prevent oral trauma and support the chin, as illustrated in Photo 5.1.8
- The anaesthetist will then command "move your right foot". If there is movement in the isolated foot, induction is not complete and a further dose may be required.
- The third time out occurs immediately before treatment is administered.
- It is important that the "treat" button is held down for the full duration of delivery of the stimulus. The MECTA spECTrum 5000 device will complete a final internal check before the stimulus is delivered. Both the Thymatron and spECTrum devices will automatically terminate the stimulus once the correct dose has been administered.
- Monitor seizure.
- When the motor seizure has stopped, deflate the blood pressure cuff on the cuff-monitored limb.
- Encourage the anaesthetist to avoid ventilation and do not touch the patient during this period until the EEG seizure has terminated and the EEG recording device has been turned off to eliminate EEG artefact.
- EEG termination is indicated with the appearance of postictal suppression on the recording paper. On the Thymatron System IV the ictal line will cease and the audible warble becomes a monotonous tone.
- The recorder should then be turned off manually.

MONITORING ELECTRODES ANATOMICAL PLACEMENT

Both ECT devices have the capacity to record four to six channels. The Thymatron System IV

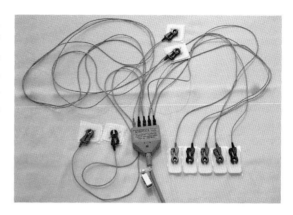

Photo 5.1.9 *Yoke and four-channel recording electrodes*

Photo 5.1.10 *Tray of recording disposable electrodes*

has four channels as standard: Channels 1 and 2 EEG, Channel 3 ECG and Channel 4 EMG (Somatics L.L.C., 2015). The base model of the MECTA spECTrum 4000M and 4000Q allows for two-channel recording only: both channels EEG or one channel EEG and one channel ECG. The speECTrum 5000M and 5000Q include four additional channels: three channels of EEG and a channel to record the motor activity via the optical motion sensor (OMS) (MECTA Corporation, 2015).

The following discussion, although specific to the Thymatron System IV, can be adapted to the MECTA spECTrum 5000 devices.

Thymatron System IV

The Thymatron has four monitoring channels that attach to the ECT device via a yoke and connect to disposable electrodes, as shown in Photos 5.1.9 and 5.1.10.

Each pair of leads is colour coded: red, black and brown. Channels 1 and 2 (red and black leads) record right and left electroencephalogram (EEG); Channel 3 (red and black leads closest to the earth (green)) records the electrocardiogram (ECG); Channel 4 (two brown electrodes) records the electromyogram (EMG) with the final lead coloured green for earth, as illustrated in Photo 5.1.9.

PLACEMENT OF ELECTRODES

EEG. The EEG electrodes are coloured red and black. Red electrodes are attached to the left and right frontal positions, two centimetres above the eyebrow in the midpoint of the orbit.

They can be attached in a horizontal or vertical position dependent upon the hairline or 5 mm apart in the midline when bifrontal or left anterior right frontal electrode placements are used, as illustrated in Photos 5.1.4 and 5.1.5. The black electrodes monitor the posterior part of the brain and are placed on the mastoid processes high up behind each ear, as shown in Photo 5.1.11.

EMG. The EMG electrodes are brown in colour and are placed on the dorsum of the right foot four centimetres apart across the muscle bulk above the cuff monitoring system. If circulation is compromised with prominent pitting oedema the cuff should be placed on the right arm, just above the wrist, with the electrodes placed two to four

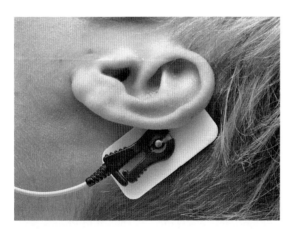

Photo 5.1.11 *Mastoid recording electrode*

CLINICAL WISDOM 5.1.1

The blood pressure cuff is usually placed directly above the right ankle, with two electromyographic electrodes Thymatron System IV device placed across the muscle bulk on the dorsal aspect of the foot, separated by four centimetres, or the optical motion sensor (OMS) attached to the MECTA spECTrum 5000 device, to the great toe to record the motor seizure. Caution is needed if circulation is compromised or there is prominent pitting oedema. In such cases it is recommended that the cuff be applied to the lower arm immediately above the wrist, usually on the right side, with electrodes placed on the muscles of the dorsum of the hand with a "stress ball" inside the hand. Flexibility is required as the intravenous access point can be located on the right arm if veins are not available on the left side.

centimetres on the dorsum of the hand across the muscle bulk shown in Photos 5.1.1 and 5.1.2. If using a MECTA device, attach the optical motion sensor to the great toe with the Velcro strap.

ECG. The ECG electrodes are coloured red and black, the same as the EEG electrodes. This can be confusing. Care needs to be taken to ensure that they are not mixed up with the EEG electrodes. If this occurs, the recorded trace will be difficult to interpret. The black recording electrode is placed on the anterior aspect of the right chest wall, while the red electrode is positioned on the left lateral side of the chest, as illustrated in Photo 5.1.5.

Earth. The earth electrode is coloured green. It is placed on the midpoint of the right clavicle. The right clavicle is chosen to eliminate artefacts from the rhythm of the heart that can occur if it is positioned towards the centre of the chest or on the left side, as shown Photo 5.1.5.

ELECTRODE SITE SKIN PREPARATION

Evidence to guide skin site preparation is limited. The aim is to produce high-quality traces and low

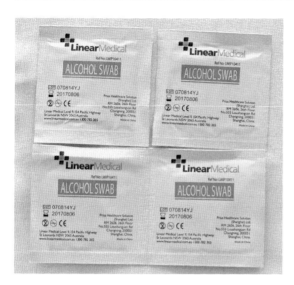

Photo 5.1.12 *Alcohol swabs*

Photo 5.1.13 *Abrasive conductive gel*

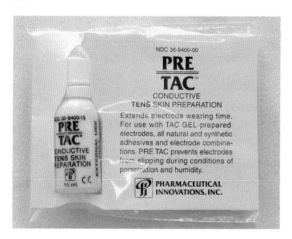

Photo 5.1.14 *Non-abrasive conductive solution*

Photo 5.1.15
Aqueous coupling conductivity gel

impedance. The following protocol is based upon years of practice-based experience using disposable treatment electrodes.

Careful attention needs to be given to skin preparation under the recording and treatment electrodes to remove skin residues, oils and make-up. Hair under the electrodes can significantly affect the quality of the recorded EEG and raise the static impedance.

Saline scrub. Each electrode site should be scrubbed with clean gauze dampened with normal saline. The gauze should be damp as excessive moisture can prevent good adhesion at all electrode sites.

Alcohol scrub. Following the saline wash, each electrode site should be scrubbed with an alcohol swab to clear the remaining skin oils and dry the skin, as shown in Photo 5.1.12.

Conduction gel/solution scrub. Impedance can be lowered considerably if the skin under the treating electrodes is scrubbed with an abrasive gel, or non-abrasive solution, as illustrated in Photos 5.1.13 and 5.1.14. The scrub is adequate if there is a red skin flare under the prepared site. Caution is needed when using the abrasive gel to prevent excoriation of the skin, particularly in the elderly. The abrasive gel should not be used under the handheld metal electrodes as it can cause skin burns. An aqueous coupling conductivity gel should be used instead, as illustrated in Photo 5.1.15.

APPLY TREATMENT ELECTRODES

Refer to Section 5.2 for details.

TESTING IMPEDANCE

Thymatron System IV

Impedance is tested by pressing the yellow impedance button, located immediately under the LCD display on the left side of the device. If there is an open circuit impedance the screen will flash "> 3000 ohm", as illustrated in Photo 5.1.16. It is recommended that skin preparation should be thorough to ensure an impedance of less than 1500 ohms to reduce the voltage administered, enhancing the quality of the stimulus that penetrates the brain tissue.

▌ *Photo 5.1.16* *Thymatron System IV open circuit*

After completion of an internal self-test, the Thymatron System IV automatically displays "No Base" in the impedance LCD window. Once the yellow impedance button has been pressed the device displays various LCD statements, including: "Baseline" and "Ready", indicating that the machine is set and treatment can commence, as illustrated in Photo 5.1.17. It changes to "Treat" when the stimulus is applied.

Once impedance has been established, it is important to complete a baseline recording to ensure that all recording electrodes are positioned correctly and are working satisfactorily by depressing the "Start/Stop" button located on the right side of the Thymatron device. The recording device will activate four recording channels on calibrated graph

CLINICAL WISDOM 5.1.2

Some Thymatron System IV devices are very sensitive to patient movement and are slow to establish "Ready". If the machine does not display "Ready", treatment will proceed but the parameters generated at the end of the trace will be incomplete. Experience has demonstrated that the "Ready" sign can be achieved more easily if the patient remains perfectly still with minimal staff contact when the impedance button is pressed.

If the problem persists and "Ready" is difficult to achieve, the button can be pushed before the circuit has been completed, giving the device more time to set up. When the stimulus circuit is incomplete the LCD display will flash ">3000 ohm" to indicate that a circuit has not been established. Treatment *should not proceed* until adequate impedance has been established to prevent an administration of an inadequate stimulus.

If the device continues to flash ">3000 ohm", a rapid assessment of the treatment electrodes should be completed to identify the fault. It is not uncommon for this fault to be a failure to insert the cable firmly into the electrode connector or lack of adequate skin preparation. If this fails to resolve the problem, it is possible that the leads are damaged and a new set should be installed.

▌ *Photo 5.1.17* *Thymatron System IV ready to treat*

paper. Turn off the recording device once the baseline has been established.

CLINICAL WISDOM 5.1.3

If disposable treatment electrodes are used, it is recommended that pressure is applied during the anaesthetic induction and muscle relaxation phases, by placing the palm of the right hand over the disposable electrode and holding the handheld electrode over the vertex for right unilateral treatment or using both hands for a bilateral technique. Experience has demonstrated that the warmth from the palm of the hand facilitates better contact. If this technique fails to lower impedance, it is recommended that the "dummy electrodes" are placed over the disposable electrode before the stimulus is administered. ECT should not proceed if impedance continues to flash ">3000 ohm".

CLINICAL WISDOM 5.1.4

Breathing through the mask can induce anxiety in some patients, as it requires firm pressure on the face to produce an adequate seal. If the patient experiences anxiety, allowing the patient to hold the mask onto their face may reduce it. In someone who is extremely anxious, the mask can be removed and the plastic tube held between the teeth or in front of their nose. In the worst-case scenario, treatment can be delayed to complete hyperventilation once unconsciousness has been achieved.

MECTA spECTrum 5000

Impedance is measured automatically on this device and is displayed as a vertical bar on the right side of the screen, as illustrated in Photo 5.1.18. It will not interfere with treatment or the recording process provided that it is below an acceptable limit of 5000 ohms. If impedance is too high the device has a default safety feature that prevents the stimulus being administered. This safety feature is not

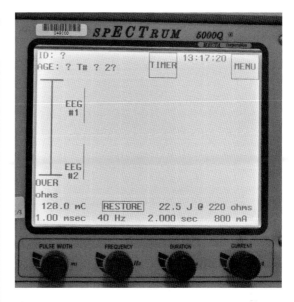

Photo 5.1.18 *MECTA spECTrum 5000 display*

available on the Thymatron System IV device where the stimulus can still be administered.

OXYGENATION/HYPERVENTILATION

Oxygenation is defined as ventilation with 100% oxygen, positive pressure and a respiratory rate between 15 to 20 breaths per minute, at five litres per minute from the onset of anaesthesia until spontaneous respirations resume (American Psychiatric Association, 2001). Best practice recommends that patients be oxygenated for a period of three to four minutes prior to induction, as shown in Photo 5.1.19.

All patients can benefit but particular care should be given to patients at risk of myocardial ischaemia, those who are obese and those who have pulmonary disease. Early work suggests that hyperventilation prior to the stimulus can improve seizure quality reduce the time to recovery and cognitive impairment (Chater and Simpson, 1988; Haeck, Gillmann, Janouschek and Grözinger, 2011; Sawayama et al., 2008).

These findings were supported in a more recent randomised controlled trial by Mayur, Bray, Fernandes, Bythe and Gilbett (2010). Twenty-five patients with major depressive disorder treated with

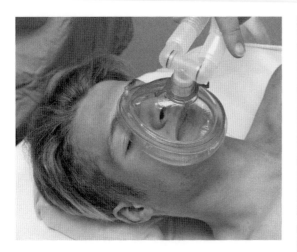

Photo 5.1.19 *Ventilation system*

right unilateral ECT 3 times above threshold were randomised to either ECT with hyperventilation or without hyperventilation from induction to the time of the stimulus. They concluded that orientation time was 30% longer among those who did not receive hyperventilation. They did not demonstrate any difference in EEG quality at the first treatment session but seizure length was longer after the second session. There was a significant increase in threshold over time across both groups.

CLINICAL WISDOM 5.1.5

Pulse oximetry is mandatory for all patients throughout the procedure to ensure adequate oxygen saturation levels. Certain patients are at risk of rapid haemoglobin oxygen desaturation during the early postictal period. Risk factors include morbid obesity, smoking and pulmonary disease. Males with beards are particularly at risk as the beard makes it difficult to achieve an adequate seal around the mask, allowing oxygen to escape. In these cases the team should discuss the best way to minimise the risks during the procedure; a laryngeal mask may offer a solution. If the patient is ventilated during the seizure, care should be taken to prevent artefacts on the EEG recording.

CLINICAL WISDOM 5.1.6

Disposable bite blocks are shaped to fit the upper and lower teeth and provide protection of the molars. Care is needed to fit them accurately as they can be difficult to insert owing to the tongue getting in the way and the frenulum exposed, subjecting it to injury. Disposable bite blocks are produced by a number of device manufacturers and add to the cost of each treatment. Generally the costs of sterilisation are less per unit, making the reusable bite blocks attractive.

The reusable bite blocks are made of soft rubber with a tube in the top to facilitate ventilation for the unconscious patient. Again, care is required to ensure that they are inserted correctly as the molar teeth may not be protected with all of the jaw pressure going through the front teeth. It is no longer acceptable practice to insert green gauze wrapped in tape between the front teeth as it does not provide sufficient protection, placing too much force on the front of the jaw and making injury more likely. All old-style non-flexible mouthguards should be avoided to minimise teeth trauma.

The anaesthetist ventilates the patient from the onset of the anaesthesia until adequate spontaneous respiration is resumed. It has been noted that cerebral oxygen consumption goes up by an order of 200% during the seizure, making ventilation prior to the treatment essential (Saito et al., 1996). Most anaesthetists do not ventilate during the seizure period; however, if it is maintained care should be taken to ensure artefacts are not transferred to the EEG. In a titration session it is recommended that the anaesthetist hyperventilate the patient between stimuli administration.

PROTECTION OF THE ORAL CAVITY

After a patient is fully relaxed, an appropriate mouthguard should be inserted between the upper and lower teeth. There are two types of bite

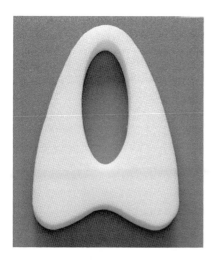

Photo 5.1.20 *Disposable bite block*

Photo 5.1.21 *Reusable bite block*

blocks commonly used, reusable or disposable, as illustrated in Photos 5.1.20 and 5.1.21.

Reusable bite blocks come in different sizes to accommodate different jaw anatomy. The bite block should be flexible to absorb the force exerted by the pterygoid, masseter and temporalis muscles of the jaw. Care should be taken to ensure that the mouthguard protects the molars deep in the jaw and that the tongue is out of the way of the teeth. Broken teeth, bites to the tongue or tears of the

frenulum are possible if careful attention is not given to this procedure.

It is recommended that dentures be removed and a mouthguard inserted to protect the gums. Once the bite block has been inserted, it is important to manually support the jaw until after the application of the stimulus to minimise jaw movement or displacement of the bite block.

An effective mouthguard should be made of flexible material and be large enough to distribute the stimulus induced pressure from the jaw clench evenly cross the teeth and allow the flow of air to enable ongoing ventilation through the mouth as nasal passages may become blocked with secretions.

It is very important that the Guedel airway be removed and replaced by a mouthguard prior to the delivery of the stimulus. Guedel airways are made of solid plastic and may cause teeth damage. A laryngeal mask is sometimes used if a patient has a difficult airway or beard or is prone to rapid desaturation. This airway is made of soft plastic and is taped into the correct position. Support of the lower jaw prevents sudden clenching and damage to the teeth.

TIME OUT

Best practice recommends that all centres administering ECT develop a time out procedure as per regional correct patient and correct procedure (NSQHS, 2012; Watts, 2016). The time out procedure should check the name, date of birth, electrode placement, stimulus dose and pulse width, and match the patient's label with the ECT order. The procedure should be completed at different times: during the course of ECT, when the patient arrives at the theatre complex and transferred into theatre, immediately before induction and immediately before treatment is administered.

A mnemonic has been developed to aid the final time out procedure. The treating team recites the following:

> "Sux away, chocks away, cross-check and arm, fire away!"

- **"Sux away"**. Check suxamethonium given and absent deep tendon knee reflex.
- **"Chocks away"**. Ensure that bite block has been inserted with adequate support of the chin.
- **"Cross-check and arm"**. Ensure that all parameters on the ECT device are set correctly and the patient does not respond to the command "move the right foot" with a final check of impedance.
- **"Fire away"**. Refers to the green light that all systems are checked and ready to treat (Weiss, Hansen, Bull and Hughes, 2017).

ANAESTHETIC TECHNIQUE

Routine anaesthetic technique is set out in Table 5.6.1.

ADMINISTRATION OF ANAESTHETIC AGENTS

Details are set out in Section 5.6.

DELIVERY OF STIMULUS

As noted, it is important that the ECT team reaches a consensus that everything is in order before treatment commences.

Thymatron System IV

It is recommended that the impedance level is checked immediately prior to treatment being administered. Once the "Ready" sign has appeared on the LCD screen, treatment can proceed. Lift protective cover and push the "Treat" button, shown in Photo 5.7.1. The device requires that the button be held down firmly throughout the delivery of the stimulus. When the button is pressed it is illuminated with a yellow light that continues until the stimulus has been delivered. The device will automatically terminate the stimulus once the energy has been delivered. It is then safe to release the button. The audible warble will begin and continue until the recording device has been stopped.

CLINICAL WISDOM 5.1.7

The audible warble is a feature of the Thymatron devices that changes in intensity and frequency during the seizure. It is not present on a MECTA device. A skilled ECT practitioner can use this sound to determine seizure quality, adequacy of skin preparation, quality of the recording, artefacts and when the seizure has ceased. It is curious that the impedance and treat buttons are both yellow in colour. The treat button is then illuminated yellow during the administration of the stimulus. This has sometimes led to potentially serious errors when a junior doctor attempts to press the treat button instead of the impedance button during the set-up period. Fortunately, the treat button has a spring-loaded plastic cover, making it more difficult to accidentally active it. Manufacturing the device with a red treat button would potentially eliminate this problem.

MECTA spECTrum 5000

The impedance is automatically calculated on the MECTA spECTrum 5000M or Q devices. To deliver the stimulus, lift the cover off the orange stimulus output button, illustrated in Photo 5.7.3. Apply firm pressure until the stimulus has been administered. During this period the device prints out the self-test result. Once this has been completed, the device administers the stimulus. The stimulus status light changes to red/orange, indicating that the stimulus is being delivered. Once this light has been extinguished the button can be released.

Premature release of the button on either device results in inadequate delivery of energy, producing an unpredictable, low-intensity stimulus that can result in an abortive seizure. The amount of charge that has been administered is displayed on the printout that is produced once the recording device has been stopped.

If a seizure has not been induced, restimulation is required. Subconvulsive stimuli result in bradycardia and may cause increased level of confusion during the recovery period.

Once the seizure has been initiated, it is important to closely monitor the patient and the seizure generated on the recording device to identify the appropriate EEG end point. Once this has been determined the monitor can be stopped.

Determining the EEG end point is assisted on the Thymatron System IV by an auditory warble. The end point is indicated by a continuous high-pitched sound.

It is recommended that the recording device on both devices be stopped eight to 10 seconds after postictal suppression has been achieved to enable calibration of the seizure adequacy algorithms that are printed at the end of the trace on both devices.

PROCEDURE POST-SEIZURE

The period immediately after the seizure has terminated is the point of greatest risk of adverse events and requires the full attention of the anaesthetist. Ventilation continues until spontaneous breathing occurs. A Hudson mask is attached to a portable oxygen cylinder and the patient is transferred to the recovery area after all recording and stimulus electrodes have been removed. The anaesthetist will determine whether to recover in a head-up or coma position. To ensure the patient's safe transfer to recovery, a mobile oximetry device is placed on the patient's finger when they leave theatre and changed to a fixed device in recovery that is maintained until the patient is orientated to time and place and is breathing spontaneously.

Appropriate entries should be made into the computer or paper record concerning the treatment that has been administered. The ECT practitioner should carefully follow the procedure specified by the relevant legislation where the treatment has been administered.

When the patient arrives in recovery the anaesthetist provides a handover to recovery staff. The recovery nurse monitors the patient's vital observations over the next hour. Once recovery has been achieved, the patient is transferred to the ward or offered a light meal and a drink prior to going home.

RECOVERY

- Ventilate the patient until spontaneous breathing re-occurs.
- Follow the anaesthetist's preference for recovery prior to transfer to the recovery area. Coma position or elevate the head of the bed.
- ECT nurse to assist anaesthetist in transferring the patient to the recovery area for more intensive monitoring by recovery staff until the patient has returned to full consciousness.
- 100% oxygen should be continued until the patient has returned to full consciousness.
- The patient is then returned to the ward to have breakfast or, if an outpatient, given a light breakfast before going home in the company of an adult.
- Remind the patient that they are not to drive or be alone for the next 24-hour period.

MISSED OR ABORTIVE SEIZURES

Missed seizures

A missed seizure is defined as the absence of any motor tonic clonic movements or EEG seizure activity after a stimulus has been administered (American Psychiatric Association, 2001; Waite and Easton, 2013)

A missed seizure may be due to insufficient stimulus intensity, excess dynamic impedance, premature stimulus termination, hypercapnia or the effect of mediations like benzodiazepines or excessive anaesthetic induction agent (Scott, 2005)

Restimulation should occur once the following procedure has been followed:

- Increasing the stimulus dose by one level: the value will depend upon the type of ECT administered (see ECT titration protocol). For example, with brief pulse using a Thymatron System IV, go from 20% (101 mC) to 30% (151 mC) or if using ultrabrief-pulse ECT go from 25% (126 mC) to 35% (176 mC).
- Recheck impedance to ensure it is the lowest value possible, preferably below 1500 ohms.

- Hyperventilate the patient during this period to prevent complications and potentially lower the seizure threshold.
- Administer the stimulus.
- Wait 10 to 15 seconds before a further stimulation is delivered to overcome the "refractory period" and allow for the development of any delayed seizure. Threshold seizures often have a very long recruitment phase and it is important to wait long enough to ensure that a seizure has not occurred.
- If no seizure activity has been established, the above procedure should be repeated.
- Once the treatment has ceased it is important to review the patient history and medication sheet to identify the possible cause of the failed seizure.

Abortive seizures

An abortive seizure is defined as a seizure that is less than 15 seconds by motor and EEG criteria (American Psychiatric Association, 2001). Abortive seizures create a challenge for the ECT practitioner, as short seizures alone may not be ineffective, making the decision to restimulate complicated and this should be made in the context of clinical response. If the decision is made to apply another stimulus the procedure note above should be followed. It may be prudent to allow a longer time interval before restimulation to overcome the sharp transient rise in seizure threshold that can occur under these circumstances.

REFERENCES

American Psychiatric Association. (2001). *The Practice of Electroconvulsive Therapy: Recommendations for Treatment, Training and Privileging: A Task Force Report*, 2nd edition. Washington, DC: American Psychiatric Association.

Chater, S.N., and Simpson, K.H. (1988). Effect of passive hyperventilation on seizure duration in patients undergoing electroconvulsive therapy. *British Journal of Anaesthesia, 60*(1), 70–73. Retrieved from www.ncbi.nlm.nih.gov/pubmed/3122811.

Fink, M., and Johnson, L. (1982). Monitoring the duration of electroconvulsive therapy seizures: 'cuff' and EEG methods compared. *Archives of General Psychiatry, 39*(10), 1189–1191. doi:10.1001/archpsyc.1982.04290100055009.

Greenberg, L.B. (1985). Detection of prolonged seizures during electroconvulsive therapy: a comparison of electroencephalogram and cuff monitoring. *Convulsive Therapy, 1*(1), 32–37. Retrieved from www.ncbi.nlm.nih.gov/pubmed/11940803.

Haeck, M., Gillmann, B., Janouschek, H., and Grözinger, M. (2011). Electroconvulsive therapy can benefit from controlled hyperventilation using a laryngeal mask. *European Archives of Psychiatry and Clinical Neuroscience, Nov*(261 Suppl 2), S173–176. doi:10.1007/s00406-011-0240-4.

Hamilton, M. (1987). Electrodermal response as a monitor in ECT. *British Journal of Psychiatry, 151*, 559.

Jayaprakash, M.S., Gangadhar, B.N., Janakiramaiah, N., and Subbakrishna, D.K. (1998). Limitations of motor seizure monitoring in ECT. *Indian Journal of Psychiatry, 40*(1), 55–59.

Mayur, P., Bray, A., Fernandes, J., Bythe, K., and Gilbett, D. (2010). Impact of hyperventilation on stimulus efficiency during the early phase of an electroconvulsive therapy course: a randomized double-blind study. *Journal of ECT, 26*, 91–94.

MECTA Corporation. (2015). spECTrum 5000Q – MECTA Corp. Retrieved from www.mectacorp.com/spectrum-5000Q.html.

NSQHS. (2012). Standard 5: Patient identification and procedure matching. *Commonweath Government*. Retrieved from www.safetyandquality.gov.au/wp-content/uploads/2012/10/Standard5_Oct_2012_WEB.pdf.

Saito, S., Miyoshi, S., Yoshikawa, D., Shimada, H., Morita, T., and Kitani, Y. (1996). Regional cerebral oxygen saturation during electroconvulsive therapy: monitoring by near-infrared spectrophotometry. *Anesthesia & Analgesia, 83*(4), 726–730. Retrieved from www.ncbi.nlm.nih.gov/pubmed/8831310.

Sawayama, E., Takahashi, M., Inoue, A., Nakajima, K., Kano, A., Sawayama, T., . . . Miyaoka, H. (2008). Moderate hyperventilation prolongs electroencephalogram seizure duration of the first electroconvulsive therapy. *Journal of ECT, 24*(3), 195–198. doi:10.1097/YCT.0b013e3181620815.

Scott, A.I.F. (2005). *The ECT Handbook*, 2nd edition. London: Royal College of Psychiatrists.

Somatics, L.L.C. (2015). Somatics, LLC – manufacturer of the Thymatron ECT machine. Retrieved from www.thymatron.com/main_home.asp.

Waite, J., and Easton, A. (2013). *The ECT Handbook*, 3rd edition. London: Royal College of Psychiatrists.

Watts, B.V. (2016). A time-out before every ECT treatment. *Journal of ECT, 32*(4), 224.

Weiss, A.M., Hansen, S., Bull, M., and Hughes, P. (2017). A time-out before every ECT procedure. *Journal of ECT, 33*(3), 218–219.

Wise, M.E., Mackie, F., Zamar, A.C., and Watson, J.P. (2000). Investigation of the "cuff" method for assessing seizure duration in electroconvulsive therapy. *Psychiatric Bulletin, 24*, 301.

Electrode placement

One of the most challenging aspects confronting an ECT practitioner is deciding the type of ECT that is suitable for the clinical situation. Over the past 25 years the decision has become considerable more complex, with the type of ECT changing from a choice of two different options to well over nine different combinations that can be used depending upon the clinical situation.

Incorporating change and new information into clinical work can be challenging, with practitioners tending to be conservative and preferring to use strategies that have been effective in the past, a phenomenon that has a long history.

HISTORY

It is best illustrated by the intense historical debate in the literature concerning the benefits of right unilateral (RUL) ECT over bitemporal (BT) ECT. From the outset the pronounced amnestic effects of bitemporal sine wave ECT drove a substantial portion of ECT research into alternatives with the introduction of a brief-pulse stimulus in the early 1940s (Kellner, Tobias and Wiegand, 2010). The advent of unilateral electrode placement was credited to Goldman (1949), with the term "unilateral electroconvulsive therapy" coined by Lancaster, Steinert and Frost (1958), as illustrated in Figure 5.2.1. The frustration of this early work, which continues today, is that attempts to reduce confusion and memory disturbance compromised efficacy, leaving the clinical impression that RUL ECT was less potent than BT ECT (Abrams, 2002). By the 1970s, studies began to show that RUL ECT was an effective form of treatment that had significant lower levels of cognitive impairment (d'Elia and Raotma, 1975), leading to the standardised electrode placement for RUL that continues to be known as the "d'Elia placement" (d'Elia, 1970, 1976), as illustrated in Figure 5.2.1.

It was not until the early work by Sackeim, Decina, Kanzler, Kerr and Malitz (1987), which showed a dose–response relationship between the antidepressant effect and electrical stimulus dose, that a better understanding as to why RUL ECT was less potent than BT was determined. Further work demonstrated that low-dose RUL ECT was ineffective compared to low-dose BT ECT, in that the generalised seizure was necessary but not sufficient to ensure a clinical response (Sackeim et al., 1993) and that high-dose RUL was necessary to have an equivalent antidepressant response rate of 62% to BT but substantially less cognitive impairment (Sackeim et al., 2000).

These findings did not stop the debate continuing until a recent meta-analysis concluded that high-dose RUL ECT does not differ from moderate-dose BT ECT in antidepressant efficacy but has significant cognitive advantages (Kolshus, Jelovac and McLoughlin, 2017).

CURRENT PRACTICE

Further confusion for the ECT practitioner has come in recent years, with evidence appearing that bifrontal ECT may be as effective as high-dose RUL and moderate-dose BT ECT (Kellner et al., 2010), and the advent of brief-pulse and ultrabrief ECT (Tor et al., 2015). These advances offer the potential for at least nine different combinations of ECT with three different electrode placements that can be delivered with three different square wave stimulus pulse widths.

Consensus is difficult to achieve using evidence alone. Following an overview of the most common electrode placements, the chapter will conclude with recommendations to guide clinical practice.

It is now well established that unilateral placement of electrodes over the non-dominant hemisphere causes fewer severe cognitive side effects than bilateral placement (Abrams, Dornbush, Feldstein, Volavka and Roubicek, 1972; Kolshus et al., 2017; Murugesan, 1994; Sackeim et al., 1993). The asymmetric placement of the electrodes in unilateral ECT results in the relative sparing of cognitive function on the contralateral hemisphere. For unilateral ECT to be effective, the intensity of the stimulus dose needs to be suprathreshold as low-energy seizures are ineffective (Sackeim et al., 1993; Sackeim et al., 2000).

Sackeim et al. (2000) highlight that increasing the stimulus dose six levels above the dose that elicited the seizure (high-dose strategy) is the most efficacious. When dosing at this energy level, the efficacy is increased and may equal the efficacy of bitemporal ECT but may lose the cognitive advantage (Kolshus et al., 2017; Sackeim et al., 2000).

The trade-off between efficacy and cognitive impairment is one of the greatest challenges in ECT treatment (Freeman, 2013).

ULTRABRIEF ECT

More recent studies have demonstrated that cognitive effects of very high dose unilateral ECT can be reduced when an ultrabrief pulse width of

0.3 ms is utilised (Sackeim et al., 2008). Since that time, this form of ECT has been extensively studied, establishing a strong evidence base that ultrabrief ECT maintains efficacy with less cognitive impairment than brief-pulse ECT (Galletly, Paterson and Burton, 2012; Loo, Katalinic, Martin and Schweitzer, 2012; Loo et al., 2014; Loo et al., 2008; Magid, Truong, Trevino and Husain, 2013; Pisvejc et al., 1998; Sienaert, Vansteelandt, Demyttenaere and Peuskens, 2009; Spaans et al., 2013; Spaans, Verwijk and Comijs, 2013).

A recent meta-analysis has summarised the data from six randomised controlled trials involving a total of 689 patients comparing ultrabrief to brief-pulse right unilateral ECT. They found that brief-pulse ECT was significantly more efficacious in treating depression than ultrabrief ECT but showed significantly more cognitive side effects in all cognitive domains examined. The mean number of treatment sessions given was 8.7 for brief-pulse ECT and 9.6 for ultrabrief ECT. Ultrabrief ECT had lower response and remission rates of 55.3% and 33.8%, compared to brief-pulse 58.1% and 44.9%, with the number of treatments needed, 12.1, in favour of brief-pulse ECT. This meta-analysis highlights the substantial cognitive advantages of ultrabrief ECT over brief-pulse ECT but was less efficient in treating depression and required one more treatment session (Tor et al., 2015; Worthington, 2015).

CLINICAL WISDOM 5.2.1

The evidence base supporting the efficacy of ECT is overwhelming with the recent publication of the PRIDE study (Kellner et al., 2016). Why is it that ECT continues to face such strong opposition and negativity, with the media very happy to present very biased and opinionated misinformation?

> There are some places where psychiatrists think it works, and they just do it lots of times, and there are some places where people think: "Bloody hell, I don't think the evidence for this is very good," so will only do it in absolutely desperate circumstances.

Davis and Duncan, 2017

Or

> Children as young as 10 are undergoing potentially deadly electroshock therapy.

Torpey, 2016

Stigma remains the single most damaging factor in ECT practice. This is reflected in the current deliberation facing the US Food & Drug Administration (2017) concerning the reclassification of ECT devices. What initially appears to be a win for ECT advocates is in fact highly restrictive, limiting the treatment to acute treatment of major depression. Other conditions like schizophrenia, schizoaffective disorder, mania, catatonia and self-injurious behaviour in autism are excluded under the ruling (Lutz, 2016).

Practice-based experience highlights that stigma begins in the ECT treatment room. This section illustrates two of the most common systems used worldwide to administer ECT. It is the author's assertion that the handheld electrodes illustrated in these photographs directly contribute to stigma each time junior eyes observe ECT for the first time. In order to achieve patient-centered care there is a call to allow family members to come into the treatment room to observe ECT being administered (Coffey and Coffey, 2016). Disposable treating electrodes turn ECT into a modern, day-only hospital procedure!

NB: The images presented in this section illustrate the difference between two different methods to administer ECT and not device manufacturers. It is not the author's intention to make judgement on the ECT devices, which are equally effective in the delivery of modern and effective ECT!

Further support for ultrabrief-pulse ECT comes from the Prolonging Remission in Depressed Elderly (PRIDE) study, which evaluated the efficacy of ultrabrief right unilateral ECT combined with venlafaxine for the treatment of a large sample of geriatric depressed patients who were over 60 years of age. As the study progressed, early release of data demonstrated efficacy with a remission rate of 63% reported following enrolment of 141 patients (Gammon, 2013) and a similar rate of remission of 62% reported two years later (Harrison, 2015).

The final results of the PRIDE study have now been published (Kellner et al., 2016). Of the 240 patients who entered phase one of the study, there were 174 who successfully completed. Overall, 61.7% (148/240) of all patients met remission criteria, 10% (24/240) did not remit and 28.3% (68/240) dropped out, with 70% (169/240) meeting response criteria. Among those who remitted, the mean decrease in the 24-item Hamilton Depression Rating Scale was 24.7 points with a mean final score of 7.3 and an average change from baseline of 79%. The average number of treatments to remission was 7.3. This data highlights the efficacy of ultrabrief RUL ECT combined with venlafaxine as a highly effective treatment option for depressed geriatric patients with excellent safety and tolerability.

These studies demonstrate that ultrabrief RUL ECT is well tolerated with significantly lower levels of cognitive side effects and only modest reduction in efficacy compared to brief-pulse ECT and bilateral ECT and should now be considered the default first-line treatment for patients who do not present with extreme risk (Tor et al., 2015).

LANDMARKS

The term fronto-temporal position has been used to describe the electrode position that is 2.5 cm above the midpoint of an imaginary line drawn between the outer tragus of the ear and the external canthus of the eye. For simplicity, the preferred term in this *Workbook* is the "temporal" position. The vertex is the intersection of the lines drawn between the nasion and inion and the right and left

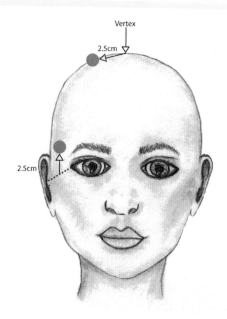

Figure 5.2.1 *Right unilateral electrode placement*

tragus of the ear. These positions are illustrated in Figures 5.1.2 and 5.2.2.

RIGHT UNILATERAL ECT NON-DOMINANT (RUL)

Right unilateral ECT (RUL) involves the placement of treatment electrodes 2.5 cm to the right of the vertex and in the right temporal areas of the head. This position is known as the d'Elia position (d'Elia, 1970, 1976; d'Elia and Raotma, 1975). Photo 5.2.1 shows the set-up for the Thymatron System IV disposable electrodes and Photo 5.2.2 is the set-up for the MECTA spECTrum 5000 handheld electrodes.

The temporal electrode (disposable or handheld) is placed over the right temporal fossa, with the centre of the electrode 2.5 cm above the midpoint of an imaginary line drawn between the tragus of the ear and the outer canthus of the eye. Photo 5.2.3 illustrates the position for RUL and Photo 5.2.4 for the left bitemporal electrode.

When using a disposable electrode, for example a Thymapad, the lower corner of the pad without

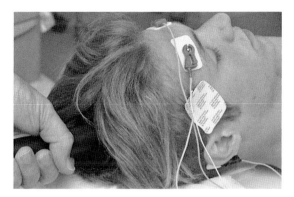

Photo 5.2.1 *RUL Thymatron handheld and disposable electrodes*

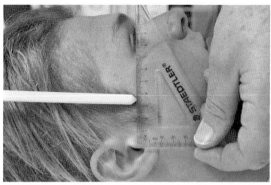

Photo 5.2.3 *Midpoint line between outer canthus eye and tragus ear RUL and LFRT*

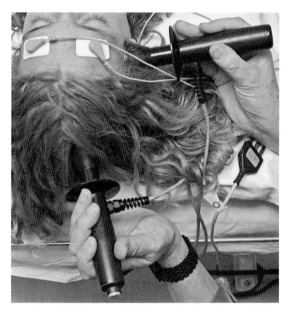

Photo 5.2.2 *RUL MECTA handheld electrodes*

the "dimple" should be placed on the midpoint of the line and slanted at a 45% angle towards the forehead with the lead superior, as illustrated in Photo 5.2.5.

Placing the index fingers of both hands on the left and right ear and touching the thumb midline behind the head, at the intersection of the lines drawn between the nasion and the inion and the tragus of each ear, can determine the vertex position, as illustrated in Photo 5.2.6.

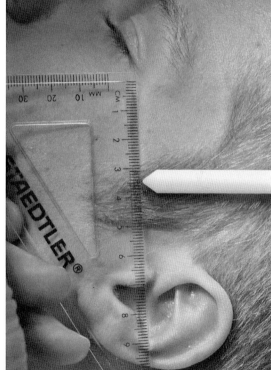

Photo 5.2.4 *Midpoint line between outer canthus eye and tragus ear BT and LUL*

In order to assist in identifying the correct anatomical location for this electrode, a doughnut-shaped pillow replaces the standard pillow as it

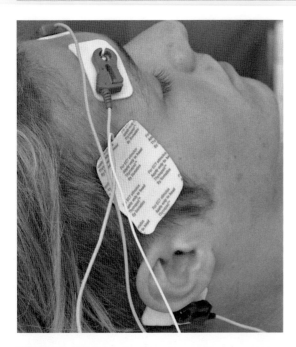

Photo 5.2.5 *Disposable and recording electrodes RUL*

Photo 5.2.6 *Vertex determination RUL and LUL*

can obscure this position when the head is hyper-extended by the anaesthetist to facilitate airway management, as illustrated in Photo 5.1.3.

Stimulation using a unilateral electrode placement initiates a pattern of neuronal recruitment within the stimulated neurons, and the pathways to which they project with the thalamocortical feedback loop are essential to this process (Coffey, 1993). For bilateral electrical stimulation, seizures generalisation appears to be elicited via direct activation of diencephalic nuclei, whereas in unilateral ECT there is initial activation of the underlying cortical circuitry with a secondary generalisation via corticothalamic pathways. This produces a well generalised seizure capable of stimulating the primary motor cortex (Staton, Hass and Brumback, 1981).

The motor cortex is particularly excitable and capable of generalisations through projections to subcortical centres. It is known that the motor cortex has the lowest seizure threshold within the cortex (Coffey, 1993). It has been suggested that the d'Elia position may result in less shunting, utilising potentially low impedance pathways through the skull offered by the sagittal sinus, thereby making it the most dependable in eliciting maximal seizure activity.

Some ECT services worldwide have adopted a moderate dosing protocol for RUL ECT that increases the stimulus at the second session by three levels above seizure threshold to minimise cognition impairment. The trade-off between less cognitive impairment and lower stimulus dose requires close monitoring of the patient to detect a lack of clinical progress. Dose above threshold for unilateral electrode placement remains a contentious area with many proponents advocating high dose protocols ranging from 5 to 8 times threshold arguing that lower doses are ineffective.

"HANDEDNESS" OR LATERALITY

The notion of handedness or laterality is a theoretically important concept for ECT. It is known that if a stimulus is applied to the dominant hemisphere there is an increased likelihood of cognitive impairment (Daniel and Crovitz, 1983). The aim of ECT is to stimulate the non-dominant hemisphere.

In practice, handedness is difficult to assess in a clinical setting. The patient's self-report of handedness, or reliance on which hand they use to write, is unreliable as many strongly left-handed people write with their right hand (Peters, 1995). It has become convention to always utilise the right hemispheric placement as the majority of people are left hemisphere-dominant even if they are left-handed (American Psychiatric Association, 2001).

It is estimated that 70% of people are left hemisphere-dominant, resulting in right-handedness. In the 30% who are left-handed, 70% of this group are lateralised for language functions in a manner similar to right-handed people (Bryden, 1982). Of the remainder, 15% have bilateral representation of language, with the other 15% being truly right hemisphere-dominant (Bryden and Steenhuis, 1991; Ramussen and Milner, 1977).

It has been shown that right unilateral ECT produces less disruption on verbal functions than left unilateral ECT or bilateral ECT in right-handed patients (Daniel and Crovitz, 1983). Clinically, most ECT practitioners prefer to administer right unilateral ECT independent of handedness.

The decision to switch from right to left unilateral electrode placement should be made when there is an unexpected severe postictal confusion, dysphasia or memory impairment soon after the course of ECT has commenced. Switching to left unilateral ECT can rapidly resolve this complication, allowing for the remainder of the course completed uneventfully. The position for left unilateral ECT is the mirror image of RUL electrode placement,

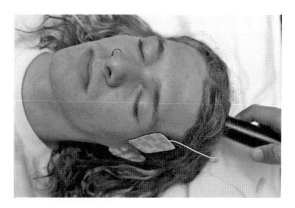

Photo 5.2.7 *LUL Thymatron handheld and disposable electrodes*

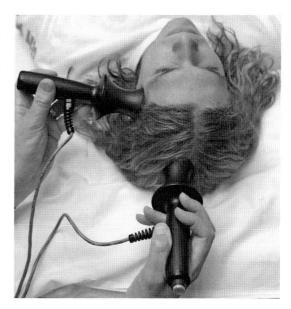

Photo 5.2.8 *LUL MECTA handheld electrodes*

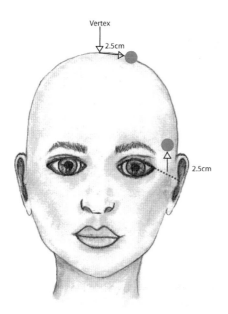

Figure 5.2.2 *Left unilateral electrode placement*

with the electrode being placed 2.5 cm to the left side of the sagittal line.

LEFT UNILATERAL ELECTRODE PLACEMENT (LUL)

Left unilateral ECT has been proposed as an alternative to RUL for left-handed patients presumed to have right-hemisphere localisation of language function. The set-up for this electrode placement is illustrated in Figure 5.2.2 and Photos 5.2.7 and 5.2.8.

There were a number of early studies that focused on the exploration of lateralisation of memory function with right- and left-sided ECT (Berent, Cohen and Silverman, 1975; Cohen, Noblin, Silverman and Penick, 1968; Costello, Belton, Abra and Dunn, 1970; Fleminger, de Horne and Nott, 1970; Jackson, 1978; Wilson and Gottlieb, 1967). The relevance of these studies has been challenged as they all used a sine wave stimulus that is known to have a substantial impact on cognitive function (Kellner, Tobias and Wiegand, 2010).

There has been one clinical trial of LUL compared to RUL (Abrams, Swartz and Vedak, 1989). In this study, 30 male patients with melancholic depression were randomised to either LUL (11 subjects) or RUL (19 subjects) at a fixed stimulus dose of 378 mC; there was a decrease in efficacy measures of 85% for LUL and 70% for RUL with no adverse cognitive effects reported.

Currently, the primary reason for electing to use LUL ECT are in left-handed individuals who develop significant postictal delirium soon after the course of ECT as commenced (Kellner, 1997) or when there is a skull defect over the right hemisphere, making RUL inadvisable (Warnell, 2004).

BITEMPORAL ECT (BT)

The set-up for bitemporal ECT is shown in Figure 5.1.3 and illustrated in Photos 5.2.9 and 5.2.10. It is generally accepted that bitemporal electrode placement has superior efficacy and is "the gold standard" for ECT (American Psychiatric Association, 2001; NSW Health, 2010; SA Health, 2014; Tiller and Lyndon, 2003; Waite and Easton, 2013). However, the improved efficacy is associated with the greatest degree of cognitive impairment, particularly retrograde autobiographical memory loss, which in some cases may not be fully reversible (Sackeim et al., 2007; Semkovska and McLoughlin, 2013). Bitemporal ECT has been shown to have a significantly faster antidepressant response early

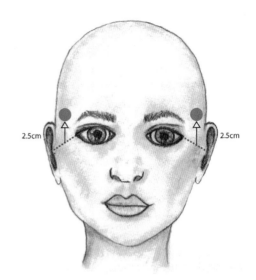

Figure 5.2.3 *Bitemporal electrode placement*

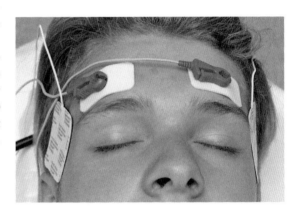

Photo 5.2.9 *BT Thymatron disposable electrode placement*

the treatment course compared to other forms of ECT (Kellner et al., 2010).

The correct position for bitemporal electrode placement is illustrated in Photo 5.2.9 for Thymatron System IV disposable electrodes and 5.2.10 for MECTA spECTrum 5000 handheld electrodes. Electrodes are placed over the right and left temporal fossa, with the centre of the electrode 2.5 cm above the midpoint of the line drawn between the tragus of the ear and the outer canthus of the eye.

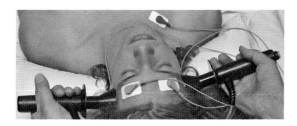

Photo 5.2.10 *BT MECTA handheld electrode placement*

Sackeim et al. (2000) demonstrated that the amount of energy needed above seizure threshold for bitemporal ECT was substantially lower than that required for effective unilateral treatment, as both high-dose and low-dose protocols were effective, with all forms of bilateral ECT having worse cognitive impairment. When this placement is utilised, there is less reliance on establishing adequate EEG parameters to ensure a robust clinical response.

As noted, a different dosing protocol is utilised following the titration session for bitemporal electrode placement. Power is increased by one and a half levels above threshold, compared to a minimum of three levels for right unilateral treatment.

For many years, bitemporal electrode placement was used routinely (Abrams, 2002). However, recent ECT minimum standards of practice guidelines note that this electrode placement should only be used when other electrode placements have been ineffective or when there is a medical emergency where a rapid response is necessary owing to a life-threatening clinical presentation (Dunne and McLoughlin, 2013; NSW Health, 2010; SA Health, 2014; Tasmanian Government, 2013; Victorian Government, 2014)

Experience demonstrates that if a patient has failed to respond to right unilateral or bifrontal electrode placement, bitemporal electrode placement should be considered. In this situation, ideally the patient should be retitrated but this potentially delays recovery; a preferable approach is to reduce the stimulus dose by one or two levels: dependent upon the quality of the EEG, low-dose

bitemporal ECT is effective (Nobler et al., 1993), with higher stimulus doses causing excessive cognitive impairment (Sackeim et al., 2007).

BIFRONTAL ECT (BF)

Bifrontal ECT has been proposed as an alternative bilateral technique with less cognitive impairment. It is thought that this position matches the efficacy of bitemporal electrode placement with fewer memory effects owing to avoidance of stimulation over the hippocampal region in the brain (Letemendia et al., 1993).

The standard for bifrontal ECT is based upon the electrode placement originally used by Letemendia et al. (1993) and replicated in a more recent trial by Bailine et al. (2000), where both electrodes are placed 5 cm about the canthus of the eye in the parasagittal plane using a line triangulated 45 degrees from the tragus of the ear. This position is illustrated in Figure 5.2.4. Photo 5.2.11 illustrates how to correctly determine the anatomical position using the triangulation method. Photo 5.2.12 shows the correct set-up for the Thymatron System IV disposable electrodes and Photo 5.2.13 demonstrates the correct set-up for the MECTA spECTrum 5000 using handheld electrodes.

Bifrontal electrode placement was first proposed by Inglis (1969), with the early trials being completed a few years later using multiple ECT (four to six seizures per treatment session up to three sessions) or daily bifrontal ECT (seven days a week until recovery) (Abrams and Fink, 1972; Abrams and Taylor, 1973). Following two attempts, the group abandoned the technique owing to a lack of clinical advantage over bitemporal ECT with an increased risk of skin burns over the forehead due to shunting of current secondary to the very short inter-electrode distance used (Abrams, 2002). These trials were further limited as the technique was utilised with high-intensity forms of ECT that had increased risks of complications and have long been abandoned.

The electrode position in these early studies was different to more recent bifrontal ECT, with the

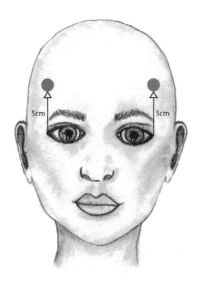

Figure 5.2.4 *Bifrontal electrode placement*

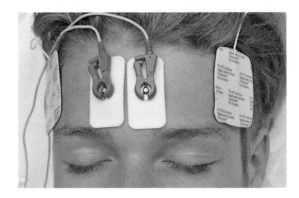

Photo 5.2.12 *BF Thymatron disposable electrodes*

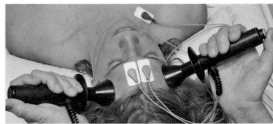

Photo 5.2.13 *BF MECTA handheld electrodes*

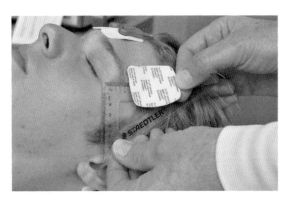

Photo 5.2.11 *Triangulation method to determine correct BF electrode position*

electrodes placed on either side of the midline, 5 cm apart and 5 cm above the nasion (Abrams, 2002). Letemendia et al. (1993) placed the electrode 5 cm above the outer canthus of the eye in the parasagittal plane, with an inter-electrode distance varying between 12 and 15 cm, depending upon the anatomy of the skull.

In their study, Letemendia et al. (1993) compared three electrode placements – right unilateral (RUL), bitemporal (BT) and bifrontal (BF) – in 59 patients with major depression, dosing all placements at 1 times threshold. They found that bifrontal ECT was the most effective method requiring less treatment sessions to gain remission, 10 sessions compared to 12 for BT and 16 for RUL with less cognitive impairment. The major criticism of the study was the very low-stimulus dose used for RUL, now known to be ineffective (Sackeim et al., 1987).

Bailine et al. (2000) replicated these findings in their study, where they randomly assigned 48 patients with major depression to either bifrontal or bitemporal ECT using the same electrode position as Letemendia et al. (1993). All patients received a brief-pulse stimulus at 1.5 times threshold. Forty-seven of 48 patients remitted by ECT number 12. There was no difference in remission rates or the number of ECT treatments to achieve remission. However, patients in the bifrontal group showed less ECT-induced cognitive impairment as measured by the Folstein Mini Mental State Examination (MMSE) (Folstein, Folstein and McHugh, 1975). A major criticism of this study was the inadequacy of the cognitive testing that was completed (MMSE alone) and the low-stimulus dose above threshold.

Heikman et al. (2002) randomised 24 patients to high-dose RUL at 4 times seizure threshold, moderate-dose RUL at 1.5 times seizure threshold to low-dose (just above threshold) bifrontal ECT. High-dose, right unilateral ECT was associated with a significantly faster response to treatment, with a mean number of seven treatments compared to low-dose, bifrontal ECT, which had a mean of 12 treatments.

Bakewell, Russo, Tanner, Avery and Neumaier (2004) completed a retrospective chart review of 76 depressed patients who had bitemporal or bifrontal ECT. The dose relative to threshold was not reported. They concluded that bitemporal was more effective but bifrontal had less memory loss and had less postictal confusion or disorientation. They noted that bifrontal patients were more likely to be readmitted to hospital within a 12-month period but experienced less cognitive impairment. Technical difficulties were more common with bifrontal electrode placement, with a higher number of failed or inadequate seizures and a high rate of switching to bitemporal ECT from this electrode position.

Little et al. (2004) completed a retrospective chart review of 14 elderly patients who received BF ECT. They reported a response rate of 86% but also noted there was a 35% rate of "cognitive adverse effects" as determined by chart notation.

Ranjkesh, Barekatain and Akuchakian (2005) compared three different types of ECT: moderate-dose BF, 50% above seizure threshold; high-dose RUL, 4 times seizure threshold; and just above seizure threshold BT in 45 randomly assigned depressed patients. In 39 patients who completed the course of treatment there was no significant difference in efficacy between the three methods, with a significant difference in cognition in favour of BF. A limitation in this study is the use of the MMSE (Folstein et al., 1975) as the only memory test.

Eschweiler et al. (2007) replicated these findings in a study of 94 medication-resistant patients who were randomly assigned to either bifrontal electrode placement at 1.5 times seizure threshold or right unilateral ECT at 2.5 times threshold. Following six treatments administered over a three-week period the study showed no difference in clinical response rates, which were 26%, or cognitive side effects between the two groups, concluding that both placements were reasonably safe and moderately efficacious. It is likely that the low response rates are due to the assessment early in the course of treatment: six sessions, low-stimulus doses and a twice-weekly schedule.

In a critical review of bifrontal ECT, Crowley, Pickle, Dale and Fattal (2008) note that seizures induced by BF affect the brain differently to RUL and BT ECT. They highlight that with BF ECT there is an increase in cerebral blood flow in the frontal lobes that is more intense than either of the other electrode placements, suggesting that cognitive impairment with this placement may be different and affects executive function more specifically, suggesting the need for more studies in this area.

Sienaert et al. (2009) challenges the notion that ultrabrief bilateral techniques were ineffective in a study in which they compared the efficacy of ultrabrief-pulse BF and RUL ECT in 81 randomly assigned medication refractory depressed patients. BF was administered at 1.5 times seizure threshold and RUL at 6 times seizure threshold. They demonstrated identical response rates of 78.1% for both groups but the high-dose RUL group required fewer treatments (eight versus 10) to achieve this outcome. This study challenges the view that an ultrabrief pulse width with bilateral ECT may be ineffective (Sackeim et al., 2008).

In a recent multicentred trial, Kellner et al. (2010) compared right unilateral electrode placement (RUL) at 6 times seizure threshold and bifrontal electrode placement (BF) and bitemporal electrode placement (BT) at 1.5 times seizure threshold in 230 patients with bipolar or unipolar major depression. A brief-pulse stimulus (1.0 ms) was applied. All patients underwent a full battery of cognitive testing and completed the Hamilton Depression Rating Scale. All electrode placements were equally efficacious, with remission rates of 55% for RUL, 61% for BF and 64% for BT. In contrast to other studies, there was no cognitive advantage for RUL or BF over BT, there was no difference in executive function and reorientation time was longer for the BF group. These results were disappointing in their inability to discriminate between the three different electrode placements. The high dose used for RUL 6 times seizure threshold compromised the cognitive advantage for this electrode placement but strengthened its capacity to achieve remission.

In 2012, a meta-analysis was published that tried to summarise the data concerning BF ECT (Dunne and McLoughlin, 2012). Eight randomised trials were included; seven studies used the MMSE as the only measure of cognitive function while two studies included more complex measures, complex-figure delayed recall, trail-making tests and verbal learning. They concluded that BF ECT was as effective as BT and RUL ECT but may have modest benefits on specific memory domains. BF MMSE scores declined less than BT but not compared to RUL. BF scored better on the complex-figure recall test than RUL but not on the impaired word recall test. They suggest that BF may have some potential advantages but requires greater characterisation owing to its shorter history compared to the other electrode placements.

In conclusion, the available data to date would suggest that the differences in efficacy for each placement are modest when each placement is optimised with proper technique. There does appear to be some cognitive advantage in using bifrontal electrode placement over bitemporal electrode placement but this finding has not been replicated in the most recent large, randomised control trial (Kellner et al., 2010). Speed of antidepressant effect, an important consideration for those patients with the most clinically acuity, is reported to be faster with BT ECT. Overall, RUL electrode placement continues to have an advantage, with fewer cognitive effects reported.

LEFT ANTERIOR RIGHT TEMPORAL (LART)/LEFT FRONTAL RIGHT TEMPORAL (LFRT) ECT

There has been some confusion with this electrode placement, with left anterior right temporal (LART) being used interchangeably with left frontal right temporal electrode placement (LFRT) when in fact the frontal electrode is positioned differently (Weiss, Hansen, Safranko and Hughes, 2015). The differences in these placements are illustrated in Figure 5.2.5. For LFRT the electrodes are placed in Position 1, right, and Position 6, left, whereas in LART the electrodes placement are placed in Position 1, right, and Position 7. These placements have rarely been studied.

Swartz (1994) first proposed this asymmetrical electrode placement based upon the belief that it would spare the memory centres of the brain, decreasing adverse cognitive effects and improving the efficacy of RUL ECT. The left electrode was placed in the anterior position away from the skull suture line, similar to the position used in bifrontal ECT, whereas the right electrode was maintained in the standard position 2.5 cm above the mid-point of the imaginary line drawn between the

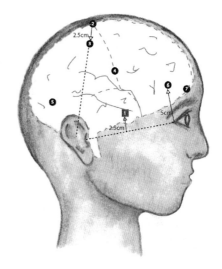

Figure 5.2.5 *Bifrontal electrode placement*

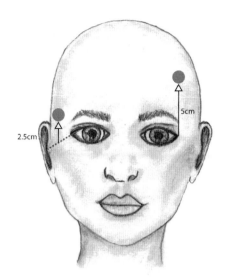

Figure 5.2.6 *Left frontal right temporal electrode placement*

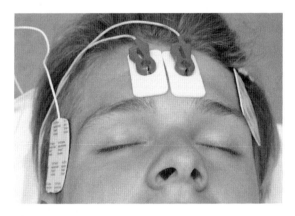

Photo 5.2.14 *Left frontal right temporal Thymatron disposable electrode placement*

Photo 5.2.15 *Left frontal right temporal MECTA handheld electrode placement*

tragus of the ear and the outer canthus of the eye. The set-up for LFRT is illustrated in Figure 5.2.6, Photo 5.2.13 for Thymatron System IV using disposable electrodes and Photo 5.2.15 for the MECTA spECTrum 5000 using handheld electrodes.

Swartz (1994) used this placement in an open trial of 10 women with depression. All met remission criteria after the course of ECT, with an average treatment number of 8.5 sessions with little change in memory at the end of the treatment course, mean MMSE scores reported as 28.4.

In a further study, Manley and Swartz (1994) trialled LART in four patients with major depression. They met remission criteria after six to 11 treatments, with no cognitive impairment using the MMSE. Three of the four patients had received a prior course of ECT with another electrode placement and were reported by family members to have experienced significant cognitive impairment that was also noted in the medical record.

A small, double-blinded study of eight patients with major depression – four randomised to BT ECT and the other four to LART – reported similar efficacy for both electrode placements with less cognitive impairment for LART (Swartz and Evans, 1996).

LART has been used for long-term maintenance ECT (m-ECT). Weiss et al. (2015) reported the successful use of LAFT in maintaining the benefits of m-ECT in three elderly patients who had a history of schizoaffective disorder and complex medical commodities that prevented the use of psychotropic medication. All three patients had become treatment-resistant to previous trials of RUL, BF and BT ECT.

LART ECT has been used successful in a recent acute setting of an 84-year-old man who had a very high seizure threshold. Using a Thymatron System IV device, ineffective threshold seizures were obtained with high-dose ultrabrief ECT. Attempts to elicit effective seizures by changing to brief-pulse RUL ECT resulted in aborted seizures after multiple stimulations at high stimulus energy of 100% (504 mC), 140% (706 mC) and 160% (806 mC) and brief-pulse BT ECT with stimulus doses of 100% (504 mC), 140% (706 mC) and 200% (1008 mC).

The patient gained remission following hyperventilation, a substantial reduction in the dose of thiopentone through the addition of remifentanil and changing to LART ECT with a titration seizure at 100% (504 mC) and four further treatments administered at 140% (706 mC).

OTHER ELECTRODE PLACEMENTS

Since ECT's inception in 1938, a range of other ECT electrode placements have been investigated and are shown in Figure 5.2.5.

These placements include:

- Position 1: temporal electrode placement used in all positions;
- Position 2: Freidman and Wilcox placement (Friedman, 1942; Friedman and Wilcox1942);
- Position 3: d'Elia placement (d'Elia, 1970);
- Position 4: Lancaster placement (Lancester et al., 1958);
- Position 5: McAndrew placement (McAndrew, Berkley and Matthews, 1967);
- Position 6: bifrontal placement (Abrams and Taylor, 1973; Letemendia et al., 1993);
- Position 7: Muller placement (Muller, 1971).

RECOMMENDATIONS FOR CLINICAL PRACTICE

The current complexity of ECT in conjunction with the discrepancies of the evidence makes it challenging for the ECT practitioner to decide how to start and what to do if there is treatment failure. There is growing evidence concerning ultrabrief ECT (0.3 ms) but it is less clear for brief-pulse ECT.

The definition of brief pulse has become a point of intense debate and uncertainty as it can range from 0.5 to 1.0 milliseconds. In part this debate highlights the difference between the evidence, which has examined 1.0 millisecond brief pulse, and practice-based experience, which has used the default setting of 0.5 milliseconds on the Thymatron System IV device since it was released. Clinical experience using the default setting on the Thymatron System IV would suggest a cognitive advantage for all electrodes' placements when used in conjunction with a combination anaesthetic regime, thiopentone and remifentanil, where the remifentanil has been used at high dose to markedly reduce the dose of thiopentone to minimise the impact of thiopentone on seizure expression.

The following practice guidance is based upon a consensus statement that was reached by a group of Australian ECT experts, organised by the Royal Australian and New Zealand College of Psychiatrists (RANZCP) (SEN, 2017).

UNIPOLAR AND BIPOLAR DEPRESSION

There are a number of options avaliable based upon the current evidence and practice-based experience:

- It is now common practice to commence treatment with ultrabrief pulse width (0.3 ms) at 6 times threshold with right unilateral electrode placement owing to the cogntive advantage of this method. Ultrabrief ECT should be considered the default for most patients who are severely unwell but not at high risk. A stronger form of ECT may be necessary in a medial emergency when a patient is under an involuntary order and not able to give informed consent.
- Brief pulse width at 3 to 6 times threshold with right unilateral electrode placement.
- Brief pulse width at 1.5 times threshold with bifrontal electrode placement.

An important consideration in this decision rests upon the need for speed of response, the patient's previous response to ECT and the need to reduce potential cognitive side effects.

Recommendations to use uinlateral ECT as the default placement for patients with unipolar and bipolar depression goes back many years (Abrams, 2002). It is now well known that bi-temporal (BT) ECT can cause retrograde amnesia that can be severe and persistent (McElhiney et al., 1995; Sackeim et al., 2007; Sobin et al., 1995; Squire, Slater and Miller, 1981; Weiner, Rogers, Davidson and Squire, 1986). The severity and risk are dependent upon patient risk factors, the stimulus used, dose above seizure threshold and the number of treatments administered.

If bitemporal ECT is chosen as a first-line treatment for a patient, the rational for this choice needs to be carefully documented in the medical record. If possible, the risk versus benefits of this choice should be discussed with the patient and their families and during the determination by the relevant review tribunal. If bitemporal ECT is choosen it should be adminstered using a brief pulse width at 1.5 times seizure threshold.

Close monitoring of the patient is vital for all forms of ECT, particularly for bitemporal electrode placement, to detect any cognitive changes early in the course of treatment so that changes can be made to the treatment schedule to limit severe and/or persistant retrogreade amnesia and assess clinical improvement. It is highly recommended that reorientation be asssessed after each treatment using scales like "time to recovery" or the brief ECT congitive screen (BECS) (Martin et al., 2013). The test results should be reviewed before the next treatment is adminstered to inform decision-making concerning continuing, altering the schedule or ending the course of ECT.

If bitemporal ECT is the preferred choice it is strongly recommended that pulse widths greater than 1.0 milliseconds wiith high stimulus doses or sine wave ECT should be avoid owing to the strong evidence that it is associated with marked cognitive impairment.

If ultrabrief unilateral ECT has been commenced, consider switching to brief-pulse unilateral or bifrontal ECT if there has been no discernable improvement after six treatments. If brief-pulse unilateral ECT has been commenced, switching to a stronger form of treatment may be considered earlier, after treatment 4. Brief-pulse bifrontal or bitemporal ECT should be considered if there is no improvement after six to eight treatments. If there is a marked deterioration in clinical severity as treatment progresses, consideration should be given to switching earlier or choosing a bilateral approach. Fully informed consent is fundamental to the administration of ECT and is particularly necessary when stronger forms of treatment are being considered.

Clinical presentations can be complicated, making it difficult to decide on the correct type of ECT to administer, taking into consideration pulse width, dosing and combination of electrode placements. Limited evidence on bifrontal and bitemporal ECT suggests lower effiacy for ultrabrief than brief-pulse. If in doubt, discussing treatment options with an experienced ECT practitioner is strongly recommended.

SCHIZOPHRENIA

ECT may be considered as a treatment option for patients with schizophrenia and is the second most common diagnosis treated in the USA, Canada, Europe and Third World countries (Chanpattana and Sackeim, 2010). ECT can be administered in combination with antipsychotic medication when a rapid clinical response is an urgent priority and in patients with treatment-resistant schizophrenia who have an inadequate response to antipsychotic medication alone (Petrides et al., 2015). Acute positive symptoms respond to ECT when used in conjunction with antipsychotic medication as well as schizophrenia associated with depression. The adverse cognitive effects of ECT in people with schizophrenia appear to be consistent with those observed in the treatment of depression.

A limited analysis of data from studies comparing bitemporal and unilateral ECT found no clear advantage for either electrode placement (Tharyan and Adams, 2005).

The clinical decision to administer ECT to a patient with schizophrenia are similar to those with depression. It is essential to balance efficacy and speed of response against side effects. Less is known about the optimal ECT electrode placement for the treatment of schizophrenia. One study suggested that bifrontal ECT may be more effective than bitemporal ECT in people with schizophrenia and schizoaffective disorder, with the added benefit of causing less cognitive impairment (Phutane, Thirthalli and Muralidharan, 2013), a finding yet to be replicated. Ultrabrief ECT is likely to have significant advantages in reducing cognitive side effects, although its efficacy in schizophrenia is unproven.

REFERENCES

Abrams, R. (2002b). *Electroconvulsive Therapy*, 4th edition. New York: Oxford University Press.

Abrams, R., Dornbush, R.L., Feldstein, S., Volavka, J., and Roubicek, J. (1972). Unilateral and bilateral electroconvulsive therapy. Effects on depression, memory, and the electroencephalogram. *Archives of General Psychiatry*, 27(1), 88–91. Retrieved from www.ncbi.nlm.nih.gov/pubmed/5032728.

Abrams, R., and Fink, M. (1972). Clinical experiences with multiple electroconvulsive treatments. *Comprehensive Psychiatry*, 13(2), 115–121. Retrieved from www.ncbi.nlm.nih.gov/pubmed/5010591.

Abrams, R., Swartz, C.M., and Vedak, C. (1989). Antidepressant effects of right versus left unilateral ECT and the lateralization theory of ECT action. *American Journal of Psychiatry*, 146(9), 1190–1192.

Abrams, R., and Taylor, M.A. (1973). Anterior bifrontal ECT: a clinical trial. *British Journal of Psychiatry*, 122(570), 587–590. Retrieved from www.ncbi.nlm.nih.gov/pubmed/4717031.

American Psychiatric Association. (2001). *The Practice of Electroconvulsive Therapy: Recommendations for Treatment, Training and Privileging: A Task Force Report*, 2nd edition. Washington, DC: American Psychiatric Association.

Bailine, S.H., Rifkin, A., Kayne, E., Selzer, J.A., Vital-Herne, J., Blieka, M., and Pollack, S. (2000). Comparison of bifrontal and bitemporal ECT for major depression. *American Journal of Psychiatry*, 157(1), 121–123. doi:10.1176/ajp.157.1.121.

Bakewell, C.J., Russo, J., Tanner, C., Avery, D.H., and Neumaier, J.F. (2004). Comparison of clinical efficacy and side effects for bitemporal and bifrontal electrode placement in electroconvulsive therapy. *Journal of ECT*, 20(3), 145–153. Retrieved from www.ncbi.nlm.nih.gov/pubmed/15342998.

Berent, S., Cohen, B.D., and Silverman, A. (1975). Changes in verbal and nonverbal learning following a single left or right unilateral electroconvulsive treatment. *Biological Psychiatry*, 10(1), 95–100.

Bryden, M. (1982). *Laterality: Functional Asymmetry in the Intact Brain*. New York: Academic Press.

Bryden, M., and Steenhuis, R.E. (1991). Issues in the assessment of handedness. In Kitterle, F.L. (Ed.), *Cerebral Laterality: Theory and Research*. Mahwah, NJ: Erlbaum.

Chanpattana, W., and Sackeim, H.A. (2010). Electroconvulsive therapy in treatment-resistant schizophrenia: prediction of response and the nature of symptomatic improvement. *Journal of ECT*, 26(4), 289–298. doi:10.1097/YCT.0b013e3181cb5e0f.

Coffey, C.E. (1993). *The Cinical Science of Electroconvulsive Therapy*. (Vol. 38). Washington, DC: American Psychiatric Press.

Cohen, B.D., Noblin, C.D., Silverman, A.J., and Penick, S.B. (1968). Functional asymmetry of the human brain. *Science*, 162(3852), 475–477. Retrieved from www.ncbi.nlm.nih.gov/pubmed/5683059.

Costello, C.G., Belton, G.P., Abra, J.C., and Dunn, B.E. (1970). The amnesic and therapeutic effects of bilateral and unilateral ECT. *British Journal of Psychiatry*, 116(530), 69–78. Retrieved from www.ncbi.nlm.nih.gov/pubmed/5411010.

Crowley, K., Pickle, J., Dale, R., and Fattal, O. (2008). A critical examination of bifrontal electroconvulsive therapy: clinical efficacy, cognitive side effects, and directions for future research. *Journal of ECT*, 24(4), 268–271. doi:10.1097/YCT.0b013e318168e72c.

d'Elia, G. (1970). Unilateral electroconvulsive therapy. *Acta Psychiatrica Scandinavica, Supplement 215*, 1–98.

d'Elia, G. (1976). Memory changes after unliateral electroconvulsive therapy with different electrode positions. *Cortex*, 12(3), 280–289.

d'Elia, G., and Raotma, H. (1975). Is unilateral ECT less effective than bilateral ECT? *British Journal of Psychiatry*, 126, 83–89.

Daniel, W.F., and Crovitz, H.F. (1983). Acute memory impairment following electroconvulsive therapy, 2: effects of electrode placement. *Acta Psychiatrica Scandinavica*, 67, 57–68.

Dunne, R.A., and McLoughlin, D.M. (2012). Systematic review and meta-analysis of bifrontal electroconvulsive therapy versus bilateral and unilateral electroconvulsive therapy in depression. *The World Journal of Biological Psychiatry, 13*(4), 248–258. doi:10.3109/15622975.2011.615863.

Dunne, R.A., and McLoughlin, D.M. (2013). ECT prescribing and practice. In Waite, J., and Easton, A. (Eds.), *The ECT Handbook,* 3rd edition (pp. 28–44). London: Royal College of Psychiatrists.

Eschweiler, G.W., Vonthein, R., Bode, R., Huell, M., Conca, A., Peters, O., . . . Schlotter, W. (2007). Clinical efficacy and cognitive side effects of bifrontal versus right unilateral electroconvulsive therapy (ECT): A short-term randomised controlled trial in pharmaco-resistant major depression. *Journal of Affective Disorders, 101*(1–3), 149–157. doi:10.1016/j.jad.2006.11.012.

Fleminger, J.J., de Horne, D.J., and Nott, P.N. (1970). Unilateral electroconvulsive therapy and cerebral dominance: effect of right- and left-sided electrode placement on verbal memory. *Journal of Neurology, Neurosurgery, and Psychiatry, 33*(3), 408–411. Retrieved from www.ncbi.nlm.nih.gov/pubmed/5431728.

Folstein, M.F., Folstein, S.E., and McHugh, P.R. (1975). "Mini-mental state": a practical method for grading the cognitive state of patients for the clinician. *Journal of Psychiatric Research, 12,* 189–198.

Freeman, C.P. (2013). Cognitive adverse effects of ECT. In Waite, J., and Easton, A. (Eds.), *The ECT Handbook, 3rd edition*. London: Royal College of Psychiatrists.

Friedman, E. (1942). Unidirectional electrostimulated convulsive therapy. *American Journal of Psychiatry, 99*(218–223).

Friedman, E., and Wilcox, P.H. (1942). Electro-stimulated Convulsive Doses in intact humans by means of unidirectional currents. *Journal of Nervous and Mental Disorders, 96,* 56–63.

Galletly, C., Paterson, T., and Burton, C. (2012). A report on the introduction of ultrabrief pulse width ECT in a private psychiatric hospital. *Journal of ECT, 28*(1), 59. doi:10.1097/YCT.0b013e318221b42e.

Gammon, K. (2013). *Ultrabrief ECT May Ease Depression in the Elderly*. Paper presented at the American Association for Geriatric Psychiatry (AAGP) 2013 Annual Meeting. Los Angeles, CA. Retrieved from www.medscape.com/viewarticle/781103.

Goldman, D. (1949). Brief stimulus electric shock therapy. *Journal of Nervous and Mental Disease, 110*(1), 36–45. Retrieved from www.ncbi.nlm.nih.gov/pubmed/18132845.

Harrison, P. (2015). *PRIDE Continues to Support ECT in Depressed Elderly*. Paper presented at the 28th European College of Neuropsychopharmacology (ECNP) Congress. Amsterdam, The Netherlands.

Heikman, P., Kalska, H., Katila, H., Sarna, S., Tuunainen, A., and Kuoppasalmi, K. (2002). Right unilateral and bifrontal electroconvulsive therapy in the treatment of depression: a preliminary study. *Journal of ECT, 18*(1), 26–30. Retrieved from www.ncbi.nlm.nih.gov/pubmed/11925518.

Inglis, J. (1969). Electrode placement and the effects of ECT on mood and memory in depression. *Canadian Journal of Psychiatry, 14,* 463–471.

Jackson, B. (1978). The effects of unilateral and bilateral ECT on verbal and visual spatial memory. *Journal of Clinical Psychology, 34*(1), 4–13. Retrieved from www.ncbi.nlm.nih.gov/pubmed/641180.

Kellner, C.H. (1997). Left unilateral ECT: still a viable option? *Convulsive Therapy, 13*(2), 65–67. Retrieved from www.ncbi.nlm.nih.gov/pubmed/9253525.

Kellner, C.H., Husain, M.M., Knapp, R.G., McCall, W.V., Petrides, G., Rudorfer, M.V., . . . Lisanby, S.H. (2016). Right unilateral ultrabrief pulse ECT in geriatric depression: phase 1 of the PRIDE study. *American Journal of Psychiatry, 173*(11), 1101–1109. doi:10.1176/appi.ajp.2016.15081101.

Kellner, C.H., Knapp, R., Husain, M.M., Rasmussen, K., Sampson, S., Cullum, M., . . . Petrides, G. (2010). Bifrontal, bitemporal and right unilateral electrode placement in ECT: randomised trial. *British Journal of Psychiatry, 196*(3), 226–234. doi:10.1192/bjp.bp.109.066183.

Kellner, C.H., Tobias, K.G., and Wiegand, J. (2010). Electrode placement in electroconvulsive therapy (ECT): a review of the literature. *Journal of ECT, 26*(3), 175–180. doi:10.1097/YCT.0b013e3181e48154.

Kolshus, E., Jelovac, A., and McLoughlin, D.M. (2017). Bitemporal v. high-dose right unilateral electroconvulsive therapy for depression: a systematic review and meta-analysis of randomized controlled trials. *Psychological Medicine, 47*(3), 518–530. doi:10.1017/S0033291716002737.

Lancester, N.P., Steinert, R.R., and Frost, I. (1958). Unilateral electro-convulsive therapy. *Journal of Mental Science, 104,* 221–227.

Letemendia, F.J.J., Delva, N.J., Rodenburg, M., Lawson, J.S., Inglis, J., Waldron, J.J., and Lywood, D.W. (1993). Therapeutic advantage of bifrontal electrode placement in ECT. *Psychological Medicine, 23*(2), 349–360. doi:10.1017/S0033291700028452.

Little, J.D., Atkins, M.R., Munday, J., Lyall, G., Greene, D., Chubb, G., and Orr, M. (2004). Bifrontal electroconvulsive therapy in the elderly: a 2-year retrospective. *Journal of ECT, 20*(3), 139–141. Retrieved from http://journals.lww.com/ectjournal/Fulltext/2004/09000/Bifrontal_Electroconvulsive_Therapy_in_the.3.aspx.

Loo, C.K., Katalinic, N., Martin, D., and Schweitzer, I. (2012). A review of ultrabrief pulse width electroconvulsive therapy. *Therapeutic Advances in Chronic Disease, 3*(2), 69–85. doi:10.1177/2040622311432493.

Loo, C.K., Katalinic, N., Smith, D.J., Ingram, A., Dowling, N., Martin, D., . . . Schweitzer, I. (2014). A randomised controlled trial of brief and ultrabrief pulse right unilateral electroconvulsive therapy. *International Journal of Neuropsychopharmacology, 18*(1).

Loo, C.K., Sainsbury, K., Sheehan, P., and Lyndon, B. (2008). A comparison of RUL ultrabrief pulse (0.3ms) ECT and standard RUL ECT. *International Journal of Neuropsychopharmacology, 11*(7), 883–890.

McAndrew, J., Berkley, B., and Matthews, C. (1967). The effect of dominant and nondominant unilateral ECT as compared to bilateral ECT. *American Journal of Psychiatry, 124*, 483–454.

McElhiney, M.C., Moody, B.J., Steif, B.L., Prudic, J., Devanand, D.P., Nobler, M.S., and Sackeim, H.A. (1995). Autobiographical memory and mood: effects of electroconvulsive therapy. *Neuropsychology Review, 9*, 501–517.

Magid, M., Truong, L., Trevino, K., and Husain, M. (2013). Efficacy of right unilateral ultrabrief pulse width ECT: a preliminary report. *Journal of ECT, 29*(4), 258–264. doi:10.1097/YCT.0000000000000080.

Manley, D.T., and Swartz, C.M. (1994). Asymmetric bilateral right fronto-temporal left frontal stimulus electrode placement: comparisons with bifronto-temporal and unilateral placements. Convulsive Therapy. *Convulsive Therapy, 10*(4), 267–270. Retrieved from www.ncbi.nlm.nih.gov/pubmed/7850396.

Martin, D.M., Katalinic, N., Ingram, A., Schweitzer, I., Smith, D.J., Hadzi-Pavlovic, D., and Loo, C.K. (2013). A new early cognitive screening measure to detect cognitive side-effects of electroconvulsive therapy? *Journal of Psychiatric Research, 47*(12), 1967–1974. doi:10.1016/j.jpsychires.2013.08.021.

Muller, D.J. (1971). Unilateral ECT. (One year's experience at a city hospital). *Diseases of the Nervous System, 32*(6), 422–424. Retrieved from www.ncbi.nlm.nih.gov/pubmed/5570697.

Murugesan, G. (1994). Electrode placement, stimulus dosing and seizure monitoring during ECT. *Australian and New Zealand Journal of Psychiatry, 28*(4), 675–683. Retrieved from www.ncbi.nlm.nih.gov/pubmed/7794211.

Nobler, M.S., Sackeim, H.A., Solomou, M., Luber, B., Devanand, D.P., and Prudic, J. (1993). EEG manifestations during ECT: effects of electrode placement and stimulus intensity. *Biological Psychiatry, 34*(5), 321–330. doi:10.1016/0006–3223(93)90089-V.

NSW Health. (2010). ECT minimum standard of practice NSW. Retrieved from www.health.nsw.gov.au/policies/pd/2011/pdf/PD2011_003.pdf.

Peters, M. (1995). Handedness and its relation to other indices of cerebral lateralization. In Davidson, R.J., and Hugdal, K. (Eds.) *Brain Asymmetry* (pp. 183–214). Cambridge, MA: MIT Press.

Petrides, G., Malur, C., Braga, R.J., Bailine, S.H., Schooler, N.R., Malhotra, A.K., . . . Mendelowitz, A. (2015). Electroconvulsive therapy augmentation in clozapine-resistant schizophrenia: a prospective, randomized study. *American Journal of Psychiatry, 172*(1), 52–58. doi:10.1176/appi.ajp.2014.13060787.

Phutane, V., Thirthalli, J., and Muralidharan, K. (2013). Double-blind randomized controlled study showing symptomatic and cognitive superiority of bifrontal over bitemporal electrode placement during electroconvulsive therapy for schizophrenia. *Brain Stimulation, 6*, 210–217.

Pisvejc, J., Hyrman, V., Sikora, J., Berankova, A., Kobeda, B., Auerova, M., and Sochorova, V. (1998). A comparison of brief and ulatrabrief pusle stimuli in unilateral ECT. *Journal of ECT, 14*(2), 68–75.

Ramussen, T., and Milner, B. (1977). The role of early left-brain injury in determining lateralization of cerebral speech functions. *Annals of the New York Academy of Science, 299*, 355–369.

Ranjkesh, F., Barekatain, M., and Akuchakian, S. (2005). Bifrontal versus right unilateral and bitemporal electroconvulsive therapy in major depressive disorder. *Journal of ECT, 21*(4), 207–210. Retrieved from www.ncbi.nlm.nih.gov/pubmed/16301878.

SA Health. (2014). South Australian guidelines for electroconvulsive therapy. Retrieved from www.sahealth.sa.gov.au/wps/wcm/connect/0608270046ad5b01b89.

Sackeim, H.A., Decina, P., Kanzler, M., Kerr, B., and Malitz, S. (1987). Effects of electrode placement on the efficacy of titrated, low-dose ECT. *American Journal of Psychiatry, 144*(11), 1449–1455. Retrieved from www.ncbi.nlm.nih.gov/pubmed/3314538.

Sackeim, H.A., Decina, P., Prohovnik, I., and Malitz, S. (1987). Seizure threshold in electroconvulsive therapy: effects of sex, age, electrode placement and the number of treatments. *Archives of General Psychiatry, 44*, 355–360.

Sackeim, H.A., Prudic, J., Devanand, D.P., Kiersky, J.E., Fitzsimons, L., Moody, B. J., . . . Settembrino, J.M. (1993). Effects of stimulus intensity and electrode placement on the efficacy and cognitive effects of electroconvulsive therapy. *New England Journal of Medicine, 328*(12). Retrieved from www.nejm.org/doi/pdf/10.1056/NEJM199303253281204.

Sackeim, H.A., Prudic, J., Devanand, D.P., Nobler, M.S., Lisanby, S.H., Peyser, S., . . . Clark, J. (2000). A prospective, randomized, double-blind comparison of bilateral and right unilateral electroconvulsive therapy at different stimulus intensities. *Archives of General Psychiatry, 57*(5), 425–434. doi:10.1001/archpsyc.57.5.425.

Sackeim, H.A., Prudic, J., Fuller, R., Keilp, J., Lavori, P.W., and Olfson, M. (2007). The cognitive effects of electroconvulsive therapy in community settings. *Neuropsycho-pharmacology, 32*(1), 244–254. doi:10.1038/sj.npp.1301 180.

Sackeim, H.A., Prudic, J., Nobler, M.S., Fitzsimons, L., Lisanby, S.H., Payne, N., . . . Devanand, D.P. (2008). Effects of pulse width and electrode placement on the efficacy and cognitive effects of electroconvulsive therapy. *Brain Stimulation 1*(2), 71–83. doi:10.1016/j.brs.2008.03.001.

Semkovska, M., and McLoughlin, D.M. (2013). Measuring retrograde autobiographical amnesia following electroconvulsive therapy: historical perspective and current issues. *Journal of ECT, 29*(2), 127–133.

SEN. (2017). RANZCP: Section for ECT and Neurostimulation. Retrieved from www.ranzcp.org/Membership/Faculties-sections/Electroconvulsive-Therapy-and-Neurostimulation.aspx.

Sienaert, P., Vansteelandt, K., Demyttenaere, K., and Peuskens, J. (2009). Randomized comparison of ultra-brief bifrontal and unilateral electroconvulsive therapy for major depression: clinical efficacy. *Journal of Affective Disorders, 116*(1–2), 106–112. doi:10.1016/j.jad.2008.11.001.

Sobin, C., Sackeim, H.A., Prudic, J., Devanand, D.P., Moody, B.J., and McElhiney, M.C. (1995). Predictors of retrograde amnesia following ECT. *American Journal of Psychiatry, 152*(7), 995–1001. Retrieved from www.ncbi.nlm.nih.gov/pubmed/7793470.

Spaans H-P, Kho, K.H., Verwijk, E., Kok, R.M., and Stek, M.L. (2013). Efficacy of ultrabrief electroconvulsive therapy for depression: a systematic review. *Journal of Affective Disorders, 150*(3), 720–726.

Spaans H-P, Verwijk, E., and Comijs, H.C. (2013). Efficacy and cognitive side effects after brief pusle and ultrabrief pulse right unilateral electroconvulsive therapy for major depression: a randomized, double-blind, controlled study. *Journal of Clinical Psychiatry, 2013*(74), 11.

Squire, L.R., Slater, P.C., and Miller, P.L. (1981). Retrograde amnesia and bilateral electroconvulsive therapy. Long-term follow-up. *Archives of General Psychiatry, 38*(1), 89–95. Retrieved from www.ncbi.nlm.nih.gov/pubmed/7458573.

Staton, R.D., Hass, P.J., and Brumback, R.A. (1981). Electroencephalographic recording during bitemporal and unilateral non-dominant hemisphere (Lancaster Position) electroconvulsive therapy. *Journal of Clinical Psychiatry, 42*(7), 264–269. Retrieved from www.ncbi.nlm.nih.gov/pubmed/7240112.

Swartz, C.M. (1994). Asymmetric bilateral right fronto-temporal left frontal stimulus electrode placement. *Neuropsychobiology, 10*(4), 174–179.

Swartz, C.M., and Evans, C.M. (1996). Beyond bitemporal and right unilateral electrode placements. *Psychiatric Annals, 26*, 705–708.

Tasmanian Government. (2013). Tasmania's Mental Health Act 2013: a guide for clinicians. Retrieved from www.dhhs.tas.gov.au/__data/assets/pdf_file/0017/152315/Clinicians Guide_CombinedAllChapters.pdf.

Tharyan, P., and Adams, C. (2005). Electroconvulsive therapy for schizophrenia. *Cochrane Database of Systematic Reviews 2 (CD00007).*

Tiller, J.W.G., and Lyndon, R.W. (2003). *Electroconvulsive Therapy: An Australian Guide.* Melbourne, Australia: Australian Post Graduate Medicine.

Tor, P.C., Bautovich, A., Wang, M.J., Martin, D., Harvey, S.B., and Loo, C. (2015). A systematic review and meta-analysis of brief versus ultrabrief right unilateral electroconvulsive therapy for depression. *Journal of Clinical Psychiatry, 10*(4088). doi:10.4088/JCP.14r09145.

Victorian Government. (2014). Victoria's Mental Health Act 2014 (the Act). Retrieved from www.health.vic.gov.au/mentalhealth/mhactreform/.

Waite, J., and Easton, A. (2013). *The ECT Handbook,* 3rd edition. London: Royal College of Psychiatrists.

Warnell, R.L. (2004). Successful use of left-unilateral electroconvulsive therapy in a right-handed male. *Journal of ECT, 20*(2), 123–126.

Weiner, R.D., Rogers, H.J., Davidson, J.R., and Squire, L.R. (1986). Effects of stimulus parameters on cognitive side effects. *Annals of the New York Academy of Science, 462,* 315–325. Retrieved from www.ncbi.nlm.nih.gov/pubmed/3458412.

Weiss, A.M., Hansen, S.M., Safranko, I., and Hughes, P. (2015). Effectiveness of left anterior right temporal electrode placement in electroconvulsive therapy: 3 case reports. *Journal of ECT, 31*(1), e1–3. doi:10.1097/YCT.0000000000000136.

Wilson, I.C., and Gottlieb, G. (1967). Unilateral electroconvulsive shock therapy. *Diseases of the Nervous System, 28*(8), 541–545. Retrieved from www.ncbi.nlm.nih.gov/pubmed/6048417.

Worthington, E. (2015). Electroconvulsive therapy: new ultra-brief depression treatment "more effective", with "fewer side effects", research shows. *ABC News.* Retrieved from www.abc.net.au/news/2015-07-22/shorter-electroshock-treatment-has-fewer-side-effects/6638302.

Stimulus dosing strategies

The work by Sackeim, Decina, Kanzler, Kerr and Malitz (1987) on seizure threshold challenged the notion that elicitation of a generalised seizure is, in and of itself, sufficient for the antidepressant properties of ECT. In order for a treatment to be effective it was necessary to determine a patient's seizure threshold by a titration method to determine the dose required to administered a suprathreshold seizure, particularly for right unilateral ECT (Sackeim, Decina, Prohovnik and Malitz, 1987). Initial clinical practice and the evidence base supporting the technique were mixed (Farah and McCall, 1993), resulting in considerable controversy. Not everyone accepted its validity, arguing that no consistent relationship had ever been detected between the clinical antidepressant response to ECT and either the threshold or the duration of the induced seizure resulting in unnecessary exposure to anaesthesia by administering an ineffective treatment leading to a number of different dosing techniques being proposed (Abrams, 2002; Kellne, 2001; Swartz, 2001).

Regardless of the criticism, the technique of stimulus dose titration gained worldwide popularity. In recent years there has been a growing body of support for this method (Chung and Wong, 2001; Heikman, Tuunainen and Kuoppasalmi, 1999), with one study demonstrating that if the age-based method had been used to determine seizure threshold 30% of females and 8% of males would have received excessive initial treatment stimuli (Tiller and Ingram, 2006). Organisations like the American Psychiatric Association (2001), the Royal College of Psychiatry (Waite and Easton, 2013) and the Royal Australian and New Zealand College of Psychiatry (2007) have recommended the use of this technique during the initial treatment session as it individualises the treatment, minimising cognitive impairment.

In Australia, most state minimum standard ECT guidelines recommend stimulus dose titration as the best method to determine the stimulus at the next treatment session (Chief Psychiatrist of Western Australia, 2015; NSW Health, 2010; Queensland Mental Health Review Tribunal, 2000; SA Health, 2014; Victorian Government, 2014).

CURRENT DEBATE CONCERNING DOSING STRATEGIES

The quest is to find the "ideal treatment". The ideal treatment can be defined as one with a good evidence base, producing a consistent, objectively measurable parameter that reliably predicts anti-depressant potency with minimal cognitive side effects. The titration method aims to identify the ideal treatment starting point, highlighting that fixed dosing strategies result in "overdose" of some patients, particularly when bitemporal ECT is administered, and "underdose" other patients when right unilateral electrode placement is utilised.

FIXED HIGH-DOSE STRATEGY

A fixed high-dose stimulus has been proposed as an alternative method for the first treatment session by Abrams (2002). A high stimulus delivered at the first session is determined by setting the continuously variable stimulation dial on the ECT device to either 70% (252 mC) or 100% (504 mC) of its maximum capacity and maintain this dose throughout the ECT course. This was the predominant technique utilised worldwide since the inception of ECT until it was challenged by the stimulus dose titration method.

The evidence

A study of 76 elderly patients with major depression compared moderately titrated dose (2.25 times seizure threshold) to fixed high-dose stimulus, 403 mC, right unilateral ECT and found that the fixed dose group responded faster and required fewer treatment sessions, but cognitive side effects

CLINICAL WISDOM 5.3.1

The original Thymatron DGx device delivered stimulus energy from 5% (25 mC) to 100% (504 mC). The stimulus was determined by a large dial located on the front left of the device dial, which was originally referred to as the "age dial". This dial was based upon the age-based dosing technique. The manufacturers proposed that age was one of the most consistent determinates of seizure threshold (Abrams, 2002). To make choosing the stimulus dose easy, they recommended that all that was needed was to adjust the dial to the number that corresponded to the patient's age. It soon became apparent that the dose of energy delivered was too strong, resulting in significant cognitive impairment. It was subsequent revised to the half-age-based dosing strategy (Petrides and Fink, 1996), making the "age dial" irrelevant and it soon became known as the stimulus dose "percentage energy dial".

Subsequently, in Europe and Australia the Thymatron DGx device was modified to "2 times dose" by plugging in a Flexi Dial device, illustrated in Photo 1.3.9, into the back of the Thymatron DGx, increasing the stimulus from 100% (504 mC) to 200% (1100 mC). Confusion occurred when MECTA released the spECTrum 5000M device, which had a continuously variable stimulus dial that delivered a stimulus from 2% (22.9 mC) to 100% (1152 mC). The description of the stimulus dose as "50% administered" is still commonly used in countries like Australia, where for many years the predominant ECT device was a Thymatron.

were not examined in detail (McCall, Farah, Reboussin and Colenda, 1995).

These findings were confirmed in a subsequent study of 72 patients with major depression treated with fixed high dose (403 mC) or moderately titrated (2.25 times, mean dose of 136 mC) RUL, with a 67% response in the high-dose group and only a 39% response in the moderately titrated group (McCall, Reboussin, Weiner and Sackeim, 2000). This study extensively tested cognitive effects, demonstrating a distinct advantage for the moderately titrated group, with less impact on autobiographical and post-ECT reorientation times. They concluded that response and cognitive side effects increase as the stimulus dose above threshold is raised.

In a more recent study, Stoppe, Louzã, Rosa, Gil, and Rigonatti (2006) examined 39 elderly in-patients with major depression who were treated with fixed high-dose RUL or fixed high-dose BT. The remission rate was 88.2% for the fixed high-dose RUL, compared to a remission rate of 68.2% for the high-dose BT group. However, there was a significant difference in cognitive outcome favouring the fixed RUL group.

AGE-BASED DOSE STRATEGY

Age-based dosing was a strategy developed by Abrams (2002). This technique aimed at simplifying the dose administered at the first treatment session by setting the continuously variable stimulus dial to the patient's age; for example, a patient who is aged 50 years would be treated with 50% energy.

HALF-AGE DOSE STRATEGY

The half-age method was proposed by Petrides and Fink (1996) in response to criticism that the age-based method resulted in overstimulation of many patients, resulting in marked cognitive impairment. The half-age dose is simple compared to the cumbersome threshold determination strategy that requires multiple stimulations. The continuously variable stimulation dial is set to correspond to half of the patient's age in years (stimulus dose [mC] = 0.5 ×

age) (Abrams, 2002). The study examined an energy estimate in 35 patients who were given bitemporal ECT at half-age in "percent of energy" or joules delivered by the Thymatron or MECTA devices. Half-age energy was 7 joules (30%) higher than titration estimates, corresponding to 55% energy of the age method. The authors concluded that energy dosing by half-age calculation in bilateral ET was simple, practical and avoided overdosing and repeated stimulation, a technique that was effective for BT ECT and a useful substitute for the more complex strategy based upon threshold estimation.

Abrams (2002) notes that the half-age method worked more effectively with a 0.5 millisecond pulse width than with a 1 millisecond or greater pulse width. The authors recommend that this method is best suited to bitemporal and bifrontal ECT.

STIMULUS DOSE TITRATION

In a study of 52 depressed patients, Sackeim et al. (1987) demonstrated that there was a 12-fold difference in the minimal electrical intensity, measured in units of charge (millicoulombs), required to illicit a seizure. The major variables identified were age, sex, electrode placement and number of treatments administered during the ECT course.

Further work challenged the claim that the elicitation of a generalised seizure is, in and of itself, sufficient to account for the antidepressant effect from ECT. Low-dose RUL was highly ineffective and dosing above threshold may be a better predictor of efficacy (Sackeim et al., 1987). Stimulus dose titration has become the standard ECT protocol utilised by many ECT services around the world and in Australia.

CHANGING THE STIMULUS DOSE

Changing the stimulus charge is a fundamental strategy that underpins stimulus dose titration. The most common method used in clinical practice is to times the seizure threshold stimulus setting by a multiple of that dose. For simplicity, the schedule that has been developed for the Thymatron System

Table 5.3.1
Ultra Brief (0.3ms)
Right Unilateral ECT

Titration Protocol - RUL Ultra Brief Pulse 0.3ms					
Titration Stimulus Settings		Go to	Treatment 6 x threshold		
Percent Energy (%)	Millicoulombs (mC)			Percent Energy (%)	Millicoulombs (mC)
2	10	→		10	50
4	20	→		25	126
8	40	→		50	252
15	76	→		90	454
25	126	→		150	756
35*	176	→		200	1008
50*	252	→		200	1008
75*	378	→		200	1008

Dosing Protocol For Subsequent Treatments	2% 10mC	4% 20mC	8% 40mC	15% 76mC	25% 126mC	35% 176mC	50% 252mC	75% 378mC	90% 454mC	150% 756mC	200% 1008mC

Commence 2% (25mC) for all patients

*It is not possible to achieve 6x threshold above this level

For use with a Thymatron System IV or MECTA spECTrum 5000M device
For MECTA spECTrum 5000Q devices refer to user manual or website

Table 5.3.2
Brief Pulse (0.5ms)
Right Unilateral ECT

Titration Protocol - RUL Brief Pulse 0.5m				
Stimulus Settings		Go to	Treatment 3 x threshold	
Percent Energy (%)	Millicoulombs (mC)		Percent Energy (%)	Millicoulombs (mC)
5	25	→	20	101
10	50	→	30	151
15	76	→	50	252
20	101	→	70	353
30	151	→	100	504
50	252	→	140	706

Dosing Protocol For Subsequent Treatments	5% 25mC	10% 50mC	15% 76mC	20% 101mC	30% 151mC	50% 252mC	70% 353mC	100% 504mC	140% 706mC	200% 1008mC

- Commence 5% (25mC) for all electrode placements, male & female younger than 60 years.
- Commence 10% (50mC) for all electrode placements, males & females older than 60 years.
- If no seizure after second stimulation, increase power by 2 levels and stimulate again.
- For the next treatment after stimulus dose titration:
  - Increase 3 levels above threshold when using a combination anaesthetic (induction agent with ultra brief narcotic)
  - Increase 5 levels above threshold when using a single anaesthetic induction agent
- Increase one level for subsequent treatments as threshold rises.

For use with a Thymatron System IV device
For MECTA devices refer to user manual or website

IV device is illustrated in this section. Equivalent dosing tables have been developed for the MECTA spECTrum 5000M and spECTrum 5000Q and can be found on the MECTA website (MECTA Corporation, 2016).

For example, if a threshold seizure were obtained at the setting of 4%, 20 mC, the dose that would be administered at the next treatment session would be 6 times the stimulus setting, 25% or 126 mC. Different dosing strategies are used for different electrode placements. Table 5.3.1 illustrates the dosing strategies for ultrabrief ECT, Table 5.3.2 shows the dosing strategies for brief-pulse right unilateral ECT and Table 5.3.3 illustrates the dosing strategies for brief-pulse bitemporal ECT.

It is of note that 0.5 millisecond is the preferred setting for brief pulse in these schedules, which are used together with a combination anaesthetic regime, thiopentone and remifentanil, where the remifentanil has been used at high dose to markedly reduce the dose of thiopentone to minimise the impact of thiopentone on seizure expression. Higher stimulus dose protocols (5 to 8 times) are recommended if traditional doses of induction agents are utilised. Careful monitoring is required to prevent a more rapid cognitive decline.

CLINICAL WISDOM 5.3.2

One of the challenges facing a junior ECT practitioner is overcoming the confusion that exists concerning dosing strategies. Early literature focused on using "dose levels" to dose above threshold or change the stimulus charge during a course of treatment. This is highlighted in Table 5.3.4, which specifies dosing increments based upon levels. This method was proposed by the Duke University ECT research group, under the leadership of Professor Richard Weiner, who completed much of the early research into ECT practice.

The alternative method to dose above threshold or change the stimulus charge that is frequently noted in the literature is "times seizure threshold". This terminology has come out of the Columbia University ECT research group, under the leadership of Professor Harold Sackeim. This terminology is associated with stimulus dose titration, a technique that is now used worldwide. " X times seizure threshold" refers to the technique of using a multiple of the stimulus setting to determine the dose used at the next treatment session, as illustrated in Tables 5.3.1 to 5.2.3.

Table 5.3.3
Brief Pulse (0.5ms)
Bitemporal (BT), Bifrontal (BT)
Left Frontal Right Temporal (LFRT) ECT

Titration Protocol – BT, BF & LFRT Brief Pulse 0.5m				
Stimulus Settings		**Go to**	**Treatment 1.5 x threshold**	
Percent Energy (%)	Millicoulombs (mC)		Percent Energy (%)	Millicoulombs (mC)
5	25	→	10	50
10	50	→	15	78
15	76	→	25	126
20	101	→	30	151
30	151	→	45	227
50	252	→	75	378

Dosing Protocol For Subsequent Treatments	5% 25mC	10% 50mC	15% 76mC	20% 101mC	30% 151mC	50% 252mC	70% 353mC	100% 504mC	140% 706mC	200% 1008mC

- Commence 5% (25mC) for all electrode placements, male & female younger than 60 years.
- Commence 10% (50mC) for all electrode placements, males & females older than 60 years.
- Increase 1.5 levels above threshold for next treatment
- By convention the *bilateral* dosing protocol is used here for LFRT even though there is limited evidence

For use with a Thymatron System IV device
For MECTA devices refer to user manual or website

Table 5.3.4 Brief-pulse bitemporal and bifrontal ECT (0.5 ms)

Titration Dosing Guide Variables	mC	(%)	Duke Uni. RUL	Level BL	Thymatron System IV mC	System IV %	MECTA SpECTrum 5000m mC	%	Level RUL	Thymatron DGx mC	%
				1			22.9	2%			
M & F RUL (<45 years)	25	5%	1	2	25	5%	34.7	3%	1	25	5%
				3			46.2	4%			
F RUL (>46);	50	10%	2	4	50	10%	57.4	5%	2	50	10%
				5			69.1	6%			
FBL;			3	6	76	15%	80.5	7%	3	76	15%
M RUL				7			92.2	8%			
& BL			4	8	101	20%	126.5	11%	4	126	20%
			5	9	151	30%	161.3	14%	5	176	30%
				10			242.3	21%			
			6	11	252	50%	322.4	28%	6	252	50%
			7	12	353	70%	438.2	38%	7	353	70%
			8	13	504	100%	575.6	50%	8	504	100%
			9	13.5	706	140%	864.6	75%	9		
					806	160%					
					907	180%					
			10	14	1008	200%	1152	100%			

M = Male F = Female   mC = Charge   % = Energy

Changing Power Levels
1. Push and hold % energy button
2. Wait for program to flash
3. Turn dial to the right two or three clicks until 2x flashes
4. Release button
5. Dial up appropriate power

Table 5.3.4 has been included as it demonstrates an older dosing strategy using levels to determine the stimulus dose above seizure threshold and subsequent stimulus doses changes.

DOSE BASED UPON MULTIPLE FACTORS

Benchmark method

An alternative method has been proposed by Swartz (2002). He argues that the stimulus dose titration method has no basis in physiology. He proposed that an alternative method should be based upon a range of other known physiological principles including:

- higher doses of energy produce greater physiological effects, and
- a strong physiological marker like peak heart rate indicates good treatment quality.

He proposed that the first session should commence with a strong stimulus that results in intense physiological effects that act as benchmarks. For subsequent treatments the electrical stimulus dose is gradually adjusted to approximate the lowest dose that produces physiological effects that are near the benchmark. If these markers deteriorate then a higher stimulus dose is required. In this way he proposes that the benchmark fulfils a similar role as a "serum drug level" does in pharmacotherapy (Swartz, 2002). This method has failed to gain acceptance in clinical practice owing to its complexity and lack of evidence base.

Other methods

Other techniques use established algorithms that make allowances for the impact that age, sex and electrode placement has on seizure threshold to guide the dose at the first treatment session. The stimulus dose is then increased by one level (usually 50% increase in energy) according to clinical progress and the quality of the EEG seizure.

REFERENCES

Abrams, R. (2002). *Electroconvulsive Therapy*, 4th edition. New York: Oxford University Press.

American Psychiatric Association. (2001). *The Practice of Electroconvulsive Therapy: Recommendations for Treatment, Training and Privileging: A Task Force Report*, 2nd edition. Washington, DC: American Psychiatric Association.

Chief Psychiatrist of Western Australia. (2015). Chief Psychiatrist's practice standards for the administration of electroconvulsive therapy. Retrieved from www.chiefpsychiatrist. wa.gov.au/wp-content/uploads/2015/12/CP_ECT_Standards_ 2015.pdf.

Chung, K.F., and Wong, S.J. (2001). Stimulus dose titration for electroconvulsive therapy. *Psychiatry and Clinical Neuroscience.*, *55*(2), 105–110. doi:10.1046/j.1440-1819.2001. 00795.x.

Farah, A., and McCall, W.V. (1993). Electroconvulsive therapy stimulus dosing: a survey of contemporary practices. *Journal of ECT*, *9*(2), 90–94. Retrieved from http://journals.lww.com/ ectjournal/Fulltext/1993/06000/Electroconvulsive_Therapy_ Stimulus_Dosing__A.2.aspx.

Heikman, P., Tuunainen, A., and Kuoppasalmi, K. (1999). Value of the initial stimulus dose in right unilateral and bifrontal electroconvulsive therapy. *Psychological Medicine*, *29*(6), 1417–1423.

Kellne, C.H. (2001). Towards the modal ECT treatment. *Journal of ECT*, *17*, 1–2.

McCall, W.V., Farah, B.A., Reboussin, D.M., and Colenda, C.C. (1995). Comparison of the eficacay of titrated, moderate-dose and fixed, high-dose right unilateral ECT in elderly patients. *American Journal of Geriatric Psychiatry*, *3*, 317–324.

McCall, W.V., Reboussin, D.M., Weiner, R.D., and Sackeim, H.A. (2000). Titrated moderately suprathreshold vs fixed high-dose right unilateral electroconvulsive therapy: acute antidepressant and cognitive effects. *Archives of General Psychiatry*, *57*(5), 438–444. doi:10.1001/archpsyc.57.5.438.

MECTA Corporation. (2016). Optical motional sensor. Retrieved from www.mectacorp.com/optical-motion-sensor.html.

NSW Health. (2010). ECT minimum standard of practice NSW. Retrieved from www.health.nsw.gov.au/policies/pd/ 2011/pdf/PD2011_003.pdf.

Petrides, G., and Fink, M. (1996). The "half-age" stimulation strategy for ECT dosing. *Convulsive Therapy*, *12*(3), 138–146. Retrieved from www.ncbi.nlm.nih.gov/pubmed/8872401.

Queensland Mental Health Review Tribunal. (2000). Electroconvulsive Therapy Guideline V2.0. Retrieved from http:// mhrt.qld.gov.au/wp-content/uploads/2010/04/Electro-convulsive-Therapy-Guideline-V2.0–150211.pdf.

RANZCP. (2007). Clinical memorandum #12 electroconvulsive therapy. Melbourne, Australia.

SA Health. (2014). South Australian guidelines for electro-convulsive therapy. Retrieved from www.sahealth.sa.gov.au/ wps/wcm/connect/0608270046ad5b01b89.

Sackeim, H.A., Decina, P., Kanzler, M., Kerr, B., and Malitz, S. (1987). Effects of electrode placement on the efficacy of titrated, low-dose ECT. *American Journal of Psychiatry*, *144*(11), 1449–1455. Retrieved from www.ncbi.nlm.nih.gov/ pubmed/3314538.

Sackeim, H.A., Decina, P., Prohovnik, I., and Malitz, S. (1987). Seizure threshold in electroconvulsive therapy: effects of sex, age, electrode placement, and number of treatments. *Archives of General Psychiatry*, *44*(4), 355–360. doi:10.1001/archpsyc. 1987.01800160067009.

Stoppe, A., Louzã, M., Rosa, M., Gil, G., and Rigonatti, S. (2006). Fixed high-dose electroconvulsive therapy in the elderly with depression: a double-blind, randomized comparison of efficacy and tolerability between unilateral and bilateral electrode placement. *Journal of ECT*, *22*(2), 92–99. Retrieved from http://journals.lww.com/ectjournal/Fulltext/2006/06000/ Fixed_High_Dose_Electroconvulsive_Therapy_in_the.3.aspx.

Swartz, C.M. (2001). Stimulus dosing in electroconvulsive therapy and the threshold multiple method. *Journal of ECT*, *17*, 87–90.

Swartz, C.M. (2002). ECT dosing by the benchmark method. *German Journal of Psychiatry*, *5*, 1–4. Retrieved from www.gjpsy.uni-goettingen.de.

Tiller, J.W.G., and Ingram, N. (2006). Seizure threshold determination for electroconvulsive therapy: stimulus dose titration versus age-based estimations. *Australian and New Zealand Journal of Psychiatry*, *40*(2), 188–192. doi:10.1080/ j.1440-1614.2006.01773.x.

Victorian Government. (2014). Mental Health Act 2014 handbook. Retrieved from www.health.vic.gov.au/mental health/mhact2014/.

Waite, J., and Easton, A. (2013). *The ECT Handbook, 3rd edition*. London: Royal College of Psychiatrists.

The stimulus

STIMULUS PARAMETERS

Identifying which attributes of the electrical stimulus are of greatest significance in producing the desired convulsions for effective ECT has been a major focus of research. Early on it was thought that the efficacy of ECT was related to the induction of a bilateral grand mal seizure, which provided a relatively distinct criterion of stimulus adequacy for the clinician (Weaver, Ravaris, Rush and Paananen, 1974).

The implication was that stimulus characteristics were largely irrelevant, provided that a bilateral convulsion was evoked. This view has been challenged with increasing evidence highlighting that not all bilateral seizures are equally efficacious (Sackeim, Decina, Kanzler, Kerr and Malitz, 1987). Clinical outcome and side effects from ECT are dependent upon not only the absolute electrical dosage administered but also the extent to which electrical dosage exceeds the seizure threshold (Sackeim et al., 1993).

Since the inception of ECT, quantification of the stimulus intensity has utilised Ohm's law, linking voltage (V), current (I) and resistance/impedance (R). The greater resistance to the flow of current, the greater is the voltage required to maintain the same current. The flow of current though a conductor varies directly with the voltage applied and inversely with the resistance (Abrams, 2002). Ohm's law, current, voltage, resistance, frequency, and other stimulus parameters are set out and defined in Table 5.4.1.

There has been considerable debate as to which of these factors should be held constant and which to vary when the stimulus is applied to

Table 5.4.1 Stimulus parameters

Parameters	Definitions
1. Ohm's law	Current is proportional to the voltage applied relative to the resistance encountered. Current = voltage/resistance Applies to direct current (DC) circuits.
1 a. Current	The number of electron per second flowing through a circuit, measured in amperes (A) or milliamperes (mA).
1 b. Voltage	The force that drives the flow of electrons during the stimulus, measured in volts (V). Voltage = current × impedance
1 c. Resistance	Measure of the obstacle to current flow in direct currents, measured in ohms.
2. Impedance	Measure of the obstacle to current flow in alternating currents. The level of resistance that needs to be overcome in order for a current to flow, measured in ohms. Used interchangeably with resistance as capacitance and inductance are not major contributors in ECT.
2 a. Capacitance	The property of being able to accumulate charge.
2 b. Inductance	The property of being able to induce an electromagnetic force or field.
3. Frequency	The number of alterations in direction, cycles of positive and negative flow of current per second, measured in hertz (Hz).
4. Sine wave	A continuous stream of electricity that flows in alternating directions.
3. Brief pulse	Shorts bursts of current interrupted by periods of electrical inactivity. Wider pulses deliver a greater charge than narrow pulses. Characterized by pulse width, frequency, duration and peak current.
3 a. Pulse width	Duration of each pulse, measured in ms.
3 b. Pulse frequency	Pulse pairs per second, measured in hertz (Hz).
3 c. Duration	The length of the entire series of pulses delivered, measured in seconds.
3 d. Peak current	Maximum intensity of each pulse, measured from the zero baseline in amperes.
4. Inter-pulse interval	Length of the electrical silence between bursts of current.
5. Stimulus train	Duration over which brief-pulses are administered.
6. Charge	The quantity of electrons flowing through a circuit over a given period of time equal to the product of the amount of current in a single pulse and the number of pulses delivered in the series, measured in millicoulombs (mC) Charge (mC) = pulse width (ms) × 2×frequency (Hz) × duration (sec) × peak current (mA)
7. Energy	The product of voltage and current over the entire stimulus duration, measured in joules (J).

Energy (J) = current (mA) × voltage (V) × duration (sec) at peak pulse amplitude
Energy= current^2 × dynamic impedance × duration at peak pulse amplitude

elicit a seizure during ECT (American Psychiatric Association, 2001). A further area of discussion has been which parameter best quantifies ECT dosage: energy or charge. Both energy and charge are composite intensity measures that allow the overall stimulus dose to be represented by a single number (Beyer, Weiner and Glenn, 1998). For many years, energy was the composite parameter utilised. The unit of charge is preferable as all of its variables are known before the stimulus is administered, whereas for energy this is not the case, with the value of dynamic impedance unknown until after the passage of the stimulus (Sackeim et al., 1994). Charge has now become the default composite intensity measure on all new devices (MECTA Corporation, 2015; Somatics L.L.C., 2015).

THE ECT ELECTRICAL CIRCUIT

The ECT electrical circuit is set out in Figure 5.4.1. The circuit includes: the ECT device, the stimulus cables, the stimulus electrodes (all low impedance), the scalp (low impedance), the skull (high impedance) and the brain (low impedance). The challenge for effective ECT is to delivering a high-quality stimulus to specific brain areas by overcoming the high resistance of the skull.

IMPEDANCE

The electrical impedance during the passage of the stimulus is a measure of the obstacle to the current flow. It can vary substantially between patients, and from treatment to treatment in the same patient (Coffey, Lucke, Weiner, Krystal and Aque, 1995; Sackeim, Devanand and Prudic, 1991). Impedance is used interchangeably with resistance, as other potential factors involved in alternative currents, capacitance and inductance are not major contributors in ECT. Impedance is the level of resistance that needs to be overcome in order for a current to flow. The greater the resistance, the greater the push or voltage needed for a fixed flow of electrons. Likewise, the lower the impedance the less voltage or push needed to move a fixed flow of electrons.

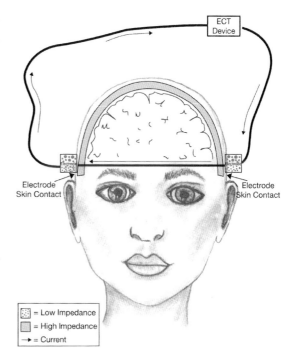

Figure 5.4.1 *Electrical circuit highlighting impedance*

Source: Adapted from Beyer et al., 1998

It is measured in ohms (Beyer et al., 1998). In ECT, high impedance is commonly encountered owing to poor skin preparation and electrode contact, requiring a higher voltage to deliver a given current, making the stimulus less efficient.

Most of the stimulus current is shunted across the scalp tissues between the electrodes without even entering the brain due the extremely high intrinsic impedance associated with the skull (see Figure 5.4.1) (Beyer et al., 1998). If the impedance is too high owing to poor contact of the stimulus electrodes with the skin, the current flows through a smaller area increasing the risk of skin burns and reducing the effectiveness of the stimulus delivered. Skin burns are very rare with modern devices and adequate skin preparation technique.

Impedance can be either static or dynamic:

- Static impedance is the impedance obtained during the test period generated by a very low voltage current through the entire system, allowing estimation before the stimulation is administered. It ranges from 300 to 3000 ohms (see Photos 5.1.16 and 5.1.18).

- Dynamic impedance is the impedance measured during the stimulus current. It can range from 130 to 350 ohms. The impedance of the scalp tissue underlying the stimulus electrode is voltage-sensitive and drops instantaneously during the passage of the stimulus current (Beyer et al., 1998).

The primary source of impedance is the scalp tissue that underlies the stimulus electrodes. In ECT the patient becomes part of a biological electrical circuit, and within this circuit they provide most of the impedance, as shown in Figure 5.4.1. Impedance is higher for women than men, greater for unilateral than bilateral electrode placement and inversely proportional to the electrode size. Impedance can vary substantially between patients and varying from treatment to treatment in the same patient (Coffey et al., 1995).

Common causes of very high static impedance are:

- failure to connect the stimulus cable to the stimulus electrodes;
- inadequate coupling of the stimulus electrode to the scalp through the use of insufficient gel, particularly when hair is in the way or there is too little pressure applied to the stimulus electrode;
- inadequate preparation of the electrode site due to failure to apply the abrasive or non-abrasive gel or lack of vigour in cleaning.

Impedance needs to be considered independently owing to the effect it has on other stimulus parameters, depending upon the design of the ECT device (see the tables). For constant-current design, Ohm's law states that voltage increases with impedance up to the design limits of the instrument (Weaver and Williams, 1986). The actual electrical energy received by the patient would therefore depend on the impedance encountered (Sackeim et al., 1994). It is therefore important to minimise impedance by adequate skin site preparation prior to placement of the electrodes (Beyer et al., 1998)

Both the Thymatron System IV and MECTA spECTrum 5000 devices enable testing of static impedance before the treatment stimulus is administered. The Thymatron System IV has an LED display that shows the impedance after the button is pushed, as shown in Photo 5.7.1, whereas the MECTA spECTrum 5000 device provides continuous updated static impedance on the touch screen as well as printing it on the paper trace at the end of the self-test, as shown in Photo 5.7.7. Both devices record the static and dynamic impedance at the end of the EEG record.

CHARGE

Charge can be defined as the quantity of electrons flowing through a circuit over a given period of time (Beyer et al., 1998; Sackeim et al., 1994). It is usually measured in coulombs or for ECT millicoulombs. For constant-current devices, current is equal to the amplitude of each pulse or peak current that is given over a fixed period of time.

Charge (in mC) is determined by current (in amps [A]) times the pulse width (in ms) multiplied by twice the frequency (in Hz) times the duration (in seconds). The stimulus pulse is biphasic, requiring the frequency to be multiplied by two. Charge is the preferred single composite intensity measure over energy as it is predictable because it is independent of impedance (Beyer et al., 1998); see Table 5.4.1.

Charge (mC) = Current (A) × pulse width (ms) × twice the frequency (Hz) × duration (s).

ENERGY

Energy is the second composite parameter to represent the stimulus dose. It is measured in joules (J), as defined in Table 5.4.1. It is defined as the capacity to do work and overcome resistance. This parameter was used in the early ECT devices before it was recognised that constant-current devices deliver a more reliable stimulus as static impedance can be determined and reduced by better skin preparation enhancing the charge delivered whereas dynamic impedance is only determined after the stimulus has been applied.

Energy relies on the value for the dynamic impedance, which cannot be determined until the passage of the stimulus has occurred, making estimations based upon the low-voltage test of static impedance before treatment inaccurate (Beyer et al., 1998).

CHARGE-RATE

Charge-rate is defined as the rate at which the total charge is delivered over time and is measured in millicoulombs per second (mC/sec). It is the product of the stimulus parameters noted above. It has been shown that lower charge-rates are consistent with greater efficacy in seizure induction and better quality seizures (Swartz, 1994; Swartz,

1994a). Low charge-rates produce better outcomes, as it is easier to induce a seizure that is of high quality with lower levels of energy, thereby minimising memory impairment. High charge-rates are ineffective and result in more pronounced side effects (Sackeim et al., 1994).

THE ACTION POTENTIAL

Familiarity with some of the basic principles of neuronal physiology is important in understanding the electrical stimulus applied in ECT. The action potential, illustrated in Figure 5.4.2, is the basic mechanism by which electrical energy travels along a neuronal axon. Action potentials are generated by specific voltage-gated ion channels embedded within the cell membrane that are shut when the membrane potential is near the resting potential. Following a stimulus they rapidly open, allowing sodium ions to rush into the neuron, which has a relative negative charge compared to the outside, changing the electrochemical gradient increasing

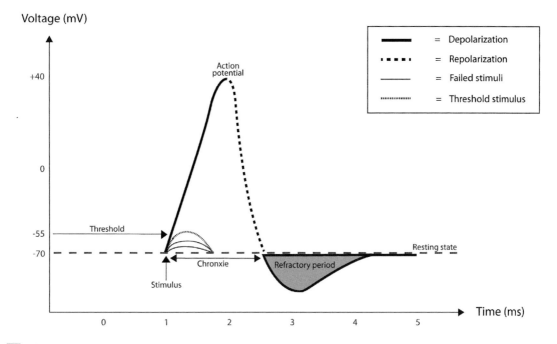

Figure 5.4.2 *Action potential*

the membrane potential causing more channels to open. The process continues rapidly until all of the ion channels have opened causing a large increase in membrane potential. The sodium ion channels close and they are actively transported out of the membrane. Potassium channels are then activated and there is an outward flow of potassium ions returning the electrochemical gradient back to the resting state after a transient negative shift during which the plasma membrane is incapable of firing. The sodium and potassium gated ion channels open and close as the membrane reaches the threshold potential in response to a signal from another neuron (Guyton and Hall, 2016).

The action potential can be divided into five phases: the rising phase, the peak phase, the falling phase, the overshoot phase and the refractory phase. It consists of:

- Depolarisation: The inward flow of sodium ions that follows a threshold stimulus increasing the concentration of positively charged cations in the cell causing the potential of the cell to be higher than the cell's resting potential leading to the rising phase.
- Repolarisation: The outward flow of cations from the cell causing a change in the membrane potential that returns it to a negative value after the depolarisation phase, the falling phase.
- Refractory period: The period of time after an action potential has been generated in which the neuron is unable to be depolarised no matter how strong the stimulus.
- Chronaxie: The optimum current duration required to produce neuronal depolarisation usually between 0.1 and 0.2 milliseconds (Sackeim et al., 1994).

INAPPROPRIATE STIMULI

Inappropriate stimuli are those that have excessive pulse width, requiring more energy to produce depolarisation, and those that have too high a frequency and are crowded too closely together.

CLINICAL WISDOM 5.4.1

Low charge-rate stimuli have low frequency (70 Hz), short pulse-width (0.2–0.5 ms) and long duration (Abrams, 2002). The introduction of the Thymatron System IV device in the early 2000s to clinical practice resulted in a striking change in the capacity to generate suprathreshold seizures at much lower energy levels when the default setting of "Low 0.5" was used during the delivery of the stimulus, with equivalent improvement in cognitive outcomes. As noted by Abrams, a lower charge-rate produced a better outcome, inducing seizures of better quality at lower levels of energy, minimising memory impairment.

While many centres used this setting, clinical practice did not conform to the evidence current at that time for brief-pulse ECT that utilised a stimulus of 1.0 milliseconds (ms). Evidence supporting the use of ultrabrief pulses is a recent phenomenon with the advent of ultrabrief ECT utilising a pulse width of 0.3 ms. This form of ECT has become the gold standard when the need for urgent treatment is not required.

Stimuli generated by sine wave devices are inappropriate as they deliver charge during the refractory period, leading to increased adverse effects.

CONSTANT CURRENT

Recent work on the neurobiological effects of electrical stimulation in neural tissue has suggested that constant-current was a more rational approach to device instrumentation than the use of constant-voltage or constant-energy principles as current was of greater physiological significance (Abrams, 2002).

A constant-current device delivers constant current and allows voltage to vary proportionally with impedance (electrical resistance) offered by the head of the patient during the application of stimulus.

In a constant-voltage device the voltage is held constant while the current varies inversely with resistance. It is therefore possible with constant-voltage devices that they may not induce an adequate seizure as high impedance levels can occur owing to poor skin preparation, resulting in decreased current intensity, with this parameter only determined after the stimulus has been delivered (Sackeim et al., 1994).

With constant-energy devices (Medcraft Corporation, 1986) the stimulus is delivered until a preset amount of stimulus energy has been reached by allowing charge to varying inversely with dynamic impedance (Beyer et al., 1998). As a result, less energy is delivered if the patient has very high impedance, reducing the intensity of the seizure elicited, making it a less effective stimulus and reducing clinical response.

The American Psychiatric Association Task Force (American Psychiatric Association, 2001) recommended that modern ECT devices be constant-current and square wave, with EEG monitoring built in. They should replace all other devices. Contemporary machines such as MECTA spECTrum 5000 and Thymatron System IV are examples of this type of device.

It is of concern that this recommendation had been ignored by some large New York hospital ECT services, where treatment continued to be delivered with sine wave devices as late as the mid-2000s (Sackeim et al., 2007).

WAVE FORM

The nature and type of waveform utilised in ECT has been the subject of considerable research over many years. Brief-pulse square waves have been extensively investigated and are illustrated in Figure 5.4.3.

These wave forms consist of a series of short bursts of current flow interrupted by longer periods of electrical inactivity, which results in considerably

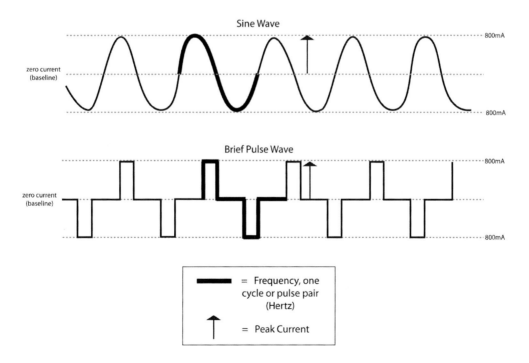

Figure 5.4.3 *Sine and brief-pulse waves*

lower energy content being delivered (Murugesan, 1994). This contrasts to the traditional sine wave-form: a slow rising current that delivers higher stimulus energy. Brief-pulse stimuli require less charge (mC) or energy (J) than a sine wave stimulus to elicit a seizure (Weiner, 1980). Studies have shown that sine wave stimulation is associated with more severe cognitive side effects than brief-pulse waveforms (Carney et al., 1976; Valentine, Keddie and Dunne, 1968; Weiner et al., 1986).

It is believed that the leading edge of the wave-form is responsible for neuronal depolarisation and seizure induction (American Psychiatric Asso-ciation, 2001). For sine waveforms, a slow rising current can increase the firing threshold of neurons through the process of accommodation. This is in contrast to a fast rising current, which can elicit the seizure at lower current intensity. A fast rising current is also known as a brief pulse (Koester, 1985).

After a neuron has depolarised, it enters a refractory period, which prevents further depolar-isation for a certain time period. In ECT, an applied stimulus needs to be of the right type; continuing to stimulate a neuron during the refractory phase contributes to a higher level of side effects.

A brief-pulse stimulus was first used for ECT in the 1940s, producing seizures with smaller amounts of electrical energy aimed at reducing adverse central nervous system effects (Liberson, 1948). Valentine et al. (1968) demonstrated the benefits of a pulse current of low-power over high-power sinusoidal current, producing less post-treatment "confusion and amnesia".

Weaver et al. (1977) showed that low-energy brief-pulse stimuli required less current and only half the total energy to produce clinically effective convulsions with no significant cognitive impair-ment. Not all agreed with this finding (Shellen-berger, Miller, Small, Milstein and Stout, 1982; Spanis and Squire, 1981; Squire and Zouzounis, 1986). Squire and Zouzounis (1986) acknowledged that there was an early advantage for a brief-pulse stimulus within the first hour after treatment but this advantage was subsequently lost. Weiner (1982)

noted in his review of the literature that many of the early papers were methodologically flawed, preventing progress.

It was not until the mid-1980s that there was convincing evidence that the cognitive impair ment associated with an interrupted brief-pulse stimulus waveform was significantly less than those linked with the more traditional sine wave stimu-lus (Coffey et al., 1995; Daniel and Crovitz, 1983; Weiner and Krystal, 1994; Weiner et al., 1986). By 1990, brief-pulse square wave stimuli were accepted into contemporary ECT practice (American Psychi-atric Association, 1990; Freeman et al., 1989).

A survey conducted in 1989 into the practice of ECT in Australia and New Zealand showed that all ECT devices used were of this type, with the majority of patients (63%) receiving RUL com-pared to practice in the United States of America, the United Kingdom and New Zealand, where the majority of patients received BT ECT (O'Dea, Mitchell and Hickie, 1991).

PULSE WIDTH

History

Wider pulses deliver a greater charge than narrow ones but are inefficient in eliciting seizures as they involve current exposure after neurons have depolarised (Sackeim et al., 1994). Swartz (1994b) commented that the much broader width of the traditional sine wave stimulus underlies its lower efficiency and greater side effects. He noted that maximum stimulus efficiency should correspond to a pulse width and frequency that most closely correspond to the times taken by neural depolarisa-tion, axonal and synaptic transmissions and repolarisation. Different pulse widths are illustrated in Figure 5.4.4.

It was believed that the optimal current duration to produce central neuronal depolarisation is between 0.1 and 0.2 ms, known as the chronaxie (Sackeim et al., 1994). Pulse widths greater than one millisecond had no advantage (Sackeim et al., 1994; Weaver et al., 1974; Weaver and Williams,

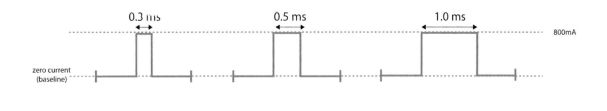

Figure 5.4.4 *Different pulse widths with positive cycle*

1986).

Hyrman, Palmer, Cernik and Jetelina (1985) suggested that the stimulus capable of producing seizures reliably with the least energy consisted of brief, unidirectional pulses, between 40 and 60 microseconds in duration, applied at a frequency between 100 Hz and 300 Hz, a finding confirmed by later work that an ultrabrief pulse width (less than 0.5 ms) was particularly efficient at eliciting a seizure (Lisanby and Sackeim, 1997). Early on there was concern that this form of stimulus may be associated with less effective seizures that required additional treatments to produce a therapeutic response (Cronholm and Ottosson, 1963; Robin and de Tissera, 1982; Weiner, 1982), creating a general reluctance to use ultrabrief pulse configurations in routine clinical practice at that time (American Psychiatric Association, 2001).

Current practice

Following the work by Sackeim et al. (2008), which demonstrated a marked cognitive advantage for ultrabrief, right unilateral ECT with only a modest reduction in efficacy, there were many randomised controlled trials confirming these results (Galletly, Paterson and Burton, 2012; Harrison, 2015; Loo, Katalinic, Martin and Schweitzer, 2012; Loo et al., 2014; Loo et al., 2008; Magid, Truong, Trevino and Husain, 2013; Sienaert, Vansteelandt, Demyttenaere and Peuskens, 2009; Spaans et al., 2013), as well as a meta-analysis (Tor et al., 2015). Ultrabrief ECT should be considered as a first-line treatment for the majority of patients with major depression owing to the marked reduction in cognitive side

CLINICAL WISDOM 5.4.2

The introduction of the Thymatron System IV device in 2002 resulted in striking changes to clinical practice when the default stimulus pulse width of 0.5 ms was utilised. Early observation highlighted that when patients were retitrated using this technique the stimulus charge required to elicit a seizure was at least 50% less than the dose of energy previously administered. Improvement occurred rapidly, with fewer cognitive side effects, a clinical observation that is now confirmed by the evidence supporting ultrabrief ECT.

effects and only a slight reduction in efficacy when urgent intervention is not required.

INTER-PULSE INTERVAL

The inter-pulse interval has not been thoroughly studied (Weaver and Williams, 1986). Seizures can be reliably induced with a stimulus that has an inter-pulse interval between 10 and 30 milliseconds, with the standard being defined as 30 milliseconds (Weaver, Ives and Williams, 1982).

STIMULUS TRAIN

The stimulus train refers to the duration over which brief pulses are delivered. Weaver, Ives and Williams (1978) noted that significantly fewer pulses were required for unilateral electrode placement compared to bilateral treatment. In further work they specified that the optimal stimulus train duration lies in the range of three to five seconds. However, this depends upon other parameters such as pulse width, frequency and peak current.

Swartz and Larson (1989) compared the seizure durations of patients who received the same absolute stimulus intensity (in charge) using either shorter or longer train duration. They concluded that the longer-duration stimulus packages were more efficient in eliciting adequate seizures than the shorter duration configuration. Sackeim et al. (1994) noted that manipulating the stimulus train duration may be a particularly efficient means of adjusting stimulus dosage relative to increasing pulse width, pulse frequency or current intensity. However, they caution that long stimulus trains might cause excessive cognitive dysfunction by applying additional stimulation after the seizure has already begun.

Abrams (1994) challenged this view, stating that long stimulus trains have been used routinely for many years by Scandinavian investigators without incurring excess cognitive dysfunction.

In a further study, Devanand, Lisanby, Nobler and Sackeim (1998) confirm that manipulating stimulus duration was more efficient than changing the frequency, resulting in a significantly lower seizure threshold, with a mean of 94 mC compared to 114 mC, and there was a trend towards fewer stimulations administered to induce a seizure for the stimulus train group.

FREQUENCY

Frequency refers to the number of electrical pulses per second delivered during the stimulus application. Murugesan (1994) noted that a frequency of 70 Hz is equal to 140 pulses per second as the pulse wave is bidirectional. Hyrman et al. (1985) showed that the seizure threshold dropped sharply as the frequency went from seven to 100 pulses per second but did not change significantly from 100 to 300 pulses per second, making a stimulus frequency between the ranges of 100 to 300 Hz the most efficient.

More recent work suggests that lower frequencies are more effective in inducing seizures than high frequencies (Peterchev, Rosa, Deng, Prudic and Lisanby, 2010). These findings have been supported by other work, where initiating stimulus dose titration to determine seizure threshold by increasing frequency was less effective than altering the stimulus train and required an increased level of charge (Devanand et al., 1998). Further study is required to determine the precise number of pulses required in a stimulus to induce an adequate seizure with good efficacy and reduced side effects.

AMPLITUDE

Pulse amplitude has been the one parameter in the ECT stimulus that has been the most neglected, with most devices holding a fixed current amplitude – 900 mA for the Thymatron System IV and 800 mA for the MECTA spECTrum 5000M, with the MECTA spECTrum Q offering a narrow range of adjustability between 500 and 800 mA (Peterchev et al., 2010). In other brain stimulation therapies like repetitive transcranial magnetic stimulation (rTMS) or deep brain stimulation (DBS), the central role of the pulse amplitude in controlling the volume of stimulated neurons is well recognised (Peterchev et al., 2010).

In ECT, the amplitude of the ECT current pulse is directly proportional to the magnitude of the induced electric field, thereby providing the most immediate control over the amount of brain tissue that is directed activated by the ECT stimulus. It is possible that low current amplitudes can trigger adequate seizures with therapeutic efficacy and reduced side effects (Peterchev et al., 2010).

Computational modelling of direct brain excitation induced by ECT demonstrated that a reduction in stimulus amplitude and pulse width led to a reduction in the spatial extent of brain activation (Bai, Loo, Al Abed and Dokos, 2012). Individualisation of pulse amplitude may compensate for anatomical head variability, leading to more consistent clinical outcomes (Deng, Lisanby and Peterchev, 2009), with other work suggesting that reduction in pulse amplitude may reduce side effects from ECT (Deng, Lisanby and Peterchev, 2011).

In a small case series, five patients with major depression were successfully stimulated with a 0.5 A current amplitude, nearly half of the conventional level of 0.8 to 0.9 A (Rosa, Abdo, Lisanby and Peterchev, 2011). Further work is required to evaluate the therapeutic efficacy and adverse effect profile of ECT with reduced and potentially individualised current amplitude.

STIMULUS DOSE

The stimulus dose refers to the dosage of charge that is applied to induce a seizure during ECT. For many years it has been asserted that, independent of dosage, the elicitation of a generalised seizure was necessary and sufficient for the antidepressant properties of ECT: "any seizure was good enough" (Sackeim, Decina, Prohovnik and Malitz, 1987). Standard practice was to administer the same electrical dose to all patients. When a fixed dose was used, many patients might receive stimulation far in excess of that necessary to elicit an adequate ictal response, resulting in significant cognitive side effects, while others might receive an insufficient dose and fail to respond (Sackeim et al., 1993).

Further, it has been shown that low-dose. bilateral ECT had a powerful antidepressant effect but low-dose unilateral therapy was ineffective (Sackeim et al., 1987). It is now known that not all symmetrical seizures are equally efficacious and the clinical outcome and side effects depend not on the absolute electrical dosage administered during ECT but upon the extent to which the electrical

dosage exceeds the seizure threshold (Sackeim et al., 1993). This has led to the concept of "suprathreshold dosing".

SEIZURE THRESHOLD

An important concept underlying the findings highlighted above is seizure threshold. Seizure threshold can be defined as the amount of charge required to induce a seizure with fixed pulse amplitude (Sackeim et al., 1987).

It is thought that each stimulus pulse initiates depolarisation in one or more neurons in close proximity to the stimulating electrodes while lowering the threshold in neurons further away. Temporal summation then occurs with further pulses, collectively lowering individual neuronal membrane potentials in a cumulative way, resulting in depolarisation (Abrams, 2002). Recruitment or inter-neuronal spatial summation also occurs, generating foci of seizure activity that join together and spread across the cortical surface into the subcortical structures, initiating a generalised seizure.

Factors that impact on seizure threshold include (Beyer et al., 1998; Mankad, Beyer, Weiner and Krystal, 2010):

- advanced age;
- male sex;
- bilateral electrode placements, bifrontal greater than bitemporal;
- stimulus parameters, namely pulse width;
- treatment number: it is known that there is progressive increase in seizure threshold during a course of ECT;
- lack of oxygenation before treatment is delivered;
- poor skin preparation;
- medications, particularly anticonvulsants;
- anaesthetic agents:
  - propofrol;
  - thiopentone;
  - methohexital (less than the others);

- seizure-neutral drugs:
  - ketamine;
  - ultrabrief acting narcotic agents;
  - muscle relaxants like suxamethonium, rocuronium and mivacurium;
  - hypoglycaemic drugs;
  - anticoagulant medications;
  - antihypertensive agents;
- antipsychotic medications, which usually reduce seizure threshold, particularly clozapine, for which a known complication is spontaneous seizures;
- neurological conditions, which may raise or lower seizure threshold.

EEG "THERAPEUTIC WINDOW"

An assumption that underlies stimulus dose titration is that, whenever the dose is increased to account for rising seizure threshold, an improvement in EEG morphology will always result. The morphology of the ictal EEG has become the means by which rises in seizure threshold are monitored

and detected. It has become common practice to increase the stimulus to overcome this phenomena to ensure effective treatment (Lyndon, 2001). Clinical wisdom would suggest that this is not always the case, particularly when the stimulus is set at high energy levels.

Lyndon (2001) notes that it is not infrequent at high energy levels, greater than 100%, for the EEG morphology to remain poor even when the energy level has been increased. This suggests that at higher doses the relationship between increased dose and improved EEG quality may be lost, suggesting that there is a "therapeutic window" effect. This phenomenon has been observed during the administration of cardioversion.

Brief, poor-quality seizures can be due to either insufficient or markedly suprathreshold stimulus intensity. Namely, short seizures can be due to stimulus parameters that are either too low or too high (Riddle, Scott, Bennie, Carroll and Fink, 1993; Sackeim et al., 1991). This means that abortive seizures caused by stimulus parameters that are too low will be ineffective, while those from para-

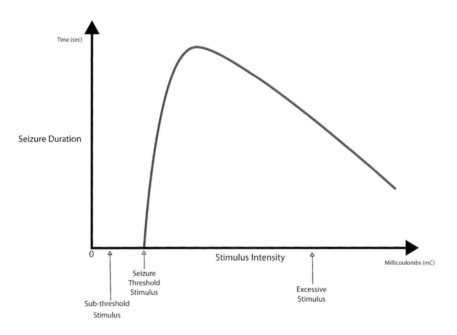

Figure 5.4.5 *Relationship between seizure duration and stimulus intensity*

meters that are set high may well be therapeutic (Sackeim et al., 1991). As a result, restimulation will be necessary in the former situation but not in the latter.

Figure 5.4.5 illustrates these phenomena. There is a complex relationship between relative stimulus intensity, namely the extent to which the stimulus exceeds seizure threshold, and seizure duration. This relationship is not linear. As shown in Figure 5.4.5, when the stimulus is barely suprathreshold increasing stimulus intensity will extend seizure duration. This is in contrast to very high stimuli, which greatly exceed seizure threshold where seizure duration typically shortens. Increased treatment numbers produce a rise in seizure threshold and seizure duration falls, shifting the curve to the right and downwards in the curve depicting the relationship between stimulus intensity and seizure duration (Mankad et al., 2010).

Lyndon (2001) recommends that retitration to determine seizure threshold may be necessary if the patient fails to respond when recent stimulus dose increases have failed to produce improvement in clinical response and the quality of the ictal EEG or the maximum of stimulus dose of 1008 mC (Thymatron) or 1152 mC (MECTA) has been reached.

Retitration often results in significant improvement in seizure parameters, which can improve therapeutic efficacy, potentially reducing cognitive impairment owing to the lower stimulus charge. The therapeutic window is more commonly encountered in patients who are having maintenance ECT, where seizure threshold rises slowly over a long period of time (Lyndon, 2001).

STIMULUS DOSE TITRATION

Stimulus dose titration is a technique that individualises the amount of energy given to a patient to prevent under- or overstimulation due to the large variation in seizure threshold between patients to improve efficacy and reduce the level of cognitive impairment (Sackeim et al., 1987). This work demonstrated that low-dose non-dominant uni-

CLINICAL WISDOM 5.4.4

It is still recognised that bitemporal electrode placement is the most efficacious ECT treatment but the technique is limited by more severe cognitive impairment. High-dose RUL six times seizure threshold, although better than BT ECT, continues to have a substantially greater risk of cognitive impairment compared to moderate-dose RUL ECT where treatment is administered 3 times above seizure threshold. Cognitive side effects were particularly less when moderate dose RUL was combined with the default Thymatron setting of 0.5 ms pulse width.

The stimulus dose titration schedule has become widely used throughout Australia. Dosing protocols have changed dramatically with the advent of ultrabrief ECT and the potential to reduce the anticonvulsant properties of the induction agent by the addition of an ultrabrief narcotic agent.

lateral ECT was ineffective (Sackeim et al., 1987). In a large study of 134 patients, stimulus dose titration was shown to be a safe and effective method for determining seizure threshold, enabling suprathreshold stimulus doses to be determined on an individual basis for subsequent treatments, thus optimising ECT technique (Beale et al., 1994).

Increasing the electrical dosage above seizure threshold (suprathreshold dosing) increases the efficacy of right unilateral ECT (RUL) to that of bitemporal ECT but maintains the benefits of less severe cognitive impairment except when the dose above seizure threshold is very high (McCall, Reboussin, Weiner and Sackeim, 2000).

Sackeim et al. (2000), in a study of 80 depressed patients, showed that RUL dosed at 500% above threshold had a response rate of 65% equivalent to BT ECT, with less severe and persistent side effects at two months follow-up. Patients treated with RUL 50% or 150% above seizure threshold had lower response rates of 35% and 30%, respectively.

COMBINED TITRATION AND TREATMENT

Tiller and Lyndon (2003) advocated that it is preferable to administer a suprathreshold stimulus (treatment) soon after threshold has been determined under the same anaesthetic to reduce the number of treatments administered during an index course of ECT. In their experience, this technique minimises the confusion and disorientation that can sometimes occur after a titration session, particularly if a number of subconvulsive stimulations have been administered.

The technique involves administering a treatment stimulus (3 to 6 times threshold) under the same general anaesthetic, a few minutes following the determination of seizure threshold by a titration method, after the patient has been hyperventilating with 100% oxygen.

In practice-based experience, administering a titration and treatment with a brief-pulse stimulus under the same anaesthetic did not minimise the confusion and disorientation but rather contributed to higher levels of postictal confusion and persistent cognitive impairment. The author does not recommend restimulation during a titration session owing to recent work highlighting that the ECT-naïve brain is very sensitive to electrical stimulation that leads to widespread neuroplasticity in neocortial, limbic and paralimbic regions with these changes related to the extent of the antidepressant response (Pirnia et al., 2016). It is unclear whether restimulation during later titration sessions may be acceptable.

SUBCONVULSIVE STIMULATION

A major concern with the stimulus dose titration method has been that it may expose the patient to unnecessary cardiac risks with repeated subconvulsive stimulation initiating a sustained parasympathetic response. The early ECT literature contained reports of adverse cardiovascular events including bradycardia, bigeminy, nodal arrhythmias and a drop in blood pressure (McCall, Reid and Ford, 1994), with other reports of sudden cardiac standstill, hypertension and tachycardia (Partridge, Weinger and Hauger, 1991; Wells, Zelcer and Treadrae, 1988; Wulfson, Askanazi and Finck, 1984). These reports lead to recommendations that "subshocks" should be avoided, particularly in clinically compromised patients (Abrams, 2002).

Cardiovascular disease

It was these concerns that prompted McCall et al. (1994) to examine the electrocardiographic (ECG) and cardiovascular effects of subconvulsive stimuli utilised in stimulus dose titration protocols for 40 consecutive inpatients with major depression. They examined the ECG, in particular heart rate (HR) and blood pressure (BP). Subconvulsive stimuli prolonged the R–R interval and decreased heart rate compared to baseline values immediately before the subconvulsive stimulus was applied. They concluded that the changes were not significant and had no clinical relevance and that subconvulsive stimuli were well tolerated in the context of titrated RUL ECT. Beale et al. (1994) replicated these findings with all patients in their study pre-medicated with glycopyrrolate prior to ECT.

Zielinski, Roose, Devanand, Woodring and Sackeim (1993) examined 40 patients with major depressive disorder and cardiac disease including left ventricular impairment, ventricular arrhythmias and conduction defects. They were matched with 40 patients with major depression who did not have cardiac disease. The study included 21 patients who had failed trials of tricyclic antidepressants owing to cardiac complications.

Patients with cardiac disease had significantly higher rates of cardiac complications than controls. The type or pre-existing cardiac abnormalities predicted the type of cardiac events that occurred during ECT. Most complications were transitory and did not prevent the completion of the course of ECT. ECT was better tolerated than tricyclic antidepressant medication, where 11 out of 21 patients were forced to discontinue drug treatment with none of them needing to withdraw from ECT. Overall, 38 out of 40 patients completed the course of ECT. The study concluded that ECT can be safely administered to patients with severe cardiovascular disease provided they are closely monitored for arrhythmias and ischaemic episodes by the anaesthetist.

Pre-medication with an anticholinergic agent to reduce the parasympathetic effects or use a beta blocker to reduce hypertension may be beneficial in high-risk patients (Zielinski et al., 1993) but routine use is not recommended (Benbow and Waite, 2013), with some reports that may increase cognitive impairment (Tiller and Lyndon, 2003).

Cognitive impairment

Early studies suggested that subconvulsive stimulation may worsen the adverse cognitive effects of ECT (Cronholm and Ottosson, 1961). This work has been challenged by a large study that randomised depressed patients to either right unilateral or bitemporal ECT, with stimulus intensity being maintained just above seizure threshold throughout the treatment course. These low-dose treatment groups were administered one or more subconvulsive stimuli as well as a grand mal seizure during 40% of the treatment sessions providing within patient comparative neurocognitive data (Prudic, Sackeim, Devanand, Krueger and Settembrino, 1994). Across a variety of neurocognitive measures, there were adverse cognitive consequences of subconvulsive stimulation prior to a convulsive stimulus. They postulated that seizure threshold may be a filter for many of the cognitive and other behavioural effects of electrical stimulation and that the crucial variable is the degree to which electrical dose exceeds threshold.

A criticism of this study was the limited number of successive subconvulsive stimuli applied, an average of one, and neurocognitive testing focused only on acute side effects and not effects that may have manifested themselves after longer time interval. A further concern raised by Swartz (1990) that subconvulsive stimuli could themselves lower seizure threshold and therefore falsely lower thresholds measured by the dose titration method

CLINICAL WISDOM 5.4.5

Practice-based experience suggests that stimulus dose titration using subconvulsive stimuli is safe and has become routine practice. Failure to elicit a seizure during a titration session may lead to an increased level of confusion and compromised cardiovascular status owing to the parasympathetic surge that is generated by the stimulus.

has not been substantiated by further seizure threshold data (Beale et al., 1994; Sackeim et al., 1993).

REFERENCES

Abrams, R. (1994). Stimulus parameters and efficacy of ECT. *Convulsive Therapy*, 10(2), 124–128; discussion 140–152. Retrieved from www.ncbi.nlm.nih.gov/pubmed/8069636.

Abrams, R. (2002). *Electroconvulsive Therapy*, 4th edition. New York: Oxford University Press.

American Psychiatric Association. (1990). *The Practice of Electroconvulsive Therapy: Recommendations for Treatment, Training and Privileging: A Task Force Report*. Washington, DC: American Psychiatric Association.

American Psychiatric Association. (2001). *The Practice of Electroconvulsive Therapy: Recommendations for Treatment, Training and Privileging: A Task Force Report*, 2nd edition. Washington, DC: American Psychiatric Association.

Bai, S., Loo, C., Al Abed, A., and Dokos, S. (2012). A computational model of direct brain excitation induced by electroconvulsive therapy: comparison among three conventional electrode placements. *Brain Stimulation*, 5(3), 408–421.

Beale, M.D., Kellner, C.H., Pritchett, J.T., Bernstein, H.J., Burns, C.M., and Knapp, R. (1994). Stimulus dose-titration in ECT: a 2-year clinical experience. *Convulsive Therapy*, 10(2), 171–176. Retrieved from www.ncbi.nlm.nih.gov/pubmed/8069643.

Benbow, S.M., and Waite, J. (2013). Safe ECT practice in people with a physical illness. In Waite, J. and Easton, A. (Eds.), *The ECT Handbook*, 3rd edition. London: Royal College of Psychiatrists.

Beyer, J.L., Weiner, R.D., and Glenn, M.D. (1998). *Electroconvulsive Therapy: A Programmed Text*, 2nd edition. Washington, DC: American Psychiatric Press.

Carney, M.W., Rogan, P.A., Sebastian, J., and Sheffield, B. (1976). A controlled comparative trial of unilateral and bilateral sinusoidal and pulse ECT in endogenous depression. *Physicians Drug Manual, 7*, 77–79.

Coffey, C.E., Lucke, J., Weiner, R.D., Krystal, A.D., and Aque, M. (1995). Seizure threshold in electroconvulsive therapy: I. Initial seizure threshold. *Biological Psychiatry, 37*(10), 713–720. doi:10.1016/0006-3223(95)00262-F.

Cronholm, B., and Ottosson, J.O. (1961). "Counter-shock" in electroconvulsive therapy. *Archives of General Psychiatry, 4*, 254–258.

Cronholm, B., and Ottosson, J.O. (1963). The experience of memory function after electroconvulsive therapy. *British Journal of Psychiatry, 109*, 251–258. Retrieved from www.ncbi.nlm.nih.gov/pubmed/14023959.

Daniel, W.F., and Crovitz, H.F. (1983). Acute memory impairment following electroconvulsive therapy. 1. Effects of electrical stimulus waveform and number of treatments. *Acta Psychiatrica Scandinavica, 67*(1), 1–7. Retrieved from www.ncbi.nlm.nih.gov/pubmed/6846033.

Deng, Z.D., Lisanby, S.H., and Peterchev, A.V. (2009). *Effect of Anatomical Variability on Neural Stimulation Strength and Focality in Electroconvulsive Therapy (ECT) and Magnetic Seizure Therapy (MST)*. Paper presented at the Annual International Conference of the IEEE, Minneapolis MN. http://ieeexplore.ieee.org/xpl/login.jsp?tp=&arnumber=5334091&url=http%3A%2F%2Fieeexplore.ieee.org%2Fxpls%2Fabs_all.jsp%3Farnumber%3D5334091.

Deng, Z.D., Lisanby, S.H., and Peterchev, A.V. (2011). Electric field strength and focality in electroconvulsive therapy and magnetic seizure therapy: a finite element simulation study. *Journal of Neural Engineering, 8*(1), 016007. doi:10.1088/1741-2560/8/1/016007.

Devanand, D.P., Lisanby, S.H., Nobler, M.S., and Sackeim, H.A. (1998). The relative efficiency of altering pulse frequency or train duration when determining seizure threshold. *Journal of ECT, 14*(4), 227–235. Retrieved from http://journals.lww.com/ectjournal/Fulltext/1998/12000/The_Relative_Efficiency_of_Altering_Pulse.2.aspx.

Freeman, C.P., Crammer, J.L., Deakin, J.F.W., McClelland, R., Mann, S.A., and Pippard, J. (1989). *The Practical Administration of Electroconvulsive Therapy (ECT)*. London: Royal College of Psychiatrists/Gaskell.

Galletly, C., Paterson, T., and Burton, C. (2012). A report on the introduction of ultrabrief pulse width ECT in a private psychiatric hospital. *Journal of ECT, 28*(1), 59. doi:10.1097/YCT.0b013e318221b42e.

Guyton, A.C., and Hall, J.E. (2016). *Textbook of Medical Physiology,* 13th edition. Philadelphia, PA: Elsevier.

Harrison, P. (2015). *PRIDE Continues to Support ECT in Depressed Elderly*. Paper presented at the 28th European College of Neuropsychopharmacology (ECNP) Congress, Amsterdam, The Netherlands.

Hyrman, V., Palmer, L.H., Cernik, J., and Jetelina, J. (1985). ECT: the search for the perfect stimulus. *Biological Psychiatry, 20*(6), 634–645. Retrieved from www.ncbi.nlm.nih.gov/pubmed/3995110.

Koester, E.R. (1985). Voltage-gated channels and the generation of the action potential In Kandel, E.R., and Schwartz, J.H. (Eds.), *Principles of Neural Science* (pp. 75–86). New York: Elsevier.

Liberson, W.T. (1948). Brief stimulus therapy. *American Journal of Psychiatry, 105*(1), 28–39. doi:10.1176/ajp.105.1.28.

Lisanby, S.H., and Sackeim, H.A. (1997). The effect of pulse width on seizure threshold during electroconvulsive shock (ECS). *Convulsive Therapy, 13*, 56.

Loo, C.K., Katalinic, N., Martin, D., and Schweitzer, I. (2012). A review of ultrabrief pulse width electroconvulsive therapy. *Therapeutic Advances in Chronic Disease, 3*(2), 69–85. doi:10.1177/2040622311432493.

Loo, C.K., Katalinic, N., Smith, D.J., Ingram, A., Dowling, N., Martin, D., . . . Schweitzer, I. (2014). A randomised controlled trial of brief and ultrabrief pulse right unilateral electroconvulsive therapy. *International Journal of Neuropsychopharmacology, 18*(1).

Loo, C.K., Sainsbury, K., Sheehan, P., and Lyndon, B. (2008). A comparison of RUL ultrabrief pulse (0.3ms) ECT and standard RUL ECT. *International Journal of Neuropsychopharmacology, 11*(7), 883–890.

Lyndon, R.W. (2001). The efficiency of high (double) dose ECT. In Little, J.D., and Petrides, G. (Eds.), *Proceedings of the first Asia Pacific ECT Conference*. Ballarat, Australia: Ballarat Health Services – Grampians Psychiatrict Services.

McCall, W.V., Reboussin, D.M., Weiner, R.D., and Sackeim, H.A. (2000). Titrated moderately suprathreshold vs fixed high-dose right unilateral electroconvulsive therapy: acute antidepressant and cognitive effects. *Archives of General Psychiatry, 57*(5), 438–444. doi:10.1001/archpsyc.57.5.438.

McCall, W.V., Reid, S., and Ford, M. (1994). Electrocardiographic and cardiovascular effects of sub-convulsive stimulation during titrated right unilateral ECT. *Convulsive Therapy, 10*(1), 25–33. Retrieved from www.ncbi.nlm.nih.gov/pubmed/8055289.

Magid, M., Truong, L., Trevino, K., and Husain, M. (2013). Efficacy of right unilateral ultrabrief pulse width ECT: a preliminary report. *Journal of ECT, 29*(4), 258–264. doi:10.1097/YCT.0000000000000080.

Mankad, M.V., Beyer, J.L., Weiner, R.D., and Krystal, A. (2010). *Clinical Manual of Electroconvulsive Therapy*. Washington, DC: American Psychiatric Publishing.

MECTA Corporation. (2015). spECTrum 5000Q – MECTA Corp. Retrieved from www.mectacorp.com/spectrum-5000Q.html.

Medcraft Corporation. (1986). *Electroshock unit neurology model B-25*. Retrieved from www.510kdecisions.com/applications/index.cfm?id=K860467.

Murugesan, G. (1994). Electrode placement, stimulus dosing and seizure monitoring during ECT. *Australian and New Zealand Journal of Psychiatry*, 28(4), 675–683. Retrieved from www.ncbi.nlm.nih.gov/pubmed/7794211.

O'Dea, J.F., Mitchell, P.B., and Hickie, I.B. (1991). Unilateral or bilateral electroconvulsive therapy for depression? A survey of practice and attitudes in Australia and New Zealand. *Medical Journal of Australia*, 155(1), 9–11. Retrieved from www.ncbi.nlm.nih.gov/pubmed/2067461.

Partridge, B.L., Weinger, M.B., and Hauger, R. (1991). Is the cardiovascular response to electroconvulsive therapy due to the electricity or the subsequent convulsion? *Anesthesia Analgesia*, 72, 706–709.

Peterchev, A.V., Rosa, M.A., Deng, Z.-D., Prudic, J., and Lisanby, S.H. (2010). ECT stimulus parameters: rethinking dosage. *Journal of ECT*, 26(3), 159–174. doi:10.1097/YCT.0b013e3181e48165.

Pirnia, T., Joshi, S.H., Leaver, A.M., Vasavada, M., Njau, S., Woods, R.P., . . . Narr, K.L. (2016). Electroconvulsive therapy and structural neuroplasticity in neocortical, limbic and paralimbic cortex. *Translational Psychiatry*, 6(6), e832. doi:10.1038/tp.2016.102.

Prudic, J., Sackeim, H.A., Devanand, D.P., Krueger, R.B., and Settembrino, J.M. (1994). Acute cognitive effects of subconvulsive electrical stimulation. *Convulsive Therapy*, 10(1), 4–12.

Riddle, W.J., Scott, A.I., Bennie, J., Carroll, S., and Fink, G. (1993). Current intensity and oxytocin release after electroconvulsive therapy. *Biological Psychiatry*, 33(11–12), 839–841. Retrieved from www.ncbi.nlm.nih.gov/pubmed/8373922.

Robin, A.A., and de Tissera, S. (1982). A double-blind controlled comparison of the therapeutic effects of low and high energy electroconvulsive therapies. *British Journal of Psychiatry*, 141, 357–366.

Rosa, M.A., Abdo, G.L., Lisanby, S.H., and Peterchev, A. (2011). Seizure induction with low-amplitude-current (0.5 A) electroconvulsive therapy. *Journal of ECT*, 27(4), 341–342. doi:10.1097/YCT.0b013e31822149db.

Sackeim, H.A., Decina, P., Kanzler, M., Kerr, B., and Malitz, S. (1987). Effects of electrode placement on the efficacy of titrated, low-dose ECT. *American Journal of Psychiatry*, 144(11), 1449–1455. Retrieved from www.ncbi.nlm.nih.gov/pubmed/3314538.

Sackeim, H.A., Decina, P., Prohovnik, I., and Malitz, S. (1987). Seizure threshold in electroconvulsive therapy: effects of sex, age, electrode placement, and number of treatments. *Archives of General Psychiatry*, 44(4), 355–360. doi:10.1001/archpsyc.1987.01800160067009.

Sackeim, H.A., Devanand, D.P., and Prudic, J. (1991). Stimulus intensity, seizure threshold, and seizure duration: impact on the efficacy and safety of electroconvulsive therapy. *Psychiatric Clinics of North America*, 14(4), 803–843. Retrieved from www.ncbi.nlm.nih.gov/pubmed/1771150.

Sackeim, H.A., Long, J., Luber, B., Moeller, J.R., Prohovnik, I., Devanand, D.P., and Nobler, M.S. (1994). Physical properties and quantification of the ECT stimulus: I. Basic principles. *Convulsive Therapy*, 10(2), 93–123. Retrieved from www.ncbi.nlm.nih.gov/pubmed/8069647.

Sackeim, H.A., Prudic, J., Devanand, D.P., Kiersky, J.E., Fitzsimons, L., Moody, B. J., . . . Settembrino, J.M. (1993). Effects of Stimulus intensity and electrode placement on the efficacy and cognitive effects of electroconvulsive therapy. *New England Journal of Medicine*, 328(12). Retrieved from www.nejm.org/doi/pdf/10.1056/NEJM199303253281204.

Sackeim, H.A., Prudic, J., Devanand, D.P., Nobler, M.S., Lisanby, S.H., . . . Clark, J. (2000). A prospective, randomized, double-blind comparison of bilateral and right unilateral electroconvulsive therapy at different stimulus intensities. *Archives of General Psychiatry*, 57(5), 425–434. doi:10.1001/archpsyc.57.5.425.

Sackeim, H.A., Prudic, J., Fuller, R., Keilp, J., Lavori, P.W., and Olfson, M. (2007). The cognitive effects of electroconvulsive therapy in community settings. *Neuropsychopharmacology*, 32(1), 244–254. doi:10.1038/sj.npp.1301180.

Sackeim, H.A., Prudic, J., Nobler, M.S., Fitzsimons, L., Lisanby, S.H., Payne, N., . . . Devanand, D.P. (2008). Effects of pulse width and electrode placement on the efficacy and cognitive effects of electroconvulsive therapy. *Brain Stimulation*, 1(2), 71–83. doi:10.1016/j.brs.2008.03.001.

Shellenberger, W., Miller, M.J., Small, I.F., Milstein, V., and Stout, J.R. (1982). Follow-up study of memory deficits after ECT. *Canadian Journal of Psychiatry*, 27(4), 325–329. Retrieved from www.ncbi.nlm.nih.gov/pubmed/7104944.

Sienaert, P., Vansteelandt, K., Demyttenaere, K., and Peuskens, J. (2009). Randomized comparison of ultra-brief bifrontal and unilateral electroconvulsive therapy for major depression: clinical efficacy. *Journal of Affective Disorders*, 116(1–2), 106–112. doi:10.1016/j.jad.2008.11.001.

Somatics, L.L.C. (2015). Somatics, LLC – manufacturer of the Thymatron ECT machine. Retrieved from www.thymatron.com/main_home.asp.

Spaans H-P, Kho, K.H., Verwijk, E., Kok, R.M., and Stek, M.L. (2013). Efficacy of ultrabrief electroconvulsive therapy for depression: a systematic review. *Journal of Affective Disorders, 150*(3), 720–726.

Spanis, C.W., and Squire, L.R. (1981). Memory and convulsive stimulation: effects of stimulus waveform. *American Journal of Psychiatry, 138*(9), 1177–1181. Retrieved from www.ncbi.nlm.nih.gov/pubmed/7270720.

Squire, L.R., and Zouzounis, J.A. (1986). ECT and memory: brief pulse versus sine wave. *American Journal of Psychiatry, 143*(5), 596–601. Retrieved from www.ncbi.nlm.nih.gov/pubmed/3963246.

Swartz, C.M. (1994). Optimising the ECT stimulus. *Convulsive Therapy, 10*(2), 132–134.

Swartz, C.M., and Larson, G. (1989). ECT stimulus duration and its efficacy. *Annals of Clinical Psychiatry, 1,* 147–152.

Swartz, C.M. (1990). Repeated ECT stimuli and the seizure threeshold. *Convulsive Therapy, 6*(2), 181–187.

Swartz, C.M. (1994a). Electroconvulsive therapy (ECT) stimulus charge rate and its efficacy. *Annals of Clinical Psychiatry, 6*(3), 205–206. Retrieved from www.ncbi.nlm.nih.gov/pubmed/7881502.

Swartz, C.M. (1994b). Optimizing the ECT stimulus. *Convulsive Therapy, 10*(2), 132–134; discussion 140–152. Retrieved from www.ncbi.nlm.nih.gov/pubmed/8069639.

Tiller, J.W.G., and Lyndon, R.W. (2003). *Electroconvulsive Therapy: An Australian Guide.* Melbourne, Australia: Australian Post Graduate Medicine.

Tor, P.C., Bautovich, A., Wang, M.J., Martin, D., Harvey, S.B., and Loo, C. (2015). A systematic review and meta-analysis of brief versus ultrabrief right unilateral electroconvulsive therapy for depression. *Journal of Clinical Psychiatry, 10*(4088). doi:10.4088/JCP.14r09145.

Valentine, S.J., Keddie, K.M., and Dunne, D. (1968). A comparison of techniques in elecrtroconvulsive therapy. *British Journal of Psychiatry, 114,* 989–996.

Weaver, L., Ives, J., and Williams, R. (1978). The threshold number of pulses in bilateral and unilateral ECT. *Biological Psychiatry, 13*(2), 227–241. Retrieved from www.ncbi.nlm.nih.gov/pubmed/667229.

Weaver, L.A., Ives, J.O., and Williams, R. (1982). Studies in brief-pulse electroconvulsive therapy: the voltage threshold, interpulse interval and pulse polarity parameters. *Biological Psychiatry, 17*(10), 1131–1143.

Weaver, L.A., Ives, J.O., Williams, R., and Nies, A. (1977). A comparison of standard alternating current and low-energy briefpulse electrotherapy. *Biological Psychiatry, 12,* 525–543.

Weaver, L., Ravaris, C., Rush, S., and Paananen, R. (1974). Stimulus parameters in electroconvulsive shock. *Journal of Psychiatric Research, 10*(3–4), 271–281. Retrieved from www.ncbi.nlm.nih.gov/pubmed/4459453.

Weaver, L.A., Jr, and Williams, R.W. (1986). Stimulus parameters and electroconvulsive therapy. *Annals of the New York Academy of Science, 462,* 174–185. Retrieved from www.ncbi.nlm.nih.gov/pubmed/3458404.

Weiner, R.D. (1980). ECT and seizure threshold: effects of stimulus waveform and electrode placement. *Biological Psychiatry, 15,* 225–241.

Weiner, R.D. (1982). The role of stimulus waveform in therapeutic and adverse effects of ECT. *Psychopharmacology Bulletin, 18*(2), 71–72. Retrieved from www.ncbi.nlm.nih.gov/pubmed/7111609.

Weiner, R.D., and Krystal, A.D. (1994). The present use of electroconvulsive therapy. *Annual Review of Medicine, 45,* 273–281.

Weiner, R.D., Rogers, H.J., Davidson, J.R., and Kahn, E.M. (1986). Effects of electroconvulsive therapy upon brain electrical activity. *Annals of the New York Academy of Science, 462,* 270–281.

Wells, D.G., Zelcer, J., and Treadrae, C. (1988). ECT-induced asystole from a sub-convulsive shock. *Anaesthesia and Intensive Care Journal, 16*(3), 368–371. Retrieved from www.ncbi.nlm.nih.gov/pubmed/3056091.

Wulfson, H.D., Askanazi, J., and Finck, A.D. (1984). Propranolol prior to ECT associated with asystole. *Anesthesiology, 60*(3), 255–256. Retrieved from www.ncbi.nlm.nih.gov/pubmed/6364891.

Zielinski, R.J., Roose, S.P., Devanand, D.P., Woodring, S., and Sackeim, H.A. (1993). Cardiovascular complications of ECT in depressed patients with cardiac disease. *American Journal of Psychiatry, 150*(6), 904–909. Retrieved from www.ncbi.nlm.nih.gov/pubmed/8494067.

Electroencephalogram (EEG)

OVERVIEW

Krystal (1998) noted that throughout the history of ECT there has been a need to objectively measure the therapeutic adequacy of an individual treatment. Originally this was done by visually monitoring the motor fit. However, if suxamethonium is given at an adequate dose, there is no visual motor fit. Placing a blood pressure cuff around the right lower leg above the ankle and inflating it before the suxamethonium is administered provides a means of maintaining visual monitoring of the motor seizure (Fink and Johnson, 1982). The isolated limb technique is illustrated in Figure 5.1.1. A limitation of this technique is that the length of a seizure does not correlate with clinical efficacy (Krystal, Coffey, Weiner and Holsinger, 1998).

The electroencephalogram (EEG) was incorporated into commercially available ECT devices in the 1990s. A striking observation was that in most cases the duration of the EEG seizure was significantly longer than the duration of the motor fit (Warmflash, Stricks and Sackeim 1987). In many cases the EEG duration could be substantially longer than 20 seconds. This observation challenged the fundamental premise that duration of the motor seizure was a significant factor in determining optimum clinical response. Very short seizures can sometimes indicate that the stimulus is too high, while a very long seizure indicates that the stimulus may be too low (Krystal et al., 1993; Sackeim, Devanand and Prudic, 1991). The relationship between seizure duration and stimulus intensity is non-linear (Mankad, Beyer, Weiner and Krystal, 2010). When the stimulus is barely suprathreshold, increasing the stimulus intensity will be associated with longer seizure duration, with the reverse being true if the stimulus greatly exceeds the seizure threshold. Likewise, as the number of ECT treatments increases seizure threshold rises and seizure duration falls with a subsequent shift to the right and downwards of the curve depicted in Figure 5.4.5.

It is now considered that EEG parameters are more closely linked to clinical response than seizure duration. The EEG should be well-developed, symmetrical and synchronous and have a high amplitude that is followed by an abrupt postictal suppression (Abrams, 2002). In addition to EEG measurements, peak heart rate has also been has been identified as a candidate to measure ECT seizure quality and provide feedback for stimulus dose regulation (Swartz, 2000).

Monitoring is now considered mandatory for all ECT treatment as therapeutic potency correlates with relative stimulus intensity. EEG monitoring provides some guidance concerning the quality of the stimulus intensity that along with careful clinical assessment can maximise the efficacy of the treatment and minimise cognitive impairment (Mankad et al., 2010; Scott and Waite, 2013).

DEFINITION

Electroencephalography is the recording of electrical activity along the scalp with electrodes placed at key positions across the head. The internationally recognised standard is known as the 10–20 system, developed to ensure reproducibility to enable comparison over time and subjects (American Electroencephalographic Society, 1991). The 10 and 20 represent the actual distances between adjacent electrodes, which are 10% to 20% of the total front to back and right to left distance of the skull (Chatrian, Lettich and Nelson, 1985). The 32-channel EEG system is commonly used in clinical practice and has recently been applied to brain control interface applications (Wang, 2012).

There are four essential anatomical landmarks on the human head used to determine the precise position of the EEG electrodes. The nasion is the intersection of the frontal bones and two nasal bones, a distinct depressed area directly between the eyes on the forehead; the inion is the midline bony prominence that is the tip of the external occipital protuberance at the back of the head and the tragus of both left and right ears. The inter-

Beta Waves

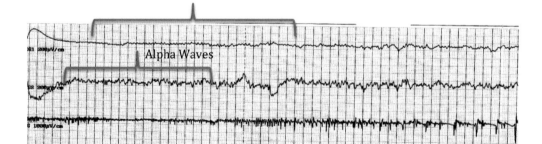

EEG 5.5.1 *Alpha and beta waves*

section of a line drawn between the tragus of both left and right ears and a line drawn between the nasion and inion determines the vertex.

The vertex is the landmark used to determine the location of the unilateral electrode placement for ECT, the resting motor threshold and EEG cap used for repetitive transcranial magnetic stimulation (rTMS) and the location of the electrodes used for transcranial direct current stimulation (tDCS).

PHYSIOLOGY

The EEG measures voltage fluctuations resulting from ionic current flows within the neuron of the brain (Mayer, 2006; Weiner, 1982). The EEG is used clinically as an investigation of brain activity. This investigation refers to the recording of the brain's spontaneous electrical activity over a short period of time, usually 20 to 40 minutes. Electrical activity is measured in up to 32 electrodes that are placed in different areas of the scalp (Mayer, 2006; Weiner, 1982). The EEG recording is acquired from surface electrodes that act as sensors. The amplitude

detected is between 10 and 30 microvolts (mV), with the bandwidth/frequency varying from 0.5 hertz (Hz) to 100 Hz. Frequency and wavelength have an inverse relationship. A frequency of 20 Hz has a wavelength of 0.2 seconds.

CATEGORISATION OF BANDWIDTHS

EEG bandwidths are categorised into slow and fast waves and high-frequency waves measured in hertz (Hz):

- slow waves:
  - delta waves from 0.5 Hz to 4 Hz;
  - theta waves from 5 Hz to 7 Hz;
- fast waves:
  - alpha waves from 8 Hz to 12 Hz;
  - beta waves from 13 Hz to 20 Hz;
- high-frequency waves:
  - frequencies greater than 20 Hz.

The most common EEG frequencies encountered in clinical practice are alpha rhythms, detected in

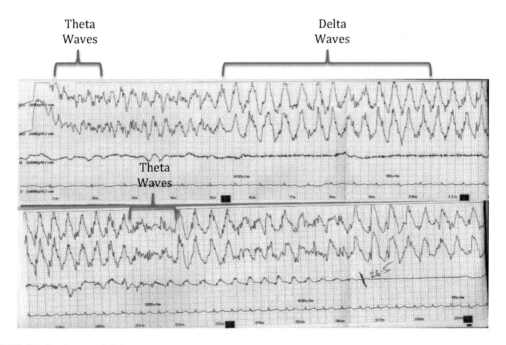

EEG 5.5.2 *Theta and delta waves*

relaxed wakeful states with eyes closed. When the eyes are open there is an increased level of arousal and beta activity is noted with desynchronisation. Drowsy states are accompanied by theta waves, while sleep and dreaming states are characterised by delta slow wave activity. Anaesthetised patients usually have alpha and beta activity.

EEG PROPERTIES

The ECT ictal EEG recording is complex, as it can be affected by various physiological and electrical "noises", reflecting the brain state, which is a non-linear process, dependent upon time, state and where the recording occurs (Mayer, 2006). In a similar way, analysis of the EEG is also complex. There are a number of methods used:

- **Manual–visual method.** Weiner (1982) first proposed using Likert scales to aided the reading of the EEG. These measures were refined into three visual scales that assisted the clinician in rating the quality of the overall ictal EEG (Krystal and Thyner, 1994):
  - Level 1: Gradual transition to seizure end, end point unclear, EEG line not flat after seizure;
  - Level 2: Gradual transition to seizure end, end point not obvious, EEG reasonably flat after seizure;
  - Level 3: Abrupt transition to seizure end, clear end point, EEG flat after seizure.
- The visual assessment was based upon dividing the ictal EEG into seven phases (Weiner, Coffey and Krystal, 1991).
- **The EEG Parameter Rating Scale.** The EEG Parameter Rating Scale (EPRS) (Edwards, Koopowitz and Harvey, 2003) was a naturalistic scale that was developed following analysis of multiple EEGs that had been recorded over a number of years. Seizure adequacy correlated most closely with an abrupt seizure end point (postictal suppression), a high amplitude rhythmic spike and wave phase (slow wave phase) of greater than 13 seconds, a seizure energy index

of greater 1000 units, and a bilateral EEG seizure length of greater than 24 seconds.
- **Linear and non-linear methods.** Linear and non-linear methods are two scientific ways of analysing the EEG with the aid of computer programs. Linear methods involve the direct measurement of a component like spectral power across non-overlapping bands, like alpha and beta, resulting in frequency content. Whereas non-linear models are more complex and include fractal dimension and Lyapunov exponent methods (Mayer, 2006).

GAIN

Gain refers to the capacity to alter the amplitude of the waveform generated on the EEG recorder. The gain could be increased, amplifying the waveform, or decreased, reducing the waveform size. The early Thymatron DGx devices had gain dials for each channel, which were located at the top of the paper recorder. This feature was discontinued with the

---

CLINICAL WISDOM 5.5.1

The EEG varies with different stimuli. Bilateral electrode placement produces more intense seizures compared to unilateral placement. Stimulus dose relative to threshold affects the EEG parameters that are generated, a factor that is particularly important with ultrabrief ECT, where seizures are often of low intensity.

It is thought that the EEG is able to predict the response to ECT. Changes in the EEG may indicate threshold changes during the course of treatment and the need to change stimulus dosing. EEG monitoring enables the detection of prolonged seizures in the absence of motor activity. In the past, such seizures were easily missed, resulting in adverse consequences to the patient. EEG monitoring is essential in determining the quality, duration and end point of a seizure generated during ECT, enabling the clinician to increase the stimulus or alter electrode placement if there is lack of clinical response with an adequate EEG.

release of the Thymatron System IV, where the gain could only be adjusted through the Flexidial programme dial. All MECTA devices that have EEG recording capacity have gain dials located to the left of the chart recorder.

Gain settings have a significant impact on accurately comparing EEGs generated after each treatment, with comparison difficult if the gain was accidently adjusted.

Optimal gain settings are those where vigorous seizure activity changes abruptly to a flat line during the postictal period. The appearance of flatness is dependent upon the gain setting on the recording device. There is still ongoing EEG activity in the brain even when the electroencephalogram appears completely flat.

WORKBOOK EEG TRACES

All of the traces featured in this *Workbook* have been recorded using a four-channel Thymatron System IV device (Somatics L.L.C., 2015):

- Channel 1: Left EEG (upper trace);
- Channel 2: Right EEG;
- Channel 3: Electromyogram (EMG); and
- Channel 4: Electrocardiogram (ECG).

PHASES OF THE ICTAL EEG

Phase 1: Baseline recording: consists of mixed fast- and slow wave activity indicative of anaesthetic effect, illustrated top left trace in EEG 5.5.3.

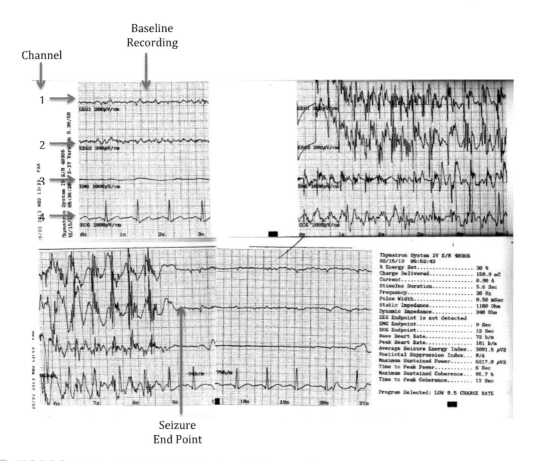

EEG 5.5.3 *Baseline short EEG with abrupt postictal suppression*

Phase 2: Application of electrical stimulus: the EEG amplifiers are blocked and recording does not occur during the stimulus.

Phase 3: Brief pre-ictal: a period of low-amplitude fast activity, illustrated in EEG 5.5.4 more noticeable on the left lead, channel 1 at the top of the trace, from 0 to 2.5 seconds.

Phase 4: Recruitment: the recruitment phase consists of low to moderate amplitude activity in the alpha to beta range associated with the synchronising of neural activity during the early stages of seizure generalisation and may be completely absent in a suprathreshold seizure as illustrated in EEG 5.5.5. In a threshold seizure the recruitment phase may lack concordance between left and right and may be very long as illustrated in EEG 5.5.4 with slow onset in the left channel that extends for greater than 11 seconds. Ideally this phase should be less than seven seconds in length.

Phase 5: Polyspike: the onset of the tonic and early components of the clonic motor response is characterised by high-frequency waves in the order of 13 to 20 Hz (beta) that may have an early and late phase lasting between 10 and 20 seconds. During the late phase the high-frequency waves are inter-spersed with lower-frequency waves in the order of 8 to 12 Hz (alpha). EEG 5.5.6 illustrates polyspike waves lasting 3.5 seconds with the early onset of slow wave activity, particularly in the right lead.

Phase 6: Polyspike and slow wave: the spike and wave phase consists of one or more spikes grouped together, followed by a slow wave, initially theta waves that emerge into delta wave formations. The spike and wave phase reflects the clonic phase of the ictal motor response and is nearly always present in a suprathreshold seizure. The absence of this phase often suggests a low-intensity seizure, common at titration or due to rising seizure threshold as treatment progresses that may be ineffective, illustrated in EEG 5.5.4.

Phase 7: Termination phase: the termination or transition phase follows immediately after the slow wave phase with a reduction in the amplitude and regularity of the seizure complexes as the seizure progresses from the ictal to postictal suppression. In threshold seizures this phase can be very long with no clear end point, illustrated in EEG 5.5.8, whereas in a suprathreshold seizure it may be completely absent as illustrated in EEGs 5.5.3 and 5.5.9.

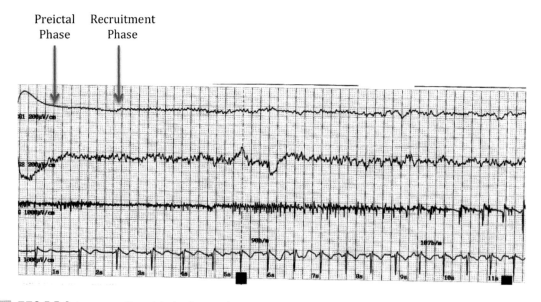

EEG 5.5.4 *Long recruitment lack of symmetry*

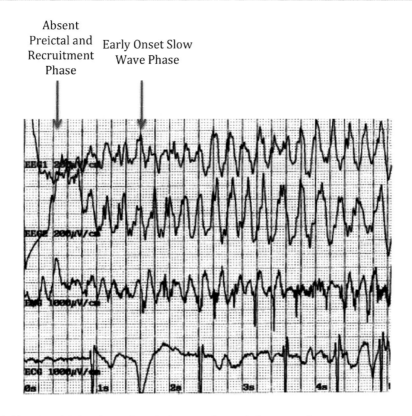

EEG 5.5.5 *Absent preictal and recruitment phases early onset slow wave phase*

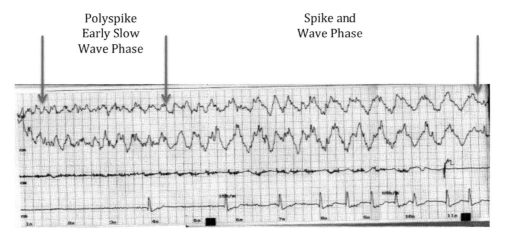

EEG 5.5.6 *Polyspike and spike and wave phases*

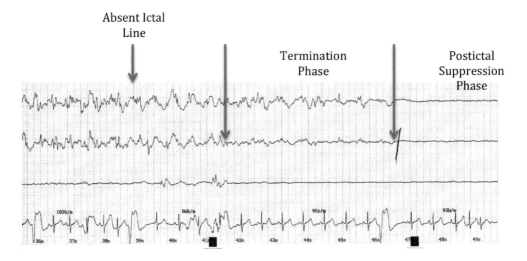

EEG 5.5.7 *Termination and postictal suppression phases absent ictal line*

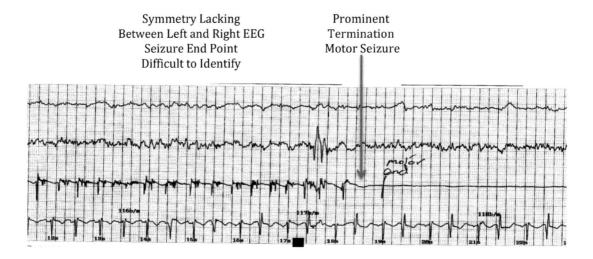

EEG 5.5.8 *Lack of EEG symmetry with EMG termination*

Phase 8: Postictal suppression: the postictal suppression phase begins immediately upon seizure termination and is characterised by electrical silence with an abrupt flattening of the EEG that persists for some time. The degree of postictal suppression varies considerably between patients and is influenced by electrode placement and rising seizure threshold (Krystal and Weiner, 1994). It is of note that when the electroencephalogram appears to be a flat line there continues to be EEG activity. This phenomenon is dependent upon the gain setting on the recording device, a feature that is not readily available on the Thymatron System IV. Abrupt postictal suppression is illustrated in EEGs 5.5.3 and 5.5.7; it is absent in EEG 5.5.8.

Absent Termination Phase
Abrupt Postictal
Suppression

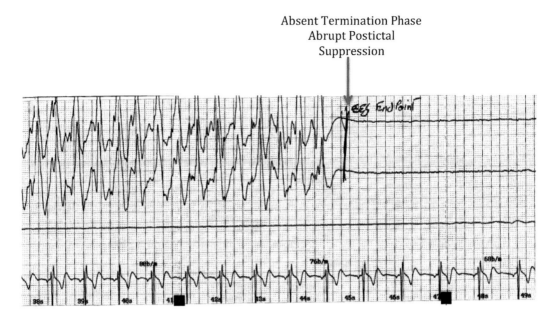

EEG 5.5.9 *Absent termination with abrupt postictal suppression phase*

Ictal Line   Symmetrical Spike and Wave
Phase with Prominent Theta
Activity

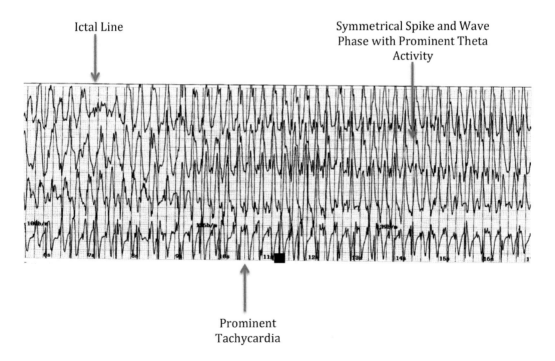

Prominent
Tachycardia

EEG 5.5.10 *Ictal line, prominent slow wave with theta waves and tachycardia*

THE ICTAL LINE

The ictal line is a feature that is unique to Thymatron devices and provides an objective measure of seizure end point. The ictal line is a fine black line printed at the top of the EEG trace, as illustrated in EEG 5.5.10. The ictal line is an objective estimation of the length of the EEG seizure. The feature can be highly variable within and between devices. EEG 5.5.7 illustrates an absent ictal line even though there is vigorous seizure activity, making the clinical usefulness of this feature uncertain.

ELECTROCARDIOGRAM (ECG)

The physiological impact of the ECT stimulus on the cardiovascular system is to cause a profound parasympathetic bradycardia that is closely followed by a sympathetic tachycardia that reverts to baseline measures following postictal suppression. EEG 5.5.11 illustrates a tachycardic state with a peak rate of 151 beats per minute during a suprathreshold seizure, while EEG 5.5.12 illustrates a profound bradycardia resulting in a cardiac pause of eight seconds before onset of the sympathetic surge.

Analysis of these changes in the ECG during the ictal motor response with different ECT stimulus doses has raised the possibility that peak heart rate may have predictive value in determining clinical efficacy. In an analysis of 24 subjects who were given standard- and higher-dose stimuli on different days using a left frontal, right temporal electrode placement, subjects who maintained peak heart rate near their individual maximum values received fewer ECT treatment than other subjects, suggesting that the peak heart rate may reflect clinical efficacy as well as stimulus dose (Swartz, 2000).

Table 5.5.1 Recommendations: phases of the EEG

- A short preictal and recruitment phase, less than seven seconds.
- A robust spike and slow wave phase, greater 13 seconds.
- Abrupt postictal suppression, flat line after terminating phase.
- A robust Postictal Suppression Index (Thymatron only):
  - Greater than 90% Thymatron DGx device,
  - Greater than 70% for the Thymatron System IV
- The Postictal Suppression Index can be highly inaccurate or absent, reducing its usefulness in clinical practice.
- Highly symmetrical, high amplitude EEG of at least 20 seconds.
- Seizures that are shorter than 15 seconds may suggest rising seizure threshold.

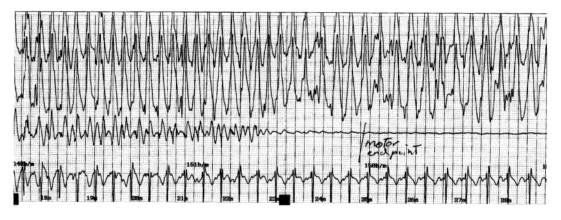

EEG 5.5.11 Peak heart rate and termination of motor seizure

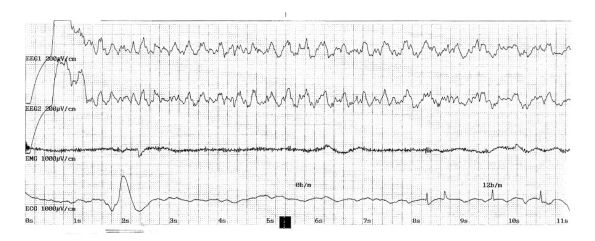

EEG 5.5.12 *Cardiac pause*

MEASUREMENT OF THE MOTOR FIT

The motor fit is measured by the Thymatron System IV using electromyogram (EMG), illustrated as Channel 3 in all of the EEG figures in this chapter, whereas the MECTA spECTrum 5000 devices measure the motor seizure by using an optical motion sensor (OMS) (MECTA Corporation, 2016). Monitoring the motor seizure alone can result in incorrect classification of treatment in at least 21.4% of ECT stimulations and may result in either unnecessary restimulation or failure to detect prolonged seizures, highlighting that monitoring the motor fit alone is unsatisfactory (Jayaprakash, Gangadhar, Janakiramaiah and Subbakrishna, 1998). Replication of this finding (Fink and Johnson, 1982; Greenberg, 1985) has led many units around the world to abandon routine measurement of the motor seizure, reserving it only for a titration session.

The motor seizure is detected using the isolated limb technique, where a cuff is placed around the lower part of the leg and inflated immediately before the suxamethonium is administered (Wise et al., 2000), as illustrated in Figure 5.1.1.

Most anaesthetic induction agents have profound anticonvulsant properties. It is now recognised that the dose of these agents should be minimised to improve seizure expression and quality that may improve clinical efficacy (Ding and White, 2002). The anaesthetist can use this technique to monitor the depth of induction by using the command "move your right foot" before the stimulation is applied. If the dose of the barbiturate is reduced through the addition of an ultrabrief narcotic agents, it is not uncommon for a patient to obey this command alerting the anaesthetist to administer a bigger dose to prevent awareness.

Awareness is a state of consciousness following induction after the administration of muscle relaxants that induce paralysis, preventing a patient communicating with the anaesthetist and leading to intense fear (Hardman and Aitkenhead, 2005; Lunn, 1987; Sandin, Enlund, Samuelsson and Lennmarken, 2000). Cuff monitoring is recommended for all treatments to minimise the dose of the induction agents administered, preventing this unpleasant phenomena.

SUMMARY

In summary, being able to understand and apply the details of the data recorded during each treatment is essential for the ECT practitioner to make clinical decisions concerning patients undergoing

CLINICAL WISDOM 5.5.2

In recent years there has been greater reliance on using the EEG as a guide to determine stimulus dose with the aid of the Likert rating scales (Nobler et al., 1993) and the electroencephalograph parameter rating scaling (EEPRS) (Edwards, Koopowitz and Harvey, 2003). Changes to practice including the introduction of brief pulse width ECT (0.5–1.0 ms), ultrabrief ECT (0.3 ms) and augmentation of the induction agent with remifentanil has meant that high-energy suprathreshold seizures can be generated at much lower stimulus levels even at the initial titration session. Trainees reflecting on the quality of the EEG have frequently raised the question:

> Why is the EEG only used to direct treatment decisions once the initial dose has been determined, independent of the quality of the EEG, particularly when the EEG at threshold is vigorous with high amplitude and good morphology?

They have suggested that in this situation a smaller incremental dose above threshold, one or two rather than three levels, could be utilised. Although this recommendation has merit, the role of the EEG in determining the stimulus dose remains unclear and its use is empirical, requiring careful monitoring to identify lack of clinical response and the need for a more aggressive approach.

Edwards, M., Koopowitz, L., and Harvey, E. (2003). A naturalistic study of the measurement of seizure adequacy in electroconvulsive therapy. *Australian and New Zealand Journal of Psychiatry, 37*(3), 312–318. Retrieved from www.ncbi.nlm.nih.gov/pubmed/12780470.

Nobler, M.S., Sackeim, H.A., Solomoub, M., Luberb, B., Devanand, D.P., and Prudic, J. (1993). EEG manifestations during ECT: effects of electrode placement and stimulus intensity. *Biological Psychiatry, 34*(5), 321–330. doi:10.1016/0006-3223(93)90089-V.

Table 5.5.2 Markers of seizure adequacy

MECTA spECTrum 5000 devices	
Charge	Composite charge value delivered
Energy	Composite energy delivered
Static impedance	Estimation of static impedance before the treatment
Dynamic impedance	Estimation of the dynamic impedance delivered during the treatment
Pulse width	Record of the pulse width used during the treatment, in milliseconds
Frequency	Measured in hertz
Duration	Duration of the seizure, measured in seconds
Current	Record of the current used during the treatment, measured in mA
EEG data analysis leading to:	Optimally combined and weighted multivariate combination of ictal EEG indices to identify treatment response, including, time to the onset of high amplitude slow waves, several measure of seizure amplitude and two measures of postictal suppression. Age, electrode placement and treatment number are important variables factored into the result for increased accuracy
1. Stimulus adequacy (SA)	An estimation of the likelihood that the ECT stimulation was sufficiently intense for efficacy
2. Stimulus level (SL)	This measure applies only to RUL. It estimates the actual amount by which the stimulus intensity exceeds seizure threshold. It attempts to estimate how suprathreshold the proceeding stimulus was

ECT. In particular, the EEG can be a valuable tool. Table 5.5.1 lists recommendations that can assist interpretation of the EEG recorded after each ECT treatment.

MARKERS OF SEIZURE ADEQUACY

There have been many attempts to identify the features of the data recorded during an ECT treatment that can predict clinical response. Tables 5.5.2, 5.5.3 and 5.5.4 list the information recorded by each ECT device and the potential markers of seizure adequacy. These values are an attempt to convey information about the type of changes that occurred during and after the seizure that may assist in determining the quality of the seizure and what should happen at the next treatment.

Markers of seizure adequacy that are thought to be linked to better clinical outcomes include: a short recruitment phase, a high level of concordance, high amplitude spike and wave activity, greater postictal suppression and peak heart rate (Folkerts, 1996; Krystal et al., 1993; Nobler et al., 1993; Swartz, 2000). A gold-standard, clinically useful ictal EEG algorithm has not yet been found even though considerable research has been undertaken.

MECTA spECTrum 5000

The data produced by the MECTA spECTrum 5000 devices is listed in Table 5.5.2. The MECTA devices offer a patented feature known as EEG data analysis that calculates parameters to aid the clinician. "Adequate" is available for all treatments and

Table 5.5.3 Markers of seizure adequacy

Thymatron System IV	
Stimulus parameters	Energy set %, charge delivered, stimulus duration, frequency, pulse width, static and dynamic impedance
EEG endpoint	Determination of EEG length after the printer has been stopped
EMG endpoint	Determination of EMG length after the printer has been stopped
ECG endpoint	Determination of EEG length after the printer has been stopped
Base heart rate	Heart rate before seizure
Peak heart rate	Highest heart rate during seizure
Average seizure energy index (ASEI)	Integrates the total ictal EEG power across the entire seizure and divides the result by the total seizure duration (automatic EEG endpoint detection program must be enabled to obtain this measure)
Postictal suppression index (PSI)	Measure of the EEG amplitude fall or flattening at the end of the seizure. PSI = Mean amplitude (beginning 0.5 seconds after seizure termination) ÷ mean 3 seconds peak amplitude × 100 / 1 = %. PSI < 70% indicates rising seizure threshold. Not always recorded
Maximum sustained power (MSP)	The mean value of a 10-second EEG segment with the highest average power recorded during the seizure
Time to peak power (TPP)	The time elapsed from stimulus termination to the point of maximum EEG power
Maximum sustained coherence (MSC)	The mean values of a five-second EEG segment with the highest average coherence recorded during the seizure
Time to peak coherence (TPC)	The time elapsed from stimulus termination to the point of maximum EEG coherence
Program selected	List program selected for this treatment (Somatics L.L.C., 2015)

Table 5.5.4 Markers Of Seizure Adequacy

Thymatron DGx	
Stimulus parameters	Energy set %, charge delivered, stimulus duration, frequency, pulse width, static and dynamic impedance
EEG endpoint	Determination of EEG length after the printer has been stopped
EMG endpoint	Determination of EMG length after the printer has been stopped
ECG endpoint	Determination of EEG length after the printer has been stopped
Base heart rate	Heart rate before seizure
Peak heart rate	Highest heart rate during seizure
Seizure energy index (SEI)	Integration of EEG amplitude throughout the duration of the seizure. SEI = Mean integrated amplitude × seizure duration. SEI < 550 suggests rising seizure threshold
Seizure concordance index (SCI) Key: EEG = Electroencephelogram EMG = Electromyogram	A measure of the correlation between the EEG and motor seizure duration, reflecting intracerebral seizure generalization. SCI = (1 − EEG − EMG) ÷ (EEG & EMG) × 100 / 1 = %. SCI < 51 suggests rising seizure threshold
Postictal suppression index (PSI)	A measure of how quickly and completely the EEG amplitude falls (flattens) just after the end of the seizure. PSI = Mean amplitude (beginning 0.5 seconds after seizure termination) ÷ mean 3 seconds peak amplitude × 100 / 1 = %. PSI < 70% suggests rising seizure threshold

"Level" is determined only for right unilateral ECT treatment. Alone these measures are of limited value and should be understood in the context of clinical recovery.

Thymatron System IV

The Thymatron System IV incorporates a range of data and measures that are automatically calculated once the seizure has been terminated are highlighted in Table 5.5.3.

Sufficient time should be allowed after the seizure end point has been determined to enable the machine to accurately and consistently calculate these stimulus parameters. Consistency in generating these parameters varies within and between devices making their usefulness in clinical practice questionable. Experience suggests that a highly intensity seizure will have the following characteristics:

1. average seizure energy index greater than 3500 microvolts^2;
2. maximum sustained power greater than 6000 microvolts^2;
3. time to peak power less than 20 seconds;
4. maximum sustained coherence greater than 90%;
5. time to peak coherence less than 20 seconds;
6. postictal suppression index greater than 90% for the Thymatron DGx device or greater than 70% for the Thymatron System IV.

A separate discussion of the Thymatron DGx device parameters, set out in Table 5.5.4, has not been included as many of them are used in the newer device.

THE FUTURE

An accurate and reliable ictal EEG algorithm that provides useful clinical information via a single index of therapeutic adequacy associated with a given seizure that enabled the practitioner to maintain the minimum effective stimulus intensity

Clipping
In Left Lead

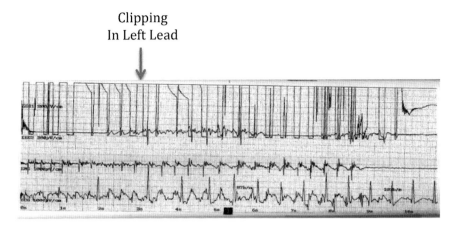

EEG 5.5.13 *Loose left monitoring lead with clipping*

Absent
Motor Fit

Loose Left
Leads

Loose Right
Leads

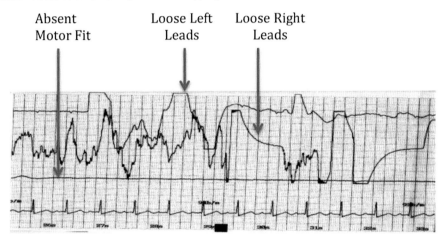

EEG 5.5.14 *Loose left and right EEG electrodes and absent motor seizure*

Ventilation
Artefact

Ventilation
Artefact

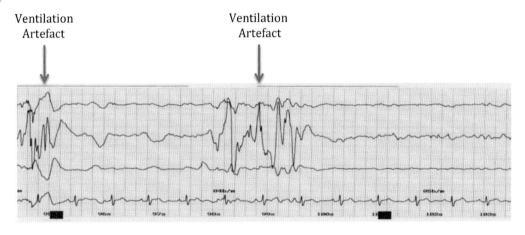

EEG 5.5.15 *Ventilation artefact*

throughout the treatment course, minimising cognitive side effects (Krystal, 1998).

EEG ARTEFACTS

EEG artefacts are frequent and can interfere with accurate recording of the EEG trace. Artefacts result in inaccurate seizure parameters and interfere with the visual assessment of the ictal trace. Common artefacts include:

- Clipping: Clipped waves are characterised by square topped waves with vertical sides of

variable duration and can be caused by movement or a loose recording lead, as illustrated in EEG 5.5.13.

- Loose recording leads, as illustrated in EEG 5.5.14.
- Ventilation: Ventilation by the anaesthetist during the procedure can result in artefact, as illustrated in EEG 5.5.15.
- Inadequate preparation of monitoring electrode sites.
- A low hairline or thick hair, particularly around the mastoid area.

Loose Motor Leads
Causing Blackout

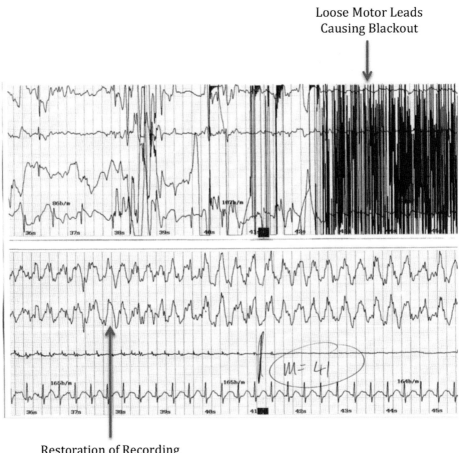

Restoration of Recording
By Manually Holding
Leads into Position

EEG 5.5.16 *Artefact from loose electrodes with recovery*

- Placement of the green earth electrode too close to the left side of the body can result in lead leakage and the EEG activity can mimic the ECG.
- Connection of the ECG leads with either left or right EEG recording electrodes.

Artefacts can be overcome by early detection and manually holding the recording electrodes into the correct position until the end of the trace, as illustrated in EEG 5.5.16.

CONCLUSION

There are many factors that can impact on the quality of the recorded ictal EEG. These include artefact, electrode placement, age, stimulus parameters, anaesthetic agents, and medications. Each of these issues need to be identified and understood by the ECT practitioner so that appropriate action can be taken to ensure the best outcome for the patient completing a course of ECT.

REFERENCES

Abrams, R. (2002). *Electroconvulsive Therapy*, 4th edition. New York: Oxford University Press.

American Electroencephalographic Society. (1991). Guidelines for standard electrode position nomenclature. *Journal of Clinical Neurophysiology, 8*, 200–202.

Chatrian, G.E., Lettich, E., and Nelson, P.L. (1985). Ten percent electrode system for topographic studies of spontaneous and evoked EEG activity. *America Journal of EEG Technology, 25*, 83–92.

Ding, Z., and White, P.F. (2002). Anesthesia for electroconvulsive therapy. *Anesthesia and Analgesia, 94*(5), 1351–1364. doi:10.1097/00000539-200205000-00057.

Edwards, M., Koopowitz, L.F., and Harvey, E.J. (2003). A naturalistic study of the measurement of seizure adequacy in electroconvulsive therapy. *Australian and New Zealand Journal of Psychiatry, 37*, 312–318.

Fink, M., and Johnson, L. (1982). Monitoring the duration of electroconvulsive therapy seizures: " cuff" and EEG methods compared. *Archives of General Psychiatry, 39*(10), 1189–1191. doi:10.1001/archpsyc.1982.04290100055009.

Folkerts, H.W. (1996). The ictal electroencephalogram as a marker for the efficacy of electroconvulsive therapy. *European Archives of Psychiatry and Clinical Neuroscience, 246*(3), 155–164.

Greenberg, L.B. (1985). Detection of prolonged seizures during electroconvulsive therapy: a comparison of electroencephalogram and cuff monitoring. *Convulsive Therapy, 1*(1), 32–37. Retrieved from www.ncbi.nlm.nih.gov/pubmed/11940803.

Hardman, J.G., and Aitkenhead, A.R. (2005). Awareness during anaesthesia. *Continuing Education in Anaesthesia, Critical Care and Pain, 5*(6), 183–186. doi:10.1093/bjaceaccp/mki049.

Jayaprakash, M.S., Gangadhar, B.N., Janakiramaiah, N., and Subbakrishna, D.K. (1998). Limitations of motor seizure monitoring in ECT. *Indian Journal of Psychiatry, 40*(1), 55–59.

Krystal, A.D., and Thyner, A.D. (1994). ECT seizure therapeutic adequacy. *Convulsive Therapy, 10*(2), 156–164. Retrieved from www.ncbi.nlm.nih.gov/pubmed/8069641.

Krystal, A.D., Weiner, R.D., McCall, W.V., Shelp, F.E., Arias, R., and Smith, P. (1993). The effects of ECT stimulus dose and electrode placement on the ictal electroencephalogram: an intraindividual crossover study. *Biological Psychiatry, 34*(11), 759–767. Retrieved from www.ncbi.nlm.nih.gov/pubmed/8292679.

Krystal, A.D. (1998). The clinical utility of ictal EEG seizure adequacy models. *Psychiatric Annals, 28*(1), 30–35.

Krystal, A.D., Coffey, C.E., Weiner, R.D., and Holsinger, T. (1998). Changes in seizure threshold over the course of electroconvulsive therapy affect therapeutic response and are detected by ictal EEG ratings. *The Journal of Neuropsychiatry and Clinical Neurosciences, 10*(2), 178–186. doi:10.1176/jnp.10.2.178.

Krystal, A.D., and Weiner, R.D. (1994). ECT seizure therapeutic adequacy. *Convulsive Therapy, 10*(2), 153–164. Retrieved from www.ncbi.nlm.nih.gov/pubmed/8069641.

Lunn, J.N. (1987). Awareness during anaesthesia. *Canadian Journal of Anaesthetics, 34 Suppl 1*, S41–42. doi:10.1007/BF03009897.

Mankad, Beyer, Weiner and Krystal, A. (2010). *Clinical Manual of electroconvulsive Therapy*. Washington, DC: American Psychiatric Publishing.

Mayer, P. (2006). Ictal electroencephalographic characteristics during electroconvulsive therapy: a review of determination and clinical relevance. *Journal of ECT, 22*(3), 213–217.

MECTA Corporation. (2016). Optical motional sensor. Retrieved from www.mectacorp.com/optical-motion-sensor.html.

Nobler, M.S., Sackeim, H.A., Solomou, M., Luber, B., Devanand, D.P., and Prudic, J. (1993). EEG manifestations during ECT: effects of electrode placement and stimulus intensity. *Biological Psychiatry, 34*(5), 321–330. doi:10.1016/0006-3223(93)90089-V.

Sackeim, H.A., Devanand, D.P., and Prudic, J. (1991). Stimulus intensity, seizure threshold, and seizure duration: impact on the efficacy and safety of electroconvulsive therapy. *Psychiatric Clinics of North America, 14*(4), 803–843. Retrieved from www.ncbi.nlm.nih.gov/pubmed/1771150.

Sandin, R.H., Enlund, G., Samuelsson, P., and Lennmarken, C. (2000). Awareness during anaesthesia: a prospective case study. *Lancet, 355*(9205), 707–711. doi:10.1016/S0140-6736(99)11010-9.

Scott, A.I., and Waite, J. (2013). Monitoring a course of ECT. In Waite, E.A. (Ed.), *The ECT Handbook,* 3rd edition (pp. 60–70). London: Royal College of Psychiatrists.

Somatics, L.L.C. (2015). *Somatics, LLC* – manufacturer of the Thymatron ECT machine. Retrieved from www.thymatron.com/main_home.asp.

Swartz, C.M. (2000). Physiological response to ECT stimulus dose. *Psychiatry Research, 97*(2–3), 229–235. Retrieved from www.ncbi.nlm.nih.gov/pubmed/11166093.

Wang, C.S. (2012). Design of a 32-channel EEG system for brain control interface applications. *Journal of Biomedicine and Biotechnology, 2012,* 274939. doi:10.1155/2012/274939.

Warmflash, V.L., Stricks, L., and Sackeim, H.A. (1987). Reliability and validity of measures of seizure duration. *Convulsive Therapy, 3,* 18–25.

Weiner, R.D., Coffey, C.E., and Krystal, A.D. (1991). The monitoring and management of electrically induced seizures. *Psychiatric Clinics of North America, 14,* 845–869.

Weiner, R.D. (1982). Electroencephalographic properties of ECT. *Psychopharmacology Bulletin, 18*(2), 78–81.

Wise, M.E., Mackie, F., Zamar, A.C., and Watson, J.P. (2000). Investigation of the "cuff" method for assessing seizure duration in electroconvulsive therapy. *Psychiatric Bulletin, 24,* 301.

Anaesthesia for ECT

ANAESTHETIC TECHNIQUE

The principles of general anaesthesia for ECT are the same as those for any other day-only procedure. They include:

- rendering the patient unconscious during the procedure, eliminating distress;
- maintaining physiological stability throughout the anaesthesia and procedure;
- protecting the patient from injury resulting from being unconscious and/or the procedure that is performed.

One principle that is unique to ECT is pre-oxygenation. This is usually given for a period of two to three minutes prior to induction, with hyperventilation administered before the treatment is administered if required. The routine anaesthetic techniques associated with ECT are set out in Table 5.6.1.

The dose and combination of anaesthetic agents utilised should be a team decision under the guidance of the anaesthetist. Due diligence is required to minimise the dose of the induction agent as most agents have anticonvulsant properties. In modern ECT practice the anaesthetist is considered to be an important member of the team, enabling routine consultation about treatment outcomes, the quality of the EEG and the potential impact that anaesthetic drugs are having on the treatment.

▌ **Table 5.6.1** Anaesthetic technique

1 Discuss previous treatments, complications, clinical response and need to change anaesthetic doses with the ECT team
2 Pre-oxygenate for two to three minutes prior to the procedure
3 Conduct time out: correct patient and procedure
4 Check vital signs
5 Administer other drugs to target specific comorbidity
6 Administer induction agents
7 Administer appropriate muscle relaxant
8 Time duration after administration of suxamethonium until the ECT stimulus to ensure maximum muscle relaxation, between 90 to 120 seconds
9 Continue airway management and ventilation with 100% oxygen until the stimulus is applied, hyperventilating if required
10 Insert bite block and support the chin
11 Demonstrate absence of deep tendon knee reflex
12 Final agreement by all team members that it is time to treat
13 Stimulus applied, passive airway management
14 Termination of seizure; active airways management; awareness that this is the most common time for complications to occur
15 Return of spontaneous respiration: apply 100% oxygen via mask and connect portable oximetry device
16 Transfer patient to the recovery area with comprehensive handover from the anaesthetist to the recovery nurse
17 Remain available to assist recovery staff in the event of complications arising

The dose of suxamethonium should also be considered. It is not uncommon for the dose to be minimised to allow for a quick turnaround between patients, resulting in partially or poorly modified seizures. Attention should be given to increasing the dose to establish more complete relaxation, ensuring the patient's safety.

Stigma is another important consideration that if often neglected by many services when it comes to the dose of suxamethonium. Poorly modified seizures are far from an ideal first experience of ECT. It is not uncommon for the procedure to be observed by students and junior staff for the first time even in private hospitals. Practice-based experience suggests that first impressions can have a lasting impact on junior staff, reinforcing stereotypes based upon misinformation gained from media or movies, who go on to become senior practitioners.

Timing of anaesthetic agents is another important consideration. Individualising the time before treatment can be particularly helpful in patients at the extremes of age. Older people have a slow circulation time delaying the action of drugs requiring longer delays compared to younger people. It is important to individualise treatment for each patient by using a stopwatch to record the length of time from the administration of suxamethonium and observing the end of muscle fasciculations. Experience suggests that two minutes is the average time required, with younger patients needing only 90 seconds and some elderly patients 150 seconds.

Recent evidence suggests that monitoring the time interval between the administration of the induction agent and time of treatment can have a significant impact on the quality of the seizure recorded at each treatment session (Galvez and Loo, 2017). Shorter time periods were association with attenuation of the EEG quality compared to longer time intervals in the same patient, a finding that may be particularly relevant when anaesthetics that are more anticonvulsant are utilised, for example propofol (Galvez, Hadzi-Pavlovic, Smith and Loo, 2015).

An ECT service should have an experienced consultant anaesthetist who provides guidance and oversight of junior consultants and anaesthetic registrars. Efforts should be made to minimise the numbers of anaesthetists providing treatment.

If this is not possible and a large number of anaesthetists are involved, it is best practice for the anaesthetic department to develop an ECT protocol standardising practice to minimise the negative effects of anaesthetic agents.

ANAESTHETIC AGENTS

Anticholinergic agents

In the past, routine pre-treatment with an anti-cholinergic agent like atropine was proposed for all titration sessions to minimise the bradycardia and excessive salivation caused by the subconvulsive stimuli (American Psychiatric Association, 2001). The advent of modern anaesthetic and ECT practice has challenged this view, reserving these agents for high-risk patients. If used, glycopyrrolate (100 to 600 micrograms) is the preferred agent over atropine (30 to 600 micrograms) as it is less likely to cross the blood–brain barrier (Walker, Bowley and Walker, 2013), causing less cognitive impairment and improving recovery (Tiller and Lyndon, 2003).

> ### CLINICAL WISDOM 5.6.1
>
> Individual sites need to develop their own policies on the use of these agents during titration or other treatment sessions. Modern anaesthetic and ECT techniques have meant that routine use of these drugs is uncommon even in the initial titration session.

Induction agents

Barbiturates

The first induction agent used in ECT was thiopentone, illustrated in Photo 5.6.1, (1.2–2.5 mg/kg) as it was the only intravenous agent available at that time and continues to be a mainstay of ECT anaesthesia. Altering the side chains of the thiopentone molecule produced methohexital a molecule that had less anticonvulsant properties,

was more potent and had a shorter duration of action; this became the preferred intravenous induction agent for this procedure (MacPherson and Loo, 2008).

Methohexital (0.5–1.0 mg/kg) remains prominent in ECT and is considered the "gold standard" against which other anaesthetic agents are compared (Ding and White, 2002). Methohexital can be difficult to administer as it is associated with pain on injection and a higher incident of involuntary movements, coughing, hiccups and laryngospasm (MacPherson and Loo, 2008). In recent years the availability of methohexital has become difficult to source and ECT services have had to revert to using thiopentone or embrace other intravenous anaesthetic agents like propofol. The frequency of sinus bradycardia and premature ventricular contractions is greater for thiopentone compared to methohexital (Ding and White, 2002).

When used thiopentone should be given as an intravenous bolus with doses maintained at the least amount necessary to maintain induction to improve seizure expression. Strategies that can assist in minimising the dose of the induction agent include adding an ultrabrief narcotic agent like

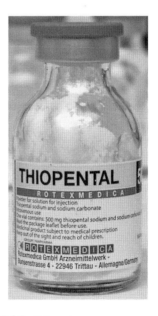

Photo 5.6.1 *Thiopentone*

remifentanil and routine monitoring of the time interval between the administration of the induction agent and treatment. Delaying the starting time of the stimulus, after infusion of the induction agent, if seizure quality is poor, can considerably improve seizure quality (Galvez and Loo, 2017).

Propofol

Since its introduction in 1980s propofol, illustrated in Photo 5.6.2, has replaced the barbiturate agents in many centres around the world. Propofol was a popular choice as an induction agent for ECT owing to its known ability to reduce the acute haemodynamic response during ECT (Ding and White, 2002). Rather than having proconvulsant properties as initially thought, it soon became apparent that propofol had more potent anticonvulsant properties compared to other intravenous anaesthetic drugs, resulting in shorter seizures that were poorly expressed with attenuated seizure qualities (Ding and White, 2002).

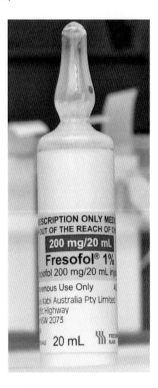

Photo 5.6.2 Propofol

Comparative studies have failed to demonstrate that shortening the length of the seizure affects the outcome of ECT treatment, suggesting that prolonged seizure duration was not absolutely necessary for successful ECT (Fear, Littlejohns, Rouse and McQuail, 1994; Geretsegger, Rochowanski, Kartnig and Unterrainer, 1998; Kirkby, Beckett, Matters and King, 1995; Malsch et al., 1994).

Recent work suggests that propofol increases seizure threshold compared to thiopentone, a finding that may have clinical implications if seizure expression is poor and there is a lack of clinical response to treatment (Galvez et al., 2015).

CLINICAL WISDOM 5.6.2

The rapid expansion in the use of propofrol as the preferred induction agent in Australia increased a number of years ago when the supply of thiopentone was affected by problems with manufacturing. The Federal Government Special Access Scheme (Australian Federal Government, 2014) provided a means to continue to use this induction agent but it did require individual applications to be made for each patient having ECT.

Opioids

Short-acting narcotic agents like alfentanil and remifentanil, illustrated in Photo 5.6.3, have the capacity to spare the dose of the induction agents like thiopentone or propofrol, minimising the haemodynamic response of ECT and reducing their anticonvulsant effect on seizure quality (Verghese and Brimacombe, 1996; Vishne, Aronov, Amiaz, Etchin and Grunhaus, 2005). It has been demonstrated that remifentanil alone does not directly improve seizure quality (Galvez et al., 2016).

Ketamine

Ketamine has unique sedative and analgesic properties with an increase in haemodynamic variables owing to its intrinsic sympathomimetic

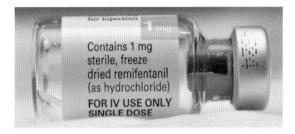

Photo 5.6.3 *Remifentanil*

activity compared to other intravenous anaesthetic agents (Ding and White, 2002). Early enthusiasm that ketamine may have intrinsic antidepressant, neuroprotective and possibly less anticonvulsant effects than other intravenous anaesthetic agents has been tempered by a recent systematic review (Galvez, McGuirk and Loo, 2016). This review showed that ketamine does speed the onset of antidepressant response early in the treatment course but to date has not produced an enhanced antidepressant response at the end of treatment with ECT. The review argues that this may be due to the development of tolerance with repeated use, a phenomenon that is well documented in the literature on abuse of and addiction to ketamine and recent animal data that shows rapid development of tolerance with repeated sub-anaesthetic ketamine injections in primates (Pouget, Wattiez, Rivaud-Pechoux and Gaymard, 2010).

Etomidate

Etomidate (0.15–0.3 mg/kg) is an intravenous anaesthetic agent that has limited worldwide availability. In countries where it is available it has been shown to be associated with longer seizure duration that may be helpful in patients with poor seizure expression despite maximal electrical stimulus applied (Avramov, Husain and White, 1995; Saffer and Berk, 1998; Trzepacz, Weniger and Greenhouse, 1993). A challenge for this agent is that it has reduced cardiovascular depressant properties, resulting in an accentuated acute haemodynamic response to ECT compared to barbiturates and propofol. In addition it may lead to increased level of postictal confusion, nausea and vomiting compared to other agents (Ding and White, 2002).

Sevoflurane

Sevoflurane is a volatile inhaled anaesthetic agent that is restricted to the operating room making it unavailable when ECT is administered in stand-alone or remote settings. There have been a number of studies that have compared the acute haemodynamic response of sevoflurane and thiopentone during ECT. Sevoflurane at high dose (3.4%) or mixed with nitrous oxide (50%) was more effective than thiopentone in blunting the cardiovascular effects during ECT (Tanaka et al., 1997). The impact on seizure quality was not recorded but seizure length and recovery time were similar to thiopentone although set-up time was longer (Tanaka et al., 1997). Volatile anaesthetic agents may have a role in providing ECT safely to women in late-stage pregnancy as it can reduce post-ECT-induced contractions (Ishikawa et al., 2001).

MUSCLE RELAXANTS

Muscle relaxants are used to modify the muscle activity during the stimulation and seizure, reducing the risk of injury (Nott and Watts, 1999; Sarpel, Togrul, Herdem, Tan and Baytok, 1996) and muscular pain after ECT (Herriot, Cowain and McLeod, 1996).

Suxamethonium or succinylcholine

Suxamethonium (0.5–1.5 mg/kg), illustrated in Photo 5.6.4, is the most common muscle relaxant used due to the rapid onset and short duration of action. Suxamethonium is administered as an intravenous bolus after complete induction has been achieved.

Best practice requires that the ECT stimulus be administered after complete relaxation has been achieved when the fasciculations in the skeletal muscles have ceased. Careful observation of the toes and the foot that has not been cuffed is required to ensure that the fine movements have ceased before treatment proceeds. Fasciculations are often not easy to observe, particularly in the elderly. Other techniques include demonstrating an absent deep tendon knee reflex, illustrated in Photo 5.1.7, using a stopwatch so that is commenced immediately after the suxamethonium has been administered with complete muscle relaxation achieved 90 and 120 seconds later. Time to treatment will depend upon a patient's age and circulation time. The ECT team should reach a consensus that muscle relaxation has been achieved before the stimulus is applied.

Depolarising muscle relaxants are not without complications in high-risk patients where there can be a risk of malignant hyperthermia and hyperkalemia following the administration of suxamethonium and non-depolarising agents may be preferable in these situations (Ding and White, 2002). Legal guidelines mandate that a suitable supply of dantrolene is kept on the emergency trolley in the event of this event (NSW Health, 2010).

Non-depolarising muscle relaxants

Mivacurium is the most common non-depolarising muscle relaxant that is used as an alternative to suxamethonium during ECT in patients who develop a malignant hyperthermia, although the later was more effective than mivacurium in preventing muscle contractions (Cheam et al., 1999).

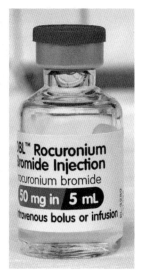

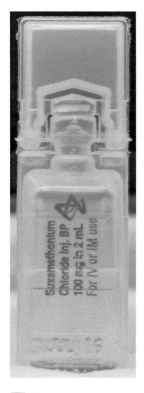

Photo 5.6.5
Rocuronium

Photo 5.6.4
Suxamethonium

Small doses of non-depolarising muscle relaxants, like vecuronium and rocuronium, illustrated in Photo 5.6.5, are administered before suxamethonium, blocking depolarisation of the muscle spindles and overcoming severe suxamethonium-induced myalgia in susceptible patients (Herriot et al., 1996).

EQUIPMENT

The minimum equipment that is required in giving anaesthesia within an operating theatre and other sites includes (ANZCA, 2015):

- a reliable source of oxygen with the appropriate backup cylinders;
- a breathing system that can deliver 100% oxygen both to a spontaneously breathing patient as well as enabling controlled ventilation when required, as illustrated Photo 5.1.19;

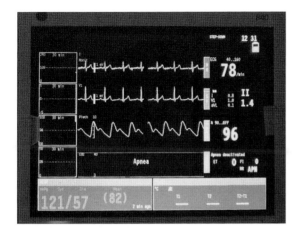

Photo 5.6.6 *Monitoring device*

- a backup device in the event of failure of the above apparatus;
- a monitoring apparatus capable of measuring and displaying arterial oxygen saturation, electrocardiograph and non-invasive arterial blood pressure, as illustrated in Photo 5.6.6;
- devices to manage the airway including: oropharyngeal, nasopharyngeal and laryngeal mask airways and endotracheal tubes;
- first-line emergency drugs;
- second-line drugs are neither necessary nor appropriate, according to most guidelines, in a stand-alone ECT suite.

CLINICAL WISDOM 5.6.4

Anecdotal observation suggest that during a course of ECT, particularly in maintenance patients, the dose of the induction agents and suxamethonium may need to be adjusted owing to slow and partial induction or increased motor activity, suggesting that there may be a tolerance effect with extended use. There is no evidence to support this observation owing to the small number of patients. Most patients have an index course of ECT with only a small number going onto a long course of maintenance treatment. ECT is the only treatment where a patient has multiple exposures to these anaesthetic agents.

DAY-ONLY PROCEDURES

All ECT services providing ambulatory patients same day ECT treatment are governed by the regulations of the local area health district in which it is administered. Most guidelines recommend:

- Fasting of sufficient duration to minimise the gastric residue to prevent respiratory inhalation, usually from the night before.
- Some flexibility in fasting duration is required if the list is long as it can make treatment of the last patient quite late in the day. Most anaesthetists would insist that there should be no solid food eaten six hours prior to the anaesthetic and clear fluids up to four hours before the procedure.
- All patients are required to undergo a pre-anaesthetic examination, with careful attention given to respiratory and cardiovascular systems.
- Dentition is very important. Most anaesthetists remove dentures prior to administering ECT.
- If there is doubt over the fitness of a patient to undergo treatment, consultation should be made with the relevant medical discipline to achieve stability.
- The use of an appropriate soft bite block to protect dentition, with hard plastic airways removed prior to treatment.
- Supervision by a responsible adult for 24 hours after ECT.
- A patient should not drive for 24 hours after the exposure to the anaesthetic agent.
- In most instances, benzodiazepines should not be given prior to ECT owing to their anticonvulsant properties. Agitation and distress should be managed with higher doses of sedative atypical antipsychotics.
- Vital signs, oximetry, non-invasive arterial blood pressure and ECG should be monitoried before, during and after the treatment until the patient is fully awake.
- Seizure quality should be routinely monitored by an EEG that is coupled to the ECT device

- "Time to recovery" should be monitored as a marker of retrograde (autobiographical) memory (Martin et al., 2013).
- There should be routine use of validated scales to assess early cognition changes (Porter, Heenan and Reeves, 2008) and therapeutic response, with results incorporated into clinical practice.

RECOVERY

Recovery of patients should be conducted in an authorised recovery area that meets the requirement specified by the local perioperative service (ANZCA, 2010). A patient is transferred to recovery by a nurse escort and the anaesthetist who provide a handover to recovery staff and ensures that they are breathing spontaneously before returning to theatre. Airway support using jaw thrust with 100% oxygen is required until the patient is fully conscious and orientated in time, place and person and can manage their own airway. The recovery nurse should monitor and record blood pressure, pulse rate, respiratory rate and oxygen saturations every five minutes for the unconscious patient and every 15 minutes for the conscious patient.

The recovery team requires a policy to manage the difficult patient who emerges from the anaesthetic in a state of agitation and arousal. The guideline should be developed by recovery, anaesthetic and ECT staff and include advice concerning pharmacological and physical techniques that could be used to maintain patient and staff safety. At-risk patients should be identified early so that these techniques can be used routine during the recovery period. Pharmacological management must include the anaesthetist.

The most effective care of the distressed patient involves one-to-one nursing support. Making the following adjustments to the electric bed can assist nursing the agitated patient:

- elevate the head of the bed so that the patient is in a sitting position;
- elevate the foot of the bed;
- once the head and foot of bed have been elevated, partially tilt the bed so that the head is a downward position and the patient is contained in a V position;
- reduce the height of the bed to the lowest setting to prevent injuries and falls.

Staff should exercise caution, be aware of safety issues at all times and recognise when it is appropriate to request assistance. Symptomatic relief should be offered for minor complaints like headache and nausea as well as a light meal and fluids to ensure that the patient's gag reflex has returned.

Inpatients can be transferred back to the ward on their bed within an hour, providing all vital signs are stable. It is essential that the transferring nurse provide a detailed handover to the nursing staff on the ward, ensuring that all data is entered into the appropriate recording system.

Outpatients can be discharged home when orientated to time, place and person and are able to ambulate without assistance. Many hospitals have a post-anaesthetic discharge scoring system (PADSS), which provides objective assessment of recovery (McMeekin, 2010). The PADSS is a clinically based, objective scoring system used to measure the home readiness of patients following day surgery. Measures include that all vital signs are within 20% of pre-ECT limits and that the patient is fully orientated and not experiencing pain, nausea or vomiting.

HYPEROXYGENATION

Oxygenation is defined as ventilation with 100% oxygen in a positive pressure environment and a respiratory rate of between to 15–20 breaths per minute. The patient is asked to take deep breaths of pure oxygen administered through a mask during the set-up process, usually two to three minutes before the treatment begins (Mankad and Weiner, 2010). In some patients the mask can induce anxiety and they should be given the option of holding it onto their face themselves or putting the plastic tube between their teeth.

Once induction has occurred, the anaesthetist should maintain oxygenation via controlled ventilation with an appropriate breathing system. Cerebral oxygen consumption during a seizure can go up by an order of 200% (Posner, Plum and Van Poznak, 1969). Some anaesthetists may ventilate during the seizure but care needs to be taken to prevent EEG artefacts, as illustrated in EEG 5.5.15.

In a titration session, where more than one stimulus is applied, it is recommended that the anaesthetist hyperventilate between stimuli. There is evidence that hyperventilation lowers seizure threshold, enhancing the expression of EEG seizure activity (Bergholm, Gran and Bleie, 1984; Chater and Simpson, 1988; Rasanen, Martin, Downs and Hodges, 1988; Swayama, Takahashi and Inoue, 2008) and may improve reorientation time by up to 34% (Mayur et al., 2010).

Particular attention needs to be given for patients who are at high risk of rapid haemoglobin oxygen desaturation. These include patients who are morbidly obese, smokers and those patients with pulmonary disease. Arterial hypoxia may develop rapidly during or after the seizure regardless of oxygen supplementation and adequate control over the airway, ventilation and pulse oximetry monitoring is essential to ensure adequate levels of saturation (Rasanen et al., 1988).

The ECT practitioner should be aware that hyperventilation decreases carbon dioxide saturation thereby diminishing the drive to breathe after the seizure and the frequency of ventilation should be gradually reduced, allowing for spontaneous breathing (Mankad and Weiner, 2010).

MOUTH PROTECTION

When the patient is fully relaxed, an appropriate bite block should be inserted between the upper and lower teeth. Once the stimulation is applied there is a direct stimulation of the pterygoid, masseter and temporalis muscles, resulting in jaw contraction. This can be very forceful as the direct stimulation prevents muscle relaxant from having a full effect on these muscles. Care should be taken

to ensure that the bite block protects the molars deep in the jaw and that the tongue is out of the way of the teeth. Broken teeth or bites to the tongue are possible if careful attention is not given to this procedure. It is dangerous for a solid plastic airway to be left in place during the application of the stimulus as it concentrates the force of the jaw over a limited number of anterior teeth. An effective bite block should be made of flexible material and be large enough to distribute the load of the jaw clench evenly across the teeth.

Bite blocks may be disposable or reusable following sterilisation. The choice depends upon the appropriate regional health policy. Disposable bite blocks can be expensive, increasing the cost of the procedure.

Most anaesthetists will remove dentures prior to the insertion of a bite block. Once inserted, it is important to manually support the jaw until after the application of the stimulus. This reduces the pressure applied to the teeth. Bite blocks should allow the flow of air to ensure adequate ventilation while the patient is unconscious.

Bite blocks

Disposable/single-use bite blocks
One of the ECT device manufacturers produces a disposable mouthguard, as illustrated in Photos 5.1.20 and 5.1.21. These guards are shaped to fit the upper and lower teeth and provide protection of the molars. Sometimes they can be difficult to insert as the tongue gets in the way. Care should be taken to ensure that the tongue is relaxed within the mouth to avoid injury.

Reusable/rubber bite blocks
These bite blocks are made of soft rubber and are sterilised before each use, illustrated in Photo 5.1.21. The limitation of these bite blocks is that they may not fully protect the molar teeth in the back of the mouth. Care should be taken to ensure that it is inserted deeply into the mouth. The mouthguard has a hole at the top to allow adequate ventilation

for the unconscious patient. All hard types of mouthguards need to be avoided to minimise teeth trauma.

REFERENCES

American Psychiatric Association. (2001). *The Practice of Electroconvulsive Therapy: Recommendations for Treatment, Training and Privileging: A Task Force Report,* 2nd edition. Washington, DC: American Psychiatric Association.

ANZCA. (2010). Recommendations for the perioperative care of patients selected for day care surgery. Retrieved from www.anzca.edu.au/resources/professional-documents/pdfs/ps15-2010-recommendations-for-the-perioperative-care-of-patients-selected-for-day-care-surgery.pdf.

ANZCA. (2015). Pre, peri and post operative guidelines. Retrieved from www.anzca.edu.au/resources/professional-documents.

Avramov, M.N., Husain, M.M., and White, P.F. (1995). The comparative effects of methohexital, propofol, and etomidate for electroconvulsive therapy. *Anesthesia & Analgesia, 81*(3), 596–602. Retrieved from www.ncbi.nlm.nih.gov/pubmed/7653829.

Bergholm, P., Gran, L., and Bleie, H. (1984). Seizure duration in unilateral electroconvulsive therapy: the effect of hypocapnia induced by hyperventilation and the effect of ventilation with oxygen. *Acta Psychiatrica Scandinavica, 69,* 121–128.

Chater, S.N., and Simpson, K.H. (1988). Effect of passive hyperventilation on seizure duration in patients undergoing electroconvulsive therapy. *British Journal of Anaesthesia, 60*(1), 70–73.

Cheam, E.W., Critchley, L.A., Chiu, P.T., Yap, J.C., and Ha, V.W. (1999). Low-dose mivacurium is less effective than succinylcholine in electroconvulsive therapy. *Canadian Journal of Anaesthetics, 46,* 49–51.

Ding, Z., and White, P.F. (2002). Anesthesia for electroconvulsive therapy. *Anesthesia and Analgesia, 94*(5), 1351–1364. doi:10.1097/00000539-200205000-00057.

Fear, C.F., Littlejohns, C.S., Rouse, E., and McQuail, P. (1994). Propofol anaesthesia in electroconvulsive therapy: reduced seizure duration may not be relevant. *British Journal of Psychiatry, 165,* 506–509.

Galvez, V., Hadzi-Pavlovic, D., Smith, D., and Loo, C.K. (2015). Predictors of seizure threshold in right unilateral ultrabrief electroconvulsive therapy: role of concomitant medications and anaesthesia used. *Brain Stimulation, 8*(3), 486–492. doi:10.1016/j.brs.2014.12.012.

Galvez, V., and Loo, C.K. (2017). Clinical applicability of monitoring the time interval between anesthesia and electro-convulsive therapy. *Journal of ECT, 33*(1), 4–6. doi:10.1097/YCT.0000000000000384.

Galvez, V., McGuirk, L., and Loo, C.K. (2016). The use of ketamine in ECT anaesthesia: A systematic review and critical commentary on efficacy, cognitive, safety and seizure outcomes. *World Journal of Biological Psychiatry, 1–21.* doi:10.1080/15622975.2016.1252464.

Galvez, V., Tor, P.C., Bassa, A., Hadzi-Pavlovic, D., MacPherson, R., Marroquin-Harris, M., and Loo, C.K. (2016). Does remifentanil improve ECT seizure quality? *European Archives of Psychiatry and Clinical Neuroscience, 266*(8), 719–724. doi:10.1007/s00406-016-0690-9.

Geretsegger, C., Rochowanski, E., Kartnig, C., and Unterrainer, A.F. (1998). Propofol and methohexital as anesthetic agents for electroconvulsive therapy (ECT): a comparison of seizure-quality measures and vital signs. *Journal of ECT, 14*(1), 28–35.

Herriot, P.M., Cowain, T., and McLeod, D. (1996). Use of vecuronium to prevent suxamethonium-induced myalgia after ECT. *British Journal of Psychiatry, 168,* 653–654.

Ishikawa, T., Kawahara, S., Saito, T., Otsuka, H., Kemmotsu, O., Hirayama, E., . . . Koyama, T. (2001). Anesthesia for electroconvulsive therapy during pregnancy – a case report. *Masui, 50*(9), 991–997. Retrieved from www.ncbi.nlm.nih.gov/pubmed/11593722.

Kirkby, K.C., Beckett, W.G., Matters, R.M., and King, T.E. (1995). Comparison of propofol and methohexitone in anaesthesia for ECT: effect on seizure duration and outcome. *Australian and New Zealand Journal of Psychiatry, 29*(2), 299–303. doi:10.1080/00048679509075925.

McMeekin, K. (2010). Post-Anaesthetic Discharge Scoring System (PADSS). *Day Surgery Australia, 9*(1), 20.

MacPherson, R., and Loo, C. (2008). Cognitive impairment following electroconvulsive therapy – does the choice of anaesthetic agent make a difference? *Journal of ECT, 24*(1), 52–56.

Malsch, E., Gratz, I., Mani, S., Backup, C., Levy, S., and Allen, E. (1994). Efficacy of electroconvulsive therapy after propofol and methohexital anesthesia. *Convulsive Therapy, 10*(3), 212–219. Retrieved from www.ncbi.nlm.nih.gov/pubmed/7834258.

Mankad, M.V., and Weiner, R.D. (2010). Anesthetics and other Medications. In Mankad, M.V., Beyer, J.L., Weiner, R.D., and Krystal, A.D. (Eds.), *Clinical Manual of Electroconvulsive Therapy* (pp. 81–93). Washington, DC: American Psychiatric Publishing.

Martin, D.M., Katalinic, N., Ingram, A., Schweitzer, I., Smith, D.J., Hadzi-Pavlovic, D., and Loo, C.K. (2013). A new early cognitive screening measure to detect cognitive side-effects of electroconvulsive therapy? *Journal of Psychiatric Research, 47*(12), 1967–1974. doi:10.1016/j.jpsychires.2013.08.021.

Nott, M.R., and Watts, J.S. (1999). A fractured hip during electroconvulsive therapy. *European Journal of Anaesthesiology, 16*(4), 265–267. Retrieved from www.ncbi.nlm.nih.gov/pubmed/10234499.

NSW Health. (2010). ECT minimum standard of practice NSW. Retrieved from www.health.nsw.gov.au/policies/pd/2011/pdf/PD2011_003.pdf.

Porter, R., Heenan, H., and Reeves, J. (2008). Early effects of electroconvulsive therapy on cognitive function. *Journal of ECT, 24*(1), 35–39. doi:10.1097/YCT.0b013e31816207f0.

Posner, J.B., Plum, F., and Van Poznak, A. (1969). Cerebral metabolism during electrically induced seizures in man. *Archives of Neurology, 20*(4), 388–395. Retrieved from www.ncbi.nlm.nih.gov/pubmed/5796727.

Pouget, P., Wattiez, N., Rivaud-Pechoux, S., and Gaymard, B. (2010). Rapid development of tolerance to sub-anaesthetic dose of ketamine: an oculomotor study in macaque monkeys. *Psychopharmacology (Berl), 209*(4), 313–318. doi:10.1007/s00213-010-1797-8.

Rasanen, J., Martin, D.J., Downs, J.B., and Hodges, M.R. (1988). Oxygen supplementation during electroconvulsive therapy. *British Journal of Anaesthesia, 61*(5), 593–597. Retrieved from www.ncbi.nlm.nih.gov/pubmed/3207530.

Saffer, S., and Berk, M. (1998). Anesthetic induction for ECT with etomidate is associated with longer seizure duration than thiopentone. *Journal of ECT, 14,* 89–93.

Sarpel, Y., Togrul, E., Herdem, M., Tan, I., and Baytok, G. (1996). Central acetabular fracture-dislocation following electroconvulsive therapy: report of two similar cases. *Journal of Trauma, 41*(2), 342–344. Retrieved from www.ncbi.nlm.nih.gov/pubmed/8760548.

Swayama, E., Takahashi, M., and Inoue, A. (2008). Moderate hyperventilation problongs electroencephalogram seizure duration of the first electroconvulsive therapy. *Journal of ECT, 24,* 195–198.

Tanaka, N., Saito, Y., Hikawa, Y., Nakazawa, K., Yasuda, K., and Amaha, K. (1997). Effects of thiopental and sevoflurane on hemodynamics during anesthetic management of electroconvulsive therapy. *Masui, 46*(12), 1575–1579. Retrieved from www.ncbi.nlm.nih.gov/pubmed/9455079.

Tiller, J.W.G., and Lyndon, R.W. (2003). *Electroconvulsive Therapy: An Australian Guide.* Melbourne, Australia: Australian Post Graduate Medicine.

Trzepacz, P.T., Weniger, F.C., and Greenhouse, J. (1993). Etomidate anesthesia increases seizure duration during ECT. A retrospective study. *General Hospital Psychiatry, 15*(2), 115–120. Retrieved from www.ncbi.nlm.nih.gov/pubmed/8472938.

Verghese, C., and Brimacombe, J.R. (1996). Survey of laryngeal mask airway usage in 11,910 patients: safety and efficacy for conventional and nonconventional usage. *Anesthesia and Analgesia, 82*(1), 129–133. Retrieved from http://journals.lww.com/anesthesia-analgesia/Fulltext/1996/01000/Survey_of_Laryngeal_Mask_Airway_Usage_in_11,910.23.aspx.

Vishne, T., Aronov, S., Amiaz, R., Etchin, A., and Grunhaus, L. (2005). Remifentanil supplementation of propofol during electroconvulsive therapy: effect on seizure duration and cardiovascular stability. *Journal of ECT, 21*(3), 235–238.

Walker, S.C., Bowley, C.J., and Walker, A.C. (2013). Anaesthesia for ECT. In Waite, J., and Easton, A. (Eds.), *The ECT Handbook.* London: Royal College of Psychiatrists.

ECT devices: set-up procedure

THYMATRON SYSTEM IV

Check that the Thymatron device has been recently inspected and certified as being safe for use, as illustrated in Photo 5.7.1.

- Check that the device completes an internal self-test.
- Complete an external test by attaching the EctoBrain II, illustrated in Photo 5.7.2.
- Depress the impedance button it should be between 200 to 220 ohms.
- Set an appropriate stimulus dose then treat observing that the green light illuminates "pass" in the output test area at the top of the EctoBrain II.
- After treatment the Thymatron should print out EEG, EMG and ECG traces generated by

the Ectobrain. How the EctoBrain is set will depend on the type of trace produced.

- Disconnect the EctoBrain II and ensure that the leads for EEG monitoring and treatment electrode cable are secured to the device before turning it on.

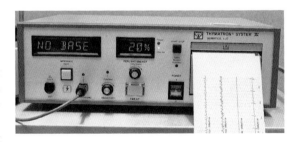

Photo 5.7.1 *Thymatron System IV ECT device*

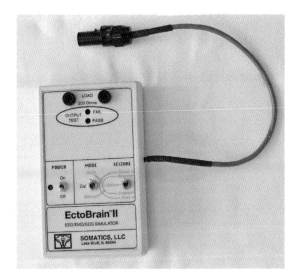

Photo 5.7.2 *EctoBrain II for use with Thymatron System IV device*

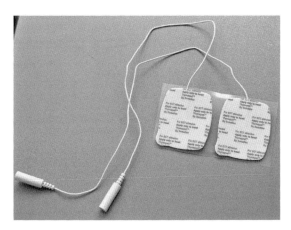

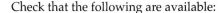

Photo 5.7.3 *Disposable electrodes (Thymapads)*

Photo 5.7.4 *Thymatron handheld electrode*

Photo 5.7.5 *Thymatron dummy electrodes*

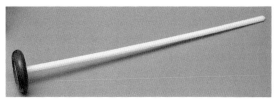

Photo 5.7.6 *Tendon hammer*

Check that the following are available:

- Thymapads, illustrated in Photo 5.7.3;
- handheld electrode, illustrated in Photo 5.7.4;
- EEG electrodes, shown in Photo 5.1.10;
- normal saline solution, warmed if possible to minimise discomfort to the patient;
- conductive gel for handheld electrode, illustrated in Photo 5.1.15;
- alcohol swabs, illustrated in Photo 5.1.12;
- abrasive gel for disposable and handheld electrodes, illustrated in Photo 5.1.13 as NeuPrep;
- conductive solution for disposable electrode, illustrated in Photo 5.1.14 as PreTac;
- blood pressure cuff for "cuff monitoring";
- dummy electrode to manually hold the Thymapad if contact is poor, illustrated in Photo 5.7.5;
- metal discs that insert into the handheld electrode (there should be concave and flat discs);
- spare paper for the EEG recorder;
- tendon hammer, illustrated in Photo 5.7.6;

- bite blocks, disposable (illustrated in Photo 5.1.20) and reusable (illustrated in Photo 5.1.21);
- intravenous cannulas;
- a dedicated doughnut-shaped pillow to allow easy access for the vertex electrode when the head is in the fully extended position, as illustrated in Photo 5.1.3;
- a timer for monitoring time from anaesthetic to treatment;
- the medical record;
- appropriate recording forms for the treatment session.

Request that the patient be brought into the suite with a nurse assistant.

Ask the patient to lie comfortably on the table.

Introduce yourself and the ECT team and briefly explain the procedure, especially if this is the patient's first session.

The anaesthetist team introduces themselves, obtains IV access and informs the patient that they will be given two or more different anaesthetic drugs through "the drip" to go to sleep.

The Thymatron System IV device is different to the DGx machine in that it has a larger yoke with four monitoring channels, illustrated in Photo 5.7.1:

- two red frontal leads, two black mastoid leads;
- green earth lead that is usually sited on the clavicle;
- two ECG leads: red placed on the left side of the chest and black placed on the right side of the chest;
- two EMG leads: both brown, place approximately 2–4 cm apart on the dorsum of foot parallel to the muscle bulk immediately below the BP cuff.

The ECT practitioner fits the EEG leads while the ECT nurse applies the ECG and EMG leads.

Set the pulse width by pressing and holding the percent energy dial – the pulse width will flash; turning clockwise or anticlockwise adjusts the pulse width. Set the percent energy dial to the correct dose after reviewing the EEG tracing from the previous treatment and noting the recommendation of the treating doctor. Then follow the procedure below:

- Wash the recording and treating electrode site with normal saline to remove skin oil.
- Repeat this procedure with an alcohol swab.
- Apply abrasive electrode gel using a light scrubbing motion and / or the conductive solution to the skin or scalp site beneath the electrode.
- Apply the five EEG leads.
- Apply the ECG and EMG electrodes.
- Clip the bulldog clip attached to the monitoring leads to the left side of the patient's gown / clothing. If the patient needs to be moved then the lead yoke moves with them preventing disruption of the set-up.
- Apply the treating electrodes; refer to Figures 5.2.1 to 5.2.6 and Photos 5.2.1 to 5.2.14 for the correct placement and correct device.
- Apply firm pressure to the disposable electrode with palm of hand to ensure adequate adhesion.
- When administering RUL, use a saline swab to douse the hair on the right vertex area and rub in electrode conduction-enhancing paste.
- If administering RUL or LUL, attach the concave disc to the black handheld electrode.
- Apply electrode cream or gel to the metal surface.
- Inform the patient that they may experience pressure on the back of their head and position the handheld electrode onto the right vertex area.
- Press impedance button "No Base" will change to "Testing" then display in the static impedance in the LED screen above the impedance button. A number ranging from 0 to 3000 ohms, representing the static impedance in ohms, follows this. Aim for a number less than 1500 ohms.
- When the impedance button is released and the message "Baseline" will appear for several seconds after the impedance test button is released. This indicates that the device is collecting the baseline EEG data.

- When baseline EEG collection has been accomplished, the word "Ready" will appear in the LED.
- Check that the percent energy dial is set at the correct energy setting. It is always best to set the percent energy before the set-up begins to ensure that the correct dose is administered to the patient.
- The charge dose in millicoulombs corresponding to any percent energy figure shown in the LED can be viewed at any time for one second by turning the percentage energy dial one click to either side then back again.
- If the LCD flashes ">3000 ohm" it indicates that an error has occurred in the set-up. Recheck the treatment electrodes to identify the source of the error. The most common cause is failure to insert the electrode cable into the Thymapad connection or the handheld electrode. Occasionally, the Thymapad or the cable may be faulty and should be replaced.
- Avoid moving the patient's head or touching or moving the recoding electrodes, lead wires or recording cables during baseline EEG collection as this can delay the process.
- A heavy (black) trace on one or more leads imply that there is a poor connection; check all leads to ensure good contact has been achieved.
- The problem is usually a loose mastoid electrode; replace or reapplies pressure to ensure adhesion. If this fails to correct the problem, check the connection between the lead wire and the yoke. Firm pressure on the coupling device can usually rectify the problem. If this fails you may need to replace the EEG, ECG or EMG leads or the yoke cable.
- The device is now ready to administer ECT.
- Complete time out procedure following the local area protocol.
- The anaesthetist begins ventilation with 100% oxygen.
- Once everything is ready, the anaesthetist administers the induction agents and muscle relaxant.
- Activate the timer when the suxamethonium is administered.

- Observe the patient closely for fasciculation. Complete relaxation is obtained once all fasciculations have ceased.
- Demonstrate an absent knee deep tendon reflex, indicating effective paralysis.
- When ready the anaesthetist inserts the bite block and supports the chin.
- Compete the final time out and check of the impedance, for more details concerning the time out procedure refer to Section 5.1.
- If the impedance is high it is useful to ask an assistant to put pressure on disposable electrodes using dummy electrodes.
- Treatment should commence once the team agrees that everything is ready to proceed.
- Lift the protective plastic cover and push the yellow button with one hand while holding the vertex electrode device with the other.
- The treatment button will glow yellow during the application of the stimulus and turn off once the stimulus has been delivered.
- Do not release the button until all of the stimulus is delivered – this is evident by the light going out, the patient's masseters releasing and the recording paper starting to print out.
- The duration of the stimulation will vary depending upon type of ECT administered with longer durations for ultrabrief.
- The recording device automatically activates generating an ictal line and audible warble that persists throughout the seizure.
- The end of the seizure is determined by postictal suppression assisted by the audible warble changing to a monotone.
- Allow the trace to continue for a further 10 seconds so that the device can calculate the seizure adequacy parameters then push the start/stop button to end recording.
- Postictal Suppression Index (PSI) can be a useful parameter that can assist in determining seizure adequacy and is used in assessing the amount of energy required for future treatments.
- Remove all treatment and recording leads.
- Record details in the appropriate medical record.

For power settings above 100% without ultrabrief pulse width (0.3 ms) modification

- Press Flexidial button once.
- Turn anticlockwise until "Programs" found on LCD display (10 clicks).
- Press Flexidial button once.
- Turn clockwise two clicks to "2x" charge-rate.
- LCD display flashes.
- Press Flexidial once.
- To set, press "start/stop" button (paper feed).
- Device prints out settings.
- Set required power level, for example 140%.

Safety monitor activated alarm

The safety monitor activated LED is a patented safety feature built into the Thymatron System IV. It is an electronic apparatus to automatically measure the electrical dosage of an ECT device at the time of stimulus to prevent delivery to the patient a dosage substantially larger than the dosage selected by the operator. When the measured dosage varies more or less than the selected limited amount from the stimulus dial setting, it triggers the visible red LED and a loud audible signal blocking the device from delivering further stimuli without first being reset (Somatics, 1995).

For power settings above 100% with ultrabrief pulse width (0.3 ms) modification

- Push and hold percent energy button.
- Wait for programme to flash.
- Turn dial to the right three clicks until "2x" flashes.
- When administering ultrabrief ECT, turn the percent energy button two clicks to the right until "2xLP" flashes (LP stands for lowest pulse width).
- Release button.
- Dial up appropriate power.

MECTA SPECTRUM 5000M AND Q

Check that the MECTA device has been recently inspected and certified as being safe for use.

Ensure that the MECTA device is plugged into a power supply.

Ensure that the leads for the EEG monitoring and are secured to the device.

The following should be available:

- handheld treatment electrodes, illustrated in Photo 5.7.8;
- optical motor sensor, a device that is connected to the great toe of the cuff-monitored foot;
- EEG skin pads;
- normal saline solution, warmed if possible for patient comfort;
- electrode gel;

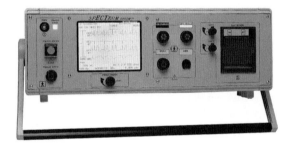

Photo 5.7.7 *MECTA spECTrum 5000Q ECT device*

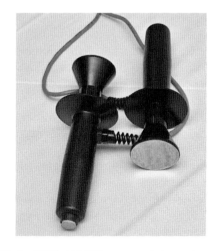

Photo 5.7.8 *MECTA treatment electrodes*

- conductive gel for handheld electrode, illustrated in Photo 5.1.15;
- abrasive gel for use under the handheld electrodes, illustrated in Photo 5.1.13 as NeuPrep;
- alcohol swabs, illustrated in Photo 5.1.12;
- blood pressure cuff for "cuff monitoring";
- spare paper for the EEG recorder;
- tendon hammer, illustrated in Photo 5.7.6;
- bite blocks, disposable (illustrated in Photo 5.2.20) and reusable (Photo 5.1.21);
- intravenous cannula;
- A dedicated doughnut-shaped pillow to allow easy access for the vertex electrode when the head is in the fully extended position, illustrated in Photo 5.1.3;
- the medical record;
- appropriate recording forms for the treatment session;

Turn on the MECTA spECTrum 5000 device. The device takes a minute or so to performing internal tests. Completion indicated when the screen reads "internal test passed", adjust contrast and "press clear to proceed".

Once "clear" has been pressed, the display indicates four channels: Channel 1, left EEG; Channel 2, right EEG; Channel 3, optical motion sensor (OMS); Channel 4, ECG.

Press the menu button located on the upper right part of the screen. Then select the "patient data" button. Add the following patient data:

- medical record number;
- patient age;
- number of treatments;
- maintenance treatment YES or NO;
- electrode placement RUL or BL;

Once this information has been recorded, press "Exit", located in the top left-hand side of the screen. Press "Exit" again to return to the recording screen.

N.B. The device can only be activated once the home screen is displayed.

Request that the patient be brought into the suite with a nursing assistant.

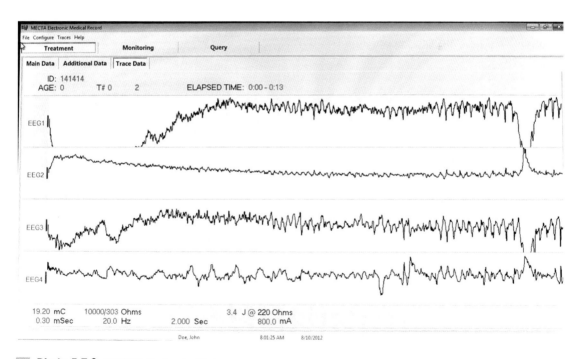

Photo 5.7.9 *MECTA electronic display*

Ask the patient to lie comfortably on the table.

Introduce yourself and the ECT team and briefly explain the procedure, especially if this is the patient's first session.

The anaesthetist team introduces themselves, obtains IV access and inform the patient that they will be given two or more different anaesthetic drugs through "the drip" to go to sleep.

The ECT practitioner fits the EEG leads while the ECT nurse applies the ECG and EMG leads.

On the MECTA spECTrum 5000M, set the percent charge dial to the correct dose after reviewing the EEG tracing from the previous treatment and noting the recommendation of the treating doctor. If using a spECTrum 5000Q device, the stimulus parameters pulse width, frequency, duration and current will need to set individually as per dosing protocol.

Then follow the procedure below:

- Wash the recording and treating electrode site with normal saline to remove skin oil.
- Repeat this procedure with an alcohol swab.
- Apply abrasive electrode gel using a light scrubbing motion and/or the conductive solution to the skin or scalp site beneath the treating electrode.
- Apply the five EEG leads.
- Apply the ECG electrodes and the OMS if fitted to the device.
- Clip the bulldog clip attached to the monitoring leads to the left side of the patient's gown/clothing. If the patient needs to be moved, the lead yoke moves with them, preventing disruption of the set-up.
- Mark the site for the treatment electrodes; refer to Figures 5.2.1 to 5.2.6 and Photos 5.2.1 to 5.2.14 for the correct placement and correct device.
- When administering RUL, use a saline swab to douse the hair on the right vertex area and rub in electrode conduction-enhancing paste.
- Apply electrode cream or gel to the metal surface of the treatment electrodes.
- Inform the patient that they may experience pressure under the treatment electrodes.

- Check that the device is set at the correct energy setting. It is best practice to set the stimulus before the set-up begins to ensure that the correct dose is administered to the patient.
- Impedance is automatically calculated and displayed as:
  "Stimulus status": an LED light to the right of the power button, illustrated in Photo 5.7.7. An indicator bar located on the left side of the touch screen, the lower the position on the bar the lower the impedance with the actual value in ohms recorded below this bar graph, illustrated in Photo 5.1.18.
- Turn on the chart recorder, activating the EEG paper, and ensure that all baseline measures are recorded.
- Left, Channel 1, and right, Channel 2, EEGs are also recorded on the screen.
- If artefact is present, check all electrodes to ensure adequate adhesion; if this fails you may need to replace the cable.
- If indicated, ensure that the OMS device is applied to the great toe below the cuff monitor with the green surface touching the skin.
- The device is now ready to administer ECT.
- Complete time out procedure following the local area protocol.
- The anaesthetist begins ventilation with 100% oxygen.
- Once everything is ready the anaesthetist administers the induction agents and muscle relaxant.
- Activate the timer when the suxamethonium is administered.
- Observe the patient closely for fasciculation. Complete relaxation is obtained once all fasciculation have ceased.
- Demonstrate an absent knee deep tendon reflex, indicating effective paralysis.
- Ensure that the handheld treatment electrodes are located in the correct anatomical site, avoid accidently putting pressure on the stimulus button, illustrated in Photo 5.7.8.
- When ready the anaesthetist inserts the bite block and supports the chin.

- Compete the final time out and check impedance.
- Treatment should commence once the team agrees that everything is ready to proceed.
- Press the orange button located at the end of one of the treatment electrodes; it will glow orange throughout the delivery of the stimulus.
- The duration of the stimulation will vary depending upon type of ECT administered with longer durations for ultrabrief.
- There is a three-second delay before the stimulus is administered; during this period the device prints out a self-test result.
- Once this has been completed, it then administers the stimulus.
- The stimulus status light changes to orange, indicating stimulus administration.
- The recording device automatically activates generating a paper and electronic record that will display on the touch screen as well as the optional electronic screen if attached, illustrated in Photo 5.7.9 as a four-channel EEG recording.
- The MECTA spECTrum device does not have an audible facility to indicate seizure activity.
- Stop recording a few seconds after postictal suppression has occurred: flat line at the end of seizure.

- The EEG recording device is de-activated by either pushing the "Off" button on the chart recorder or the square labelled "Done" at the top left-hand corner of the touch screen.
- For RUL ECT, the device will calculate seizure adequacy and seizure-level parameters that are printed with other parameters at the end of the EEG trace.
- Seizure adequacy and seizure-level parameters provide information that can assist with decision-making regarding the adequacy of the seizure generated in the context of clinical response, determining what stimulus should be applied at the next treatment session.

THYMATRON DGX

The set-up for the Thymatron DGx is similar to the set-up for the Thymatron System IV, which has not been modified to administer an ultrabrief (0.3 millisecond) stimulus listed above and will not be repeated.

REFERENCE

Somatics, L.L.C. (1995). Safety monitor circuit for an ECT device and method: US 5470347 A. Retrieved from www.google.com/patents/US5470347.

CHAPTER 6

Ambulatory ECT, continuation ECT and maintenance ECT

ECT after completion of the index course

AMBULATORY ECT

Ambulatory or outpatient ECT is organised once a patient has improved enough to return home but further treatment is required to gain remission. Factors that favour returning home include:

- the patient or carer's preference;
- minimising the disruption to family life;
- greater normalisation away from the sick role;
- better use of community resources;
- continuation and maintenance ECT

A flexible approach is recommended to meet the broad needs of patients as well as referring physicians.

If the acuity of the patient is low, ambulatory ECT can be organised for an index course of treat-ment and the patient remains at maintained at home. There are a number of obstacles that need to be overcome:

- lack of priority over more acute patients who are currently inpatients, resulting in lengthy delays in commencing treatment;
- carer and family fatigue;
- worries about the patient's risk to self and others;
- mounting anxiety and dread within the patient each time they have to present to the hospital that can lead to worsening their clinical state and make ECT less effective;
- managing complex medical problems that require regular monitoring.

Maintaining the patient within the community improves communication between the ECT team and community services, including private psychiatrists and community teams enhancing continued care. Community psychiatrists and private psychiatrists as well as the relevant mental health team are able to refer patients for a course of ECT. Within a public setting it is recommended that private psychiatrists refer the patient to the local community mental health team for a second opinion and ongoing management of the patient during the course of ECT treatment.

There are a number of other criteria that should be satisfied in order for a patient to be eligible for ambulatory ECT. The treating team / clinician should be confident that the patient:

- will have a responsible and reliable adult available at home to supervise them according to the local day-only surgical procedure requirements;
- has an adult who can assist them with transport to and from hospital;
- will take essential medication such as antiarrhythmic and antihypertensive medication, if required prior to the ECT with a sip of water;
- can reliably fast for a specific duration, usually eight to 10 hours before the procedure;
- can arrive promptly before the scheduled time of the ECT treatment;
- will not drive, use other machinery or do anything else hazardous on the day of treatment;
- is monitored regularly by the treating consultant psychiatrist, who can review their progress during the course of ECT;
- has a psychiatrist who together with the ECT team makes decisions concerning clinical progress;
- is not a danger to themselves or to other people, is not at risk of suicide or self-harm and is not influenced by psychotic phenomena.

There are a number of relative contraindications for outpatient ECT. These include:

- where there is poor compliance;
- absence of support for 24 hours after the anaesthetic;
- patients who are an acute suicide risk;
- medical conditions requiring more intensive monitoring;
- a history of ECT-related states of confusion beyond the immediate recovery period;
- insufficient resources available for outpatient ECT to be administered safely;
- poor oral intake after treatment;
- high anaesthetic risk;
- ongoing abuse of alcohol and other substances.

Patient monitoring

Patients undergoing outpatient ECT need to be carefully monitored. All legal requirements should be completed before treatment is administered. It is recommended that the treating team or psychiatrist review the patient and meet with the family regularly during the course of treatment. It is not unusual for patients' physical, mental and legal status to change positively or negatively during treatment. Careful monitoring, discussion with family and carers and clear documentation are required early on during the course of treatment as the vegetative symptoms of depression often improve before the negative cognitions. The patient, still depressed, has been "freed up" enough to carry out their suicide plan. If the family or staff are concerned, urgent assessment and hospitalisation may be required.

The ECT team should liaise directly with the community psychiatrist if they are concerned about lack of progression or cognitive impairment so that changes can be made to the treatment plan. It is best practice to monitor with measures that are completed before, during and after the course of treatment to guide management. Time to recovery has become an important assessment that should be undertaken after each treatment, with recent data linking this finding to more enduring retrograde amnesia (Martin et al., 2013; Porter, Douglas and Knight, 2008).

TAPERING OR STEP-DOWN ECT

It is now common practice to taper or step down the index course of ECT. Tapering ECT is a protocol of gradually reducing the frequency of treatment immediately following an index course of ECT. The schedule varies and must be individualised with steps down to twice a week, weekly, two-weekly or even three-weekly. It is during this phase that medication is maximised to ensure that remission is maintained as the frequency of ECT is slowly reduced and ceased. The aim is to prevent a "clinical dip", which was very common in the past when the index course of ECT was suddenly ceased prior to initiating treatment with a tricyclic antidepressant.

CLINICAL WISDOM 6.1.1

Too often general practitioners are left out of the loop. Their involvement as an active participant in ongoing care ensures that changes in a patient's physical state are detected and appropriate investigations initiated, with treatment initiated as clinically indicated. GPs provide a different perspective that can be helpful in assessing the patient's mental state and the benefits of maintenance ECT.

Effective m-ECT requires clear communication between the patient, family, treatment team and the psychiatric team prescribing the ECT. It is important to involve the patient's general practitioner in coordinating six-monthly physicals with appropriate investigations and details forwarded to the ECT service.

CONTINUATION ECT

Continuation ECT (c-ECT) refers to ECT that is given after an episode of depression to prevent a relapse of the same episode over a six-month period. It is administered on a one-, two-, three- or four-weekly basis over a six-month period dependent upon clinical need.

MAINTENANCE ECT

Maintenance ECT (m-ECT) is defined as ECT that is administered after a six-month period to prevent recurrence of a new episode of depression and may last for years or indefinitely. The patient and doctor agree that this is the preferred treatment option often owing to a long period of treatment resistance and relapse. If the person is not capable of providing informed consent the relevant mental health tribunal should regularly review the patient to determine the necessity of ongoing ECT.

The transition from continuation to maintenance ECT is arbitrary and the two terms are often used interchangeably, with both terms referring the use of ECT as prophylaxis to prevent relapse and a return of symptoms.

Best practice requires that a second opinion, by a suitably qualified psychiatrist, be completed on a 12-monthly basis or before if there are complications with the treatment.

INDICATIONS FOR CONTINUATION AND MAINTENANCE ECT

The decision to proceed to continuation/maintenance ECT is complex and is often based upon a number of factors (Trevino, McClintock and Husain, 2010; NSW Health, 2010):

- the clinical presentation and response to the index course;
- minimal cognitive impairment during the index course;
- a clear history of relapse/recurrence despite having an adequate trials of medications and combinations;
- intolerance to pharmacotherapy and other maintenance therapy;
- severity of illness;
- the patient's request;
- close consultation with the patient, carers and family.

Maintenance ECT has been used successfully in patients with recurrent episodes of major depression or bipolar disorder to control recurrent depressive or manic swings, and treatment-resistant schizophrenia, where ECT is used in conjunction with ongoing antipsychotic medication.

CURRENT STATE OF THE EVIDENCE

Brown, Lee, Scott and Cummings (2014) conducted a systematic review of all the available evidence and found 103 abstracts and 36 articles, with only six studies meeting the criteria for inclusion. Of these studies, three were randomised controlled trials (RCT), one was a non-randomised comparison trial, one a retrospective case control study and one a matched design pre- and post-intervention study. All of the studies followed patients who were given m-ECT after an index course of treatment and compared them to a group of patients who did not receive ongoing ECT. A meta-analysis was not conducted owing to the heterogeneous nature of the sample but the authors did conclude that c/m-ECT was efficacious for the prevention of relapse/recurrence of major depression and that the efficacy was increased when combined with antidepressant medication and flexible treatment intervals that were responsive to early signs of recurrence.

The evidence supporting the use of continuation and maintenance ECT has been strengthened with the recent publication of the Prolonging Remission in Depressed Elderly (PRIDE) study (Kellner et al., 2016). PRIDE demonstrated superiority of the continuation ECT arm over pharmacotherapy only in preventing relapse after ECT over a six-month follow-up period. These results are in contrast to the first prospective RCT, which compared maintenance ECT monotherapy (bilateral electrode placement) against maintenance medication only following a successful index course of ECT (CORE) (Kellner et al., 2006). The CORE study failed to demonstrate a significant difference between maintenance ECT and pharmacotherapy (lithium plus antidepressant) in preventing relapse post-ECT, with relapse rates of about a third of patients in each group.

The PRIDE study recruited 240 elderly patients with major depressive disorder for an acute course or right unilateral ultrabrief ECT combined with venlafaxine. Remission was achieved in 148 (61.7%) of participants. Of these, 120 consented to Phase 2 of the trial and were randomised to pharmacotherapy (venlafaxine plus lithium) or pharmacotherapy plus c-ECT for four weeks with additional ECT as needed. Continuation ECT following a successful course of ECT, treatments being at least weekly for one month-post index course and then as clinically indicated combined with antidepressant medication and lithium, was more effective in preventing relapse than mediation alone at six months post-ECT (Kellner et al., 2016).

There is strong evidence that lithium in combination with antidepressant medication can help prevent depressive relapse during the first six months after a successful course of ECT and should be considered when contemplating c-ECT. The use of lithium may be one reason for the success of the PRIDE study, with the dose of lithium withheld the night before treatment to prevent postictal confusion. Rasmussen (2015) reviewed the literature concerning the use of lithium in preventing relapse post-ECT, highlighting the benefits but also raising a number of important questions that need to be answered, including the optimal blood level, duration of use and concomitant antidepressant choice.

THE LITERATURE

Case reports and smaller studies remain an important source of information that can guide clinical practice. The following review highlights the effectiveness of ECT when it is continued after a successful course of treatment.

Frederikse, Petrides and Kellner (2006) summarised the literature and concluded that published and emerging data supports the use of ECT in specific populations. These include medication refractory patients, those who have been ECT-responsive in the past and those who are prone to relapses of depression. This view was supported by Andrade and Kurinji (2002), who also noted that m-ECT was useful to reduce the risk of relapse in patients after a successful index course of treatment. It was particularly useful in those patients who had a poor response or could not tolerate medication. They noted that, despite the potential value of m-ECT, it is often neglected in clinical practice.

Vaidya, Mahableshwarkar and Shahid (2003) noted that m-ECT was safe and more tolerated and efficacious in response prevention. Maintenance ECT reduced hospitalisation rates, particularly in the elderly and patients who were treatment-resistant to medication. They echo the sentiments that m-ECT was an underutilised treatment, even though the overwhelming majority of studies highlighted the efficacy of m-ECT in bipolar disorder. They urged clinicians to seriously consider using this strategy in clinical practice.

Rabheru (2012) reviewed the literature and noted that there was a high risk of relapse after ECT was discontinued and that m-ECT was an underused treatment option. Using m-ECT substantially reduced the risk of relapse in patients with major depressive disorder as well as bipolar disorder and schizophrenia.

One of the concerns surrounding m-ECT is the potential for long-term cognitive impairment, particularly if used for greater than one year. Russell et al. (2003), in a retrospective study of 43 patients who suffered from unipolar and bipolar depression and schizoaffective disorder who had m-ECT for greater than 12 months, concluded that the benefits were present in all patients regardless of their diagnosis. All of the patients in the study had been on multiple medications and required frequent hospitalisations before m-ECT was commenced. Following m-ECT, they noted improvement in the broad range of areas including improvements in level of function, reduction in persistent and troubling symptoms and a reduced need for hospitalisation. In this study they noted that there was little change in the cognitive function of the group.

This finding was supported by Vothknecht et al. (2003), Rami et al. (2004) and Abraham, Milev, Delva

and Zaheer (2006), who demonstrated that cognitive function remained stable in patients who had m-ECT. If cognitive difficulties were experienced they were noted to be limited and tolerable.

Dew and McCall (2004) noted that m-ECT is highly effective and well tolerated in acutely ill patients. It is a useful and cost-effective modality that reduces the need for rehospitalisation. Sartorius and Henn (2005) emphasised that ECT was a prudent tool for keeping patients with major depression in remission. It is the only treatment that yields extended periods of euthymia in patients with treatment-resistant mania (Tsao, Jain, Gibson, Guedet and Lehrmann., 2004). and that m-ECT was a safe alternative to medication alone (Swoboda, Colnca, Konig, Waanders and Hansen, 2001).

Studies of patients who have been managed with medication alone have had disappointing results with high rates of relapse. In a study of response to medication after an effective index course of ECT, Sackeim et al. (2001) noted that 60% of patients on nortriptyline alone relapsed within five weeks of ECT termination. When combined with lithium the rate improved, with 61% remaining well over a six-month period, a finding that has been supported by others (Serra et al., 2006; Navarro et al., 2008).

The combination of neuroleptic medication and m-ECT improves quality of life and level of function in the long term for patients with schizophrenia and schizoaffective disorder (Chanpattana and Kramer, 2003; Swoboda et al., 2001).

Levy-Rueff, Jurgens, Loo, Olie and Amado (2008) reported on 19 patients who underwent m-ECT for schizophrenia between 1991 to 2005, with a mean age of 47.5 years at the beginning of treatment and a mean duration of illness of 24 years. They noted that the indications for m-ECT were an increase of symptom intensity, increase of acute episodes, inefficiency or intolerance of medications or early relapse after the index course of ECT was ceased following a good outcome. All were given bilateral electrode placement. The results were positive, with a mean reduction of yearly hospitalisations of 80%. There was a 40% reduction in duration of hospitalisation and improved ability to take part in activities around the ward or return home. Other improvements included a better quality of life, moving to a day-care facility or living in a halfway house. Maintenance ECT was effective in treating mood symptoms, delusions, anorexia, suicidal ideation, anxiety symptoms and increasing cooperation and treatment compliance. Finally they note that there was no consensus on the rate and number of m-ECT as it varied from patient to patient and was dependent upon the clinical symptoms, compliance and tolerability, with combining m-ECT with medication more effective than either alone.

Wjikstra et al. (2005) reported on a case of a patient who had recurrent episodes of major depressive disorder with psychosis. Prior to the implementation of ECT, the patient had spent 29 months in hospital over a four-year period. Following the commencement of ECT there had been no further admissions to hospital over the next seven and a half years, with 244 treatments administered and no evidence of cognitive decline.

Shimizu et al. (2007) report on a patient with treatment-resistant schizophrenia who had spent seven years continuously in hospital prior to the implementation of ECT. ECT resulted in a dramatic improvement in psychotic symptoms, improving his safety and well-being, enabling him to return home to live with his family.

In conclusion, smaller studies and case reports support the finding of the RCT that m-ECT is effective in preventing relapse after a successful index course of ECT. Despite the potential value of maintenance ECT in improving quality of life and reducing hospitalisation, it is a treatment that is neglected in clinical practice (Andrade and Kurinji, 2002).

MAINTENANCE ECT SCHEDULE

Two approaches – fast or slow transition – have been proposed to move from an index course of treatment to m-ECT (NSW Health, 2010), with a third, more effective method emerging from a recently published randomised clinical trial.

Fast transition involves moving from the index course of treatment to monthly treatment by reducing the frequency of treatment every week. The first maintenance treatment is given one week after the completion of the index course, then two-weekly, then three-weekly before moving to monthly.

Slow transition is a more cautious approach, maintaining treatment more frequently at one and two weeks before moving to monthly. The Consortium for Research in ECT (CORE) used a slow transition method in their multisite randomised control trial involving 201 patients (Kellner et al., 2006). All patients had an index course of bitemporal ECT and were then streamed into continuation ECT or continuation medication groups. The latter involved lithium plus nortriptyline and both were continued for a six-month period. As noted above, the results were disappointing, with each arm having high dropout rates of 16% for the c-ECT and 22% for the continuation medication group, with the overall efficacy similar for both groups.

The discussion noted that one of the challenges they faced in this study was an inability to adjust the treatment schedule for the continuation ECT group, this being in marked contrast to clinical practice, where a flexible, patient-focused ECT schedule was common (Lisanby et al., 2008). Neither a fast or slow transition are best practice with the benefit of a more cautious, flexible approach to m-ECT superior, an approach that has been highlighted in the recent PRIDE study (Kellner et al., 2016).

In phase two of the PRIDE study, 120 remitters from Phase 1 were randomised into two treatment arms, continuing venlafaxine with the addition of lithium or continuing ECT plus medication (venlafaxine plus lithium) weekly for four weeks plus additional ECT as required using the Symptoms Titrated Algorithm-Based Longitudinal ECT (STABLE) algorithm. At 24 weeks, the ECT plus medication group had statistically significant lower Hamilton Depression Rating Scale for Depression (HAM-D) (Hamilton, 1960) scores than the mediation-only group and significantly more were rated "not at all" on the Clinical Global Impression Scale (CGI-S) (Busner and Targum, 2007), with only 32% requiring additional ECT during the period.

THE END POINT FOR MAINTENANCE ECT

There is no clearly defined end point. It is recommended that the treating team review the patient every month, with a more extensive review every six months or more frequently if clinically indicated. Involuntary patients are usually reviewed by the relevant mental health review every six months, which will determine what other investigations are required. Best practice suggests that voluntary patients reconsent for maintenance ECT every 12 months, complete a physical examination and relevant blood investigations and have a second opinion from a suitable trained physician.

Physical assessment

Physical assessment should include:

- physical examination;
- blood investigations including: electrolytes, full blood count, liver function tests, thyroid function, blood sugar levels and any other relevant blood investigations;
- electrocardiogram (ECG) or Echocardiogram if the patient is on clozapine;
- chest X-ray if elderly or a smoker;
- any other clinical investigations that are indicated.

Cognitive assessment

Instruments like the Mini Mental State Examination (MMSE) are not sensitive and often fail to show any change when used to assess cognitive change over a long period of time. Rami-Gonzalez et al. (2003) monitored 11 patients with neuropsychological testing over a three-year period who were

having m-ECT every one to two months for major depression. They demonstrated deficits in learning and other frontal lobe function during this period. Best practice suggests that cognitive testing should occur every three months or more frequently if clinically indicated in patients having continuation or maintenance ECT (NSW Health, 2010; SA Health, 2014). These guidelines recommended using a range of different tests, which are discussed in more detail in Section 4.2 (Adverse events).

A number of things can be done if cognitive decline is detected:

- Review electrode placement and switching back to a unilateral electrode placement with careful monitoring of clinical decline.
- Narrow the pulse width of the treatment.
- Extend the inter-treatment interval to as long as possible.
- Review and adjust of psychotropic medication with the ultimate aim of ceasing ongoing ECT.

There are marked differences in opinion between the lengths that treatment should be maintained. In a recent review of the literature, Rabheru (2012) noted there is a high relapse rate when ECT is ceased and m-ECT should be considered for high-risk patients and families. This group may benefit from treatment over many years, with the duration determined empirically.

Case conference

Practice-based experience indicates that a case conference with all relevant parties should be held regularly for patients having maintenance ECT. The case conference should focus on all treatment options, including trials of new medications or new combinations of medications, psychosocial interventions and continuing maintenance ECT.

Participants should include: the treating team (psychiatrist and case manager), family, carers, members of the ECT service and any other person deemed to be significant to the case.

Day of treatment

The patient should arrive punctually, with adequate time to complete admission requirements. The ECT team, theatre and recovery staff are responsible for the care of the patient throughout the treatment session, with the duty of care continuing until the patient is fit to leave. The ECT team should ensure that the patient has been compliant with the minimum requirements for treatment: fasting from midnight, swallowing essential medications with a small quantity of water, being accompanied to the hospital by family and friends and a responsible adult remaining with the patient for 24 hours after the anaesthetic has been administered.

CLINICAL WISDOM 6.1.2

Continuation and maintenance ECT can be a very effective treatment for patients who fail to remain well with pharmacotherapy and psychological interventions but is often underutilised. ECT practitioners often lack confidence in prescribing the treatment and third-party payers are reluctant to pay owing to a lack of sufficient evidence supporting its use (McCall, 2016) and other groups arguing that ECT should only be used as a last resort (NICE, 2003, modified 2009). The PRIDE study goes a long way to addressing this dilemma, not only by demonstrating that continuation ECT is superior to pharmacotherapy alone but also by providing the practitioner with a Symptom-Titrated, Algorithm-Based Longitudinal ECT (STABLE) algorithm to guide the frequency of further ECT treatments (Kellner et al., 2016).

REFERENCES

Abraham, G., Milev, R., Delva, N., and Zaheer, J. (2006). Clinical outcome and memory function with maintenance electroconvulsive therapy: a retrospective study. *Journal of ECT, March 22* (1), 43–45.

Andrade, C., and Kurinji, S. (2002). Continuation and maintenance ECT: a review of recent research. *Journal of ECT, 18*(3), 149–158.

Brown, D.E., Lee, H., Scott, D., and Cummings, G.G. (2014). Efficacy of continuation/maintenance electroconvulsive therapy for the prevention of recurrence of a major depressive episode in adults with unipolar depression: a systematic review. *Journal of ECT, 30*(3), 195–202.

Busner, J., and Targum, S.D. (2007). The Clinical Global Impressions Scale: applying a research tool in clinical practice. *Psychiatry (Edgmont), 4*(7), 28–37.

Chanpattana, W., and Kramer, B.A. (2003). Acute and maintenance ECT with flupenthixol in refractory schizophrenia: sustained improvements in psychopathology, quality of life, and social outcomes. *Schizophrenia Research, September, 1 63*(1–2), 189–193.

Dew, R., and McCall, V. (2004). Efficiency of outpatient ECT. *Journal of ECT, March 20*(1), 24–25.

Frederikse, M., Petrides, G., and Kellner, C. (2006). Continuation and maintenance electroconvulsive therapy for the treatment of depressive illness: a response to the National Institute for Clinical Excellence report. *Journal of ECT, 22*(1), 13–17.

Hamilton, M. (1960). A rating scale for depression. *Journal of Neurology, Neurosurgery, and Psychiatry, 23*, 56–62. Retrieved from www.ncbi.nlm.nih.gov/pubmed/14399272.

Kellner, C.H., Knapp, R.G., Petrides, G., Rummans, T.A., Husain, M.M., Rasmussen, K., . . . M., F. (2006). Continuation electroconvulsive therapy vs pharmacotherapy for relapse prevention in major depression: a multisite study from the Consortium for Research in Electroconvulsive Therapy (CORE). *Archives of General Psychiatry, 63*(12), 1337–1344.

Kellner, C.H., Husain, M.M., Knapp, R.G., McCall, W.V., Petrides, G., Rudorfer, M.V., . . . Lisanby, S.H. (2016). Right unilateral ultrabrief pulse ECT in geriatric depression: phase 1 of the PRIDE study. *American Journal of Psychiatry, 173*(11), 1101–1109. doi:10.1176/appi.ajp.2016.15081101.

Kellner, C.H., Husain, M.M., Knapp, R.G., McCall, W.V., Petrides, G., Rudorfer, M.V., . . . Lisanby, S.H. (2016). A novel strategy for continuation ECT in geriatric depression: phase 2 of the PRIDE study. *American Journal of Psychiatry, 173*(11), 1110–1118. doi:10.1176/appi.ajp.2016.16010118.

Kellner, C.H., Knapp, R.G., Petrides, G., Rummans, T.A., Husain, M.M., Rasmussen, K., . . . Fink, M. (2006). Continuation electroconvulsive therapy vs pharmacotherapy for relapse prevention in major depression: a multisite study from the Consortium for Research in Electroconvulsive Therapy (CORE). *Archives of General Psychiatry, 63*(12), 1337–1344. doi:10.1001/archpsyc.63.12.1337.

Levy-Rueff, M., Jurgens, A., Loo, H., Olie, J.P., and Amado, I. (2008). Maintenance electroconvulsive therapy and treatment of refractory schizophrenia. *Encephale, October 34*(5), 526–533.

Lisanby, S.H., Sampson, S., Husain, M.M., Petrides, G., Knapp, R.G., McCall, V., . . . Kellner, C.H. (2008). Toward individualized post-electroconvulsive therapy care: piloting the Symptom-Titrated, Algorithm-Based Longitudinal ECT (STABLE) intervention. *Journal of ECT, 24*(3), 179–182. doi:10.1097/YCT.0b013e318185fa6b.

Martin, D.M., Katalinic, N., Ingram, A., Schweitzer, I., Smith, D.J., Hadzi-Pavlovic, D., and Loo, C.K. (2013). A new early cognitive screening measure to detect cognitive side-effects of electroconvulsive therapy? *Journal of Psychiatric Research, 47*(12), 1967–1974. doi:10.1016/j.jpsychires.2013.08.021.

NSW Health. (2010). ECT minimum standard of practice NSW. Retrieved from www.health.nsw.gov.au/policies/pd/2011/pdf/PD2011_003.pdf.

Porter, R.J., Douglas, K., and Knight, R.G. (2008). Monitoring of cognitive effects during a course of electroconvulsive therapy: recommendations for clinical practice. *Journal of ECT, 24*(1), 25–34. doi:10.1097/YCT.0b013e31815d9627.

Rabheru, K. (2012). Maintenance electroconvulsive therapy (M-ECT) after acute response: examining the evidence for who, what, when, and how? *Journal of ECT, 28*(1), 39–47. doi:10.1097/YCT.0b013e3182455758.

Rami, L., Bernardo, M., Boget, T., Ferrer, J., Portella, M.J., Gil-Verona, J.A., and M., S. (2004). Cognitive status of psychiatric patients under maintenance electroconvulsive therapy: a one-year longitudinal study. *Neuropsychiatry Clinical Neuroscience, 16*(4), 465–471.

Rami-Gonzalez, L., Salamero, M., Boget, T., Catalan, R., Ferrer, J., and Bernardo, M. (2003). Pattern of cognitive dysfunction in depressive patients during maintenance electroconvulsive therapy. *Psychological Medicine, 33*(2), 345–350. Retrieved from www.ncbi.nlm.nih.gov/pubmed/12622313.

Rasmussen, K.G. (2015). Lithium for post-electroconvulsive therapy depressive relapse prevention: a consideration of the evidence. *Journal of ECT, 31*(2), 87–90. doi:10.1097/YCT.0000000000000203.

Russell, J.C., Rasmussen, K.G., O'Connor, M.K., Copeman, C.A., Ryan, D.A., and Rummans, T.A. (2003). Long-term maintenance ECT: a retrospective review of efficacy and cognitive outcome. *Journal of ECT, March 19*(1), 4–9.

SA Health. (2014). South Australian guidelines for electroconvulsive therapy, Retrieved from www.sahealth.sa.gov.au/wps/wcm/connect/0608270046ad5b01b89.

Sackeim, H.A., Haskett, R.F., Mulsant, B.H., Thase, M.E., Mann, J.J., Pettinati, H.M., . . . Prudic, J. (2001). Continuation pharmacotherapy in the prevention of relapse following electroconvulsive therapy: a randomized controlled trial. *Journal of the American Medical Association, 285*(10), 1299–1307. Retrieved from www.ncbi.nlm.nih.gov/pubmed/11255384.

Sartorius, A., and Henn, F.A. (2005). Continuation ECT. *Psychiatrische Praxis, November 32*(8), 408–411.

Serra, M., Gastó, C., Navarro, V., Torres, X., Blanch, J., and G., M. (2006). [Maintenance electroconvulsive therapy in elderly psychotic unipolar depression] *Medical Clinics (Barcelona), April 8 126*(13), 491–492.

Shimizu, E., Imai, M., Fujisaki, M., Shinoda, N., Handa, S., Watanabe, H., . . . Iyo, M. (2007). Maintenance electro-convulsive therapy (ECT) for treatment-resistant disorganized schizophrenia. *Progress in Neuropsychopharmacology & Biological Psychiatry, 31*(2), 571–573. doi:10.1016/j.pnpbp.2006.11.014.

Swoboda, E., Colnca, A., Konig, P., Waanders, R., and Hansen, M. (2001). Maintenance ECT in affective and schizoaffective disorder. *Neuropsychobiology, January 43*(1), 23–28.

Trevino, K., McClintock, S.M., and Husain, M.M. (2010). A review of continuation electroconvulsive therapy: application, safety, and efficacy. *Journal of ECT, 26*(3), 186–195.

Tsao, C.I., Jain, S., Gibson, R.H., Guedet, P.J., and Lehrmann, J.A. (2004). Maintenance ECT for recurrent medication-refractory mania. *Journal of ECT, 20*(2), 118–119.

Vaidya, N.A., Mahableshwarkar, A.R., and Shahid, R. (2003). Continuation and maintenance ECT in treatment-resistant bipolar disorder. *Journal of ECT, 19*(1), 10–16.

Victor Navarro, Cristóbal Gastó, Xavier Torres, Guillem Masana, Rafael Penadés, Joana Guarch, . . . Rosa Catalán. (2008). Continuation/maintenance treatment with nortriptyline versus combined nortriptyline and ect in late-life psychotic depression: a two-year randomized study. *The American Journal of Geriatric Psychiatry, 16*(6), 498–505.

Vothknecht, S., Kho, K.H., van Schaick, H.W., Zwinderman, A.H., Middelkoop, H., and BA., B. (2003). Effects of main-tenance electroconvulsive therapy on cognitive functions ECT. *Journal of ECT, 19*(3), 151–157.

CHAPTER 7

The **ECT** nurse and the **ECT** coordinator

Nurses: key members of the ECT team

Nurses have been involved in the care of patients undergoing ECT since its inception in 1937. Research into the role of the ECT nurse has not kept pace with new developments in ECT practice. There is little direction or understanding from the literature as to how nurses are involved with patients and the treating team during the pre-, peri- and post-ECT treatment phases (Victorian Department of Health, 2013). As ECT evolved over the years, incorporating many new developments, the responsibility of the nurse in the delivery of ECT has increased considerably.

NURSING INVOLVEMENT IN THE ECT JOURNEY

A modern ECT service has a strong patient focus. Understanding the role of the nurse in ECT in this context facilitates good clinical outcomes by emphasising the importance of best practice to enhance the lived experience. Sensitivity of the nurse to the patient experience during the assessment of the pre-treatment plan, preparation, monitoring during the procedure, recovery and return to the ward or home is essential to this process.

Five components have been identified as crucial to best nursing practice in the delivery of ECT:

- provision of emotional and educational support to the patient, family and carers;
- orientation of patients and families to the ECT suite and/or theatre complex;
- reassurance that ECT is a safe and effective treatment that produces a rapid clinical response;
- refuting false beliefs and stigma about the procedure;

- provision of an independent objective review of information obtained by the patient and carers from their psychiatrist answering any questions that may arise (Finch, 2005).

Specifically the nurse has a role in all aspects of the patient's journey through each treatment cycle, resulting in a course of ECT that can range from seven to 12 or more treatments. The repeated exposure to anaesthesia, theatre, potential complications in recovery and return to the ward can take its toll on the patient's continued consent and belief that they will recover. Active support from regular nursing staff who remain empathic but also have a high level of expertise is crucial to the success of the treatment.

Nurses play a significant role in ECT at a number of different levels, starting with the ward and admissions nurse though to the more experienced ECT nurse and ECT coordinator. Nurses and coordinators are part of the ECT team, working alongside psychiatrists and anaesthetists in the delivery of ECT. Over the years they have developed specialist skills in ECT (Hardy et al., 2015; Rosedale and Knight, 2015).

The ECT coordinator is the most significant nursing role in the delivery of the treatment (Victorian Department of Health, 2013). They have responsibility for managing all aspects of the service and are the "powerhouse" of the ECT team, keeping the whole service functioning when psychiatrists and junior registrars have "taken their eye off the ball" owing to heavy clinical demands.

ECT WARD NURSE

Ward nurses are responsible for preparing patients for ECT and anaesthetics. This includes documenting vital observations like pulse and blood pressure, through to checking legal documentation and the administration of pre-procedure medication. They are also responsible for the patient when they return to the ward from the recovery area. Table 7.1.1 lists the duties and responsibilities of the ward nurse.

▌ **Table 7.1.1** Ward nurse

Pre-ECT

- Provide education and emotional support for the patient and their family/carer.
- Check correct patient and procedure, and ensure identification and allergy bands are placed on the patients wrist and ankle as per hospital policy, procedure and the director.
- Complete pre-ECT vital observation and associated documentation.
- Administer required pre-ECT mediations, such as blood pressure, cardiac, anti-reflux medications and sedating antipsychotics for anxious patients.
- Liaise with the treating psychiatrist and the ECT team regarding any special requirements prior to ECT, such as withholding certain medications like anti-epileptics and benzodiazepines.
- Check legal and hospital specific forms have been completed and up to date, including the medication chart.
- Ensure that the patient is dressed in appropriate clothing (such as a hospital gown or loose fitting clothing) as per hospital policies.
- Liaise with the ECT porter and ECT team regarding transfer to the ECT suite and time of the treatment.
- Provide a clinical handover of the patient to the ECT admissions nurse as per hospital policy, procedure and directives.

On return to the ward

- The ward nurse accepts clinical handover from the admissions nurse before escorting the patient back to the ward.
- Complete vital observations and associated documentation.
- Assess gag reflex and provide food and fluids.
- Observe for signs of adverse effects such as headache or confusion.
- Document and report any adverse effects to the treating psychiatry team.

ECT ADMISSIONS NURSE

The ECT admissions nurse works within a general hospital theatre. They are responsible for greeting patients from the ward and admitting outpatients for ECT treatment. They are the first person to ensure the correct patient and correct procedure, ensuring that all statutory and hospital forms are complete and up to date before the treatment. Another important role is to coordinate patients through the ECT theatre and assist the recovery nurses. Duties of the ECT admissions nurse are listed in Table 7.1.2.

ECT RECOVERY NURSE

Another important role for the nurse during ECT is recovering patients after the treatment has been completed. The duties of the ECT recovery nurse are listed in Table 7.1.3. In most general hospitals specialist recovery nurses fulfil this role for all patients who have had a procedure on that day. These nurses, along with all perioperative staff,

need support from the ECT team to help them deal with patients who have a severe mental illness.

As noted in an earlier section, when a new ECT service is established in a general hospital the ECT team needs to provide regular in-service training to help staff overcome stigma associated with mental illness and ECT specifically. They will need support to handle patients who develop a postictal

Photo 7.1.1 *Correct bed position to restrain the difficult patient in recovery*

Table 7.1.2 ECT admissions nurse

Inpatients

- Liaise with the ECT nurse/ECT coordinator regarding any patient issues and plan the day.
- Liaise with ward nurses regarding patients' medications, specific patient requirements and time of treatment.
- Liaise with the ECT porter regarding transfers to and from the ECT suite.
- Accept clinical handover from the ward nurse.
- Check vital observations, medication charts, legal and required hospital documentation has been completed with the ward nurse.
- Check correct patient and procedure, and ensure identification and allergy bands are placed on the patients' wrist and ankle as per hospital policy.
- Ask the patient about any issues regarding adverse effects from previous treatment and report findings to the treating psychiatrist, anaesthetist and ECT nurse/coordinator.
- Enquire about any changes in the patient's health status, such as cold and flu-like symptoms and report findings to the anaesthetist and ECT nurse/coordinator.

Ambulatory patients

- Follow guidelines above as per patient preparation pre-ECT and admission to the ECT treatment area.
- Check that the patient has organised a responsible adult to pick them up and stay with them for 25 hours post-anaesthetic as per local health district and state health policy/guidelines directive.
- Inform the patient and carer that following the anaesthetic that they should not make legal decisions or drive a motor vehicle within 24 hours of ECT treatment.
- Liaise with the patient's psychiatric treating team, case manager and GP to ensure continuity of care.
- Give the patient a follow-up card with the next treatment date.

Table 7.1.3 ECT recovery nurse

- The nurse should follow the recovery observation guidelines as specified by the local health district.
- The recovery nurse should take a handover from the anaesthetist.
- The recovery nurse must ensure that the patient has regained consciousness, is orientated in time, place and person and is fit to return to the ward and be discharged home according to local health district policy.
- It is best practice for the recovery nurse to complete time to recovery measures that are recorded in the medical record.
- Due care should be given to ensure that patients' privacy, respect and dignity are maintained at all times.
- Ensure that there is a patent airway in the unconscious patient by using jaw thrust until the patient is conscious and can manage his or her own airway.
- Observe and record blood pressure, pulse and respiratory rates and oxygen saturation levels every five minutes for the unconscious patient and every 15 minutes for the conscious patient.
- It is not uncommon for patients to emerge from anaesthesia in a state of agitation and arousal. When detected the anaesthetist should be consulted who can initiate the appropriated intervention.
- Headache and myalgia can be treated with paracetamol or non-steroidal anti-inflammatory drugs (NSAID) in consultation with the anaesthetist.
- If the myalgia remains a problem the nurse needs to inform the anaesthetist, who can administer a non-depolarising muscle relaxant prior to the administration of suxamethonium at the time of the next treatment, to prevent the suxamethonium induced myalgia.
- Offer outpatients food and fluid after the nurse has assessed that the patient's gag reflex has returned.
- Outpatients can be discharged from recovery when:
  - orientated to time, place and person and are able to ambulate without assistance;
  - all vital signs are within 20% of pre-ECT limits;
  - the patient is not experiencing any pain, nausea or vomiting, scoring zero on the post-anaesthetic discharge scoring system.
- Inpatients can be transferred back to their ward on their bed within an hour provided that all vital signs are stable.
- Ensure that all data entered into the computer record is printed and placed in the ECT file before returning to the ward.

Table 7.1.4 Managing the agitated patient

- Ensure one to one nursing with adequate support if things deteriorate.
- Alert the ECT team and ask for assistance if needed.
- Alert the anaesthetist who can organise pharmacological intervention.
- The agitated patient should be nursed in the following position, illustrated in Photo 7.1.1:
  - adjust the head of the bed so that the patient is in a sitting position;
  - elevate the foot of the bed;
  - tilt the bed so that the head is in a downward position and the foot of the bed is in an upward position;
  - reduce the height of the bed to the lowest setting to prevent injury.
- Staff should exercise caution, ensuring their own and patients' safety.

delirium in recovery after the treatment. Details on how to manage a difficult patient are listed in Table 7.1.4 and illustrated in Photo 7.1.1. If done well, the service can function very efficiently with a high level of morale, ensuring the best outcome for patients having ECT.

Stigma among perioperative staff can be high, with ECT seen as being less important and not "life-threatening". If this attitude is not addressed through active collaboration, ECT can be marginalised. Marginalisation of ECT can lead to the treatment relegated to a recovery area, where it is often administered behind a screen with minimal privacy or placed on the "emergency list" with low priority, administered after long periods of fasting, facing frequent cancellations.

CLINICAL WISDOM 7.1.1

Dedicated hours for ECT nurses are required to ensure a patient-focused and efficient service that provides high-quality ECT treatment. Services that have nurses who share this role with other responsibilities often fail to ensure best practice. The amount of hours required is dependent upon the size of the region and the volume of patients requiring ECT. Very busy services may benefit from separating the role of the ECT theatre nurse and the ECT coordinator.

A dedicated, enthusiastic and experienced ECT coordinator can work closely with the medical ECT clinical director, providing momentum to an ECT service that is difficult to achieve without the appointment of this position. The ECT coordinator can advocate for ECT patients, families and carers at many levels of hospital administration and ward management, areas of a hospital that can be dominated by senior nurses who may not have the same relationship with the medical clinical director of ECT services.

ECT NURSE

The ECT nurse and ECT coordinator can be either stand-alone or dual roles dependent upon the volume of ECT that is delivered within a local health region. In a busy unit, the responsibilities of the nurse fulfilling both roles can be large and separate positions are preferable. The treatment room duties and responsibilities of the ECT nurse are listed in Table 7.1.5.

ECT COORDINATOR

Busy services need to appoint an ECT coordinator with appropriate hours depending on service demand. The coordinator is a vital part of the ECT team. They form the "powerhouse" of an ECT service and provide a vital administrative and coordinating role at all points along the ECT clinical pathway (Tiller and Lyndon, 2003). Throughout this process, the ECT coordinator needs to remind the team to remain patient-focused, gently reassuring and encouraging the patient along what can be a frightening and challenging journey.

Table 7.1.5 ECT nurse

In theatre

- Set up and prepare ECT equipment and theatre.
- Test ECT device.
- Liaise with admission regarding patient flow.
- Accept patient clinical handover from the admissions nurse.
- Check patient identification.
- Check medications given/withheld.
- Check all legal and hospital required documents have been completed.
- Liaise with the anaesthetist and anaesthetic nurse regarding any patient medical concerns.
- Liaise with the treating psychiatric consultant/registrar regarding patient's mental health status and if the current ECT treatment modality has been effective or ineffective.
- Enter and manage ECT in-theatre electronic data collection.
- Assist treating psychiatric consultant/registrar with monitoring leads.
- Complete correct patient/correct procedure time out with the treating psychiatric consultant/egistrar and the anaesthetist as per hospital policies.
- When treatment is complete remove leads and prepare equipment for the next patient.
- Assist the anaesthetist and anaesthetic nurse where required.
- Assist the anaesthetist to transfer patient to recovery.
- Give clinical handover to admissions nurse and recovery staff including any mental health issues or risks.
- Ensure correct documentation has been completed by all parties responsible according to hospital policy, for example the ECT register, schedule drug book and electronic database.

Table 7.1.6 ECT coordinator

Powerhouse of the ECT team

- Work closely with the medical director of ECT services.
- Liaise with hospital administrators about all aspects of the ECT service.
- Coordinate nursing practices throughout the delivery of ECT within the hospital and the local health region.
- Provide advocacy for patients, family and carers.
- Provide education about all facets of ECT to the patient and their family and carers.
- Coordinate and manage patient appointment schedules for both inpatients and outpatients.
- Liaise with the ward psychiatry team regarding current patients and new referrals.
- Liaise with the theatre anaesthetic team regarding anaesthetic reviews and current patient medical concerns.
- Liaise with other allied health teams such as cardiologists and neurologists when required.
- Provide support and education to ward and recovery nursing staff and nursing students.
- Coordinate and participate in the ECT training programme.
- Participate in research projects.
- Maintain accurate statistical information reports for service evaluation and research.
- Coordinate the collection of cognitive and rating measure data.
- Participate in relevant committees, like the ECT committee.
- Participate in the formulation of standards, policies, protocols and clinical guidelines.
- Participate in quality improvement programmes.
- Promote quality improvement in all facets of care and evaluate nursing standards.
- Ensure compliance with the relevant regional mental health legislation.
- Provide and maintain the ECT medical record.

The ECT coordinator may be a nurse or other health care professional with a particular interest and expertise in ECT. They should work in close consultation with the psychiatrist who is the clinical director of the ECT service and the director of anaesthesia to coordinate anaesthetists. Table 7.1.6 list the duties and responsibilities of the ECT Coordinator.

REFERENCES

Finch, S. (2005). *Nurse Guidance for ECT*. Glasgow, UK: The Glasgow ECT Nurses Forum.

Tiller, J.W.G., and Lyndon, R.W. (2003). *Electroconvulsive Therapy: An Australian Guide*. Melbourne, Australia: Australian Post Graduate Medicine.

CHAPTER 8

ECT: the lived experience

Consumer perspectives

Increasingly, the role of the consumer in the delivery of ECT services has become an important development in modern practice. In part this has arisen owing to an increasing demand for accountability and an inability of services to change. The results of the third large-scale audit into Electroconvulsive Therapy services in England and Wales were disappointing. The audit examined the impact of the activity of the Royal College of Psychiatrists over a 20-year period, highlighting that only one third of clinics meet the minimum standards of practice (Duffett and Lelliott, 1998). This led to sharp criticism and increased demand for accountability of services delivering ECT.

An independent review was conducted by the National Institute for Health and Care Excellence (NICE), which released the *Guidance on the use of Electroconvulsive Therapy* in 2003 (NICE, 2003). The document was based on two large-scale reviews of ECT practice (Rose, Fleischmann, Wykes, Leese and Bindman, 2003; UK ECT Review Group, 2003). Rose et al. (2003) concluded that ECT services were out of touch with consumers and carers and challenged the Royal College of Psychiatrist's statement that over 80% of patients were satisfied

with electroconvulsive therapy and memory loss was not clinically important. Their study showed that over a third of patients reported persistent problems with memory (Carney and Geddes, 2003). A further study highlighted problems with consent, with nearly a third of consumers stating that they did not freely consent for ECT even though they had signed the consent form (Rose, Wykes, Bindman and Fleischmann, 2005). In a more recent study, which collected qualitative data from the internet, a video archive and consumer publications, identified that twice as many testimonies were very negative about the experience of receiving ECT, with the most significant side effect persistent memory loss (Rose, Fleischmann and Wykes, 2009).

Learned colleges and societies have responded to these reports through the development of consumer affiliations and networks (ISEN, 2016; SEN, 2015), recognising the important role that consumers can play in service delivery and patient engagement. Over recent years these groups have dedicated more resources to consumers supporting their attendance and encouraging them to present at conferences and other learned discussions about the delivery of ECT.

Listening to the lived experience and working closely with consumers improves a patient's journey through multiple treatment sessions, enabling them to better embrace the positive outcomes, more easily identified by staff and carers. Many consumers are overwhelmed with fear and trepidation when their psychiatrist first proposes the treatment. Patients frequently have a vivid image of Randall P. McMurphy, immortalised by Jack Nicholson in the movie *One Flew Over the Cuckoo's Nest*, being pushed down onto a narrow bed and told "This won't hurt and it will just last a moment" as a set of electrodes were clamped over his ears (Filmsite Movie Review, 1975; Solovitich, 2006).

Kivler (2010) strongly echoes these sentiments in her book *Shock Therapy? Are you kidding me? No Way*, even though the book strongly advocates the benefits of ECT. Thoughts of this movie filled her mind: "people who get that treatment end up staring into space forever. . . . They sit and rock and drool." Solovitich (2006) also reflected on the negative impact of this movie in a patient contemplating ECT for the first time:

> more than two decades after the movie's release, the image remained so vivid that Rachel nearly backed out. . . . Having ECT must mean she really was crazy. But it wasn't anything like the movie. Instead it turned out to be more like day surgery.

Fifty patients and their relatives from India were recruited into a survey examining their satisfaction with ECT. 54% stated that they were overall satisfied with the treatment, 65% felt that it had a positive outcome in reducing symptoms and another 22% to 50% were unsure. Clear disapproval was uncommon (Rajagopal, Chakrabarti and Grover, 2013). Relatives were significantly more satisfied with all aspects of treatment. However, this study confirms other findings that patients continued to have strong fears of ECT, lacked sufficient information about the treatment and were concerned about the possibility of enduring cognitive problems (Rajagopal et al., 2013).

Despite these ongoing concerns, the weight of evidence supports the notion that patients undergoing ECT are well disposed towards the treatment (Chakrabarti, Grover and Rajagopal, 2010).

Consumers have provided a strong voice supporting groups like the National Network of Depression Centres (NNDC) (Weiner et al., 2013) and provided opposition to the US Food and Drug Administration (FDA) reclassification of Electroconvulsive Therapy (ECT) devices (US FDA, 2015). The determination by the FDA was discriminatory, with potentially wide-reaching ramifications not just for device manufacturers, who will be required to produce costly high-quality evidence to justify their devices, but also restricting the use of ECT from the current six diagnostic categories to major depression alone, thereby underestimating the efficacy of ECT as a means to produce large clinical improvement for individuals suffering from severe psychiatric disorders (Lutz, 2016; Weiner et al., 2013).

In 2016 the Royal Australian and New Zealand College of Psychiatrists (RANZCP), Section for ECT and Neurostimulation (SEN), formed a network for consumers and carers. The aims of the network were to:

* inform the College of carer and consumer perspectives on ECT and neurostimulation;
* inform the general public through various media about carer and consumer perspectives on ECT and neurostimulation;
* inform prospective consumers of neurostimulation services and their carers by providing access to first-hand perspectives;
* involve consumers in submissions to professional and government bodies about relevant matters concerning ECT and neurostimulation (SEN, 2015).

In the same year, RANZCP released a revised pamphlet for consumers and carers that was written in plain English addressing key questions and concerns illustrated with patient testimonials (RANZCP, 2016).

For ECT to withstand strong criticism in the future and remain an effective treatment for patients with severe mental illness, much needs to be done to improve the practice of ECT and enhance patient satisfaction with the experience of treatment through active involvement of consumers and carers (Chakrabarti et al., 2010). Patients want clinicians to be the voice of hope, point out their potential and celebrate their victories, no matter how small, and always talk about recovery (Kivler, 2010):

> Accept us, not reject us, respect us, not pity us, admire us, not fear us.
>
> (Kivler, 2010)

WOW I HAVE MY LIFE BACK!
BY ALIRRA

Wow I have my life back is a frank and open account of how ECT changed one person's life. Alirra has written a moving and honest story about the impact that ECT has had on her life, from the early fears before the first treatment to accepting that ongoing ECT was necessary to remain well. She has now had 72 treatments and has become a passion advocate for mental health and ECT in particular!

WOW I HAVE MY LIFE BACK!

They say "what doesn't kill you only makes you stronger". If that were the case you would have thought I'd be strong enough to face my demons head on. I wasn't strong enough to see tomorrow. I cringed tomorrow would be like today and the day before that. In fact I couldn't remember the last time I looked forward to tomorrow.

I had struggled with depression before but this was different.

I was in a low period of my mood disorder and it resulted in my inability to function in the "real" world. I had no strength to do this yet I tried so hard to wear a smile, but the smile quickly faded.

I relied on those around me to be the stability I needed to make it to the next day. I hated knowing that I was relying on others and avoided it for as long as possible. I didn't want those close to me to know what was really going on inside my head. I wanted to save them from the person I had become.

I despised my feeling of weakness!

I despised myself for being unwell again!

I have struggled before with anxiety, mania and depression but this time it was different. The thing is it was slowly killing me. You can't see a mental illness but I felt it. I felt it so strongly that urges to harm myself become more frequent. I become more tired and I couldn't ignore the torment that had been playing on my mind constantly. Any ability to rationalise within myself at that stage was no longer possible.

I missed the feeling of a clear mind instead I felt a thick black fog that stopped me seeing the positives. Each day the fog was getting lower and lower, the visibility of each day became worse and from this my ability to function becomes non-existent.

The words of others rolled around in my head for days. Worrying about the judgment. At this stage I panicked and pushed people away in the fear of judgment and ridicule.

I asked myself what is wrong with me and it sent my mind into over drive wanting to hide my true feelings from the world. I didn't want people to think that something wasn't right with me. I wanted to conform to society with uncertainties of myself hidden. It takes a lot of effort to keep your head above water trying to stay afloat.

I was drowning in the words others had spoken!

I was drowning in my own fears!

I was drowning by my self-enforced isolation!

I was drowning in the stigma society has created!

I was drowning because stability felt so far away!

How simple it would have been to let myself drown in the sea of emotions. Then I was introduced to Electroconvulsive Therapy (ECT). ECT saved me, it gave me the strength to pick up my broken pieces and put myself back together.

So here I am telling a section of my mental journey.

As a child and teenager life was very rocky dealing with depression, anxiety and ADHD. I still believe these have made me into a much stronger person and accepting person. My family struggled with my symptoms of ADHD such as hyperactivity, difficulties focusing, emotional out bursts and carless behaviours.

From the age of four my family tried many different avenues to get answers as to why I was different to other children my age.

When I was seven I was diagnosed with Attention Deficit Hyperactivity Disorder (ADHD). This diagnosis was such a relief to my family; they had finally found an answer. It was decided I'd try medication to help manage my ADHD, the medication was successful and things became easier for my family and myself.

This began to fade in my early teens. I felt anxious, was easily emotional, overwhelmed with sadness and I began to withdraw. These feelings scared me and I didn't know who I was anymore.

I was diagnosed with depression and anxiety. I felt a sense of relief now knowing I wasn't imaging what I was experiencing, having a label helped me realise I wasn't the only one who felt this way. After trying other treatments for my depression I was again put on medication to assist with a stable mood and less anxiety.

In my late teens my symptoms of ADHD, anxiety and depression began to change. My moods of depression and mania swung from one extreme to another. Again I felt alone and I couldn't understand or explain the changes that I was experiencing.

Luckily I was diagnosed early as having bipolar. Again having a diagnosis made acceptance of this mental illness much easier. I'm also very thankful to have been diagnosed early.

From being on medication at an early age I had always thought medication was the answer to my wellbeing. I believed taking my tablets every day, regular doctor visits and at times stays at a mental health clinic was the key to stability. Previously when I've been unwell with my bipolar, these have been the things that have pulled me out of depression or mania.

My view on medication changed when I fell into the deepest and darkest depression I have experienced. I spent more than three months in a mental health clinic trying so hard to get myself well. At that point in my life, I didn't think stability of my mood was possible any more and I had forgot what happiness felt like, I was empty inside.

What had got me well previously wasn't helping and I was ready to give up, I was planning how to take my life until Electroconvulsive Therapy saved me.

When ECT treatment was first suggested I was petrified but willing to try anything to get back to the person I once was. I spoke it over with my family and psychiatrist and it was decided I would start Electroconvulsive Therapy.

Like many people I had a horrible image in my head of what I thought the procedure would entail. I had fears because of the out dated stigma, media portrayals and stereotypes that still surrounds this effective treatment. My mind went back to the early years of the 50s where ECT was misused and barbaric to those having the treatment.

I can assure you ECT is no longer like that!

While staying in the mental health clinic I was lucky to have met other patients who have had or were having treatment and happy to share their own ECT experiences with me. Hearing that it was successful for others lifted my spirits, that if it can work for them then it can work for me. I felt hope for the first time in months.

Those sharing also told me about the negative experiences they have had from ECT.

I was made fully aware of the side effects of ECT and it did worry me such as memory loss, confusion, tiredness, aches, and nausea. I was particularly anxious about memory loss, but the more I spoke about it the less I worried.

I felt the side effects were a small price to pay for having my life back!

I'm glad to have heard the positives and negatives of the treatment by those who know it the best, the patients. A doctor and nurse can tell you all about Electroconvulsive Therapy, but getting feedback and support from those who've been in your situation I believe is always more powerful and uplifting.

My first ECT treatment was life changing. It was the start of my recovery!

I was woken early and given a hospital gown to wear. The wait was on for my turn, the longer I waited the more anxious I became. When it was finally my turn I slowly walked down the corridor with a nurse, through the big plastic doors and into the theatre where the treatment was taking place. At that moment I had so many thoughts running around in my mind. Should I do this? What if it doesn't work? Is it going to hurt? What will I be like when I wake up? What are people going to think of me? Am I strong enough? What side effects will I experience? How long will I have to do this?

I didn't think it was possible to get any more anxious but I did after seeing the nurses and doctors in their scrubs. Although the small room was full of people I felt alone. I lay down on the cold, uncomfortable bed and the process began.

This was the start of my many ECT treatments. When I woke up in recovery I felt nauseas, anxious, tired and emotional. But I had done it! I got through my first ECT.

As I woke and looked around to see others who had ECT treatment I realised it was the start of becoming me again. Although I needed multiple treatments my anxiety around the process including pads placed on my head, pads being placed on my chest and having an IV inserted still frightened me. During the start of my ECT I didn't feel strong enough within myself to continue but thankfully I had great supports to boost me up when I was at my lowest.

The side effects that I had experienced on my first ECT were easily fixed with taking medication the morning before my next treatment. On a whole I was extremely lucky to have had minimal side effects through my ECT journey. My memory loss was much less than expected and I was able to wake up after the procedure reasonably well, like waking up from a normal sleep. At times I was tired but functioned easily enough throughout the day. I felt little to no confusion. My emotions were still a mess at times, but as the treatment continued this became much less.

As time went on and I had more treatments I began to notice a positive step-by-step difference within myself that I hadn't felt for months. Others including nurses, doctors and family also began to see the change. I am so grateful for these people who supported and encouraged me to become well again.

I had stability back in my life and I was able to function again, I owed this to ECT. I stepped back into the real world and began to enjoy life again.

My first course of Electroconvulsive Therapy honestly saved my life. It helped give me the ability to smile again. A real smile of happiness not a mask that I had been shakily holding for months.

All was going well until the black dog decided to make an appearance five months later. I had hit rock bottom and was again overcome with hopelessness and emotional hatred towards myself. So it was decided I was too unwell and was in need of another stay at the clinic. Again ECT was suggested, it worked so well last time so I was keen to try it a second.

After this I had three more clinic stays where I received ECT treatments each time. My life had become a permanent roller coaster ride of highs and lows my bipolar was in full swing. Each clinic stay my world had started to crumble down around me and I couldn't see a way out, each time ECT was the answer. All I knew was ECT was helping me to achieve stability but this only lasted for so long. With each course of the ECT I needed more treatments to become well again.

Medication was not holding me any more than a few months. I felt like stability was only achieved by ECT and I was slowly giving up hope on that as well. The highs and lows again became too much and I had yet another clinic stay. But this stay turned out to be a big turning point in my life.

It was decided I would continue to have maintenance ECT once home. This involves regular outpatient ECT treatments to maintain mood stability, for me this is once a fortnight. I respond well to the ECT treatments and my side effects are still minimal in comparison to others who've had the amount of ECTs I've had. Because of these things the decision to have maintenance ECT was easy.

I believe a big part of staying well with bipolar is to create a routine and continue to follow it a closely as possible. Maintenance ECT has become part of life. This treatment and routine I feel has made my life a lot less stressful. Because of maintenance ECT I've achieved stability and wellness. I now rarely experience the roller coaster ride I'd been on previously and believe this is due to my fortnightly treatment.

I often wonder where my life would be for me if it weren't for maintenance. I do know I wouldn't be the determined stigma fighting person I am today. Life is not always smooth sailing but because of maintenance ECT it has made things much easier to handle and has helped me in many different areas of my life that I thought were out of reach. I can now function in society without fear of embarrassment or feeling like the odd one out. I've taken hold of my emotions and developed strategies on how to overcome what had once thrown me into a state of ruin.

I've achieved the longest level of stability in 10 years. My goals of studying have become achievable. Something that had always seemed too difficult was now in reach. My relationships with family and friends have become a lot less strained. I'm able to better communicate with them on how I'm feeling instead of putting up a wall.

Negative side effects that I have experienced during my maintenance ECT is memory loss that ranges from next to nothing, forgetting conversations or at times not remembering what I had learnt in class the day before. I now struggle more with my concentration also. But I believe these things are a small price to pay to maintain my stability in life. After having 72 treatments my anxiety is now much less when it comes to the ECT process. I no longer worry about side effects because I know what I am doing now is the right thing for my wellbeing.

Now I can walk through those once dreaded plastic doors that held so much fear with more confidence and reassurance within myself that yes this is helping and will continue to. I believe some of this confidence comes from knowing the routine of what was about to happen so well and seeing the same familiar faces. The anaesthetist often triggers the small amount of anxiety that I do feel. The longer they are at finding a big juicy vein the more my anxiety grows.

I've been asked would I recommend ECT to others? My answer to this is yes. If a person is unwell, other options have failed and they are suitable for the treatment, I believe ECT should be looked at so that person can live again without the struggle of a mental illness weighing them down.

The stigma and stereotypes attached to Electroconvulsive Therapy can be debilitating within itself before adding other personal worries from the patient on top of it!

Electroconvulsive Therapy is not spoken about and some aren't even aware that it's still being used or how successful the treatment really is. Because of this and the misleading factors associated with ECT I am proactive in the fight to change society's views and misunderstandings of mental illness and ECT. I don't want others to feel the awful emotional pain of what's associated with having ECT because it is still so stigmatised. I hope by sharing my experiences others will see that ECT and having a mental illness is no longer something to fear.

I now look back and amaze myself with how far I have come in my ECT journey. From the lowest I had ever felt, to the roller coaster ride of stability and now to great opportunities and achieving things I would never had imagined was possible.

I choose to be thankful of my mental health journey, it has made me into the strong, companionate and resilient person I am today!

Alirra, April 2017

REFERENCES

Carney, S., and Geddes, J. (2003). Electroconvulsive therapy: recent recommendations are likely to improve standards and uniformity of use. *British Medical Journal, 326*(7403), 1343–1344.

Chakrabarti, S., Grover, S., and Rajagopal, R. (2010). Electroconvulsive therapy: a review of knowledge, experience and attitudes of patients concerning the treatment. *World Journal of Biological Psychiatry, 11*(3), 525–537. doi:10.3109/15622970903559925.

Duffett, R., and Lelliott, P. (1998). Auditing electroconvulsive therapy. The third cycle. *British Journal of Psychiatry, 172*(5), 401–405. Retrieved from www.ncbi.nlm.nih.gov/pubmed/9747401.

Filmsite Movie Review. (1975). One Flew Over the Cuckoo's Nest (1975). Retrieved from www.filmsite.org/onef.html.

ISEN. (2016). Resources for patients. Retrieved from www.isen-ect.org/educational-content.

Kivler, C.A. (2010). *Will I Ever Be the Same Again? Transforming the Face of ECT (Shock Therapy)*. New York: Three Gem/Kivler.

Lutz, A.S.F. (2016). Why the FDA's move to restrict ECT should alarm us all. *Psychology Today*. Retrieved from www.psychologytoday.com/blog/inspectrum/201601/why-the-fdas-move-restrict-ect-should-alarm-us-all.

NICE. (2003). *Guidance on the Use of Electroconvulsive Therapy. (Vol. Guidance Number 59)*. London: National Institute for Health and Care Excellence; National Health Service.

Rajagopal, R., Chakrabarti, S., and Grover, S. (2013). Satisfaction with electroconvulsive therapy among patients and their relatives. *Journal of ECT, 29*(4), 279–286. doi:10.1097/YCT.0b013e318292b010.

RANZCP. (2016). Electroconvulsive therapy – ECT. Retrieved from www.ranzcp.org/ect.

Rose, D.S., Fleischmann, P., Wykes, T., Leese, M., and Bindman, J. (2003). Patients' perspectives on electroconvulsive therapy: systematic review. *British Medical Journal, 326*(7403), 1363. doi:10.1136/bmj.326.7403.1363.

Rose, D.S., Fleischmann. P, and Wykes, T.H. (2009). Consumers' views of electroconvulsive therapy: a qualitative analysis. *Journal of Mental Health, 13*(3), 285–293. doi:10.1080/09638230410001700916.

Rose. D, S., Wykes, T.H., Bindman, J.P., and Fleischmann, P.S. (2005). Information, consent and perceived coercion: patients' perspectives on electroconvulsive therapy. *British Journal of Psychiatry, 186*(1), 54–59. Retrieved from http://bjp.rcpsych.org/content/186/1/54.abstract.

SEN. (2015). The RANZCP Section for Electroconvulsive Therapy and Neurostimulation (SEN). Retrieved from www.ranzcp.org/. . ./Electroconvulsive-Therapy-and-Neuro-stimulation.

Solovitich, S. (2006). ECT: When all else fails. *BP Magazine*.

UK ECT Review Group. (2003). Efficacy and safety of electro-convulsive therapy in depressive disorders: a systematic review and meta-analysis. *Lancet, 361*, 799–808.

US Center for Devices and Radiological Health (2016). *Electroconvulsive Therapy (ECT) Devices for Class II Intended Uses: Draft Guidance for Industry, Clinicians and Food and Drug Administration Staff.*

Weiner, R., Lisanby, S.H., Husain, M.M., Morales, O.G., Maixner, D.F., Hall, S.E., ... Greden, J.F. (2013). Electroconvulsive therapy device classification: response to FDA advisory panel hearing and recommendations. *Journal of Clinical Psychiatry, 74*(1), 38–42. doi:10.4088/JCP.12cs 08260.

CHAPTER 9

Scenario-based problems

Postictal delirium and ECT

You have been asked to assess LP, a 74-year-old woman, for a course of ECT. She has a past history of recurrent episodes of major depressive disorder with melancholia and psychosis. Her medical history includes hypertension and there have been reports in the past of metabolic changes that have complicated treatment with medication. She has already been in hospital for six weeks.

1 Describe the next steps in your workup to commence ECT.

- Conduct a comprehensive physical examination and undertake appropriate investigations including an electrocardiogram.
- Corroborate the history by contact with the family and other medical facilities.
- Comprehensively assess LP's cognition and her ability to provide informed consent.
- Consider application to the appropriate mental health tribunal if LP lacks capacity.

PROGRESS

The treating team identified that her physical state is stable and does not require any further investigations but her psychiatric condition has not responded to escitalopram 20 mg a day and she is slowly deteriorating as she is not eating or drinking and she is losing weight.

2 What type of ECT should you propose?

1 Ultrabrief ECT?
2 Brief-pulse, right unilateral ECT?
3 Bifrontal ECT?
4 Bilateral ECT
5 Left anterior right temporal?

3 Explain your reasoning behind your choice.

- Ultrabrief ECT may be the treatment of choice following the recently published PRIDE studies that demonstrated a robust response with reduced cognitive impairment in the elderly (Kellner et al., 2016).
- Each of the other forms of ECT offer the benefit of a more rapid response as they are stronger and are worth considering as LP is not eating or drinking.
- The risk of this decision at this early point in her treatment is that LP may experience more cognitive impairment, something that may have been avoided by choosing ultrabrief ECT.

PROGRESS

You decided to go with brief-pulse RUL ECT as there is a degree of urgency but it is not a medical emergency requiring a very strong form of ECT like bitemporal electrode placement.

TREATMENT 1

The set-up for ECT has gone very well and LP had a titration threshold seizure at 10% (50 mC) energy.

4 What is your recommendation for the stimulus energy at the next treatment session? And why?

1 Continue 10% (50 mC) energy.
2 Increase one level to 15% (76 mC).
3 Increase six levels to 100% (504 mC).
4 Increasing three levels to 30% (151 mC).
5 Increase four levels 50% (252 mC).
6 Increase six times rather than levels to 60% (302 mC).
- Your decision at this time should follow the protocol that your ECT suite has developed to guide treatment.
- Some centres around the world have adopted a moderate dosing approach when using RUL, increasing by three levels above threshold, Option 4, a strategy that is memory sparing compared to high-dose strategies, Options 3, 5 and 6.
- Options 1 and 2 are likely to be ineffective.
- There is general confusion in clinical practice between increasing dose above threshold by levels, first proposed by the Duke University group (Beyer, Weiner and Glenn, 1998), and times threshold, a concept adopted by the Columbia University group (Sackeim et al., 2000).

PROGRESS

Following your patient's transfer to recovery, the anaesthetist receives an urgent call from the recovery staff, who are worried that your patient is highly agitated and distressed. You accompany the anaesthetist to the bedside and note that she is disorientated in time, place and person and is trying to crawl out of bed.

5   What interventions are required at this time?

- Safety must come first!
- To make LP safe you feel that you will need:
  - pharmacological restraints;
  - more staff to supervise limbs and trunk;
  - mechanical restraint by manipulating the hospital bed.

PROGRESS

On this occasion the anaesthetist suggests that you give clonidine, which is administered intravenously with a good effect. The patient gradually settles over the next 10 to 15 minutes. The anaesthetist recommends that clonidine be given routinely after the next treatment to facilitate a smooth recovery after the next session.

At the next treatment session you elect to increase the stimulus energy to by three levels (moderate dose). The set-up and the administration of the stimulus go very smoothly. You review the EEG and are satisfied that it is satisfactory as it has the classic characteristics of a suprathreshold seizure.

6   A suprathreshold seizure is characterised by which of the following features?

1   Very long recruitment and termination.
2   Short recruitment, poor symmetry with an abrupt end.
3   Short recruitment, high level of symmetry with slow termination and postictal suppression.
4   Short recruitment, high level of symmetry between left and right EEG, long period polyspike slow waves phase with an abrupt postictal suppression.
5   Very good polyspike and slow wave phase (>13 seconds) with an asymmetrical end.

The correct answer is option 4.

You recommend a stimulus dose of 30% (151 mC) for the next treatment and that clonidine is administered as per the protocol determined by the anaesthetist to prevent another episode of postictal delirium.

PROGRESS

On this occasion the clonidine provides little benefit. The patient quickly becomes agitated and distressed preventing transfer. Another dose of clonidine is administered, with only partial benefit. The patient remains agitated and failure to respond to commands. After a few minutes the anaesthetist administers intravenous midazolam, allowing transfer to recovery.

7   You are concerned that the patient may again become agitated in recovery. What factors should you be considering at this stage?

Some of the factors that can lead to a postictal delirium include:
- handedness;
- other medications such as lithium;
- oxygen saturation;
- concurrent illness;
- sensitivity to anaesthetic agents.

PROGRESS

You return to theatre but soon receive an urgent call from recovery to attend quickly as your patient has become increasingly agitated and distressed.

8   What do you do next?

- On this occasion you altered the bed into a V shape head and feet up with trunk down to provide a higher level of restraint.
- You ask for assistance from theatre staff forming a team to supporting the patient.
- You discuss with the anaesthetist other pharmacotherapy treatment options.
- You administer a further dose of midazolam.
- However, the patient has not settled and following discussion the anaesthetist considers administering a small dose of an induction agent.

It is not uncommon for an anaesthetist to administer a small dose of propofol 20 mg to 40 mg to contain the patient. The anaesthetist is not able to administer a higher dose of this anaesthetic agent, as it requires constant supervision by the anaesthetist preventing them from returning to theatre. The anaesthetist administers 40 mg of propofol in addition to the extra midazolam, with partial benefit.

9   Pharmacologically, what are the risks and which other strategies would you consider at this point concerning the best management of this patient?

- The risk of respiratory suppression limits administering any further doses of midazolam.
- Further doses of clonidine are also limited owing to potential cardiovascular adverse events.
- Ensure that LP has been given 100% oxygen through a mask and that her saturations are 100%.
- It is important to remain calm and talk to LP in a soothing reassuring manner.
- The patient is expressing delusional statements in the context of disorientation and you consider administering a small dose of haloperidol after discussion with the anaesthetist.
- Once LP's condition has stabilised it is imperative that a cause of this severe postictal delirium is found before the next treatment session.

PROGRESS

It is now 40 minutes since treatment and the patient is slowly improving. You review the medical record and discover that the patient was commenced on a selective serotonin reuptake inhibitor, escitalopram, one week earlier. An urgent set of electrolytes is requested and you identify that LP has a sodium level of 130 mmol/L. It is likely that her delirium is secondary to hyponatraemia (low sodium).

10 What is your next step?

1 Correct the underlying sodium abnormality and proceed with treatment.
2 Correct the underlying sodium abnormality; cease escitalopram and delay further ECT treatments until after a multidisciplinary case review.
3 Correct the underlying sodium abnormality; continue escitalopram but delay further ECT treatments until after a multidisciplinary case review.
4 Discuss the complications noted above with the treating team and proceed with ECT.
5 Cease escitalopram and continue with ECT.
6 Discuss with treating team, ensure switching to alternative non-SSRI antidepressant correct sodium and continue ECT.

The correct answer is option 6.

LITERATURE

Hyponatremia is an electrolyte disturbance in which the sodium iron concentration is lower than the normal range, 135 to 145 millemoles per litre (mmol/L) and may be caused by psychotropic medications, although the mechanism is unknown (Madhusoodanan et al., 2002).

Symptoms of hyponatremia can mimic depression, psychosis, confusion, agitation and lethargy. Early recognition of this state is important and periodic monitoring of serum electrolytes is necessary. Treatment involves stopping the medication and assuring normal extracellular fluid volume. Infrequently, an intravenous infusion of hypertonic saline is required (Madhusoodanan et al., 2002; Sharma and Pompei, 1996).

Hyponatremia needs to be corrected prior to commencing ECT, as it can lower seizure threshold leading to an increased risk of spontaneous seizures (Finlayson, Vieweg, Wilkey and Cooper, 1989), prolonged seizures or a severe postical delirium (Greer and Stewart, 1993).

REFERENCES

Beyer, J.L., Weiner, R.D., and Glenn, M.D. (1998). *Electroconvulsive Therapy: A Programmed Text*, 2nd edition. Washington, DC: American Psychiatric Press.

Finlayson, A.J., Vieweg, W.V., Wilkey, W.D., and Cooper, A.J. (1989). Hyponatremic seizure following ECT. *Canadian Journal of Psychiatry, 34*(5), 463–464. Retrieved from www.ncbi.nlm.nih.gov/pubmed/2504479.

Greer, R.A., and Stewart, R.B. (1993). Hyponatremia and ECT. *American Journal of Psychiatry, 150*(8), 1272. doi:10.1176/ajp.150.8.1272.

Kellner, C.H., Husain, M.M., Knapp, R.G., McCall, W.V., Petrides, G., Rudorfer, M.V., ... Lisanby, S.H. (2016). Right unilateral ultrabrief pulse ECT in geriatric depression: phase 1 of the PRIDE study. *American Journal of Psychiatry, 173*(11), 1101–1109. doi:10.1176/appi.ajp.2016.15081101.

Madhusoodanan, S., Bogunovic, O.J., Moise, D., Brenner, R., Markowitz, S., and Sotelo, J. (2002). Hyponatraemia associated with psychotropic medications. *Adverse Drug Reactions and Toxicological Reviews, 21*(1–2), 17–29. doi:10.1007/BF03256181.

Sackeim, H.A., Prudic, J., Devanand, D.P., Nobler, M.S., Lisanby, S.H., Peyser, S., ... Clark, J. (2000). A prospective, randomized, double-blind comparison of bilateral and right unilateral electroconvulsive therapy at different stimulus intensities. *Archives of General Psychiatry, 57*(5), 425–434. doi:10.1001/archpsyc.57.5.425.

Sharma, H., and Pompei, P. (1996). Antidepressant-induced hyponatraemia in the aged. Avoidance and management strategies. *Drugs & Aging, 8*(6), 430–435. Retrieved from www.ncbi.nlm.nih.gov/pubmed/8736626.

ECT, the elderly and a high seizure threshold

An 82-year-old married man, AD, presents with a supportive wife and two daughters, aged 52 and 55, both married with adult children.

Retired from a large mining company, AD began as an apprentice, rising to become superintendent of training (2400 personnel under his care) at the Division of Worker Compensation, noted to be extremely capable owing to his meticulous and organised approach to work.

---

1 Is it common for some one very capable and organised to develop mental health problems?

Yes, patients with an obsessional, iconoclastic personality style lack flexibility and capacity to adjust and adapt to the challenges life presents, making them vulnerable to depression (Boyce and Mason, 1996; Charney, Nelson and Quinlan, 1981; Kendell and Discipio, 1970).

PRESENTATION

AD first presented to a psychiatrist at the age of 72 years. He retired aged 65 but found it difficult to adjust to retirement after holding a prominent job and failing to make adequate plans for retirement.

* described him as a "fickle eater" and his wife spoiled him;
* atrial fibrillation, treated with warfarin and a beta blocker for many years.

DIAGNOSES

* major depressive disorder with prominent ruminations/delusions;
* generalised anxiety disorder;
* obsessional personality style;
* polio aged 18/12 left him with weakness in leg muscles and a lifetime difficulty with eating. Speculation that the poliovirus affected his gag reflex making swallowing difficult. His family

PROGRESS

AD gained remission after two-year treatment with private psychiatrist following trials of different medications with psychotherapy focusing on cognitive behaviour therapy.

Remission achieved with venlafaxine 375 mg and quetiapine 200 mg twice daily and 400 mg at night and regularly psychotherapy two- to four-weekly.

2   Please comment on the choice of drugs and the doses used to achieve remission. Highlight the pros, cons and factors that need to be in place to ensure best practice.

- Ensure fully informed consent of patient and his family.
- Monitor for common side effects including: postural hypotension or hypertension, ensure normal QTc interval by completing EEG and other serotonergic symptoms.
- Family report that the psychiatrist was surprised that AD tolerated high doses of medications extremely well and was able to achieve remission.

PROGRESS

AD was lost to follow-up and managed by his GP. He was able to maintain a high level of function: driving, playing bowls each week, socialising and enjoying going shopping with family.

PRESENTATION 10 YEARS LATER

AD, now aged 82, drove himself to the accident and emergency department of a large public hospital, as he felt dizzy playing bowls. On examination he appeared fit and well with all investigations coming back normal, except for postural hypotension with a blood pressure of 140/80 sitting and 125/70 standing. Staff "alarmed "by high doses of medication involved psychiatry liaison service. Kept in hospital for two nights, where the dose of venlafaxine was dropped to 150 mg and quetiapine to 200 mg at night and sent home.

3   Is this the best management plan?

4   Could it have been done differently?

Doses of medication appear high for someone in this age group!

But good tolerability except for BP; he had been on these doses for 11 years.

Doses of psychotropic medications are best to be altered slowly not dramatically and then sent home.

MARKED DETERIORATION IN FUNCTION

Within a few days AD started to deteriorate, with increasing levels of agitation, anxiety and intense ruminations with delusional intensity and inability to cope with routine activities of daily living, increasing dependence on family.

To the family's dismay they had recently decided to save money and downgraded their private health insurance, excluding admission to a psychiatric hospital for a two-month period.

RETURNED TO PRIVATE PSYCHIATRIST

Recommended quetiapine 100 mg three times a day and 200 mg at night and venlafaxine changed to desvenlafaxine; dose increased to 200 mg a day. Over the next four months, mental state continued to rapidly decline. Admitted to a private psychiatric hospital, desvenlafaxine changed to high-dose escitalopram and quetiapine switched to high-dose olanzapine. Achieved a partial response and discharged home for Christmas.

At the next review in January, psychiatrist alarmed at the marked deterioration.

AD was not eating and drinking only small amounts. There was marked weight loss and loss of muscle tone. GP hospital referral stated that he was alarmed by the rapid changes that occurred; AD was in "total system shut down".

---

5 What is the next step?

Now a medical emergency, all investigations and urgent cardiology review revealed no abnormalities except postural hypotension that was thought to be due to dehydration. AD had lost 10 kg in weight and was now 65 kg.

---

6 Is ECT appropriate in this setting?

ECT has been shown to be the treatment of choice for the frail elderly (Burke, Rubin, Zorumski and Wetzel, 1987; Karlinsky and Shulman, 1984; Manly, Oakley and Bloch, 2000; Rabheru, 2001; van der Wurff et al., 2003).

CONSENT FOR ECT

Complex and potentially life-threatening situation patient and family consented for ECT (Rajkumar, Saravanan and Jacob, 2006).

DIAGNOSIS

Major depressive disorder, recurrent episode, with melancholia and marked psychomotor agitation.

Treating team had a strong belief that AD would have a robust response to ECT (Kellner et al., 2016).

ECT CHALLENGES

Treatment commenced with ultrabrief RUL ECT.

TITRATION SESSION USING A THYMATRON SYSTEM IV

- Stimulated 2% (10 mC), 4% (20 mC): no seizure.
- Threshold seizure at 8% (40 mC) with motor fit: 19 seconds and EEG: low amplitude with poor symmetry and lack of electrical silence.

TREATMENT 2

Stimulus dose increased to 50% (252 mC).

- Motor fit: 24 seconds, partially modified by suxamethonium.
- EEG: 43 seconds, reasonable quality but end point poor.

TREATMENT 3

Stimulus dose continued at 50% (252 mC).

- Motor fit: 17 seconds.
- EEG: 19 seconds.

AD continues to deteriorate; family worried.

7   What is happening?

Seizure threshold is known to increase during the course of ECT, making the stimulus less effective (Sackeim et al., 1993; Sackeim et al., 1994). Age and sex are some of the significant variables thought to impact on the seizure quality (Boylan et al., 2000).

8   What would you do next?

1   Continue stimulus dose and increase suxamethonium.
2   Continue stimulus dose and decrease suxamethonium.
3   Increase stimulus dose.
4   Decease stimulus dose.
5   Change electrode placement.

9   Is it too early to change electrode placement?

No: patient markedly deteriorating; staff share the worries of the family.

TREATMENT 4

- Changed to BT ECT 50% (252 mC), brief pulse width (0.5 ms).
- No seizure at 50% (252 mC), 70% (438 mC) or 100% (575 mC).

- Seizure at 140% (865 mC).
  - Motor fit: 27 seconds.
  - EEG: 50 seconds, with poor quality with lack of symmetry and clear end point.

10 Please comment on this decision.

11 Should the pulse width have been altered beyond 0.5 ms?

12 Are there any other options?

13 What would you do next?

Missed or aborted seizure during the course of ECT can be a problem and may preclude completion of an effective course of treatment (Datto, Rai, Ilivicky and Caroff, 2002). Seizure augmentation and use of pro-convulsant agents have been used to overcome resistance to the induction and continuation of seizure activity (Datto et al., 2002; Loo, Simpson and MacPherson, 2010; Loo, Kaill, Paton and Simpson, 2010; Nobler and Sackeim, 1993). There has also been some suggestion that changing from thiopentone to ketamine may be a useful strategy (Kranaster, Kammerer-Ciernioch, Hoyer and Sartorius, 2011).

TREATMENT 5

Anaesthetic agents altered:

Bitemporal ECT continued.

- The dose of thiopentone reduced from 200 mg to125 mg and the dose of remifentanil increased to 200 microgram.
- Carefully monitoring that full induction has been achieving using the isolated limb technique and shouting "AD, move your right foot".

- Stimulus dose 140% (865 mC), 160% (806 mC) and 200% (1008 mC).

No seizure at 200% despite significant reduction in thiopentone dose.

14 Where to from here?

Discuss augmentation strategies.
- Caffeine (Coffey, Figel, Weiner and Saunders, 1990; Coffey et al., 1987; McCall, Reid, Rosenquist, Foreman and Kiesow-Webb, 1993; Sawynok, 1995).
- Theophylline (Nobler and Sackeim, 1993).
- Hyperventilation (Mayur, Bray, Fernandes, Bythe and Gilbett, 2010).

15 Other options?

Bifrontal ECT?
- Tends to have a higher seizure threshold, making it harder to elicit a seizure.

Increasing stimulus pulse width and continue bitemporal ECT?
- May be an effective strategy; altering pulse width should always be considered. The evidence base for bilateral ECT shows that it is most effective with a brief pulse of 1.0 millisecond. Shorter pulse widths are more effective at eliciting seizures, a factor that is relevant in this case example. A complication in changing the pulse width is the potential for more substantial cognitive impairment but it may be at this point that it is more important to get him better.

TREATMENT 6

- Switched to left frontal, right temporal (LART).
- Stimulus dose 100% (504 mC), pulse width maintained at 0.5 ms.
- Stimulus dose was not titrated but estimated owing to an urgent need to reverse the deteriorating clinical situation. Urgent need to elicit a seizure.
- Motor fit: 23 seconds.
- EEG: 25 seconds, lacking symmetry and a post ictal suppression.

- Equivocal seizure.
- Early clinical response noted by family after this treatment; able to walk to café at front of hospital for milkshake and cake.

TREATMENTS 7–9

- Doses of anaesthesia and electrode placement remained unchanged. Hyperventilation with 40 rapid breaths administered before each treatment.

- Equivocal seizures with motor fits ranging from 17 to 25 seconds and EEG ranging from 25 to 37 seconds.
- Clinical response noted after each treatment by family and staff.
- Increased motor activity, eating and drinking, weight increasing, able to engage in eye contact with increased reactivity of affect and less anxiety and agitation.

AD continued to improve with ECT and was able to return home, family optimistic that he would be able to regain a quality of life. One further ECT treatment was scheduled as an outpatient, while the dose of medication was maximised.

Further improvement was evident at the time of AD's first appointment with his private psychiatrist.

REFERENCES

Boyce, P., and Mason, C. (1996). An overview of depression-prone personality traits and the role of interpersonal sensitivity. *Australian and New Zealand Journal of Psychiatry*, 30(1), 90–103.

Boylan, L., Haskett, R.F., Mulsant, B.F., Greenberg, R.M., Prudic, J., Spicknall, K., . . . Sackeim, H.A. (2000). Determinants of seizure threshold in ECT: benzodiazepine use, anaesthetic dosage and other factors. *Journal of ECT*, 16, 3–16.

Burke, W.J., Rubin, E.H., Zorumski, C.F., and Wetzel, R.D. (1987). The safety of ECT in geriatric psychiatry. *Journal of the American Geriatrics Society*, 35(6), 516–521. Retrieved from www.ncbi.nlm.nih.gov/pubmed/3571804.

Charney, D.S., Nelson, J.C., and Quinlan, D.M. (1981). Personality traits and disorder in depression. *American Journal of Psychiatry*, 138(12), 1601–1604. doi:10.1176/ajp. 138.12.1601.

Coffey, C.E., Figel, G.S., Weiner, R.D., and Saunders, W.B. (1990). Caffeine augmentation of ECT. *American Journal of Psychiatry*, 147(5), 579–585. Retrieved from www.ncbi.nlm.nih.gov/pubmed/2183632.

Coffey, C.E., Weiner, R.D., Hinkle, P.E., Cress, N., Daughtry, G., and Wilson, W.H. (1987). Augmentation of ECT seizures with caffeine. *Biological Psychiatry*, 22(5), 637–649. Retrieved from www.ncbi.nlm.nih.gov/pubmed/3580438.

Datto, C., Rai, A.K., Ilivicky, H.J., and Caroff, S.N. (2002). Augmentation of seizure induction in electroconvulsive therapy:

a clinical reappraisal. *Journal of ECT, 18*(3), 118–125. Retrieved from www.ncbi.nlm.nih.gov/pubmed/12394529.

Karlinsky, H., and Shulman, K.T. (1984). The clinical use of electroconvulsive therapy in old age. *Journal of the American Geriatrics Society, 32*, 183–186.

Kellner, C.H., Husain, M.M., Knapp, R.G., McCall, W.V., Petrides, G., Rudorfer, M.V., . . . Lisanby, S.H. (2016). Right unilateral ultrabrief pulse ECT in geriatric depression: phase 1 of the PRIDE study. *American Journal of Psychiatry, 173*(11), 1101–1109. doi:10.1176/appi.ajp.2016.15081101.

Kendell, R.E., and Discipio, W.J. (1970). Obsessional symptoms and obsessional personality traits in patients with depressive illnesses. *Psychological Medicine, 1*(1), 65–72. doi:10.1017/S0033291700040022.

Kranaster, L., Kammerer-Ciernioch, J., Hoyer, C., and Sartorius, A. (2011). Clinically favourable effects of ketamine as an anaesthetic for electroconvulsive therapy: a retrospective study. *European Archives of Psychiatry and Clinical Neuroscience, 261*(8), 575–582. doi:10.1007/s00406-011-0205-7.

Loo, C., Simpson, B., and MacPherson, R. (2010). Augmentation strategies in electroconvulsive therapy. *Journal of ECT, 26*(3), 202–207. doi:10.1097/YCT.0b013e3181e48143.

Loo, C.K., Kaill, A., Paton, P., and Simpson, B. (2010). The difficult-to-treat electroconvulsive therapy patient – strategies for augmenting outcomes. *Journal of Affective Disorders, 124*(3), 219–227. doi:10.1016/j.jad.2009.07.011.

McCall, W.V., Reid, S., Rosenquist, P., Foreman, A., and Kiesow-Webb, N. (1993). A reappraisal of the role of caffeine in ECT. *American Journal of Psychiatry, 150*(10), 1543–1545. Retrieved from www.ncbi.nlm.nih.gov/pubmed/8379563.

Manly, D.T., Oakley, S.P., Jr, and Bloch, R.M. (2000). Electroconvulsive Therapy in Old-Old Patients. *The American Journal of Geriatric Psychiatry, 8*(3), 232–236. doi:10.1097/00019442-200008000-00009.

Mayur, P., Bray, A., Fernandes, J., Bythe, K., and Gilbett, D. (2010). Impact of hyperventilation on stimulus efficiency during the early phase of an electroconvulsive therapy course: a randomized double-blind study. *Journal of ECT, 26*, 91–94.

Nobler, M.S., and Sackeim, H.A. (1993). Augmentation strategies in electroconvulsive therapy: a synthesis. *Convulsive Therapy, 9*(4), 331–351. Retrieved from www.ncbi.nlm.nih.gov/pubmed/11941229.

Rabheru, K. (2001). The use of electroconvulsive therapy in special patient populations. *Canadian Journal of Psychiatry, 46*(8), 710–719. doi:10.1177/070674370104600803.

Rajkumar, A.P., Saravanan, B., and Jacob, K.S. (2006). Perspectives of patients and relatives about electroconvulsive therapy: a qualitative study from Vellore, India. *Journal of ECT, 22*(4), 253–258.

Sackeim, H.A., Long, J., Luber, B., Moeller, J.R., Prohovnik, I., Devanand, D.P., and Nobler, M.S. (1994). Physical properties and quantification of the ECT stimulus: I. Basic principles. *Convulsive Therapy, 10*(2), 93–123. Retrieved from www.ncbi.nlm.nih.gov/pubmed/8069647.

Sackeim, H.A., Prudic, J., Devanand, D.P., Kiersky, J.E., Fitzsimons, L., Moody, B.J., . . . Settembrino, J.M. (1993). Effects of Stimulus intensity and electrode placement on the efficacy and cognitive effects of electroconvulsive therapy. *New England Journal of Medicine, 328*(12). Retrieved from www.nejm.org/doi/pdf/10.1056/NEJM199303253281204.

Sawynok, J. (1995). Pharmacological rationale for the clinical use of caffeine. *Drugs, 49*, 37–50.

van der Wurff, F.B., Stek, M.L., Hoogendijk, W.J., and Beekman, A.T. (2003). The efficacy and safety of ECT in depressed older adults: a literature review. *International Journal Geriatric Psychiatry, 18*, 894–904.

ECT, epilepsy and obsessional personality style

You are referred a 66-year-old woman, ST, married to a war veteran who was on an army pension. ST has a supportive daughter and son who are both married with children. There is no clear family history of mood disorders or epilepsy. ST developed late onset grand mal epilepsy in her early 50s. The condition was very responsive to anticonvulsant medication, lamotrigine 50 mg twice a day, and she had been stable for 10 years. ST had an obsessional personality style and was described by her family as a perfectionistic, meticulous person who could not rest until the job was completed. ST said, "I have always been in control all my life".

the slow death of her 10-year-old granddaughter (daughter's child) from leukaemia. ST said that she was not able to grieve and developed "pathological grief" that was hidden by her obsessional personality style. There was no past psychiatric history of mental health problems in ST or in the family. ST felt down all of the time, was not sleeping, had lost her appetite and was losing weight. She was frustrated that she was a bad person for not doing enough for her granddaughter. ST said that she felt anxious all of the time and could not look after her house as she had done before. The GP had commenced sertraline 100 mg a day but this had not helped her symptoms.

PRESENTATION

ST described the onset of major depressive symptoms 18 months before presentation, following

---

1 Are people with obsessional personality styles more at risk of depression than others? What would you do next?

- Yes there is good evidence that people with an obsessional, anankastic personality styles have less capacity to grieve and have a greater risk of developing depression (Boyce and Mason, 1996; Charney, Nelson and Quinlan, 1981; Kendell and Discipio, 1970).
- ST is steadily getting worse and requires admission to a private hospital to reassess.

FIRST ADMISSION

Following ST's admission to a private hospital, the diagnosis of major depressive disorder with

prominent anxiety symptoms was made in the context of an obsessional personality style. ST had a partial response to desvenlafaxine 100 mg a day and quetiapine 100 mg at night. Initially ST found it challenging to engage in the psychological group programmes, preferring treatment individually. At the time of discharge she accepted a referral to the hospital day programme and follow-up with the psychiatrist.

THREE WEEKS LATER

Within days ST had a catastrophic "melt down" that she defined as an adverse reaction to desvenlafaxine. It was evident that she had some side effects to the medication; however, the first admission unmasked deep-seated memories from the past that ST had not spoken about for many years, bringing on intense and overwhelming symptoms of post-traumatic stress disorder (PTSD) that compounded the other diagnoses made during the first admission. ST described a history of child sexual abuse from the age of four to10 years by her paternal grandfather. These events had been hidden for many years by ST's controlling personality style and were unmasked by the death of her granddaughter.

---

2   What is your next step? What are the options available? Are medication needed or should the focus primarily be psychological?

- ST requires a further admission to hospital and cannot be managed at home.
- Attempts to talk about the past events creates intense levels of agitation and distress, making it necessary to focus on the here and now.
- She was unable to accept that some of the symptoms that she attributed totally on the desvenlafaxine may have been secondary to emerging PTSD.
- ST feels shattered that her previous coping strategies had failed, causing intense loss of confidence and low self-esteem making her want to die due to guilt that she had let everyone down.
- ST is at high risk of self-harm.

SECOND ADMISSION

Desvenlafaxine was ceased and changed to dothiepin, with the dose gradually increased to 250 mg at night. The dose of lamotrigine strengthened to 100 mg in the morning and 150 mg at night, with daytime quetiapine added to control the agitation. She engaged with a psychologist but found talking about her and the loss hard work, often feeling exhausted and anxious by the end of the session. The interventions were helpful and ST was discharged home with follow-up in your rooms.

PROGRESS AFTER DISCHARGE

After an early response to dothiepin and an intensive psychotherapy ST dramatically deteriorated. You get an urgent phone call from her GP, who was concerned about the rapid decline and requested an urgent review. ST now had generalised anxiety with daily panic attacks. She felt overwhelmed, had lost her confidence and had low self-esteem and intense guilt that she was no longer the strong person she had been before her granddaughter died. ST felt helpless and hopeless and just wanted to die.

3 What would you do next? What are the challenges you may encounter during the admission?

- ST requires urgent admission to hospital.
- ST's obsessional personality style will make it challenging for her to engage with a psychologist or nursing staff during this crisis admission; you have to be in charge and make some difficult decisions.
- You have considered the possibility of an involuntary order due to ST's high risk of self-harm; however, you are confident that can manage her in a private hospital.
- You have a close therapeutic relationship with ST that will enable you to manage her high level of distress by setting firm boundaries within a trusting alliance, active engagement with the family and close nursing observation.
- ECT has become the treatment of choice.

THIRD ADMISSION

It is evident that ST has responded only partially to medication and she requires ECT. ST struggles during the consent process owing to her fear of the treatment but more importantly that she has to give up her sense of control in order to get better.

4 How would you proceed?

5 What are the issues that need to be considered to ensure ST consents for this potentially life-saving treatment?

6 If ST fails to consent, would you consider administering ECT in an involuntary capacity?

- You need to give adequate time for the consent process.
- Engagement of the family is important during this time.
- Encourage ST and the family to discuss the treatment with your experienced nursing staff.
- You need to remain confident that you can contain ST's level of distress and that ECT is the treatment of choice.
- It is very important not to let your own fears and stigma impose at this point as it can undermine your therapeutic alliance, intensifying ST's sense of hopelessness and need to die.

PROGRESS

ST agreed to a course of ECT after involving her husband and two children in the consent process. Each person highlighted his or her concerns about the treatment as the only exposure to ECT was via the media and film. You listen to their concern and provide objective information about modern ECT, giving them time to consider the various treatment options available to ST. It is important not to rush the consent process. A second opinion was organised with an independent psychiatrist to provide a further avenue for the patient and family to discuss their concerns. ST consented to a course of ultrabrief ECT. MADRS completed: 38/60.

TITRATION SESSION USING A THYMATRON SYSTEM IV

- Stimulus dose 2% (10 mC), 4% (20 mC), no seizure.

- Stimulus dose 8% (40 mC), threshold seizure short.
- Motor fit: 5 seconds detected by the isolated limb technique.
- EEG: end point difficult to determine, with low-amplitude asymmetric wave form that lacked postictal suppression.

The ECT practitioner noted that she was still taking lamotrigine 100 mg in the morning and 150 mg at night.

---

7 What would you do next?

---

8 Can ECT have a successful outcome?

---

9 What do you tell your patient and their family?

- It is likely that lamotrigine has raised the seizure threshold.
- You are surprised as in your experience this drug has minimal impact on seizure threshold when the dose is kept low 200 mg a day, with various case reports supporting this view (Sienaert and Peuskens, 2007).
- You make a note in the ECT record, requesting the anaesthetist to reduce the dose of thiopentone, which can also raise the seizure threshold.
- You are aware that the dose is routinely higher for the titration session.

ECT PROCEEDS

You reduce the dose of lamotrigine by 50 mg a day to being it into line with the evidence noted above, and withhold it the night before treatment.

TREATMENT 2: INCREASE STIMULUS DOSE SIX TIMES TO 50% (252 MC) AS PER PROTOCOL

- The dose of thiopentone reduced by 50 mg to 150 mg and the dose of remifentanil increased to 250 micrograms.

- Carefully monitoring that full induction has been achieving using the isolated limb technique and shouting "ST, move your right foot".
- Stimulus dose 50% (252 mC).
- Motor fit: 10 seconds.
- EEG: 10 seconds, poor quality low amplitude, lacking symmetry and abrupt termination.

10 What would you do next?

- You are concerned about the poor quality seizure.
- It is likely that if you do nothing there may be an abortive seizure at the next session requiring escalation of the stimulus.
- You therefore decide to drastically reduce the dose of lamotrigine, recalling that ST had had no seizure for 10 years when taking a dose of 50 mg twice a day.

SUBSEQUENT ECT TREATMENTS

Lamotrigine dose reduced to 50 mg bd and withheld the night and morning before treatment.

TREATMENT 3

- Stimulus increased to 75% (378 mC).
- Motor fit: 31 seconds.
- EEG: 67 seconds, significant improvement in EEG quality, continues to have a poor termination.

TREATMENTS 4–8

- Stimulus increased to 90% (454 mC).
- Motor fit: ranges between 32 and 45 seconds.
- EEG: robust with improved post ictal suppression.

PROGRESS

ST began to respond after the fourth treatment, gaining remission by Treatment 7, as reflected in the MADRS score from 38/60 to 6/60. ST continued to express her concerns that she was not the same person as before. Gentle encouragement was required to reassure her that she had to find a "new form of her old self". ST began to apply mindfulness techniques and was open to psychotherapy with a focus on grief work and loss. Medication was further adjusted. Dothiepin was ceased and a trial of amitriptyline caused side effects. ST tolerated a combination of nortriptyline 150 mg at night with lithium slow release 450 mg a day.

11 What other options were there for ST?

12 What is the trade-off with administering a higher stimulus dose?

13 Is your patient a candidate for continuation ECT?

- You have considered other options prior to commencing ECT, all of which had failed.
- The higher stimulus dose is necessary to gain remission but carries the risk of more cognitive impairment.
- The high stimulus dose also reflects a rise in seizure threshold that will be protective of any break through spontaneous seizures occurring between treatments (Ragab and Elaghoury, 2017).

- It is important at this time to discuss with ST the role of ECT as a continuation or maintenance treatment but you do not consider it necessary as she has only had one index course of treatment.
- You reassure her that the changes made to medication have a strong evidence base to keep her well without the need for ECT.
- The focus of treatment should now shift to psychotherapy to help ST deal with issues of grief, loss and trauma to help her find a new sense of self and prevent relapse.

LITERATURE

Anticonvulsants (AC) During Electroconvulsive Therapy: Review and Recommendations (Sienaert and Peuskens, 2007):

- lack of RCT regarding safety and outcome;
- existing data from case reports for patients with epilepsy or those with depression and comorbid epilepsy;
- occasional difficulty in eliciting seizures;
- no severe ADR or complications;
- no evidence that AC augment therapeutic efficacy of ECT;
- need to simplify anticonvulsants and reduce dose;
- ECT is anticonvulsant; combination exacerbates a rise in seizure threshold that can usually be overcome by raising stimulus intensity.

There is a high risk of relapse after a course of ECT, particularly if the antidepressant medication is not altered. It is important that medications are altered during the course of ECT to maintain remission. Evidence supports the use of nortriptyline and lithium (Kellner et al., 2006) and venlafaxine and lithium (Kellner et al., 2016; McCall, 2016).

REFERENCES

Boyce, P., and Mason, C. (1996). An overview of depression-prone personality traits and the role of interpersonal sensitivity. *Australian and New Zealand Journal of Psychiatry, 30*(1), 90–103.

Charney, D.S., Nelson, J.C., and Quinlan, D.M. (1981). Personality traits and disorder in depression. *American Journal of Psychiatry, 138*(12), 1601–1604. doi:10.1176/ajp.138.12.1601.

Kellner, C.H., Knapp, R.G., Petrides, G., Rummans, T.A., Husain, M.M., Rasmussen, K., ... M., F. (2006). Continuation electroconvulsive therapy vs pharmacotherapy for relapse prevention in major depression: a multisite study from the Consortium for Research in Electroconvulsive Therapy (CORE). *Archives of General Psychiatry, 63*(12), 1337–1344.

Kellner, C.H., Husain, M.M., Knapp, R.G., McCall, W.V., Petrides, G., Rudorfer, M.V., ... Lisanby, S.H. (2016). A novel strategy for continuation ECT in geriatric depression: phase 2 of the PRIDE study. *American Journal of Psychiatry, 173*(11), 1110–1118. doi:10.1176/appi.ajp.2016.16010118.

Kendell, R.E., and Discipio, W.J. (1970). Obsessional symptoms and obsessional personality traits in patients with depressive illnesses. *Psychological Medicine, 1*(1), 65–72. doi:10.1017/S0033291700040022.

McCall, W.V. (2016). Finally, evidence for continuation electroconvulsive therapy in major depressive disorder. *Journal of ECT, 32*(4), 221. doi:10.1097/yct.0000000000000368.

Ragab, A., and Elaghoury, A. (2017). Electroconvulsive therapy as a treatment option for intractable epilepsy: a care report. *Brain Stimulation, 10*, 393.

Sienaert, P., and Peuskens, J. (2007). Anticonvulsants during electroconvulsive therapy: review and recommendations. *Journal of ECT, 23*(2), 120–123. doi:10.1097/YCT.0b013e3180330059.

Fear of ECT

FC is a 27-year-old female referred to you for treatment. She has lived with her partner for five years and has completed a Bachelor of Arts (major in international studies) degree. FC is currently studying law but her degree has been challenged over the last few years by worsening symptoms of bipolar disorder with strong suicidal ideation. FC met her treating psychiatrist at the age of 15, when she had prominent anxiety symptoms soon after being diagnosed with an eating disorder. FC has been seeing him regularly since that time. They have established a close therapeutic alliance.

DIAGNOSES

FC has had a number of diagnoses over the years, with an eating disorder in her early teens and then severe anxiety disorder with panic attacks that was managed by the local public child and adolescent mental health service with only partial benefit. She met her private psychiatrist at the age of 15, when she had her first major depressive epi sode with a suicide attempt by overdose. FC was treated with selective serotonin reuptake inhibitors (SSRI) including sertraline and fluoxetine, providing partial relief that was short-lived. Fluvoxamine made her feel worse, with more intense mood swings and suicidal ideation. FC's partner confirmed the recent deterioration in FC's mental state as she had become difficult to live with and he was worried about her safety.

1   What other diagnoses should be considered?

- Borderline personality disorder (BPD) is a common differential diagnosis that should be excluded in this setting (Benazzi, 2000).
- BPD is unlikely as there was no history of trauma and FC had a supportive family who reinforced her obsessional personality style driven to achieve in the context of low self-esteem and self-worth and a strong fear of failure.

FAMILY HISTORY

FC had a supportive mother; father and sister aged 22 (no illness). There was a strong family history of mental illness, with a number of relatives on both sides suffering from anxiety and depression and a paternal uncle who had bipolar disorder and who committed suicide aged 24.

DEVELOPMENTAL HISTORY

There was no history of trauma. FC was very bright, topping her class in primary school. High school was challenging owing to the onset of depression and anxiety symptoms. FC completed school, earning a high entrance score for university. She was accepted into arts and law degrees. Over the years her performance has been variable owing to the impact of the bipolar disorder.

PROGRESS

Bipolar disorder, Type 2, diagnosed when FC was aged 18 by her psychiatrist. Antidepressant medications were minimised as they were contributing to her instability. Different mood stabilisers were trailed; lamotrigine produced an early clinical response at a dose of 75 mg a day before causing a body rash and the drug was ceased; sodium valproate had limited clinical effect but caused weight gain) and was ceased; and topiramate led to some improvement in mood stability but also to nausea and weight loss, exacerbating her eating disorder, and had to be ceased.

FC tolerated lithium carbonate slow release (SR) 900 mg a day, which reduced the mood swings but did not prevent the depressive symptoms with suicidal ideation, which became more pervasive over the last three years. Immediately prior to the admission, FC was commenced on mirtazapine 30 mg at night, providing improvement in her sleep but not mood state.

---

2   What other options are available? What else would you consider?

- The psychiatrist had frequent discussions about the benefits of ECT.
- FC repeatedly expressed her fear of the treatment and would not consider it as a treatment option.
- FC was reluctant to engage with a psychologist owing to a negative experience she had while attending the public child and adolescent service in her teenage years.
- FC now had a close alliance with her treating psychiatrist and did not feel the need to "start all over".

THE ECT JOURNEY

FC's strong fears of ECT were evident very early on, with concerns about stigma, shame and cognitive impairment that were confounded by an irrational fear that it may not work. If it does not work, then "I would have nothing left but to kill myself".

---

3   What is your duty of care? Should you stop talking about ECT?

- FC's treating psychiatrist did not look after inpatients and she had been managed by different psychiatrists during each admission. Ensure the same treating psychiatrist for all future admissions.
- It is likely that this was another barrier that hindered FC consenting for ECT.
- It is important to consider the ethics that underpins your duty of care and available treatment options (Fox, 2009; Mankad, 2015).

ADMISSIONS TO A PRIVATE HOSPITAL

2015 – Admitted for ECT but failed to give consent. Partial response to venlafaxine, lithium SR 900 mg and quetiapine 75 mg at night; quetiapine dose kept low owing to FC's concerns about weight gain.

2016 – Admitted for ECT but failed to give consent. Good initial response to dothiepin 250 mg, lithium SR 900 mg, and quetiapine 75 mg.

2017 – Admitted for ECT and on this occasion consented. Dothiepin had been ceased a few months before the admission owing to multiple side effects. Desvenlafaxine 100 mg had been added to lithium and quetiapine with minimal benefit. Parents stated that her treating psychiatrist was very impressed that she was able to move forward. MADRS completed: 48/60.

---

4   How would you proceed from here? Are there potential problems?

- Mother involved in the session to provide increased support.
- Mother was very keen for FC to try ECT as she had been in a dark place for a long time.
- FC freely consented for ECT without coercion and agreed to commence with ultrabrief ECT.
- FC's fears eased after an independent psychiatrist who also worked in the private hospital was organised to provide a third opinion.
- Decision made to halve the dose of lithium SR to 450 mg a day to avoid delirium and mirtazapine 30 mg at night was ceased owing to FC's fear of weight gain.

INITIAL ECT SESSION

ECT staff commented about FC's high level of anxiety on the morning of first treatment, blood pressure (BP) 180 mmHg/90 mmHg with tachycardia, compared to a resting BP of 130 mmHg/75 mmHg.

TITRATION SESSION USING A THYMATRON SYSTEM IV

Stimulus dose 2% (5 mC) energy resulted in a motor fit with duration of 38 seconds and an EEG of 38 seconds; adequate symmetry and reasonable postictal suppression.

FC experienced a mild headache and muscle pain after the treatment but was very relieved that the first session was over.

COURSE OF ECT

Treatment 2

- Stimulus dose increased as per protocol to 10% (50 mC).
- Motor fit: 42 seconds.
- EEG: 50 seconds; robust seizure with high level of symmetry and postictal suppression.

Treatment 3

- Stimulus dose 10% (50 mC).
- Motor fit: 32 seconds.
- EEG: 55 seconds, robust seizure with high level of symmetry and postictal suppression.

Treatment 4

- Stimulus dose 10% (50 mC).
- Motor fit: 36 seconds.
- EEG: 36 seconds, robust seizure with high level of symmetry and postictal suppression.

Early signs of improvement were noted by staff but FC stated that she was exactly the same, with worsening anxiety and fear that the treatment would not work.

Treatment 5

- Stimulus dose maintained at 10% (50 mC).
- Motor fit: 17 seconds.
- EEG: 17 seconds; decline in seizure quality with short duration, lacking symmetry with poor termination and postictal suppression.

---

5 Are you concerned about this change in the quality of the EEG?

---

6 Should you make changes to your technique?

---

7 Consider the following options:

1 Stay with ultrabrief and increase to 15%.
This is a reasonable option as there was objective evidence that ECT was working.

2 Continue with current dose.
It is evident that seizure threshold is rising. Remaining at the same dose of energy may lead to marked deterioration in seizure quality, reducing efficacy.

3 Change to bifrontal ECT and retitrate the stimulus dose.
It would be premature to change electrode placement after Treatment 5, particularly when there has been objective evidence of clinical improvement. Practice wisdom for ultrabrief ECT suggests that a change in electrode placement should be considered between Treatments 6 and 8 if there has been limited clinical improvement.

4 Change to bifrontal at 15%.
See discussion above. It is usual practice to reduce the stimulus dose for a bilateral electrode placement. There may be an argument for this dose as BF has a higher seizure threshold than bitemporal ECT.

5 Change to brief-pulse RUL at 10%.
There may be some advantage in changing to brief pulse if the stimulus dose is increased to 1 milliseconds but this carries the potential for more cognitive impairment. Based upon the discussion above, it is premature to change the way the stimulus is delivered at this point.

Treatment 6

FC frustrated by the lack of progress with ECT and fearful that she may be right and the treatment will not work.

Treatment continued with ultrabrief and the stimulus dose increased to 15% (76 mC) to overcome the rise in seizure threshold:

- Motor fit: 27 seconds.
- EEG: 50 seconds, short recruitment phase, high level of symmetry and postictal suppression.

Treatment 7

Parameters continued as above.

Treatment 8

Decision made to change the stimulus to brief pulse and strengthened the dose to 20% (101 mC) owing to worsening subjective complaints about lack of improvement.

- Motor fit: 42 seconds.
- EEG: 42 seconds, robust morphology with high level of postictal suppression.

---

8   What will you do next? Do you abandon further treatment?

- You are concerned about the lack of progress and reassess FC's clinical state after discussing how she has been on the ward with nursing staff.
- At this point it is very important to corroborate the history from family and engage them in the treatment alliance.
- It would be helpful to repeat the depression rating scale and repeat cognitive screen.
- It would be easy to be overwhelmed with FC's counter-transference that ECT has not worked and that there are no further options available, Leaving her very vulnerable and at high risk of suicide.

PROGRESS

Nursing staff handover expressed increasing concern that FC had not left her darkened room for a number of days and was rarely eating or interacting with other patients and was difficult to engage with staff.

The psychiatrist invited FC's mother to the next clinical review in an attempt to enhance clinical rapport.

FC expressed intense feeling of hopelessness with strong suicidal ideation with plans.

Difference between patient's view and staff observations highlighted over the last two weeks of treatment.

Mum reported that daughter had always been a "glass half-empty" person since she was a young girl. FC was high-achieving but had immense self-doubt and lack of confidence and often failed to complete activities owing to her fear of failure. Mum felt that the lack of improvement with medication was a "self-fulfilling prophecy".

The psychiatrist noted the emerging failure in treatment alliance as FC had given up and lost her desire to get better. Recovery overwhelmed by a strong fear that ECT would fail, "Just like all of the other treatments!"

ECT ceased until the next clinical review. FC agreed to talk to her mother over the next few days to find ways to overcome her negative thinking and loss of confidence in her psychiatrist (McCall, 2008).

---

9   What is the next step?

10 What are the possible options?

1   Abandon treatment.
    The risk of this option is that it could fulfil her belief that ECT is another treatment that has failed and would provide an impetus for suicide.
2   Make FC involuntary with the aim of continuing treatment.
    This strategy should be considered as FC is at high risk. However, you already have a fragile therapeutic relationship with FC. Placing her under an order would require transfer to another facility, further damaging your capacity to continue care of this patient.
3   Attempt re-engagement and build rapport with the aim of continuing treatment.
    This is the preferred strategy. FC has strong suicidal ideation with loose plans but she still feels safe and supported by nursing staff in your unit.
4   Build alliance with patient by enhancing the fragile relationship she has with mother with the aim of enhancing treatment.
    FC's mother's involvement in FC's management throughout the admission has enabled FC to become closer to her. Further engagement of mum will ensure FC's safety and may make further treatment with ECT possible.
5   Continue treatment.
    The risk of this decision is that the cost of clinical improvement would be to further damage the therapeutic alliance, making any potential treatment after discharge very difficult.

NEXT CLINICAL REVIEW

A further session was held with mum, who stated that FC had become increasingly upset over the weekend, as she felt very helpless that she had nothing further to offer her daughter and had to leave prematurely.

FC said that the session held with her psychiatrist during the previous session followed by the events that happened with her mum proved to be a turning point in her recovery.

Staff reports over the weekend highlighted that there was a significant shift in FC's behaviour. She began to come out of her room, eat more regular meals, started to exercise again and interacted with staff. All staff reported that her affect remained flat and depressed with minimal reactivity.

FC expressed a desire to re-establish a therapeutic alliance with her psychiatrist. She said that although she still found it hard to accept that ECT would work for her she was able to put her fears about recovery and memory impairment on hold: "You Win!" (McCall, 2008).

MEDICATION DECISIONS REVERSED

There was some concern that the halving the dose of lithium and ceasing mirtazapine may have contributed to FC's marked decline:

- Lithium SR increased from 450 to 900 mg nocte.
- Mirtazapine increased from 30 to 60 mg nocte.

ECT RECOMMENCED

Decision to use a stronger form of treatment, brief-pulse bifrontal (BF) ECT, dose strengthened to 20% (101 mC)

- FC recovered well from the treatment, with no delirium reported.
- FC agreed to monitor her appetite.

Treatments 8–12

BF ECT continued at 20% (101 mC) with excellent seizure quality, high amplitude, and symmetry with an abrupt termination and robust postictal suppression.

PROGRESS

FC remitted by Treatment 10; two further treatments administered to consolidate improvement before discharge.

Montgomery Asberg Depression Rating Scale (MADRS) changed from 48/60 before ECT to 8/60 after Treatment 10.

At the time of discharge, FC was hopeful and optimistic about her future. She had reengaged with study, exercised regularly and was communicating freely with staff. FC re-established an active therapeutic alliance with her psychiatrist and was regularly using the memory control diary to manage cognitive changes. The diary helped FC overcome her fear by providing options to minimise the day-to-day impact of these cognitive changes.

There was a considerable shift in FC's relationship with her family and partner, who were initially kept at arm's length, increasing FC's sense of isolation and despair. The engagement of the family was a fundamental part of the treatment alliance, contributing to the improvement.

It is evident that at discharge FC's recovery was superior to the two previous admissions using medication and psychotherapy alone and that her quality of life should continue to improve over the next three months after discharge (McCall, Reboussin, Cohen and Lawton, 2001).

LITERATURE

The literature concerning fear and ECT is limited, as featured in some editorials and case reports, with a literature review presented at a recent international conference (Obbels, Verwijk, Bouckaert and Sienaert, 2017). In this review the prevalence of ECT-related anxiety from 22 studies was broad, ranging from 14% to 75% of all cases. There was a wide range of subjects included in the studies, with the most commonly reported fear associated with memory loss and brain damage (Obbels et al., 2017).

Pathological fear and apprehension concerning ECT has been described as a "side effect" of treatment (Sackeim, 1992) and was first described by Gallineck (1956), who noted that there was often a second level of fear in addition to the usual fear found in other surgical procedures. Fox (1993) described three case reports, speculating that this level of fear may be due to a sense of disconnectedness, a loss of control and disorientation in recovery.

There are many reasons for disliking ECT:

- burden on family carer(s);
- inconvenience; forgoing a whole day;
- displeasure owing to the long wait
- apprehension regarding having repeated anaesthetics;
- recovery – period of confusion disorientation;
- troublesome burden of cognitive impairment;
- failure to recognise the potential life-saving aspect of ECT (Fox, 2009).

Fear is common in relatives and family (McCall, 2007). Engaging their support is essential to enable patients to overcome their fear by saying "you win!" (McCall, 2008) so that they can recognise the potential life-saving aspect of ECT (Kivler 2010).

Fear is common in involuntary patients and may be exacerbated by a lack of insight, the severity of the illness and the strong resistance of carers. Surprisingly, this group are not at high risk of bitter ECT complaint (Rasmussen, 2015).

> The ECT practitioner may be on solid legal ground to pursue ECT over the wishes of the family, particularly if the patient is in a potentially life threatening condition, however, there may be a difference between what legally can be done versus what should be done.
>
> (McCall, 2007)

IN SUMMARY

Many patients dislike ECT and are often the last to appreciate its benefits (McCall, 2007). Fear can be reduced by the involvement of family and carers.

There are some that suggest that both patient and family sign written consent forms (Rajkumar, Saravanan and Jacob, 2006), while others go further and suggest that carers routinely be present during each ECT session (Evans and Staudenmier, 2005). Other strategies to minimise fear and anxiety such as music and an aquarium in the waiting room as well as emotional support were not helpful; however, talking-through techniques, information leaflets and animal-assisted therapy may have some merit (Obbels et al., 2017).

REFERENCES

Benazzi, F. (2000). Borderline personality disorder and bipolar II disorder in private practice depressed outpatients. *Comprehensive Psychiatry, 41*(2), 106–110. Retrieved from www.ncbi.nlm.nih.gov/pubmed/10741888.

Evans, G., and Staudenmier, J.J. (2005). Family member presence during electroconvulsive therapy: patient rights versus medical culture. *Journal of ECT, 21*(1), 48–50. Retrieved from www.ncbi.nlm.nih.gov/pubmed/15791179.

Fox, H.A. (1993). Patients' fear of and objection to electroconvulsive therapy. *Hospital and Community Psychiatry, 44*(4), 357–360. Retrieved from www.ncbi.nlm.nih.gov/pubmed/8462942.

Fox, H.A. (2009). Patients' objections to electroconvulsive therapy. *Journal of ECT, 25*(4), 288. doi:10.1097/YCT.0b013e31819fe012.

Gallineck, A. (1956). Fear and anxiety in the course of electroshock therapy. *American Journal of Psychiatry, 113*, 428–434.

Kivler, C.A. (2010). *Will I Ever Be the Same Again? Transforming the Face of ECT (Shock Therapy)*. New York: Three Gem/Kivler.

Mankad, M. (2015). Informed consent for electroconvulsive therapy – finding balance. *Journal of ECT, 31*(3), 143–146. doi:10.1097/YCT.0000000000000241.

McCall, W.V. (2007). Electroconvulsive therapy: all in the family. *Journal of ECT, 23*(4), 213–214.

McCall, W.V. (2008). You win. *Journal of ECT, 24*(4), 243.

McCall, W.V., Reboussin, B.A., Cohen, W., and Lawton, P. (2001). Electroconvulsive therapy is associated with superior symptomatic and functional change in depressed patients after psychiatric hospitalization. *Journal of Affective Disorders, 63*(1), 17–25. doi:10.1016/S0165-0327(00)00167-1.

Obbels, J., Verwijk, E., Bouckaert, F., and Sienaert, P. (2017). ECT-related fear: what have we (not) learned? *Brain Stimulation, 10*(2), 325–326.

Rajkumar, A.P., Saravanan, B., and Jacob, K.S. (2006). Perspectives of patients and relatives about electroconvulsive therapy: a qualitative study from Vellore, India. *Journal of ECT, 22*(4), 253–258.

Rasmussen, K.G. (2015). Rage against the (ECT) machine. *Journal of ECT, 31*(1), 1–2. doi:10.1097/YCT.0000000000000171.

Sackeim, H.A. (1992). The cognitive effects of electroconvulsive therapy. In Moos, W.H., Ganzu, E.R., and Thal, L.J. (Eds.), *Cognitive Disorders: Pathophysiology and Treatment* (pp. 183–228). New York: Marcel Dekker.

Complex **ECT** treatment: identify errors and make recommendations for improvement

Table 9.5.1 Complex ECT treatments

Name	Date	Impedance	EMG	EEG	Energy	ECT Number
John Doe	7/09/2016	>3000	not detected	not detected	200% (1008 mC)	12
	3/09/2016	2100	not detected	8 sec	180% (907 mC)	11
	31/08/2016	>3000	not detected	not detected	160% (806 mC)	10
	24/08/2016	>3000	not detected	8 sec	140% (504 mC)	9
	21/08/2016	2740	5 sec	17 sec	100% (353 mC)	8
	17/08/2016	>3000	6 sec	12 sec	70% (353 mC)	7
	14/08/2016	1570	8 sec	12 sec	50% (252 mC)	6
	10/08/2016	>3000	23 sec	23 sec	50% (252 mC)	5
	6/08/2016	1570	8 sec	10 sec	20% (101 mC)	4
	3/08/2016	1870	24 sec	not detected	20% (101 mC)	3
	24/07/2016	2720	22 sec	32 sec	20% (101 mC)	2
	20/07/2016	>3000	N/A	not detected	5% (25 mC)	1

Brief-pulse, right unilateral (RUL) ECT using a Thymatron System IV
The course of treatment progresses from bottom to top

Answer these questions about the course of brief-pulse right unilateral (RUL) ECT using a Thymatron System IV with the information provided in Table 9.5.1.

QUESTIONS

1 Identify at least five errors with this course of ECT.

a. _____

b. _____

c. _____

d. _____

e. _____

2　List and discuss four potential causes of the errors in this case.

a. _____

b. _____

c. _____

d. _____

3　What are the potential consequences/outcomes for this patient having **ECT**?

Table 9.5.2 Complex ECT treatments second course

Name	Date	Impedance	EMG	EEG	Energy	ECT #
John Doe	12/11/2016	>3000	5 sec	12 sec	140%	5
	7/11/2016	>3000	8 sec	14 sec	100%	4
	28/10/2016	>3000	not detected	9 sec	200%	3
	23/10/2016	2990	5 sec	not detected	140%	2
	14/10/2016	>3000	17 sec	not detected	100%	1

Brief-pulse, right unilateral (RUL) ECT using a Thymatron System IV
The course of treatment progresses from bottom to top

4　Following your review of the first course, you are then presented with further data about this patient's second course of ECT one month later, as set out in Table 9.5.2. Critically review and comment.

ANSWERS

1　Identify at least five errors with this course of ECT.

The errors in this course of treatment are many. They include:

a　The rapid escalation in the stimulus dose from 5% (25 mC) to 200% (1008 mC).

b　Four treatments failed to detect an EMG seizure. Visual motor fit not recorded.

c　Four treatments did not have an EEG seizure (Treatments 1, 3, 10 and 12).

d　Treatments 1, 10 and 12 did not have a motor or EEG seizure.

e　The impedance was inadequate throughout the course of treatment, with the lowest being 1570 ohms for Treatments 4 and 6. On the Thymatron device impedance should ideally be below 1500 ohms.

f　Treatment should not have proceeded on half the treatments owing to a very high impedance ">3000 ohm" (Treatments 1, 7, 9, 10 and 12). This is a major problem with the Thymatron device. The ECT stimulus can still be administered even when the impedance is highly inadequate. ">3000 ohm" usually occurs when there is an open circuit. MECTA devices will not deliver a stimulus in this situation.

g   Duration is no longer a significant parameter that correlates with clinical response; however, in this course of treatment only Treatment 2 met the early requirement of a motor fit greater than 24 seconds.

h   Increasing the dose of energy did not overcome the lack of seizure quality and clinical improvement due to very poor set-up technique.

i   A clinical review was not conducted until the end of the course of treatment. Advice from a skilled ECT practitioner should have been sought after Treatment 5.

j   Alternative strategies were not considered.

2   **What are the potential causes of this problem?**

a   ECT device not working properly.
It is essential that the ECT device is tested before each ECT list. If using a Thymatron System IV, use of the "EctoBrain" provides objective confirmation that the device is ready for use.

b   Lack of preparation of electrode sites.
Inadequate preparation of treatment electrode sites can cause very high impedance and may account for some of the difficulties noted in this case.

c   Very high and variable doses of anaesthetic agents.
This patient was male and weighed 75 kg. The anaesthetists changed with every treatment each administering their own formula. Doses of thiopentone ranged from 350 mg to 450 mg and the dose of propofol ranged from 250 to 350 mg. The recommended doses when using these drugs during ECT are thiopentone between 1.5 to a maximum of 2.5 mg/kg and propofol 0.75 to a maximum of 1.5 mg/kg (Ding and White, 2002).
In ECT the aim is to utilise the smallest dose possible owing to the anticonvulsant

properties of these agents. The use of an ultra-short-acting opioid like remifentanil (0.5 microgram to 1.0 microgram) can act as a sparing agent, enabling the dose of the primary induction agent to be markedly lowered, thereby reducing the anticonvulsant properties of the anaesthetic medication (MacPherson and Loo, 2008). Delaying treatment until two to three minutes is another strategy that can be very effective with recent evidence (Galvez and Loo, 2017).

d   Lack of communication between the ECT and anaesthetic team.
Communication between staff working in the treatment room is essential to prevent errors and inappropriate dosages of anaesthetic agents. An ECT service should aim to develop a cohesive team that discusses the impact of anaesthesia on clinical progress to see if adjustment can be made.

e   Poor knowledge and experience in ECT.
It is clear in this case that the ECT practitioner lacked understanding of the technical aspects of ECT.

f   Lack of clinical review.
The ECT practitioner did not complete a clinical review until the end of the course of treatment. It is essential for patients to be reviewed regularly during the course of treatment and implement objective outcome measures to assist with clinical management.

g   Failure to ask for help until very late in the course of treatment.
It is essential to ask for assistance early if there is lack of clinical progress and inexperience.

3   **What are the potential consequences/outcomes for this patient having ECT?**

Potential consequences of this case include:

a   Potential for severe cognitive impairment.
b   Lack of clinical progression.
c   Unnecessary exposure to 12 anaesthetics.

d Long period of hospitalisation.

e Strong belief that ECT is a bad treatment that does not work.

f Potential for anger and frustration by family and carers about the poor treatment and consequence for the patient.

g Reinforcement of the belief by mental health and perioperative staff that ECT is an archaic treatment that should be banned.

h Lack of priority for ECT within the service.

i ECT can be done badly, particularly when using disposable electrodes. Attention to the preparation is essential. Firm pressure applied by the dummy electrodes can reduce impedance substantially increasing the clinical response.

4 Following your review of the first course, you are then presented with further data about this patient's second course of ECT one month later, set out in Figure 9.5.2. Critically review and comment.

You are shocked by this new information reinforcing all of the above points, raising more questions than answers.

Why is it that it has taken 17 ineffective treatments before someone asked for help?

How could this patient be recommenced with ECT with nothing changing leading to another ineffective course of treatment?

CONCLUSION

This case highlights how easily ECT practice can fail owing to a lack of implementation of minimum standards of practice and regular credentialing of ECT practitioners.

REFERENCES

Ding, Z., and White, P.F. (2002). Anesthesia for electroconvulsive therapy. *Anesthesia and Analgesia, 94*(5), 1351–1364. doi:10.1097/00000539-200205000-00057.

Galvez, V., and Loo, C.K. (2017). Clinical applicability of monitoring the time interval between anesthesia and electroconvulsive therapy. *Journal of ECT, 33*(1), 4–6. doi:10.1097/YCT.0000000000000384.

MacPherson, R., and Loo, C. (2008). Cognitive impairment following electroconvulsive therapy – does the choice of anaesthetic agent make a difference? *Journal of ECT, 24*(1), 52–56.

EEG challenges: what should you do next?

CASE 1: 19-YEAR-OLD FEMALE, SUPRATHRESHOLD SEIZURE

You are asked to comment on EEG 9.6.1 following the third RUL ultrabrief ECT treatment in a 19-year-old female, TC, who developed a severe major depressive disorder in the context of a relationship break up. She presented to your hospital after a high-lethality suicide attempt by overdose of prescription medication.

There was a strong family history of depression on the maternal side and a paternal uncle suicide a number of years ago. The treating psychiatrist is concerned that she has had only a partial response to ECT with persistent suicidal ideation.

1   Describe the features of the EEG.

2   What is your advice to the treating psychiatrist?

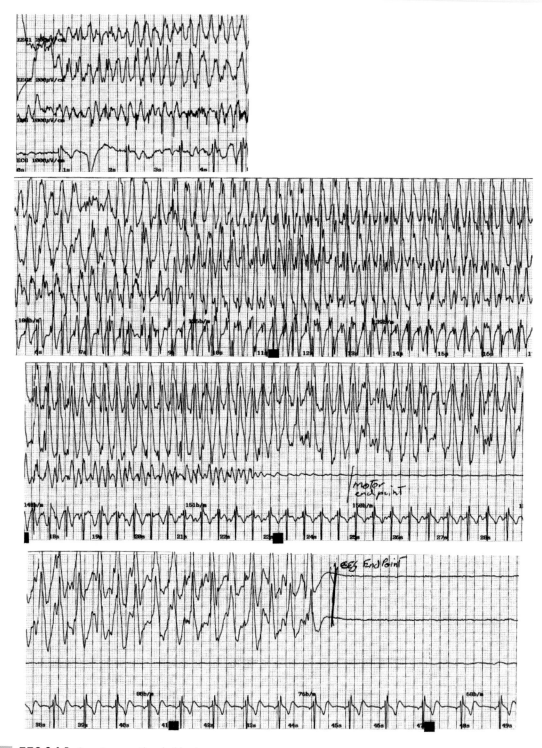

EEG 9.6.1 Case 1: suprathreshold seizure

ANSWERS

1 Features of EEG 9.6.1:

  a Short recruitment phase, one second.

  b High concordance and symmetry between left and right.

  c Early onset of polyspike waveforms between one and three seconds on the left but almost absent on the right side owing to the early intrusion of slow waveforms.

  d High amplitude in both left and right.

  e Robust spike and wave phase (slow wave phase) that dominate the recording.

  f Motor fit ends between 23 to 25 seconds but the EEG persists for much longer.

  g Abrupt postictal suppression that is highly symmetrical with sustained electrical silence.

  h Bradycardia for the first two seconds that is rapidly followed by a tachycardia, 156 beats per minute (bpm) returning to a resting level of 68 bpm by the end of the seizure.

2 What is your advice to the treating psychiatrist?

  a You tell the psychiatrist not to be too concerned.

  b TC is having ultrabrief ECT that can have a slower onset of action.

  c The EEG is suprathreshold, fulfilling all requirements for an effective treatment.

  d There are some early signs of improvement that is an excellent predictor of TC gaining remission.

  e You reassure the psychiatrist that suicidal ideation and negative cognitions are often late to remit. TC may go through a period of high risk over the next few days as the vegetative symptoms improve. Vigilance is required until these symptoms resolve.

  f You highlight the recent evidence from the PRIDE study that ECT is anti-suicidal.

CASE 2: 42-YEAR-OLD MALE, THRESHOLD SEIZURE

You are the treating psychiatrist for AB, a 42-year-old male with a diagnosis of severe major depressive disorder, recurrent episode with psychosis and melancholia. AB had a robust respond to bitemporal ECT five years ago at a different facility. He had some memory loss but it returned about six weeks later.

AB's family are keen to commence ECT as quickly as possible to stop further deterioration as he has lost weight and was being consumed with delusions of guilt and poverty. He has been on a combination of venlafaxine 225 mg and quetiapine 300 mg at night since that time and remained well until his father died six months ago. He was recently commenced on diazepam 5 mg twice a day by his GP owing to agitation.

1 What medication adjustments would you make in preparation for ECT?

You have recently introduced ultrabrief ECT into your hospital.

2 Describe the issues that need to be addressed during your consent about the pros and cons of ultrabrief compared to bitemporal ECT. Would you involve his family in this session?

AB agrees to proceed with ultrabrief ECT, keen to try the new form of ECT owing to memory problems experienced last time.

You follow the stimulus dosing protocol in this *Workbook*, Table 5.3.1, during the initial titration session. AB had a seizure on the second attempt at 4% (20 mC).

---

3 What stimulus dose would you set at the next treatment?

---

4 Describe the EEG shown in EEG 9.6.2.

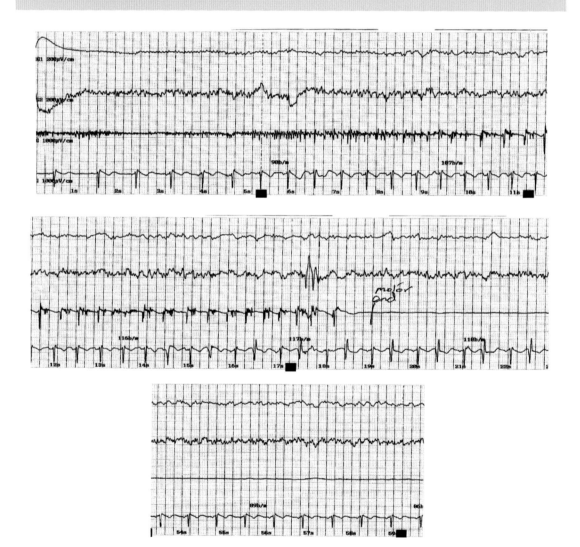

EEG 9.6.2 *Case 2: threshold seizure*

There was a marked improvement in the EEG quality with subsequent treatments and the stimulus dose was maintained at 25% (126 mC). AB had a robust response and gained remission by

Treatment 8. You give him three more treatments, tapered over the next few weeks after discharge, to ensure stability. AB had minimal cognitive impairment.

ANSWERS

1 What medication adjustments would you make in preparation for ECT?

  a Antidepressant:
    i   Venlafaxine dose could be increased during course. of ECT if tolerated.
    ii Change to a different class of medication: an SSRI, like escitalopram, or a tricyclic antidepressant, like nortriptyline, at high dose. Nortriptyline would facilitate sleep something that has been troublesome in the past.
    iii You are aware of the PRIDE study and consider augmenting with lithium (Kellner et al., 2016).
  b Antipsychotic medication:
    i   The seroquel may need to be strengthened by adding doses during the day to prevent agitation and allow the removal of diazepam.
    ii A more potent atypical antipsychotic may need to be considered, like paliperidone.
  c Benzodiazepine:
    i   The diazepam needs to be ceased 24–48 hours before ECT is commenced as it has strong anticonvulsant properties.
    ii This class of medication needs to be avoided during the course of ECT.

2 Describe the issues that need to be addressed during your consent about the pros and cons of ultrabrief compared to bitemporal ECT. Would you involve his family in this session? Some of the issues that need to be addressed are:

  a Discuss the latest evidence that supports ultrabrief ECT, RCTs (Galletly, Clarke and Paterson, 2014; Galletly, Paterson and Burton, 2012; Loo, Katalinic, Martin and Schweitzer, 2012; Loo et al., 2014; Loo

et al., 2008; Mayer, Byth and Harris, 2013; Niemantsverdriet, Birkenhager and van den Broek, 2011; Sackeim et al., 2008; Sienaert, Vansteelandt, Demyttenaere and Peuskens, 2009; Sienaert, Vansteelandt, Demyttenaere and Peuskens, 2010; Tor et al., 2015).
  b May have a slower onset of action.
  c Substantially better cognitive impairment profile.
  d It would be essential to involve the family in the consent process, gaining their support for the new treatment approach.
  e Highlight that you use low doses of anaesthetic induction agents to minimise the anticonvulsant effects on the seizure and monitor for awareness using the isolated limb technique.

3 What stimulus dose would you set at the next treatment?

The stimulus dose required for the next treatment would be 25% (126 mC), 6 times seizure threshold.

4 The features of EEG 9.6.2 include:

  a Threshold seizure.
  b Lacks symmetry and concordance, particularly over the first 8 seconds.
  c Very long recruitment phase.
  d More polyspike waveforms on the right, almost absent in the left lead.
  e A seizure has occurred with a motor fit of 19 seconds.
  f Absence of spike and wave phase.
  g Poor postictal suppression with end point difficult to determine.
  h Compare seizure quality with baseline EEG (not shown in EEG 9.6.2).
  i This seizure is unlikely to have therapeutic benefit.

CASE 3: 84-YEAR-OLD FEMALE, POOR-QUALITY EEG

You are the ECT practitioner who has been asked to consult an 84-year-old woman who has been receiving right unilateral brief-pulse (RUL) maintenance ECT (m-ECT) every three to four weeks for five years. She has treatment-resistant schizoaffective disorder that has required multiple hospitalisations in the past. She is unable to tolerate a range of medications.

Since m-ECT she has only had two brief admissions to hospital. Her symptoms remitted after three ECT treatments during the first admission four years ago and the second two years later where she had four tapered treatments before returning to a monthly schedule over the last 12 months.

The team are concerned that her mental state has dipped, with some psychotic symptoms returning. They wonder if this may be due to deterioration in the quality of the ECT that she has been receiving.

---

1 Comment on EEG 9.6.3.

---

2 Is the treating team correct in their assertion that the quality of ECT has deteriorated?

---

3 What suggestions can you make to maintain m-ECT for this patient?

ANSWERS

1 Comment on EEG 9.6.3.

   a The EEG is highly inadequate with poor seizure expression, reduced length motor second seconds and EEG 18 seconds.
   b There are considerable artefacts from the EMG.
   c Most features of a good EEG are absent except:
      i   Short recruitment of two seconds.
      ii Symmetrical left and right EEGs.
      iii Clear postictal suppression.
   d You note that over the last six treatments seizure quality has steadily deteriorated.
   e The treating team has tried to overcome the deterioration by increasing the stimulus dose.
   f For many years treatment was administered at a dose of 100% (576 mC).
   g You note that it is now 200% (1016 mC).

2 Is the treating team correct in their assertion that the quality of ECT has deteriorated?

   Yes, it is evident that this low-quality EEG is ineffective, accounting for the clinical deterioration noted by the team.

3 What suggestions can you make to maintain m-ECT for this patient?

   a Treatment options include:
      i   Retitration at the next ECT session, as it is likely that the stimulus dose is well above seizure threshold (refer to Figure 5.4.5). It is likely that the EEG will improve dramatic improving the effectiveness of the treatment.
      ii Changing to a different electrode placement should only be considered if there is no response to retitration.

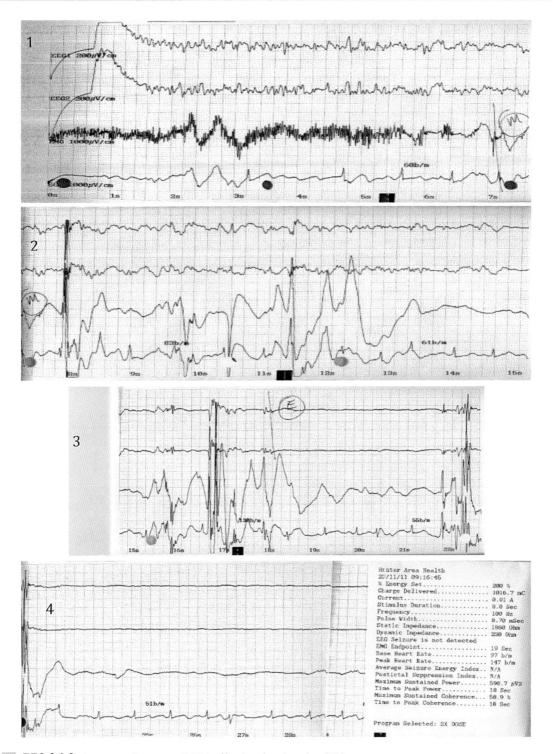

EEG 9.6.3 *Case 3: maintenance ECT ineffective, deteriorating EEG*

CASE 4: 36-YEAR-OLD FEMALE, FIFTH TREATMENT WITH SHORT EEG

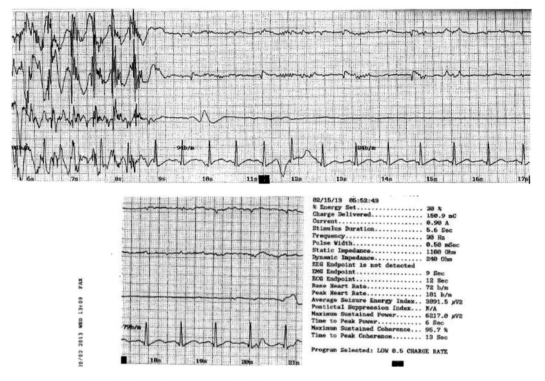

02/15/13 05:52:43
% Energy Set..................... 30 %
Charge Delivered............... 150.9 mC
Current........................ 0.90 A
Stimulus Duration.............. 5.6 Sec
Frequency...................... 30 Hz
Pulse Width.................... 0.50 mSec
Static Impedance............... 1100 Ohm
Dynamic Impedance.............. 240 Ohm
EEG Endpoint is not detected
EMG Endpoint................... 9 Sec
ECG Endpoint................... 12 Sec
Base Heart Rate................ 72 b/m
Peak Heart Rate................ 101 b/m
Average Seizure Energy Index.. 3891.5 μV2
Postictal Suppression Index... N/A
Maximum Sustained Power....... 6217.0 μV2
Time to Peak Power............ 6 Sec
Maximum Sustained Coherence... 95.7 %
Time to Peak Coherence........ 13 Sec

Program Selected: LOW 0.5 CHARGE RATE

EEG 9.6.4 *Case 4: short EEG; what should you do?*

1 Comment on EEG 9.6.4.

2 What are the treatment options available?

ANSWERS

1 Comment on EEG 9.6.4.

a The EEG shows a highly symmetrical EEG that is very short with all parameters terminating after eight seconds.

b There is some ECG artefact in the subsequent recording, reflected in both left and right channels.

c In many ways it fulfils many of the features of an ideal trace.

2 What are the treatment options available?

a Options will depend upon the clinical context including electrode placement and if there has been improvement.

b Continuing the same dose of 30% (151 mC) over subsequent treatment may result in an aborted or missed seizure due to rising seizure threshold, making increasing the dose advisable.

REFERENCES

Galletly, C., Clarke, P., and Paterson, T. (2014). Practical considerations in the use of ultrabrief ECT in clinical practice. *Journal of ECT, 30*(1), 10–14.

Galletly, C., Paterson, T., and Burton, C. (2012). A report on the introduction of ultrabrief pulse width ECT in a private psychiatric hospital. *Journal of ECT, 28*(1), *59*. doi:10.1097/YCT.0b013e318221b42e.

Kellner, C.H., Husain, M.M., Knapp, R.G., McCall, W.V., Petrides, G., Rudorfer, M.V., . . . Lisanby, S.H. (2016). Right unilateral ultrabrief pulse ECT in geriatric depression: phase 1 of the PRIDE study. *American Journal of Psychiatry, 173*(11), 1101–1109. doi:10.1176/appi.ajp.2016.15081101.

Loo, C.K., Katalinic, N., Martin, D., and Schweitzer, I. (2012). A review of ultrabrief pulse width electroconvulsive therapy. *Therapeutic Advances in Chronic Disease, 3*(2), 69–85. doi:10.1177/2040622311432493.

Loo, C.K., Katalinic, N., Smith, D.J., Ingram, A., Dowling, N., Martin, D., . . . Schweitzer, I. (2014). A randomised controlled trial of brief and ultrabrief pulse right unilateral electroconvulsive therapy. *International Journal of Neuropsychopharmacology, 18*(1).

Loo, C.K., Sainsbury, K., Sheehan, P., and Lyndon, B. (2008). A comparison of RUL ultrabrief pulse (0.3ms) ECT and standard RUL ECT. *International Journal of Neuropsychopharmacology, 11*(7), 883–890.

Mayer, P., Byth, K., and Harris, A. (2013). Acute antidepressant effects of right unilateral ultra-brief ECT: a double-blind randomised controlled trial. *Journal of Affective Disorders, 13*(149(1–3)), 426–429.

Niemantsverdriet, L., Birkenhager, T.K., and van den Broek, W.W. (2011). The efficacy of ultrabrief-pulse (0.25 millisecond) versus brief-pulse (0.50 millisecond) bilateral electroconvulsive therapy in major depression. *Journal of ECT, 27*(1), 55–58. doi:10.1097/YCT.0b013e3181da8412.

Sackeim, H.A., Prudic, J., Nobler, M.S., Fitzsimons, L., Lisanby, S.H., Payne, N., . . . Devanand, D.P. (2008). Effects of pulse width and electrode placement on the efficacy and cognitive effects of electroconvulsive therapy. *Brain Stimulation, 1*(2), 71–83. doi:10.1016/j.brs.2008.03.001.

Sienaert, P., Vansteelandt, K., Demyttenaere, K., and Peuskens, J. (2009). Randomized comparison of ultra-brief bifrontal and unilateral electroconvulsive therapy for major depression: clinical efficacy. *Journal of Affective Disorders, 116*(1–2), 106–112. doi:10.1016/j.jad.2008.11.001.

Sienaert, P., Vansteelandt, K., Demyttenaere, K., and Peuskens, J. (2010). Randomized comparison of ultra-brief bifrontal and unilateral electroconvulsive therapy for major depression: cognitive side-effects. *Journal of Affective Disorders, 122*(1–2), 60–67. doi:10.1016/j.jad.2009.06.011.

Tor, P.C., Bautovich, A., Wang, M.J., Martin, D., Harvey, S.B., and Loo, C. (2015). A systematic review and meta-analysis of brief versus ultrabrief right unilateral electroconvulsive therapy for depression. *Journal of Clinical Psychiatry, 10*(4088). doi:10.4088/JCP.14r09145.

Index

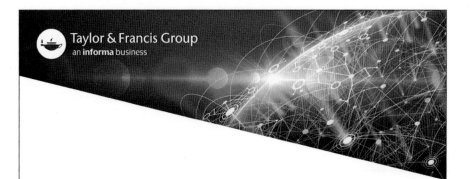